INDIA DEVELOPMENT REPORT

INDIA DEVELOPMENT REPORT
2004–05

edited by
KIRIT S. PARIKH • R. RADHAKRISHNA

OXFORD
UNIVERSITY PRESS

YMCA Library Building, Jai Singh Road, New Delhi 110 001

Oxford University Press is a department of the University of Oxford. It furthers the
University's objective of excellence in research, scholarship, and education
by publishing worldwide in

Oxford   New York

Auckland   Cape Town   Dar es Salaam   Hong Kong   Karac
Kuala Lumpur   Madrid   Melbourne   Mexico City   Nairobi
New Delhi   Shanghai   Taipei   Toronto

With offices in

Argentina   Austria   Brazil   Chile   Czech Republic   France   Greece
Guatemala   Hungary   Italy   Japan   Poland   Portugal   Singapore
South Korea Switzerland   Thailand   Turkey   Ukraine   Vietnam

Oxford is a registered trademark of Oxford University Press
in the UK and in certain other countries

Published in India by Oxford University Press, New Delhi

© Oxford University Press and Indira Gandhi Institute of Development Research 2005

The moral rights of the author have been asserted
Database right Oxford University Press (maker)

First published 2005

All rights reserved. No part of this publication may be reproduced,
or transmitted in any form or by any means, electronic or mechanical,
including photocopying, recording or by any information storage and
retrieval system, without permission in writing from Oxford University Press.
Enquiries concerning reproduction outside the scope of the above should be
sent to the Rights Department, Oxford University Press, at the address above

You must not circulate this book in any other binding or cover
and you must impose this same condition on any acquirer

ISBN 019 566873 1

Typeset in Garamond in 10.5/12.5
by Excellent Laser Typesetters, Pitampura, Delhi 110 034
Printed by Roopak Printers, New Delhi 110 032
and published by Manzar Khan, Oxford University Press
YMCA Library Building, Jai Singh Road, New Delhi 110 001

Preface

The Indian economy has experienced dramatic turnaround in the last two years since the *India Development Report 2002* (IDR) was published. It has made a vigorous recovery from the unprecedented drought in 2002–3 and attained a high growth rate of 8.1 per cent in 2003–04. There are signs that India is on its way to becoming an economic power. The previous government had started nurturing the business constituency to fire the animal spirit of entrepreneurs. As pointed out in our previous report, social exclusion, growing regional disparities, and a high incidence of poverty and unemployment are stark realities. The current growth process is showing signs of social disarticulation. Achieving high growth is one thing, making it pro poor is quite another.

The IDR 2004–05 looks at the macroeconomic scene from both growth and human development aspects as well as from the poverty perspective. It analyses issues such as poverty reduction, state of healthcare, public expenditure in social sectors, agricultural R&D, corporate sector performance, intellectual property rights (IPR) policy, and urban transportation; it also discusses policy options related to these issues and suggests possible solutions. While the presentation is kept lucid and non-technical so as to make it accessible to the general reader, we try not to compromise analytical rigour. We hope that the IDR will contribute to the on going debate on various issues of inclusive development.

This is the fourth in the IDR series and as before almost all the papers are written by the faculty and research scholars of Indira Gandhi Institute of Development Research (IGIDR), Mumbai. The Statistical Appendices have been contributed by S. L. Shetty of EPW Research Foundation. Through IDR, the faculty of IGIDR communicates to the larger community the results of its research with a view to initiate debate and discussion, and hopefully to improve policy. The views expressed here are the views of the individual authors.

In such a report many people contribute in a variety of ways. Their support and enthusiastic participation are critical in bringing out such a report. Patrick Lewis has co-ordinated the production and ably kept track of drafts of various authors, queries from editors, responses and other details. Rohit Mutatkar, our PhD student, has provided research assistance. We are also grateful for the editorial support and help provided by Oxford University Press, Delhi. We thank them all.

KIRIT S. PARIKH
R. RADHAKRISHNA

Contents

List of Tables x
List of Figures xiii
List of Boxes xiv
List of Statistical Appendices xv
List of Abbreviations xvii

1. **Overview: Ten Years of Reforms, What Next?** 1
   Kirit S. Parikh • R. Radhakrishna

   How Rapidly is the Indian Economy Growing?
   How Sustainable is our Growth Performance?   1
   What is the State of Poverty in the Country and its Character?
   How do we Make Growth Inclusive?   3
   What is the State of Health in India?   6
   What have We Done for the Social Sector? How has the Social
   Sector Expenditure Grown?   8
   How are We Facing the IPR Challenge?   10
   Importance of New Agricultural Varieties   11
   Importance of Transaction Costs: How can We Facilitate Trade?   12
   A Healthy Banking Sector   14
   Why has not High Fiscal Deficit Led to Inflation and Disasters?   15
   What are the Emerging Issues and Possible Solutions to the
   Urban Transport Challenge?   16
   India's Strengths and Weaknesses   16
   Is Bharat Wilting? The Challenges   18

2. **Macroeconomic Scene: Growth and Equity Perspectives** 21
   Manoj Panda

   Macroeconomic Performance   21
   Fluctuations in the Incidence of Poverty   33
   Interstate Growth Performance   35
   Summary and Conclusions   37

3. **Poverty in India: Dimensions and Character** 40
   R. Radhakrishna • Shovan Ray

   Poverty in the Post-reform Period   42
   Profiles of the Poor   45
   Malnutrition   52
   The Emerging Scenario   55

4. **Public Health Scenario in India** — 62
   Srijit Mishra

   Burden of Diseases   62
   Infant and Child Mortality   64
   Maternal Health   64
   Some Infectious and Parasitic Diseases   67
   Lifestyle Diseases   69
   Morbidity and Physical Disability   70
   Outpatient and Inpatient Treatment   72
   Health Care Expenditure   74
   Some Other Emerging Issues   77
   Conclusions   81

5. **Lack of Energy, Water, and Sanitation and its Impact on Rural India** — 84
   Jyoti Parikh • Kirit Parikh • Vijay Laxmi

   Estimation of Drain on Human Resources due to Cooking Fuels   85
   Recommendations for Energy Supply and Utilization   93
   Recommendations for Action for Gender Equity   93
   Recommendations for Water and Sanitation Facilities   94
   Recommendations for Health Care Facilities   95
   Recommendations for Transportation Facilities   95

6. **Patterns in Social Sector Expenditure: Pre- and Post-reform Periods** — 96
   S. Mahendra Dev • Jos Mooij

   Trends in Social Sector Expenditure   96
   Trends in Expenditures by the Central Government   98
   Trends in Expenditure by the States   101
   Comparisons with Other Countries and International Norms   102
   Effectiveness of Social Sector Expenditure   104
   Experiences of Some States   105
   How to Improve Effectiveness in Social Sector Policy Implementation   106
   By Way of Conclusion   107

7. **India's Patent Policy and Political Economy of Development** — 112
   Anitha Ramanna

   Economic Costs and Benefits of Patents   113
   Patent System in India   113
   India's Patent Policy Shift   114
   Explaining India's Patent Policy Reforms   115
   Opposition to Patent Reform   116
   Rise of Actors that Promoted Reform   116
   Public Sector Research Institutions and Patent Policy Shift   117
   Promoting Patent Activity   117
   Defeating the Bio-Piracy Argument Against Patent Reform   118
   Building Coalitions for Reform   118
   Public Sector Research Institutions and Patent Activity   119
   Public Sector Research Institutions and Development Strategy   120

8. **New Technologies for India's Development** — 126
   Jayan Jose Thomas

   Opportunities from New Technologies   127
   Challenges to Technology-aided Growth   132

The Urgent Need to Create New Technologies   135
Human Development and Diffusion of New Technologies   136
Complementarities between Policy Interventions for Economic Growth and
Diffusion of New Technologies   138

9. **Hybrid Rice: The Indian Experience and Comparison with the Rest of Asia**   141
   Aldas Janaiah

   Rice production in Asia and India   141
   Hybrid Rice: Viewed as an Innovative Technology   144
   Insights from the Farm Level Experiences in India   144
   Comparison with the Chinese Experience   146
   Some Policy Issues   150
   Conclusions   151

10. **Trade Facilitation**   154
    Nirmal Sengupta • Moana Bhagabati

    Trade Facilitation in India   155
    Conclusions   168

11. **The New Basel Capital Accord: Rationale, Design, and Tentative Implications for India**   171
    D. M. Nachane • Partha Ray • Saibal Ghosh

    Regulation of Banks   173
    The New Basel Accord: Genesis and Major Features   174
    Possible Implications for Emerging Market Economies   179
    Reactions from the Developing Countries   182
    Emerging Scenario   187

12. **Puzzles in Indian Performance: Deficits without Disasters**   191
    Ashima Goyal

    Trend or Shocks   191
    Openness and the Current Account   197
    The Twin Deficits   198
    Investment Fluctuations   201
    Monetary Policy, the Term Structure of Interest Rates, and Expectations   202
    Credit and Finance   205
    Conclusions   207

13. **Urban Transportation Trends, Alternatives, and Policy Issues**   209
    Sudhakar Yedla

    Growth of Vehicular Stock   209
    Projection of Vehicular Stock   212
    Travel Demand Projection   214
    Trends in Environmental Emissions and Ambient Air Quality   215
    Technological and Management Alternatives   217
    Policy Initiative and Measures   222

Statistical Appendices   227

Tables

2.1	Average Annual Growth in GDP	22
2.2	Annual Growth Rates in Index of Agricultural Production	23
2.3	Growth Rates in Index Number of Industrial Production	24
2.4	Growth in Index Number of Industrial Production by used based sectors	25
2.5	Growth of Employment (Usual Status)	27
2.6	Elasticity of Employment with Respect to Income	28
2.7	Savings and Capital Formation	29
2.8	Major Foreign Trade Parameters	30
2.9	Growth in Monetary Variables	31
2.10	Fiscal Parameters of Central Government	32
2.11	Fiscal Parameters of State Government	32
2.12	Head Count Ratio of Rural Poverty for Major States in India: 1999–2000	35
2.13	Coefficient of Variations in Growth Rates of State Income	36
3.1	Growth Rates of Total Expenditure at 1990–1 Prices and Poverty	45
3.2	Incidence of Poverty Level—Social and Occupational Group	45
3.3	Percentage Distribution of Persons Below Poverty Line by Occupation Groups—Statewise, 1993–4 and 1999–2000	47
3.4	Percentage Distribution of Persons Below Poverty Line by Caste—Statewise 1993–4 and 1999–2000	49
3.5a	Incidence of Chronic Poverty—Statewise, 1993–4 and 1999–2000 (Rural)	50
3.5b	Incidence of Poverty—Statewise 1993–4 and 1999–2000 (Urban)	51
3.6	Under-nutrition (Height-for-age) among Poor and Incidence of Chronic Poverty: 1997–8	52
3.7	Under-nutrition among Children (aged 1–5 years) and CED among Adults in Rural Areas of Selected States	53
3.8	NFHS Estimates of Malnutrition among Children (Weight-for-age) and CED among Ever-married Women	54
3.9	Malnutrition and Poverty	54
3.10	NNMB (2000–1) and NFHS-2 Estimates of Under-nutrition in Rural Areas based on Standard Deviation	55
4.1	Distribution of Causes of Death in India, 1998	63
4.2	Neonatal, Infant and Under-five Mortality Rates, 1998–9	65
4.3	Maternal Mortality Rate (Indirect estimates, 1987–96 and SRS estimates 1998) and Some Aspects of Maternal Care in Rural and Urban India, 1998–9	66
4.4	Availability of Equipment and Supplies to Facilitate Maternal and Childcare in Primary Health Centres	67
4.5	Proportion of Households with access to Piped Water, Bathroom, Latrine, and Drainage, and Female Literacy: 2001	69
4.6	Age- and Caste-wise Incidence of Regular Consumers of Tobacco by Males and Females in Rural and Urban Areas, 1993–4	70

4.7	Morbidity Prevalence, Infant Mortality, and Life Expectation across 15 Major States in Rural and Urban India	71
4.8	Prevalence of Acute and Chronic Ailment and Hospitalization per 1000 Persons across Expenditure Decile/Quintile, Caste, and Age by Sex for Rural/Urban regions, 1995–6	71
4.9	Short Duration Morbidity (30 Day Recall) and Major Morbidity (Previous Year) across States, 1994	72
4.10	Physical (Visual, Hearing, Speech, or Locomotor) Disability per 100,000 Persons, 1991	73
4.11	Share of Public and Private Sectors in Inpatient Care	74
4.12	Medical Expenditure per Treatment in Outpatient and Inpatient Care, 1986–7 and 1995–6	75
4.13	Average Expenditure (in Rupees) per Treated Ailment in Private Sector and Ratio of Private to Public in Rural/Urban India for Outpatient/Inpatient Care across Major States, 1995–6	76
4.14	Per Capita Public Expenditure on Health (1999–2000) and Income-class Bias in Public Expenditure (1995–6) across 14 Major States	77
4.15	Health Expenditure and Health Personnel (Comparing India with other SAARC Countries, China, and Developed Countries of Germany, the UK, and the USA), 2000	78
5.1	District, Village, Household and IAQ Monitoring Sample Sizes	85
5.2	Share of the Sampled States in RNI and share of RNI in RAI	86
5.3	Estimates of Energy Consumption Pattern and Time and Efforts for Gathering	88
5.4	Estimates of Access to Drinking Water, Sewerage, and Toilet Facility	88
5.5	Economic Burden of Respiratory and Eye Diseases	90
5.6	Total Economic Losses due to Water Related Diseases	91
5.7	Total Economic Burden	92
5.8	Households Willing to Pay for Improvement (million)	93
6.1	Social Sector (Social Services and Rural Development) Expenditure by Centre and States	97
6.2	Social Sector Exp. of Centre and States (%), 1990–1 and 2000–1	98
6.3	Expenditure on Education (in Rs Crores current prices) and its Composition 1990–1 to 1998–9	99
6.4	Social Sector Expenditure (Social services + Rural Dev) by Centre	99
6.5	Intrasectoral Allocation (%) in Education, Health, and Rural Development: Central Government Expenditure 1992–3 to 2002–3	100
6.6	Share of External Aid in Sectoral Spending on Children (Union Budget) (%)	101
6.7	Trend Growth Rates of Social Sector Expenditure of All States (% per annum)	101
6.8	Per capita Expenditure in Social Services and Rural Development at Current Prices (in Rs): 1999–2000, 2000–1	102
6.9	Index of Per capita Real Expenditure on Social Services and Rural Development (at 1993–4 prices) at State Level	102
6.10	Composition of Public Expenditure in India and Developing Countries	103
6.11	Public Expenditure on Education and Health: International Comparisons	103
6.12	Social Sector Ratios	104
6.13	Composition of Social Sector Expenditure	105
6.A1	All State Social Sector Expenditures as per cent of GDP	110
6.A2	All States Social Sector Expenditure as per cent of Total Expenditure	110
6.A3	All States Per Capita Real Expenditure (at 1993–4 prices) on Social Sector	111
7.1	Major Changes to India's Patent Law	115
7.2	Patenting Record of the CSIR in India 1990–1 to 1998–9	120
7.3	Department of Biotechnology: Patent Applications Filed in India According to TIFAC Database, 1995–2002	121
7.4	DBT Patents Granted so far	122
7.5	Indian Council of Agricultural Research: Patent Applications According to TIFAC Database, 1995–2002	123
8.1	Production of IT Products and Services in India: Projections for the year 2008	127
8.2	Employment Generation in India by IT Sector, Projections for 2008	128
8.3	Diffusion of ICTs, India and Selected Countries	132

8.4	Growth of Telecommunication Network and Internet in India, over the Years	133
8.5	Variations in Diffusion of Technologies Across Indian States	134
8.6	Investment and Achievements in the Creation of New Technologies, India and Selected Countries	136
8.7	Indicators for Educational Achievements across Indian States	137
9.1	Changes in Growth of Rice Yield in Major Countries in Asia, 1968–90 and 1991–2002	142
9.2	Compound Growth Rates of Yield for Rice in Major States of India	143
9.3	Comparative Cost–Return Profile for the Cultivation of Hybrid and Inbred Rice Varieties Over the Period in India	146
9.4	Comparative Cost-Return Profile for the Cultivation of Hybrid and Inbred Rice Varieties in Bangladesh, the Philippines, and Vietnam	149
9.5	Sensitivity analysis on how much subsidy is required for hybrid seed for commercial cultivators of hybrid rice in India	150
9.6	Sensitivity Analysis on How Much Market Price is Required for Hybrid Rice Grain in India	151
10.1	The Customs' EDI Trading Partners	158
11.1	Proposed New Accord versus 1988 Accord: Salient Features	176
11.2	Variants of Risk Calculation in Basel II	176
11.3	Risk-weights of Basel II: Exemplified with Standard and Poor's Rating	177
11.4	Timetable for Implementing Basel II	180
11.5	Capital Requirements for Unsecured Corporate Borrowers	181
11.6	Capital Requirements By Emerging Market	183
12.1	Price and Output Trends (per cent per year)	193
12.2	Shocks hitting the Economy after the mid-1990s	194
12.3	Percentage Changes in the Parameters of the Model in One Simulation Period Compared to the Previous One	195
12.4	Items in India's BOP as a percentage of GDP	198
12.5	Averages and Deviations from Average	201
12.6	Correlations among private investment (PI), interest, exchange, and inflation rates	202
12.7	Arbitrage in Currency Markets	204
12.8	Indicators of Credit and Financial Markets as % of GDP	206
12.9	Household Savings Choices	206
12.10	Credit to Selected Sectors as a Percentage of Non-food Gross Bank Credit	207
13.1	Annual Growth Rates of Motor Vehicles (Cars, Taxis, Buses, Trucks, Three Wheelers, and Two Wheelers) in Major Indian Cities from 1985 to 2002 (%)	210
13.2	Total Registered Motor Vehicles in Major Cities of India in the Year 2002	211
13.3	Projected Vehicular Stock in Delhi	212
13.4	Projected Vehicular Stock in Mumbai	213
13.5	On-road Vehicles in Different Cities as a Percentage of Registered Vehicles (2002)	213
13.6	Estimated Vehicle Kilometers of Travel in 2010 for All Major Cities (million)	214
13.7	Share of Air Pollution from Different Sectors	217
13.8	Garaging Status of Vehicle Type in Different Cities	217
13.9	Natural Gas Vehicles (NGVs) in the World (2001–2)	218
13.10	CNG City Buses in Different Cities Around the World (2000)	218
13.11	Cost Comparison of Conventional Vehicles vis-à-vis CNG Vehicles in Delhi	218
13.12	Comparison of Various Auto Technologies in India	220

Figures

2.1	Average Growth Rates in Various Service Sectors	26
2.2	Annualized Inflation Rate	29
2.3	Movement of Head Count Ratio of Poverty in Rural and Urban India	34
2.4	Per Capita Income and Average Growth Rate for Major Indian States	35
2.5	Gini Coefficient for Real Per Capita GSDP across States	36
3.1	Trends in Poverty in India	41
3.2	Share of Poverty—Statewise.	46
4.1	Proportion of Households Reporting Consumption of Tobacco, 1999–2000	69
4.2	Share of Public and Private in Hospitalized Care across Expenditure Quintile and Caste in Rural and Urban India, 1995–6	73
4.3	Share of Outpatient and Inpatient Public and Private Care, 1986–7 and 1995–6	75
5.1	Total economic losses due to diseases caused because of lack of access to clean energy, water and, sanitation	92
7.1	Patent Applications Filed in India by the CSIR	120
8.1	Annual Rates of Growth of Software Production and GDP (both at current prices) in India, 1992–3 to 2001–2	127
8.2	Annual Rates of Growth of Central Government Expenditure on R&D, and National Expenditure on R&D as Proportion of GNP: India, 1980–1 to 1998–9 (in per cent)	136
9.1	Trends in rice yield for irrigated and rainfed ecosystems, India, 1967–99	143
9.2	Trend in the adoption of hybrid rice in China	147
11.1	Risk Decomposition of a Typical Commercial/Investment Bank	177
12.1	Sector-wise contribution to inflation	196
12.2	Is the primary deficit as large as it seems?	200
12.3	Contribution of growth and real interest rates to the fiscal deficit	200
12.4	The risk premium in Indian currency markets	204
13.1	Pattern of vehicular stock in different cities from 1985 to 2002	211
13.2	Percentage share of travel modes in different cities in the year 2002	212
13.3	Percentage difference in registered vehicles and on-road vehicles	214
13.4	Pollutant load from transport sector in different cities in India (2002)	215
13.5	Changes in SPM concentration over the period 1995–2001	216
13.6	Changes in NOx concentration over the period 1995–2001	216
13.7	Consumer price of various auto fuels in Indian cities (2000–2 average prices)	219

Boxes

2.1	India Vision 2020	27
2.2	Can India Rise to Become a Major Economic Power?	38
3.1	Socio-Economic Status, Perceptions and Aspirations of the Poor in Three Contrasting States	43
3.2	Profile of Scheduled Tribes	48
4.1	Changing Demographic Profile and Epidemiological Transition	63
4.2	Home-based Neonatal Care (HBNC)	65
4.3	Corporate Sector in Health Care: The Case of Apollo	80
5.1	Some Relevant Million Development Goals (MDG) up to 2015	85
5.2	Survey Design	86
5.3	Household Enery—Rural India	87
5.4	Water and Sanitation—Rural India	88
5.5	Respiratory and Eye Diseases	89
5.6	Water-related Diseases	91
8.1	The Outcry Against Outsourcing	129
10.1	The WTO	155
11.1	Capital Adequacy	175
11.2	Major Features of the Third Consultative Document (2003)	180
12.1	The Structure of the Argument and the Main Conclusions	192
12.2	Modelling India's Openness to the Rest of the World	195
12.3	What is the Government's Primary Deficit?	199
12.4	Arbitrage at the short end	204
13.1	Directives of the Supreme Court aiming at Environmental Emission Control	223
13.2	Gasoline Lead Phase-out Programme in India	224
13.3	Recommendations Made by the Committee Constituted by the Mumbai High Court	225

Statistical Appendices

I(1)	Key National Accounts Aggregrates at 1993–4 Prices	229
I(2)	Gross and Net Domestic Savings by Type of Institutions (at Current Prices)	233
I(3)	Gross Capital Formation by Type of Institutions at Current Prices	235
I(4)	Net Capital Stock by Type of Institutions and Capital-Output Ratios	237
II(1)	Production Trends in Major Agricultural Crops	239
II(2)	Trends in Yields of Major Crops	241
II(3)	Structural Changes in Indian Industry and Decadal Growth	242
II(4)	Index of Industrial Production for Major Groups and Sub-groups	243
III(1)	Budgetary Position of Government of India	247
III(2)	Consolidated Budgetary Position of State Governments at a Glance	248
IV(1)	Select Aggregates:Scheduled Commercial Banks (Outstandings and Growth Rates)	249
IV(2)	Components of Money Stock (Outstandings and Growth Rates)	250
V(1)	Business Growth of Capital Market Segment of National Stock Exchange (NSE)	251
V(2)	Trade and Settlement Statistics of Bombay Stock Exchange (BSE)	252
V(3)	Growth of Derivative Segment in National Stock Exchange (NSE)	253
V(4)	Growth of Derivative Segment in Bombay Stock Exchange (BSE)	254
VI(1)	Wholesale Price Index: Point-to-Point and Average Annual Variations	255
VI(2)	Cost of Living Indices	
	(A) Consumer Price Index for Industrial Workers: Point-to-Point and Average Annual Variations	257
	(B) Consumer Price Index for Urban Non Manual Employees: Point-to-Point and Average Annual Variations	259
	(C) Consumer Price Index for Agricultural Labourers: Point-to-Point and Average Annual Variations	260
VII(1)	India's Balance of Payments: 1990–1 to 2002–3	261
VII(2)	Indices of Real Effective Exchange Rate (REER) and Nominal Effective Exchange Rate (NEER) for the Indian Rupee	264
VII(3)	Exchange Rate for the Indian Rupee vis-à-vis Some Select Currencies	266
VIII(1)	State-Wise Population:1951–2001	268
VIII(2)	State-Wise Rural and Urban Population: 1951–2001	269
VIII(3)	State-Wise Sex ratio (females per 1000 males)	270
VIII(4)	State-Wise Literacy Rate 1951 to 2001	271
VIII(5)	State-Wise Infant Mortality Rate: 1961, 1981, 1991 and 2001	272
VIII(6)	Human Development Index for India by State: 1981, 1991, and 2001	273
IX(1)	Poverty Estimates: Statewise (Headcount Ratio)	275
IX(2)	Annual Growth Rate of Employment By Agricultural and Non-Agricultural Sectors, 1950–1 to 1999–2000	276
IX(3)	Number of Workers and Worker-Population Ratios	
	(A) Number of Workers (in Terms of Usual Status) by Sex and Rural-Urban Residence 1951 to 1999–2000	277
	(B) Worker Population Ratios by Sex and Rural-Urban Residence, 1951 to 1999–2000	277

Contributed by EPW Research Foundation.

xvi STATISTICAL APPENDICES

IX(4)	Macro Scenario on Employment and Sectoral Employment Growth	
	(A) Past and Present Macro-Scenario on Employment and Unemployment (CDS Basis) (Person years)	278
	(B) Sectoral Employment Growth (CDS Basis)	278
IX(5)	Growth of Employment :Statewise and Rural and Urban in the 1980s and 1990s	279
X(1)	Rank of States in Descending Order of Per Capita NSDP and GSDP (Three-Yearly Annual Averages)	280
X(2)	Trends in Statewise Bank Deposits and Credit and Credit-Deposit Ratios	282
X(3)	Trends in Districtwise Deposits and Credit and Credit-Deposit Ratios	283

Abbreviations

AAI	Airports Authority of India
ADB	Asian Development Bank
AES	Agro-ecological System
APEC	Asia-Pacific Economic cooperation
ASI	Annual Survey of Industries
BCBS	Basel Committee on Banking Supervision
BHEL	Bharat Heavy Electricals Limited
BIS	Bank of International Settlements
BIS	Bureau of Indian Standards
BJP	Bharatiya Janata Party
BMI	Body Mass Index
BOI	Bank of India
BOP	Balance of Payment
BOV	Battery-operated vehicle
BSE	Bombay (Brihanmumbai) Stock Exchange
BSNL	Bharat Sanchar Nigam Limited
CA	Current Account
CAD	Current Account Deficit
CAS	Current Account Surplus
CBEC	Central Board of Excise and Customs
CBO	Community-based Organization
CED	Chronic Energy Deficiency
CFFACT	United Nations Centre for Trade Facilitation and Electronic Business
CEPA	Comprehensive Economic Partnership Agreement
CFS	Container Freight Station
CII	Confederation of Indian Industries
CMNMP	Chief Minister's Nutrition Meal Programme
CNG	Compressed Natural Gas
CO	Carbon Monoxide
CO_2	Carbon Dioxide
CPCB	Central Pollution Control Board
CPR	Common Pool Resources
CRR	Cash Reserve Ratio
CRRI	Central Road research Institute
CSIR	Indian council for Scientific and Industrial Research
CSS	Centrally Sponsored Schemes
CV	Coefficient of Variation
DALYS	Disability Adjusted Light Years
DATES	Diet, Alchohol, Tobacco, Exercise Stress
DBT	Department of Biotechnology

DCA	Department of Company Affairs
DEL	Direct Exchange Telephone Line
DFI	Development Financial Institution
DFID	Department for International Development
DGFT	Directorate General of Foreign Trade
DNA	Deoxyribonucleic Acid
DOTS	Directly Observed Treatment-Short Course
DPEP	District Primary Education Programme
EC	European Commission
EDI	Electronic Data Interchange
EDIFACT	United Nations Electronic Data Interchange Administration, Commerce and Transport
EERC	Environmental Economics Research Committees
EM	Equity Multiplier
EMRS	Exclusive Marketing Rates
EOC	Emergency Obstetric Case
EPWRF	EPW Research Foundation
EU	European Union
EV	Electric Vehicle
FAO	Food and Agriculture Organization
FDI	Foreign Direct Investment
FGT	Foster-Greer-Thorbeck
FICCI	Federation of Indian Chambers of Commerce and Industry
FII	Foreign Institutional Investors
FPI	Foreign Portfolio Investment
FRLHT	Foundation for Revitalization of Local Health Trade
GDP	Gross Domestic Product
GFD	Gross Fiscal Deficit
GNP	Gross National Product
GNS	Gross National Saving
GOI	Government of India
GSOP	Gross State Domestic Product
GBNC	Home-based Neonatal Care
HC	Hydrocarbons
HCR	Head Count Ratio
HEV	Hybrid Electric Vehicle
HIV/AIDS	Human Immuno-deficiency Virus/Acquired Immune Deficiency Syndrome
IAP	Indoor Air Pollution
ICAR	Indian Council for Agricultural Research
ICC	The International Chamber of Commerce
ICD	Inland Container Depot
ICEGATE	Indian Customs and Central Excise Electronic Commerce/Electronic Data Interchange Gateway
ICENET	Indian Customs and Central Excise Network
ICMR	Indian Council of Medical Research
ICT	Information and Communication Technology
IDBI	Industrial Development Bank of India
IDR	India Development Report
IGIDR	The Indira Gandhi Institute of Development Research
IIT	Indian Institute of Technology
I&M	Inspection and Maintenance
IMR	Infant Mortality Rate
IPO	Initial Public Offering
IPR	Intellectual Property Rights

IRB	International Rating Based Model
IRDA	Insurance Regulatory and Development Authority
ISP	Internet Service Provider
IT	Information Technology
ITC	International Trade Centre
ITES	Information Technology Enabled Services
JGSY	Jawahar Gram Samridhi Yojana
JNPT	Jawaharlal Nehru Port Trust
JRY	Jawahar Rozgar Yojana
LCC	Life Cycle Operating Cost
LCL	Less than Container Load
LCS	Land Customs Station
LDC	Less Developed Countries
LIBOR	London Inter Bank Offer Rate
LPG	Liquefied Petroleum Gas
LRI/ARI	Lower Respiratory Infection/Acute Respiratory Infection
Mbps	Megabits per Second
MDG	Millennium Development Goal
MFN	Most Favoured Nation
MHz	Mega Hertz
MMT	Multimodal Transport
MNES	Ministry of Non-Conventional Energy Sources
MPTA	Major Port Trusts Act
MSSRF	MS Swaminathan Research Foundation
MTD	Multimodal Transport Document
MTO	Multimodal Transport Operator
MTNL	Mahanagar Telephone Nigam Limited
MV	Modern Varieties
NACO	National Aids Control Organization
NAMP	National Air Quality Monitoring Programme
NCA	Net Cropped Area
NCAER	National Council of Applied Economic Research
NCL	National Chemical Laboratory
NDA	National Democratic Alliance
NFA	Net Foreign Asset
NFHS	National Family Health Survey
NGO	Non-Government Organization
NGV	Natural Gas Vehicles
NHDP	National Highways Development Programme
NIF	National Innovation Foundation
NHP	National Health Policy
NMR	Neonatal Mortality Rate
NNMB	National Nutrition Monitoring Bureau
NOx	Nitrogen Oxide
NPA	Non-Performing Asset
NRI	Non-Resident Indian
NSS	National Sample Survey
NSSO	National Sample Survey Organization
NTB	Non-Traff Barrier
NTP	National Telecom Policy
OECD	Organization for Economic Corporation and Development
ORS	Oral Rehydration Salts
PAN	Permanent Account Number

PCE	Per Capita (total) Expenditure
PCO	Public Call Office
PD	Primary Deficit
PD	Probability of Default
PDS	Public Distribution System
PHC	Primary Health Centre
PLR	Prime Lending Rate
PMGSY	Prime Minister's Gram Samridhi Yojana
POL	Petroleum, Oil, and Lubricants
PROBE	Public Report on Basic Education
PSU	Public Sector Undertaking
PUC	Pollution Under Control
RBI	Reserve Bank of India
R&D	Research and Development
RNTCP	Revised National Tuberculosis Control Programme
ROA	Return on Equity
RSPM	Respirable Suspended Particulate Matter
SAARC	South Asian Association for Regional Cooperation
SAD	Single Administrative Document
SAFTA	South Asian Free Trade Area
SAPAP	South Asia Poverty Alleviation Programme
SC	Scheduled Caste
SCD(R)	Survey of Causes of Death (Rural)
SDP	State-level Domestic Product
SEARCH	Society for Education, Action, and Research in Community Health
SEBI	Securities and Exchange Board of India
SEZ	Special Economic Zone
SIA	Supplementary Immunization Activities
SLI	Standard of Living Index
SME	Small and Medium Enterprises
SNP	Single Nucleotide Polymorphism
SO_2	Sulpher Dioxide
SPCB	State Pollution Control Board
SPM	Suspended Particulate Matter
SPS	Sanitary and Phyto-Sanitary Measures
Sristi	Society for Research and Initiation for sustainable Technologies and Institutions
SSI	Small-Scale Industry
ST	Scheduled Tribe
S&T	Science and Technology
STD	Subscriber Trunk Dialling
TAMP	Tariff Authority for Major Ports
TBA	Traditional Birth Attendant
TCS	Tata Consultancy Services
TFP	Total Factor Productivity
TNIP	Tamil Nadu Integrated Nutrition Project
TPA	Third Party Administrator
TRAI	Telecom Regulatory Authority of India
TRIPs	Trade Related Intellectual Property Rights Agreement
TRS	Trade Registration System
UA	Urban Agglomeration
UNCTAD	United Nations Conference on Trade and Development
UNDP	United Nations Development Programme
UNESCAP	United Nations Economic and Social Commission for Asia and Pacific

USPTO	United States Patent and Trademark Office
VaR	Value of Risk
VHS	Voluntary Health Service
VHW	Village Health Worker
VoIP	Voice over Internet Protocol
VPT	Village Public Telephone
VRS	Voluntary Retirement Scheme
WEHAB	Water, Energy, Health, Agriculture and Biodiversity
WIPO	World Intellectual Property Organization
WLL	Wireless in Local Loop
WPI	Wholesale Price Index
WPR	Work Participation Rate
WSSO	World Summit on Sustainable Development
WTO	World Trade Organization

1 Overview
Ten Years of Reforms, What Next?

Kirit S. Parikh • R. Radhakrishna

In January 2004 the Indian economy appeared to be growing rapidly and on the verge of take-off. The National Democratic Alliance (NDA) government claimed that the Indian economy was shining. The dramatic election results of May 2004 that swept away the Bharatiaya Janata Party (BJP)-led NDA coalition government and the state elections that deposed many state chief ministers with large reputations raise the question that if the economy was shining where did the shine go?

This India Development Report (IDR) 2004 looks at some aspects of the Indian economy, raises some questions and shows why these are important, what has been our response, and what options exist. We look at the macro scene from economic growth, human development, and poverty perspectives. The questions addressed are:

1. How rapidly is the Indian economy growing?
2. How sustainable is our growth performance?
3. What are the prospects of the Indian economy?
4. What is the state of poverty in the country and its character?
5. How do we make growth inclusive?
6. What is the access to clean water and fuels in rural India?
7. What is the state of health in India?
8. What have we done for the social sector?
9. How are we facing the intellectual property rights (IPR) challenge?
10. What is the role of new and emerging technologies?
11. What can we expect from new agricultural varieties?
12. How can we facilitate trade to boost it further?
13. How do we get a healthy banking sector—a precondition for convertibility? Are the international norms the best for Indian banks? What should be our approach?
14. Why has high fiscal deficit not led to inflation and disasters?
15. What are the emerging issues and possible solutions to the urban transport challenge?
16. Is the Bharat, that lives in India's villages and urban slums, wilting? Is India a shining star or a passing comet?
17. What lessons are there for the new government?

How Rapidly is the Indian Economy Growing? How Sustainable is our Growth Performance?

After the initiation of economic reforms in 1991, the gross domestic product (GDP) grew at a high rate till 1996–7. But the optimism generated during the mid-1990s did not last long. The growth rate in the economy has returned to about 5.5 per cent since 1997–8. In 2003–4 the growth rate is estimated to exceed 8 per cent. A sense of economic optimism prevails in some quarters. Manoj Panda examines the country's macroeconomic scene in Chapter 2, 'Macroeconomic Scene: Growth and Equity Perspectives'.

Even though the growth rate had slowed down in the late 1990s, it is possible to draw attention to several strong features of the economy at present. Unlike the growth experience of the 1980s, the GDP growth process of the 1990s seems sustainable. There are at least three reasons for this:

(1) In recent years, the economy has withstood, without any major disruption, several shocks like the

East Asian crisis, global depression, border tension, the Iraq war, oil price fluctuations, and a major drought. The sustenance of an average GDP growth rate of 5.5 per cent per annum in such an environment is commendable and points towards the new strength of the economy.

(2) The growth process of the 1980s took place in a more protected environment and neglected microeconomic efficiency. Even though agricultural growth was lower in the 1990s than in the 1980s the growth rates of aggregate GDP were comparable. The service sector boom in the mid-1990s took place when the nominal interest rate was 17 to 18 per cent. The growth rates recorded in the post-liberalization era, though quantitatively not very different, have taken place in a fairly competitive environment.

(3) At present there is macroeconomic stability on several counts compared to the 1980s. Inflation is low, there is abundant liquidity at low interest rate, exchange rate is reasonably stable under a managed float regime, foreign exchange reserves have been rising, short-term external debt is low, and food grain stocks are adequate even after a drought year.

On the weakness side, however, high fiscal deficit of about 10 per cent of GDP causes concern about medium-term fiscal stability. The deficit level is worse than that in several countries, which went through macroeconomic crisis. India has avoided the crisis due to its strong external and monetary positions. Rising current expenditure of the government has put pressure on revenue deficit and government savings have turned into dissavings. This has contributed to a fall in overall savings and investment rate in the economy. The need for correction of primary and revenue deficits and restoration of the structure of government expenditure in favour of capital formation and the social sector cannot be overemphasized.

The high growth rate of 8 per cent obtained during 2003–4 is the outcome of a growth rate of 9.0 per cent of the agricultural GDP. Agricultural GDP has a trend growth rate of 3 per cent. A fall of 3 per cent in the previous year meant that agricultural GDP was 6 per cent below the trend value. Thus, just to get back on the trend line would mean a growth rate of 9 per cent. To sustain a high growth rate the other sectors would have to grow faster. The service sector has been the principal driver of the GDP growth during the 1990s. It would be difficult to maintain a high GDP growth of 8 per cent without a strong manufacturing revival. The Indian industrial sector is going through a process of restructuring, consolidation, adoption of cost cutting measures, foreign collaboration, and technology upgradation. Some of these sectors, such as automobile, pharmaceuticals, etc., have already become quite competitive in the world market on cost and quality considerations. There has been a distinct broad-based improvement in industrial activity during the last one year. The emerging demand pattern would call for agricultural diversification in favour of vegetables, horticulture, livestock, afforestation, and agro-processing. These sectors would also have more employment potential to absorb a good part of the increasing labour force. Trade, tourism, and construction are other sectors that could play an important role in employment generation.

The Indian economy has been steadily moving towards integration with the global economy. Imports and exports together currently account for 23 per cent of GDP compared to just 15 per cent in 1990–1. A major recent development on the trade front has been that the current account balance has turned surplus in the last two years from a deficit of 3.1 per cent of GDP in 1990–1. This implies that the current external receipts are good enough to pay for current external liabilities. This transformation has been achieved primarily due to the rise in net invisible earnings by about 3 per cent of GDP, reflecting substantial expansion of transfers (remittances) from abroad as well as software and other service exports. In absolute terms, the transfers were of the order of about US$ 15 billion while software exports were close to US$ 10 billion.

India currently has huge stocks of foreign exchange reserves and foodgrains. Stock accumulation beyond an optimal level is not without cost. It would be beneficial to absorb the capital flows in future to increase investment. Similarly, stocks of foodgrains could partly be used for expanding public employment generation programmes for the poor.

Reduction of the bank rate by the Reserve Bank of India (RBI) led to a fall in the spectrum of interest rates charged by the commercial banks. Commercial banks held government securities at 39 per cent of their net demand and time liabilities which was far in excess of the statutory minimum limits of 25 per cent. Government securities have been attractive instruments for the banks to meet prudential norms imposed during financial reforms.

In recent years, the RBI has been sterilizing the excess primary liquidity generated by the large increase in net foreign exchange assets through open market sales of government securities. Net domestic assets of the RBI as a proportion of the reserve money have fallen from about 90 per cent in the early 1990s to as low as 3 per cent by the end of March 2003. The RBI would need to manage surplus on the balance of payments by resorting to other instruments.

Acceleration of the GDP growth would critically depend on public finance management and the continuation of the reform process in order to achieve more efficient resource allocation. Benefits of trade reforms for growth cannot be reaped in the face of policy restrictions on resource movement within the domestic economy. While product market reforms have brought in competition in availability of goods and services, the gains of the reform measures cannot be realized fully unless substantial factor market reforms also take place.

The economic reform process has caused major structural changes in the Indian economy. Redeployment of resources often causes transitional problems, as there are gainers and losers in resource reallocation. Quick redeployment of resources could shorten the transition period without postponing the benefits further. At the same time, helping the losers for redeployment and retraining, where necessary, needs to be an integral part of the reform package.

While poverty has been reduced in all major states during the 1990s, the process has been very much uneven. Poverty reduction has been fast in the states which have experienced reasonable growth during the 1990s. There are also strong indications that interstate inequality has been rising during the post-reform period and poverty has become concentrated in the backward regions in central and eastern India. Adequate attention must be given to make the growth process more balanced across regions. The government's role in physical and social capital formation needs to be stepped up in the slow growing backward regions. Significant poverty reduction at the national level would require higher growth in the backward areas in the near future.

WHAT IS THE STATE OF POVERTY IN THE COUNTRY AND ITS CHARACTER? HOW DO WE MAKE GROWTH INCLUSIVE?

Economic growth is, after all, for the people. If the people are poor, if they remain unemployed, or their livelihoods are threatened, if they don't have access to clean water and clean fuel, if they do not have adequate health services, and if rural and urban development remains unsatisfactory, then growth loses its lustre. What has been the status of human development in India? Radhakrishna and Ray look at the progress in poverty removal in the country in Chapter 3, 'Poverty in India: Its Dimensions and Character'.

How much has Poverty Reduced?

During the past two decades, the process of poverty reduction has been significant. This has been well documented. The proportion of the population below the poverty line remained constant (at about 50 per cent) till the mid-1970s but registered a decline thereafter with yearly fluctuations. The decline was remarkable in the 1980s and the 1990s—from 51 per cent in 1977–8 to 39 per cent in 1987–8 and further to 26 per cent in 1999–2001 (*Economic Survey*, 2001–2). This can be attributed to higher economic growth, improvement in real wages, and proliferation of poverty alleviation programmes. The severity of poverty, reflected in the percentage of the very poor—defined as those whose total consumption expenditure is less than 75 per cent of the poverty line—has declined at a faster rate than income poverty in both rural and urban areas (Radhakrishna and Ravi 2004). It is likely that the incidence of poverty continues to decline and will become residual by the end of this decade. Despite the favourable declining trend, poverty remains a serious concern since children constitute close to half of the poor.

How are Growth and Poverty Related?

The strength of the trickle-down effect is usually measured by the elasticity of headcount poverty with respect to income. Our estimate of poverty elasticity with respect to income (per capita total expenditure) is –1.68 for rural and –1.87 for urban. Clearly, the rural–urban differences in poverty reduction cannot be attributed to the differences in the growth elasticity of poverty but to the differences in their income growth. During 1990–2001, the per capita expenditure has increased at 1.31 per cent per annum in rural areas, while it is 3.06 per cent in urban regions. Since the poor are predominant in rural areas and depend mainly on agriculture for their livelihood, achieving the goal of poverty reduction depends on the growth of agriculture. To achieve more than 3 per cent reduction rate of rural poverty, it is essential that agriculture grows at 4 to 5 per cent per annum, especially in the regions with a high concentration of poor.

Who Gained from Poverty Reduction in the 1990s?

A number of findings follow from the analysis of Radhakrishna and Ray.

(1) All the states, with the exception of Assam and Orissa, and all socio-economic groups have experienced poverty reduction between 1993–4 and 1999–2000. Assam, Orissa, Madhya Pradesh, and Uttar Pradesh have remained behind in poverty reduction. Structural factors and inadequate growth might be the major causes underlying their poor performance. In this context, it is worth mentioning that Rajasthan, a resource-poor state, performed better in poverty reduction and may have lessons to offer from its experience.

(2) Due to uneven poverty reduction across states and social groups, the poor got concentrated in less developed states and among a few vulnerable social groups. In the all-India context of rural poor, the relative share of underdeveloped states such as Bihar, Orissa, Madhya Pradesh, and Uttar Pradesh increased from 53 per cent in 1993-4 to 61 per cent in 1999-2000 and the share of the developed north-western states such as Punjab, Haryana, and Himachal Pradesh declined from 3 to 1 per cent. Interestingly, some of the better developed states such as Maharashtra, Gujarat, and West Bengal have a relatively higher share of rural poverty. The urban poor are getting concentrated in Uttar Pradesh, Maharashtra, West Bengal, Madhya Pradesh, and Andhra Pradesh.

(3) The occupational composition of the poor has also been changing. Rural poverty is getting concentrated mostly in the agricultural labour and artisan households and urban poverty in the casual labour households. It is likely that the poor will be increasingly vulnerable to risks in the labour market and suffer from transient poverty since their dependence on the casual labour market for their livelihood is rising fast in both rural and urban areas. In the agriculturally prosperous states, agricultural labour households account for the bulk of the rural poor while in less developed regions, rural poverty has extended to other occupational groups including those that are self employed in agriculture.

(4) Urban poverty reduced faster than rural poverty and was concentrated among casual labour households. This is due to faster economic growth in urban areas. But interquintile urban inequality and rural–urban inequality has been on the rise.

(5) Poverty is not merely an economic phenomenon but also a social one. Poverty is disproportionately high among scheduled castes (SCs) and scheduled tribes (STs). It is noteworthy that the share of STs in all-India poor has been on the rise. Reduction in poverty among the tribals is slower. It is noteworthy that tribals in states where they are in the minority (for example, Orissa, Madhya Pradesh) experience the worst forms of poverty. In rural areas, STs were located mainly in four states, namely, Madhya Pradesh, Orissa, Bihar, and Maharashtra. However, tribal communities in the north-east of India have performed relatively better than those from other social groups. Meghalaya, Mizoram and Nagaland had no incidence of the very poor. Poverty reduction in the north-east region of India provides a different perspective. In this region, literacy rates are high and other social indicators of development are sanguine. Despite large tribal habitations, the incidence and severity of poverty among the tribal groups are remarkably low—an achievement rarely observed elsewhere in the country.

(6) The poor among the SCs were concentrated in Uttar Pradesh, Bihar, Madhya Pradesh, and West Bengal. Also, in states where substantial poverty reduction has been achieved, those who remain poor belong to either of these disadvantaged groups. They are the last ones to benefit from poverty reduction. For instance, in 1999–2000, Punjab had 6 per cent of its rural population below the poverty line. Seventy eight per cent of them belonged to the SCs, although their share in rural population was only 38 per cent.

What have We Done to Reduce Poverty?
The Government of India has all along been giving importance to direct poverty alleviation programmes. It currently commits Rs 11,000 crore per annum on centrally sponsored schemes (CSS) including self-employment and wage-employment programmes and direct cash transfers. There are about 180 CSS administered by the Ministry of Rural Development, and implemented by states that contribute about 25 per cent to the total fiscal cost. In addition, some state governments have their own poverty alleviation schemes. The multiciplicity of the programmes is advocated on the grounds of multidimensionality of poverty and regional variations in the efficacy of the delivery system. In addition, the Government of India, through its public distribution system (PDS), supplies six essential commodities at below the market prices through 450,000 nationwide fair price shops. It commits about Rs 28,000 crore per annum for PDS. The expenditures for CSS and PDS together account for about 2 per cent of the GDP and 20 per cent of the central tax revenue. While the potential impact of a public expenditure of this magnitude on poverty reduction could be high, various surveys and evaluation studies have pointed out that the actual impact on poverty has been modest. A number of evaluation studies show that poor states benefit the least from the CSS and PDS. There are leakages in the numerous CSS which lie between 20 per cent and 70 per cent (Farrington et al. 2003). The causes of leakages were extensively analysed by various researchers. According to them, a major weakness of the CSS and PDS is their supply-driven and top-down approach with little concern for the complexities at the grassroots. The recent restructuring of schemes, including the merging of a number of schemes, focusing more attention on community/group and client-oriented schemes, and involving more panchayati raj institutions, especially gram panchayats and community-based organizations in the implementation, may, to some extent, plug the loopholes. The suggestion to identify the delivery systems that work and design schemes around them is worth exploring (Farrington et al. 2003).

What should be Done to Accelerate the Process of Poverty Reduction?

While we have seen that growth of average income leads to significant reduction in poverty, we have also seen that such trickle-down does not reach all groups and sections. Safety nets to protect the groups that are excluded or are marginalized by the process of growth are needed. There is, however, a need to go beyond the establishment of social safety nets; focus directly on providing employment and raising the income of the poor through explicit policy interventions. The experience, by and large, is that countries which are the most successful in reducing poverty are the ones which have combined rapid growth with equity promoting growth. In such a strategy public policies influence both the distribution of income and the process of income generation. It needs to be emphasized, however, that the importance of growth cannot be ignored. A strategy which focuses primarly on reducing inequality through redistribution of assets or incomes, but ignores growth, is unlikely to lead to a sustained process of poverty reduction. It may undermine the incentive system and, also, impose serious constraints in finding the resources necessary to finance targeted anti-poverty interventions in the absence of growth. Therefore, growth needs to be rapid enough to significantly improve the absolute conditions of the poor. And to have the maximum impact, there should also be an improvement in the relative position of the poor, and the share of the poor in the incremental income should be more than their share in the average.

Poverty reduction in rural areas has been less impressive in the 1990s. The reasons include: (i) poor performance of agriculture, which is a major source of livelihood for the poor; (ii) slowdown in the expansion of rural employment—high growth has, neither directly nor indirectly, created unskilled and semi-skilled jobs which benefit the poor most; and (iii) skewed spatial pattern of growth—less growth in areas in which the poor are mostly located, that is, Bihar, Orissa, Uttar Pradesh, and Madhya Pradesh. What is needed is a development strategy which results in excess supply in the product market and excess demand in the labour market. The sectors which meet the criteria are agricultural and rural non-farm sectors. Agricultural productivity improvements and growth of the non-farm sector are essential for long-term poverty eradication. This has been the process of transition from an agrarian economy towards an industrial one—adopted by many East and South East Asian countries, which resulted in a sharp decline in poverty (Barker and Dawe 2001).

What is India's Record in Improving the Nutritional Status of its Population?

Poverty, as exists in India, results in under-nutrition. While estimates of poverty from consumer expenditure surveys provide an indirect measure of poverty, a direct measure of nutritional status can provide an alternative measure of welfare. Therefore, Radhakrishna and Ray also look at the nutritional status of people in India.

Child Nutrition

They examine India's performance in the reduction of malnutrition and find it less impressive than its performance in poverty reduction. The incidence of child malnutrition is higher than that of poverty, with the highest incidence in the poorest states, and the lowest, not in the richest, but in the middle-income states with progressive, social, and food security policies.

The percentage of children suffering from malnutrition in the rural areas of the eight states covered by the National Nutrition Monitoring Bureau (NNMB) declined from 62.5 per cent in 1975–9 to 47.7 per cent in 2000–1. The annual rate of decline is less than one percentage point. Hence, about half of the children of India have not reached their physical or mental potential and a majority of them might be functionally impaired. Under these circumstances, the children of the poor communities suffering from malnutriton face a greater risk of child mortality and cannot achieve full genetic growth potential and end up as adults with small body size. Malnutrition, by virtue of its synergistic relationship with infectious diseases, has a powerful impact on child mortality and morbidity. Such a high level of wasting away of human resources should be a matter of shame for the country and, therefore, unacceptable.

The interstate variations in malnutrition levels of children are pervasive. In terms of the nutritional status of children, middle-income states such as Kerala and Tamil Nadu performed better than high income states like Maharashtra and middle income states like West Bengal. The better performances from Kerala and Tamil Nadu could be attributed to their interventions in health and nutrition programmes. Not surprisingly, poor states such as Madhya Pradesh and Orissa showed the worst performances. The north-eastern states are comparatively better in peformance than many other states and some of them have out-performed Kerala.

Household-level analysis of child malnutrition data shows that the risk of malnutrition decreases with increased household income. However, the relation between malnutrition and income is weak and, surprisingly, malnutrition persists even if poverty is eliminated. Child malnutrition is generally high among households where mothers are illiterate and have poor nutritional levels. Birth order and leafy vegetable consumption are the other important factors and so also is medical care during pregnancy.

Adult Malnutrition

The NNMB data show that in rural areas 37.4 per cent of adult males and 39.4 per cent of adult females suffered from chronic energy deficiency (CED) in 2000–1. This is largely due to poor diet and infection during childhood. Iron deficiency is widely prevalent among pregnant women. According to the latest National Family Health Survey (NFHS-2), about half of the pregnant women suffer from iron deficiency and consequent anaemia. The interstate variations are similar to those of child malnutrition. The prevalance of CED is low in Kerala and high in Gujarat, Maharashtra, and Madhya Pradesh.

How do We Change the Outcome?

Concerted efforts should be made to bridge the food energy gap of the poor. This has to be supplemented with efforts to eradicate micro-nutrient deficiency. Nutrition intervention programmes such as Integrated Child Development Services and Midday Meal Schemes should be scaled up. Nutritional status also depends on factors outside the food sector, including social, economic, and environmental conditions. Sukhatme, in his pioneering study on malnutrition, explained that conversion efficiency of food depends on the access to safe drinking water, health care, and environmental hygiene.

Srijit Mishra addresses the issue of improving the health status of the poor in Chapter 4, 'Public Health Scenario in India', and Parikh et al. address issues related to access to safe drinking water and environmental hygiene in Chapter 5, 'Lack of Energy, Water, and Sanitation and its Impact on Rural India'.

WHAT IS THE STATE OF HEALTH IN INDIA?

The expenditure on health accounts for 5.6 per cent of the total GDP while the public health expenditure is at 0.9 per cent. India has, over the years, built up a vast health infrastructure and manpower at primary, secondary, and tertiary care in the government, voluntary, and private sectors. Technological advances have made deep inroads into health services. Consequently, there has been a significant expansion in the physical provision of health services. During 1951–96, the number of hospitals and dispensaries increased from 9209 to 43,322 and hospital beds from 1.17 to 8.70 million; and during 1951–99 nursing personnel increased from 0.18 to 8.7 lakh and allopathic doctors from 0.62 to 5.0 lakhs (*Economic Survey* 2002-3). Such a massive expansion on the supply side has resulted in the eradication of leprosy, smallpox, guineaworms, and in the near eradication of polio.

However, India is far from realizing the 1978 Alma Ata declaration of 'Health for All by 2000' incorporated as certain goals into its National Health Policy, 1983. Many goals remain elusive—infant mortality at 66 per 1000 live births in 2001 falls short of the goal of 60, maternal mortality rate at 479 per 100,000 live births in 1992-3 is well above the goal of below 200, the percentage of babies with birth weight below 2.5 kg at 30 per cent (in 1993) falls short of 10 per cent, and immunization status at 42 per cent in 1998-9 is far from attaining universal coverage. Presently, less than 20 per cent of the population utilize public health facilities. What is disquieting is that about 2.2 million children die every year, and most of these are preventable. Major causes are malnutrition and inadequate supply of vaccines. Preventable and treatable diseases take a huge toll among the poor.

The health gap between the rich and the poor is large. For example, in 1998-9 the under-five mortality rate (deaths of children under five years per 1000 live births) was 46 for the richest quintile while it was 141 for the poorest. (Carr 2004). Poverty makes people vulnerable to diseases. The poor–rich gap is largely due to non accessibility of health care to the poor. To illustrate, in 1998-9, among the children aged 12 to 23 months, only 21 per cent were vaccinated in the poorest quintile, while in the richest it was 61 per cent. Among women, 16 per cent in the poorest quintile received delivery assistance from a doctor or a nurse or a midwife in contrast to 84 per cent of the women in the richest quintile who received such assistance. The poor carry disproportionately more of the burden of infectious diseases, non-communicable diseases, and death and disability due to injury. The major causes of avoidable excess deaths among the poor are malaria and TB; maternal and parental conditions with childhood diseases such as measles, tetanus, diphtheria, acute respiratory infection, and diarrhoea; malnutrition and tobacco related diseases.

There exists significant rural–urban differences. In 1998-9, the under-five mortality rate for rural areas was 104 as compared to 63 in urban India. Child mortality (death between the first and fifth birthdays) among girls was 47 per cent more than boys. Addressing this inequity will significantly reduce overall child deaths.

The health care gap is substantial across states. The bottom four states in terms of public provisioning are

Madhya Pradesh, Orissa, Uttar Pradesh, and Bihar. These states, together with Rajasthan, account for two-thirds of the infant/child deaths. Kerala, Gujarat, and Tamil Nadu have better provisioning. For example, the percentage of deliveries assisted by health professionals vary between 94 per cent in Kerala, 60 per cent in Maharashtra, 23 per cent in Bihar, and 22 per cent in Uttar Pradesh. Differences in health care spending contribute to interstate disparities. Per capita annual public expenditure on health care in 1999–2000 in Punjab was Rs 256 per annum as against Rs 50 per annum in Bihar.

How do We Improve Access to Health Care?

Strengthening health care infrastructure especially in rural areas should be of paramount importance. This can be done by augmenting equipment, supplies of medicines and manpower at primary health centres (PHCs), and improving road network. Telemedicine can be a cost-effective way of providing specialist care in rural areas—a successful example is the linking of the Apollo's secondary care centre at Aragonda, Andhra Pradesh to hospitals in Hyderabad and Chennai.

One major concern that requires immediate attention is the health care needs of the poor. The emerging private health insurance market does not provide solutions for the poor and high-risk segments of the population. Initiatives taken by some non-government organizations (NGOs) such as voluntary health service (VHS), established in 1958 in Chennai, and home-based neonatal care (HBNC) intervention in a tribal region of Maharashtra are based on community participation that include the poor and the vulnerable. Initiatives of this type emphasize preventive care and have positive health impacts. Replicating such successes on a larger scale requires a group of committed workers.

India is moving towards a market-driven health care system. There is a trend towards greater utilization of health care from private providers. Poor access/quality of public facilities may be one reason, but an outcome of this is an excessive use of diagnostic medical services. This may increase cost and also lead to misallocation of scarce resources. It is not only inefficient and iniquitous, but also compromises on the quality of care. There is also a possibility of slackening in the research and development (R&D) efforts associated with the diseases that most commonly afflict the poor. A necessary precondition for the success of private sector participation is an effective regulation of cost and quality that include clinical and non-clinical services. It should go beyond health care providers and address issues relating to the pharmaceutical industry and insurance sectors. The NGOs working in health care should also be brought under its ambit.

What is the Access to Clean Water and Fuels in Rural India?

A vast number of persons in rural India do not have easy access to clean energy, safe drinking water, and sanitation facilities. This takes a heavy toll of human health and drains much human resources. Jyoti Parikh, Kirit Parikh, and Vijay Laxmi examine these issues in Chapter 5, entitled, 'Lack of Energy, Water, and Sanitation, and its Impact on Rural India', based on a large integrated sample survey involving some 18,000 households and 80,000 persons.

What is the Drain on Human Resources due to Dirty Cooking Fuels?

Rural households in the country consume about 310 million tonnes of biofuels in a year only for cooking purposes and these biofuels are procured mostly through gathering. It is estimated that 85 million households are spending 30 billion hours per annum in gathering these fuels. While this provides livelihood to some of the poor who sell these in local markets, most households gather these for self-consumption.

Besides the drudgery of collection and transportation of these fuels, about 174 million females are exposed to an average 6.8mg/cum of respirable suspended particulate matter (RSPM) during cooking. Those who are in close proximity to the stove are sometimes exposed to even higher levels of pollution (9.2 mg/cum) than the person doing the cooking.

What is the Drain on Resources due to the Lack of Proper Access to Clean Water and Sanitation?

In rural India about 71 million households fetch water from outside by spending some 102 billion hours in a year. Further, only 7 per cent of rural households are connected to the sewerage system and only 9 per cent households have in-house toilet facilities. The opportunity cost of the time thus spent is high, particularly in terms of schooling for girls and social and economic opportunities for women.

What is the Toll on Human Health and the Economic Burden

Approximately 24 million rural adults have symptoms of respiratory diseases and around 17 million adults have serious respiratory health problems due to the use of biofuels. Moreover, 12 million children below five years of age suffer from lower respiratory infection/acute respiratory infection (LRI/ARI). Risk of respiratory diseases in women above 30 years of age is about four times higher than in younger women. Other things being equal, literacy seems to help reduce the adverse impact.

Illiterate women are at three to six times higher risk of contracting respiratory diseases compared to literate ones. The benefits of literacy impacts on the occurrence of respiratory diseases show at the primary level of education itself. Risk of respiratory and eye diseases are positively associated with lifetime exposure to the biofuels.

The economic burden due to treatment of respiratory diseases is approximately Rs 45 billion a year at 2000 prices. This is in addition to government subsidy provided to various health centres. The illnesses also lead to loss of working days, worth around Rs 47 billion per year.

Due to unsafe drinking water about 42 million adults and 27 million children in rural India suffer from water-related diseases. The expenditure incurred due to these diseases is approximately Rs 42 billion a year. The cost of human workdays lost due to water-related diseases is around Rs 131 billion in a year. Thus the total economic loss due to inadequate energy and water facilities come to over Rs 1042 billion per annum.

Rural households are willing to pay for improving the condition of their kitchens by reducing smoke, for clean drinking water, and for better sanitation. The amount they are willing to pay may be small compared to what is needed but it provides the kernel required for programmes to grow.

Access to clean energy, water, sanitation, and health services needs to be stressed for social and economic development. There are strong poverty–gender–environment linkages here. We need a holistic view to reach a consensus to set and achieve common goals in these areas.

Energy Supply and Utilization

The cooking fuel requirements of poor households in terms of fossil fuels are minuscule compared to the import of petroleum products for transportation and industries. Greater political commitment and cooperation among government ministries, development agencies, and community organizations are needed to ensure that rural women can choose from a range of cleaner fuels and energy technologies, in order to reduce their daily burdens and increase their social and economic opportunities.

We need to develop new, more effective strategies to reach the poorest households. Subsidies could be given directly to consumers (rather than suppliers), empowering them to make their own energy decisions. In addition, subsidies for rural electrification and renewable energy technologies should go to promote income-producing activities that benefit women as well as men.

It is now time to shift from academic studies on how many deaths take place due to dirty fuels and unsafe water to prevention and treatment of diseases.

Water and Sanitation Facilities

Providing access to safe drinking water upon which the health of individuals and the welfare of the people depend requires an integrated approach for comprehensive and sustainable solutions. The aim of the policy should be to provide safe sources of drinking water within peoples' reach and to minimize the hardship they face in collecting water. Priorities in sanitation should be to provide people with sanitation facilities so that water sources do not get contaminated. Human excreta are the most important disease-carrying agents due to the practice of defecation in open spaces. In some villages community toilets can be popularized, with adequate awareness programme's about the reasons to keep them clean.

Policy measures and interventions should ensure that open water sources are restricted in their use and water testing and monitoring should be done regularly at delivery points. Alternative water sources should be strengthened. The way water is stored and handled in the house significantly affects the occurrence of water-borne diseases. Awareness programmes on safe and simple techniques of handling and storing water should be promoted.

Health Care Facilities

Training of health care professionals is needed to spot the problems relating to pollution and to sensitize them to be alert. Improvement in housing design, provision for ventilation in the kitchen, and increase in female literacy can help in reducing the adverse health impacts. Health centres should be networked with information systems so that they can communicate with each other for better implementation of public health policy.

Village level cooperative transport facilities can also be developed to reduce the burden of carrying heavy loads of fuel and water over long distances.

There is a need for a comprehensive policy and programme that can integrate energy, water, sanitation, and health with other development goals such as employment generation, poverty alleviation, and sustainable livelihood so as to bring about a cohesive development in all arenas of life of the rural people, especially the rural women.

WHAT HAVE WE DONE FOR THE SOCIAL SECTOR? HOW HAS THE SOCIAL SECTOR EXPENDITURE GROWN?

The poor lack access to safe drinking water, decent housing, adequate sanitation, health care, and so on. They depend mostly on public services for their needs.

The public spending on the social sector is well short of the international norms. Even this low spending seems to have been adversely affected during the economic reform period and what is disquieting is that, due to fiscal crisis, the poor states fared badly. Mahendra Dev and Mooij have analysed the patterns in social sector expenditures, during the pre- and post-reform periods in Chapter 6, 'Patterns in Social Sector Expenditures: Pre- and Post-Reform Periods'. They review the trends in the expenditure of the centre as well as the states and address the following four questions:

(1) Has the social sector expenditure declined/increased in the post-reform period (after 1992–3) as compared to the pre-reform period (the 1980s)? The social sector expenditure of both the centre and the states, as a proportion of GDP, has not increased during the reform period except in 1999–2000. The percentages were lower in the 1990s than in the late 1980s. However, social sector expenditure as a proportion of total public expenditure has been on the higher side since the mid-1990s than in the late 1980s. In terms of per capita real expenditure, social sector expenditure has also been more since the mid-1990s than what it had been in the latter half of 1980s. Since 1993–4, the social sector expenditure by the central government, as a proportion of the GDP, was higher than that of 1990–1, although not very much different from the shares in the late 1980s. As a proportion of public expenditure and in terms of real per capita expenditure, there has been a significant increase in social sector spending since the mid-1990s. However, the growth rates per annum for the pre- and post-reform periods show that the pace of growth was much lower in the 1990s than in the 1980s. This is true for all the three measures of social expenditure development. If the state government expenditure (combining for all the 25 states) is taken as a proportion of aggregate expenditure, then the social sector spending comes down. As a proportion of GDP the increase has been marginal. In terms of per capita real expenditure, there has been some increase, and that too only in the second half of the 1990s. Again, the pace of growth was much lower in the post-reform period than in the pre-reform period.

(2) What have been the developments in education and health expenditure patterns? Neither the centre nor the states increased the expenditure on health to any considerably extent. The situation in the first half of the 1990s was especially bleak. During the the second half the per capita real expenditure on health by the states increased (no change in terms of proportion of GDP or gross state domestic product (GSDP)). Intrasectoral allocations show that there has been a shift towards maternal and child health which is a move towards social priority. With regard to education, expenditure from all the departments declined from 4.1 per cent of GDP in 1990–1 to 3.8 per cent in 1998–9. This is mainly due to the decline at the state level. The centre increased its expenditure after 1995–6. This increase is entirely due to increases in spending on elementary education and, to a large extent, (but not completely) related to the introduction and expansion of the midday meal programme. The shift within education is also towards social priority areas.

(3) What are the interstate disparities in social sector expenditures? In the first half of the 1990s, the social sector expenditure by majority of the states has not increased significantly, but in the latter half there has been an increase (in terms of per capita real expenditure). The rich and middle-income states have done better than the poor states, but there are huge variations within the groups of rich, middle, and poor states. Within the group of rich states, social sector spending is the highest in Goa. Within the group of middle-income states, West Bengal is an outlier, in the sense that its social spending has increased much less than that of the other middle-income states, while at the absolute level, it is also not very high. Within the group of poor states, the performance (in terms of spending) of Madhya Pradesh, Orissa, and Rajasthan has improved considerably, especially in the late 1990s, while Bihar and Uttar Pradesh fared less well.

(4) How does social sector expenditure in India compare with expenditure levels in other countries and with international norms? Social sector expenditure in India in the 1990s was low (according to the United Nations Development Programme (UNDP) recommended ratio) as compared to the other developing countries, and certainly as compared to East Asian countries. It is not always low as compared to what India spent in the 1980s which depends on the indicator chosen to assess social expenditure trends. But what is clear is that the pace of growth in social sector expenditure has slowed down in the post-reform period and that it is true with regard to all three indicators. The performance of various states is much worse than that of the centre.

Tasks Ahead

There are quite a few tasks ahead to achieve the goals of reducing poverty levels and providing health care for all. First, there is an urgent need for stepping up social sector expenditure. A substantial increase in the allocation for the social sector is likely to happen only when there are changes in the budget-making process. In that respect, movement towards decentralized planning and increasing awareness among the public about budgets are to be welcomed. Such type of movements can play a very important role in involving a wider group of people in the budget-making process.

Second, there is an obvious need for better utilization of the allocated resources. Poor implementation, misuse of funds, and corruption are acknowledged in various policy documents. Some of these problems have been briefly discussed in the preceeding sections while discussing the leakages in CSS and PDS. The delivery systems need to be reformed as in the case of poverty alleviation programmes.

HOW ARE WE FACING THE IPR CHALLENGE?

Comparative advantage is being determined increasingly by technological knowledge. The IPR regime thus becomes of vital importance. There is a new proactive stance of the science and technology (S&T) establishment on the IPR regime. We are eager and confident to face the challenge. A transformation of the R&D paradigm from 'publish or perish' to 'patent and prosper' has taken place. Anitha Ramanna examines the issues in Chapter 7, 'India's Patent Policy and Political Economy of Development'.

Economic reforms, liberalization, deregulation, and privatization have been opposed by people for a variety of reasons. Many public sector enterprises and institutions have not particularly welcomed the reforms. However, their response to IPR has been different.

Public sector research institutions in India adopted a proactive role on patents. The Indian Council for Scientific and Industrial Research (CSIR), the coordinating body for over 40 scientific institutes in India, was instrumental in setting the framework for patent reform. The CSIR and other public sector research institutions are part of a strong pro-patent lobby that has emerged in India who point out that greater patent protection would lead to an increase in foreign direct investment (FDI), transfer of technology, and R&D by foreign companies, and would enable domestic actors to become more innovative and acquire patents.

From 'Publish or Perish' to 'Patent and Prosper'

The CSIR promoted reforms in India's patent policy in several ways. First, through shifting the focus from publishing to patenting in research institutions; second, through the formulation of a strategy to counter the perceived negative implications of patents on traditional knowledge; third, by forging links with NGOs and international organizations on IPR issues and promoting a patent culture among scientists both inside and outside the industry.

Public sector research institutions including CSIR, the Department of Biotechnology, and the Indian Council of Agricultural Research (ICAR) are changing their focus from publishing to patenting and are increasing their patent filings in India. These institutions have also set up offices to enable them to increase their IPR activities. The Department of Biotechnology established a Patent Facilitating Cell in July 1999. The Indian Council of Medical Research (ICMR) has also created an IPR cell. The ICAR established an Intellectual Property Section that began functioning in 1998.

What Led to this Proactive Stance?

It is clear that on certain aspects of liberalization, public sector institutions may take the lead in promoting change, and may be crucial for promoting and consolidating reform. The interests of the public sector cannot be easily defined based on assigning to the public sector the objective function of maximization of social welfare or the bureaucrats' objective function. Public sector institutions could have defined their interests in terms of opposition to patent reforms and built coalitions with actors who advocated resistance to change. The fact that these institutions shifted their interests and no longer believed that reverse engineering was the best strategy was strongly shaped by how the interests of the public sector were defined. Patents, in one sense, were perceived as a means for earning revenue as old sources of funding were being reduced. This points to the fact that preferences and interests of the public sector institutions cannot be presumed, are subject to change, and are influenced by external factors and the role of other actors.

Who will do Socially Relevant Research?

As public sector institutions take on a greater commercial orientation, they may become internally competitive and may also become competitors of the private sector. While competition may increase efficiency, there are continued difficulties in defining what socially useful research objectives the public sector should adopt. Concerns are also being currently expressed internationally regarding the impact of IPR on the direction of public sector research. There is a need to evolve a crucial balance between promoting patentable innovations and directing research towards social objectives to correct for market failures.

WHAT IS THE ROLE OF EMERGING TECHNOLOGIES IN INDIA'S DEVELOPMENT?

The global economy is increasingly and rapidly becoming a knowledge economy. Technological developments are taking place at an ever-increasing pace. While we have benefited from the information and communication technologies (ICTs), we still have many more opportunities coming our way. Way back in 1999, in IDR: 1999–2001, we had pointed out the tremendous scope for growth of the information technology enabled services (ITES) sector. The growth of ITES has been spectacular. Yet more is possible. What role the emerging technologies, especially ICTs, can play in India's development and how their potential may be realized, is examined by Jayan Thomas in Chapter 8, 'New Technologies for India's Development'.

New technologies promise great opportunities for India's development. Between 1992–3 and 2001–2, India's software industry has been growing at an average annual rate of approximately 50 per cent—a rate more than three times faster than the rate of growth of the country's whole economy (both the growth rates at current prices) during the same period. In recent years, there has been a significant increase in outsourcing of all kinds of knowledge-based activities to India from firms in developed countries. It is estimated that, by 2008, exports by India's information technology (IT) industry will form 35 per cent of India's total exports and 6 per cent of the total global IT exports. It is also estimated that the IT industry will generate 2.2 million jobs in India by 2008. The fast growth of the software industry and ITES in India in recent years is driven, largely, by the relatively low wage levels of the country's English-speaking professionals.

New technologies are also potent tools for the development of the people in rural areas and people belonging to disadvantaged sections of society—as a few of the ongoing experiments in various Indian states attest. ICTs have been used to enhance effectiveness in the delivery of health services in rural and remote locations; in programmes to impart literacy among adults; and as a tool for improving efficiency in agriculture and traditional industries. ICTs have been used in governance to speed up the processes of interaction between citizens and the administration. In many ways, ICTs can be sources of empowerment to the poor and to those sections of the population, including women, who are traditionally excluded from development. Biotechnology can ensure low-cost and efficient health care to India's population, and can come up with agricultural techniques suited for small farmers in the country.

There are, however, important hurdles to reaping such opportunities promised by the new technologies. India is far behind most countries with respect to the physical infrastructure for the spread of digital technologies. In 2001, the total number of subscribers of telephone mainlines and cellular phones per 100 persons was 4.4 in India, compared with 110.6 in South Korea and 111.8 in the United States of America (USA). The number of Internet subscribers per 100 population was 0.7 in India, compared with 4.7 in Brazil and 50.1 in the USA in that year. There exist large variations in telephone density across different Indian states. Rural areas of the country lag far behind urban areas with respect to the physical infrastructure for telecommunications network. In 2003, telephone density (mainlines per 1000 people) varied from 268.5 in Delhi to 13.2 in Bihar. Telephone density in India's rural areas was 14.9 and telephone density in the country's urban areas was 151.6 at that point in time. In India, Internet users are heavily concentrated in urban areas. Limited availability of bandwidth and the near non-availability of content in the Indian languages are among the important constraints to the effective use of the Internet in India's rural areas.

The most difficult hurdle to development aided by the new technologies in India is the high level of illiteracy and social inequalities that continue to prevail in the country. In India, educational achievements are low in rural areas, among females, among members of the socially disadvantaged castes, and in the states of Bihar, Madhya Pradesh, Orissa, Rajasthan, and Uttar Pradesh. The Indian states have not been committed enough in ensuring basic education of the country's population.

For new technologies to make their impact felt across wider sections of India's population, there is an urgent need to step up investment in physical infrastructure, particularly telecom infrastructure. More importantly, public policy in India should realize that benefits from investment in primary education are ever so great in this emerging era of knowledge-based growth—and the costs of under-investment are ever so high.

To meet the challenges from the emerging knowledge economy, it is also important to enhance domestic investment in India in R&D. Research efforts in ICTs should primarily focus attention on the needs of the domestic market. Similarly, there is a need to enhance domestic research in biotechnology, addressing India's problems and concerns, particularly food security.

Lastly, public policy in India must also realize that the new technologies can only be very efficient tools for development and that they cannot replace the much needed policy interventions in income growth and redistribution.

IMPORTANCE OF NEW AGRICULTURAL VARIETIES

The importance of higher agricultural growth for both poverty redressal and sustaining high overall growth is well recognized. High yielding varieties have played a critical role in our agricultural development in the past.

Poverty ratios are lower in states such as Punjab, Haryana, Andhra Pradesh, and Tamil Nadu that have higher adoption rates of modern varieties of rice. The modern rice technology and reliable irrigation are crucial inputs for improving the rice sector. Aldas Janaiah in Chapter 9, 'Hybrid Rice: The Indian Experience and Comparison with the Rest of Asia', examines the role of hybrid rice.

Is Food Security under Threat?

The sense of complacency in the demand–supply balance of food grains began disappearing since the early 1990s, when it was observed that rice production growth was lower than population growth in many Asian countries reversing the upward trend in the per capita availability of rice from domestic production. Yield increases in rice, achieved during the green revolution era, started to erode for intensive irrigated rice systems. Most of the rice-land for this eco-system are already cultivated with modern varieties (MVs), and the yield has reached almost 6.0 tonnes per hectare, a level at which the yield has remained stagnant in Japan and Korea over the last two decades. On the other hand, crop yields are very low in the poverty-ridden rain-fed areas of eastern India.

Is Hybrid Rice an Alternative?

The policy-makers and research managers in tropical Asia considered the hybrid rice as a readily available technology to bring another rice revolution by reversing the yield-declining trend in irrigated environments, and raising crop yields in the rain-fed regions. Further, China's miraculous success in the popularization of hybrid rice in the late 1970s and the 1980s has motivated some countries in tropical Asia to invest more resources for hybrid rice R&D since the early 1990s. Hybrid rice R&D programmes over the past one decade resulted in the development and release of some promising hybrid varieties for farmers in tropical Asian countries including India. However, many farmers who grew hybrid rice initially for one or two seasons have started dropping out from hybrid rice cultivation in the irrigated regions, while hybrid rice was found non-suitable for rain-fed regions in India and in other countries. Therefore, the rate of hybrid rice adoption by the farmers is too limited and scattered in these countries, except in Vietnam.

Why Don't Farmers Accept Hybrid Rice?

Concern has been raised whether the yield gain of current rice hybrids over the best popular inbred varieties is adequate to induce farmers for adoption of this technology. Hybrid rice had higher yield under farmers' fields in all study-sites except in Tamil Nadu. Yield gains of hybrid rice were associated with additional production costs in all study sites, and lower market price for output in some study sites. Thus, many farmers are dropping out from hybrid rice cultivation after one or two seasons of experience. However, Vietnam,—which has agro-ecological, political, socio-economic, and institutional features very similar to those of south China—is the only country in tropical Asia where hybrid rice adoption has been growing.

Lack of consumer acceptance of hybrid rice grain due to poor cooking, eating, and keeping qualities leading to lower market price (especially in India), lower head-rice recovery, more broken rice after milling, higher costs of hybrid rice seed, formation of sterile grains in the productive tillers were serious constraints that led to the discontinuance of hybrid rice cultivation. Thus, the next generation of rice technology for the Asian tropics ought to focus on farmer–consumer acceptable new hybrids with improved grain quality.

An important policy implication is that we need to strengthen our agricultural research establishment if we want to step up agricultural growth and accelerate poverty reduction.

IMPORTANCE OF TRANSACTION COSTS: HOW CAN WE FACILITATE TRADE?

The Indian economy is fast globalizing in the sense that it is getting integrated with the world economy. Trade and technical progress are important elements of this process. How can we stimulate trade? So far we have concentrated on tariff reduction and exchange rate regimes for it. Our trade has been constrained not just by the tariff regime but also by high transaction costs, which can play an important role here. Nirmal Sengupta and Moana Bhagabati examine the issues connected with trade facilitation in Chapter 10, 'Trade Facilitation'.

An import/export transaction involves a series of processes which translate into costs, both in time and money. This adds to the cost of doing business and ultimately affects a country's growth rates in international trade. The term 'trade facilitation' is used for a set of tasks designed to reduce the transaction cost incurred in trade. It includes numerous areas like simplification of data and documentation, faster clearance, dwell time reduction, efficient risk management, facilitation by financial agencies, transparency and due process in judicial and administrative matters, simplification of cross-border procedures for movement of goods, etc. Trade facilitation applies for domestic trade too but is more important in international trade where procedures and regulations are higher. As tariff levels have declined over the years, transaction costs have acquired increasing importance in international trade. Several international agencies are working on trade facilitation. In World Trade Organization (WTO) agenda, this is one of the new (Singapore) issues under consideration.

Consistent with liberalization and opening up of the economy in the early 1990s, India has initiated trade facilitation at various fronts. To cope with a significant increase in its maritime trade after 1990, India has made considerable improvements in roads, port facilities, berthing capacity, facilities for storage and movement of goods and vehicular traffic, containerization of general cargo, etc. But there are still large gaps between what is needed and what is in existence. Turnaround time at the ports fell to 2.5 days in 2002–3 from 4.1 days the year before, but is still well below international standards. New procedures for better capacity utilization of coastal vessels have resulted in reduction of freight costs. To develop Indian ports as consolidation hub ports, the government has allowed consolidation of Less than Container Load (LCL) cargoes at Indian ports. Electronic Data Interchange (EDI) has been introduced at almost all the major ports and air cargo complexes. The Chennai Port Trust is moving towards facilitating paperless transaction for port users. An EDI gateway project is being introduced to enable remote filing of customs declarations and communications with trading partners, by the importers and exporters, from their offices. Special attention is given to the speedy handling of cargo for reducing its dwell time. The objective is to reduce dwell time of exports to 12 hours, and of imports to 24 hours to conform to internationally accepted norms. An EXIM Bank study estimated that in 1998 Indian firms perceived avoidable transaction costs as about 10.78 per cent of export revenues. A re-survey found that several reforms succeeded in eliminating about 60 per cent of this in just five years. It is claimed that approximately 80 per cent of daily air cargo shipments are assessed on the same day by customs.

Significant improvements have been made in other spheres of trade facilitation. Task Force on Indirect Taxes (Kelkar Committee) dealt with trade facilitation alongside tariff reduction. All the rules and notifications are available real time on the Directorate General of Foreign Trade (DGFT) website and 75 per cent of the licence applications are being filed and processed online. Several attempts were made in the past to simplify documents, but few have been pursued further. The present format of the Shipping Bill, evolved in 1991, is the only notable success in simplification of data and documentation. The simplification in tariff structure in the past few years has, in turn, simplified the customs clearance procedures to a great extent. The government has reduced the scale of examination for export goods considerably and also simplified the procedure for examination. A codified risk management module has been tested recently for import consignments. Efforts are being made to replace the existing system of concurrent audit of import documents by post-clearance audit. Regulations have been framed to allow import and export through the courier mode. As a step towards modernization, the major and minor ports are being privatized and corporatized. A Tariff Authority for Major Ports (TAMP) was established for regulation of tariffs. The financial agencies related to export and import and banking institutions are involved at all stages of the export–import business cycle. International standard practices are being introduced in these spheres. Further improvements have been made in review and appeal procedures, and other spheres of judicial and administrative systems. Steps have been taken to introduce advance rulings procedure.

However, many of these reforms have not made much impact because of some serious bottlenecks. Infrastructures and equipments are either insufficient, obsolete, or poorly maintained. Legal changes that are needed to make many facilitation measures effective, are slow. A serious problem is that the measures taken in India are not always in harmony with international systems. Problems are also the result of a lack of positive approach and service orientation on the part of the officers and the staff. Even after success, pilot projects are not extended for a long time. The readiness of agencies and companies to move into a different environment is constrained by a number of factors. Policies and programmes are needed to overcome these problems.

India is a natural hub for the trade activities of several of its neighbours. Though it has taken a number of steps towards forging free trade agreements with its neighbouring countries, the success achieved has not been uniform. Excessive border dwell times are common. With some neighbours there is a thriving cross-border trade through informal channels which need to be contained by further facilitation of formal trade. With some others there are considerable delays in processing at the borders. Infrastructure conditions and bilateral agreements regulating trade with neighbouring countries need a lot of improvement.

Benefits of trade facilitation arise both directly and indirectly, from reduction of time and cost of transactions and, in turn, from increased volume of trade. Excessive regulation curtails private sector participation and competition, thereby stifling entrepreneurship and private investment. Lack of predictability entails significant disadvantages for Small and Medium Enterprises (SMEs) and enterprises in developing countries. Also, for India to benefit from trade facilitation, domestic reforms must match with trade facilitation in international trade. Otherwise, domestic traders will be at a disadvantage while global trade will be privileged. Similarly, if restrictive Non-Tariff Barriers (NTBs) like Sanitary and Phytosanitary Measures (SPS) prevail in developed countries they reduce the benefits of trade facilitation undertaken by countries like India.

A Healthy Banking Sector

Along with integration with global trade, manufacturing, and services (which we had elaborated in past IDRs), financial integration is also a part of globalization. The Capital Account Convertibility Committee had recommended that an important precondition was the health of the banking sector. We have made significant progress in this direction. For example, we require the banks to follow international norms of capital adequacy and risk management. The latter has become particularly important now as the derivatives and options markets develop. The norms for banks, however, have to be set in a consistent manner across countries so that Indian banks do not suffer from a competitive disadvantage. Dilip Nachane, Partha Ray and Saibal Ghosh examine these issues in Chapter 11, 'The New Basel Capital Accord: Rationale, Design, and Tentative Implications for India'.

The Switzerland-based Bank for International Settlement (BIS) sets up norms for international harmonization of financial regulation. In recent years, the international harmonization of financial regulation has been the subject of considerable attention from academics and policy-makers alike. The Basel Capital Accord of 1988 was the outcome of a long-drawn-out initiative to strive for greater international uniformity in prudential capital standards for banks' credit risks. However, in the wake of considerable dissatisfaction with the provisions of the 1988 Accord, a revised accord (Basel II) was proposed in 1999 which addressed several of the shortcomings of the earlier accord. Nachane, Roy, and Ghosh also examine the implication for India of the new Basel Capital Accord.

What is the New Basel Accord?

The Basel II rests on three pillars: (a) minimum capital requirement, (b) supervisory review process, and (c) market discipline.

Much of the concern about the Basel II comes from the first pillar of minimum capital requirements. Banks have to maintain adequate capital to account for different risks. How the risk is measured becomes critical. Banks, under the new accord, can choose from the following three variants to measure risks, namely, (a) a basic standardized model (modified version of the existing approach); (b) an internal rating-based (IRB) foundation model; and (c) an advanced IRB model. While the basic standardized model is based on the ratings of the external rating agencies like Moody's or Standard and Poor's, a basic requirement for the foundation or advanced IRB model is to develop the bank's own internal rating system. It may be noted that, depending on which model is chosen, the capital requirement will vary—a fact having important implications for the emerging market economies. A noteworthy feature of the Basel II is that it allows for a separate treatment of credit risk, market risk, and operational risk.

Much of the discussion stimulated by the Basel II has focused on its standardized approach to the risk weighting of different elements among the assets of a bank. This is because of the proposed reliance on external credit assessment institutions in delineating risk weights. While the standardized approach is, in principle, close to the existing arrangement, under the IRB approach, banks will be allowed to use their internal estimates of borrowers' creditworthiness, subject to supervisory validation. A crucial role in the IRB approach is assigned to Value-at-Risk (VaR) models, which are estimates of the extent of loss of the value of a bank's portfolio for a given probability.

The new Basel accord also provides a menu of approaches towards measurement of operational risk, that is, risks arising from management failures. The second pillar of the new Basel accord focuses on improving the supervisory review process and views the role of supervisory review as a critical complement to capital requirement and market discipline. It emphasizes that, despite improving the risk sensitivity of the minimum capital requirements, supervisors need to take a comprehensive view on how banks handle their risk management and internal capital allocation process. Subject to shortcomings in these, supervisors could require higher than the minimum capital target from a given institution.

The potential of market discipline (the third pillar of the Basel II) to reinforce capital regulation depends on the disclosure of reliable and timely information with a view to enabling banks' counter parties to make well-founded risk assessments. The information needs to be supplemented by an analysis of factors affecting the banks' capital position. Moreover, banks are encouraged to disclose ways in which they allocate capital among their different activities. The disclosures envisaged under this pillar need to be made on a semi-annual basis.

What would be the Impact on India?

As far as the impact of the Basel II on banking systems of less developed countries (LDCs) is concerned, three major concerns have been voiced. First, that the application of IRB is costly and discriminates against the smaller banks. Second, capital requirements, unless adjusted for cyclical fluctuations, are very likely to exacerbate these fluctuations. Third, a problem of adverse selection arises, because only those banks which are likely to benefit from IRB will adopt the approach, while other banks will hold on to the standardized approach. Overall, the amount of banking capital is liable to decrease below the safe limits.

What is Our Reaction?

The RBI, in its comments on the Second Consultative Document, pointed out that the Basel II would involve a shift in direct supervisory focus to the implementation issues, and that banks and the supervisors would be required to invest large resources in upgrading their technology and human resources to meet the minimum standards. It came down forcefully on the increasing reliance on external rating agencies in the regulatory process on the ground that such a move would undermine the initiative of banks in enhancing their risk management policies and practices and in upgrading internal control systems.

While the RBI agreed with the view that the focus of the Basel II might be primarily on internationally active banks, it contended that, after a period of time, all 'significant' banks would be expected to adhere to it. It was, however, pointed out that the standardized approach might not suit the needs of the smaller banks. As a consequence, it suggested a simplified standardized approach for those banks that are not internationally active.

The Basel II is thus likely to pose profound challenges for the Indian banking system. Some of these consequences could force considerable internal adjustment on banks—a realization which has been gradually dawning among banking circles in India.

WHY HAS NOT HIGH FISCAL DEFICIT LED TO INFLATION AND DISASTERS?

Apart from the challenges from globalization, the persistent high fiscal deficit is a cause for concern. The rating agencies downgrade us and we have to pay more for money in the international market. Many economists feel strongly that this is not sustainable and that it will come home to roost. There are, however, some puzzles here that are addressed by Ashima Goyal in Chapter 12, 'Puzzles in Indian Performance: Deficits without Disasters'.

Uneven behaviour of investment in the post-reform period was a major factor that was keeping Indian growth below potential in the late 1990s. Perceived increase in risk and adverse expectations prevented investment from rising.

The fiscal deficit is expected to raise interest rates as demand for funds rise. Excess demand raises expected inflation, and expected depreciation of the currency. Since sufficient domestic and foreign savings were available to compensate for government borrowing, the high fiscal deficit did not crowd out private investment or raise risk and interest rates. A sign of the absence of excess demand was that the fiscal deficit did not lead to a current account deficit. Foreign exchange reserves accumulated. Adequate domestic supply of goods and imports were important explanations of low inflation.

The factors that have shown much larger relative variation in the reform period are nominal interest and exchange rates. A steep rise in nominal interest rates reduces the net worth of firms. Since Indian firms did not have access to instruments in the capital market to fully diversify risk, a fall in net worth raised risk aversion and reduced activity. High and fluctuating nominal rates may have added to exogenous shocks. Thus policies and imperfect capital markets amplified the shocks. These kept business expectations at low growth paths, and thus reduced private investment. In the 1990s, short-term nominal interest rates were raised in periods of expected depreciation of the currency, and affected long-term rates with a lag that is reducing. Reducing volatility in nominal exchange rates through monetary tightening was achieved initially at too great a cost in terms of foregone growth and adverse expectations. Macro policies need to be designed to lower volatility in key macroeconomic variables and market mechanisms developed to lower the impact of volatility faced by firms and households.

The second factor raising uncertainty was that exposing manufacture to international competition had been delayed too long. The fear of future competition initially caused paralysis from perceived risk, but by 2003, through lowered cost and improved quality, competitiveness was attained. The fall in bank loans and slump in stock markets also contributed to perceptions of higher risk, but this may have been part cause and part effect of the slowdown.

A reduction in real interest rates and a rise in growth is an effective way to reduce government deficits. It was the contrary movements in these two variables that were responsible for rising fiscal deficits in the late 1990s. Indian nominal interest rates fell smoothly, especially since 2001, despite high government deficits, and aggressive sterilization, showing the opportunities that had existed to reduce interest rates. But inflation fell even faster so that real interest rates remained high, even as growth continued to be low. However, the stable softening nominal interest rate regime, and rise in infrastructure spending, succeeded in stimulating higher industrial growth by 2003. Lower interest rates encouraged housing construction and consumer expenditure, which, along with road building, stimulated industry.

The analysis suggests that macro policies can stimulate growth, make it easier to undertake deep reform, and the latter can reinforce growth, allowing it to reach potential.

What are the Emerging Issues and Possible Solutions to the Urban Transport Challenge?

Urbanization takes place along with economic development. The automobile culture is spreading rapidly in the country. Transport problem in the cities has become a major problem for its implications on the efficient functioning of a city, the quality of urban life, and for energy sector policies. Sudhakar Yedla looks at these problems in Chapter 13, 'Urban Transportation: Trends, Alternatives, and Policy Issues'.

The vehicular stock is on the rise in all urban centres. However, class I cities like Hyderabad and Ahmedabad are fast catching up with the mega cities with respect to the vehicular stock as well as with the level of pollution.

There is a considerable difference between the registered vehicles and on-road vehicles. Hence, it was suggested that on-road vehicles rather than registered vehicles, be considered for traffic management plans and emission control strategies.

Garaging was noted to be another major issue affecting transport planning in urban centres. About 70 per cent of commercial vehicles filling fuel in fuel stations in Delhi were found to be garaging outside the city. In the case of Hyderabad, the 2-wheelers garaging outside were found to be very high (around 25 per cent). This essentially leads to an under-estimation of pollution, because these vehicles plying on city roads are not considered in the calculation as they are registered elsewhere. Similar problem is noticed with traffic that could be bypassed.

Trends in ambient air quality were analyzed and it was found that some cities like Delhi have been experiencing improved air quality because of certain initiatives taken over the past few years. However, class I cities like Hyderabad and Ahmedabad have been experiencing rising environmental emissions.

Lack of infrastructure and additional costs were found to be major barriers for the implementation of alternative transport options like compressed natural gas (CNG).

An integrated approach is needed to address the various issues concerning urban transportation, namely, fuels, technology, adaptability, social costs, policy solutions, and institutional arrangement. From the efforts made in this chapter it is evident that various issues need to be addressed in integration to achieve sustainable transportation. Certain critical issues like the difference of on-road stock from the registered stock, garaging differences, and barriers to the adaptation of alternative technologies have been brought out in the debate. The present 'reactive' approach to urban transportation problems needs to be substantiated with proper planning of urban transportation systems and management techniques in class I cities to control the rising traffic problems and the resulting environmental pollution.

India's Strengths and Weaknesses

The Indian economy is showing signs of health. The growth rate in the fiscal year April 2003–March 2004 is expected to exceed 8.0 per cent. The inflation rate is a modest 5 per cent, Foreign exchange reserves have crossed the US$ 100 billion mark. The interest rates are low. The half-yearly results of the corporate sectors show robust profits. Exports are growing at 10 per cent in US dollar terms. The BJP ruled government had launched a loud campaign to spread the 'feel-good factor' and to persuade the people that India is shining. However, the Indian economy has been so many times on the verge of take-off that one tends to be skeptical that this time will be any different. Moreover, the stunning defeat of the BJP at the May 2004 elections indicates that something is wrong in the country. Also there have been warnings that while India may be shining, Bharat, that lives in rural areas and urban slums, is wilting.

We feel that the Indian economy has a number of strengths and that it can have sustained high growth for some years to come. It can be a shining star in the heavens and not a passing comet. However, this will depend on what we do to prevent Bharat from wilting. India can shine only if Bharat also glows.

Prospects of Growth for The Year 2003–4

Was the 8.0 per cent growth in 2003–4 over 2002–3 'just an outcome of good monsoon and can we continue to do as well or better next year?' The 9 per cent growth rate of agriculture certainly contributed to the high growth rate. However, a substantial part of the impact of high growth rate of agriculture is usually realized in the following year. In 10 out of 12 years since 1970 when agriculture grew by more than 5 per cent, the growth rate of non-agriculture in the year following the good agricultural year was higher than in the same year. Also the meteorological department has predicted a 100 per cent normal monsoon. Thus domestic demand for non-agriculture will be healthy this year. Also the export demand is likely to grow. Moreover, the excess capacity in industries created in the mid-1990s seems to have been exhausted and new investments in the industrial sector are required. A pick up in the demand for capital goods seems to confirm this. A higher growth in the industry and services sectors can be expected. Thus, at least for the next year, even a reasonable monsoon and a 3 per cent growth in agriculture and 8.5 per cent growth in non-agriculture will keep us going at the rate of 7 per cent.

Trade

The major reforms over the past decade have been in the area of trade and domestic deregulation. Openness of the economy has led to increase in the level of trade. In 2002–3 India's exports showed a growth rate of 17.9 per cent and reached a level of US$ 51 billion.

Export growth this year seems to have done as well if not better, despite an appreciation of the rupee against the US dollar of more than 5 per cent, on the average. What is even more noteworthy is that India is now exporting engineering goods such as automobiles and motorbikes all over the world, including industrialized countries, competing on both quality and price. Exports of manufactures now constitute 75 per cent of India's exports. With the expected buoyancy in the global economy this year, India's exports should continue to do well. To some extent India's exports have boomed due to the pump priming President Bush had done in the US economy. Yet this will continue till the US elections in November 2004, so, at least for the coming year, we should do well. Also, India's trade with the developing countries of Asia is growing rapidly. It has reached a level of US$ 20 billion. Since the Asian countries are growing rapidly, this is a good sign for India's growth prospect.

Indian Software and Services Market

A large part of the export earnings come from invisibles, which include software and ITES. These have been growing rapidly. India's IT market has grown rapidly from Rs 5450 crores in 1994–5 to Rs 79,337 crores in 2002–3. The boom is continuing. Suddenly, the advantage of software services, in IT-enabled back-office services, as well as in designing, entertainment, and creative literature are all now seen as drivers of further rapid growth. After all, services are the ultimate luxury goods. When your stomach is full, you want to eat in a gourmet restaurant. When your closet is full, you desire designer clothes. When you have leisure you want to be entertained. One can look at the growth of the software sector and its growing importance. This market has grown from 0.72 per cent of GDP in 1997–8 to 2.38 per cent of GDP by 2002–3. Employment has also risen dramatically in this sector. The importance of this development goes beyond the numbers. The sense of 'we can do anything' that it has generated is precious. Suddenly Indians are willing to take the risk and venture into new areas. Also important is that the English-speaking non-specialized graduate is no longer only fit to be just a clerk in a boring bureaucracy. She has an asset that earns good salary. The uneasiness that job loss due to outsourcing creates in industrialized countries is reflected in the stance taken by the USA's Presidential candidate, John Kerry. Yet the benefits of outsourcing to firms in industrialized countries is so large that these firms cannot neglect outsourcing if they are to remain competitive. We can thus expect ITES to keep growing, though there may be some hiccups on the way.

Industrial Growth

Industrial growth is now picking up. The dramatic fall in interest rate and the ability to borrow at low rates in the international markets have increased the profitability of Indian industries. Instead of credit at 14 per cent or more, large companies are able to raise money at 6 per cent to 8 per cent. Even net of the non-business income the profits have been good. Non-food credit off-take has increased and so has the production of investment goods. The industry is also showing productivity growth. In a number of industries we have become globally competitive. These include steel, pharmaceuticals, and automobile industries. Thus industrial growth is on the upswing.

For the small-scale units, however, credit is somewhat hard to get. Banks find it easier and less risky to lend to the government whose appetite seems to be endless.

Roads

The infrastructure scene has witnessed dramatic improvements in the last few years. The then prime minister, Atal Behari Vajpayee's National Highways Development Programme (NHDP) has been a roaring success. Some recent slippages notwithstanding, it is already benefiting the Indian economy. The NHDP was followed up with a Gram Sadak Yojana that will connect all the villages with all-weather roads. Such connectivity is vital for rural development, for markets to be integrated, and for farmer-producers to get better prices.

Communication

In today's world of ICT, communication connectivity is critical for competitiveness. Telephone was considered a luxury good by Indian planners. Rajiv Gandhi and Sam Pitroda changed that mindset. They introduced the Subscriber Trunk Dialling (STD) booths that dot our cities and countryside. Their ubiquitousness is a proof of the need, demand, and usefulness of communication. It used to be that to get a landline one had to wait for 10 years in some cities. Liberalization has seen a dramatic improvement. Today you can get a phone, certainly a mobile phone, on demand. Finally, we have woken up to the fact that telecommunication is a vital factor of production and critical for efficiency.

Power—The Most Critical Infrastructure

Power shortages have been endemic in India. They persist even today. In Delhi, in May 2004, a year after privatization, outages and power cuts are almost a daily affair. What to speak of the problems faced by Bharat? Even after 10 years of reforms by stealth, we have not yet got our act together. The regulators are still learning and experimenting. Privatization should improve efficiency and reduce cost. It should give cheaper power to consumers. Instead we see increase in prices even for those who were not subsidized earlier, without any improvement in the quality of supply. A promising development, however, is the development of power trading on the availability-based tariff. Under this system power is traded by 15 minute blocks and the price depends on the frequency. With the frequency of 50 cycles per second the price is Rs 1.40 per unit. When there is excess supply and frequency increases, the price drops and when there is excess demand and frequency decreases, the price rises steeply. Anyone can sell power to anyone on this market. If we can make the power market function well we can feel optimistic that the power situation will see a dramatic change in the near future. It will bring in the large number of captive power plants amounting to nearly 20 per cent of installed capacity in the country, to supplement power supply. (Parikh 2003). This can remove a very important bottleneck that has stifled India's growth in the past.

Resilience

The Indian economy has acquired a lot of resilience. Its ability to withstand shocks has improved. With a reserve exceeding US$ 100 billion, oil price swings do not paralyse the economy. A buffer stock of food grains large enough—perhaps too large—to withstand any weather sequence gives further confidence that growth would not be easily interrupted.

IS BHARAT WILTING? THE CHALLENGES

The Indian economy is indeed shining but is Bharat, that lives in villages and urban slums, wilting? The election results would seem to indicate so.

Poverty, Inequity, and Employment

Some concerns that throw a shadow on all the shine of India are the slowdown in the growth rate of employment and the rising inequities in a number of ways. Employment growth in rural areas has slowed down to 1.3 per cent per annum over 1993–4 to 1999–2000 compared to 1.8 per cent over 1983 to 1993–4. This rate is much below the growth rate of the labour force. In urban areas too the rate has slowed down over these periods to 2.4 per cent from 2.6 per cent. Thus reforms do not seem to have led to labour intensive development. This is not too surprising as the over-staffed public sector expansion slowed down during the 1990s, many voluntary retirement schemes were introduced, and, as we still have not carried out labour law reforms nor abolished completely small scale reservation, employment expansion in the private sector has not been as fast as might have been expected. With the growth in trade, the economy would have expanded activities in labour intensive sectors with these reforms.

Yet the poverty indicators do show improvement. From 1993–4 to 1999–2000 the percentage of the very poor (defined as those below 75 per cent of state specific poverty line) fell from 14.7 per cent to 8.2 per cent at the all-India level. In almost all states except Assam and Orissa, there have been significant reductions, and even Bihar and Uttar Pradesh show more than 50 per cent reduction.

There is also some reduction in under-nutrition in rural areas. The incidence of under-nutrition has come down from 56.2 per cent in 1991–2 to 50.5 per cent in 2000–1. Under-nutrition is here defined in terms of weight for age, which is below two standard deviations from the median. While the reduction may be welcome the high incidence is indeed shameful.

The feeling of inequity also seems to be growing at many levels. If we look at the rate of growth of per capita consumption expenditure, we find that in rural areas it was higher for the bottom 30 per cent than for the middle 40 per cent or for the top 30 per cent over the 1990s. This means that rural inequity has gone down. However, the growth rate of per capita urban consumption expenditure was 2.27 per cent per year—much higher compared to 1.40 per cent for rural people. Within urban population too the growth rate of the top 30 per cent was 2.55 per cent compared to 1.49 per cent for the bottom 30 per cent. The inequity between rural and urban areas and within urban population has indeed increased. Perhaps the sense of inequity is further aggravated by the constant exposure to the lifestyle of the rich and famous, reported daily on 'Page 3' of national newspapers, creating a sense of deprivation and jealousy in people.

Bharat is not wilting as the improvement in poverty figures show, but if we do not take care it may. With the growing inequity Bharat may look lustreless. We may also lose the shine off India.

We have yet to overcome many obstacles—some of which are of our own creation—to ensure a broad-based growth that is inclusive and which can pull Bharat up side by side with India. Among these are the following: employment generation, labour laws, small-scale industry (SSI) reservation, provision of *Bijlee–Pani–Sadak* (electricity–water–roads) to all, poor human development, a large educational backlog which is becoming ever more important for Bharat, a slow judicial system, fiscal deficit, and political problems of Ram Mandir and Kashmir.

Employment Generation

Employment generation has to have one of the highest priority for the new government. Of course, employment has to be in productive activities that earn good wages. We have seen that economic growth does not generate the needed employment in an environment where the public sector is contracting and the private sector does not have the incentives to employ labour-intensive techniques. The most effective measures for sustained and remunerative employment generation are, ironically, labour law reforms and abolition of SSI reservations. At the same time we should promote agricultural growth and launch a nationwide employment guarantee scheme that is designed to build rural infrastructure and improve land productivity.

Labour Laws and SSI Reservation

Protection of organized labour had been carried to extremes in the past and it had stifled growth of employment. There is now a greater appreciation of this. Yet we have still some way to go to provide flexibility to production units while protecting reasonable rights of workers. Some of the promises made by past budgets have yet to be fulfilled.

Even today SSIs are protected from domestic large-scale manufacturers by reserving certain products for the small-scale units. There is, however, a serious anomaly as the same products manufactured by a large-scale product can be easily imported. We need to scrap this reservation policy. These two are vital reforms to stimulate labour intensive growth and employment.

Bijlee–Pani–Sadak and Shiksha

Once Bijlee, Pani, and Sadak are provided, people demand *Shiksha* (education). Our performance in primary education has been very poor. The literacy level of only 65 per cent attained after 57 years of independence is a shame. For an economy that aspires to grow rapidly in today's global knowledge economy, it is a great handicap. India must educate all her people to their best potential. It is not enough to see that all children get quality education for at least eight years—they need to be educated till Class 12. Education till that level must be made free and compulsory. Today many states do not provide public schools beyond Class 8, thus depriving the poor and rural children from high school education. We also need a drive for near 100 per cent adult literacy. The burden of poor-quality education is borne by all but more so by the rural and urban poor.

Poor Human Development

In spite of the shine of economic growth, poverty still persists in India. India spends large amount of resources on anti-poverty programmes. Unfortunately, the targeting effectiveness is very low and efficiency poor. A whole new approach is needed to make them effective. The poor also suffer from poor access to health facilities, poor sanitation, and unsafe drinking water. Like illiteracy these will also drag down India's economic growth and what is the worth of economic growth if we cannot take care of these problems for all Indians.

Fiscal Deficit

The high fiscal deficit persists. The high growth of the economy should have brought down the deficit and the government could have used the surplus to retire some debt or make much needed investments and public outlay on the social sector. Hopefully, the new government will rationalize revenue expenditure and also raise tax–GDP ratio and further growth next year will help moderate the problem. Better enforcement and tax collection can also help. Continued high deficit poses a real threat to sustained high growth. Unless growth momentum is continued and more jobs are created Bharat may wilt.

Slow Judicial System

The person who wins a civil suit in India loses and one who loses is ruined, goes a popular saying. This is because the judicial system takes years to resolve disputes. Justice delayed is justice denied. Also justice delayed is justice that is expensive. It is justice for India but not Bharat. This puts an enormous burden on the economic system too. For example, without quick justice, banks cannot effectively deal with recalcitrant borrowers. Governance also can be greatly improved with a faster judicial system. Right to information and civil society vigilance could be made effective. A proposal to limit the number of adjournments that may be granted in a case, was resisted by the lawyers, who charge fees based on number of appearances. The proposal ought to be adopted immediately.

Privatization

The new government has promised that only privatization that is in the national interest will be carried out. Clearly loss-making units should be privatized if public sector reforms to inject professionalism, autonomy, accountability fail to make them strong enough to compete in the open market. Option of units owned by the government but under private management may also be considered. Even some profit-making units may be privatized if the rate of social return earned is not adequate and the resources may give higher return in other uses. The case for privatizing units that are earning hefty returns is not obvious. It rests on the danger of political interference that public sector units face—that may easily and quickly turn a profit-making unit into a loss-making one. If these are not to be privatized, then political discipline and mechanisms of substantive accountability without interference in management are required. Similarly, unless we develop appropriate regulatory mechanisms privatizing public sector monopolies and replacing them with private sector monopolies will most likely not be in social interest. Privatization should not be an ideological stance but a strategic option.

Political Uncertainty

To us, the biggest uncertainty concerning sustaining the momentum of growth is political. How we resolve the *Mandir–Masjid* (temple–mosque) problem and how we maintain the secular fabric of the society are critical. The recent moves for peace in Kashmir and with Pakistan are thus most welcome. The stability and effectiveness of a multi-party coalition government is important for sustaining inclusive development. India has reasonably good experience in managing coalition governments. We have seen that the former prime minister, Atal Bihari Vajpayee, could give stability to such a government. The present prime minister, Manmohan Singh, not only has the required statesmanship to provide stability to the coalition, but also the sensitivity and sagacity to give direction for inclusive and rapid development.

REFERENCES

Barker, R. and David Dawe (2001), 'The Asian Rice Economy in Transition: Challenges Ahead', International Workshop on Medium and Long Term Prospects of Rice Supply and Demand in the 21st Century, International Rice Research Institute, Los Banos, Philippines, 3–5 December.

Carr, D. (2004), 'Improving the Health of the World's Poorest People', Health Bulletin No. 1, Population Reference Bureau.

Farrington, John, N. C. Saxena, T. Barton, and R. Nayak (2003), 'Post Offices, Pensions, and Computers: New Opportunities for Combining Growth and Social Protection in Weekly Integrated Rural Areas', *National Resources Perspectives No. 8*, June 2003.

Parikh, Kirit (2003), 'A Market for Electrons', *Business Standard*, 21 October 2003.

Radhakrishna, R. and C. Ravi (2004), 'Measurement of Changer in Economic Welfare in India: 1970–2001', forthcoming in the *Journal of Quantitative Economics*.

2 Macroeconomic Scene
Growth and Equity Perspectives

Manoj Panda[1]

It is about 12 years now since the initiation of the economic reform process in 1991. The scope of the reforms undertaken has been wide ranging, covering such spheres as international trade, industrial production, financial markets, and foreign investment. The system of state control on economic activities has gradually been dismantled and replaced by a more market friendly economic system where economic decisions of private agents respond to market signals. The reforms related to two major components: (a) trade liberalization aiming at outward orientation and integration with rest of the world, and (b) deregulation and privatization of industrial production aimed at putting the private sector as the dominant driver in this sphere. The first component involved abolition of import quotas and reduction of tariff rates to moderate levels, devaluation of the Indian rupee to correct for 'bias' against exports, introduction of market determined foreign exchange rate, and current account convertibility. The major components in the sphere of industrial deregulation and promotion were abolition of the system of industrial licensing, promotion of foreign investment including majority share holding in several industries, interest rate deregulation, and disinvestment by the government of its equity in public sector enterprises. The primary objective of the reform was to put the economy on a sustainable high growth path by establishing an incentive framework that helps movement towards the best possible allocation of factors of production across various sectors in the economy and the most efficient input combination within a production sector. It was expected that the higher growth path would be broad based enough to improve welfare of various sections of the population, particularly that of the poor class.

This chapter reviews the macroeconomic developments since the reforms from growth and equity perspectives.

MACROECONOMIC PERFORMANCE

GDP Growth

After initiation of the development planning process in 1951, the Indian economy grew at an average rate of about 3.5 per cent for about three decades. It accelerated thereafter and grew at 5.6 per cent during the period 1981–90. While this higher average growth was commendable, it was accompanied by large macroeconomic imbalances as reflected in fiscal deficit, current account deficit, foreign debt, and debt service ratio. The unsustainable nature of this growth process was evident from the 1991 crisis when it could not meet the oil price rise and other shocks arising from the Gulf War. The reform measures undertaken since 1991 aimed at placing the economy on a sustainable higher growth path. After a period of adjustment, the economy witnessed an excellent growth performance in GDP of about 7.5 per cent for three consecutive years—1994–5 to 1996–7. But the optimism generated during the mid-1990s did not last long. The average annual growth rates in GDP during 1992–3 to 2001–2 turns out to be 6.1 per cent per annum. In fact, the growth rate in the economy has returned to about 5.5 per cent since 1997–8 (Table 2.1). This GDP growth rate, however, seems sustainable on a long-term basis. There are at least three reasons for this:

• In recent years, the economy has withstood several shocks like the East Asian crisis, global depression,

---

[1] The author is thankful to A. Ganesh Kumar and the editors of this volume for comments on an earlier version of the paper and to Vijaya Pawar for data related help.

TABLE 2.1
Average Annual Growth in GDP

	1981-2 to 1990-1	1992-3 to 2001-2	1992-3 to 2002-3	1997-8 to 2001-2	1997-8 to 2002-3
GDP	5.6	6.1	5.9	5.5	5.3
Agriculture	3.8	3.3	2.7	2.0	1.2
Industry	7.0	6.3	6.4	4.6	5.0
Service	6.7	7.8	7.8	8.1	8.0

border tension, the war in Iraq, oil price fluctuations, and a major drought without any large-scale disruption. The sustenance of an average GDP growth rate of 5.5 per cent per annum under such environment is commendable and points towards the new strength of the economy.

- The growth process of the 1980s took place under a more protected environment[2] and neglected microeconomic efficiency. The growth rates recorded in the post-liberalization era, though quantitatively not very different, have taken place in a fairly competitive environment.

- As we shall be discussing later, there is macroeconomic stability on several counts compared to the 1980s. Inflation is low, exchange rate is reasonably stable under a managed float regime, foreign exchange reserves have been rising, short-term external debt is low, and foodgrain stocks are adequate even after a drought year.

Looking at the sectoral composition of growth, the source of higher growth since 1992 has been the service sector. In fact, average annual growth rates in both the agriculture and industry sectors seem to be lower by about half a per cent during the post-liberalization era compared to the pre-liberalization period. It is only the service sector that has accelerated to 7.8 per cent during 1992–2002 from 6.7 per cent during 1981–90 and has been the principal driver of the GDP growth.

Revival of industry seems to be the key to achieve a higher growth target. It would be difficult to maintain a high GDP growth of 7–8 per cent without a strong manufacturing expansion. It is worth noting that the strong performance of the economy during the mid-1990s was broad based. It was led by the industrial sector which grew by about 10 per cent followed by the service sector growth of about 8 per cent. Agriculture too performed fairly well with a growth rate of about 4.5 per cent during 1994–6.

Agricultural GDP fell by 3.2 per cent in the year 2002–3 due to one of the worst drought conditions in recent decades. But the improved performance of the industrial and service sectors at about 6 and 7 per cent respectively helped to maintain a GDP growth of 4.3 per cent. The intensity of the drought was comparable to 1987–8 when the real GDP registered an absolute fall. Looked at from this angle, the overall performance in 2002–3 should be viewed as a satisfactory one. The structural changes in the economy, particularly the falling share of agriculture in GDP, have led to reduced effect of agricultural fluctuations on the GDP. Also, as the economy gets more integrated with the rest of the world, external demand can substitute fall in domestic demand for the tradable sectors and help in the development of more resilience in one sector to shocks in another sector in the domestic economy.

The economy has bounced back during 2003–4 with an expected GDP growth of about 8 per cent. Agriculture is likely to attain a growth of 9–10 per cent indicating recovery from the low base of the previous year and placing it back near the trend. More remarkable is the partial revival of the industrial sector which is expected to grow at about 6 per cent. The service sector is estimated to continue its average growth rate of about 8 per cent.

Agriculture

Rainfall for the country as a whole was 19 per cent below normal and as many as 21 out of 36 meteorological subdivisions had rainfall deficiency of more than 20 per cent. In some parts of the country, the deficiency was as high as 60 per cent. As a result, production of foodgrains fell by about 14 per cent (to 183 million tonnes) and non-food grain crops by 9 per cent with oilseeds output fall being as high as 24 per cent. The adverse effect on agriculture was more intense than in any other year during the last two decades.

It is natural to expect the structure of production within agriculture to change from foodgrain to non-foodgrain crops over the years in response to Engel elasticities of demand. But there has clearly been a fall in output growth rate of non-foodgrain crops led by oilseeds in recent years with the result that foodgrain output growth exceeds non-foodgrain output growth even if we leave aside the drought year 2002–3 (Table 2.2). As far as the edible oil sector is concerned, an increased proportion of demand for edible oils is now met by imports because of domestic output decline in edible oilseeds since the liberalization.

The bias in agricultural price support policy in favour of rice and wheat in the green revolution areas has distorted the cropping pattern. Huge buffer stocks of foodgrains built up in recent years indicate limited sustainable future growth potential in this sector and the

---

[2] The reform process in a limited scale started in the mid-1980s when Rajiv Gandhi was the prime minister.

TABLE 2.2
Annual Growth Rates in Index of Agricultural Production
(per cent per annum)

Year	All crops	Foodgrains	Non-foodgrains	Oilseeds	Cotton	Sugarcane
1981–2	7.0	2.6	14.8	22.4	12.5	20.8
1982–3	–4.0	–3.6	–4.7	–12.5	–4.4	1.7
1983–4	13.2	18.4	4.6	18.1	–15.2	–8.1
1984–5	–0.6	–4.3	6.4	5.4	33.2	–2.2
1985–6	1.4	5.0	–4.7	–13.3	2.6	0.2
1986–7	–3.6	–5.3	–0.4	0.9	–20.9	9.0
1987–8	0.1	–2.8	5.2	13.4	–7.6	5.8
1988–9	21.4	21.7	21.0	35.8	37.0	3.2
1989–90	2.1	0.7	4.5	–2.7	30.6	11.1
1990–1	3.8	3.3	4.4	8.1	–35.8	–18.4
1991–2	–2.0	–4.2	1.6	1.3	–1.3	5.4
1992–3	4.2	4.7	3.5	6.4	17.3	–10.3
1993–4	3.8	4.2	3.1	5.1	–5.8	0.8
1994–5	4.9	3.7	6.8	2.5	10.7	19.9
1995–6	–2.6	–6.2	2.5	1.8	8.2	2.0
1996–7	9.3	10.1	8.4	9.1	10.6	–1.3
1997–8	–5.9	–3.2	–9.6	–14.3	–23.7	0.7
1998–9	7.6	6.1	9.8	13.5	13.2	3.3
1999–2000	–0.6	2.7	–5.2	–14.1	–6.2	3.9
2000–1	–6.3	–6.7	–5.7	–8.7	–17.4	–1.1
2001–2	7.0	8.4	4.8	9.3	6.2	1.4
2002–3	–12.6	–14.6	–9.5	–24.0	–7.9	–7.2
Average growth rates						
1981–90	3.5	2.9	4.8	7.0	2.8	2.6
1992–2001	2.1	2.4	1.8	1.1	1.3	1.9
1992–2002	0.8	0.8	0.8	–1.2	0.5	1.1

need for agricultural diversification. The closing stocks reached 65 million tonnes in June 2002, but got moderated to 40 million tonnes in May 2003 and further to 22 million tonnes in November 2003 due to foodgrains exports of about 10 million tonnes in 2002–3 and higher domestic off-take through public distribution and release to the market in the wake of drought conditions.

India has become the largest producer of milk in the world in recent years. The livestock and fisheries sector has recently emerged as the most important sub-sector in agriculture and allied category and contributes to about 7 per cent of GDP and provides employment opportunities to 11 million people in principal status category and to another 8 million in subsidiary status. Livestock ownership being skewed in favour of small farmers in India, the income generated in this sector gets more equitably distributed. Another important attribute of this sector is that women account for a majority of the workforce.

Given the large variability in climate and soil conditions in the country, India is capable of producing a wide range of high value horticultural crops with good profit opportunities for farmers. Only about 1 per cent of the estimated 140 million tones of fruits and vegetables produced in the country goes to the processing stage at present. Commercial horticulture aiming at supplying to the exports market or feeding the food processing plants could potentially attract educated entrepreneurs to agriculture in a large scale. Floriculture provides another potentially profitable agro-business opportunity. Both horticulture and floriculture are employment-intensive activities. The government could help in providing the necessary modern infrastructure like cold storage for preservation, refrigerated transportation, grading and quality control for these emerging sectors. Absence of proper marketing network is another bottleneck for the development of this sector.

Investment in agriculture has fallen to 1.3 per cent of GDP in recent years. This decline, attributed to stagnation in public investment, has been a matter of concern in several quarters. It may be noted that only around 40 per cent of the cultivated area in the country is currently under irrigation. Most of the remaining 60 per cent of area falls under arid and semi-arid zones. Taking into account current trends in irrigation expansion of less than 1 million hectares per year on an average, more than half of the cultivated land would remain unirrigated even after a decade. Increased focus is needed in rainfed areas for realizing future agricultural growth potential through new programmes like watershed development which aims at soil and water conservation. Agricultural research and extension could play a role in adopting suitable cropping pattern and seed varieties.

Industry

Industrial deregulation and trade reforms introduced changes in the overall environment and organizational structure in Indian industry. The Indian corporate sector is going through structural changes in response to the new policy regime. After the reforms, industrial output positively responded with a time lag and remained high for a couple of years with a peak growth rate of 13 per cent during 1995–6. Industrial growth rate has remained sluggish since then ranging between 2.7 and 6.7 per cent. On the whole, the performance of the industrial sector during the post-reform period 1992–2002 has not been as good as that in the pre-reform period 1982–90 (Table 2.3). While the industrial growth process was led by the capital goods sector in most of the years in the 1980s, it had not been so in the 1990s when consumer goods, capital goods, and intermediates played the lead role in different years. As a result, the dispersion in average growth rates across the use based sectors has fallen in the post-liberalization period (Table 2.4).

There was distinct broad-based improvement in industrial activity during 2002–3 driven by domestic and exports demand. Exports demand expansion could be traced to the revival of the world economy during the year. Despite the fall in agricultural output, the domestic demand expansion that started in the early part of 2002 could be maintained by autonomous government expenditures in the form of investment on national highways construction and the drought relief measures. We might note in this context the significant growth of the capital goods sector and the consumer non-durables by more than 10 per cent in 2002–3 (Table 2.4). However, the consumer durable goods sector, which had been quite buoyant since 1999, did suffer a downturn in 2002–3 with an absolute fall in output by 6 per cent.

The infrastructure industries grew on an average by about 5 per cent during 2002–3. Electricity, coal, and crude petroleum sectors grew at moderate rates. The accelerated growth of cement and finished steel was largely due to domestic and external demand respectively. The NHDP is being undertaken to improve road connectivity across major cities. Unless the infrastructure sectors grow and close the gaps in estimated requirement and availability, bottlenecks might arise for future growth in the economy.

TABLE 2.3
Growth Rates in Index Number of Industrial Production
(per cent per annum)

Year	Mining and quarrying	Manufacturing	Electricity	General
1982–3	12.4	1.3	5.7	3.2
1983–4	11.8	5.7	7.6	6.7
1984–5	8.8	8.0	12.0	8.6
1985–6	4.1	9.7	8.5	8.7
1986–7	6.2	9.4	10.3	9.2
1987–8	3.7	7.9	7.6	7.3
1988–9	7.9	8.7	9.5	8.7
1989–90	6.3	8.6	10.9	8.6
1990–1	4.5	8.9	7.8	8.2
1991–2	0.6	–0.8	8.5	0.6
1992–3	0.6	2.2	5.0	2.3
1993–4	3.5	6.1	7.5	6.0
1994–5	9.8	9.1	8.5	9.1
1995–6	9.7	14.1	8.1	13.0
1996–7	–1.9	7.3	4.0	6.1
1997–8	6.9	6.6	6.6	6.7
1998–9	–0.8	4.4	6.4	4.1
1999–2000	1.0	7.1	7.3	6.7
2000–1	2.8	5.3	4.0	5.0
2001–2	1.2	2.9	3.1	2.7
2002–3	5.8	6.0	3.2	5.8
Average growth rates				
1982–90	7.3	7.6	8.9	7.7
1994–2002	3.8	7.0	5.7	6.6
1996–2002	2.1	5.7	4.9	5.3

Economic reforms were meant to promote industrial productivity through more efficient resource use by easing out restrictions on investment decisions, choice of technology and factor combination, and by exposing them to greater competition in the domestic and world markets. Yet, attempts to estimate total factor productivity (TFP) in the post-reform period do not suggest unambiguous results. The evidence is mixed with TFP growth changing in either direction depending on the method used during the post-reform years compared to the pre-reform period in Indian manufacturing.[3] In an interesting analysis, Balakrishnan and Babu (2003) attribute the principal cause of industrial output growth during the post-liberalization period to an increase in share of investment to output across the board possibly in response to rise in profit rate. The ratio rose to 0.7 during 1991–9 from 0.4 during 1973–90 for the manufacturing sector as

---
[3] See Goldar (2000) for a discussion of various studies.

TABLE 2.4
Growth in Index Number of Industrial Production by Used Based Sectors
(per cent per annum)

Year	Basic goods	Capital goods	Intermediate goods	Consumer goods	Consumer durables	Consumer non-durables
1982–3	7.0	3.7	1.0	–1.6	9.1	–2.8
1983–4	6.0	11.7	9.8	1.6	16.1	–0.4
1984–5	11.1	3.0	9.7	7.2	27.3	5.1
1985–6	6.8	10.6	7.5	12.5	18.7	11.5
1986–7	9.3	18.2	4.1	6.1	13.7	3.6
1987–8	5.5	15.9	2.7	9.8	7.6	10.3
1988–9	9.9	7.1	11.7	3.9	22.3	0.1
1989–90	5.4	21.9	4.3	6.5	2.4	7.5
1990–1	6.9	16.0	4.7	6.8	10.7	5.8
1991–2	6.5	–8.5	–2.1	1.0	–10.9	4.0
1992–3	2.6	–0.1	5.4	1.8	–0.7	2.4
1993–4	9.4	–4.1	11.7	4.0	16.1	1.3
1994–5	5.5	24.8	3.7	8.7	10.2	8.4
1995–6	10.7	5.4	19.3	12.8	25.8	9.8
1996–7	3.0	11.4	8.1	6.2	4.6	6.6
1997–8	6.8	5.8	8.0	5.5	7.8	4.9
1998–9	1.7	12.6	6.1	2.2	5.6	1.1
1999–2000	5.5	6.9	8.8	5.7	14.1	3.2
2000–1	3.9	1.7	4.7	8.0	14.6	5.8
2001–2	2.6	–3.4	1.5	6.0	11.5	4.1
2002–3	4.9	10.5	3.9	7.1	–6.3	12.0
Averages						
1982–90	7.5	12.0	6.2	5.9	14.2	4.5
1994–2002	7.5	10.6	5.8	6.2	12.0	5.3
1996–2002	7.1	9.3	5.3	6.2	10.1	5.6

a whole. They view this rise as a reflection of the success of reforms from the supply side. Dholakia (2002), on the other hand, finds that the growth rate of the private non-agricultural sector doubled during 1985–2000 compared to the period 1960–85 accompanied by increased flow of factor inputs. He finds about 40 per cent of the growth could be attributed to TFP growth which means that the efficiency of the non-agricultural private sector improved significantly after 1985. In fact, he also finds increase in efficiency of factor inputs employed in agriculture and non-agricultural public sector during 1985–2000.

The Indian industrial sector is going through a process of restructuring and consolidation after liberalization. The industries have responded to the reforms through mergers and acquisitions, adoption of cost cutting measures, foreign collaboration, technology upgradation, and outward orientation in sectors such as cement, steel, aluminium, pharmaceuticals, and automobiles. Some of them have become quite competitive in the world market on cost and quality considerations. Certain rigidities continue to constrain firm choices in resource allocation. Choice of the least cost input mix and further reforms in the left-out areas could help to remove some of these rigidities. We turn to them later.

Service

During recent decades the service sector has been growing at a rate faster than that of the agriculture or industry sectors. It now accounts for about half of the total GDP generated in the country. Figure 2.1 depicts the average growth rates for the various components of the service sector during the 1980s and the 1990s. Communication has been the fastest growing component during the 1990s. Other service sectors that have recorded higher growth after liberalization compared to the 1980s include construction, trade, hotels and restaurants, and transport (other than railways). On the other hand, there was deceleration in the growth of the public

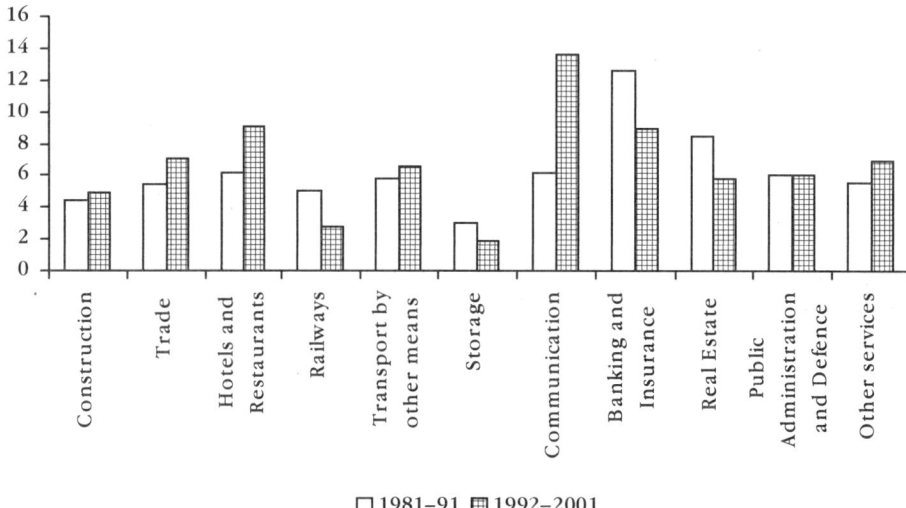

Figure 2.1: Average Growth Rates in Various Service Sectors

sector dominated areas like railways and banking and insurance. Despite the deceleration, the banking and insurance sector has experienced the second highest growth mainly because liberalization facilitated entry of private players in the financial markets. Note that the public administration and defence sector continued to grow in the 1990s at about the same rate as it had done in the 1980s. While the government placed restrictions on expansion of new government jobs in the 1990s to curb overstaffing, it had to spend more in real terms on existing employees because of the salary hike that followed the recommendations of the Fifth Pay Commission.

Employment

Agriculture continues to be the dominant source of employment in India. It employs about 60 per cent of the total workforce, even though its share in GDP has fallen to about a quarter. This implies that the productivity of a typical worker in agriculture is one-forth that of his counterpart in non-agriculture. As per the National Sample Survey Organization (NSSO) data, the incidence of open unemployment has increased from 1.96 per cent in 1993-4 to 2.25 per cent in 1999-2000. In absolute terms, more than 9 million persons remained unemployed in 1999-2000. The volume of total unemployment that takes into account the existence of substantial underemployment and seasonal variations in work availability has been estimated at 35 million persons in 2002 according to the Vision 2020 report prepared by the Planning Commission.[4] The size of the labour force according to this document was 375 million in 2002 and it is expected to grow at approximately 2 per cent per annum over the next two decades.

The NSSO data indicate that employment growth had decelerated in the Indian economy in the 1990s. The growth rates in both rural and urban segments had been about 1 percentage point less from 1993-4 to 1999-2000 than those witnessed from 1983-4 to 1993-4 (Table 2.5).[5] Since agriculture and allied sectors account for most of the employment in India, the fall in employment growth was driven by this sector. Crop output increase has been largely due to yield rather than area expansion in recent decades leading to a fall in labour absorption capacity. Employment volume has fallen in absolute terms in mining and quarrying and public utilities which are mostly in the public sector and associated with over-employment. In contrast, there was acceleration in employment growth in construction, transport, financial services, and real estate business—sectors which also had high income growth.

Employment growth relative to income growth has fallen sharply in recent years (Table 2.6). There has hardly been any employment growth, particularly in the agricultural sector. Another feature of the labour market that raises concern is the increasing casualization of the labour force as revealed by an increase in the share of casual workers in total employment. The casual workers are among the most vulnerable sections of the society.

Given the low employment–income elasticities, a very high income growth rate would be needed for solving the unemployment problem within a reasonable time

---

[4] See Box 2.1 for some salient features of the Vision 2020 report.

[5] These data are taken from Chadha and Sahu (2002). The NSSO quenquennial round data for 1987-8 is not used by the authors for comparison because it happened to be a drought year with abnormally low volume of employment.

> **Box 2.1**
> **India Vision 2020**
>
> A report entitled 'India Vision 2020' (Planning Commission, 2004) has recently formulated a set of long-term economic goals for the nation realizable by proper utilization of untapped potentials. Prepared by a committee of the Planning Commission, the report recognizes the changing environment and the wide range of new possibilities open before the nation—rapid rise in educational levels, technological advancement, cheaper and faster communication, quick availability of information, and access to world market due to globalization. Some salient features of the Indian economy as visualized in the report over the next two decades are:
>
> - India could aspire to attain an average level of living of the current upper middle income countries such as Argentina, Malaysia, and South Africa.
> - The nation would be able to produce food needed for the projected population of 1.3 billion and generate some exportable surplus. But this by itself would not ensure eradication of under-nutrition due to lack of purchasing power of the poor.
> - A comprehensive national food security strategy must include security of livelihood. Labour force is expected to expand by 45 per cent and generation of about 200 million new jobs over the next 20 years would be a major challenge before the nation.
> - A significant departure from earlier government statements is the report's advocacy of access to gainful employment as a constitutional right for the citizens to enable them 'to exercise their economic rights in a market economy'.
> - Changing demographic composition would double the number of senior citizens necessitating adoption of special measures for them.
> - The report describes the knowledge revolution as an uncommon opportunity and human resource as the most important determinant of future output and employment growth. It recommends school education as 'an essential prerequisite for citizens to adapt and succeed economically'.
> - Future growth is likely to concentrate in big cities of one million or more population and urban population is expected to reach 40 per cent of the total. This would put more strain on urban infrastructure development calling for innovative solutions.
> - Establishment of links among the major rivers could channel surplus water from flood-prone areas to drought-prone areas and help increase the irrigation potential.
> - India has to meet the challenge of global competition and seize upon the global capital flows destinations by providing secure and attractive returns.
>
> Several aspects in the report need deeper probe at both analytical and empirical levels. For example, will provision of purchasing power be adequate to ensure removal of under-nutrition? Does the state possess sufficient means and mechanisms to ensure employment as a constitutional right?

TABLE 2.5
Growth of Employment (Usual Status)

(per cent per annum)

	Rural		Urban	
	1983–93	1993–2000	1983–93	1993–2000
Agriculture and allied	1.38	0.18	1.54	–3.4
Mining and quarrying	3.84	–2.28	4.15	–3.71
Manufacturing	2.14	1.78	2.21	1.83
Electricity, gas, and water supply	4.7	–5.65	4.46	–4.19
Construction	5.18	6.43	6.2	6.26
Trade, hotels, and restaurants	3.72	1.18	3.94	5.54
Transport, storage, and communication	4.58	7.29	2.9	3.91
Finance, insurance, real estate	5.99	2.51	5.63	7.05
Public administration, community and personal services	3.13	0.32	4.16	0.13
Total non-agriculture	3.23	2.31	3.54	2.96
All sectors	1.75	0.66	3.27	2.27

Source: Chadha and Sahu, EPW, 25 May 2002.

TABLE 2.6
Elasticity of Employment with Respect to Income

	1983–93	1993–9
Agriculture and allied	0.48	0.01
Mining and quarrying	0.61	–0.49
Manufacturing	0.32	0.20
Electricity, gas, and water supply	0.48	–0.52
Construction	1.27	1.00
Trade, hotels, and restaurants	0.67	0.38
Transport, storage, and communication	0.55	0.56
Finance, insurance, real estate	0.49	0.68
Public administration, community services	0.63	0.02
All sectors	0.36	0.13

Source: Chadha and Sahu, EPW, 25 May 2002.

horizon. A task force set up by the government had suggested a 9 per cent GDP growth target per annum to generate adequate employment. But it might be difficult to realize above 7 per cent GDP growth without drastic policy changes. Against this background, it would be important to promote agricultural growth for employment generation. Bhalla and Hazell (2003) suggest agricultural growth in rainfed areas would be particularly beneficial for meeting employment expansion targets.

Given the limited employment potential contribution of the organized sector, most of the new jobs would be generated in the unorganized sector. The Vision 2020 document lays emphasis on the growth of the vegetables, horticulture, agro-processing, garment, SSI, afforestation, trade, tourism, and construction sectors from the employment point of view. The primary sector would continue to employ most of the workforce for at least another decade. There is large scope for employment generation in crop diversification and afforestation. But a proper strategy of non-farm employment growth must be devised to shift workforce from agriculture and to reduce the gap in labour productivity between agricultural and non-agricultural sectors.

Balakrishnan and Babu (2003) find that apprehensions about a jobless growth process do not seem to hold true for the sectors covered by the Annual Survey of Industries (ASI) with average annual growth rate in industrial employment rising to 1.51 per cent per annum during 1991–9 from 1.28 per cent during 1973–90. It is worth noting in this context another interesting study by Hasan, Mitra, and Ramaswamy (2003) that provides evidence of an inverse relationship between labour demand elasticities and the extent of protection in the industrial sector in India. On the basis of interindustry analysis for 15 major states, they find that the labour demand elasticities have gone up after the reforms. There are two implications of this result: (i) productivity growth, if any, could be expected to lead to higher growth in employment and wage, and (ii) output volatility could potentially cause larger wage and employment volatility in future. Policy-makers need to strike a balance between these two opposing effects on labour welfare.

On the whole, the employment scenario does not look bright enough to reduce the current stock of unemployment in the short run. Designing mechanism for reorientation of growth strategy in favour of labour intensive sectors in a competitive market economy is not an easy task. It looks like the government would need to expand the volume of employment generation programmes being undertaken as part of poverty alleviation measures in order to protect the poor.

Inflation

The annual inflation rate had generally remained low at less than 5 per cent since the mid-1990s except for 1998–9 and 2000–1. It rose during 2002–3 on the face of the rise in world prices of petroleum, oil, and lubricants (POL) and domestic shortages due to drought conditions. The annual point-to-point inflation rate for all commodities stood at 6.5 per cent by the end of March 2003 as against 1.6 per cent during the same period in the previous year (Figure 2.2). Two groups, fuel–power–light–lubricants and fruits–vegetables, have contributed the most to recent volatility in prices. One noteworthy feature is that foodgrain prices remained under control, despite the drought, thanks to effective supply management involving higher off-take from the PDS, larger allocation for public works programmes, and open market sales.

The drought conditions did have upward effects in prices of oilseeds and sugarcane as well as the corresponding end products, like, edible oils and sugar. Higher inflation during the year in certain other commodities like petroleum products, cotton textiles, and iron and steel reflected volatility in world market prices. Domestic prices can no longer be insulated from world prices in a liberalized open economy environment. It is also worth noting in this context that India is a large importer of vegetable oils and the standard small country assumption does not hold in this case. A significant upward change in India's import demand—caused by a shortfall in domestic production of oilseeds—would itself push up the world price of edible oils and calls for strategic behaviour on the part of Indian importers. A similar response is needed in case of foodgrains trade too, specially in the case of rice where the world market is very thin.[6]

---

[6] See Parikh et al. (1997) for an analytical discussion on this point.

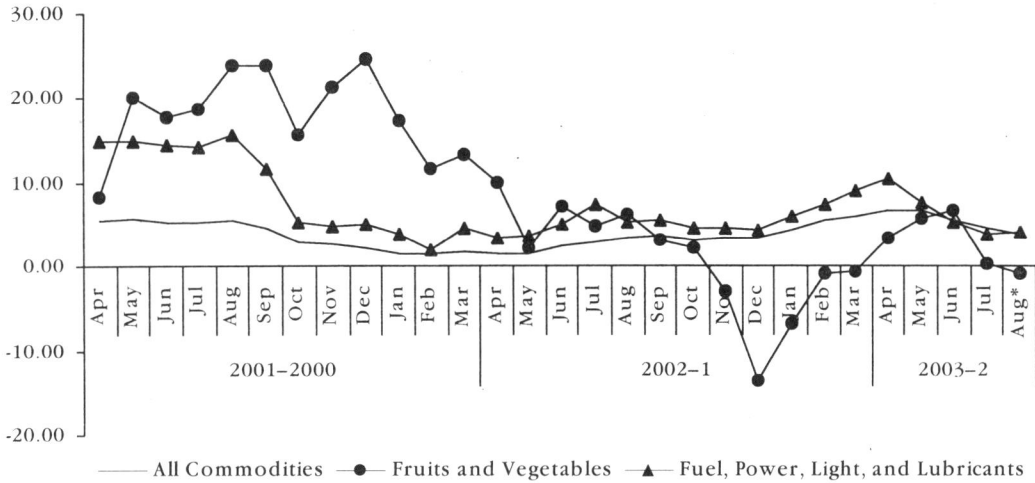

Figure 2.2: Annualized Inflation Rate

Savings and Investment

Gross domestic savings rose from 23.1 per cent of GDP in 1990–1 to 25.1 per cent in 1995–6. This trend, however, got reversed later and the savings rate fell to 21.5 per cent in 1998–9 driven by fall in savings from the public sector and the private corporate sector. Savings by the household sector, which accounts for the bulk of the total savings in India, had declined to 17 per cent of GDP in 1996–7. It has been rising since then and reached a peak of 22.5 per cent of GDP in 2001–2. Savings by the private corporate sector increased from below 3 per cent of GDP before 1990–1 to 4.9 per cent in 1995–6 but has fallen back to about 4 per cent in recent years. The household sector and the private corporate sector together accounted for a savings rate of 26.5 per cent of GDP in 2001–2. Aggregate domestic savings, however, remained lower at 24.0 per cent because of negative public sector savings by as much as 2.5 per cent of GDP. The public sector, which used to have positive savings during the 1980s and most of the 1990s, has generated negative savings since 1998–9.

Gross domestic capital formation rates used to be higher than gross domestic savings with the investment-

TABLE 2.7
Savings and Capital Formation

Year	Gross domestic savings				Gross capital formation				
	Household sector	Private corporate sector	Public sector	Total savings	Private sector	Household sector	Private corporate Sector	Public sector	Gross domestic capital formation (GDCF)
1990–1	19.3	2.7	1.1	23.1	15.5	10.6	4.1	9.4	26.3
1991–2	17.0	3.1	2.0	22.1	13.5	7.5	5.7	8.8	22.6
1992–3	17.5	2.7	1.6	21.8	15.5	8.8	6.5	8.6	23.6
1993–4	18.4	3.5	0.6	22.5	13.0	7.4	5.6	8.2	23.1
1994–5	19.7	3.5	1.7	24.9	14.7	7.8	6.9	8.7	26.0
1995–6	18.2	4.9	2.0	25.1	18.9	9.3	9.6	7.7	26.9
1996–7	17.0	4.5	1.7	23.2	14.7	6.7	8.4	7.0	24.5
1997–8	17.6	4.2	1.3	23.1	16.0	8.0	8.4	6.6	24.6
1998–9	18.8	3.7	–1.0	21.5	14.8	8.2	6.6	6.6	22.6
1999–2000	20.8	4.4	–1.0	24.2	16.7	9.2	6.4	6.9	25.2
2000–1	21.6	4.1	–2.3	23.4	16.1	11.2	4.9	6.4	24.0
2001–2	22.5	4.0	–2.5	24.0	16.1	11.3	4.8	6.3	23.7

savings gap accounting for foreign savings.[7] The situation got reversed since 2001–2 with the emergence of a surplus current account of balance of payments (BOP) (discussed below). Gross domestic capital formation at current prices, adjusted for errors and omissions, stood at 23.7 per cent in 2001–2 which was more than 3 percentage points lower than the 1995–6 level. Capital formation in the public sector has fallen by about 3 percentage points since 1990–1 to 6.3 per cent in 2001–2. Investment by the corporate sector has decelerated to 4.8 per cent of GDP in 2001–2 from 9.6 per cent in 1995–6 reflecting gloom in industrial outlook. Capital formation in the private household sector had fallen after the mid-1990s but has picked up in recent years to remain at about 11 per cent of GDP. Increasing the investment and savings rate by 4–5 per cent of GDP would be crucial for attaining a higher GDP growth rate of 7–8 per cent.[8]

International Trade

The world trade volume recovered modestly in 2002 and 2003 after an absolute fall in 2001. India's exports growth at about 19 per cent during 2002–3 far exceeded world trade expansion. This helped exports value as a percentage of GDP to reach the two digit level for the first time. Imports too grew sharply to 12.8 per cent of GDP in 2002–3 from 12.0 per cent in the previous year. Imports and exports together currently account for 23 per cent of GDP compared to just 15 per cent in 1990–1 (Table 2.8) and reflects the steady movement towards integration with the global economy.

A major development in the last two years on the trade front has been that the current account balance has turned surplus from a deficit of 3.1 per cent of GDP in 1990–1 to a surplus of 0.3 per cent of GDP in 2001–2 and further improved to 0.7 per cent in 2002–3. The surplus on current account means that we have entered, after about three decades, a phase where current external receipts are good enough to pay for current external liabilities. This transformation has been achieved primarily due to the rise in invisible earnings by about 6 per cent of GDP reflecting substantial expansion of transfers (remittances) from abroad as well as software and other service exports. In absolute terms, the transfers were of the order of about US$ 15 billion while software exports were close to US$ 10 billion. The net gain on the invisibles account has been about 3 per cent of GDP since invisible payments involving travel, transport, dividends, and other service-related payments too rose due to progressive liberalization of the exchange regime.

Foreign direct investment (FDI) and portfolio investment, however, declined by about US$ 1 billion each to US$ 4.6 billion during 2002–3 reflecting similar trends at the global level. FDI could play a critical role in manufacturing exports promotions, market diversification, technology transfer, and productivity increase. India needs to increase its share of high technology manufactured products in its export basket.

The overall surge in capital flows continued and led to further build up of the RBI's net foreign assets (NFA) which crossed US$ 100 billion by the end of 2003. The reserves at present are adequate to pay for imports bill

TABLE 2.8
Major Foreign Trade Parameters

(as per cent of GDP)

	1990–1	1994–5	1995–6	1996–7	1997–8	1998–9	1999–2000	2000–1	2001–2	2002–3
Export	5.8	8.8	9.7	9.5	8.7	8.2	8.4	9.8	9.3	10.4
Import	8.8	11.7	13.1	13.6	12.5	11.4	12.4	12.9	12	12.8
Trade deficit	3	2.9	3.4	4.1	3.8	3.2	4	3.1	2.7	2.4
Current receipts	8	13.7	14.9	15.4	14.3	14.3	15.1	17.3	16.9	18.7
Current account balance	–3.1	–1.1	–1.7	–1.2	–1.4	–1.0	–1.1	–0.5	0.3	
Net invisibles	–0.1	1.9	1.6	2.9	2.5	2.2	3	2.4	2.8	3.1
Foreign investment	0.03	1.6	1.4	1.6	1.3	0.6	1.1	1.3	1.4	0.9
Debt–GDP ratio	28.7	32.3	28.3	26.2	24.3	23.4	22.2	22.4	21	20
Debt reserve ratio	35.3	26.2	24.3	21.2	18.9	17.8	16.2	17.2	13.9	14.7

[7] Foreign savings account for above 5 per cent of GDP in China and several East Asian economies and contribute substantially to raise investment above domestic savings.

[8] The Tenth Plan targets for an investment rate of 28.4 per cent of GDP and a savings rate of 26.8 per cent.

of close to one and half years. Given that the current level of forex reserves are good enough to meet precautionary motives, there is a need to examine the continuation of the policy of accumulation of the reserves. Net capital flows in future could partly be absorbed by the economy by enhancing investment and future growth potential.[9] Reserve built up beyond an optimal level could be costly for the economy. Further liberalization of the capital account and prepayment of high cost debt would benefit the economy. The government could also take this opportunity to reduce the import tariff rates, which are still high, to comparable levels in East Asia.

Money and Credit

Consistent with the reduced overall growth, both reserve money and broad money (M_3) grew by 9 and 14 per cent respectively during 2002–3 on a monthly average basis—about 2 percentage points less than corresponding figures in the previous year (Table 2.9). The non-food component of the bank credit to the commercial sector, on the other hand, accelerated by about 5 percentage points, mainly reflecting the recovery in industrial activity. The RBI cut down the bank rate, the repo rate and the cash reserve ratio (CRR) leading to a fall in the spectrum of the interest rates charged by the commercial banks. Commercial banks held government securities at 39 per cent of their net demand and time liabilities which was far in excess of the statutory minimum limits of 25 per cent. Government securities have been attractive instruments for the banks to meet prudential norms imposed during financial reforms.

Net domestic assets of the RBI as a proportion of the reserve money have fallen from about 90 per cent in the early 1990s to as low as 3 per cent by the end of March 2003. The limit to the sterilization process seems to be fast approaching. The RBI would need to manage surplus on the balance of payments by resorting to other instruments. Further liberalization of the capital account and prepayment of high cost debt are obvious candidates in this context as noted above.

Public Finance

The overall fiscal position of the governments continues to be under stress. After the initiation of the economic reforms in 1991, the combined gross fiscal deficit of the central and state governments had considerably improved by 3 percentage points to 6.4 per cent of GDP in 1996–7. But it has continuously slipped back since then and stood at 10 per cent of GDP in 2002–3 which was higher than even the 1990–1 level. The combined total expenditure of the governments turns out to be as much as 30 per cent of GDP and thus plays an important role in macroeconomic developments. Taken together, the governments raise about half of the total expenditure as tax revenue, another one-sixth as non-tax revenue, and meet the remaining one-third through capital receipts most of which are borrowings.

TABLE 2.9
Growth in Monetary Variables

Variable	Growth rate on monthly average basis				Outstanding as on 31 March 2003 (rupees crore)
	1999–2000	2000–1	2001–2	2002–3	
1. Reserve money	12	7.8	11.1	9.3	369,061
2. Broad money (M_3)	17.2	15.7	16.1	14	1,695,551
Net bank credit to government	15.1	13.8	16.7	13.7	678,059
Net reserve bank credit to government	5.3	0.9	1.5	−17.4	120,679
Bank credit to commercial sector	16.4	19.7	12.8	12.6	862,068
Scheduled commercial banks' non-food credit	15.5	15.4	11.8	16.5	635,192
Net foreign exchange assets of banking sector	21.1	17.9	24.5	31.4	393,715

The RBI's liquidity management activity operates through various policy options aiming at controlling the reserve money. In recent years, the RBI has been sterilizing the excess primary liquidity generated by the large increase in net foreign exchange assets through open market sales of government securities and repos.

[9] Lal, Bery, and Pant (2003) carry out counterfactual experiments under certain assumptions and find that large volumes of GDP had been foregone during the 1990s due to failure to absorb the capital inflows.

Revenue deficit increased in the second half of the 1990s by about 3 per cent of GDP due to increase in salary bills and other government consumption expenditures and stood close to 7 per cent in 2002–3. The burden of expenditure reduction mostly fell on capital outlays during the 1990s and distorted the structure of government expenditure in favour of current expenditure and away from investment. In particular, the central government capital outlays fell from 2.1 per cent of GDP to 1.2 per cent during the first half of the 1990s and have nearly remained constant since then. This had adverse implications on the expansion of the productive capacity of the economy, particularly because public investment on economic and social infrastructure crowds in private investment in India.

While the tax–GDP ratio improved a bit for the state governments taken together, it had deteriorated for the central government over the last decade (Tables 2.10 and 2.11). Factors contributing to the deterioration in indirect tax to GDP ratio include reduction in customs and excise duty rates to more competitive levels as part of the fiscal reform process and the continued shift in the composition of GDP in favour of the less taxed service sector. The recent efforts made to widen the tax base to the service sector in a comprehensive manner no doubt need to be pursued further.

Direct taxes have been buoyant and exhibited increasing trend in relation to GDP from 1.8 per cent in 1990–1 to 3.3 per cent in 2002–3. As a result, there has been a marked shift in the composition of central tax revenue in favour of direct taxes whose share rose from 18 per cent to 37 per cent over the same period. These developments have led to make the central government's tax structure less regressive.

Non-tax revenue receipts of both central and state governments increased in the first half of the 1990s, but have stagnated after that at around 4 per cent of GDP.

TABLE 2.10
Fiscal Parameters of Central Government

(as per cent of GDP)

Years	1970–9	1980–91	1996–7	1997–8	1998–9	1999–2000	2000–1	2001–2	2002–3 (BE)	2002–03 (RE)	2003–4 (BE)
Total expenditure	14.40	17.70	14.69	15.24	16.04	15.39	15.47	15.79	16.05	16.34	15.99
Revenue expenditure	8.40	11.70	11.62	11.84	12.43	12.86	13.20	13.14	13.32	13.82	13.35
Interest payments	1.50	2.80	4.35	4.31	4.47	4.66	4.72	4.68	4.59	4.68	4.49
Subsidies	0.80	1.70	1.13	1.22	1.36	1.26	1.28	1.36	1.56	1.81	1.82
Capital disbursements	6.00	6.00	3.08	3.40	3.61	2.53	2.27	2.65	2.73	2.52	2.65
Total tax	8.70	10.00	9.40	9.10	8.30	8.90	9.0	8.10	9.2	9.0	9.2
Direct tax	2.30	2.00	2.80	3.20	2.70	3.00	3.20	3.00	3.60	3.30	3.50
Indirect tax	6.40	7.90	6.60	6.00	5.60	5.90	5.70	5.10	5.60	5.60	5.70
Non-tax revenue	2.00	2.40	2.38	2.51	2.58	2.75	2.66	2.95	2.82	2.94	2.54
Gross fiscal deficit	3.80	6.80	4.11	4.81	5.14	5.41	5.65	6.14		5.88	5.60
Gross primary deficit	2.30	3.90	–0.24	0.50	0.67	0.75	0.93	1.46		1.21	1.11
Revenue deficit	–0.30	1.90	48.93	52.23	59.09	64.55	71.74	71.06	70.38	71.98	73.09

TABLE 2.11
Fiscal Parameters of State Governments

(as percentage to GDP)

Year	1994–5	1995–6	1996–7	1997–8	1998–9	1999–2000	2000–1	2001–2 (RE)
Total expenditure	13.6	12.98	13.32	16.55	13.75	14.92	15.12	16.38
Developmental expenditure	8.78	8.39	8.67	8.34	8.49	8.90	9.17	9.64
Economic services	4.67	4.16	4.37	4.12	3.95	4.01	4.22	4.35
Social services	4.11	4.23	4.3	4.22	4.55	4.89	4.95	5.29
Non-developmental expenditure	4.17	4.05	4.08	4.12	4.46	5.24	5.18	5.86
Interest payments	1.63	1.6	1.68	1.73	1.85	2.15	2.25	2.63
Administration and general services	1.99	1.92	1.87	1.84	1.97	2.31	2.35	2.45
Total tax	5.5	5.4	5.2	5.1	5.1	5.3	5.6	5.6
Direct tax	0.7	0.7	0.6	0.4	0.6	0.6	0.6	0.6
Indirect tax	4.8	4.7	4.6	4.7	4.5	4.7	5	4.9
Non-tax revenue	4.1	3.7	3.4	3.2	2.7	3.09	3.5	3.3
Grants	0.2	1.8	1.7	1.6	1.4	1.6	1.8	2.2
States own non-taxes	3.9	1.9	1.7	1.6	1.3	1.5	1.7	1.1
Gross fiscal deficit	2.7	2.6	2.7	2.9	4.3	4.7	4.3	4.2
Gross primary deficit	0.8	0.8	0.9	0.9	2.2	2.4	1.8	1.5
Revenue deficit	0.6	0.7	1.2	1.1	2.5	2.8	2.5	2.6

The persistently loss-making public sector undertakings (PSUs) constitute a problem area and their restructuring has not been an easy task. The authorities have slipped in meeting the disinvestment targets for a variety of reasons. Imposition of proper user charges is another step needed for expanding non-tax revenue. Admittedly, the process of rationalization of user charges must be a continuous process in utilities such as power, transport, and irrigation. Implementation of such measures would require establishment of credible independent regulatory authorities to ensure to the public that cost recoveries are reasonable and users are not paying for increasing inefficiency of the PSUs.

Public debt has risen sharply from 58 per cent of GDP in 1995–6 to 76 per cent in 2002–3. This has led to continued increase in interest payments as a percentage of GDP despite a fall in the interest rate of outstanding liabilities.[10] Debt servicing currently accounts for the bulk of the market borrowings of the governments. Further deterioration in debt position could put the governments in a debt trap where current borrowings are used only to pay back past loans. A decomposition analysis by Rangarajan and Srivastava (2003) draws attention to the fact that the cushion provided by the excess of growth rate over interest rate in the past may not continue to be available with the end of the regime of financial repression. They note that growth rates have been lower than interest rates for three years starting from 2000–1. A primary surplus on a sustained basis would be needed to reduce debt–GDP ratio in the liberalized context. Another important emerging issue in this context is the growth in outstanding government guarantees to loans raised by PSUs, specially at the state level. When part of such contingent liabilities turn out to be actual liability, it puts further stress on the already hard budget situation.

The wide fiscal deficit and skewed government expenditure towards salaries, pensions, and interest payments provide limited scope for the government to allocate resources towards developmental and productive activities. Notwithstanding this constraint, the government did play an important role in arresting adverse welfare effects of the drought in 2002–3 by the provision of adequate relief measures. To a lesser extent, government policies also helped the revival of the industrial activities through extensive road construction activities.

FLUCTUATIONS IN THE INCIDENCE OF POVERTY

A per capita real income growth of about 4 per cent after the initiation of the reforms translates to about 50 per cent rise over a period of 11 years, that is, from about Rs 7400 in 1992–3 to about Rs 11,200 in 2002–3. The question that naturally arises then is whether the growth process in the post-reform era has been widespread enough to make an impact on the poor and the rich alike. This is important particularly because one of the major arguments for economic reform was that higher growth would accelerate the removal of absolute poverty.

Poverty is commonly measured with the help of a poverty line which is a benchmark income or consumption level to distinguish the poor from the non-poor. The Planning Commission has defined the poverty lines as Rs 49 and Rs 56 for rural and urban India respectively for the base year 1973–4. These lines meet the nutritional norms in the base year and are updated for other years using suitable price indices. The most commonly used poverty index is the 'headcount ratio' (HCR) which refers to the proportion of the total population that falls below the poverty line.

Figure 2.3 shows the long-term trends in the HCR of poverty in rural and urban areas during the period 1960–1 to 1999–2000. The figure is based on the estimates made by the World Bank[11] till 1993–4 and updated by us to 1999–2000. Incidence of poverty fluctuated till the early 1970s without any upward or downward trend. There was, however, a clear declining trend in both rural and urban areas during 1973–4 to 1989–90 when the HCR fell from 56 per cent to 34 per cent in rural India and from 48 per cent to 33 per cent in urban India.

The developments during the 1990s indicate that poverty rose a bit immediately after the reforms. But the benefits of the reform measures on the poor were clearly visible by 1999–2000. Poverty ratio in both rural and urban India fell considerably by then compared to the pre-reform period.[12] The proportion of the population below the poverty line came down to 26 per cent in 1999–2000 from 34 per cent prior to the reforms.[13]

---

[10] The fall in interest rate has been small due to outstanding liabilities contracted at high interest rates in the past.

[11] The World Bank has adopted the official poverty line for 1973–4. The price indices used for updating are close to, but not exactly the same as, the official ones in so far as the Bank corrects for the constant price used for fuel wood over the years in the consumer price indices.

[12] Alternative measures of poverty like poverty gap or squared poverty gap that take into account depth and intensity also confirm this result. The official estimates for 1999–2000 are not strictly comparable with those in the previous rounds due to changes in questionnaire design and attempts have been made to correct for this by Deaton and Dreze (2002) and Sundaram and Tendulkar (2003). The alternative estimates do confirm that poverty has fallen between 1993–4 and 1999–2000, though by reduced magnitudes.

[13] The 56th round NSSO data for 2000–1 have been released on some variables towards completion of this paper. A quick check indicates the HCR of poverty to be about 25 per cent in both rural and urban areas at the all-India level for 2000–1.

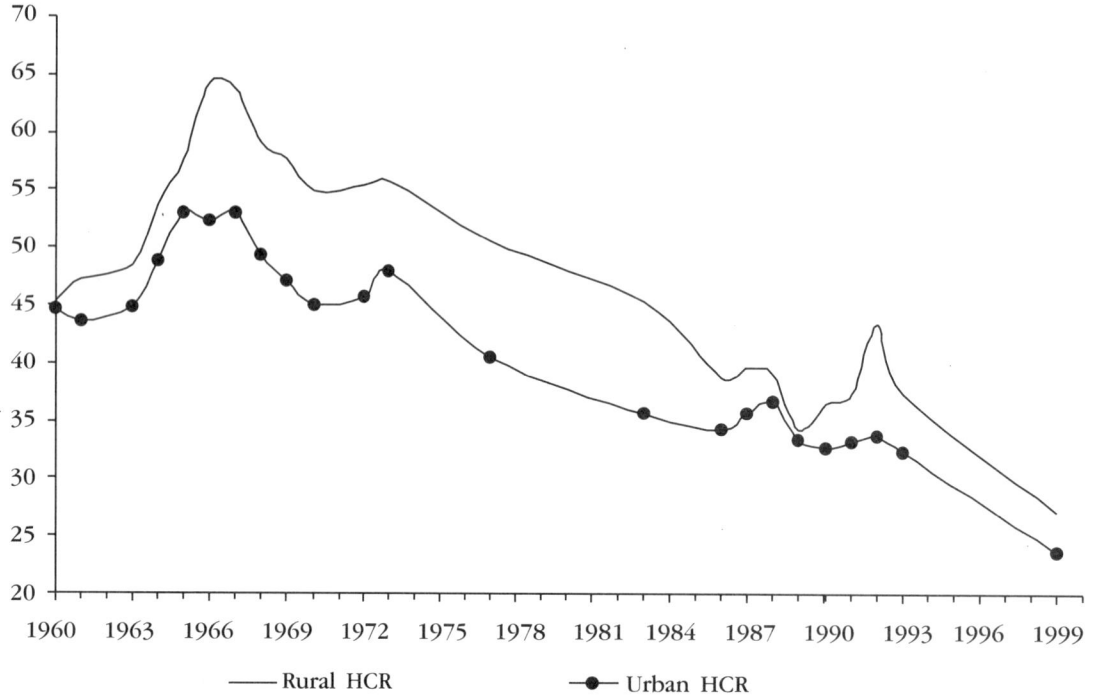

Figure 2.3: Movement of Head Count Ratio of Poverty in Rural and Urban India

Incidence of poverty is affected by two factors—growth in average income and distribution. Poverty reduction is fast when average income rises and inequality falls. While the poor have benefited from both growth and distribution effects in India over a period of about four decades, most of the poverty reduction has been driven by economic growth (Ravallion and Datt 1996). The Indian growth process has been more or less distribution neutral on a long-term basis.[14] The distribution parameter has changed within a narrow range over about four decades with small year-to-year changes in either direction. Given this feature, the fluctuations in poverty incidence till the early 1970s, noted above, are primarily explained by slow per capita income growth. Incidence of poverty started to fall after the mid-1970s when there was a marked acceleration in the per capita GDP growth rate to above 3 per cent (Figure 2.3). Hence, the importance of a critical minimum steady growth in per capita income for poverty reduction could not be overemphasized in the Indian context (Panda 1999).

Table 2.12 presents the HCR of rural poverty for 1993–4 and 1999–2000 for 15 major states in India accounting for about 90 per cent of the total population. Poverty has fallen by about 10 percentage points in 1999–2000 over 1993–4 for all the states taken together. But the performance of the states on the poverty front has not been uniform. Some states like Gujarat, Haryana, Karnataka, Kerala, Punjab, and Rajasthan have been able to reduce the proportion of poor in their states faster than others. These states are also doing reasonably well on the growth front. On the other hand, states like Orissa, Assam, and Bihar have been lagging behind on both growth as well as poverty counts.

Regional Concentration of Poverty

While poverty had fallen at the national level during the 1990s, it is increasingly getting concentrated in certain states. Table 2.12 reveals that there are considerable variations in the incidence of poverty across states and spreads from as low as 6–8 per cent for Punjab and Haryana to as high as 47 per cent for Orissa and 37 per cent for Bihar. Among the 15 major states, six states have HCRs which are higher than the national level of 26 per cent. These states are Orissa, Bihar, Madhya Pradesh, Assam, Uttar Pradesh, and West Bengal and together account for as high as two-thirds of the total number of poor in the country. Three other states—Maharashtra, Tamil Nadu, and Karnataka—exhibit moderate levels of poverty varying between 19–25 per cent. The nine states with high and moderate incidence of poverty contain as much as 85 per cent of India's total poor. Poverty alleviation efforts, henceforth, must be

---

[14] Deaton and Dreze (2002) draw attention to increasing inequality between rural and urban areas and within urban areas during the 1990s.

concentrated in these states so as to make a significant difference at the national level.[15]

TABLE 2.12
Head Count Ratio of Rural Poverty for Major States in India: 1999–2000

State	HCR 1993–4	HCR 1999–2000	Est. number of poor in 1999–2000	Percentage contribution to total poor in 1999–2000
Andhra Pradesh	22.19	15.37	11.27	4.67
Assam	40.86	36.79	8.29	3.44
Bihar	54.96	42.7	39.02	16.18
Gujarat	24.21	13.13	5.67	2.35
Haryana	25.05	8.12	1.54	0.64
Karnataka	33.16	19.02	9.12	3.78
Kerala	25.43	12.12	3.32	1.38
Madhya Pradesh	42.52	37.52	28.79	11.94
Maharashtra	36.86	24.58	22.00	9.12
Orissa	48.56	47.38	16.64	6.9
Punjab	11.77	5.83	1.28	0.53
Rajasthan	27.41	14.78	6.89	2.86
Tamil Nadu	35.03	20.88	12.11	5.02
Uttar Pradesh	40.85	30.99	49.92	20.7
West Bengal	35.66	28.03	20.47	8.49
Total	35.97	26.1	241.21	100

Source: Own estimates based on NSSO unit level data available on CDs.

INTERSTATE GROWTH PERFORMANCE

This brings us to disparities across states in India. As per the new series in national income with 1993–4 base, the per capita GSDP in 1993–4 varied from Rs 19,960 in Delhi to Rs 3400 for Bihar which was roughly in the ratio of 5.9 to 1. Such large interstate variations got further aggravated in 2000–1 when Goa recorded the highest per capita income at Rs 31,000 and Bihar the lowest at Rs 3700 at 1993–4 prices which implied a ratio of 8.4 to 1. Thus, the growth rate of about 6 per cent registered at the national level in the post-liberalization period has not been shared equally across the regions or states in the country.

Figure 2.4 depicts the states arranged in descending order of per capita income in 1993–4 and also plots the average growth rates witnessed by them during 1993–4 to 2000–1. It indicates that, in general, richer states have increased their income faster than poorer states. It could be seen that Delhi and Goa, the two richest states in the base year (1993–4) are also the two fastest growing states in the post-liberalization period. On the other hand, states like Assam, Orissa, Uttar Pradesh, and Bihar, which were at the bottom of the per capita income scale in 1993–4, are among the slowest growing states. The other fast growing states are Karnataka, West Bengal, and Rajasthan from the middle income rung. Punjab, Maharashtra, Haryana, and Gujarat, which had high per capita income to begin with, have been able to maintain moderate to high growth rates in their GSDP. The high-income states have attained moderate to high income

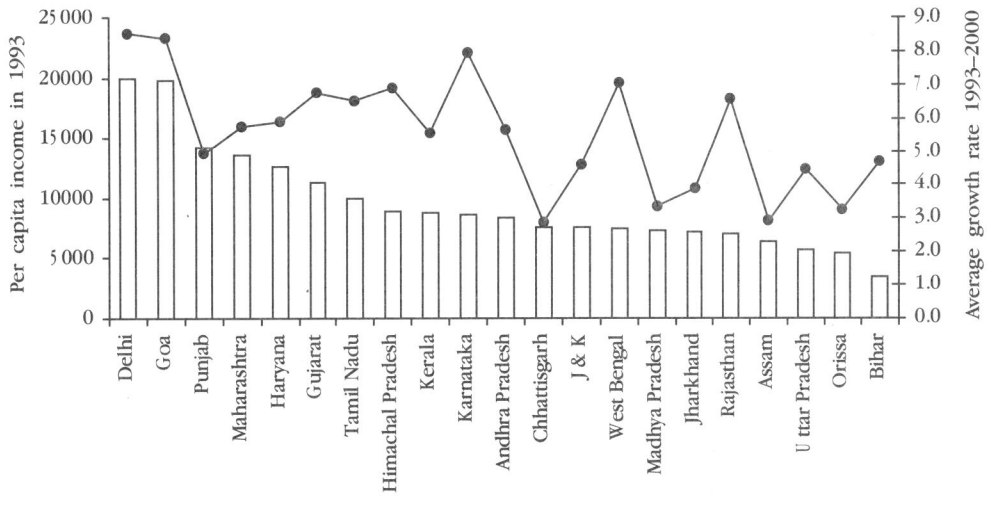

Figure 2.4: Per Capita Income and Average Growth Rate for Major Indian States

[15] Chapter 3, 'Poverty in India: Its Dimensions and Character', in this volume by Radhakrishna and Ray draws attention to this aspect.

growth rates while the low-income states—with the exception of West Bengal and Rajasthan—have attained low income growth rates.

Did the overall degree of interstate disparity increase after liberalization? To answer this question, we take the help of two indices calculated by EPW Research Foundation (EPWRF) (2003). The first relates to the coefficient of variation (CV) in growth rates of GSDP and the second to the Gini coefficient. The CV rose from 30.52 per cent between 1980–1 and 1990–1 to 41.1 per cent between 1993–4 and 2000–1 and that of per capita GSDP from 50.20 to 68.04 during the same period[16] (Table 2.13). The Gini coefficient, a popular measure of inequality, has been rising over the years (Figure 2.5). Taking all the states together, it moved up slowly from 20.9 in 1980–1 to 22.8 in 1991–2, but has moved sharply thereafter to reach 29.2 in 2000–1. Similar movements are noticed even when we consider 16 major states, though the extent of inequality is lower among the major states. Future policy attention must focus on the divergence in per capita income across states.

One might be of the opinion that if realization of maximum growth potential at the national level involves an increase in regional concentration, so be it. Why bother about it? Is it not natural to have regions or states above or below the national level growth rates? However, it would indeed be a matter of concern if interstate disparities get widened over time. Such a concern may arise on several grounds. First, labour is not perfectly

TABLE 2.13
Coefficient of Variations in Growth Rates of State Income

(Percentage)

	Period	For all states	For 16 major states
GSDP at 1980–1 prices	1980–93	29.61	18.12
GSDP at 1993–4 prices	1993–2000	41.09	27.17
Per capita GSDP at 1980–1 prices	1980–93	51.06	29.99
Per capita GSDP at 1993–4 prices	1993–2000	68.04	43.25
GSDP at 1980–1 prices	1980–90	30.52	17.12
GSDP at 1993–4 prices	1990–2000	28.14	27.94
Per capita GSDP at 1980–1 prices	1980–90	50.20	25.36
Per capita GSDP at 1993–4 prices	1990–2000	52.19	48.02

Source: EPWRF (2003).

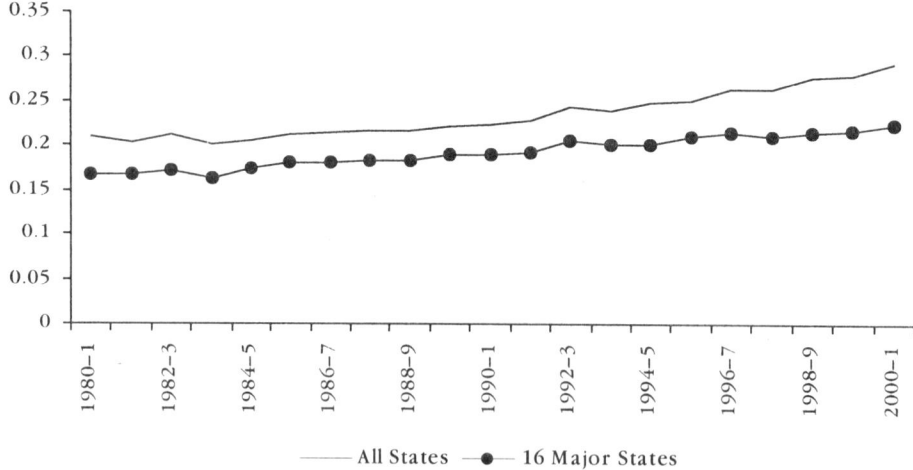

Figure 2.5: Gini Coefficient for Real Per Capita GSDP across States
Source: Based on EPWRF (2003).

[16] EPWRF also notes that if the new GSDP series is extended backwards to cover the period 1990–1 to 2000–1, the CVs in the 1980s and 1990s do not differ significantly. Our emphasis has been on the period 1993–4 onwards since it reflects the developments in the post-liberalization era, while the whole of the 1990s includes the years of crisis and transition.

mobile across regions in India where there are strong sub-national sentiments. Second, there are limits on the part of the central government to undertake large-scale redistributive measures after realizing maximum growth potential at the national level. Third, if some states are deriving benefits of high growth now because of deliberate heavy public investment undertaken by the central government in the past, it is only fair that similar benefits be passed on to their less privileged sister states in the form of infrastructural investment to correct for intertemporal bias.

Thus, recent developments do cause concern about increasing regional disparities and point towards the need for higher growth in the central and eastern regions of the country. These regions are characterized by low per capita income, slow income growth, and a high concentration of poor. The national poverty reduction target would call for fast expansion of state income in the poorer states. Incidentally, the number of total poor in central and eastern India would account for over 20 per cent of the total poor in the world.[17] Unless there is substantial reduction in the incidence of poverty in these regions, it would be difficult to achieve the MDG of the United Nations. It is undoubtedly time to shift the focus of agricultural and rural growth to the central and eastern regions of the country.

The pattern of growth—and not just grown itself—has also been found to be important for poverty reduction. Agricultural growth has a larger effect on poverty reduction than non-agricultural growth.[18] In any case, it would be only natural to focus initial attention on agriculture in the central and eastern regions which have been left out of the green revolution. A strong agricultural base would subsequently develop the rural non-farm sector. The design of policy and incentive mechanisms for spreading growth to the poor regions should be consistent with the national need for diversification towards non-food grains crops and allied activities.

SUMMARY AND CONCLUSIONS

In summary, we find that even 12 years after the initiation of the economic reform measures in 1991, it is admittedly not possible to claim that the Indian economy has been put on a higher growth path compared to the 1980s. However, it is possible to draw attention to several strong features of the economy at present. First, the sustenance of the average GDP growth rate of 5.5 per cent under adverse environments should be viewed as reasonable performance. The economy has withstood rather comfortably several shocks like the East Asian crisis, global depression, border tension, severe natural calamities, the Iraq War, fluctuations in international oil prices, and a major drought during the last five years. Second, constraints on trade and industrial operations prior to the reform meant that the growth process of the 1980s took place under a protected environment and neglected microeconomic efficiency. The growth rates recorded in the post-liberalization era, though quantitatively not very different, have taken place in a competitive environment.[19] Third, there is macroeconomic stability on several counts compared to the 1980s. Inflation is low. The exchange rate is reasonably stable under a managed float regime, foreign exchange reserves have been rising, short-term external debt is low and food grain stocks are adequate even after a drought year.

On the weakness side, high fiscal deficit of about 10 per cent of GDP causes concern about medium-term fiscal stability. The deficit level is worse than that in several countries which went through macroeconomic crisis. India has avoided the crisis due to its strong external and monetary positions noted above.[20] Rising government current expenditure has put pressure on revenue deficit and government savings have turned into dissavings. This has contributed to a fall in overall savings and investment rate in the economy. Acceleration of the GDP growth would critically depend on public finance management to correct primary and revenue deficits and restoring structure of government expenditure in favour of capital formation.

India currently has huge stocks of foreign exchange reserves and foodgrains. These are more than adequate to meet the precautionary needs by conventional wisdom. Stock accumulation is not without cost and, hence, it is time to explore alternative uses to keep the stocks at their optimal levels. It would be beneficial to absorb the capital flows to increase investment so that maximum growth potential of the economy is realized. Similarly, stocks of foodgrains beyond an optimal level are best used for expanding public employment generation programmes for the poor. After all, increasing food stocks is partly due to the lack of purchasing power of the poor.

It now seems certain now that the Tenth Plan's average growth target of 8 per cent during 2002–6 cannot be realized. The Plan's starting point turned out to be a drought year with a growth rate of about 4 per cent and the expected growth during 2003–4 has been about 8 per cent. Realization of the target would thus imply an average growth of 9 per cent during the next three years (2004–6) which is clearly beyond the feasible range on considerations of savings and investment. One might suggest that the Tenth Plan could target to attain about

---

[17] According to World Bank (2003) India accounts for one-third of the total poor in the world.

[18] See Ravallion and Datt (1996).

[19] Indeed, India could emerge as a major economic power if the current growth rate continues for a few more decades (See Box 2.2).

[20] World Bank (2003) describes the overall framework as 'loose fiscal-tight monetary' policy since it puts additional burden on monetary policy to achieve the stabilization goals.

> **Box 2.2**
> **Can India Rise to Become a Major Economic Power?**
>
> This question has recently begged attention of analysts. With an average GDP growth rate of 5.5 per cent per annum since 1980–1, India's per capita income has tripled during the last two decades. Can this trend continue for another half a century? An influential report prepared by Goldman Sachs (Wilson and Purushothaman 2003) answers this question in the affirmative.
>
> The report raised eyebrows because of its striking inference that the economic gravity of the world is likely to change by the middle of this century. The report pointed out that Brazil, Russia, India, and China—the BRICs economies—could become a large force in the world economy by 2050. These four economies would be among the largest six in the world in terms of GDP. For example, India's GDP would be more than that of Italy, France, and Germany by 2025 and that of Japan by 2035. The BRICs could together surpass the G6 countries in US dollar terms in another four decades. If so, the face of the world economy would dramatically change over the next five decades.
>
> The report makes projections from simple but economically plausible growth accounting rules. The numbers are based on projections of labour and capital stocks for the future. It assumes that (a) developing countries catch up with the developed countries on the technology front but witness slower total factor productivity growth as they approach income levels of developed countries, and (b) productivity differential leads to an appreciation of equilibrium exchange rate. The calculations indicate growth potential of the countries if they continue to follow policies broadly favourable to growth like macroeconomic stability, development of efficient economic institutions, openness and high level of education. It notes, 'Of the BRICs, India has the most work to do in expanding education'.
>
> The large absolute size, of course, does not mean that they would be the richest in per capita terms. For example, India's projected per capita income of about US$ 17,000 in 2050 would still be way behind that of the US which is likely to reach US$ 83,000 by then. Moreover, so far as average standard of living in India is concerned, the per capita GDP currently stands at 2840 in PPP US$ terms in 2001, though it is 462 US$ without PPP adjustment. Thus, the purchasing power of the people would not rise as dramatically as the nominal dollar figures indicate.

7 per cent growth during the remaining three years. This would not be possible without a step up in the overall savings and investment rate in the economy and the continuation of the reform process further in order to achieve more efficient resource allocation.

The trade reforms could be continued further to bring down the tariff rates to internationally competitive levels. Freer imports are the best instruments available to put pressure on domestic industry to survive in a competitive environment. However, benefits of trade reforms for growth cannot be reaped in the face of policy restrictions on resource movement within the domestic economy. While product market reforms have brought in competition in availability of goods and services, the gains of the reform measures cannot be realized fully unless substantial factor market reforms also take place. The key areas that call for reforms in the domestic sector in the Indian economy are:

- Labour market
- Land market
- Bankruptcy procedures
- Small Scale Reservation

It is widely recognized that the labour market in organized industry is too restrictive in India. Flexibility in labour laws must be introduced so that producers can reallocate factors to take advantage of new technology and respond to relative price movements across sectors. Moreover, while safeguarding fair interests of labourers, labour laws must not stand in the way of closure of non-viable industries. We need to introduce proper institutional framework through which labour and capital locked up in failed firms are rapidly redeployed into productive uses. In the absence of a reasonable labour laws and bankruptcy procedure, adequate internal and external capital would not flow into productive use.

Land market reforms are necessary for responding to the changing market conditions in agriculture. Land market in India is very thin. For better resource reallocation, the rental market should be activated as a first step with a proper regulatory mechanism that ensures ownership rights of small farmers. For example, it is now recognized that institutional changes like permitting contract farming would be necessary in order that a viable and efficient food processing sector takes off on a large scale in India. Growth in several sectors is also hindered by reservation for SSI which makes no sense in a regime where goods produced outside the country are freely available. Indian industries subject to small scale reservation would find it difficult to derive benefits of economies of scale, even though they would be expected to compete with externally produced goods not subject to constraints of scale.

The economic reform process has caused major structural changes in the Indian economy. This, in turn, provides new livelihood opportunities for the poor. While efficient market-based allocation can provide new employment opportunities to the poor, cases of market failures due to absence of proper institutional mechanisms could adversely affect the poor. The state or other social institutions should ensure in such cases that the poor have access to the market on fair terms.

Redeployment of resources often causes transitional problems. As a rule, there would be gainers and losers in resource reallocation. Quick redeployment of resources could shorten the transition period without postponing the benefits further. At the same time, helping the losers for redeployment and retraining where necessary need to be an integral part of the game. An effective safety net policy that provides short-term income support and access to basic social services during the transition phase could make the reform process more acceptable to the working class. The proper design of such a policy that is broadly consistent with the primary objectives of reform constitutes a major challenge in taking the reform process further into labour and land markets.

Lastly, while poverty has reduced in all major states during the 1990s, the process has been very much uneven. Poverty reduction has been fast in the states which have experienced reasonable growth during the 1990s. There are also strong indications that interstate inequality has been rising during the post-reform period and poverty has become concentrated in the backward regions in central and eastern India. Adequate attention must be given to make the growth process more balanced across regions. The government's role in physical and social capital formation needs to be stepped up in the slow growing backward regions. Significant poverty reduction at the national level would require higher growth in the backward areas in the near future. It is time to shift the focus of growth-oriented public policies to the central and eastern regions of the country on grounds of both higher growth and lower poverty.

References

Balakrishnan, Pulapre and M. Suresh Babu (2003), 'Growth and Distribution in Indian Industry in the Nineties', *Economic and Political Weekly*, Vol. 38, No. 38.

Bhalla, G. S. and Peter Hazell (2003), 'Rural Employment and Poverty: Strategies to Eliminate Rural Poverty', *Economic and Political Weekly*, Vol. 38, No. 33.

Chadha and Sahu (2002), 'Post-reform Setbacks in Rural Employment: Issues that need Further Scrutiny', *Economic and Political Weekly*, Vol. 37, No. 21.

Deaton, Angus and Jean Dreze (2002), 'Poverty and Inequality in India: A re-examination', *Economic and Political Weekly*, Vol. 37, No. 36.

Dholakia, Bakul H. (2002), 'Sources of India's Accelerated Growth and the Vision of Indian Economy in 2020', *Indian Economic Journal*, Vol. 49, No. 4.

EPW Research Foundation (2003), 'Domestic Product of States of India 1960-1 to 2000-1', Mumbai.

Goldar, Bishwanath (2000), 'Productivity Growth in Indian Manufacturing in the 1980s and 1990s', Institute of Economic Growth, New Delhi.

Hasan, Rana, Devashish Mitra, and K. V. Ramaswamy (2003), 'Trade Reforms, Labour Regulations and Labour-demand Elasticities: Empirical Evidence from India', NBER Working Paper No. 9879, National Bureau of Economic Research, Cambridge, MA.

Lal, Deepak, Suman Bery, and Devendra Kumar Pant (2003), 'The Real Exchange Rate, Fiscal Deficits and Capital Flows India: 1981-2000', *Economic and Political Weekly*, Vol. 38, No. 47.

Panda, Manoj (1999), 'Growth with Equity: Policy Lessons from the Experience of India', in *Growth with Equity: Policy Lessons from the Experiences of Selected Asian Countries*, United Nations, New York, 1999 (ST/ESCAP/2007).

Parikh, K., N. S. S. Narayana, M. Panda, and A. Ganesh Kumar (1997), 'Agricultural Liberalization: Growth, Welfare and Large Country Effects', *Agricultural Economics*, Vol. 17, No. 1.

Planning Commission (2004), 'India Vision 2020', Report of the Committee of India Vision 2020, GOI, New Delhi.

——— (2002), 'Tenth Five Year Plan 2002-7, Volume-I', Government of India, New Delhi.

Radhakrishna R. and S. Ray (2004), 'Poverty in India: Its Dimensions and Character', this volume, chapter 3.

Rangarajan, C. and D. K. Srivastava (2003), 'Dynamics of Debt Accumulation in India: Impact of Primary Deficit, Growth and Interest Rate', *Economic and Political Weekly*, Vol. 38, No. 46.

Ravallion, M. and G. Datt (1996), 'India's checkered history in fight against poverty', *Economic and Political Weekly*, Vol. 31, Special Number.

Reserve Bank of India (2003), 'Annual Report 2002-3', Mumbai.

Sundaram, K. and S. D. Tendulkar (2003), 'Poverty Has Declined in the 1990s: A Resolution of Comparability Problems In NSS Consumption Expenditure Data', *Economic and Political Weekly*, Vol. 38, No. 4.

Wilson, Dominic and Roopa Purushothaman (2003), 'Dreaming with BRICs: The Path to 2050; Global Economics Paper No. 99, Goldman Sachs.

World Bank (2003), 'India: Sustaining Reform, Reducing Poverty', Oxford University Press, New Delhi.

3 Poverty in India
Dimensions and Character

R. Radhakrishna • Shovan Ray

Poverty reduction has been a major goal of development policy in India since the country became independent and the achievement of a minimum standard of living for all within a reasonable period has been the implicit or explicit objective of all socio-economic endeavours initiated under the various five-year plans. This was sought to be achieved by attaining higher growth—raising through the purchasing power of the poor with the endowment of land and non-land assets and generating employment opportunities and through public intervention for consumption smoothening by undertaking large scale food-for-work programmes. Poverty alleviation programmes targeted at the poor are supplementing market forces and generic growth strategies. There are by now well laid down procedures for measuring income poverty, for monitoring changes over time and across space, and for identifying the poor, and for evaluating the impact and outcomes of different policies and programmes. There is also extensive literature on different aspects of poverty reduction and also a better understanding of the efficacy of different policies. The recent body of literature highlights the multi-dimensionality of poverty and the conceptual problems involved in aggregation across the dimensions and the inadequacy of operationalizing poverty in terms of income. It also highlights that the poor are not a single homogenous lot.

The proportion of people below the poverty line (BPL) remained above 50 per cent with no declining trend till the mid-1970s but registered thereafter a declining trend with yearly fluctuations. It declined perceptively in the late 1970s and 1980s from 51 per cent in 1977–8 to 39 per cent in 1987–8 (Planning Commission). The intensity of poverty has also declined considerably in both rural and urban areas. The declining long-term trend has been sustained in the 1990s although with sharp year to year variations (Figure 3.1). Yet, 260 million Indians (193 million in rural and 67 million in urban India) remained below the poverty line in 1999–2000.[1] It is clear that even with the reduction in the poverty level, absolute poverty in India, even in income terms, remains unacceptably large. Economic growth and improvement in real wages, particularly with growth in agriculture which supports a considerable part of the population, has impacted upon the proportion of persons in poverty. It is not just income growth alone that has brought about poverty reduction through the trickledown process. There have been direct interventions too in a major way for poverty alleviation in India. The major poverty alleviation programmes include self-employment programmes, wage employment programmes, PDS and nutrition programmes, and social security programmes.[2] Employment creation through investment in infrastructure development and pension schemes for the elderly are the recent initiatives. There has also been some shift in strategy from individual and household-centred approach to community/group-based approach and, what is more, social mobilization for improving the livelihood of the poor is gaining some prominence.

The poverty situation today is markedly different from that which prevailed three decades back. The

---

[1] There has been an interesting debate on the measurement of poverty in the 55th Round (1999–2000) of NSS and adjustments have been made to suggest alternative figures of poverty. See Sen (2000), Deaton and Dreze (2002).

[2] A recent study by the Indira Gandhi Institute of Development Research (IGIDR) prepared for UNDP/UNOPS on South Asia Poverty Alleviation Programme (SAPAP, 2003), provides a detailed account of programmes and policies for direct and related interventions in India.

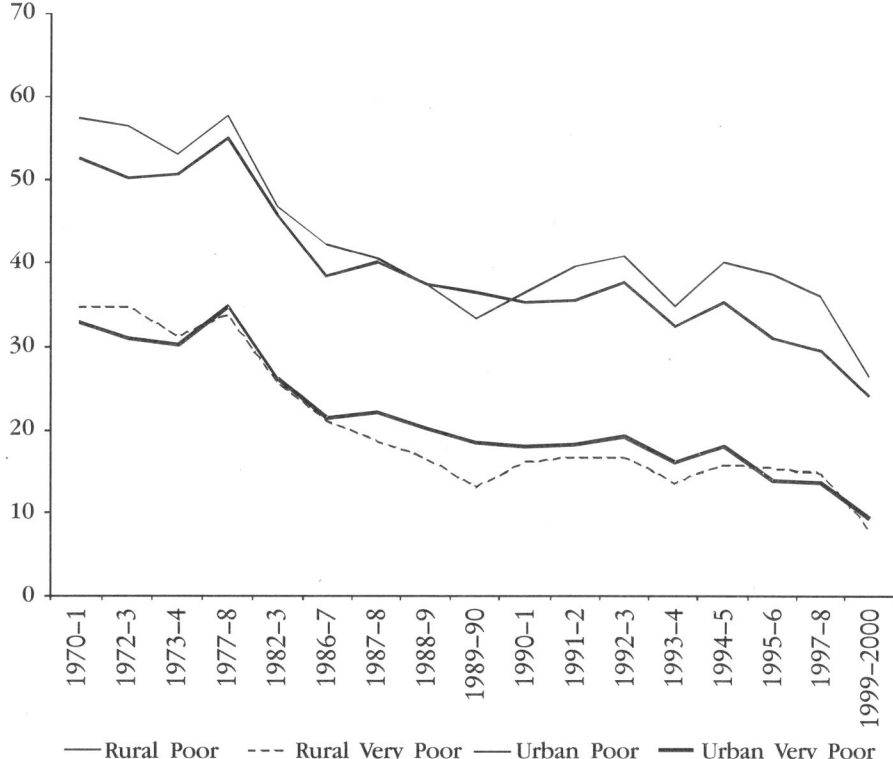

Figure 3.1: Trends in Poverty in India

spatial map and social base of poverty have significantly changed over time, and poverty is increasingly getting concentrated in a few geographical locations and among specific social groups. The geographical divide can be illustrated by the increased relative share of the undeveloped states such as Bihar, Orissa, Madhya Pradesh, and Uttar Pradesh in the all-India rural poor from 53 per cent in 1993–4 to 61 per cent in 1999–2000 and a reduced share of the developed north-western states (Punjab, Haryana, and Himachal Pradesh) from 3 to 1 per cent (SAPAP 2003).

Poverty in India is not merely an economic phenomenon but also a social one. It is disproportionately high among SCs and STs.[3] Whether one considers the Planning Commission's estimates or those of individual scholars, the share of the STs in poverty had gone up during the 1990s and that of SCs remained more or less the same. The tribal communities in the north-east of India have done relatively better for themselves. But as a group, tribals in India are poor and deprived. Also, in states which achieved substantial poverty reduction, the remaining poor belong to either of these two disadvantaged groups. For instance, in 1999–2000, Punjab had

6 per cent of its rural population below poverty line, but SCs alone accounted for 76 per cent of the poor while their share in rural population was 38 per cent (Radhakrishna et al. 2003).

For a long time anti-poverty strategies have looked at poverty reduction in minimalist terms of bringing the poor above the poverty line by focusing on their income improvement through employment programmes targeted at the individual. The poor near the poverty line might indeed cross the poverty line and leave behind the hard core poor who suffer from multiple deprivation. It is now widely recognized that while income poverty reduction is relatively easy, elimination of multiple deprivation is more difficult to achieve. The magnitude of deprivation has been brought out by two recent large-scale nationwide surveys. The NFHS (1998) reveals that 47 per cent of children are malnourished and 74 per cent are anaemic; 36 per cent of ever-married women aged 15–49 years have chronic energy deficiency; 54 per cent of women aged 15–49 years in rural areas have no education; about 50 per cent of the pregnant women suffer from iron deficiency; 71 per cent of rural households do not have any toilet facility; 19 per cent of villages do not have any health facility, and 51 per cent of the villages do not have any drainage facility—either underground or open. The National Council of Applied Economic Research (NCAER) survey of human development in India

---

[3] Recently, two journals dedicated a special number each to the deliberations on Scheduled Castes in India—*Artha Vijnana*, Mar–June (2001) and *Journal of Indian School of Political Economy*, July–December (2000).

has also tended to reveal a similar picture—50 per cent of the rural population suffer from 'capability poverty'; 43 per cent of rural households have domestic lighting, only 25 per cent have access to tap water, and a mere 33 per cent utilize the public distribution facilities (Shariff 1999). Clearly, poverty reduction strategy should go beyond income poverty and inadequacy of basic needs and rights as well as inadequate access to both productive assets and social infrastructure.

Poverty is seen today as an outcome of multiple deprivations, and empowerment of the poor is considered a critical factor in accelerating poverty reduction. Empowerment is sought to be achieved by giving a role to the poor in governance and development decisions. At present, NGOs, activists, and donor agencies have a substantial presence in the field exerting pressure on policy-makers to involve the stakeholder in the project cycle of poverty alleviation programmes, activate the panchayats and promote institutions like self-help groups and user groups, and mobilize the poor for collective action. SAPAP (2003) notes that poverty is a product of livelihood systems and the socio-political and economic forces that shape them, and argues that multi-dimensional interventions revolving around land and other property rights, bargaining power for improved wage rate, holistic health care, micro insurance, and physical and social security are needed for accelerating poverty reduction.[4] The key issue is to weaken the strong hold of the rich in the governance of local institutions and facilitate the participation of the poor. The route to poverty reduction differs across states. Box 3.1 presents some contrasting situations.

In this chapter we cover mainly the post-reform period and argue for the need for a perspective that views the poor as part of a wider society with links and relationships that affect their economic conditions.[5]

POVERTY IN THE POST-REFORM PERIOD

During the 1990s, the tendencies of slowing down of rural employment growth and slowdown in the growth momentum of rural non-agricultural activities seem to have affected the pace of decline in rural poverty and aggravated rural–urban disparities. We review in this context the trends in total expenditure utilizing the NSSO Consumer Expenditure data of the last three decades.[6]

Rural per capita total expenditure (PCE) per month at 1990–1 prices which was Rs 158 in 1970–1, increased steadily to Rs 213 by 1989–90 and declined sharply by 5 per cent to Rs 202 in 1990–1 (The NSSO Consumer Expenditure Data). During the 1990s, it fluctuated between Rs 202–14, except in 1997 when it reached the highest level of Rs 235. Its annual trend growth rate fell to 1.17 per cent (1.40 per cent if the 55th Round is included) from 1.54 per cent during 1970–89 (Table 3.1). In contrast, the urban annual growth rate accelerated from 1.45 per cent during 1970–89, to about 2.77 per cent (2.27 per cent if the 55th NSS Round is included). Clearly, rural–urban disparity widened during the 1990s. There had been no significant change in the ratio of urban to rural per capita expenditure during 1970–89, but it increased thereafter at the rate of 1.6 per cent per annum. The 1990s growth benefited urban areas the most and aggravated the rural–urban divide. Our results are robust whether we include or exclude the 55th Round from the analysis. The widening rural–urban disparity has coincided with widening inequality in the urban expenditure distribution: Gini coefficient of urban consumer expenditure which had no trend increase during 1970–89 has increased at an annual rate of 1.4 per cent per annum during the 1990s (The NSSO Consumer Expenditure Data). The widening inequality is also reflected in the differential growth across the urban expenditure groups. The per capita expenditure of the top 30 per cent increased at 3.31 per cent (2.55 per cent if the 55th Round is included) per annum while that of the bottom 30 per cent increased at 1.70 per cent (1.47 per cent if the 55th Round is included). On the other hand, rural inequality tended to decline in the 1990s. The rural bottom 30 per cent experienced a decline in the annual growth rate of per capita expenditure during the 1990s. It dropped from 1.71 per cent during 1970–89 to 1.19 per cent during 1990–8 (1.49 per cent if the 55th Round is included). However, even in this decline the rate of growth for the bottom 30 per cent was higher in comparison to the middle and top groups. Our analysis conclusively shows that in the

---

[4] 'The micro finance and social development and social protection policies and programmes hold great potential. The GO, NGO, CBO, SHG, and PRI partnership and network for information exchange, resource sharing, negotiations, bargaining and lobbying should be strengthened further for sustainable development'. It also notes: 'while we want the institutional change to help the poor, institutions including the state and NGO tend to be controlled by the powerful non-poor. Often those who control one institution also control others'.

[5] Tables included in this paper are drawn from the IGIDR–IIPA project on Chronic Poverty (2003).

[6] This review is based on the detailed study of Ravi (2000) for the period 1970–1 to 1998. Ravi has updated his study and shared with us his estimates for 1999–2000. Leaving aside the conceptual problems created by changes in methodologies in the 55th NSS round, its data have been utilized for checking the robustness of the findings based on Ravi's earlier estimates which includes those of thin samples.

Box 3.1

Socio-Economic Status, Perceptions and Aspirations of the Poor
in Three Contrasting States

Kerala

Kerala's achievements in social development and reduction in poverty are very impressive. It is topmost among the states in the ranking based on composite index of socio-economic and demographic indicators. Out of its 14 districts, seven are among the first 10 districts and 13 among the first 100 districts. Kerala has also experienced substantial rural diversification driven by commercialization rather than rural industrial enterprises. The share of non-agriculture in the rural workforce was 71.3 per cent as against 26.7 per cent for all-India. However, Kerala's impressive social development has not been matched by adequate employment generation. Despite high remittances sustained over a long period (about 30 per cent of state-level domestic product (SDP)), industrial investment has remained low. Kerala's impressive development has also not been matched by adequate employment generation.

The percentage of poor in rural areas declined from 50 per cent in 1973–4 to 12.7 per cent in 1999–2000. Kerala's record of overcoming poverty even with moderate economic growth has been attributed to its effective implementation of land reforms, comprehensive social and food security coverage and public action—of democratically elected state governments, decentralized system of governance and a highly conscious civil society. Recent *Peoples' campaign* and *Kutambashree* programmes have also impacted upon poverty. However, the state has been affected during the last three years by the sharp fall in the prices of cash crops in the world market which might have aggravated transient poverty.

Poverty gets increasingly concentrated among casual labour, particularly those engaged in agricultural activities; casual labour (agricultura + non-agricultural) accounts for 72 per cent and agricultural labour 47 per cent of the rural poor. Poverty has spread across caste groups; SCs and STs constitute 21 per cent of the poor, much less compared to other states.

Despite a moderate level of economic development, Kerala could make a significant dent on poverty during the last three decades. Sustainability of low levels of poverty assumes importance in the wake of trade liberalization, a stagnant agriculture, and a highly unionized labour.

Poverty and unemployment has one to one relationship among low income groups in Kerala. The number of days of unemployment for the very poor exceeds 200 days in a year. Occasional hunger is prevalent among the poor. Migration and indebtedness are some of the coping mechanisms.

The poor perceive poverty to be a situation where a household fails to make both ends meet and forces it to indulge in borrowings. Poverty makes them vulnerable to 'shocks'. The very poor are those who can hardly afford more than one meal a day and depend exclusively on a single source of income and also depend on others for daily needs. The poorest, are the tribals living in remote areas, the SCs who depend exclusively on forests for livelihood and the fisher-folk. These groups are often deprived of access to health and education. For the reduction of poverty, the suggestions of the poor include: reorganization of labour and development of infrastructure, quality of education, market oriented skills, and increased access to health services. The poor also indicated that decentralized governance would be an effective intervention for the supply of social goods and services to the poor.

Gujarat

Gujarat has been on the forefront of economic growth in the last two decades and as a leading state in terms of private investment and foreign capital inflows. However, it is comparatively a laggard in sectors such as population and demography, agriculture, health and nutrition, education, environment and natural resources. The contribution of agriculture to growth has been very limited and the state has suffered from shocks due to drought towards the end of the 1990s. Employment growth has been dismal due to low employment elasticity. This has been due to the sectoral pattern of growth biased against agriculture and the type of industries chosen. Both out-migration from rural areas and in-migration into rural and urban areas from both within the state and from other states impose enormous social costs on migrant households.

The economic growth impacted upon income poverty, which declined in rural areas from 46.4 per cent in 1973–4 to 13.7 per cent in 1999–2000. Poverty is concentrated among SC/ST communities and casual wage labour. Casual labour constitutes 70 per cent of the rural poor and SC and ST account for 57 per cent of the poor. High dependency rates, lack of skills and asset-less-ness are the basic characteristics of most of the poor. Seasonal hunger though prevails in poor households is not a wide spread phenomenon. The poor have not benefitted much either from Rural Development or Poverty Alleviation Programmes. Agriculture is the major source of employment for the

(contd.)

Box 3.1 (contd.)

poor. The earning members of SC/ST communities were unemployed for periods extending upto four months. High incidence of child labour has been observed among the severe poor (landless labour households). Seasonal migration is less common among the poorer sections compared to the non-poor and borrowing is the main coping mechanism. Access to safety nets is weak for the poor.

The poor in Gujarat perceive poverty more as an economic deprivation. The major causes of poverty as perceived by the poor are inadequate employment opportunities (86 per cent); low levels of literacy (83 per cent); low wages (81 per cent) and less occupational diversification (68 per cent).

The poor strongly consider that provision of wage and self-employment are the most appropriate interventions for poverty reduction. The other public support systems include: wide and effective coverage of PDS, social assistance, enforcement of minimum wages and distribution of surplus land. They have stated that development of economic infrastructure (irrigation and transport network) and location of industries would help the poor.

Madhya Pradesh

Madhya Pradesh is characterized by a high incidence of poverty, the lowest literacy rate and the highest rate of child mortality. It is at the bottom of the ranking based on composite index of socio-economic and demographic indicators. None of the districts figure among the first 100 districts. Lack of diversification is the chief characteristic of its economy—86 per cent of its rural workers (72 per cent of the total workers) depend on agriculture for their livelihood. Unirrigated agriculture which account for two-thirds of the cultivated land is highly degraded and characterized by low agricultural productivity, low wages, high distressed seasonal migration and high incidence of child and bonded labour.

Most of the poor in Madhya Pradesh are SCs and STs. Together they account for about 60 per cent of the rural poor. Close to 70 per cent of the poor are engaged in agricultural activities. Child labour is a widespread phenomenon and is also one of the coping mechanisms of the poor to avert distress—the other coping mechanisms being indebtedness and migration. Occasional hunger is prevalent among the poor households'. Social exclusion due to caste hierarchy prevents the poor to gain from development process. The degradation of land and water resources and a poor communication network are also responsible for high levels of poverty. The gender disparities further compounded the complex problem of multiple deprivation.

The SCs and STs own less land and generally poor quality land. In the land reform process, the land distributed was government wasteland which is generally of poor quality. In some cases, the poor were denied the allotted land which was under the illegal possession of the dominant castes. However, in some locations, land reform was found to have strengthened the livelihoods of the poor and made them credit-worthy. Second round of land reforms and improvements in land records are necessary for poverty reduction.

The poor men perceive lack of wealth and ability to accumulate as the reason for poverty. Poor women feel that inability to cope with distress and daily struggle for survival is poverty. The poor have observed that fragmentation of assets like land and low productivity of resources accentuates poverty. Instances of displacement and access restriction to common pool research (CPRs) are also identified as major sources of insecurity to them. The poor in the forest area have attributed their poverty to the degradation of forests. The poor feel that basic minimum services provided by the local bodies are of low quality and have led to poor quality of life.

The poor have observed that more thrust on programmes which enhance the rural livelihoods and direct anti-poverty initiatives would help them. Improved access of the poor to assets, natural resources, public goods, and political institutions suggested for poverty reduction. Quality of governance and its sensitivity to the problems of the poor is considered equally important.

Source: Asian Development Bank sponsored study in 'Poverty Assessment in Gujarat, Kerala, and Madhya Pradesh' undertaken by the National Institute of Rural Development and NGOs. For details see Radhakrishna et al. (2003), *Chronic Poverty Report (Draft).*

1990s, urban areas gained substantially from growth and the top 30 per cent the most and the relative position of rural areas turned adverse. Due to methodological controversies relating to the 55th Round, it cannot be said decisively whether the PCE growth in rural areas has slowed, but acceleration, as observed in the case of urban areas, is ruled out. It is, however, seen that the rate of decline in poverty was much slower in rural areas as compared to urban areas.

Rural poverty ratio declined at an annual rate of 2.5 per cent during the 1970s and 1980s (The NSSO Consumer Expenditure Data). The inclusion and exclusion of the 55th Round produces varying results relating to poverty reduction in the 1990s. There was deceleration in the rate of reduction in rural poverty if the 55th Round data was excluded and, in fact, during 1990–8, the rate has dropped to 0.73. However, there may not be such a drop in the growth rate if the 55th Round data

TABLE 3.1
Growth Rates of Total Expenditure at 1990–1 Prices and Poverty

(per cent per annum)

Annualized growth rates

Rural

Per capita total expenditure

	Bottom 30%	Middle 40%	Top 30%	All classes
1970–89	1.71	1.40	1.45	1.54
1990–8	1.19	1.11	1.23	1.18
1990–2000*	1.49	1.32	1.41	1.40

Urban

Per capita total expenditure

	Bottom 30%	Middle 40%	Top 30%	All classes
1970–89	1.44	1.50	1.40	1.45
1990–8	1.70	2.27	3.31	2.77
1990–2000*	1.49	2.11	2.55	2.27

* Includes 55th Round

Annual growth of poverty

Rural

	Head count	Poverty gap ratio	Squared poverty gap
1970–89	–2.50	–4.14	–5.78
1990–8	–0.73	–1.30	–2.09

Urban

	Head count	Poverty gap ratio	Squared poverty gap
1970–89	–1.96	–2.90	–4.09
1990–8	–3.05	–4.39	–6.59

Source: Ravi (2000).

are included. On the other hand, urban poverty declined at the rate of 2 per cent per annum during the 1970s and the 1980s and at 3.05 per cent during 1990–8.

PROFILES OF THE POOR

The composition of the poor has been changing and rural poverty is getting mostly concentrated in the agricultural labour and artisan households and urban poverty in the casual labour households (Tables 3.2–3.3). Agricultural labour households which accounted for 41 per cent of rural poor in 1993–4 increased to 47 per cent in 1999–2000 (Table 3.3). In contrast, the share of the self-employed in agriculture among rural poor dropped from 33 to 28 per cent. The relative size of agricultural labour households among the poor has increased from 28 to 31 per cent due to the increased dependency of rural households on agricultural labour for livelihood as well as higher incidence of poverty among agricultural labour households—40 per cent in 1999–2000 in contrast to 26 per cent in all rural households (Table 3.2). Casual labour households constituted 32 per cent of urban poor in 1999–2000 increasing from 25 per cent in 1993–4. The increase in its share was both due to the increased dependency of urban households on urban casual labour market from 25 per cent in 1993–4 to 32 per cent in 1999–2000 as well as higher incidence of poverty among urban casual labour households. It needs to be recognized that growing dependency of rural and urban households on casual labour market exposes the poor to market risks and tends to increase transient poverty, whereby households move in and out of poverty due to fluctuations in the labour market.

The geographical landscape of rural poverty has been changing (Figure 3.2). The percentage share of backward states such as Bihar, Orissa, Madhya Pradesh, and Uttar Pradesh in the rural poor rose from 53 in 1993–4 to 61 in 1999, whereas the share of the agriculturally prosperous north-western states of Punjab, Haryana, and Himachal Pradesh declined from 3.03 to 1.26 per cent and that of the southern states from 15.12 to 11.23 per cent (SAPAP 2003). Interestingly, some of the better-off states such as Maharashtra, Gujarat, and West Bengal had a relatively higher share in rural poverty. These three states accounted for one-fifth of the rural poor in 1999–2000. The urban poor were getting concentrated in Uttar Pradesh, Maharashtra, West Bengal, Madhya Pradesh, and Andhra Pradesh. Their share in all-India urban poverty rose from 56 per cent in 1993–4 to 60 per cent in 1999–2001.

TABLE 3.2
Incidence of Poverty Level—Social and Occupational Group

Category	Incidence (%)			
	Very poor		Poor	
	1993–4	1999–2000	1993–4	1999–2000
Rural				
Caste				
ST	22.1	17.0	50.2	44.2
SC	21.7	11.5	48.3	35.3
OBC	NA	7.0	NA	25.5
Occupation				
Agricultural labour	26.2	14.1	54.4	39.7
Non-agricultural labour	15.2	8.7	42.2	27.2
Urban				
Caste				
ST	24.0	17.5	43.0	37.5
SC	26.1	16.4	50.9	39.1
OBC	–	10.7	–	30.2
Occupation				
Casual labour	36.6	26.0	64.5	53.0

Source: Computed using NSS 50th and 55th Round data on Household Consumer Expenditure.

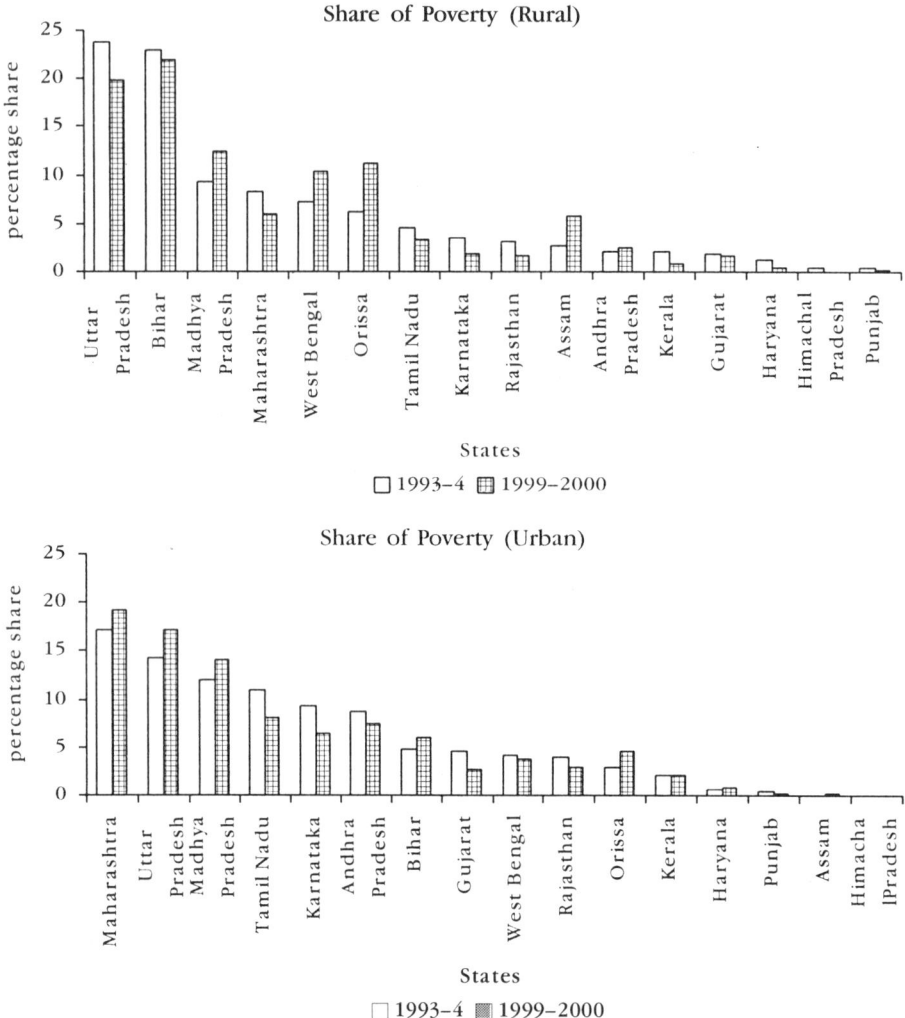

Figure 3.2: Share of Poverty—Statewise.

The occupational composition of the rural poor varied across the states. In general, in the developed states poverty was highly concentrated among agricultural labour households and, in contrast, in the backward states poverty extended to other occupational groups, including the self-employed in agriculture (Table 3.3). For instance, in Punjab, Haryana, Maharashtra, and Andhra Pradesh agricultural labour households constituted more than 60 per cent of the rural poor in 1999–2000, but they constituted less than 16 per cent in Rajasthan and 28 per cent in Assam.

Among the social groups, SCs, STs, and backward castes accounted for 81 per cent of the rural poor in 1999–2000 (Table 3.4) whereas they were considerably less among the rural population. The poor among the SCs in rural areas were concentrated in Uttar Pradesh, Bihar, and West Bengal. They comprised 58 per cent of the poor among SCs. In urban areas, Madhya Pradesh and Uttar Pradesh accounted for 41 per cent of the poor among the SCs. The incidence of poverty among SCs was high in Bihar, Madhya Pradesh, and Uttar Pradesh in both rural and urban areas. In terms of income poverty and other indicators of human development also such as education, health, etc., the STs are at the bottom. The increasing concentration of poverty among tribals who suffer from multiple deprivations is a matter of concern (see Box 3.2).

The percentage of ST population among the rural poor has been increasing fast. It increased from 14.8 in 1993–4 to 17.5 in 1999–2000 (Table 3.4). The increase was mainly on account of the comparatively slower reduction in the incidence of poverty among the STs. The percentage of poor among the STs declined from 50 in 1993–4 to 44.2 in 1999–2000 whereas for all rural population it declined from 37 to 27. Bihar, Gujarat, Madhya Pradesh, and Maharashtra together accounted for 75.5 per cent of the poor among STs in 1999–2000. It is noteworthy that nearly 30 per cent of the poor were located in Madhya Pradesh. The poverty levels of STs in rural areas were high in Orissa (73 per cent), Bihar

TABLE 3.3
Percentage Distribution of Persons Below Poverty Line by Occupation Groups—Statewise, 1993-4 and 1999-2000

(Rural)

State	Year	Artisans	Agricultural labour	Non-agricultural labour	Self-employed in agriculture	Others	Total
Andhra Pradesh	1993-4	7.8	51.3	7.3	19.2	14.3	100.0
	1999-2000	10.5	63.9	4.6	18.5	2.5	
Assam	1993-4	9.6	28.7	15.5	40.2	6.0	100.0
	1999-2000	15.2	27.8	20.6	28.6	7.8	
Bihar	1993-4	11.0	46.9	3.7	32.2	6.3	100.0
	1999-2000	12.3	46.5	6.3	26.4	8.5	
Gujarat	1993-4	7.6	49.2	9.1	18.8	15.3	100.0
	1999-2000	7.1	59.1	10.8	19.1	3.8	
Haryana	1993-4	14.3	32.1	18.8	29.4	5.4	100.0
	1999-2000	17.2	50.3	22.2	6.6	3.8	
Himachal Pradesh	1993-4	7.9	4.3	17.6	65.8	4.4	100.0
	1999-2000	12.5	8.0	34.1	40.6	4.8	
Karnataka	1993-4	12.6	54.2	2.9	28.5	1.8	100.0
	1999-2000	8.8	59.7	4.2	24.7	2.7	
Kerala	1993-4	13.3	35.0	23.2	11.2	17.3	100.0
	1999-2000	14.6	46.7	25.4	7.6	5.8	
Madhya Pradesh	1993-4	5.2	45.2	4.8	42.8	1.9	100.0
	1999-2000	6.2	51.2	6.1	34.0	2.4	
Maharashtra	1993-4	5.1	48.9	6.6	19.1	20.4	100.0
	1999-2000	5.5	66.4	4.1	20.6	3.3	
Orissa	1993-4	14.2	45.2	5.3	30.8	4.4	100.0
	1999-2000	8.2	55.9	4.2	26.6	5.1	
Punjab	1993-4	12.4	64.3	11.2	7.7	4.4	100.0
	1999-2000	11.1	66.0	10.5	5.2	7.1	
Rajasthan	1993-4	9.4	14.1	27.9	42.4	6.2	100.0
	1999-2000	9.2	16.0	22.3	47.8	4.7	
Tamil Nadu	1993-4	8.2	61.4	9.5	16.0	4.8	100.0
	1999-2000	10.0	65.5	9.5	9.7	5.4	
Uttar Pradesh	1993-4	14.1	26.5	6.0	49.5	3.9	100.0
	1999-2000	17.2	29.9	6.9	40.1	5.9	
West Bengal	1993-4	18.3	44.1	13.7	21.5	2.5	100.0
	1999-2000	20.4	55.4	5.5	15.4	3.3	
Other States and Union Territories	1993-4	9.6	21.1	16.8	43.6	8.9	100.0
	1999-2000	3.2	33.2	13.5	38.7	11.4	
All India	1993-4	11.2	40.7	8.4	33.2	6.5	100.0
	1999-2000	12.3	46.8	7.6	28.1	5.3	

Source: Computed from NSS 50th and 55th Rounds data on Household Consumer Expenditure.

(59 per cent), Madhya Pradesh (57 per cent), and West Bengal (50 per cent) and in urban areas, in Orissa (59 per cent), Karnataka (52 per cent), Andhra Pradesh (46 per cent), and Bihar (43 per cent).

Severity of Poverty

The percentage of the very poor in rural areas declined from 15 in 1993-4 to 8 in 1999-2000 and in urban areas from 15 to 9—a decline by about 1 percentage point per year (Table 3.5). The data show faster decline in the case of the very poor as compared to the poor. For instance, Ravi (2000) shows that during 1970-89, the percentage of the very poor declined at an annual rate of 4.15 per cent in rural areas and 2.86 per cent in urban areas, whereas the percentage of poor declined at 2.50 per cent in rural areas and 1.96 per cent in urban areas. If the historical trends persist the percentage of the very poor

> **BOX 3.2**
> **Profile of Scheduled Tribes**
>
> There are more than 400 ST communities spread across the country and they constitute about 8 per cent of the total population. Certain geographical areas are, however, characterized by large tribal habitats. Across the states, they live in areas of difficult access such as hills, forests, deserts, perpetually snowbound areas and in small and scattered hamlets. These also contribute to their social exclusion and economic marginalization. The STs are mostly located in central and eastern parts of India besides the north-east, where they constitute the numerically, socially, and politically dominant communities in most states except Assam.
>
> Among the various factors responsible for the persistence of hard core poverty and marginalization of tribals, land alienation is one of the most important ones. This has been mainly caused by large development projects, increasing urbanization, acquisition of tribal lands, etc. Although a number of legislations have been enacted to preserve the rights of the tribal community over land, in recent years, landlessness among them has considerably increased. The discrimination in the labour markets is another important reason. Compared to other social groups, a substantially higher portion of the ST population is involved in low-quality employment such as agricultural and non-agricultural labour with low productivity. The level of occupational diversification is also very low—more than 70 per cent of them are dependent on agriculture either as self-employed or casual labourers. The acute shortage of employment opportunities in tribal regions has led to some kind of forced out-migration of tribal workers who get working opportunities only in low-quality occupations.
>
> In terms of indicators of human development such as education and health also, STs are at the bottom of the pile. Literacy levels are much lower than that of other social groups like SCs, OBCs, etc., and gender disparity in literacy is also very high among STs. Female literacy is as low as 32 per cent in rural areas and 60 per cent in urban areas. The education status of their children is also quite deplorable—61 per cent in the age group 5–14 years are currently enrolled in school. This leads to a substantially higher concentration of child labour within the community. In terms of health indicators also STs are ranked at the bottom. NFHS II shows that the IMR among STs is as high as 84 as against 62 in other categories per thousand live births.

will reduce to insignificant levels by the end of this decade in most of the states.

Interstate variations in the incidence of the very poor were significant—the incidence of the very poor in rural areas varied between 0 and 21.7 per cent in 1999–2000 and in urban areas between 0 and 21.6 per cent (Table 3.5). Meghalaya, Mizoram, Nagaland, Delhi, Chandigarh, Andaman and Nicobar Islands, Lakshadweep, Goa, and Daman and Diu had no incidence of the very poor. Almost all of them had either no or very low incidence of very poor even in 1993–4. All these union territories and small states performed extremely well in reducing the severity of poverty. It is worth noting that Rajasthan, a less developed state, performed well in the reduction of incidence of the very poor.

Orissa had the highest incidence of the very poor in rural as well as urban areas in 1999–2000, and presented a different picture in the 1990s in reducing the incidence of the very poor (Table 3.5). Assam is in league with Orissa in terms of poor performance. The incidence of the very poor increased in Assam between 1993–4 and 1999–2000 in both rural and urban areas despite a reduction in the percentage of the poor, implying worsening of inequality among the poor. Bihar and Madhya Pradesh had a high incidence of the very poor in rural as well as urban areas, Assam and West Bengal had a high incidence of the very poor in rural areas, as did Maharashtra, Uttar Pradesh, and Pondicherry in urban areas (See Table 3.5).

In rural areas, very poor STs were located mainly in four states, namely, Madhya Pradesh, Orissa, Bihar and Maharashtra (Radhakrishna et al. 2003). They comprised 77 per cent of the very poor STs in 1999–2000 (ibid.). In the case of SCs, the very poor were concentrated in Uttar Pradesh, Bihar, and West Bengal—they together accounted for 63 per cent of the very poor SCs in 1999–2000. In urban areas, the very poor among SCs and STs were mostly located in these states (ibid.). It is worth noting that the concentration of the very poor in these states tended to be somewhat higher than the concentration of the poor.

Chronic Poverty

How can chronically poor households be identified among the poor? The sub-category of poor persons who are below the poverty line for a long duration, usually five years, constitute the chronic poor. In practice, the availability of data dictates the norm chosen for duration. In the National Sample Surveys (NSS), the duration does not extend beyond a year and also specific household consumption is available for a reference period of usually one month. Hence, it is not possible to identify the chronic poor from the NSS data.

TABLE 3.4
Percentage Distribution of Persons Below Poverty Line by Caste—Statewise 1993-4 and 1999-2000

(Rural)

State	Year	ST	SC	OBC	Others	Total
Andhra Pradesh	1993-4	15.4	31.6		53.0	
	1999-2000	15.6	35.0	41.3	(49.4) 8.1	100.0
Assam	1993-4	13.3	9.3		77.5	
	1999-2000	15.4	12.5	18.8	(72.1) 53.3	100.0
Bihar	1993-4	10.1	26.5		63.4	
	1999-2000	9.5	28.1	50.4	(62.4) 12.0	100.0
Gujarat	1993-4	30.8	18.0		51.1	
	1999-2000	43.1	13.8	29.3	(43.1) 13.8	100.0
Haryana	1993-4	–	47.2		52.8	
	1999-2000	–	55.4	36.9	(44.6) 7.7	100.0
Himachal Pradesh	1993-4	9.2	29.1		61.7	
	1999-2000	2.7	41.9	10.7	(55.4) 44.7	100.0
Karnataka	1993-4	11.7	32.5		57.0	
	1999-2000	11.6	30.0	36.6	(58.8) 21.9	100.0
Kerala	1993-4	2.2	14.9		83.0	
	1999-2000	4.5	16.4	59.3	(79.1) 19.8	100.0
Madhya Pradesh	1993-4	41.4	19.5		39.2	
	1999-2000	42.9	16.0	36.0	(41.0) 5.0	100.0
Maharashtra	1993-4	18.1	22.0		59.9	
	1999-2000	31.7	17.7	28.5	(50.6) 22.1	100.0
Orissa	1993-4	36.0	18.5		45.5	
	1999-2000	41.1	22.4	26.4	(36.4) 10.0	100.0
Punjab	1993-4	–	74.9		25.1	
	1999-2000	–	78.7	17.1	(21.4) 4.3	100.0
Rajasthan	1993-4	28.8	26.4		44.9	
	1999-2000	36.5	23.7	27.5	(39.8) 12.3	100.0
Tamil Nadu	1993-4	2.7	34.6		62.7	
	1999-2000	2.6	48.5	46.1	(48.8) 2.7	100.0
Uttar Pradesh	1993-4	0.8	33.7		65.5	
	1999-2000	1.4	34.6	47.6	(64.1) 16.5	100.0
West Bengal	1993-4	12.4	36.1		51.5	
	1999-2000	10.6	30.1	4.3	(59.3) 55.0	100.0
Other States and Union Territories	1993-4	52.7	12.6		34.7	
	1999-2000	39.4	13.5	13.3	(47.1) 33.8	100.0
All India	1993-4	14.8	27.6		57.6	
	1999-2000	17.5	27.3	36.3	(55.2) 18.9	100.0

Note: Figures in the parentheses include 'OBC' also.
Source: Computed from NSS 50th and 55th Rounds data on Household Consumer Expenditure.

Radhakrishna et al. (2003) have attempted to identify the chronic poor in an indirect manner by establishing correspondence between NSS and NFHS data. NFHS has not collected any information on income/consumption. However, it has collected information on households' possession of durables, ownership of assets, amenities, etc. Using this information, a standard of living index has been computed for each sample household of NFHS. Correspondence between the poverty line and standard of living index (SLI) has been established by equating the percentage of persons below the poverty line computed from the NSS data with the percentage of persons below the standard of living index. The percentage of persons below cut off point of the standard of living index will be equal to the percentage of persons below the poverty line of the NSS. A poor household with a malnourished child is considered as chronically poor. Among the three measures of malnutrition, height-for-age index

TABLE 3.5a
Incidence of Chronic Poverty—Statewise, 1993–4 and 1999–2000 (Rural)

(percentages)

NSS code	State/Union Territories	1993–4				1999–2000			
		Extremely poor	Very poor	Moderately poor	Poor (below poverty line)	Extremely poor	Very poor	Moderately poor	Poor (below poverty line)
1	All-India	2.0	14.7	22.1	36.8	0.8	8.2	18.3	26.5
2	Andhra Pradesh	0.6	4.1	11.8	15.9	0.4	2.7	7.8	10.5
3	Arunachal Pradesh	2.5	16.1	25.3	41.4	0.0	6.3	17.1	23.4
4	Assam	0.7	12.3	33.0	45.3	1.9	14.8	25.4	40.2
5	Bihar	4.0	27.6	30.3	57.9	1.1	14.1	29.9	44.0
6	Goa	0.2	1.9	3.1	5.0	0.0	0.0	0.0	0.0
7	Gujarat	0.5	6.5	15.6	22.1	0.2	3.3	9.1	12.4
8	Haryana	1.1	8.8	19.5	28.3	0.6	1.5	5.9	7.4
9	Himchal Pradesh	0.9	8.9	21.4	30.3	0.0	1.3	6.2	7.5
10	Jammu and Kashmir	0.4	4.9	13.3	18.2	0.0	0.5	4.2	4.7
11	Karnataka	1.4	11.2	19.0	30.2	0.3	3.3	13.6	16.9
12	Kerala	1.5	9.4	16.0	25.4	0.2	1.9	7.5	9.4
13	Madhya Pradesh	2.6	16.9	23.8	40.7	1.2	12.3	24.9	37.2
14	Maharashtra	3.2	16.0	21.9	37.9	0.7	6.5	16.8	23.3
15	Manipur	0.1	2.3	16.9	19.2	0.0	2.4	11.7	14.1
16	Meghalaya	0.2	2.9	21.4	24.3	0.0	0.2	5.8	6.0
17	Mizoram	0	1.3	4.9	6.2	0.0	0.1	2.7	2.8
18	Nagaland	0	0.0	1.9	1.9	0.0	0.0	0.2	0.2
19	Orissa	3.1	21.7	28.1	49.8	2.8	21.7	26.1	47.8
20	Punjab	0.1	3.0	8.7	11.7	0.0	1.1	4.9	6.0
21	Rajasthan	0.7	8.6	17.8	26.4	0.1	2.4	11.0	13.4
22	Sikkim	0	8.1	23.2	31.3	0.2	3.2	18.5	21.7
23	Tamil Nadu	1.9	12.4	20.6	33.0	0.6	5.7	14.4	20.1
24	Tripura	0.9	8.7	14.6	23.3	0.2	3.2	13.5	16.7
25	Uttar Pradesh	2.6	19.4	23	42.4	0.5	8.7	22.3	31.0
26	West Bengal	1.4	13.6	27.6	41.2	1.1	10.8	20.9	31.7
27	Andaman and Nicobar Islands	0	0.0	1.1	1.1	0.0	0.0	0.3	0.3
28	Chandigarh	0	0.0	11.8	11.8	0.1	0.1	7.6	7.7
29	Dadra and Nagar Haveli	0.1	18.5	33.2	51.7	0.0	4.7	11.9	16.6
30	Daman and Diu	0	1.6	0	1.6	0.0	0.0	0.0	0.0
31	Delhi	0	0.0	2	2.0	0.0	0.0	0.7	0.7
32	Lakshadweep	0	0.0	0	0.0	0.0	0.0	0.0	0.0
33	Pondicherry	0	5.3	13.6	18.9	0.5	2.9	8.6	11.5

Notes: Extremely Poor: Persons whose per capita total expenditure is less than 50 per cent of state-specific poverty line.
Very poor: All those persons whose per capita total expenditure is less than 75 per cent of the state-specific poverty line.
Moderately poor: Persons whose per capita expenditure lies between 75 per cent and 100 per cent of state-specific poverty lines.
Source: Computed from NSS 50th and 55th Rounds data on Household Consumer Expenditure.

is an indicator of chronic under-nutrition (stunted), weight-for-height index (wasted) reflects acute under-nutrition and weight-for-age (under weight) is a composite measure of both chronic and acute under-nutrition. Radhakrishna et al. (2003) have chosen height-for-age since deficiency in food energy intake over a long duration gets reflected in stunting.

The standard of living index data revealed that 57 per cent of children belonging to poor households in rural areas and 50 per cent of children belonging to poor

TABLE 3.5b
Incidence of Poverty—Statewise 1993-4 and 1999-2000 (Urban)

(percentages)

NSS code	State/Union Territories	1993-4				1999-2000			
		Extremely poor	Very poor	Moderately poor	Poor (below poverty line)	Extremely poor	Very poor	Moderately poor	Poor (below poverty line)
1	All-India	2.9	15.1	17.7	32.8	1.2	9.2	14.8	24.0
2	Andhra Pradesh	2.2	16.8	22.0	38.8	1.2	9.3	17.9	27.2
3	Arunachal Pradesh	0.4	1.9	3.9	5.8	2.2	4.1	0.9	5.0
4	Assam	0.2	1.2	6.8	8.0	0.2	2.1	5.1	7.2
5	Bihar	1.6	13.9	20.9	34.8	1.4	10.5	23.0	33.5
6	Goa	0.3	7.6	20.6	28.2	0.0	3.8	2.5	6.3
7	Gujarat	1.2	10.7	17.6	28.3	0.4	3.7	11.1	14.8
8	Haryana	0.2	4.9	11.5	16.4	1.2	3.6	6.4	10.0
9	Himachal Pradesh	0	1.1	8.2	9.3	0.0	0.9	3.7	4.6
10	Jammu and Kashmir	0	1.9	3.2	5.1	0.0	0.0	2.0	2.0
11	Karnataka	4.9	21.7	18.1	39.8	1.9	9.3	15.3	24.6
12	Kerala	2.0	9.8	14.5	24.3	0.9	6.2	13.7	19.9
13	Madhya Pradesh	5.3	25.3	22.8	48.1	2.7	18.2	20.4	38.6
14	Maharashtra	5.9	18.4	16.6	35.0	2.4	12.4	14.4	26.8
15	Manipur	0.2	0.4	6.5	6.9	0.0	0.0	0.5	0.5
16	Meghalaya	0	0.1	1.7	1.8	0.0	0.0	0.0	0.0
17	Mizoram	0	0	0	0	0.0	0.0	0.0	0.0
18	Nagaland	0	0	0	0	0.0	0.0	0.0	0.0
19	Orissa	4.2	21.7	18.9	40.6	3.0	21.6	21.9	43.5
20	Punjab	0	2.2	8.6	10.8	0.0	0.9	4.5	5.4
21	Rajasthan	1.3	12.7	18.3	31.0	0.1	5.6	13.8	19.4
22	Sikkim	0	0	1.0	1.0	0.0	1.2	3.6	4.8
23	Tamil Nadu	3.7	18.2	21.7	39.9	1.2	7.9	14.6	22.5
24	Tripura	0.1	1.8	4.2	6.0	0	0.4	1.0	1.4
25	Uttar Pradesj	2.9	17.0	18.1	35.1	1.0	12.3	18.4	30.7
26	West Bengal	0.8	7.4	15.6	23	0.2	4.2	10.5	14.7
27	Andaman and Nicobar Islands	0.1	1.2	4.0	5.2	0.0	0.5	0.0	0.5
28	Chandigarh	0.2	0.2	1.9	2.1	0.0	0.9	2.2	3.1
29	Dadra and Nagar Haveli	4.0	28.3	10.7	39.0	0.0	2.0	10.3	12.3
30	Daman and Diu	0	2.1	19.6	21.7	0.0	1.4	9.5	10.9
31	Delhi	1	6.9	9.2	16.1	0.0	1.7	7.5	9.2
32	Lakshadweep	0	4.7	11.2	15.9	0.0	0.1	3.2	3.3
33	Pondicherry	3.2	16.1	20.3	36.4	2.2	12.7	9.7	22.4

Notes: Extremely poor: Persons whose per capita total expenditure is less than 50 per cent of state-specific poverty line.
Very poor: All those persons whose per capita total expenditure is less than 75 per cent of the state-specific poverty line.
Moderately poor: Persons whose per capita expenditure lies between 75 per cent and 100 per cent of state-specific poverty lines.
Source: Computed using NSS 50th and 55th Rounds data on Household Consumer Expenditure.

households in urban areas were stunted. The percentage of stunted children among the poor varied between 32 (in Kerala) and 63 (in West Bengal) in rural areas and between 31 (in Kerala) and 64 (in Haryana) in urban areas. It is worth observing that in some of the states with low incidence of poverty, such as Haryana and Jammu and Kashmir, the percentage of stunted children among the poor was higher.

The incidence of chronic poverty has been estimated by multiplying the percentage of malnourished among the poor with the proportion of the poor. The estimates of incidence of the chronically poor are presented in Table 3.6. The percentage of the chronically poor in 1997–8 is estimated to be 15 per cent in rural areas and 14 per cent in urban areas. The incidence of chronic poverty is higher than the incidence of very poor but lower than the severe malnutrition levels (weight-for-age/height-for-age less than median—3 SD).

The percentage of the chronically poor is quite high in Bihar (25.3 per cent in rural and 19.3 in urban areas), Orissa (24.4 per cent in rural and 22.2 in urban areas), Madhya Pradesh (21.4 per cent in rural and 22.2 in urban areas) and Uttar Pradesh (19.6 per cent in rural and 19.4 per cent in urban areas). It is also high in the rural areas of Assam and West Bengal. Chronic poverty is very low in Jammu and Kashmir, the north-western states of Punjab, Haryana, and Himachal Pradesh, and Kerala.

The profiles of the very poor are likely to reflect those of the chronically poor. Although levels differ, chronic poverty and incidence of the very poor are correlated. Since the probability of a very poor household moving out of poverty in some good years is likely to be very low, the incidence of chronic poverty may be high among the very poor. It may be noted that profiles of the very poor are not very sensitive to marginal changes in the cut-off point.

MALNUTRITION

Malnutrition among Children

The National Nutrition Monitoring Bureau (NNMB) Reports provide data on the nutritional status of the general population as well as certain vulnerable groups in rural areas based on large-scale periodic diet and nutritional surveys in nine states. These reports use the Gomez classification for children and the body-mass index (BMI) classification for adults. The NNMB data show that the incidence of under-nutrition among children, even though slowly declining, was still alarmingly high during the late 1990s and their incidence is much higher than that of income poverty. About half of the children and slightly over a third of the adults were undernourished in 2000–1.

The proportion of malnourished children (1–5 years) declined from 62.5 per cent in 1975–9 to 56.2 per cent in 1991–2 and further to 47.7 per cent in 2000–1 (Table 3.7). The decline is visible across all NNMB sample states except Madhya Pradesh and Orissa, and is very striking

TABLE 3.6
Under-nutrition (Height-for-age) among
Poor and Incidence of Chronic Poverty: 1997–8

State	Rural		Urban	
	Percentage of stunted children among poor	Percentage of chronically poor	Percentage of stunted children among poor	Percentage of chronically poor
Andhra Pradesh	49.6	5.2	34.3	13.5
Assam	52.4	21.1	49.1	3.8
Bihar	57.5	25.3	63.0	19.3
Gujarat	49.5	6.1	51.2	7.3
Haryana	60.5	4.5	64.2	6.1
Himachal Pradesh	58.8	4.4	54.8	2.7
Jammu and Kashmir	59.9	2.8	51.6	1.2
Karnataka	56.5	9.6	49.7	13.9
Kerala	32.4	3.1	30.9	6.5
Madhya Pradesh	57.4	21.4	56.9	22.2
Maharashtra	55.8	13.0	30.9	15.0
Orissa	51.1	24.4	49.1	22.2
Punjab	56.9	3.4	46.4	3.1
Rajasthan	60.1	8.1	57.2	11.7
Tamil Nadu	41.6	8.4	46.5	9.4
West Bengal	60.0	19.0	53.5	8.8
Uttar Pradesh	63.1	19.6	59.6	19.4
Other States	43.1	5.3	46.4	3.9
All-India	57.1	15.1	49.6	13.7

Note: Stunted children among the poor are estimated by matching NSS and NFHS data at unit level.

in Kerala and Tamil Nadu—declining from 56.8 to 28.8 per cent in Kerala and from 59.6 to 39.0 per cent in Tamil Nadu during 1975–2001. Malnutrition levels in Madhya Pradesh and Orissa in 2000–1 was about the same as in the early 1970s.

TABLE 3.7
Under-nutrition among Children (aged 1–5 years) and CED among Adults in Rural Areas of Selected States*

State	Period	Under-nutrition (%)	CED Males	CED Females
Kerala	1975–9	56.8		
	1991–2	35.6		
	2000–1	28.8	22.4	18.7
Tamil Nadu	1975–9	59.6		
	1991–2	47.4		
	2000–1	39.0	26.7	38.2
Karnataka	1975–9	64.3		
	1991–2	62.8		
	2000–1	47.7	36.2	41.7
Andhra Pradesh	1975–9	61.5		
	1991–2	50.8		
	2000–1	39.9	37.4	42.0
Maharashtra	1975–9	71.4		
	1991–1	62.2		
	2000–1	55.2	41.3	45.1
Gujarat	1975–9	68.1		
	1991–1	62.3		
	2000–1	48.9	37.1	33.3
Madhya Pradesh	1975–9	61.3		
	2000–1	63.9	42.8	41.9
Orissa	1975–9	56.6		
	1991–1	58.8		
	2000–1	54.4	38.6	46.0
West Bengal	1975–9	60.6		
	2000–1	49.6	40.5	45.9
All-States	1975–9	62.5		
	1991–1	56.2		
	2000–1	50.5	37.4	39.4

Notes: Under-nutrition (severe plus moderate) estimates are based on Gomez classification and CED is the percentage of adults whose BMI is less than 18.5.
* Pooled estimates of Kerala, Tamil Nadu, Karnataka, Andhra Pradesh, Maharashtra, Gujarat, and Orissa for 1975–9; Kerala, Tamil Nadu, Andhra Pradesh, Maharashtra, Gujarat, and Orissa for 1991–2 and all the nine for 2000–1.
Source: National Nutritional Monitoring Bureau, National Institute of Nutrition, Hyderabad.
(i) Second Report Survey, 1999—Rural NNMB Technical Report No. 18.
(ii) Diet Nutritional Status of Rural population, 2002—NNMB Technical Report No. 21.

There are substantial interstate variations in the malnutrition levels of children under five years. In 2000–1, the percentage of moderately and severely malnourished children varied between 28.8 in Kerala and 63.9 in Madhya Pradesh (see the under-nutrition percentage column in Table 3.7). In terms of the nutritional status of children, middle-income states such as Kerala, Tamil Nadu, and Andhra Pradesh performed better than higher-income states like Maharashtra, Gujarat, and West Bengal. Not surprisingly, poorer states such as Madhya Pradesh and Orissa showed the worst performance. It is worth noting that even with low food energy intake Kerala and Tamil Nadu could perform better (see Box 3.1 for the factors underlying the better performance of Kerala). NFHS estimates of malnutrition based on standard deviation classification also reveal a similar pattern (Table 3.8).

Chronic Energy Deficiency among Adults

NNMB data show that 37.4 per cent of adult males and 39.4 per cent of adult females in 2000–1 suffered from Chronic Energy Deficiency (CED) in eight sample states (Table 3.7). The interstate variations in CED are similar to those of malnutrition among children. CED was found to be lower in Kerala (22.4 per cent for males and 18.7 per cent for females) and in Tamil Nadu (26.7 per cent for males and 38.7 per cent for females) and higher in Madhya Pradesh, Maharashtra, and West Bengal (above 50 per cent). Gender differences seem to exist in some states, particularly in Tamil Nadu.

NFHS-II shows that 36 per cent of ever-married women aged 15–49 years have chronic energy deficiency (Table 3.8). It is more pronounced for rural women, illiterate women, and women surviving in a low standard of living situation (Arnold et al. 2003).[7] CED levels are higher in Maharashtra, Gujarat, and West Bengal and are closer to that of less developed states like Bihar, Madhya Pradesh, and Orissa. Punjab, Kerala, Arunachal Pradesh, Manipur, and Nagaland have lower incidence of female malnutrition.

Poverty and Malnutrition

What is the impact of poverty reduction on malnutrition? Is the reduction in malnutrition commensurate with poverty reduction? Some exercises were made to statistically connect the two variables but due to data limitations the purpose is limited to being only indicative. Rural malnutrition based on weight-for-age NFHS statewise data is regressed on rural poverty estimates based on the NSS 55th Round. Semi-log type of specification is chosen to allow for the existence of malnutrition at zero level of poverty. The coefficients are statistically

---

[7] Women who consume milk or curd daily are, however, less prone to CED than women who do not (Arnold et al. 2003).

TABLE 3.8
NFHS Estimates of Malnutrition among Children (Weight-for-age) and CED among Ever-married Women

State	1993 (children under four years)			1998–9 (children under three years)	CED among ever-married women (age 15–49 years)
	Rural	Urban	All	All (Rural + Urban)	(Rural + Urban)
Andhra Pradesh	52.1	40.2	49.1	37.7	37.8
Bihar	64.1	53.8	62.6	54.4	39.7
Gujarat	45.8	40.5	44.1	45.1	37.6
Haryana	39.4	33.0	37.9	34.6	26.1
Himachal Pradesh	48.3	30.2	47.0	43.6	29.9
Jammu and Kashmir	NA	NA	44.5	34.5	26.6
Karnataka	NA	NA	NA	43.9	39.4
Kerala	30.6	22.9	28.5	26.9	18.9
Madhya Pradesh	59.4	50.1	57.4	55.1	38.6
Maharashtra	57.5	45.5	52.6	49.6	40.2
Orissa	NA	NA	55.3	54.4	48.4
Punjab	47.4	40.0	45.9	28.7	17.0
Rajasthan	41.1	43.9	41.6	50.6	36.6
Tamil Nadu	52.1	32.3	46.6	36.7	29.3
Uttar Pradesh	NA	NA	49.8	51.7	36.2
West Bengal	NA	NA	56.8	48.7	44.4
North East					
Arunachal Pradesh	40.3	36.2	39.7	24.3	11.1
Assam	51.8	37.3	50.4	36.0	27.1
Manipur	31.6	25.9	30.1	27.5	19.3
Meghalaya	47.2	37.5	45.5	37.9	25.7
Mizoram	34.5	22.0	28.1	27.7	22.8
Nagaland	30.5	19.7	28.7	24.1	18.7
Tripura	53.0	31.6	48.8	NA	35.7
All-India	59.9	45.2	53.4	47.0	36.2

Notes: Children below 2 SD from the international reference population median are treated as suffering from malnutrition.
Source: NFHS 1993 and 1998–9.
CED among ever-married women are from (Arnold et al. 2003).

significant, but the goodness of fit is not very high (Table 3.9). It seems that factors other than income poverty also influence malnutrition. The intercept coefficients are statistically significant indicating the prevalence of

TABLE 3.9
Malnutrition and Poverty
(NSS-NFHS)

$$Ln\ m_1 = 2.08 + 0.026\ P$$
$$t = (13.36)\ \ (3.83)$$
$$\bar{R}^2 = 0.39\ \ df = 20$$

$$Ln\ m_2 = 3.49 + 0.011\ P$$
$$t = (11.37)\ \ (3.57)$$
$$\bar{R}^2 = 0.33\ \ df = 20$$

Notes: m_1 = Percentage of children with severe underweight (< Median–3 SD)
m_2 = Percentage of children with underweight (< Median–2 SD)
P = Percentge of people below the poverty line.

malnutrition even when poverty is completely eradicated. The poverty coefficients are positive and significant. They show that a 10 per cent reduction in poverty reduces malnutrition by 6 per cent and severe malnutrition by 5 per cent. The malnutrition for 20 quintiles formed on the basis of standard of living index also revealed that malnutrition declines with improvement in the standard of living but it persists even among the top quintiles. For example, 10 per cent of rural children in the top quintile class suffer from severe malnutrition and another 18 per cent from moderate to mild malnutrition—in all, 28 per cent. In urban areas 7 per cent of children suffer from severe malnutrition and 14 per cent from moderate to mild malnutrition—21 per cent in all.

Targeting

Estimates of the undernourished show that 20–5 per cent of rural children are severely malnourished and another

30–9 per cent are mild to moderately malnourished based on weight-for-age criterion. According to the height-for-age criterion (Table 3.10). 25 per cent are severely and another 24 per cent are mild to moderately malnourished. Eradication of severe malnutrition should be the first priority of any nutrition policy and the feeding programmes should be targeted towards them.

TABLE 3.10
NNMB (2000–1) and NFHS–2 Estimates of Under-nutrition in Rural Areas based on Standard Deviation

Severe under-nutrition (< median–3 SD)		
NNMB :	21 per cent	Weight-for-age
NFHS :	20 per cent	Weight-for-age
NNMB :	25 per cent	Height-for-age
NFHS :	25 per cent	Height-for-age
Under-nutrition (< Median–2 SD)		
NNMB :	60 per cent	Weight-for-age
NFHS :	49.6 per cent	Weight-for-age
NNMB :	49 per cent	Height-for-age
NFHS :	48.5 per cent	Height-for-age

Note: NNMB age group—1–5 years.
NFHS age group—< 3 years (Estimated from unit level data).

THE EMERGING SCENARIO

A few observations can be made from the preceding analysis of poverty reduction in the states. First, all states with the exception of Assam and Orissa experienced poverty reduction between 1993–4 and 1999–2000. In Assam and Orissa the reduction was not unequivocal and increased among the very poor. However, due to uneven poverty reduction across states and social groups, the poor are getting concentrated in less developed states as well as among a few vulnerable social groups. In the agriculturally prosperous states, agricultural labour households accounted for the bulk of the rural poor and in the less developed regions rural poverty extended to other occupational groups, including the self-employed in agriculture. In the urban areas, poverty tends to be concentrated more among the casual labour households. Second, Assam, Orissa, Madhya Pradesh, and Uttar Pradesh have remained laggards in poverty reduction. In this context, it is worth mentioning that Rajasthan, a resource poor and erstwhile laggard state could perform well in poverty reduction and may have lessons to offer from its experience. Third, the poor are likely to be vulnerable to risks in the labour market and may increasingly suffer from transient poverty since their dependence on the casual labour market for livelihood is rising both in rural and urban areas. Backward regions and disadvantaged social groups are afflicted by chronic as well as transient poverty.

Poverty has declined considerably over the last three decades, but the magnitude and characteristics of decline show some patterns. The decline was sharp in states where agricultural growth is higher in comparison to states where income growth has been low. It is also seen that during the 1990s, the decline in poverty had percolated to the bottom in all the states, albeit in varied measures. As a result, both the incidence of poverty and the proportion of the very poor have declined in urban as well as rural areas and also across social groups. It is also noteworthy that the decline seems to be greater among the very poor compared with the poor. However, data analysis suggest that the income gap between poor and rich expenditure groups has widened in the relatively advanced regions. This is not generally the case in the stagnant regions of the country.

Interestingly, due to growth momentum the position of SCs in terms of per capita consumption was better in Punjab than in the backward states. But in terms of income/consumption, the gap between socially backward groups and the rest was greater in Punjab than in other states. Thus income, and particularly agricultural income growth is an important channel for alleviating poverty across regions, social groups, economic status, and the occupational group of the household.[8]

It seems that while growth may not be equalizing, there is good empirical support to claim that the poor and the very poor have been better off with growth than without it.[9] Growth is also beneficial to those who are socially excluded in India, such as STs and SCs. Since malnutrition and chronic poverty are closely associated with persistent inadequacy in attaining the minimum income status, income growth, ceteris paribus, has a pervasive influence over time on multi-dimensional poverty. This generally requires other supportive measures to be successful. The most important complementing factors are certain aspects of human development such as education and health and conducive public

---

[8] The relationship between agricultural growth and income poverty reduction has been extensively studied in India. See Datt and Ravallion (1998a, b), Fan, Hazell, and Thorat (2000) among others. This was also further investigated in the IGIDR study for FAO, Roles of Agriculture (2003), wherein it was seen that the elasticity of poverty reduction has remained high and significant with respect to output growth in all major sectors and particularly with respect to agricultural growth. The study further showed with recent data the linkages through relative food prices, real wage rate, irrigation, and development expenditure. The access to water for irrigation is very important in this endeavour.

[9] In fact, data analysis for the 1970s and 1980s cited above show that the decline in the proportion of the very poor occurred at a faster rate than the decline in the proportion of the poor in both rural and urban areas.

policy interventions. These are seen to be efficacious in Kerala and several other north-eastern states. As argued later, participatory growth processes would strengthen the poverty reduction link further.

It has been established earlier in this chapter that the rural–urban divide is widening. The average rural per capita household expenditure, which increased at a little over 1.5 per cent from 1970 to 1989 had experienced a deceleration in the 1990s. In contrast, the urban average per capita expendiure growth has accelerated over the period, thereby widening the existing rural–urban disparity. Nevertheless, observed facts show that the rate of decline in urban poverty has been faster than that of rural poverty However, while urban India is doing better, with even its bottom 30 per cent experiencing growth, there is greater inequality emerging in urban expenditure groups. It is thus easier to escape absolute poverty with a foothold in urban areas and away from the rural abyss, though the relative position of such a household may be quite dismal in comparison.

The worsening rural–urban disparity in the last decade is to a good measure the result of deceleration in agricultural growth, which is itself a matter of concern in employment generation and poverty reduction. This is the result of the focus shifting away from agriculture in general and in land augmenting public investment such as irrigation. There is also low priority given to R&D in the spread of agricultural growth. This is a matter of concern as agricultural technology's cutting edge is getting blunted and the source of growth exhausted since the last green revolution. Even where agricultural growth is happening, employment generation has been low, though real wage rates are increasing. There is also slowdown in rural non-farm employment growth although this is partly the result of decelerating agricultural prosperity itself. Data show a likely increase in annual growth rate in agriculture but that is a separate matter and is not discussed here.

The regional variation of poverty reduction through income growth noted earlier has a strong agricultural link. This has been established by researchers in a series of empirical studies.[10] The agricultural prosperity that has swept India as a whole is known to be mostly region and agro-ecological zone specific. The upper Indo-Gangetic plains of Punjab, Haryana, and west Uttar Pradesh that have experienced growth through the green revolution, is a zone identified as 'irrigated' part of agriculture[11] and this area, along with parts of the southern peninsular delta covering certain districts of Andhra Pradesh, Tamil Nadu, and Karnataka, have seen agricultural prosperity even among small holder cultivators. These are also the areas where the incidence and severity of poverty are the least. In contrast, vast areas of the country described as 'rainfed' agro-ecological zones remain largely agriculturally backward. Parts of this vast agro-ecological zone are also characterized as semi-arid (parts of Andhra Pradesh like the Telengana region and its contiguous Marathwada region of Maharashtra). The number of poor and the depth of poverty are found in abundance in the regions of central and eastern India and cover mainly the states of Madhya Pradesh, Bihar, Orissa, Assam, and parts of Andhra Pradesh, Maharashtra, and West Bengal. Some parts of the rain-shadow areas that comprise Maharashtra and Tamil Nadu are also afflicted by endemic poverty. It may be recalled that several socially excluded groups in India, particularly the STs and SCs also inhabit these poor regions. Parts of the 'arid' agro-ecological system (AES) areas of Gujarat and Rajasthan also provide a picture of deprivation, and support several socially excluded groups.[12]

It has been observed earlier that some of the better-off states like Maharashtra, Gujarat, and West Bengal bore a relatively higher share in rural poverty. It is also seen that CED levels are higher in these so called better-off states, and are not very different in this respect from Bihar, Madhya Pradesh, and Orissa. This observation can be explained in the following way to see why prosperity coexists with poverty in these states. It may be noted that high proportions of the most excluded social groups like the STs live in the rural areas of these states. These states also belong to the agro-ecological zones like 'rainfed' areas (West Bengal, Maharashtra), 'semi-arid' areas (Maharashtra), and 'arid' areas (Gujarat)

---

[10] The same has emerged from the FAO, Roles of Agriculture (2003) study conducted at IGIDR for the FAO.

[11] There are several classifications of agricultural systems into different agro-ecological zones, including those by Food and Agriculture Organization (FAO), ICAR, Planning Commission, etc. We adopt the NCAP classification of Indian agriculture into five mutually exclusive and exhaustive zones of which 'irrigated' is one. The Indo-Gangetic Plain extends to parts of Bihar and West Bengal but these parts belong to the 'rainfed' system as opposed to the 'irrigated' AES. The other three AES by NCAP classification are 'coastal', 'arid', and 'hill and mountain' covering different parts of India.

[12] It is true that differences in terrain and natural resource base could form important factors in relative backwardness. It is, however, the case that these areas are rich in natural resources and thus growth induced poverty reduction possibilities are considerable. Though some of these areas are more suited to robust industrial development due to their resource endowments, agricultural growth prospects are still enormous, and that is being emphasized here. The case for industrial development and their effect on poverty reduction is not discussed here—though it is by no means considered insignificant.

which have seen low agricultural prosperity. These cross-cutting influences of terrain, social groups and economic opportunities together contribute substantially to rural poverty in these states.[13]

An important clue that emerges from the regional profile of poverty is the scope for agricultural growth. If it were possible to refocus agricultural growth to extend to the vast geographical areas under the 'rainfed' AES, considerable progress could be made on poverty reduction even with the existing structure of asset-holding and property rights.[14] Growth in agriculture has been focused on the 'irrigated' agro-ecological zone (upper Indo-Gangetic plain), which has seen progress and has virtually removed poverty in that region and in parts of the southern peninsular India. It has, however, bypassed much of 'mainland' India that is characterized as a 'rainfed' agro-ecological zone and contains several areas of semi-arid agriculture.[15] These are the major pockets of poverty identified above. It is this map of agricultural growth that could be modified with considerable mileage for poverty reduction. It may be noted here that the 'rainfed' AES covers about 54 per cent of land area and 60 per cent of the net-cropped area (NCA) of the country and supports about 44 per cent of the population.[16]

It is imperative, therefore, that agricultural growth be stepped up and its thrust should be on the hitherto bypassed regions of central and eastern India in order that the resultant poverty reduction be sustained.[17] In the medium term an emphasis on irrigation development—which is in some sense difficult but crucial in parts of these regions[18]—agricultural technology—to sustain growth in them—and requisite policy support—to spur growth—would be critical in this quest. A recent initiative at the highest level to connect all major parts of the country through high quality surface transport infrastructure (the golden quadrilateral and the east–west and north–south corridors) is a good measure to improve livelihood opportunities of rural and deprived areas.

However, India is a country of small farmers with more than 80 per cent of farm operations done by marginal (62.8 per cent) and small (17.8 per cent) holders (less than 1 hectare of land, and somewhat more in dryland areas) operating about 34 per cent (15.6 per cent plus 18.7 per cent, respectively) of land area in the country.[19] It is the integration of these small holders in the development process that provides a major leverage to growth and poverty reduction in India. It has been noted earlier that in relatively prosperous areas, agricultural labour is the principal occupational group among the poor but in backward parts even the small holder is quite frequently poor. The latter occurrence is understandable with low agricultural prosperity. In the more prosperous regions, a considerable pool of agricultural labour is drawn from migrating groups of labour from the backward regions and certain other excluded and marginalized groups from within and outside, to whom prosperity does not percolate down in the desired measure. A good part of the casual labour of urban India—which is also identified among the principal components of the poverty pool—is also drawn from the less prosperous rural hinterland due to the widening disparity in growth, as discussed earlier. It is to the hinterland of poverty that attention should be directed. Reversing the decelerating agricultural growth and extending it to the hitherto laggard states would address the multiple problems of aggravating disparity noted earlier besides the problem of faster poverty reduction.

---

[13] In a study done by the authors for ADB/NIRD (2002) on poverty and deprivation in three selected states of India, it was found that despite vibrant growth in Gujarat in the 1990s, employment generation in rural areas were scanty. Income growth, therefore, did not have commensurate trickledown effects. There was migration in search of livelihood in all regions of Gujarat, into small urban areas where a lot of the poor were concentrated and to other states. While the Saurashtra region had the least incidence of poverty, tribal regions were the worst hit—in this prosperous state. See Box 3.1 for further issues.

[14] Growth is inescapable in any strategy for poverty reduction. As Bhalla and Hazell (2003) have concluded, 'accelerating overall growth of the economy…is essential to make a meaningful dent on underemployment and poverty'.

[15] The policy imperatives for 'semi-arid tropical' or other agro-ecological areas for agricultural development and livelihood prospects for poverty reduction would be different. See for example, Singh and Hazell (1993). No attempt is made to list these imperatives here.

[16] By comparison the 'coastal' system covers 6 per cent and the 'irrigated' system 23 per cent of NCA. The irrigation intensity in the 'rainfed' system is only 26 per cent as opposed to 47 per cent in the 'coastal' system and 64 per cent in the 'irrigated' system areas. There is thus much scope for extending prosperity and reducing poverty in this way, though we are quite aware that a 'linear' logic does not extend to prosperity and poverty alleviation.

[17] It may be added in this context that states are at different stages of development and that would impinge on the outcome. It is also true that the processes which strengthen or weaken the growth poverty reduction links differ across states and geographical regions. The combination of policies that accelerate and retard poverty reduction strategies also differ across states. These caveats are important and should be noted.

[18] It is not necessary that irrigation of the large multi-purpose variety be envisaged. Solutions through alternative irrigation methods, watershed programmes could be contemplated several of them having been very successful in all these terrains.

[19] National Sample Survey, 48th Round: Land and Livestock Holdings Survey (1991–2).

With prosperity trickling down and small holders more secure the pool of poverty may yet contain several socially excluded groups. It is also likely that, with agricultural growth, rural non-farm employment and income would be buoyed up. From the character of poverty reduction noted earlier, it is likely that such agriculture income growth may still increase income inequality even when it reduces Foster-Greer-Thorbeck (FGT) indices of poverty. But that is a separate matter.

Another dimension of poverty that requires careful consideration is the gender aspect of poverty. While evidence is available at aggregative levels on the gender discrimination against women in the labour market, particularly in rural and unorganized sectors, there is less knowledge and reliable information at the household level. While all members in a poor household may suffer, it is possible that women and girls in the family suffer disproportionately more; and it is also possible that while a household may not be counted among those suffering from poverty, the female members in it may display all the characteristics of poverty and deprivation. Tables 3.7 and 3.8 give some inkling of it. Table 3.7 shows that CED among females is generally significantly higher than males in most states and for India as a whole. Table 3.8 shows that married women in their reproductive (and working) age cohort who suffer from CED are considerably more than the proportions of poor population—more than 36 per cent of ever-married women in that age cohort were seen to be suffering from CED in 2003. However, gender discrimination at the household level to reflect poverty among girls and women is not discussed here though there is ample circumstantial evidence of its existence, as reflected in gender differences in malnutrition status, infant and child mortality, etc. Unfortunately, this issue cannot be discussed more elaborately here.

While that is unfortunate, it is recognized that women in general are more vulnerable and face discrimination and marginalization in the labour markets. Although they work for much longer hours than men and their work contributes significantly to the family's income, their work gets less recognition in terms of visibility and official statistics relating to work participation rates (WPR).[20] NSS surveys do not capture all work done by women and, hence, there may be discrepancy between official participation and time actually spent at work. Time use surveys may reveal this discrepancy. The pilot time use survey (1998-9) measures several activities done by the poor, particularly women, in these 'difficult to measure' and less visible sectors (Hirway 2002). Even when they are in the workforce, most of them work as marginal workers and do not have independent earnings. Further, there has been a decline in their workforce participation, particularly in rural areas, in the last decade—between 1993-4 and 1999-2000 there has been near stagnation in the number of female workers in the country as a whole and an absolute decline in the number of female workers in rural India leading to considerable decline of female WPR as a percentage of male WPR. During that period the WPR ratio for females declined from 59.3 to 55.3 in rural India and from 29.8 to 26.8 in urban India.[21] An overwhelmingly large percentage of women workers are illiterates and in the unorganized sectors where working conditions and compensations are less secure. They are usually less endowed, by social customs and rigidities, with human capital resources and suffer comparatively greater as a consequence (see World Bank (1991) for a discussion on several of these aspects).

Yet another aspect of labour market discrimination against women is revealed by the differentials in male and female wage rates for identical work. Although in some sectors small improvements are visible, wage rates of females continue to be considerably less than those for male workers. During the period referred to above, Sundaram (2001), on the basis of NSS data, shows that female wage as percentage of male wage has remained more or less locked at 70 for casual labour in agriculture, though they have improved from about 58 to 63 per cent for casual labour in non-agriculture. All these have manifested as somewhat greater poverty among female workers as compared with male workers.

NSS data show that the ratio of female-headed households (FHH) varies considerably between states. Meenakshi and Ray (2003), after making adjustments for demographic characteristics of households, show that FHH continue to register higher poverty rates than the general population for most states, and India as a whole, for both the 50th (1993-4) and 55th (1999-2000) Rounds of NSS. The suffering of widows in India is discussed in Dreze (1990). He argues that there are close links between widowhood and a range of other social problems and that the status of widowhood itself reduces the quality of life of most Indian women. A whole range of patriarchal institutions contribute to the deprivation of widows, including patrilineal inheritance, patrilocal residence, and the sexual division of labour (see Narayan

---

[20] A higher share of marginal workers and greater extent of involvement in the collection of free goods and unpaid domestic duties, etc., denote lower 'visibility'.

[21] See Sundaram (2001) and Hirway (2002). The same sources show that while an employment setback has hit every section of the workforce in India during that period, rural women record the most decline. It is possible that their participation in sectors not captured by official statistics could account for the severe setback for the poor, especially the women among them.

et al. (2000) for an assessment of several aspects of deprivation among widows in India and elsewhere).

We now turn to another possible route to effective poverty reduction. As distinct from the sustained income growth route, poverty reduction in the north-east of India provides a different perspective. The states (other than Assam) in the region now boast of separate statehoods with large tribal populations. In these states, literacy rates are high and many other social indicators of development are sanguine. This state of affairs has been partly contributed by history, whereby education to the masses has been imparted with a missionary zeal as a separate and autonomous process. Despite large tribal habitations, the incidence and severity of poverty among these tribal groups are remarkably low, an achievement rarely encountered among the tribal population in the other states considered. For instance, there is no incidence of the 'very poor' in the tribal states of Meghalaya, Mizoram, and Nagaland. Here, besides better indicators of human development, they have inalienable rights that they exercise on various assets including land and these tribals are not displaced and dispossessed as easily as their counterparts elsewhere. Perhaps it is their dominant status and the political power that they have enjoyed over long years, that ensured their escape from poverty beyond simple income measures. There is ample evidence that tribal communities in other regions have been deprived of similar privileges. The contribution that education, imparted to the tribal groups in this region, has made to this outcome cannot be ignored. Education is an important component of health, nutrition, and material well-being and this may not be easily short-circuited by others gaining political power.

The creation of the new states of Chhattisgarh, Jharkhand, and Uttaranchal have provided interesting laboratories for case studies on this prognosis for the future. Tribal population groups from erstwhile Madhya Pradesh and Bihar dominate the first two of the new states and Uttaranchal contains large areas of deprived livelihood opportunities in the hill areas of Kumaon and Garhwal. These groups could attain 'self-rule', and it would be interesting to see if the poor among them attain the capacity to live with sustainable livelihood and dignity. The social movements and increasing awareness among the dalits in the states of Madhya Pradesh, Bihar, and Uttar Pradesh provide interesting insights into possible scenarios of escape from poverty en bloc.

Other changes accompany the development experience. India has been facing a major demographic transition in the last few decades and this is likely to continue for a few more decades. Demographic transition is change from a stable population with high mortality and fertility to a stable population with low mortality and fertility and this brings about a perceptible change in the age structure of the population. This is happening in India and the transition would put several million elderly persons in the grip of poverty and deprivation. Old age is when people's earning capabilities diminish and extending that phase with greater longevity may make them more vulnerable in that sense. In India, changes in the age cohort would occur in a way that between the years 1996 to 2016, the number of persons above the age group of 60 years is expected to increase from 62.3 to 112.9 million. Though the population of the working age group of 15–59 years will substantially increase and that of children stabilize during that phase and these adjustments would decrease the dependency ratio, the poverty and vulnerability of the old would increase in several dimensions. This is due to the increase in size and life expectancy of the population. It may be noted here that some of the new senior citizens will provide for themselves through provisions made during their working lives, but there are many who cannot do so.[22]

In this context the situation of the elderly women is likely to be worse because they typically outlive men and their period of widowhood is prolonged due to their advancing longevity. There are also groups of disabled persons—not all of advanced age—who fall into the trap of poverty at different stages of their lives. There are those who face single deprivations but many also face multiple deprivations (for example, old age, widowhood, low assets, etc.) and are thus in the worst possible situation. State welfare support in their favour are possibly the only methods of providing them with minimum economic support. Economic growth and prosperity would have no leverage in providing them with a hope of a better life. The Government of India, in token recognition of this vulnerable group, has provided for their pensions in a limited way recently, but it is far from meeting the challenge in hand.

The picture that is emerging in the various states of India shows different patterns partly due to differences in the onset of demographic transition and partly due to differences in rates of transition. While the population pyramid of India in transition resembles that of the world as a whole, the pyramid of Kerala is approaching the shape of the developed world and that of Uttar Pradesh resembles the group of less developed countries. Population pyramids of other states lie in between these two typologies of transition. In 1971 those above 60 years of age constituted a little over 5 per cent of the

---

[22] Several innovative financial engineering schemes can be cited to show the feasibility of paying for old age from earnings during the working age. However, this is not the concern that is expressed here.

population in India, but in 2001 they were 7 per cent, and in 2016 men and women above 60 years would be 8.8 and 9.0 per cent of their total numbers. It is worth noting that in the world as a whole (in 1998), men above 60 constituted 8.41 per cent and women 10.67 per cent of their respective gender totals as opposed to 6.61 and 6.67 for India as a whole. In that year, the estimated men and women in the developed countries in that age cohort were 15.47 and 21.13 per cent, respectively. These figures underline the emerging scenarios of poverty and deprivation among a section of the old in India and widowed women among them in particular. While Kerala and Goa may be there sooner, others, such as Uttar Pradesh, Bihar, and Orissa, may reach there eventually.[23]

While unsupported old age is a matter of concern, a group of younger persons is emerging in the category of vulnerables in all classes of the society. Among diseases that have afflicted the world in recent years the most devastating and debilitating has been the human immunodeficiency virus/acquired immune deficiency syndrome (HIV/AIDS). Due to their transmission mechanisms this affects the population more typically during their working age or earlier. This process could transform the population pyramid in the development transition mentioned earlier. Some states like Andhra Pradesh, Karnataka, Kerala, Tamil Nadu, Gujarat, and Maharashtra and several areas in the north-east are relatively more affected by the disease. Although data on HIV and AIDS are emerging from the states and the National Aids Control Organization (NACO), data on this dreaded disease face problems of credibility due to non-reporting and suppression in view of social sanctions and ostracism and the consequent lack of mainstreaming of the issue in society. For instance, till October 2003 Andhra Pradesh had reported 4339 cases, Gujarat 3488 cases, Tamil Nadu 24667 cases, Maharashtra 9234 and so on, making the total number of reported cases 56,151 for India. As opposed to this the total number of HIV cases estimated for the country by NACO with an Expert Group for the year 2002 has been worked out as 3.82 million HIV infections in the adult population (15–49 years age group in the country). These estimates have been pegged up for 20 per cent as range to take care of the unaccounted number of high-risk groups and other age groups to provide the upper range at 4.58 million HIV infections. Their disaggregated estimates also suggest that prevalence varies across the country, with the highest levels of infection reported in Maharashtra, Tamil Nadu, Andhra Pradesh, Karnataka, Manipur, and Nagaland. states where HIV prevalence in antenatal women is 1 per cent or more are considered high prevalence states. The concern that this affliction brings about is its effect on able-bodied men, in particular those whose debility and death traps their young families into poverty together with lack of guidance and support to their children. These, very often, are vulnerable female-headed households and, while the control of AIDS is a health and social problem, it has a potential poverty connotation. This has been seen clearly in the context of several countries in sub-Saharan Africa. Fortuitously for India the situation is not considered so alarming in the world map on AIDS but the number of households that may be rendered poor in the process may not be trifling. Data on various household characteristics of HIV affected persons in India are not available now but are clearly warranted for policy interventions in the future.

This chapter has highlighted the multi-dimensional character of poverty and this is borne out by case studies analysed from different states of India. The experience of Kerala sheds light on a variety of intervention factors in its quest for poverty reduction.[24] Combined with income growth, human development in the form of education and health contributes to reduction in poverty. Human development has allowed a lot of unemployed people to escape poverty through migration,[25] but they have also given the natives of Kerala livelihood opportunities and vigilant governance. Experience from this state as well as others show that the poor have gained considerably by direct influence on poverty reduction through decentralized participation in governance including that by women. In this context the 73rd and 74th Amendments of the Constitution of India on local self-governance has provided a tremendous opportunity which enables an educated and empowered people to make a difference to their lives. Decentralized governance is successful through the active participation of educated and socially aware citizens. An empowered people, men and women, contribute a lot to poverty reduction even with moderate income growth. Thus robust growth has reduced poverty in India but moderate growth has also reduced multi-dimensional poverty with an empowered population, in the south and in the north-east of India.

---

[23] The figures mentioned above are age related and may include all economic classes, social groups, and professional categories. Figures quoted above are drawn from *Planning Commission*, July 2000 estimates.

[24] Our study for ADB/NIRD (2002) supports this view, though we found that even in the case of Kerala social exclusion of some forest based backward castes and of tribal groups is prevalent. See Box 3.1.

[25] Zachariah, Mathew, and Rajan (2003) state that migration and the resultant earnings and remittances by migrants have been the most important determinant of poverty reduction in Kerala. This may be an extreme position, but its contribution to livelihood support cannot be denied.

REFERENCES

ADB/NIRD (2002), 'Poverty and the Poor in Selected States of India: Gujarat, Kerala, and Madhya Pradesh', project report submitted to Asian Development Bank/National Institute of Rural Development, Hyderabad.

Arnold, Fred, Parveen Nangia, and Uma Kapila (2003), 'Indicators of Nutrition for Women and Children in India: Current Status and Programme Recommendations', presented at workshop on National Family Health Survey, Centre for Economic and Social Studies, Hyderabad.

Bhalla, G. S. and Peter Hazell (2003), 'Rural Employment and Poverty Strategies to Stimulate Rural Poverty within a Generation', *Economic & Political Weekly*, August 2003.

Datt, Gaurav and Martin Ravallion (1998a), 'Why have some Indian States done better than others at Reducing Rural Poverty?', *Economica*, Vol. 65.

Datt, Gaurav and Martin Ravallion (1998b), 'Farm Productivity and Rural Poverty in India', *Journal of Developmental Studies*, Vol. 34, No. 4.

Deaton, Angus and Jean Dreze (2002), 'Poverty and Inequality in India: A Re-examination', *Economic Political Weekly*, 7 September.

Dreze, Jean (1990), 'Windows in Rural India', STICERD, *London School of Economics*, London.

Economic Survey, 2001–2.

Fan, Shenggen, Peter Hazell, and Sukhadeo Thorat (2000), 'Government Spending, Growth and Poverty in Rural India', *American Journal of Agricultural Economics*, Vol. 82, No. 4.

FAO, Roles of Agriculture (2003), *Socio-Economic Analysis and Policy Implications of the Roles of Agriculture in Developing Countries*, project report prepared for Food and Agriculture Organization of the United Nations, Rome.

Hirway, Indira (2002), 'Employment and Unemployment Situation in 1990's—How Good are NSS Data?', *Economic and Political Weekly*, May.

Meenakshi, J. V. and Ranjan Ray (2003), 'How have the disadvantaged fared in India after the economic reforms?', in K. Sharma (ed.) *Trade policy, growth and poverty in Asian developing countries*, Routledge, London.

Narayan, Deepa, Raj Patel, Keri Schafft, Anne Rudemacher, and Sura Koch-Schulte (2000), *Voices of the Poor—Can Anyone hear Us?*, Oxford University Press for World Bank, Washington, D.C.

National Institute of Nutrition (2002), *Diet and Nutritional Status of Rural Population*, NNMB Technical Report No. 21.

——— (2000), *Diet and Nutritional Status of Tribal Population*, Report of First Repeat Survey, NNMB Technical Report No. 19.

——— (1999), Report of Second Repeat Survey, Rural NNMB Technical Report No. 18.

——— (1993), Report of NNMB Repeat Surveys (1991-2).

——— (1991), Report of NNMB Repeat Surveys (1988-90).

NFHS (1998-9), International Institute of Population Studies and ORC Macro (2000) National Family Health Survey (NFHS-2).

Radhakrishna, R., K. Hanumantha Rao, C. Ravi, and B. Sambi Reddy (2003), 'Food Security and Malnutrition', Indian Institute of Public Administration—Chronic Poverty Research Centre Seminar on Chronic Poverty and Development Policy in India, 4–5 November 2003.

Ravi, C. (2000), 'Complete Demand Systems, Welfare and Nutrition: An Analysis of Indian Consumption Data', unpublished Ph.D. thesis.

SAPAP (2003), *South Asia Poverty Alleviation Programme*, project report submitted to UNDP/UNOPS.

Sen, Abhijit (2000), 'Estimates of Consumer Expenditure and its Distribution: Statistical Priorities after NSS 55th Round', *Economic and Political Weekly*, 16 December.

Shariff, A. (1999), *India: Human Development Report*, Oxord university Press, New Delhi.

Singh, R. B. and P. B. R. Hazell (1993), 'Rural Poverty in the Semi-Arid Tropics of India: Identification, Determinants and Policy Interventions', *Economic and Political Weekly*, March 1993.

Sundaram, K. (2001), 'Employment–Unemployment Situation in the Nineties—Some Results from NSS 55th Round Survey', *Economic and Political Weekly*, March.

World Bank (1991), 'Gender and Poverty in India', *World Bank*, Washington, D.C.

Zacharia, K. C., E. T. Mathew, and S. Irudaya Rajan (2003), *Dynamics of Migration in Kerala*, Orient Longman, India.

4 Public Health Scenario in India

Srijit Mishra[1]

This chapter evaluates some aspects of the contemporary public health scenario in India. First, with increasing life expectancy the epidemiological transition points towards greater incidence of non-communicable or lifestyle diseases.[2] This goes hand in hand with the continuing serious problem of communicable and preventable diseases.[3] Second, there is a lot of variation in the public provisioning of health care—a state subject. Poor states are hard pressed for funds. Third, India is an exception across countries in that nearly four-fifths of its health care expenditure is out of pocket. Coupled with the burgeoning growth of unregulated private sector care-givers, this has serious implications. These three issues open up a number of policy questions on access to, utilization, and quality of health care. However, the most important one among them is the one which will specifically address the concerns of the poor and the sick.

An increase in longevity is, unfortunately, associated with a greater incidence of sickness. It assumes serious dimension in India, which is burdened by both communicable and preventable as well as non-communicable or lifestyle diseases. International consensus in the fight against communicable and preventable diseases find mention in the Millennium Development Goals (MDGs) and also in India's new National Health Policy (NHP) 2002 as well as in India Vision 2020.

Epidemiological variations across states suggest that poorer states have a relatively greater burden of communicable and preventable diseases whereas the demographically and economically well-off states have a relatively greater burden of non-communicable diseases. However, poorer states/groups/regions are also vulnerable to some non-communicable diseases.

BURDEN OF DISEASES

In India, reduction in mortality has doubled life expectancy at birth in the last 50 years and almost trebled it in the last 100 years,[4] but this comes with a greater incidence of sickness (morbidity).[5] An epidemiological transition seems to suggest a shift from communicable to non-communicable diseases (Box 4.1).

Recent World Health Organization (WHO) estimates for 1998 (Table 4.1) show that all sub-groups of communicable and preventable diseases have more proportion of deaths than population proportion when compared with world (column 4) or low- and middle-income countries (column 5). Diabetes mellitus, neuropsychiatric disorders (not when compared with world), cardiovascular disorders, congenital abnormalities, and oral diseases in non-communicable diseases, and unintentional injuries put greater burden. Infectious and parasitic diseases, respiratory infections, perinatal conditions, cardiovascular disorders, malignant neoplasm, and unintentional injuries together account for more than four-fifth of deaths

---

[1] The author thanks K. Srinivasan for offering insightful comments and Barnita Bagchi for her suggestions.

[2] We identify lifestyle diseases with no dietary check (full of fat and cholesterol), excess of alcohol, consumption of tobacco, no exercise, and a stressful life and refer to these as no control over DATES.

[3] Here preventable diseases refer to those identified with maternal and perinatal conditions and nutritional deficiencies (see Table 4.1).

[4] Life expectation at birth in India is as follows: 1901—female 24.0, male 23.6; 1951—female 31.7, male 32.5; and 1993–7—female 61.8, male 60.4, Central Bureau of Health Intelligence (CBHI) 2002, p. 53.

[5] Comparable estimates of NSS 28th round (1973–4), 42nd Round (1986–97) and 52nd Round (1995–6) confirm this increasing trend National Sample Survey Organisation (NSSO) 1998b, p. 18.

> Box 4.1
>
> **Changing Demographic Profile and Epidemiological Transition**
>
> Medical technology advances in disease control have, on the one hand, postponed death and, on the other hand, prolonged the average duration of certain diseases and disabilities. Thus, what seems as success in terms of increased longevity is failure in terms of greater incidence of sickness. This is also accompanied by change in the pattern of sickness.
>
> In India, Survey of Causes of Death (Rural) (SCD (R)), suggests an epidemiological transition with a decline in proportions of deaths from communicable disease (47.7 per cent in 1969–71 to 22.1 per cent in 1994–5) and an increase in that of non-communicable diseases (35.9 per cent in 1969–71 to 54.9 per cent in 1994–5). These trends are broadly indicative as the survey collects information through 'lay diagnosis reporting' (Visaria 2004).
>
> At a broader level the inter-state variation across 13 states based on years-of-life lost (YLL) per 1000 population calculated from SCD(R) (1995) also shows this epidemiological transition. The states of Bihar, Madhya Pradesh (with maximum YLL of 276), Orissa, Rajasthan, and Uttar Pradesh with YLL greater than the national average (207) have communicable and preventable diseases as predominant cause. Whereas the two states with least YLL, Kerala (74) and Punjab (141), have non-communicable disease as the predominant cause. However, a closer look at specific causes of death show that burden from cancers (non-communicable disease) is uniform across states; suicides have a heavy burden in Andhra Pradesh; and vehicular accidents have greater burden in Haryana and Rajasthan (Indrayan et al. 2002). This and our subsequent discussions in this chapter indicate that our understanding of epidemiological pattern has to go beyond changing demographic profile.

TABLE 4.1
Distribution of Causes of Death in India, 1998

Causes of death (excluding 1st row, distribution of population)	Number in thousands	Per cent of deaths (excluding 1st row, population)	Percentage of world	Percentage of low and middle income countries
Distribution of population	982223	–	16.7	19.7
Total deaths	9337	100.0	17.3	20.3
Communicable and preventable diseases	3944	42.2	24.0	24.7
Infectious and parasitic diseases	2121	22.7	21.6	21.9
Respiratory infections	987	10.6	28.1	30.9
Maternal conditions	125	1.3	25.3	25.4
Perinatal conditions	612	6.6	28.4	29.1
Nutritional deficiencies	100	1.1	20.4	21.4
Non-communicable conditions	4470	47.9	14.1	18.1
Malignant neoplasms	653	7.0	9.0	12.5
Other neoplasms	5	0.1	4.6	7.2
Diabetes mellitus	102	1.1	17.0	23.2
Nutritional/Endocrine disorders	2	0.0	1.4	2.1
Neuropsychiatric disorders	104	1.1	14.4	21.0
Sense organ disorders	0	0.0	0.2	0.2
Cardiovascular disorders	2820	30.2	16.9	21.5
Respiratory diseases	284	3.0	9.5	10.9
Digestive diseases	240	2.6	13.4	16.4
Diseases of the genito-urinary system	102	1.1	13.4	16.3
Skin diseases	2	0.0	5.4	7.7
Musculo-skeletal diseases	3	0.0	2.5	3.8
Congenital abnormalities	153	1.6	29.8	32.1
Oral diseases	0	0.0	18.7	23.0
Injuries	923	9.9	16.0	17.5
Unintentional	723	7.7	20.7	22.8
Intentional	200	2.1	8.8	9.5

Source: Peters et al. (2002, pp. 310–15).

in terms of major causes (columns 2 or 3).[6] India faces the dual burden of communicable as well as non-communicable diseases.

International consensus has emerged to reduce incidences/deaths arising out of communicable and preventable diseases, as indicated by three of the eight MDGs directly identified with health. Keeping 1990 as the benchmark, the three goals and targets therein that have to be achieved by 2015 are: (i) to reduce under-five (infant/child) mortality by two-thirds; (ii) to reduce maternal mortality rate by three-fourths; and (iii) to combat human immunodeficiency virus/acquired immune deficiency syndrome (HIV/AIDS), malaria, tuberculosis (TB), and other diseases by not only halting their rising incidences but also by reversing their spread.

India Vision 2020 in some sense concurs or even goes beyond these by stating that the current situation in upper middle-income countries is to be achieved. It envisages increasing access to health care for women and children, eliminating childhood deaths from diarrhoea by 2010, effective targeting of undernourished children, restructuring malaria workforce to reduce incidence by 50 per cent, and improving diagnostics and treatment of TB. It also seeks to address the state of under-equipped, under-staffed, and under-financed health care infrastructure, and suggests increasing public spending from 0.8 per cent to 3.4 per cent of gross domestic product (GDP) (Planning Commission 2002b, pp. 52–5).

Infant and Child Mortality

From among the 10.8 million under-five (infant and child) deaths per year in the world, 2.4 million (22.2 per cent) are in India (Black, Morris, and Bryce 2003). Within India, there are wide interstate variations. National Family Health Survey 1998–9 (NFHS-2) data show that under-five mortality per thousand live births ranges from a minimum of 18.9 in Kerala to a maximum of 137.6 in Madhya Pradesh (Table 4.2). There are only seven states with under-five mortality above the national average of 94.9. The four states of Bihar, Madhya Pradesh, Rajasthan, and Uttar Pradesh account for more than three-fifths of under-five deaths and after including Orissa they account for two-thirds of under-five deaths in India.

Under-five death is associated with socio-economic

[6] In the Indian context, there is a comprehensive exercise about burden of disease for Andhra Pradesh. It shows that lower respiratory tract infection, diarrhoeal diseases, low birth weight, tuberculosis, and falls were the five top causes of disease burden. The first three are strongly associated with infants and child deaths. Besides, falls (among younger age groups), suicides (among adolescents and young adults), fires (mostly women, perhaps due to bridal harassment), and road accidents raise important public policy questions (Institute of Health Systems (IHS) undated).

characteristics—being higher in rural as against urban and among Scheduled Tribes (STs) and Scheduled Castes (SCs), and inversely related with the mother's education and Standard of Living Index (SLI). It is also associated with medico-demographic characteristics—higher when the mother's age is below 20 years (least for the 20–9 age group), for the female child (male child for neonatal mortality), for lower birth intervals, and when birth size is lower. It decreases with birth order up to the third issue (thereafter it increases) and with medical care (antenatal, delivery assistance, and postnatal), and is lowest when all the three have been availed of (International Institute for Population Sciences (IIPS) and ORC Macro 2000, pp. 186–7, 189–91).

Almost 70 per cent of under-five deaths are infants (below one year) and about 65 per cent of infant deaths are neonates (below 30 days).[7] As per NFHS-2, 74 per cent of neonatal deaths are in the first seven days (early neonatal deaths) and more than one-third of this is on the day of birth. These proportions have been increasing over time (IIPS and ORC Macro 2000, p. 362).

Under-five deaths worldwide can reduce by 63 per cent because there exists (i) sufficient evidence for preventive intervention with regard to major causes of infant/child death such as diarrhoea, pneumonia, measles, malaria, neonatal sepsis, preterm delivery, neonatal tetanus, and mother-to-child transmission of HIV/AIDS; (ii) sufficient evidence of treatment intervention for the first five causes noted under (i); and (iii) limited evidence for treatment intervention for birth asphyxia (Jones et al. 2003). Successful intervention requires access to such knowledge and transfer of this into action. It is also necessary to go beyond biological and behavioural intervention to understand local health delivery system including possibility for community participation and availability of real-time data to identify local variations. A successful initiative in India in this regard is the cost-effective home-based neonatal care (Box 4.2).

Maternal Health

Maternal mortality rate (maternal deaths per 100000 live births) estimated by Bhat (2002) is highest in Assam (984) and lowest in Tamil Nadu (195) (Table 4.3, column 2a). It could be lower in Punjab and Kerala where estimates are not available because of low occurrence. States with high maternal mortality rate are Uttar Pradesh, Madhya Pradesh, Orissa, Gujarat, Rajasthan, and Bihar. There exists a correspondence with high infant/child mortality

[7] Another area of concern is perinatal mortality (foetal loss beyond 28 weeks of gestation till end of seventh day after birth—still birth plus early neonatal mortality) that would reflect the state of antenatal care.

TABLE 4.2
Neonatal, Infant, and Under-five Mortality Rates, 1998–9

India/States	Total			Rural			Urban		
	NMR	IMR	U5M	NMR	IMR	U5M	NMR	IMR	U5M
Andhra Pradesh	43.8	65.8	85.5	46.1	71.4	93.1	36.8	49.2	62.6
Arunachal Pradesh	41.8	63.1	98.1	NA	NA	NA	NA	NA	NA
Assam	44.6	69.5	89.5	45.2	70.9	91.6	36.0	47.1	55.0
Bihar	46.5	72.9	105.1	47.8	74.8	108.6	32.8	53.3	68.3
Chhattisgarh	54.7	80.9	122.7	NA	NA	NA	NA	NA	NA
Delhi	29.5	46.8	55.4	NA	NA	NA	NA	NA	NA
Goa	31.2	36.7	46.8	NA	NA	NA	NA	NA	NA
Gujarat	39.6	62.6	85.1	46.0	74.4	94.7	28.6	42.2	68.3
Haryana	34.9	56.8	76.8	35.6	61.5	81.9	32.6	41.6	60.4
Himachal Pradesh	22.1	34.4	42.4	22.3	34.1	42.2	19.0	37.5	45.3
Jammu and Kashmir	40.3	65.0	80.1	40.0	66.5	82.3	41.6	57.6	69.2
Jharkhand	36.6	54.3	78.3	NA	NA	NA	NA	NA	NA
Karnataka	37.1	51.5	69.8	39.3	56.5	79.0	32.1	40.1	48.8
Kerala	13.8	16.3	18.8	14.2	16.5	18.9	12.5	15.5	18.6
Madhya Pradesh	54.9	86.1	137.6	57.8	92.5	152.2	44.0	61.9	82.9
Maharashtra	32.0	43.7	58.1	36.7	50.6	67.8	24.7	33.0	42.8
Manipur	18.6	37.0	56.1	NA	NA	NA	NA	NA	NA
Meghalaya	50.7	89.0	122.0	NA	NA	NA	NA	NA	NA
Mizoram	18.8	37.0	54.7	NA	NA	NA	NA	NA	NA
Nagaland	20.1	42.1	63.8	NA	NA	NA	NA	NA	NA
Orissa	48.6	81.0	104.4	48.6	80.9	104.8	49.3	81.1	102.0
Punjab	34.3	57.1	72.1	39.3	63.3	79.4	18.6	37.7	49.7
Rajasthan	49.5	80.4	114.9	50.6	83.0	120.6	45.2	69.7	92.3
Sikkim	26.3	43.9	71.0	NA	NA	NA	NA	NA	NA
Tamil Nadu	34.8	48.2	63.3	38.1	52.1	70.4	28.5	40.6	49.7
Tripura	28.6	44.2	51.3	NA	NA	NA	NA	NA	NA
Uttar Pradesh	53.6	86.7	122.5	56.6	91.7	129.5	38.3	60.4	85.8
Uttaranchal	25.7	37.6	56.1	NA	NA	NA	NA	NA	NA
West Bengal	31.9	48.7	67.6	36.7	53.3	73.4	9.9	27.6	40.8
India	43.4	67.6	94.9	46.7	73.3	103.7	31.7	47.0	63.1

Note: NMR, IMR, and U5M denote neonatal, infant and under-five mortality rates (deaths for 1000 live births) respectively and calculation of these estimates use data for five years preceding the survey. NA denotes not available. The new states of Chhattisgarh, Jharkhand, and Uttaranchal formed part of Madhya Pradesh, Bihar, and Uttar Pradesh respectively when the survey was carried out and, hence, estimates for the latter states are inclusive of the former but independent estimates for the new states are also given.

Source: NFHS-2 final report of states and that of India (http://www.nfhsindia.org/pnfhs2.html, accessed 4 November 2003).

Box 4.2
Home-based Neonatal Care (HBNC)

HBNC is the outcome of a five-year (1993–8) field trial in the predominantly tribal district of Gadchiroli, Maharashtra by the Society for Education, Action, and Research in Community Health (SEARCH) working in this region since 1986. First, a baseline survey in 1993–5 identified major causes of neonatal death and found that two-fifths of mothers suffered from morbidity during postpartum period. Subsequently, traditional birth attendants (TBAs) and village health workers (VHWs) were trained, mothers were given health education, all neonates were given care and sick neonates were given extra attention at home. Care included resuscitating newborns not breathing regularly, supporting breastfeeding, and maintaining infant body temperature, recognizing symptoms that suggest infections and treating them with antibiotics (note that village health workers administered antibiotics). These measures reduced neonatal morbidity and mortality and maternal mortality considerably. In 39 intervention villages, IMR (death before first birthday for 1000 live births) showed a steady decline from about 80 in 1995 to 40 in 1998 whereas in 47 control villages IMR fluctuated in the range of 70–90. In HBNC, cost in 1997–8 was about Rs 200 per neonate and Rs 9000 per village whereas a study on hospital-based neonate care of Chennai showed cost to be in the range of Rs 650–1750 per neonate. Further, from 1999 SEARCH has also introduced a scheme of first-referral level care to small rural hospitals for very sick neonates.

Source: Bang et al. (1999).

states (Table 4.2). A recent survey on availability of equipment and supplies to facilitate maternal and childcare in Primary Health Centres (PHCs) shows substantial deficiencies in Bihar, Orissa, and Uttar Pradesh (Table 4.4). Low availability of obstetric care equipment in Kerala indicates availability and utilization of other medical institutions for childbirth.

NFHS-2 data show that Bihar, Madhya Pradesh, Rajasthan, and Uttar Pradesh perform worse than the low socio-economic group of all-India in antenatal care, delivery, and postpartum care (Table 4.3). The four southern states, Goa, and the urban regions of some other states seem to perform better than the high socio-economic group of all-India. The relatively poor

TABLE 4.3
Maternal Mortality Rate (Indirect estimates, 1987–96 and SRS estimates 1998) and Some Aspects of Maternal Care in Rural and Urban India, 1998–9

States/India	Maternal mortality rate		Percentage of pregnant women who did not seek any antenatal care		Institutional Delivery		Women with non-institutional deliveries seeking postpartum care within two months of delivery	
	1987–96	1998	Rural	Urban	Rural	Urban	Rural	Urban
(1)	(2a)	(2b)	(3a)	(3b)	(4a)	(4b)	(5a)	(5b)
Andhra Pradesh	283	159	9.5	0.7	40.2	78.6	45.2	42.1
Arunachal Pradesh	NA	NA	38.4*		31.2*		10.5*	
Assam	984	409	40.7	9.5	15.0	59.9	25.0	44.7
Bihar	513	452	65.6	30.6	12.1	40.1	10.1	10.0
Delhi	NA	NA	29.2	12.7	34.1	61.8	19.5*	
Goa	NA	NA	0.0	1.6	90.7	90.9	NA	NA
Gujarat	596	28	16.1	9.4	33.0	69.2	10.7	9.5
Harayana	472	103	48.0	21.6	14.9	47.1	14.6	21.8
Himachal Pradesh	NA	NA	14.1	2.8	25.4	72.0	21.0	27.0
Jammu and Kashmir	NA	NA	18.1	3.0	28.4	74.4	26.9	38.4
Karnataka	480	195	0.1	0.0	38.5	78.8	34.3	41.9
Kerala	NA	198	0.4	0.0	91.5	99.4	NA	NA
Madhya Pradesh	700	498	44.2	17.9	12.1	49.1	8.1	21.6
Maharashtra	380	135	12.5	5.2	34.5	80.8	28.0	39.3
Manipur	NA	NA	19.8*		34.5*		27.1*	
Meghalaya	NA	NA	46.4*		17.3*		20.8*	
Mizoram	NA	NA	8.2*		57.6*		20.9*	
Nagaland	NA	NA	39.6*		12.1*		4.3*	
Orissa	597	367	21.2	12.7	19.0	54.7	19.3	18.2
Punjab	NA	199	30.8	9.7	31.9	56.1	16.4	40.9
Rajasthan	580	670	58.2	30.3	14.8	47.6	5.7	10.6
Sikkim	NA	NA	1.2	0.0	28.0	58.2	38.0*	
Tripura	NA	NA	29.2*		45.2*		24.1*	
Tamil Nadu	195	79	1.3	0.8	72.5	92.5	51.4	63.8
Uttar Pradesh	737	707	69.6	34.1	11.3	36.9	7.3	5.9
West Bengal	458	266	10.8	3.6	31.3	79.7	31.7	30.4
Low SLI	NA	NA	45.1*		18.5*		15.5*	
Medium SLI	NA	NA	32.8*		34.9*		16.5*	
High SLI	NA	NA	12.4*		64.6*		20.5*	
All-India	479	407	39.8	13.6	24.6	65.1	16.1	19.6

Note: Maternal mortality rate is for 100,000 live births. NA implies not available. SLI implies standard of living index for all-India computed from asset scores. Figure in column 2a are indirect estimates. For columns 3–5, * indicates total data since rural and urban break up is not available.

Source: Bhat (2002) for column 2a, Planning Commission (2002a, p. 239) for column 2b, and NFHS-2 final report of states and that of India (http://www.nfhsindia.org/pnfhs2.html, accessed 5 November 2003) for columns 3–5.

PUBLIC HEALTH SCENARIO IN INDIA 67

TABLE 4.4
Availability of Equipment and Supplies to Facilitate Maternal and Childcare in Primary Health Centres

States	No of PHCs surveyed	Equipment				Supplies				
		Vaccine carrier	Labor room equipment	IUD insertion kit	Normal delivery kit	EOC drug	Oral pills	Measles vaccine	IFA tablets	ORS packets
Andhra Pradesh	622	96.9	73.0	32.0	45.0	5.9	62.1	83.9	25.1	58.0
Assam	333	94.9	24.9	27.0	36.9	21.0	79.0	60.1	41.1	67.9
Bihar	339	54.0	30.1	4.1	8.0	0.9	12.1	12.1	4.1	18.9
Gujarat	614	99.0	71.0	16.9	16.9	6.0	59.9	95.0	11.1	85.0
Haryana	73	97.3	31.5	98.6	97.3	93.2	95.9	80.8	98.6	97.3
Karnataka	854	95.0	61.9	73.0	52.0	26.0	80.0	68.0	34.0	70.0
Kerala	790	93.0	29.0	18.0	11.0	1.0	77.0	74.1	64.1	92.0
Madhya Pradesh	386	87.0	22.0	35.0	29.0	3.9	51.0	25.9	50.0	59.1
Maharashtra	645	100.0	93.0	98.0	98.0	77.1	75.0	97.1	42.9	80.0
Orissa	505	31.1	34.1	5.0	10.1	1.0	16.0	18.0	12.1	71.1
Punjab	26	96.2	88.5	92.3	88.5	57.7	80.8	88.5	57.7	57.7
Rajasthan	484	93.0	65.9	81.0	71.1	14.0	86.0	53.9	40.9	74.0
Tamil Nadu	672	98.1	49.0	87.1	85.0	60.0	65.0	90.0	28.0	78.0
Uttar Pradesh	486	53.9	39.9	8.0	14.0	3.9	16.0	16.0	10.1	17.1
West Bengal	825	81.0	51.0	68.0	62.1	6.1	49.0	35.0	23.0	33.0
India	7654	85.3	52.2	47.5	45.1	19.8	59.3	60.7	31.5	64.3

Note: PHC = Primary Health Centre, IUD = Intrauterine Device, EOC = Emergency Obstetric Care, IFA = Iron and Folic Acid, ORS = Oral Rehydration Salt. Data based on facilities survey (year of survey could not be obtained from the source).
Source: Rajya Sabha Unstarred Question No. 2162, dated 10 December 2001 (as obtained from www.indiastat.com, accessed 14 December 2003).

performance of economically better-off Haryana and Punjab (particularly, in terms of institutional deliveries) is intriguing. National Sample Survey (NSS) 52nd Round data suggest that a large proportion of deliveries in these states (particularly in Punjab) were at home under the supervision of professional medical care (Mishra 2003).

SOME INFECTIOUS AND PARASITIC DISEASES

HIV/AIDS

HIV infected persons in India as per an estimate for 2002 were in the range of 3.82–4.58 million, but only 68,809 cases were reported to National Aids Control Organisations (NACO) until March 2004. The proportion of women among reported cases seems to be increasing—23.1 per cent until December 2000, 25.8 per cent until May 2003, 26.8 per cent until March 2004, and 32.1 per cent in the month of March 2004 alone (CBHI 2002, NACO undated1).

Cumulative figures till March 2004 show that the proportion of women among reported cases declines with age: 0–14 years—38.5 per cent, 15–29 years—35.9 per cent, 30–44 years—21.3 per cent, and 45+ years—19.9 per cent. Among women, nearly 90 per cent are in the reproductive age group. This is a serious public policy concern more so because 85.9 per cent of the reported cases are through sexual transmission (NACO undated1). The high-risk groups are sex workers, truck drivers,[8] men having sex with men (MSM),[9] intravenous drug users, migrant labourers, and vulnerable children. However, the danger is that it has started spreading into non-risk general population. One possible reason for this is interaction of the high-risk groups with their spouses.[10]

TB

In 1998 almost 7.6 million disability adjusted life years (DALYs) and 0.42 million lives were lost (Peters et al. 2002). This puts India with little more than one-fourth

---

[8] Bryan et al. (2002) analysis observes that Indian truck drivers had substantial deficits with respect to HIV prevention information, motivation, and behaviour.

[9] The social and cultural context of MSM in India differs from that in the West not only in their sexual identities and circuits, but also in their partnerships and practices (Asthana and Oostvogels 2001).

[10] The nature of interaction is what Menezes (2003) refers to as egoistic sexual behaviour by males. Knowledge of infection with HIV/AIDS brings about altruistic sexual behaviour with spouses, but this is less likely with presence of son preference. Those who behave egoistically are also less likely to confide with their spouses about their risk status.

of the world TB burden. TB is a major killer of adults (more so for females) and with greater prevalence among the poor and the malnourished. It is commendable that research in India has introduced the directly observed treatment, short-course (DOTS)—'the most important public health breakthrough of the decade, in terms of lives which will be saved' (Director General, WHO, 24 March 1997) (DGHS (Director General of Health Services) undated1).[11]

The revised national TB control programme (RNTCP) introduced on 2 October 1993 was till February 2004 implemented in 455 districts covering 829 million people. This scheme increases case detection through compulsory three-sputum examination of any individual coughing for more than three weeks. Once the disease is identified, availability of medicine is guaranteed and DOTS ensures compliance and, hence, greater chance of a cure. In fact, success of treatment has been more than 80 per cent (note that accountability of failure lies with the health system, not with the individual). Besides, introduction of RNTCP in a phased manner is a deliberate step so as to guard against poor performance because discontinuance of treatment will not only have a poor success rate but also lead to multi-drug resistant TB. DOTS can also be very effective among HIV/AIDS infected patients who are highly susceptible to TB (DGHS undated1).

Polio

After global initiatives led to the eradication of smallpox in the mid-1970s, a contemporary initiative is to eradicate polio by 2005. It was contained to 268 cases in 2001, but there has been a resurgence to 1600 cases in India in 2002. This accounts for 83 per cent of cases worldwide with the epicentre in the state of Uttar Pradesh (65 per cent of worldwide cases). A major reason for the epidemic is reduction in supplementary immunization activities (SIAs) from 10 in 1999–2000 to only three in 2002. Efforts are already under way to increase SIAs in Uttar Pradesh and other states to make a polio-free India, nay world (WHO 2003).

Malaria

Efforts to control/eradicate malaria have been on from the early 1950s. Consequently, from 1953 to mid-1960s incidence of the disease reduced from 75 million to 0.1 million and death from malaria reduced from 0.8 million to zero. Thereafter, incidences surged to peak at 6.47 million in 1976 (CBHI 2002).

Two schemes of modified operation plan to reduce mortality and morbidity from malaria and Plasmodium falciparum containment programme were launched in 1977. Barring the period 1988–96, incidences have been declining. The twin programmes were perhaps more effective in reducing the Plasmodium vivax parasite. The proportion of the killer parasite Plasmodium falciparum, instead of declining, increased from 26 per cent in 1965 to about 52 per cent in 2000. Another startling fact is that the proportion of malaria has increased in the poorer states. In the year 2000 almost 50 per cent of Plasmodium vivax and 90 per cent of Plasmodium falciparum related cases occurred in 12 of the poorer states (Sharma 2003).[12] Further, as the malaria vector becomes insecticide-resistant and the parasite becomes drug-resistant, the disease becomes increasingly virulent and this perhaps explains the disturbing state of 200 people dying of cerebral malaria in a single district of Orissa in 2002 (personal communication from Arnab Acharya).

Diarrhoea

One-third of the deaths from parasitic and infectious diseases in India in 1998 were from diarrhoeal diseases (Peters et al. 2002), which mostly affected children below five years of age. On the curative side oral rehydration salt (ORS) and administration of intravenous fluids have been very effective, but on the preventive side inadequate sanitation and unavailability of drinking water need attention. Availability of piped water and other socio-economic aspects such as female (in particular, mother's) literacy is associated with lower incidence of diarrhoea among children (Jalan and Ravallion 2001). Access to piped water and other aspects relevant with sanitation are less than one-fourth in rural areas and nearly three-fourth in urban areas (Table 4.5).

As per NFHS-2, only 29 per cent of mothers reported that a child should be given more fluids during an episode of diarrhoea whereas 34 per cent said that the child should be given less fluids, reflecting lack of awareness (IIPS and ORC Macro 2000, pp. 221–2).

---

[11] Until 7 April 2004, lives saved through DOTS is estimated at 0.52 million. Based on a conservative calculation, this is an additional 18 per cent of the patients treated when compared with the earlier National Tuberculosis Programme. This does not account for the increase in detection due to DOTS (DGHS undated1).

[12] The poorer states are those where proportion of population below poverty line in 1999–2000 is above the national average of 26.1 per cent. The states are Arunachal Pradesh, Assam, Bihar (includes Jharkhand), Madhya Pradesh (includes Chhattisgarh), Manipur, Meghalaya, Nagaland, Orissa, Sikkim, Tripura, and Uttar Pradesh (includes Uttaranchal), and West Bengal. These states (rather, only the six major states) account for three-fifth (1991 census) of India's scheduled caste and scheduled tribe population.

TABLE 4.5
Proportion of Households with access to Piped Water, Bathroom,
Latrine, and Drainage, and Female Literacy: 2001

Characteristics	Rural	Urban	Total
Households with source of drinking water, tap (piped)	24.3	68.7	36.7
Households with bathroom	22.8	70.4	36.1
Households with latrine: pit, water closet, and other	21.9	73.7	36.4
Households with drainage: open and closed	34.2	77.9	46.4
Female literacy	46.6	73.0	54.1

Source: Census of India (2001a, Table 1; and 2001b, Tables S00–015 and S00–017).

LIFESTYLE DISEASES

As mentioned earlier in footnote 2, we identify lifestyle diseases with 'no control over DATES (diet, alcohol, tobacco, exercise, and stress)'. Table 4.1 shows that cardiovascular diseases account for nearly two-thirds of the deaths due to non-communicable diseases, which account for half of the overall deaths. Mortality from non-communicable diseases is likely to increase further.

Lifestyle diseases need not afflict the rich alone. To have an idea of the risk factor for non-communicable diseases across socio-economic groups we draw some indirect inferences from some recent environmental risk assessment studies. Parikh et al. (2003) study based on three major states of rural north India calculates risk factor for four respiratory diseases (bronchitis, asthma, chest infection, and TB—the first two being non-communicable diseases) and eye irritation (can also be non-communicable). It shows greater health risk for illiterates over literates, for those who have higher lifetime exposure to cooking (mostly females), for the poor (low asset index), for those who use biofuel as against clean fuel, or for those with fewer number of rooms in their houses. The adverse impact of biofuel on health is also true of rural Tamil Nadu (Parikh and Laxmi 2000). Another recent study analyses ambient/indoor air pollution in rural/urban areas of Lucknow (Kumar et al. 2003). It suggests that 'polycyclic aromatic hydrocarbons', a hazardous carcinogenic leading to non-communicable diseases, emitted from auto-exhaust and fuel biomass puts the economically underprivileged at greater risk.

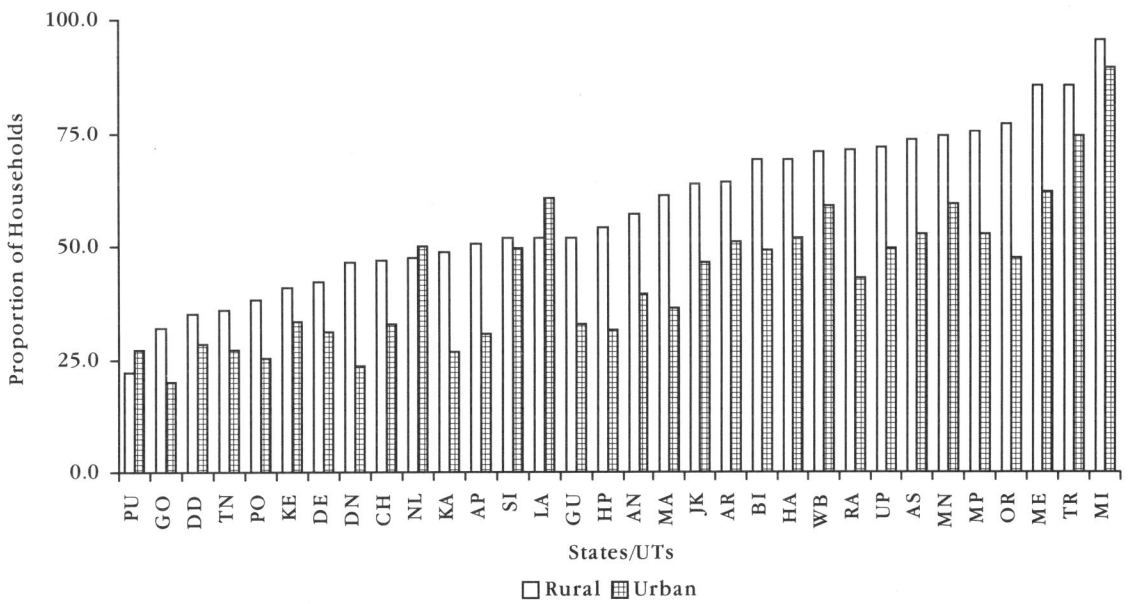

Figure 4.1: Proportion of Households Reporting Consumption of Tobacco, 1999–2000

Note: Code for states/union territories (UTs) are as follows: Andaman and Nicobar Islands (AN), Andhra Pradesh (AP), Arunachal Pradesh (AR), Assam (AS), Bihar (BI), Chandigarh (CH), Dadar and Nagar Haveli (DN), Daman and Diu (DD), Delhi (DE), Goa (GO), Gujarat (GU), Haryana (HA), Himachal Pradesh (HP), Jammu and Kashmir (JK), Karnataka (KA), Kerala (KE), Lakshadweep (LA), Madhya Pradesh (MP), Maharashtra (MA), Manipur (MN), Meghalaya (ME), Mizoram (MI), Nagaland (NL), Orissa (OR), Pondicherry (PO), Punjab (PU), Rajasthan (RA), Sikkim (SI), Tamil Nadu (TN), Tripura (TR), Uttar Pradesh (UP), and West Bengal (WB).

Source: NSSO (2001).

Figure 4.1 shows greater incidence of tobacco consumption in poorer states and in rural areas as compared to urban areas. This perhaps explains morbidity from cancer across states being highest in the north-east region followed by Orissa (Table 4.9). Besides, individual consumption data of 1993–4 reveals caste divide. It is highest among STs, SCs lie in between, and 'others' have the lowest incidence (Table 4.6). When disaggregated across states, STs still have the highest incidence in most rural areas, but SCs have the highest incidence in many urban areas. Females have much lower incidence than males. Compared across states, incidence of morbidity from cancer among females is much higher in Orissa because of chewing tobacco. The overall incidence for the country also seems to increase with age—except for males in the 60 plus age group—probably indicating the cumulative impact of higher fatality among tobacco users.[13]

Tobacco's adverse health impact is mostly through cancer-related diseases. Cancer-related mortality is much higher in developed countries. However, for cervical cancer among women and for oral cancer India's share of the global burden is much higher. India bears one-fifth of the world burden in cervical cancer that is predominantly a problem of women from poor socio-economic backgrounds (Shanta 2002–3). Because of tobacco chewing (including *gutka*) and reverse smoking, oral cancer is a serious health problem in India.

MORBIDITY AND PHYSICAL DISABILITY

Higher self-perceived morbidity in Kerala when contrasted with that of Bihar would be a reflection of epidemiological transition indicating that reduced mortality is consistent with higher morbidity and greater health consciousness (Murray 1996). Cross-section analysis across 15 major states (after excluding Assam, Orissa, and Uttar Pradesh that seem to have a relatively greater morbidity burden) shows an inverse relationship between morbidity prevalence and infant mortality (a robust indicator of health status) and a positive relationship between morbidity prevalence and life expectation (Table 4.7).

Morbidity prevalence is highest in the 60 plus age group and then among children in the 0–14 age group—the least sick being the 15–39 age group. Females seem to have greater acute and chronic morbidity prevalence across all decile/quintile (excluding 1st decile for all cases and also 2nd decile for rural chronic) and caste groups. This difference, observed more in the 15–39 and 40–59 age groups, indicates its association with reproductive health (Table 4.8). This, however, is not entirely because of childbirth-related complications. Some specific ailments most significant in terms of greater female morbidity prevalence are fevers of short duration, oral diseases, and 'others' from acute ailments and high/low blood pressure and pain in the joints from chronic

TABLE 4.6
Age- and Caste-wise Incidence of Regular Consumers of Tobacco by
Males and Females in Rural and Urban Areas, 1993–4

Rural/Urban Gender	Age group						Social group/caste			
	10–14	15–24	25–44	45–59	60 +	10 +	ST	SC	Others	All
Rural male	1.3	19.1	61.3	72.3	65.0	43.0	40.7	34.8	29.7	31.9
Rural female	0.9	4.6	12.2	20.4	21.2	10.9	15.3	8.9	6.8	8.2
Urban male	0.4	8.7	40.7	50.9	39.5	27.7	30.4	28.4	20.2	21.7
Urban female	0.2	1.2	4.5	11.4	13.0	4.7	8.4	5.8	3.2	3.7

Note: ST and SC denote scheduled tribe and scheduled caste respectively.
Source: NSSO (1998a, pp. 277–387).

[13] A recent retrospective case-control study (Gajalakshmi et al. 2003) of adult males (25–69 years) in Tamil Nadu suggests that risk of dying for 'ever-smokers' is more than double those of 'never- smokers'. One-third of excess mortality is due to respiratory diseases (chiefly TB), another one-third to vascular diseases and more than one-tenth to cancer (chiefly respiratory and digestive tract). The study also indicates that 'ever-smokers' death among older men (69+) would be one-fifth of that in the 25–69 age group. A Mumbai based study (Gupta and Mehta 2000) that followed up and traced adults (35+ years) after 5–6 years found *bidi* smokers at a greater relative-risk than that of cigarette smokers.

ailments (NSSO 1998b, pp. A22–36, A127–41). The greater morbidity prevalence among females is not obvious from the proportions that underwent hospitalization (excluding 1st decile and the 15–39 age group).

Short duration morbidity of diarrhoea (mostly afflicts children) shows relatively greater prevalence in states with higher infant/under-five mortality (Table 4.9). Morbidity from communicable diseases like leprosy and TB has the highest prevalence in Madhya Pradesh. Some other poorer states and some southern states are above the national average. Similarly, non-communicable

Table 4.7
Morbidity Prevalence, Infant Mortality, and Life Expectation across 15 Major States in Rural and Urban India

States/India	Rural			Urban		
	Morbidity prevalence 1995–6	Infant mortality 1995–6	Life expectation 1992–6	Morbidity prevalence 1995–6	Infant mortality 1995–6	Life expectation 1992–6
Andhra Pradesh	64.00	74.00	61.00	61.00	41.00	65.50
Assam	80.00	78.00	55.60	86.00	48.00	64.60
Bihar	36.00	74.00	58.70	41.00	56.00	66.00
Gujarat	46.00	68.00	60.50	36.00	47.00	63.70
Haryana	61.00	70.00	62.90	63.00	63.00	67.60
Karnataka	45.00	66.00	61.30	40.00	34.00	67.10
Kerala	118.00	15.00	72.80	88.00	15.00	73.60
Madhya Pradesh	41.00	103.00	53.70	38.00	61.00	63.00
Maharashtra	52.00	62.00	62.80	48.00	33.00	69.40
Orissa	62.00	103.00	56.10	62.00	65.00	64.70
Punjab	76.00	56.00	66.70	85.00	40.00	70.40
Rajasthan	28.00	90.00	57.50	33.00	61.00	64.40
Tamil Nadu	52.00	61.00	62.20	58.00	41.00	67.50
Uttar Pradesh	61.00	89.00	56.30	72.00	67.00	61.60
West Bengal	65.00	60.00	60.80	65.00	45.00	67.90
India	55.00	79.00	59.40	54.00	30.00	66.30
Correlation		Col. 2 & 3	Col. 2 & 4		Col. 5 & 6	Col. 5 & 7
15 states		−0.66	0.64		−0.30	0.43
Ex AS, OR, & UP		−0.87	0.89		−0.56	0.83

Note: Col. denotes column, Ex denotes excludes and AS, OR, and UP denote Assam, Orissa and Uttar Pradesh respectively.
Source: NSSO (1998b, pp. 15–16) and Planning Commission (2002a, pp. 219–20).

Table 4.8
Prevalence of Acute and Chronic Ailment and Hospitalization per 1000 Persons across Expenditure Decile/Quintile, Caste, and Age by Sex for Rural/Urban regions, 1995–6

Sub-groups		Acute				Chronic				Hospitalization			
		Rural		Urban		Rural		Urban		Rural		Urban	
		Male	Female	Male	Female	Male	Female	Male	Female	Male	Female	Male	Female
(1a)	(1b)	(2)	(3)	(4)	(5)	(6)	(7)	(8)	(9)	(10)	(11)	(12)	(13)
Decile/ Quintile	D1	34	33	34	33	9	8	8	7	3	4	12	13
	D2	32	33	34	39	8	7	8	9	6	5	13	13
	Q2	36	40	37	42	9	9	9	12	8	8	17	15
	Q3	41	45	39	42	9	11	11	13	10	9	19	20
	Q4	43	47	38	46	14	15	13	18	16	15	20	22
	D9	49	53	40	51	17	20	18	25	22	21	26	28
	D10	55	57	48	45	29	34	23	26	39	34	39	36
Caste	ST	37	38	35	43	5	5	7	10	9	8	21	22
	SC	41	43	39	37	12	12	10	12	13	11	19	19
	Others	42	45	39	45	14	16	13	16	15	14	21	20
Age	0–14	46	43	51	47	3	3	3	3	9	6	15	10
	15–39	27	36	28	37	8	9	7	9	11	14	14	19
	40–59	42	48	36	42	22	27	24	31	22	19	31	30
	60+	95	90	65	73	86	73	85	94	47	28	75	57
India		41	44	39	43	13	14	13	15	14	13	20	20

Note: D1, D2, D9, and D10 refer to 1st, 2nd, 9th, and 10th decile respectively and Q2, Q3 and Q4 refer to 2nd, 3rd, and 4th quintile respectively. ST and SC denote scheduled tribe and scheduled caste respectively.
Source: NSSO (1998b, pp. A2-169).

TABLE 4.9
Short Duration Morbidity (30 Day Recall) and Major Morbidity (Previous Year) across States, 1994

States	Short duration morbidity (30 day recall)			Major morbidity (previous year)							
				Communicable diseases		Non-communicable diseases					
	Cold/ cough	Diarrhoea	Fever	Leprosy	TB	Cancer	Diabetes	Heart disease	Epilepsy	Hyper-tension	Mental disease
Andhra Pradesh	68	36	31	63	580	66	545	676	129	1295	163
Bihar	83	39	19	29	496	19	143	443	78	481	169
Gujarat	33	9	18	30	276	7	215	188	103	381	160
Haryana	48	29	84	NA	322	34	100	230	103	372	143
Kerala	75	6	8	NA	504	39	980	914	81	1433	283
Madhya Pradesh	79	63	60	313	686	57	138	160	74	366	136
Maharashtra	48	14	26	65	282	62	130	151	147	241	84
North-east region	60	35	3	74	189	127	226	502	50	732	105
Orissa	85	54	22	31	206	74	116	245	369	863	99
Punjab	104	16	36	NA	230	28	196	166	103	1475	268
Rajasthan	72	19	26	NA	303	37	55	84	60	64	79
Tamil Nadu	125	19	27	83	583	15	377	949	205	1191	80
Uttar Pradesh	51	31	26	27	370	34	158	231	120	221	120
West Bengal	114	45	11	22	636	32	207	795	133	1049	151
India	72	31	25	57	423	43	221	385	120	589	132

Note: NA implies not available.
Source: Shariff (1999, pp. 136–41).

diseases generally have a greater prevalence in the southern states. It is also high in some of the poorer states (particularly the north-east region, Orissa and, to some extent, Bihar). This points out that epidemiological differences across states need not go hand in hand with demographic or established socio-economic patterns.

An estimate (NSS 47th Round 1991) puts 16.15 million people with physical disability (visual, hearing, speech, or locomotor) and nearly 5 per cent of these incidences (0.74 million people) having been disabled the previous year. The prevalence rate was higher in rural than in urban (Table 4.10). In rural regions of Andhra Pradesh and Orissa there is greater visual impairment, Himachal Pradesh has greater hearing and speech impairment, and Punjab has greater locomotor disability. Thus, there exists variation across type of disabilities and across states/regions and one ought to factor this into state-specific health policies/programmes.

OUTPATIENT AND INPATIENT TREATMENT

A comparison of NSS 42nd Round (1986–7) with 52nd Round (1995–6) shows that morbidity prevalence has increased from 64 to 86 in rural areas and from 31 to 84 in urban areas.[14] The proportion of those seeking treatment is more than four-fifths in rural and around nine-tenths in urban. A major reason for not seeking care relates to the ailment not being considered serious. This attitude has reduced considerably (from 75 per cent to 52 per cent in rural and from 81 per cent to 60 per cent in urban) whereas financial constraints, lack of health facility, and other reasons have increased. Financial constraint is also borne out by the proportions seeking care being higher for higher expenditure decile/quintile groups. Lower hospitalization among lower expenditure groups, STs and SCs, rural regions, and females explain some kind of divide in terms of access to and utilization of inpatient care (Table 4.8, columns 10–13).

Lower expenditure quintile groups (excluding 1st quintile in rural) as well as SCs and STs seek relatively less of hospitalization, but rely more on public health facilities (Figure 4.2). However, it is the rich who benefit more on a per capita basis because of relatively greater

[14] Morbidity prevalence refers to number ailing per 1000 persons for a 30-day recall period. Data exists for 42nd Round. For 52nd Round, we add 15-day recall period data with commencement of ailment in the last 15 days. This addition assumes that proportion falling sick in the last 15 days will be the same for the next 15 days. This and subsequent discussions in this section are based on NSSO (1998b).

TABLE 4.10
Physical (Visual, Hearing, Speech, or Locomotor) Disability per 100,000 Persons, 1991

States	Rural					Urban				
	Visual	Hearing (5+years)	Speech (5+years)	Loco-motor	Physical	Visual	Hearing (5+years)	Speech (5+years)	Loco-motor	Physical
Andhra Pradesh	806	660	345	1260	2498	385	501	359	1098	1903
Assam	382	319	261	419	1200	451	364	191	424	1186
Bihar	341	260	255	926	1573	225	215	224	932	1436
Gujarat	373	370	171	979	1676	266	317	213	1092	1648
Haryana	621	469	162	1077	1988	364	384	112	716	1374
Himachal Pradesh	629	1108	457	1356	2870	326	237	200	1106	1144
Karnataka	562	594	353	1091	2131	338	332	231	895	1494
Kerala	418	506	414	1037	1945	338	376	327	1203	1755
Madhya Pradesh	529	452	229	1207	2051	239	282	181	975	1475
Maharashtra	549	529	266	1206	2700	264	372	226	1037	1610
Orissa	820	698	256	970	2306	444	548	274	1112	2049
Punjab	599	435	259	1974	2936	325	230	264	1197	1807
Rajasthan	435	271	199	1063	1767	253	196	156	916	1126
Tamil Nadu	625	723	343	1116	2372	377	518	306	1007	1874
Uttar Pradesh	518	288	231	1083	1879	310	226	181	978	1519
West Bengal	395	570	322	890	1788	321	361	230	844	1505
India	525	467	273	1074	1995	302	339	237	962	1579
India-onset previous year	25	15	5	53	90	25	12	5	52	75

Note: Onset previous year indicates disabled during 365 days preceding the date of survey.
Source: NSSO (1994, pp. 75–117).

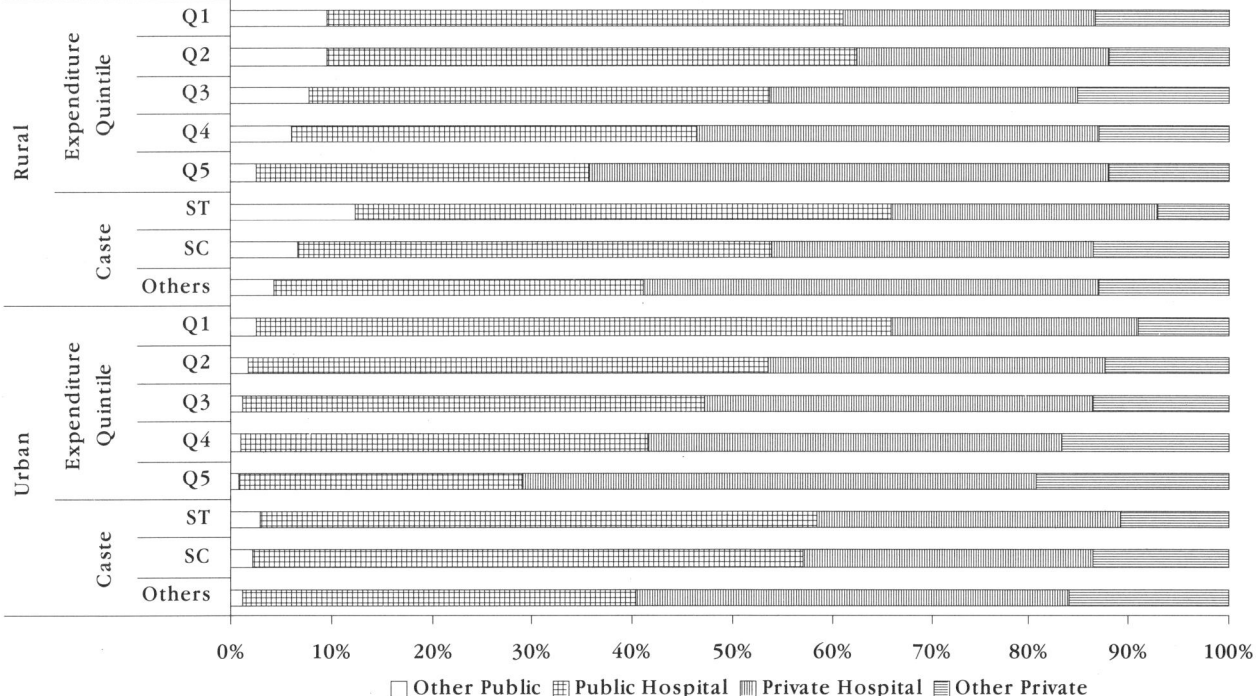

Figure 4.2: Share of Public and Private in Hospitalized Care across Expenditure Quintile and Caste in Rural and Urban India, 1995–6
Note: Other Public includes Primary/Community Health Centre, Public Dispensary, Other Private includes Nursing Home, Charitable Institutions and Others. Q1, Q2, Q3, Q4, and Q5 denote 1st, 2nd, 3rd, 4th, and 5th quintile respectively. ST and SC denote scheduled tribe and scheduled caste respectively.
Source: NSSO (1998b, pp. A65, A170).

incidence of using the public health care facilities (Mahal et al. 2000).

Public/private divide in seeking inpatient care has some interesting patterns (Table 4.11). Private sector share is below 10 per cent in the Andaman and Nicobar Islands, Himachal Pradesh, Jammu and Kashmir, most north-east states, and Orissa. A common feature perhaps is that they are either mountainous/hilly or tribal regions.

TABLE 4.11
Share of Public and Private Sectors in Inpatient Care

States	Rural		Urban	
	Public	Private	Public	Private
Andhra Pradesh	22.2	76.3	35.4	62.4
Arunachal Pradesh	65.5	25.2	89.6	8.4
Assam	69.2	24.6	63.0	33.6
Bihar	24.1	73.3	31.9	60.4
Goa	45.4	54.6	39.6	58.2
Gujarat	31.4	66.5	36.3	62.1
Haryana	30.3	69.0	37.0	62.3
Himachal Pradesh	86.5	11.5	91.3	8.0
Jammu and Kashmir	97.7	1.7	95.9	3.2
Karnataka	45.0	53.3	29.3	69.1
Kerala	39.5	59.0	37.3	59.8
Madhya Pradesh	40.4	35.4	54.7	42.9
Maharashtra	30.9	68.0	30.7	65.7
Manipur	89.2	10.4	78.3	12.2
Meghalaya	94.3	5.6	52.0	37.7
Mizoram	92.5	3.2	84.0	5.0
Nagaland	84.1	14.5	50.4	44.9
Orissa	84.2	8.7	77.9	18.3
Punjab	37.7	57.9	26.5	69.6
Rajasthan	63.3	34.3	72.1	26.5
Sikkim	96.1	3.1	80.9	19.1
Tamil Nadu	40.4	57.9	34.2	61.6
Tripura	92.5	0.1	73.0	6.4
Uttar Pradesh	46.1	51.7	39.0	59.1
West Bengal	79.9	17.5	71.3	27.6
Andaman and Nicobar Island	99.8	0.0	93.8	6.2
Chandigarh	78.8	21.2	67.0	31.7
Dadra and Nagar Haveli	48.0	52.0	23.4	76.6
Daman and Diu	26.2	73.8	61.8	34.4
Delhi	25.1	74.9	51.0	47.7
Lakshadweep	73.9	26.1	71.8	28.2
Pondicherry	81.8	0.0	76.1	23.9
India	43.8	52.9	41.9	55.3

Note: Share of public and private sectors does not add up to 100 per cent because of 'not reported cases'. Not reported cases are less than 10 per cent for all except Madhya Pradesh rural—25.2 per cent, Mizoram urban—11.0 per cent, Meghalaya urban—10.3 per cent, Pondicherry rural—18.2 per cent, and Tripura urban—20.6 per cent.
Source: NSSO (1998b, pp. A66–172).

Private share of more than 50 per cent in the economically well-off States of Gujarat, Haryana, Maharashtra, and Punjab, the demographically well-off four southern states, and Goa can be explained by greater health demand arising out of paying capacity or consciousness—whereas in Bihar and Uttar Pradesh it is more an indication of the poor state of public care facilities.

Kerala's share of private sector health care facilities (particularly across urban regions), is among the lowest—even lower than Bihar. This is because access to public health care facilities is much better in Kerala. It also raises a question on a dimension of quality—possibility of overuse being higher in the other states. In other words, excess private care indicates supplier-induced demand in the fee-for-service private sector. Equally worrisome is the fact that the growth and functioning of the private sector is totally unregulated.[15] This gives rise to unnecessary surgical interventions and one serious outcome of this is on maternal health—caesarean section deliveries are higher among affluent groups (healthy and well-nourished mothers). Medically speaking it should have been higher for the poor and malnourished mothers.[16] Such misallocation of scarce health resources makes it costlier for the rich and denies access for the poor.

The reliance on the private sector for outpatient as well as inpatient care is increasing and the share of public hospitals is decreasing over time (Figure 4.3). Gains in outpatient care are mostly to private doctors and 'others'. In inpatient care, gains are largely to private hospitals and, to a lesser extent, to nursing homes and charitable institutions.

HEALTH CARE EXPENDITURE

The gap in expenditure (per treatment) between poorest-to-richest decile has been widening—more so for inpatient care (Table 4.12). Along with a shift towards private care-givers (Figure 4.3), this has serious implications for public policy.

As expected, average expenditure per treatment in the private sector is higher and even more than twice that of the public sector in some states. There are some exceptions, particularly inpatient care in urban Haryana.

---

[15] For an annotated bibliography on private sector care and its implications, see Nandraj et al. (2001).

[16] Caesarean section deliveries were reported in 45 per cent cases (39.1–51.3, 95 per cent confidence interval) by mothers of 210 children aged 12–36 months from urban, educated, middle/upper class population of Chennai (Pai 2000). Mishra and Ramanathan (2002) use NFHS-1 (1992–3) to estimate that in Andhra Pradesh, Bihar, Gujarat, Karnataka, Punjab, and Uttar Pradesh the risk of undergoing caesarean section in the private sector is four times that in the public sector.

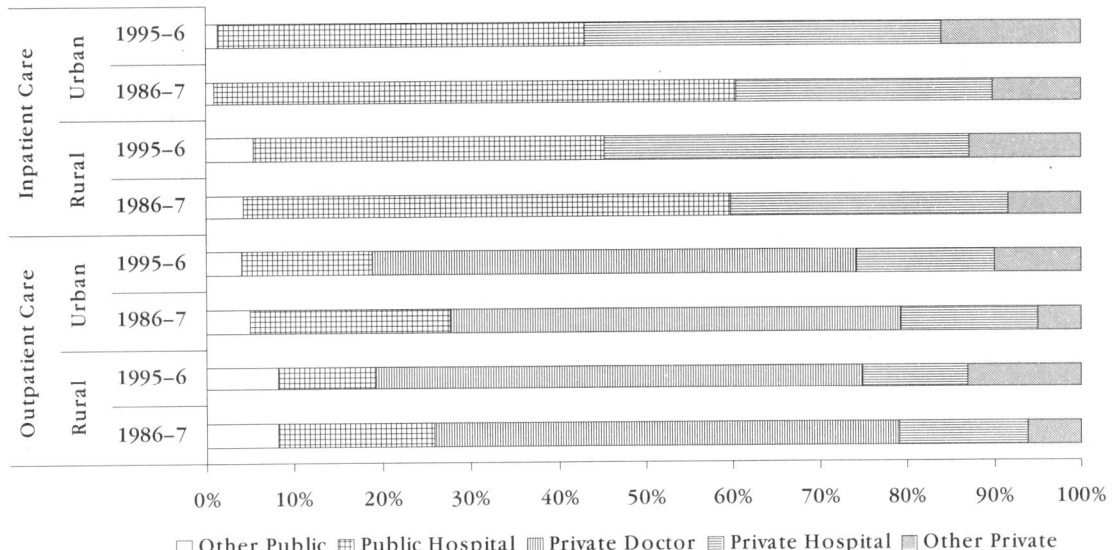

Figure 4.3: Share of Outpatient and Inpatient Public and Private Care, 1986–7 and 1995–6
Note: Other Public includes Primary/Community Health Centre, Public Dispensary, Employee State Insurance Doctors, etc. Other Private includes Nursing Home, Charitable Institutions and Others.
Source: NSSO (1998b, pp. 22, 28).

TABLE 4.12
Medical Expenditure per Treatment in Outpatient and Inpatient Care, 1986-7 and 1995-6

Out/In patient care	Average medical expenditure	Rural			Urban		
		1986–87	1995–6	% growth	1986–7	1995–6	% growth
Out patient care	Average expenditure—all	76.3	128.0	67.7	78.7	160.0	103.4
	Average expenditure—poorest decile	48.5	60.0	23.7	48.0	77.0	60.5
	Average expenditure—richest decile	98.5	203.0	106.1	128.0	261.0	103.9
	Ratio of richest/poorest decile	2.0	3.4		2.7	3.4	
In patient care	Average expenditure—all	597.1	3202.0	436.3	933.3	3921.0	320.1
	Average expenditure—poorest decile	393.5	1030.0	161.7	506.4	724.0	43.0
	Average expenditure—richest decile	882.3	6628.0	651.3	2049.1	10842.0	429.1
	Ratio of richest/poorest decile	2.2	6.4		4.0	15.0	

Note: % growth is as per current expenditure/prices. An approximate calculation of monthly per capita expenditure for the 50th percentile between the two NSS rounds suggest an increase of about 142 per cent in rural and 150 per cent in urban regions.
Source: NSSO (1992, pp. S418, S516), NSSO (1998b, pp. 5, A103, A208).

This is because almost one-third of the hospitalized (all-India average is about 4 per cent) sought care in the special paying ward of public sector services where the average expenditure turns out to Rs 19,591. People admitting themselves to the special paying ward could be doing so for some specific ailments/treatment not available in the private sector,[17] but it also reflects dual pricing in public sector health services.

Average expenditure for total inpatient care in the private sector when compared across states is the lowest in Kerala and highest in Andhra Pradesh (Table 4.13).

In the absence of information on itemwise expenditure for each disease, type of treatment, and the quality of care we can only speculate possible reasons. One reason that also partially explains the differential morbidity prevalence is that people in Kerala, being more conscious/aware, seek early medical attention and hospitalization. Hence, medical treatment would generally be less expensive. In Andhra Pradesh there is a greater reliance on the private sector—in fact, it is the highest in rural India (Table 4.11). Economic prosperity of the region (particularly, the developed districts of the coastal and Telengana regions (Narayana 2003)), as also of Punjab, could reflect some overuse and unregulated private practice (Baru 1998).

[17] On better availability of equipment and supplies with regard to maternal and child care in PHCs of Haryana see Table 4.4.

TABLE 4.13
Average Expenditure (in Rupees) per Treated Ailment in Private Sector and Ratio of Private to
Public in Rural/Urban India for Outpatient/Inpatient Care across Major States, 1995–6

States	Outpatient care				Inpatient care					
	Rural		Urban		Rural		Urban		Total	
	PVT	PVT/PUB	PVT	PVT/PUB	PVT	PVT/PUB	PVT	PVT/PUB	PVT	PVT/PUB
Andhra Pradesh	210	4.12	192	2.31	7822	3.78	7080	5.40	7642	4.30
Assam	115	0.56	166	0.86	2003	0.96	7102	3.23	3048	1.45
Bihar	220	1.18	237	2.96	4069	1.17	4512	1.61	4157	1.26
Gujarat	175	2.30	230	1.65	3285	2.24	4185	2.21	3640	2.20
Haryana	186	0.85	337	0.47	3496	1.31	5087	0.57	3819	0.90
Karnataka	142	2.03	184	1.35	4100	2.29	4502	2.88	4245	2.44
Kerala	163	1.58	140	1.56	2805	1.74	2254	1.48	2677	1.68
Madhya Pradesh	177	1.70	279	0.54	3482	1.58	3889	2.32	3644	1.84
Maharashtra	179	1.99	195	1.56	3836	2.51	5345	3.71	4528	3.04
Orissa	158	1.22	133	0.93	2583	1.54	1,1829	5.52	5211	2.98
Punjab	179	1.17	160	0.78	6171	1.69	6130	1.13	6154	1.48
Rajasthan	156	0.79	223	1.32	3971	1.51	4949	1.95	4239	1.63
Tamil Nadu	143	7.53	164	4.97	4333	5.77	5827	6.24	4928	6.05
Uttar Pradesh	225	0.55	232	0.89	4521	1.07	6515	1.26	5062	1.14
West Bengal	135	0.80	153	1.91	4303	2.87	7836	5.81	6188	4.30
India	186	1.44	200	1.20	4300	2.07	5344	2.43	4650	2.20

Note: PVT and PUB denote average expenditure in rupees per treated ailment in private and public sector respectively. PVT/PUB refers to ratio of private to public. Required data for calculating total (rural+urban) for outpatient care are not available.
Source: NSSO (1998b, pp. 32, 34, A66–199).

Another aspect of inequality across states is that per capita public expenditure is not only higher in better performing states (Table 4.14, column 2) but the real per capita expenditure has also been increasing at relatively lower rates in the poorer states. It even declined in Uttar Pradesh (Table 4.14, column 3). Exceptions are Bihar and Madhya Pradesh, but after correcting for the lower bases of these states in 1990–1 it will still not reduce the absolute differences in per capita public health expenditure with better performing states. The increasing divergence is because public health expenditure (excluding centrally sponsored schemes) is a state subject and public spending is by respective state governments. Added to this is the fact that the rich benefit relatively more from public subsidies in low performing states (Table 4.14, column 4). This means that the size of public health care is less in poorer states and the poor there get even less of it.

Further, public expenditure on health as per cent of total government expenditure has been declining over the years. There is serious mismatch with allocation biased against rural areas (nearly three-fourths of the population have merely one-tenth of budget allocation). A major share of allocation is towards family welfare (read as female family planning) and other national programmes. Even within that, more than four-fifths of the expenditure is towards salaries. This leaves hardly any scope for expenditure on infrastructure, equipment and supplies, and other requirements necessary for providing basic provision of health care. The rural population has no option but to rely on quacks and the fee-for-service private sector leading to sickness-triggered indebtedness. In fact, after dowry, the most important reason for indebtedness in rural India is health treatment (Patil, Somasundaram, and Goyal 2002).

The proportion of out-of-pocket expenditure at four-fifths of the total expenditure is the highest in India when compared with China, Germany, the United Kingdom (UK), the United States of America (USA), or even other SAARC countries (Table 4.15).[18] Out-of-pocket expenses in communist China is about 60 per cent and, what could be even worrying, is that it has increased by about 10 percentage points in five years. Equally noteworthy is the fact that public spending share is much higher in Germany, the UK, and the USA. Further, in Germany and the USA a substantial portion

[18] In fact, out of 191 countries only 30 countries have more than 50 per cent out-of-pocket expenses and of these India is only below Georgia (89.5 per cent) and Myanmar (82.6 per cent).

TABLE 4.14
Per Capita Public Expenditure on Health (1999–2000) and Income-class Bias in
Public Expenditure (1995–6) across 14 Major States

States	Per capita public expenditure on health (Rs), 1999–2000 (current prices)		Index of per capita public expenditure on Health, 1999–2000 (at 1993–4 prices with 1990–1=100)		Concentration index, 1995–6		Subsidy, ratio of richest to poorest quintile, 1995–6	
	Value	Rank	Value	Rank	Value	Rank	Value	Rank
(1)	(2a)	(2b)	(3a)	(3b)	(4a)	(4b)	(5a)	(5b)
Andhra Pradesh	128	10	159	4	0.116	6	1.85	5
Bihar	50	14	165	3	0.419	14	10.30	14
Gujarat	192	3	159	4	0.001	2	1.14	2
Haryana	169	6	136	11	0.201	8	2.98	8
Karnataka	150	9	173	1	0.208	9	3.58	9
Kerala	253	2	151	6	−0.041	1	1.10	1
Madhya Pradesh	110	11	171	2	0.292	11	4.16	11
Maharashtra	163	7	118	13	0.060	4	1.21	3
Orissa	109	12	137	10	0.282	10	4.87	12
Punjab	256	1	141	8	0.102	5	2.93	7
Rajasthan	163	7	139	9	0.334	13	4.95	13
Tamil Nadu	189	4	143	7	0.059	3	1.46	4
Uttar Pradesh	79	13	85	14	0.304	12	4.09	12
West Bengal	175	5	124	12	0.157	7	2.73	6
India	162	–	127	–	0.214	–	3.28	–

Note: Calculation of concentration index is from Lorenz curve with cumulative per cent of population across income class in the horizontal axis and cumulative per cent of population accruing benefits in the vertical axis. Unlike the usual poverty Lorenz curve that either coincides or is below the line of equality, the concentration index can also be above it. Thus, its value ranges from -1 (all benefits accrue to the poorest) to 1 (all benefits accrue to the richest). NA implies not available.
Source: Lok Sabha Unstarred Question No. 2642 dated 20 March 2002 (as obtained from www.indiastat.com, accessed 9 November 2003) for column 2; Dev (2003) for column 3, and Peters et al. (2002, p. 224) for columns 4–5.

of the private expenditure is through pre-paid plans/insurance policies.

The magnitude of health care in Germany, the UK, and the USA is portrayed by the per capita health expenditure of these three countries being greater than India's by 105, 76, and 196 times respectively (Table 4.15, column 7). Total expenditure on health as per cent of GDP, a measure that controls for size of economy, is also higher in these three countries (Table 4.15, column 2). Public spending as per cent of GDP in India is less than 1 per cent (0.87 per cent). Further, if one excludes the states of Gujarat, Kerala, Punjab, and Tamil Nadu (Table 4.14, column 2) the share of public expenditure will be lower and out-of-pocket expenses much higher.

Some Other Emerging Issues

Given the inherent uncertainty of falling sick, an excessive reliance on out-of-pocket expenses may not be a viable financing strategy and that too in a scenario where the share of the unregulated private sector is increasing. Insurance can not only act as a risk pooling strategy but also regulate cost and quality in the private health care sector. The (health) insurance market in India has opened up to the private sector only recently in 1999. To ensure coordination between the insured, the insurers, and the care-givers the insurance development regulatory authority has also paved the way for intermediaries (third party administrators or TPAs) in 2001. However, the initial impression indicates that TPAs are more involved in claims and reimbursement rather than regulating cost and quality (Bhat and Babu 2003). In any case, the private insurance market will not provide policies for the poorer and high-risk segments of the population.

Another method of risk pooling is through community participation. Voluntary Health Service (VHS) established in 1958 provides community health care through holistic medicine to the poor people in areas

TABLE 4.15
Health Expenditure and Health Personnel (Comparing India with other SAARC Countries, China, and Developed Countries of Germany, the UK, and the USA), 2000

Countries	Total expenditure on health as % of GDP	Total expenditure on health as % of total government expenditure	From total expenditure on health			Per capita expenditure on health in international dollars	Physicians for 100,000 population per year*	Nurses for 100,000 population per year*
			% public expenditure	% out of pocket	% pre-paid plans			
Bangladesh	3.8	7.1	36.4	59.7	0.0	47	20	11
Bhutan	4.1	9.2	90.6	9.4	0.0	64	16	39
China	5.3	11.0	36.6	60.4	0.3	205	162	99
Germany	10.6	17.3	75.1	10.6	12.5	2754	350	957
India	4.9	5.3	17.8	82.2	0.0	71	48	45
Maldives	7.6	10.2	83.4	16.6	0.0	254	40	113
Nepal	5.4	9.0	29.3	64.0	0.0	66	4	5
Pakistan	4.1	4.0	22.9	77.1	0.0	76	57	34
Sri Lanka	3.6	6.1	49.0	50.0	0.6	120	37	103
UK	7.3	14.9	81.0	10.6	3.2	1774	164	497
USA	13.0	16.7	44.3	15.3	34.8	4499	279	972

Note: * The estimates are for different years: Bangladesh—1997; Bhutan, Maldives, and Nepal—1995; China and Germany—1998, India—1992, Pakistan (physicians—1997 and nurses—1996), Sri Lanka—1999, UK (physicians—1993 and nurses—1989), and the USA (physicians—1995 and nurses—1996).

Source: WHO (2002, pp. 202-17) for columns 2-7; http://www3.who.int/whosis/health_personnel/ health_personnel.cfm (accessed 28 November 2003) for columns 8-9.

close to Chennai.[19] Our earlier reference to HBNC (Box 4.2) is also an outcome of community participation. Such exercises also require the involvement of non governmental organisations (NGOs).[20] However the involvement of NGOs in health care can be in different forms. They can be part of a public–private partnership to attain some public policy goals, like universal immunization, but efforts are also necessary to regulate NGOs and make them accountable. In 1994, NGOs involved in health services had substantial presence in Maharashtra (34.4 per cent villages) and Andhra Pradesh (21.2 per cent villages) while in other major states it was below 15 per cent (in Bihar, Rajasthan, and Uttar Pradesh it was even below 5 per cent) of villages. Their concentration is likely to be more in developed parts of the state. For instance, in Andhra Pradesh there were few NGO takers for the state government's call to take up management of PHCs in tribal areas. This indicates that NGO presence is least where it matters most (Misra, Chatterjee, and Rao 2003, pp. 105–6). It also suggests that efforts of the state should concentrate in providing facilities in less developed parts.

At the government level, one of the important sources of finance is from external agencies. This has also been instrumental in widespread systemic changes. The most important being the introduction of World Bank initiated health systems projects (HSPs) in Andhra Pradesh, Karnataka, Maharashtra, Orissa, Punjab, Uttar Pradesh (35 districts), and West Bengal. This was through contracts made directly with the state governments. The HSPs broadly aimed at improving: (i) efficiency in allocation and use of resources through policy and institutional development and (ii) performance through improvements in quality, effectiveness, and coverage (effective referral system as well as basic services at

---

[19] The principles of VHS are simple—greater importance to preventive over curative care based on insurance scheme for the entire family. It also emphasizes on medical education, research, and making care available in the villages. At present, VHS has 14 mini-health centres in rural areas and a 450-bed referral community hospital, nursing school, community health department, and dental college. The current premium rates of VHS per annum are in the range of Rs 50–350. The premium renewal has a serious problem (Bhagat 2003).

[20] Successful community participation has a larger focus on preventive, as against the costly curative approach, and integrates health care with other aspects of human development such as literacy/education and livelihood. For instance, community involvement in maintenance of irrigation networks will not only enhance livelihood opportunities, but also help prevent vector breeding.

primary level). The HSPs also came up with stipulation of some policy conditions (user fees, contracting out service, and institutional autonomy).[21] This has brought about a massive infusion of capital in secondary care that had almost stopped over the years. The donors were also instrumental in focusing on issues such as cooption of the private sector and NGOs, civil society participation, decentralization, and client satisfaction (Misra, Chatterjee, and Rao 2003, pp. 162, 169).

The existing public delivery system is effective in top-down reactive situations like disease outbreaks. To make the system more proactive Das Gupta, Khaleghian, and Sarwal (2003) assess governance and administration of service delivery using survey data from administrators, frontline workers, and local respondents. They suggest four measures: (i) integrate central command with some managerial autonomy that allows for experimentation/innovation and monitoring by end-users; (ii) introduce a system of incentives (not necessarily financial); (iii) make coordination of the formal health sector with those relating to food hygiene, availability of potable water, sewage, and sanitation a more permanent feature; and (iv) increase public participation through public awareness on the relevance of preventive care and public health regulation.[22]

Another related development in recent years is the growth of the pharmaceutical industry that has spread its net beyond the domestic market. The recent Pharmaceutical Policy 2002 also supports the industry's growth. It suggests reducing the span of price control and even provides for price increase in the guise of facilitating investment in research and development (R&D) and helping small firms comply with good manufacturing practices. In a sense, it overrules the Drug Price Control Review Committee 1999 that was in favour of continuing price control because of low government expenditure in health (Table 4.15) and the majority of the population being without health cover. There are no clear guidelines to ensure that R&D will emphasize on the health needs of the society. This new policy addresses business interests but fails to reflect public health concerns. It is silent on drug production where domestic supply is less than demand (TB, malarial, or leprotic drugs), improving availability of essential off-patented drugs, weeding out irrational combination, and adopting generic sales (Lalitha 2002). Creating market incentives without safeguarding against inefficiencies such as supplier-induced-demand and collusion between pharmaceutical producers and care-givers cannot be a healthy prescription.

The health care sector will also have serious implications due to globalization. In particular, through four possible modes of trade in health services—cross-border delivery, consumption abroad, commercial presence, and movement of health personnel.[23] Conventionally, cross-border delivery was largely through shipment of laboratory samples or diagnosis and clinical consultation done through traditional mail channels. Integrating cross-border delivery with the electronic or telecommunication system through interactive audiovisual mode and other forms of data communication has increased the scope for direct clinical services (diagnosis, surveillance, consultation, and second opinion). It has also taken it into new dimensions—professional backup (transmission of/access to specialized information), consumer health information, continuing professional education, and management of health care delivery. Two notable spin-offs in the Indian context are medical transcription and telepathological services by Indian doctors to hospitals in Bangladesh and Nepal. Frequent technological advances in the telecom sector will further increase the possibilities of such trade. This electronic mode can also be a cost-effective method of providing health care to remote underserved regions within the country and thereby improving access and equity, but only if the infrastructure already exists. If putting in place such a cost-intensive infrastructure is not feasible then the gap in terms of access/utilization of care is likely to further increase.

---

[21] User costs are generally below the prevailing market rate. It is supposed to supplement (not substitute) the public health budget and improve quality by way of expenditure on non-salary recurrent items such as drugs, consumables and basic maintenance. The major sources of user charges come from paying beds, outpatient charges, surgery charges, and contracting out equipment to private sector. There are no fees for preventive services such as immunization and exemptions are to be there for the poor. Exemptions may not mean much because the overall economic restructuring also suggests on reducing the number of white-card holders (poor eligible for exemption). In addition, the paying beds/wards are indicative of dual pricing and differentiated services. The rationale for institutional autonomy to facilitate innovation, reduce red tape, and help take locally relevant decisions has not come by (Narayana 2003, p. 370). The public sector can also contract out services to the private sector. In particular, health services that are highly contestable (non-clinical activities like management support, laundry and catering; routine diagnostics; and ambulatory care) and input factor markets that are highly measurable (production of consumables, equipment, pharmaceuticals, and high technology; retail and wholesale of drugs, equipment and other consumables; and capital stock) ought to be left to the private sector (Peters et al. 2002, pp. 145–6).

[22] Analysing reproductive health services Mavalankar, Ramani, and Shaw (2003) identify some of the major problems as staff non-availability, weak referral, funding shortage, and lack of accountability for quality of care. They suggest that better management through systemic changes can reduce some of these deficiencies.

[23] For an instructive write-up that also helped in our subsequent discussions on the four modes of trade see Chanda (2001).

Consumption abroad can be in the form of patients going to seek treatment or individuals going to receive professional education. Quality considerations may make richer patients in poorer countries seek treatment outside the country. This not only means patients from India are going to developed countries for treatment, but also includes patients from Bangladesh, Bhutan, Maldives, Nepal, and Pakistan who are coming to India for a similar reason. On the other hand, patients from developed countries come to India either because this turns out to be cost effective or for some alternative medicine. To tap this segment of the market some Multinational Corporations (MNCs) and the corporate sector are gearing up to provide health services that maintain quality as per international norms (combining it with electronic delivery), but at a much reduced cost (Box 4.3).

developed countries. Differences in wage and working conditions induce migration from developing to developed countries with the latter even providing special packages to fill domestic shortages. The irony is that presence of health personnel is much lower in developing countries than in developed countries (Table 4.15, columns 8 and 9). The situation for nurses (who ought to spend more time with patients) is even poignant because, as per 1992 WHO estimates for India, their numbers are less than that of doctors. With the establishment of multinational hospitals, one will also get international experts coming and offering their services in India. However, demand for care-givers (doctors and nurses) internationally as well as for the emerging private corporate sector is likely to pre-empt their availability in the public sector. This requires serious

---

Box 4.3

Corporate Sector in Health Care: The Case of Apollo

In 1983 Apollo was the first to start corporate health care delivery in India. Some other prominent names are Escorts, Fortis, Max, and Wockhardt, but Apollo's growth has given it the status of the largest hospital network of Asia and the third largest in the world. Their expansion is not just restricted to owning new units, but also through contracts to manage existing local hospitals. They have 13 owned and 22 managed hospitals with over 6000 beds in tertiary care and having presence in Bangladesh, Ghana, Nepal, Nigeria, Saudi Arabia, Sri Lanka, the United Arab Emirates, and the United Kingdom. In India, their presence is in about 35 locations. Its Delhi hospital, set up jointly with the Government of New Delhi, is the largest corporate hospital outside the USA. Its Kolkata venture is a tie-up with Parkway, a leading health care provider in Singapore. It is also the first one to initiate telemedicine facilities to rural areas by linking its secondary care centre at Aragonda to hospitals in Hyderabad and Chennai. Further, residents of about 52 villages in and around Aragonda have become part of a health insurance scheme of Re 1 per person per month. The group has now entered primary health care and have started setting up franchisee neighbourhood clinics, which will maintain international-quality norms and will have telemedicine links to its secondary and tertiary care facilities. Its pharmacy operation is in more than 120 owned and franchisee outlets. It provides international-quality care in heart surgery, bone marrow transplant, liver transplant, and orthopaedic surgery is less than three-tenths of the cost compared to their estimated cost in the USA. Such cost-effective care in Apollo as well as other corporate hospitals opens up the option for health tourism attracting patients from developed as well as our other neighbouring countries.

Source: www.apollohospitalsgroup.com and other links therein (accessed 28 February 2004) and personal communication.

Besides multinational involvement in hospitals, foreign commercial presence is now feasible in health insurance, management of health facilities, overseeing accreditation, and regulating medical standards. In fact, all aspects of health service delivery and input factor market that can involve the private sector can also have foreign commercial presence. Further, global concern identified in MDGs that has led to waiver of trade restrictions to poorer countries on essential drugs like antiretroviral for HIV/AIDS will help some Indian generic drug manufacturers make their commercial presence felt in African countries.

Conventionally, a matter of concern for developing countries is the outflow of trained care-givers to

introspection. There is a need to increase investments (perhaps through private participation under regulation and quality control) to increase the number of trained care-givers and improve wage and working condition in the public sector (more so in rural/tribal regions).

One of the most significant developments in recent years is research in genomics that identifies variation between individuals through single nucleotide polymorphisms (SNPs, or 'snips' for the lay reader).[24] Variations in gene sequence can help understand susceptibility to, protection from, age-of-onset, and severity of diseases

[24] If fragment of two genome sequences depict '...AGAGTTCT...' and '...AGGGTTAT...' then the third and seventh combinations are single base differences or SNPs.

and response to treatment. Comparing patterns and frequencies between patients and controls will help arrive at gene–disease relationship and bring about an effective 'genetic medicine'. However, some further research is necessary before it can be successfully utilized in improving the quality of life (Chakravarti 2001).

Conclusions

In summary, we find that decline in mortality increases longevity, but it also increases morbidity. This is associated with epidemiological transition from communicable to non-communicable diseases, but as it now stands, India faces the dual burden of both these groups of diseases. The NHP 2002 has rightly prioritized reduction of under-five mortality, maternal mortality and other communicable diseases, but it is silent on non-communicable diseases—the cause of nearly half of the deaths in India.

Although communicable and preventable diseases are largely concentrated in poorer states and non-communicable diseases in demographically or economically well-off states, some specific non-communicable diseases do exist in poorer states/regions/groups. Our disease-specific analysis showed that the north-east region has the highest incidence of cancer, Orissa that of epilepsy, and Bihar has the third highest incidence of mental illness across all states. Similarly, one observes greater visual impairment in Andhra Pradesh and Orissa, hearing and speech impairment in Himachal Pradesh, and locomotor disability in Punjab. These suggest that variations in epidemiological patterns need not match with our existing understanding of demographic or socio-economic patterns. Thus, diseases- or disability-wise specificity in states or even districts/blocks with emphasis on seasonal and sub-group (age, caste, gender, or income) differences will help attune public policy to improve access and utilization.

Effective public health measures also need to address issues of food hygiene, availability of clean air and water, and proper sanitation. Designing of public policy should factor in local specificities (including financial and manpower constraints/requirements). With decentralization and devolution of power, the local bodies will have a greater role. Addressing state-, district-, or block-specific public policy does not mean doing away with the role of the central government. It requires the centre to be more proactive in addressing inequities across states and to ensure appropriate regulatory and monitoring mechanisms. The ongoing centrally sponsored programmes can continue. New schemes like the launch of a national programme to provide potable water and improve environmental sanitation need urgent thinking.

The question of access to and utilization of care also needs to address the availability of care-givers. The outflow of trained care-givers (referred to as brain drain) and the growing private corporate sector will reduce their availability in the public sector. Of those available, there are fewer postings in rural/tribal regions and, among these, many remain absent for long periods. The presence of NGOs is also lower in poorer regions/villages. There is a need to increase the number of care-givers and create suitable working conditions to ensure their availability in remote areas. Again, as a large proportion of public expenditure (nearly four-fifths in PHCs) on health is on salaries, there is not much scope for improving provision of basic services.

With four-fifths of health care expenses being out-of-pocket, the increasing usage of private unregulated care that gives rise to supplier-induced demand (unnecessary medical intervention) is worrying. This, on one hand, increases cost and, on the other, leads to misallocation of scarce health resources. It is not only inefficient and iniquitous but, medically speaking, it compromises an important aspect—quality. There are two straightforward policy implications—to increase public expenditure in health (to 3.5–4.0 per cent of GDP in the next 10–15 years and to 2.0–2.5 per cent of GDP in the current plan) and to ensure maintenance of standards in quality of care.

Regulation of cost and quality in the private sector should not be restricted to care-givers. It should extend to private players involved in non-clinical services and diagnostics, the pharmaceutical industry, insurance providers, NGOs, and public care-givers. A prerequisite for the success of privatization is effective regulation. Policies that encourage privatization but give regulation the go by will be detrimental. For instance, although the new Pharmaceutical Policy 2002 is set to propel the industry further, it fails to make provision for providing essential off-patented drugs, curbing irrational combinations, encouraging generic sales, or devising a direction for research. Regulation should also keep a strict watch against possible collusion between care-givers, the pharmaceutical industry, and the insurance providers.

Be it regulation or monitoring of cost and quality, access to or utilization of health care, or analysis of epidemiological patterns, public health has to get out of anecdotal evidence and increasingly rely on scrutiny of 'hard facts'. This requires the availability of real-time data in the public domain. Its analysis will help design locally relevant public policy.

References

Asthana, S. and R. Oostvogels (2001), 'The Social Construction of Male "Homosexuality" in India: Implications for HIV Transmission and Prevention', *Social Science & Medicine*, Vol. 52, No. 5, pp. 707–21.

Bang, A. T., R. A. Bang, S. B. Baitule, M. H. Reddy, and M. D. Deshmukh (1999), 'Effect of Home-based Neonatal Care and Management of Sepsis on Neonatal Mortality: Field Trial in Rural India', *Lancet*, Vol. 354, No. 9194, pp. 1955–61.

Baru, R. (1998), *Private Health Care in India: Social Characteristics and Trends*, Sage, New Delhi.

Bhagat, R. (2003), 'Tribute: The Great "Little" Man', *The Hindu*, 28 December.

Bhat, P. N. M. (2002), 'Maternal Mortality in India: An Update', *Studies In Family Planning*, Vol. 33, No. 3, pp. 227–36.

Bhat, R., S. K. Babu (2003), 'Health Insurance and Third Party Administrators: Issues and Challenges', Working Paper No. 2003-05-02, Indian Institute of Management, Ahmedabad.

Black, R. E., S. S. Morris, and J. Bryce (2003), 'Where and Why Are 10 Million Children Dying Every Year?', *Lancet*, Vol. 361, No. 9376, pp. 2226–34.

Bryan, A. D., J. D. Fisher, and T. J. Benziger (2001), 'Determinants of HIV Risk Among Indian Truck Drivers', *Social Science & Medicine*, Vol. 53, No. 11, pp. 1413–26.

CBHI (2002), *Health Information of India 1999*, Government of India, New Delhi.

Census of India (2001a), *Provisional Population Totals*, http://www.censusindia.net/results/state.php?stad=A (accessed 20 July 2003).

——— (2001b), *Data on Houses, Household Amenities and Assets*, http://www.censusindia.net/2001housing/ (accessed 20 July 2003).

Chakravarti, A. (2001), 'Single Nucleotide Polymorphisms: To a Future of Genetic Medicine', *Nature*, Vol. 409, No. 6822, pp. 822–3.

Chanda, R. (2001), 'Trade in Health Services', Working Paper No. 70, Indian Council for Research on International Economic Relations, New Delhi.

Das Gupta, M., P. Khaleghian, and R. Sarwal (2003), 'Governance of Communicable Disease Control Services: A Case Study and Lessons from India', World Bank Policy Research Working Paper 3100, The World Bank, Washington, D.C.

Dev, S. M. (2003), 'Public Expenditure on Social Services and Poverty Alleviation Programmes: Trends and Cost Effectiveness', mimeo (paper submitted for UNDP-SAPAP study to IGIDR), Centre for Economic and Social Studies, Hyderabad.

DGHS (undated1), 'Tuberculosis Control—India', http://www.tbcindia.org/ (accessed 7 April 2004).

Gajalakshmi, V., R. Peto, T. S. Kanaka, and P. Jha (2003), 'Smoking and Mortality from Tuberculosis and Other Diseases in India: Retrospective Study of 43000 Adult Male Deaths and 35000 Controls', *Lancet*, Vol. 362, No. 9383, pp. 507–15.

Gupta, P. C. and H. C. Mehta (2000), 'A Cohort Study of All cause Mortality among Tobacco users in Mumbai', India, *Bulletin of the World Health Organization*, Vol. 78, No. 7, pp. 877–83.

IHS (undated1), *Andhra Pradesh Burden of Disease Study Results and Important Causes of Disease Burden*, http://www.ihsnet.org.in/BurdenOfDisease/APBurdenofDiseaseStudy.htm (accessed 13 November 2003).

IIPS and ORC Macro (2000), *National Family Health Survey (NFHS-2), 1998–1999, India*, IIPS, Mumbai.

Indrayan, A., M. J. Wysocki, R. Kumar, A. Chawla, and N. Singh (2002), 'Estimates of the Years-of-Life-Lost due to the Top Nine Causes of Death in Rural Areas of Major States in India in 1995', *National Medical Journal of India*, Vol. 51, No. 1, pp. 7–13.

Jalan, J. and M. Ravallion (2001), 'Does Piped Water Reduce Diarrhoea for Children in Rural India?', Policy Research Working Paper No. 2664, The World Bank, Washington, D.C.

Jones, G., R. W. Steketee, R. E. Black, Z. A. Bhutta, S. S. Morris, and the Bellagio Child Survival Study Group (2003), 'How Many Child Deaths Can We Prevent This Year?', *Lancet*, Vol. 362, No. 9377, pp. 65–71.

Kumar, S., S. K. Bhargava, N. Mathur, and A.K. Srivastava (2003), *A Study of Environmental Exposure to PAHs in Economically Underprivileged Population of Urban/Rural Areas of Uttar Pradesh*, EERC Working Paper Series: EHE-3, IGIDR, Mumbai.

Lalitha, N. (2002), 'Drug Policy 2002: Prescriptions for Symptoms', *Economic and Political Weekly*, Vol. 37, No. 30, pp. 3102–4.

Mahal, A., J. Singh, F. Afridi, V. Lamba, A. Gumber, V. Selvaraju (2000), 'Who Benefits from Public Health Spending in India? Results of a Benefit Incidence Analysis for India', NCAER, New Delhi.

Mavalankar, D., K. V. Ramani, and J. Shaw (2003), 'Management of RH Services in India and the Need for Health System Reform', Working Paper No. 2003-09-04, Indian Institute of Management, Ahmedabad.

Menezes, L. (2003), *Economic Epidemiology Modeling of HIV/AIDS Transmission Dynamics: A New Analytical Approach to Studying the HIV Epidemic in Maharashtra, India*, Synopsis of Unpublished PhD thesis submitted, IIPS, Mumbai.

Mishra, S. (2003), 'Access to Knowledge with Physical and Financial Access will Improve Child Survival', *Lancet*, Vol. 362, No. 9381, http://www.thelancet.com/journal/vol362/iss9381/full/llan.362.9381.child_survival.26716.1 (accessed 2 August 2003).

Mishra, U. S. and M. Ramanathan (2002), 'Delivery-related Complications and Determinants of Caesarean Section Rates in India', *Health Policy and Planning*, Vol. 17, No. 1, pp. 90–8.

Misra, R., R. Chatterjee, and S. Rao (2003), *India Health Report*, Oxford University Press, New Delhi.

Murray. C. J. L. (1996), 'Epidemiologic and Morbidity Transitions in India', in M. Das Gupta, T.N. Krishnan, and L. Chen (eds) *Health Poverty and Development in India*, Oxford University Press, New Delhi, pp. 122–47.

NACO (undated1), 'HIV/AIDS Indian Scenario', *http://www.naco.nic.in/indianscene/welcome.html* (accessed 7 April 2004).

Nandraj, S., V. R. Muraleedharan, R. Baru, I. Qadeer, and R. Priya (2001), *Private Health Sector in India, Review and Annotated Bibliography*, Centre for Enquiry into Health and Allied Themes, Mumbai.

Narayana, K. V. (2003), 'Size and Nature of Healthcare System', in C. H. Hanumantha Rao and S. Mahendra Dev (eds), *Andhra Pradesh Development: Economic Reforms and Challenges Ahead*, Centre for Economic and Social Studies, Hyderabad. pp. 341–72.

NSSO (2001), *Consumption of Some Important Commodities in India 1999-2000, NSS 5th Round (July 1999–June 2000)*, Report No. 461 (55/1.0/4), Government of India, New Delhi.

——— (1998a), 'Survey Results on Consumption of Tobacco in India, NSS 50th Round (1993–4)', *Sarvekshana*, Vol. 21, No. 3, pp. 261–387.

——— (1998b), *Morbidity and Treatment of Ailments: NSS 52nd Round, July 1995–June 1996*, Report No. 441 (52/25.0/1), Government of India, New Delhi.

——— (1994), 'Disability in India: NSS 47th Round (July–December 1991)', *Sarvekshana*, Vol. 18, No. 2, 69–124.

——— (1992), 'Results on Morbidity and Utilization of Medical Services NSS 42nd Round (July 1986–June 1987)', *Sarvekshana*, Vol. 15, No. 4, pp. S131–571.

Pai, M. (2000), 'Unnecessary Medical Interventions: Caesarean Sections as a Case Study', *Economic and Political Weekly*, Vol. 35, No. 31, pp. 2755–61.

Parikh, J. and V. Laxmi (2000), 'Biofuels, Pollution and Health Linkages: A Survey of Rural Tamil Nadu', *Economic and Political Weekly*, Vol. 35, No. 47, pp. 4125–37.

Parikh, J., K. Parikh, V. Laxmi, S. Karmakar, and P. Dabrase (2003), *Exonomic Analysis of Rural Pollution and Health Impacts in Northern India: A Multi-institutional Project*, EERC Working Paper Series: EHE-1, IGIDR, Mumbai.

Patil, A. V., K. V. Somasundaram, and R. C. Goyal (2002), 'Current Health Scenario in Rural India', *Australian Journal of Rural Health*, Vol. 10, No. 2, pp. 129–35.

Peters, D. H., K. S. Rao, and R. Fryatt (2003), 'Lumping and Splitting: The Health Policy Agenda in India', *Health Policy and Planning*, Vol. 18, No. 3, pp. 249–60.

Peters, D. H., A. S. Yazbeck, R. R. Sharma, G. N. V. Ramana, L. H. Pritchett, and A. Wagstaff (2002), *Better Health Systems for India's Poor: Findings, Analysis, and Options*, The World Bank, Washington, D.C.

Planning Commission (2002a), *National Human Development Report 2001*, Oxford University Press, New Delhi.

——— (2002b), *Report of the Committee on India Vision 2020*, Government of India, New Delhi.

Shanta, V. (2002–3), 'Perspectives in Cervical Cancer Prevention in India', *INCTR Newsletter*, Vol. 3, No. 3, *http://www.inctr.org/publications/2003_v03_n03_w02.shtml* (3 August 2003).

Shariff, A. (1999), *India Human Development Report: A Profile of Indian States in the 1990s*, Oxford University Press, New Delhi.

Sharma, V. P. (2003), 'Malaria and Poverty in India', *Current Science*, Vol. 84, No. 4, pp. 513–15.

Visaria, L. (2004), 'Mortality Trends and the Health Transition', in T. Dyson, R. Cassen, and L. Visaria (eds), *Twenty-first Century India: Population, Economy, Human Development, and the Environment*, Oxford University Press, Oxford, pp. 32–56.

WHO (2003), 'Global Polio Eradication Initiative—Progress 2002', WHO, Geneva.

——— (2002), *The World Health Report 2002: Reducing Risks, Promoting Healthy Life*, WHO, Geneva.

5 Lack of Energy, Water, and Sanitation and its Impact on Rural India[1]

Jyoti Parikh • Kirit Parikh • Vijay Laxmi

Despite much technical progress in the world, rural women in developing countries still use biofuels such as crop residues, dung, and fuel wood—collectively called traditional biofuels. They walk long distances to fetch fuels (Parikh and Vijay Laxmi 2000), water, and other basic needs. The time spent thus is not available for any productive activities or human resource development or self-fulfilment. This situation has serious consequences on women's health due to the physical burden involved in gathering and transporting heavy loads of fuel (Wickramsinghe 2001) and water, as well as due to the indoor air pollution (IAP) resulting from the use of biofuels. Traditional biofuels emit a large number of pollutants (Balakrishana et al. 2002, ESMAP 2001) that cause acute respiratory infections, chronic lung diseases and heart diseases, cancers, and eye problems (Vijay Laxmi et al. 2003). Unsafe drinking water and lack of sanitation facilities add considerably to these diseases. Obviously, this would have an impact on life expectancy and mortality rates. The prime sufferers are women and children. Adverse pregnancy outcomes such as stillbirths, premature births, and low birth weights are also associated with IAP affecting under-five mortality rates (Parikh et al. 1999). A life free from hunger and diseases is what is required to improve the human development index.

The Census 2001 shows that in rural India only 56 per cent households have electricity connection for lighting and 43.3 per cent still use kerosene for this purpose. Biofuels are used by 90 per cent of the rural households for cooking. Tap water availability is limited to only 24 per cent of the rural households. About 76 per cent of the population drink water from open sources such as wells, tanks, ponds, lakes, rivers, canals, etc. As per 1996 NSS, access to improved sanitation in the rural areas is only 6 per cent. This raises a number of questions:

• What types of domestic fuels are used in rural India?
• How much is the exposure to IAP? What are the consequences on health and what is the economic burden of ill health and the time spent gathering fuels?
• What is the current situation concerning access to safe drinking water and improved sanitation?
• How much time do women spend in fetching water?
• What are the consequences of the use of impure water on health and what is the economic burden of ill health and the time spent fetching water?

Easy access to energy, water sources, and sanitation should be an important goal of national development. Industrialized countries, and even some of the urban households in developing countries, have long ago reached these goals. Yet, so far, no one is willing to set a target date for when this should happen in the rural areas of developing countries. Only then can millions of rural and urban poor be mainstreamed into the economic growth process. At the World Summit on Sustainable Development (WSSD), some MDGs have been announced for this purpose. However, no action plans have yet been drawn. Moreover, access to clean energy is not included among these goals (Box 5.1).

---

[1] This chapter is based on the work done for Environmental Economics Research Committee (EERC) supported by the Ministry of Environment and Forests and World Bank and capacity 2L project of UNDP. We are grateful for the contribution of Pramod Dabrase and Shyam Karmakar. We have received comments on previous drafts from a number of experts that include Gerald Leach, J. N. Pande, P. Satsangi, S. K. Chhabra, J. Samet, Carter Brandon and others to whom we are grateful.

> BOX 5.1
>
> **Some Relevant Million Development Goals (MDG) up to 2015**
>
> A. Reduce the proportion of people who suffer from extreme poverty by 50 per cent;
> B. Achieve universal primary education;
> C. Eliminate gender disparity in primary and secondary education;
> D. Ensure environmental sustainability, in particular, reduce by 50 per cent, the proportion of people without sustainable access to safe drinking water and basic sanitation; and
> E. Reduce by two-thirds the under-five mortality rate and by three-quarters the maternal mortality ratio.
>
> This shows some of the selected MDG relevant for this chapter. The issues concern poor rural infrastructure for poverty, gender education, maternity health, child mortality rate, and life expectancy. Along with MDG, WSSD also focused specific attention on WEHAB themes that emphasized water, energy, health, agriculture, and biodiversity.

Past approaches to rural development have often relied on outside experts for delivering technologies that they considered efficient, such as improved stoves, biogas digesters, solar cookers, different types of toilets, water delivery systems and so on. Sometimes these technologies do not conform to the field conditions and are not 'appropriate' for the users. Only recently attention is being given to involve women in choosing, accessing, and adapting fuel and technologies. Participatory approaches for this are being developed.

Based on a survey, we address the questions posed earlier as well as the following ones:

• How much are rural people willing to pay for clean fuels, safe water, and toilets?

• What are the policy implications of these findings?

THE SURVEY

The study included an integrated survey covering 15,293 households (HHs) from 148 villages in the rural areas of three states of north India and one state of south India (Tables 5.1 and 5.2 shows sample size and its share in rural India). The survey was aimed at addressing issues of energy, water, sanitation, and health. Data relating to use of different fuels, access to safe drinking water, sanitation facilities, symptoms of diseases related to both air and water pollution, expenditure on health and person days loss, demographic and socio-economic information were collected from the households and individuals. At the same time measurements of air quality in and outside the kitchen and the home were carried out in Uttar Pradesh and Tamil Nadu, and water quality measurement at the source and inside the house were also carried out. Indicators for lung functions were measured for most of the adults present at the time of the survey. The doctors examined a sub-sample of individuals for confirmation of diseases. The details of the sample are given in Box 5.2.

ESTIMATION OF DRAIN ON HUMAN RESOURCES DUE TO COOKING FUELS

Estimates from the survey data show that about 96 per cent (that is, about 126 million) rural Indian households use biofuels in some form or the other for their cooking needs. This consumption estimate from the survey data seems to be higher than the Census 2001 estimates as the

TABLE 5.1
District, Village, Household and IAQ Monitoring Sample Sizes

Sample/State	Total	Uttar Pradesh	Rajasthan	Himachal Pradesh	Tamil Nadu
District	22	6	3	9	4
Villages	148	51	13	54	30
Households	15,293	7564	1989	712	5028
Individual health record (direct and proxy)	81,019	42,713	11,955	4100	22,251
Direct response	33,151	16,264	3308	1580	12,000
Proxy response	37,617	26,449	8647		
PEF record (Direct)	18,400	14,115	2705	2520	12,000
Health centre surveyed	51	36	4	2	9
Indoor air quality monitoring households	1019	519	–	–	500

TABLE 5.2
Share of the Sampled States in RNI and share of RNI in RAI

Description	Share of sampled states in RNI	North India (total)	Share of RNI in RAI
Land area (Sq Km)	68.50%	1.01 Mn Sq Km	30.75% (3.29 Mn Sq Km)
Estimated inhabited villages	86.78%	0.19 Mn	33.02% (0.59 Mn)
Total population as per 2001 census (urban + rural)	77.17%	307.21 Mn	29.91% (1027.02 Mn)
Rural population as per 2001 census	82.48%	226.23 Mn	30.50% (741.66 Mn)
Rural households 2001 (estimated)	82.71%	36.73 Mn	27.88% (131.73 Mn)
Net domestic product at current prices (1998–9)	62.75%	Rs 3,487,620 Mn	24.31%

Box 5.2
Survey Design

The survey was designed in such a way that it represents various socio-economic and geo-ecological and locational zones. At *stage one*, stratification of each state was done on the basis of its socio-cultural regions (SCRs). Accordingly, districts from each state were selected.[a] At *stage two*, allocation of number of households to each district was made based on the universal distribution of rural households in these districts. At *stage three*, stratification of districts was done by village population sizes. The villages were selected by using multistage stratified sampling design to have a representative sample. The villages were divided into four strata on the basis of population data available from Census 1991. In stratum 1, villages with population less than 1000 were included; stratum 2 had villages with population 1000–3000, whereas in stratum 3, villages with population between 3000–5000 were included. The fourth stratum with population more than 5000 was excluded from the sample because these villages resemble semi-urban areas. The selection of the villages from each stratum was done using probability proportion to size (PPS) sampling method. Selection of households (*stage four*) within selected villages was done using systematic random sampling.

The survey was conducted at three levels, namely, individual level, household level, and village level. The individual level data included physiological characteristics, namely, age, sex, height, and weight and behavioural characteristics such as smoking habit, literacy, occupation, activity time pattern, cooking involving, years of cooking, and other behaviour. Village level surveys were performed to validate the data acquired at household and individual level, and also to get an overall picture of the village. The household level data were collected to get a comprehensive picture of socio-economic conditions, energy use pattern, water and sanitation related facilities, housing characteristics, cooking behaviour, environmental priorities of women, willingness to pay to reduce kitchen smoke and to improve water and sanitation facilities.

Energy use pattern included information on consumption of biofuels and commercial fuels for cooking, place of procurement of cooking fuel, time, distance, and effort involved in procurement, progress along the energy ladder, etc. Housing characteristics included information on number of rooms, type of house and type of kitchen, location of kitchen, number of door and windows in the kitchen. Further information was collected on cooking behaviour which included number of meals cooked using different fuels in a day, hours of cooking, cooking involvement in different age groups and type of involvement. People's willingness to reduce the impact of indoor air pollution included information on people's choice of fuel, type of intervention, reason for not using clean fuels, willingness to pay for additional amount of clean fuel and additional demand for kerosene in the area.

At the individual level, the Medical Research Council (MRC) questionnaire, 1986, UK, for respiratory symptoms was followed which included questions regarding six symptom categories. The inquiry was made directly to those who were present during the survey for the analysis according to MRC protocol. In addition, proxy responses for those who were absent during the survey were obtained from the chief cook and other respondent for household survey and mother's responses for children below 15 years. According to MRC protocol only these direct responses could be analysed for the respiratory diseases. Therefore, the information collected for absent members and children are analysed separately. This gave us a picture of overall prevalence of respiratory diseases for the adults and also for the children (proxy responses of mothers). Measurement of PEF (peak expiratory flow), an indicator of airways obstruction, which reflects lung functions and the extent to which it is impaired, was conducted for direct responses.

Data on water availability, source of collection, efforts required to fetch water, problems faced in collection, type of problems, water quality, water storage and filtering practices, etc., were obtained. Symptoms of diseases such as worms in stool, diarrhoea, and jaundice were recorded. Data on availability of sanitation, and sewerage facilities and willingness to contribute to improve water, sanitation, and sewerage facilities were also collected through the survey.

[a] The State Surveyed were Uttar Pradesh (including Uttranchal), Himachal Pradesh, Rajasthan and Tamil Nadu.

census information is only about the exclusive use of fuel whereas our estimates also include the households that use mixed fuels (both commercial fuels and biofuels). In the biofuels category the use of fuelwood (79 per cent) and dungcake (63 per cent) predominate. Rural households consume about 314 million tonnes of biofuels in a year only for cooking. These biofuels are mostly procured through gathering. In a year about 352 hours are spent per household on gathering of biofuels. An estimated 85 million households spent 30 billion hours on gathering 314 million tonnes of biofuels per annum. In addition to the human days spent for this purpose the rural people have to spend a substantial number of human days to collect drinking water also.

The use of clean fuels like kerosene, liquefied petroleum gas (LPG), and biogas is rare, especially in Uttar Pradesh and Rajasthan. Only about 11 per cent households (that is, 15 million households) in rural India use kerosene for cooking (exclusively and as mixed fuels). This figure is 1.6 per cent from Census 2001 as it includes the exclusive use of kerosene. Similarly, around 5 per cent households use LPG for cooking. However, in Himachal Pradesh 55 per cent have LPG and 31 per cent use kerosene.

Kerosene using households are, on an average, consuming 179 litres of kerosene in a year for exclusive cooking. As against this consumption, mixed fuel users and users of kerosene for lighting consume about 89 litres and 56 litres respectively per year. This, in other words, means that basic requirement of kerosene for illumination and lighting fires is about 56 litres per household per year. Over and above the lighting needs, the results show that households require about 33 litres per annum to partially shift to kerosene for cooking and another 90 litres per annum is needed to switch completely by 5 per cent households. However, many households prefer to switch to LPG instead of kerosene if it is available.

Exposure to Kitchen Smokes

Besides undergoing the drudgery of collecting and transporting the fuel, about half of the total females above 10 years of age serve as chief cooks. Thus, about 174 million females are directly exposed to kitchen pollution in rural India. The extent of exposure is about three hours a day to cook all the meals (mostly two meals) in a day. Thus, a chief cook is exposed to smoke for more than 1000 hours in a year. It was also found that other family members who stay inside the poorly ventilated kitchen and house during the cooking are also exposed to a high level of pollution due to the smoke. Further, cooks are exposed to an average of 6.8 mg/m^3 of Respirable Suspended Particulate Matter (RSPM) while cooking using biofuels. Cooking with biofuels causes mean concentration of RSPM to be 9.2 mg/m^3 in the kitchen about two meters away from a stove. This shows that those who assist or are in close proximity to the stove are exposed to even higher levels of pollution as compared to the cook, especially if they are in the plume of smoke.

Drain on Resources due to Water, Sewerage, and Sanitation Facilities

Table 5.4 shows that a substantial proportion (62 per cent) of households in India collects drinking water from outside their premises and spends about 1410 hours per household in a year on this task. This, in other words, means that 71 million households fetch water from outside by spending about 102 billion hours in a year. Perhaps the same hours could be used to improve water

---

Box 5.3

Household Energy—Rural India

- 96 per cent of households use *biofuels*, 11 per cent use *kerosene* and 5 per cent use *LPG* for cooking. Most of them, however, use multiple fuels.
- Forests contribute 39 per cent of the fuelwood needs.
- 314 million tonnes of biofuels are *gathered* annually.
- 85 million households spend 30 billion hours annually in fuel wood gathering.
- 15 million households use kerosene for cooking and lighting.
- 34 per cent of households (out of the households using kerosene for cooking) procure kerosene from the open market and 97 per cent procure it from fair price shops.
- 49 per cent of households are willing to pay more than the market price to purchase kerosene for cooking.
- 0.2 per cent households use Biogas for cooking.
- 63 per cent of households are electrified.
- 33 per cent of households are willing to contribute to reduce kitchen smoke by modifying kitchen characteristics and installing ventilators, etc.

TABLE 5.3
Estimates of Energy Consumption Pattern and Time and Efforts for Gathering

Items	Estimates
Use of any biofuel (households in Mn #)	125.9
Fuelwood using households (Mn)	103.9
Dungcake using households (Mn)	83.1
Crop residue using households (Mn)	53.6
Quantity of biofuels used per year (Mn tonnes)	314
Time and effort in biofuel gathering	
Biofuels gathering households (Mn)	85.1
Time spent on biofuel collection (Mn Hrs per year)	29,998
Households using Petroleum products for cooking	
Households using kerosene for cooking (Mn)	14.9
LPG/Biogas using households (Mn)	7.4
Qty. of kerosene used for cooking exclusively, starting the fire and lighting per year (Mn Ltrs p.a.)	211
Qty. of kerosene used for cooking as mixed fuel, starting the fire and lighting per year (Mn Ltrs p.a.)	1233
Qty. of kerosene used only for lighting and starting the fire per year (Mn Ltrs p.a.)	6561
Cooking Involvement	
Involvement as chief cooks (Mn females)	173.8
Exposure for cook (no. of hrs of cooking)	Approx. 1000 hrs exposure per cook p.a.

Note: # Multiple fuel in use.

supply in the region. Low economic development is both a cause and effect of low accessibility to clean drinking water, sanitation, and sewerage facilities.

TABLE 5.4
Estimates of Access to Drinking Water, Sewerage, and Toilet Facility

Items	Estimates
Time and effort in drinking water collection	
HHs collecting water from outside (Mn)	71.27
Time spent on water collection (Mn hrs per year)	102,218
HHs having sewerage connection (Mn)	9.6
HHs having in-house toilet facility (Mn)	12.1
HHs using public toilet facility (Mn)	1.6

The study estimates that only 7 per cent of households in rural India are connected to the sewerage system. The rest of the rural households have no other option but to dispose of the waste water in the puddle next to the house, in the kitchen garden, or in the open field. Further, only 9 per cent of households (12 million) have in-house toilet facility and another 1 per cent use public toilet facility. The remaining 90 per cent of households use the nearby open space for defecation. This again deteriorates the quality of life of the people living in the rural areas. Thus, there is need to take measures to improve the supply of drinking water and sanitation as a priority issue at the village level.

Box 5.4
Water and Sanitation—Rural India

- 62 per cent of HHs do not have water supply in or near their homes.
- 71 million HHs spend 102 billion hours per year to collect water from outside home.
- Only 7 per cent of HHs are connected with sewerage facility.
- 9 per cent of HHs have toilet facility inside the house.
- 1 per cent of HHs use community toilets.

Proportion of households *willing to pay* for:
- Clean drinking water: 7%
- Community based drinking water supply: 25%
- Sewerage facilities: 28%
- In-house toilets: 29%
- Community toilets: 25%

Toll on Human Health and the Economic Burden
Health Impact of Respiratory and Eye Diseases
At an all-India level, it is estimated that out of 452 million rural adults about 73 million have some form of respiratory symptoms, out of which about 16 million are affected with bronchitis, 5 million with bronchial asthma, about 9 million with pulmonary TB, and 8 million with

chest infection. Moreover, 12 million children out of 94 million children below five years are suffering from LRI/ARI. About 44 million adults are estimated to have some eye irritation problems.

Analysis of risk factors through odd ratios show that women above 30 years of age are at a higher risk than younger women by a factor of 3.99 for bronchitis, 4.05 for asthma, 2.64 for chest infection, and 2.85 for TB. Illiterate women are at 3 to 6 times higher risk compared to literate women for all respiratory diseases. It was also observed that the odds ratio falls sharply with primary education, that is, most benefits of literacy occurs at the primary level education itself. The fuel index constructed to capture the lifetime exposure shows that with increase in the fuel index, risk from all respiratory diseases and eye diseases increases. Whereas, the asset index had a negative impact on respiratory and eye related diseases.

Economic Burden of Respiratory and Eye Diseases

Respiratory diseases have caused considerable economic burden and out of 30 million adult sufferers from respiratory diseases, a large number have spent some money for treatment or special diets. An adult sufferer, on an average, spends about Rs 1503 in a year (or Rs 125 per month) towards total health care expenses including doctor's fees, medicines, hospitalization charges, and/or special diets for respiratory diseases. This leads to an economic burden of Rs 45 billion for treatment of respiratory diseases in addition to government subsidy provided to various health centres and another Rs 47 billion for human days lost due to illness (Table 5.5).

If villages with a population greater than 5000 were included in our survey then it is quite likely that though the prevalence rates would have been less, the average cost per sick person would have been higher.

Health Impact of Water-related Diseases

Estimates show that at all-India level, about 42 million adults and 27 million children are estimated to be suffering from some form of intestinal disease. About 16 million adults and 12 million children are estimated to be affected by worms in stool, about 22 million adults and 13 million children are affected by diarrhoea, and about 8 million adults and 5 million children are affected by jaundice.

Box 5.5

Respiratory and Eye Diseases

- Respiratory symptoms are prevalent among 24 million adults, of which 17 million have serious symptoms
- Adults suffer from various respiratory diseases as given in the figure below:

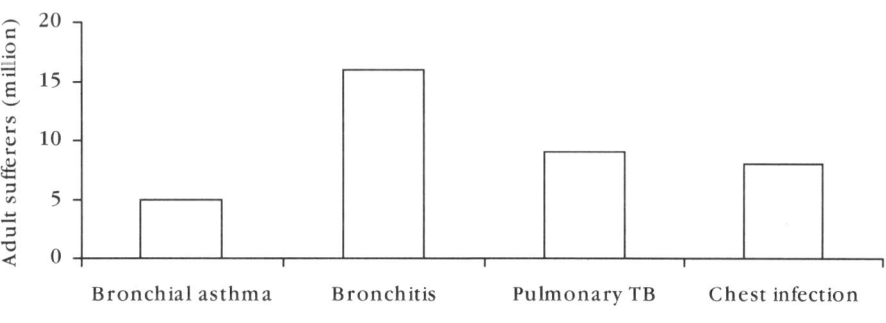

Occurance of Respirtary Diseases

LRI/ARI prevalence among children below 5 years: 12 million (13 per cent)

Expenditure on Respiratory Diseases
- Total private expenditure on health:
  o Rs 45 billion per year for respiratory diseases
  o Rs 17 billion per year for eye related diseases
- Of the total expenditure incurred on:
  o *Respiratory diseases:* 56 per cent is spent on medicine, 19 per cent on special diet and doctor's fee each and 6 per cent on hospitalization
  o *Eye related diseases:* 70 per cent is spent on medicine and 30 per cent on doctor's fee.

TABLE 5.5
Economic Burden of Respiratory and Eye Diseases

Items	Estimates
Adults	
Respiratory diseases (adults: 15 years and above age)* (Mn)	
Self-reported any respiratory symptoms	72.6
Self-reported any serious respiratory disease symptoms	54.1
Respiratory disease cases identified as per MRC symptoms (Mn)	30.5
Bronchial asthma	4.5
Bronchitis	15.6
Pulmonary TB	9.0
Chest Infection	8.1
Economic burden of respiratory diseases (Rs Mn)	45,399
Expenditure on doctor's fee of adult sufferer per year	8977
Expenditure on medicines of adult sufferer per year	25,503
Expenditure on hospitalization of adult sufferer per year	2876
Expenditure on special diets of adult sufferer per year (Rs Mn)	8043
Days lost due to illness of adult sufferer in a year (Mn Days)	777
Valuation of adult days lost (Rs Mn)	46,597
Reported eye irritation in past 1 year (adults—direct response) (Mn)	44
Expenditure on doctor's fee adult per year (Rs Mn)	5700
Expenditure on medicines adult per year (Rs Mn)	11,106
Prevalence of LRI/ARI among children below 5 years (Mn)	12.22

Note: * Not all symptoms are due to biofuels. This may be the upper limit or one can say it may be due to all causes. However, our work on risk factors gives further clues.

Economic Burden of Water-related Diseases

Water-related diseases have caused a very heavy economic burden. All the 42 million adults and 27 million children suffering from water-related diseases, took some treatment or special diets. These affected persons on an average spend about Rs 611 in a year (or Rs 51 per month) towards total expenses including doctor's fees, medicines, hospitalization charges, and/or special diets. This leads to an expenditure of about Rs 42 billion, in addition to subsidy provided to various health centres towards treatment of water-related diseases.

If we also account for the cost of human days lost due to illness (which is around 22 days in a year including days lost by other family members) taking an average cost of Rs 60 per day, the total economic burden comes to around Rs 89 billion for human days lost due to these illnesses. Thus the total loss is of Rs 131 billion per year (Table 5.6).

Total Economic Burden

Total economic loss due to lack of energy, water, and sanitation and its impact on health and human resources is summarized in Table 5.7, which shows that 15.5 billion days per year are spent or lost due to inadequate facilities and resources. The total economic loss due to the health impact of dirty fuel and unsafe water is over Rs 103 billion per year in rural areas (Table 5.7). Availability of clean energy and water sources and accessibility to better sanitation and health facilities can improve economic and social conditions of the rural poor.

Loss of 2 to 3 days per adult per year due to respiratory and water-related diseases leads to loss of Rs 147 billion per annum, if calculated using normal wages. The total economic loss due to inadequate energy and water facilities leads to loss of over Rs 1042 billion.

Better access to energy and water resources could improve efficiency of agriculture and allied activities that can create opportunities for better employment and better livelihood. When such a large human resource is spent just to meet basic needs for survival, how can people improve their living conditions and participate in the economic growth process? An integrated approach and participation from various ministries, government departments, NGOs, and village communities is required to achieve the sustainable economic development of rural India.

Willingness to Pay

A small proportion of households has shown willingness to participate in reducing kitchen smoke and improving

> Box 5.6
> **Water-related Diseases**
>
> 42 million adults (9 per cent of total adults) and 27 million children (9 per cent of total children) in rural India suffered from some water related diseases in the past. Occurrence of major diseases are as given in the figure below:
>
>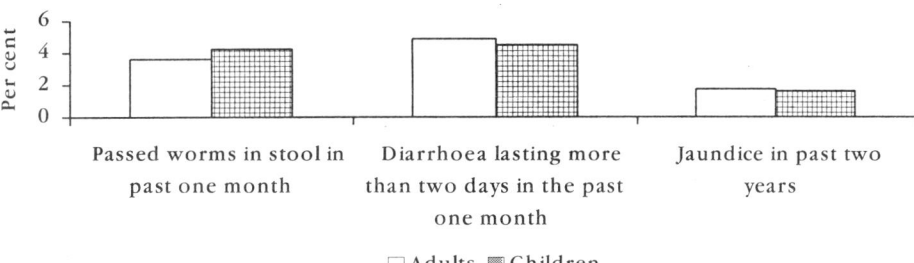
>
> - Passing of worms in stool in past one month was high among children below 5 years (in 4 per cent children).
>
> *Expenditure*
>
> Total expenditure for water related diseases for adults and children: Rs 42 billion per year
>
> - Of the total expenditure incurred, 37 per cent is spent on special diet, 33 per cent on doctor's fee, 17 per cent on hospitalization and 13 per cent on medicine.

TABLE 5.6
Total Economic Losses due to Water Related Diseases

Diseases	Estimates
Adult sufferers of water related diseases (based on direct responses) (Mn)	41.7
• Passed worms in stool in past one month	16.2
• Diarrhoea lasting more than two days in past one month	22.4
• Jaundice in past two years	7.7
Children (below 15 years) sufferers of water related diseases (based on proxy responses) (Mn)	26.8
• Passed worms in stool in past one month	12.1
• Diarrhoea lasting more than two days in past one month	13
• Jaundice in past two years	4.6
Economic burden of water related diseases (Rs Mn)	41,850
• Expenditure on doctor's fee per year	17,571
• Expenditure on medicines per year	6190
• Expenditure on hospitalization per year	5988
• Expenditure on special diets per year	12,101
Average days lost in a year due to illness (Mn days)	1484
• Valuation of days lost (Rs Mn)	89,046

the supply of clean drinking water, a sewerage system, and/or better sanitation facility. About 15 per cent (20 million households in rural India) have shown willingness to reduce smoke in their kitchen. Although about 8 per cent (11 million households) have shown willingness to contribute for clean drinking water, 71 million households in rural India spend 102 billion hours per annum in collecting water from outside the house premises.

With respect to sewerage and sanitation facilities about 29 per cent (38 million households) have shown willingness to contribute for a sewerage system. About 26 per cent (34 million households) have shown their willingness to contribute for sanitation facilities. Details of the amount people are willing to contribute to improve the facilities around them is given in Table 5.8.

Table 5.8 indicates willingness of households of households to pay collectively Rs 1.3 billion for drinking water, Rs 3.4 billion for water purification, Rs 5.1 billion for community toilets, and Rs 44 billion for in-house toilets. These amounts are small in comparison to that

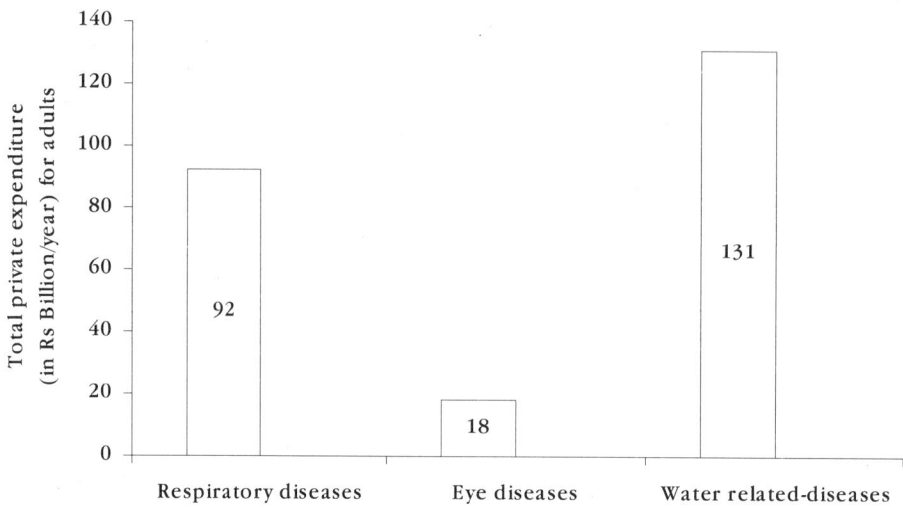

Figure 5.1: Total economic losses due to diseases caused because of lack of access to clean energy, water and, sanitation

TABLE 5.7
Total Economic Burden

	Energy (a)	Water (b)	Total (a + b)
Working days spent in fuel and water collection and work days lost due to ill health (billion)			
No. of adult working days[+] spent in fuelwood gathering and water collection	3	10.2	13.2
Adult working days lost due to diseases	0.78 (Respiratory & eye related)	1.5 (Water & sanitation related)	2.28
Direct expenditure on health by adults (billions)			
Expenditure on health by adults[$] due to various diseases	61 (Respiratory & eye related)	42 (Water & sanitation related)	103
Economic value of working days spent/lost due to energy, water, sanitation, and health (Rs billion)			
Monetary value[@] of working days spent for fuelwood gathering and water collection	180	612	792
Monetary value[@] of working day lost due to diseases	57.6 (Respiratory & eye related)	89 (Water & sanitation related)	146.6
Total economic loss due to diseases (includes direct cost and imputed cost of working days lost due to ill health)	118.6 (Respiratory & eye related)	131 (Water & sanitation related)	249.6
Total economic loss due to improper energy and water facilities and due to health impacts of their procurement and use	298.6	743	1041.6

Notes: [+] Taking 10 hrs as the standard working hours per day, number of working days lost was estimated.
[$] Estimated only for individuals above 15 years of age.
[@] This is estimated by taking Rs 60 per day as wage rate prevailing in Rajasthan.

which is required. But it is the kernel needed for the growth of programmes by the government and aid agencies. More can be mobilized as the momentum grows and benefits are felt. As against this, the cost of water-related diseases is Rs 42 billion per year privately paid for and Rs 89 billion lost due to foregone income owing to illness. About 20 million households are willing to pay for the reduction of smoke in the kitchen.

TABLE 5.8
Households Willing to Pay for Improvement (million)

HHs willing to pay for reduced kitchen smoke (HHs) (10^6)	20.3
HHs willing to pay for clean drinking water (HHs) (10^6)	10.7
Total amount willing to pay for clean drinking water (Rs)	1336
HHs willing to pay for community based water purifying facility (HHs) (10^6)	32.1
Total amount willing to pay for community based water purifying facility (Rs)	3408
HHs willing to pay for sewerage system (HHs) (10^6)	38.1
Total amount willing to contribute for sewerage system (Rs)	4278
HHs willing to pay for sanitation (HHs)	34.3
Total amount willing to contribute for in-house toilet (Rs)	44,238
Total amount willing to contribute for community toilet (Rs)	5114

We have described in this chapter the current status of energy, water, sanitation, and people's priorities, health impacts of exposure to pollutants owing to cooking with biofuels and of lack of clean drinking water. We have seen that use of dirty biofuels leads to economic loss of about Rs 299 billion per year in rural India. Therefore, access to clean energy, water, sanitation, and health services needs to be stressed for social and economic development. There are strong poverty–gender–environment linkages here. We need a holistic approach to reach a consensus to set and achieve common goals in these areas.

RECOMMENDATIONS FOR ENERGY SUPPLY AND UTILIZATION

There are two potential ways toward energy transition: (a) the one adopted by industrialized countries, and urban or wealthier households in developing countries based on the use of petroleum products; and (b) a way that uses cleaner energy technologies, including biogas, solar, wind, and micro-hydro, and cooking equipment, such as solar cookers, pressure cookers, and improved stoves. It is important that women have a say in the choice of possible energy solutions.

When the issue of providing rural women with access to petroleum products comes up, several questions are generally raised:

• Why should they use fossil fuels when they can use renewables?

• Won't there be increased foreign exchange burden from imported petroleum products?

• What about increases in greenhouse gas emissions?

These questions need to be put in a proper context. The available and practical renewable biofuels are not clean fuels. The harmful consequences of biofuels use described here should answer the first question. For the second question it is important to realize that the demand for household cooking fuels is not large. It could be satisfied with approximately 15 to 20 litres of kerosene a month per household. Globally, about 200 million tonnes of petroleum-based fuels could completely replace current household use of traditional biofuels all over the world, compared to total global energy use of 10 billion tonnes of oil equivalent.

The problem of foreign exchange burdens is also exaggerated. These household demands are very small compared to other demands on foreign exchange unrelated to satisfying basic needs. They are small even compared to the imports of other petroleum products such as diesel or gasoline. In the long run, a transition to non-polluting renewable energy technologies will benefit people in developing and industrialized countries alike. But, in the meantime, why should millions of poor women suffer so much for want of so little? For the third question concerning greenhouse gas emission by relatively clean fossil fuels, it is important to recognize that those who are answerable for fossil fuel consumption and greenhouse gas emissions are mostly people in industrialized countries and elite groups in developing countries, not these poor households whose requirements are minuscule.

RECOMMENDATIONS FOR ACTION FOR GENDER EQUITY

Greater political will is needed and cooperation among government ministries, development agencies, and community organizations, to ensure that rural women can choose from a range of cleaner fuels and energy technologies, in order to reduce their daily burdens and increase their social and economic opportunities. Unfortunately, the gender and energy issue is not specifically mentioned in the UN's MDGs. A transition to sustainable rural energy sources needs to be an important element of national development goals.

As women are the primary sufferers of the adverse impact of use of biofuels, there is a close linkage between gender and energy. Gender and energy issues have remained on the periphery of development policy, and require greater political attention and backing. Because women are particularly impacted by the continued use of traditional fuels, a special commitment is necessary to provide them with cleaner fuel choices, as well as rural electrification options that can provide better opportunities for income generation through agriculture and SSIs. Only recently has increased attention been given to involving women in assessing and adapting fuel and technology choices, and to the problems of technology diffusion among illiterate or semi-literate women. It is now time to shift from academic studies on the number of deaths taking place to the actual prevention and treatment of diseases. Newer experiments emphasize community mobilization, good governance, transparency and accountability, capacity building, and gender sensitivity. New community-level institutional arrangements include fuelwood growing associations, joint forest management projects, and associations of entrepreneurs. These measures promote replicability and propagation of programmes that previous isolated experiments did not.

In some areas, current government energy policies, including subsidies, are insufficiently responsive to women's needs. In India, for example, subsidies for kerosene are limited to amounts sufficient for lighting homes and are not adequate for meeting the cooking requirements of poor women. Universal subsidies for LPG amounted to US$ 1 billion in the last fiscal year, but much of the subsidized fuel went to affluent urban households, or was diverted to commercial sectors. There is a clear need for developing new, more effective strategies to reach the poorest households. Subsidies could be given directly to consumers (rather than suppliers), empowering them to make their own energy decisions. In addition, subsidies for rural electrification and renewable energy technologies should go to promote income-producing activities that benefit women as well as men.

Recommendations for Water and Sanitation Facilities

Water scarcity is a very important issue that leads to many other related problems. Providing access to safe drinking water upon which the health of individuals and the welfare of the people depend, requires an integrated approach for comprehensive and sustainable solutions.

The aim of the policy should be to provide safe sources of drinking water within peoples' reach and to minimize the hardship that people face in collecting water. Priorities in sanitation should be to provide people with sanitation facilities so that water does not get contaminated and does not harm health. We recommend the following policy measures and interventions.

(1) In many villages people use surface water sources such as ponds and lakes. These sources are prone to contamination from poor sanitation, agriculture run off, etc. that contain harmful disease causing agents, which affect human health. Therefore, such open sources should be restricted in their use and alternative water sources should be strengthened. If these sources are used water testing and monitoring should be done regularly at delivery points.

On an average 2774 km is walked per year per household to collect 73 kilolitres of water. This takes substantial time and hard work. Therefore it is necessary to improve the local water resource base by various methods:

• Improving groundwater resource and rainwater harvesting and storing the water for use during scarcity seasons;

• Tapping rainwater by various rainwater harvesting techniques can minimize water shortage. The advantages with rainwater harvesting are that it provides safe water supply and helps in groundwater recharge. Therefore area-specific rainwater harvesting should be promoted with community, government, and NGO participation. Watershed management programmes can play a crucial role in improving the water resource base.

(2) It is observed that water is contaminated further in the households due to poor storage methods and unhygienic means of handling the water. Contamination occurs mainly due to lack of awareness about simple methods which if practised, can influence health outcome in a positive way.

• Methods such as covering water storage pots and use of a ladle with a long handle to take out the water (this would avoid contamination of water by dirty hands and dirt in the air) need to be popularized.

• The water pots should be kept above ground level so that dust does not enter into the pots.

• Use of a simple cloth filter kept clean with regular washing helps to avoid many water-related diseases.

• Water should be boiled before drinking.

(3) Awareness programmes (especially for women) based on these simple techniques should be popularized in villages so that people practise these methods. NGOs can play a crucial role in this endeavour.

(4) As stressed in India's National Water Policy document of 2001, a village-level information system needs to be developed so that information about various water related issues may be more easily available to the people.

(5) Human excreta are the most important disease-carrying agents due to the practice of defecation in open spaces. In villages community toilets can be popularized, with adequate awareness programmes for keeping them clean. Survey suggests that people are willing to contribute for the construction of in-house and community toilets. This contribution can substantially reduce the burden on the government treasury for providing the required facility.

RECOMMENDATIONS FOR HEALTH CARE FACILITIES

- Training of health care professionals is needed to spot the problems relating to pollution and to sensitize them to be alert. Many villages either do not have convenient health centre facilities or even if they do, these centres are not equipped with the basic instruments/infrastructure required for simple treatment.

- Many diseases are spread due to a negligence and due to a lack of awareness. Most of these diseases can be avoided by simple precautions such as cleaning hands and utensils properly and by avoiding delay in treatment. Awareness about such techniques can be promoted with support from NGOs, the health ministry, and the rural development ministry.

- Exposure to air pollutants can be minimized by structural changes in housing, for example, by improving the ventilation of the kitchen and the house, or having a separate kitchen, or installing chimneys.

- Study shows that with improvement in female literacy, adverse health impacts of respiratory and water related diseases can be reduced.

- Health centres should be networked with information systems to enable them to communicate with each other for better implementation of public health policy.

- It is reported that due to lack of medical facilities nearby sick people and pregnant women suffer as they have to travel long distances to reach the health centres. To minimize their suffering and to support them with health care access, mobile vans can be introduced that go around villages.

RECOMMENDATIONS FOR TRANSPORTATION FACILITIES

- Village level cooperative transport facility such as trolleys or wheel/barrows to carry water pots and fuelwood loads could be made available to reduce the hardship and loss of productive time.

- Alternatively, collectively financed, small motorized vehicles could be provided to communities to carry fuelwood and water on a cooperative basis.

A comprehensive policy and programme is needed that can integrate energy, water, sanitation, and health with development goals such as employment generation, poverty alleviation, and sustainable livelihood so as to bring cohesive development in all arenas of life of the rural people, especially the rural women. This requires focused linkages, participatory, collective, and coordinated efforts of the different ministries such as the Ministry of Education, the Ministry of Environment and Forests, the Ministry of Petroleum, the Ministry of Rural Development, the Ministry of Health, the Ministry of Agriculture, the Ministry of Non-conventional Energy Sources, and the Central Water Commission along with local government and non-government organizations.

REFERENCES

Balakrishana, K., K. Parikh, S. Sankar, R. Padmavathi, K. Srividya, V. Venugopal, S. Prasad, and Vijay Laxmi (2002). 'Daily average exposure to respirable particulate matter from combustion of biomass fuels in rural households of southern India', *Environmental Health Perspective*, Vol. 110, No. 11.

Census of India (2001), Office of Registrar-General Commissioner, Government of India, New Delhi.

Parikh, J. (1995), 'Gender issues in energy policy', *Energy Policy*, Vol. 23, No. 5, p. 745.

Parikh, J., K. Smith, and Vijay Laxmi (1999), 'Indoor air pollution: a reflection on gender bias', *Economic and Political Weekly*, Vol. 34, No. 9, pp. 539–44.

Parikh, J. and Vijay Laxmi (2000), 'Biofuels, pollution and health linkages: a survey of rural Tamil Nadu', *Economic and Political Weekly*, Vol. 35, No. 7, pp. 4125–38.

UNDP/World Bank Energy Sector Management Assistance Program (ESMAP) (2001), 'Energy and Health for the Poor', Indoor Air Pollution News Letter.

Vijay Laxmi, J. Parikh, S. Karmakar, P. Dabrase (2003), 'Household energy, women's hardship and health impacts in rural Rajasthan, India: need for sustainable energy solutions', *Energy for Sustainable Development*, Vol. 7, No. 1, pp. 50–68.

Wickramsinghe, A. (2001), 'Gender sights and health issues in paradigm of biofuel in Sri Lanka', *Energia News*, Vol. 4, No. 4.

6 Patterns in Social Sector Expenditure Pre- and Post-reform Periods[1]

S. Mahendra Dev • Jos Mooij

Throughout the history of independent India, the Indian government has claimed that it works towards social development and the eradication of poverty. On the eve of independence, Jawaharlal Nehru, addressing the Constituent Assembly, declared that independence meant the redemption of a pledge. But he also stated that this achievement 'is but a step, an opening of opportunity, to the great triumphs and achievements that await us...the ending of poverty and ignorance and disease and inequality of opportunity'.[2]

A lot has been achieved in the past half a century. The incidence of poverty has declined from over 50 per cent in the 1950s to less than 30 per cent in the late 1990s.[3] The literacy rate has increased from less than 20 per cent in 1951 to 65 per cent in 2001. According to recent Human Development Reports published by the United Nations Development Programme (UNDP), India moved from the category of 'low' human development to that of 'medium' human development and its rank in 2003 was 127 (out of 175 countries). Nevertheless, the performance of India in the social sector is far from satisfactory and could have been much better (Dreze and Sen 1995).

The claims of the government that poverty eradication/alleviation and social development are the main challenges and that it is fully committed to address these issues have continued over time. Today, if we have to believe the government, the prime objective of most policies is to help the poor and reduce their numbers. But how genuine is this claim?

In this chapter we analyse patterns in social sector expenditures. Our focus is on the centre as well as the states. Both have their separate responsibilities, which are laid down in the Constitution. Health and most rural development issues are the responsibility of the states. Education, welfare, and employment issues come under the concurrent list—meaning that both the centre and the states are responsible. So the role of the states is much more important than that of the centre when it comes to the social sector.

We define the social sector as the total of expenditure on 'Social Services' and 'Rural Development' as given in central and state budgets. 'Social Services' includes, among other things, education, health and family welfare, water supply, and sanitation. 'Rural Development' (listed under 'Economic Services' in the budget classification) relates mostly to anti-poverty programmes. Social sector expenditure is of two kinds. First, there are social and economic expenditures that have the broader objective of expanding social opportunities and improving the social indicators of education, health, and nutritional standards of the general population; second, there are programmes that are primarily meant to alleviate poverty. Apart from (wage and self-) employment programmes for the rural and urban poor, there are specific health and nutritional programmes for women and children which largely target the poorer segments of the population.

TRENDS IN SOCIAL SECTOR EXPENDITURE

In this section we analyse the trends in social sector expenditure, defined as the total of expenditure on 'Social Services' and 'Rural Development' as given in central

---

[1] We would like to thank N. Sreedevi of the Centre for Economic and Social Studies, Hyderabad, for excellent research assistance.

[2] Jawaharlal Nehru's speech at the Constituent Assembly, New Delhi, on 14 August 1947. Quoted from Dreze and Sen (1995), p. 1.

[3] There is a controversy on the estimates based on NSS data for 1999–2000.

and state budgets. The trends are examined at three levels: (a) combined centre and states, (b) centre, and (c) states. The expenditure refers to both plan and non-plan.

Combined Expenditure by the Centre and the States

The combined social sector expenditure of the centre and the states provides the best picture of India's commitment towards the social sector.[4] There are different ways of examining the trends in budget expenditure. One way is to look at social sector expenditure as a proportion of GDP, or GSDP in the case of the states. A second way is to calculate social sector expenditure as a percentage of the aggregate budget expenditure. The third option is to look at the real per capita expenditure (at constant prices) for the social sector. Table 6.1 utilizes all these three methods for the period 1987–8 to 2000–2. India spends around 6 to 7.5 per cent of its GDP on the social sector. In 1990–1, the share in GDP was 6.78 per cent. Only in 1998–9 a higher level was reached. Throughout the 1990s social sector expenditure, in terms of percentage of GDP, was lower than the value just before the onset of the reforms, which was 7.17 per cent. This percentage was, however, reached in 2000–1 and 2001–2.

TABLE 6.1
Social Sector (Social Services and Rural Development) Expenditure by Centre and States

	Social sector expenditure (revenue and capital)		
	As % of GDP	As % of agg. pub. exp. (rev.+capital)	Per capita exp. (in Rs) in 1993–4 prices
1987–8	7.26	25.29	564
1988–9	6.95	25.22	585
1989–90	7.17	25.19	635
1990–1	6.78	24.85	623
1991–2	6.58	24.28	599
1992–3	6.38	24.06	594
1993–4	6.46	24.58	622
1994–5	6.39	25.01	632
1995–6	6.40	25.95	674
1996–7	6.30	26.46	716
1997–8	6.41	26.18	763
1998–9	7.01	27.36	882
1999–2000	7.14	26.75	951
2000–1	7.45	26.56	988
2001–2(B)	7.18	25.31	986

Source: Computed from the data available in *Indian Public Finance Statistics*, Ministry of Finance, GOI, 1995, 2002.

[4] It is difficult to get the information on combined expenditure from the budgets. Simply aggregating the expenditure by the centre and by the states gives an inflated picture because the budget information does not adjust for central transfers to states. We used data from the *Indian Public Finance Statistics* (Ministry of Finance, GOI), which is adjusted for transfer of funds. It may be noted that the classification for major heads in this source is slightly different from that in the budget tables and RBI Bulletins.

As a proportion of aggregate expenditure, India spends between 24 to 27 per cent on the social sector. The percentage started to increase in the middle of the 1990s. Since 1995–6, the percentage has been higher than what it was in the 1980s. In other words, a higher percentage of government expenditure goes to the social sector now than it used to when the reforms started or even during the last years preceding the reforms.

In terms of per capita real expenditure, social sector expenditure has continued to increase after 1993–4. Per capita expenditure has risen from Rs 623 in 1990–1 to Rs 988 in 2000–1—an increase of 75 per cent in 11 years.

On the basis of Table 6.1, different arguments can be made. Advocates of the reforms can claim that they are proved right when they say that the reforms are meant to reduce state intervention in certain sectors in order to increase expenditure on the social sector. After all, after the mid-1990s, there was an increase in social sector expenditure as percentages of overall government expenditure. Opponents of the reforms, on the other hand, can claim that the social sector has suffered because, as a percentage of GDP, social sector expenditure after 1991 was generally less than what it was in the late 1980s.

Table 6.2 disaggregates social sector expenditure, and shows that education is by far the largest head.

Share of States in Combined Social Sector Expenditure

Table 6.2 also gives information about the share of the centre and the states in overall social sector spending. It is clear that the states contribute the lion's share. In 1990–1, share of the states for the total social sector was around 85 per cent. However, the share of the states declined for most of the major heads in the course of the 1990s. In 2000–1, their share of the total social sector had been 80.7 per cent, almost 5 per cent less than what it had been a decade earlier. This reflects the severe fiscal crisis many states are experiencing at present (Saxena and Farrington 2002), but it also suggests that the commitment of the states to social development has declined during the reform period. In the area of health and family welfare, the shift from the states towards the centre is a cause for concern, as it means more emphasis on vertical disease-related interventions—which is what the centre mainly does—and less on primary health care.

Expenditure on Education and Its Components

Table 6.3 provides more information on education expenditure. It shows that in 1998–9, around Rs 50,200

TABLE 6.2
Social Sector Exp. of Centre and States (%), 1990-1 and 2000-1

Major heads	1990-1 expenditures (Rs in billion current prices)	2000-1 expenditures (Rs in billion current prices)	share of states in total spending (%)	
			1990-1	2000-1
1. Education, art and culture	173.8	690.1	90.3	89.1
2. Medical and public health, water supply, and sanitation	65.6	264.4	90.7	88.8
3. Family welfare	9.3	34.4	93.5	71.5
4. Housing	7.7	44.5	71.4	53.5
5. Urban development	7.7	45.0	85.7	94.4
6. Labour and employment	7.3	22.9	60.3	57.7
7. Social security and welfare	38.7	162.9	92.3	89.5
8. Others*	23.9	69.4	18.4	21.9
9. Social and community services (1–8)	334.1	1333.7	84.4	83.2
10. Rural development	51.5	182.6	90.3	61.0
11. Total (9–10)	385.6	1516.3	85.2	80.7

Note: * Others include scientific services and research, broadcasting, information and publicity.
The information given in the table relates to actual expenditure for 1990-1 and revised expenditure for 2000-1.
Source: Computed from the data available in *Indian Public Finance Statistics*, Ministry of Finance, GOI, 1995, 2002.

crores were allocated to education from the Education Department (col. 7). Out of this amount, Rs 24,500 crores (around 49 per cent) were allocated to elementary education. As proportion of gross national product (GNP), the share of education declined from 3.4 per cent in 1990-1 to around 3.1 per cent in the late 1990s. It may be noted that other departments also spend some part of their departmental expenditures on education. If we add this expenditure, the share of education comes to around 4.1 per cent in 1990-1 (col. 10). This share declined over time to 3.6 and 3.8 in the mid- and late 1990s, respectively. This percentage is well below the international norm of 6 per cent of GNP on education.

Table 6.3 also provides intrasectoral percentages on education for the 1990s. These expenditure relate to the funds spent by the education department only. The table shows that the share of elementary education increased from around 46 per cent in the early 1990s to 49 per cent in the late 1990s. There has been a decline in the shares of secondary, higher, and technical education during this period. As will be shown later, the shift to elementary education is mainly due to a significant increase in the share for elementary education in central government expenditure since the mid-1990s.

TRENDS IN EXPENDITURES BY THE CENTRAL GOVERNMENT

Table 6.4 gives an overview of central government expenditure for the pre-reform (1980-1 to 1989-90) and the post-reform periods (1992-3 to 2002-3). As a proportion of GDP, central government expenditure for the social sector was less than 1 per cent in the early 1980s, but this increased to around 1.55 per cent in 1989-90. This percentage declined in the first three years of the reform period, but increased afterwards to about 1.6 per cent. As a proportion of aggregate expenditure, social sector expenditure increased from 5.48 per cent in 1980-1 to 8.18 per cent in 1989-90, to more than 10 per cent in the 1990s. In terms of per capita real expenditure, social sector spending increased from Rs 48 in 1980-1 to Rs 137 in 1989-90 and to Rs 247 in 2002-3. With regard to all these three indicators, it is clear that the trend growth rate per annum was much higher in the pre-reform period than in the post-reform period. So although social sector expenditure continued to increase in the 1990s (as per cent of GDP, as per cent of aggregate expenditure, and in terms of per capita expenditure), it was at a much lower pace than in the 1980s.

Intrasectoral Allocations in Education, Health, and Rural Development

Table 6.5 provides intrasectoral allocations for education, health and family welfare, and rural development for the post-reform period. It shows that the 1990s witnessed significant shifts within these sectors.

(1) In education, there has been a sharp increase in the share of elementary education, particularly since 1995-6. This share increased from about 18 per cent in 1992-3 to 40 per cent in 1995-6 and to 48 per cent in 1997-8. Since 1998-9, however, the share has declined and it was 42 per cent in 2002-3. A further disaggregation showed that

TABLE 6.3
Expenditure on Education (in Rs Crores current prices) and its Composition 1990-1 to 1998-9

Year	Expenditure on education (in crores)							As % of GNP	
	Elementary	Secondary	Technical	Higher	Others	Total exp. on edu. from Edu. Dept.	Total exp. on edu. including other dpts	Total exp. on edu. from Edu. Dept	Total exp. on edu. including other dpts
(1)	(2)	(3)	(4)	(5)	(6)	(7)	(8)	(9)	(10)
1990-1	7955.5	5631.1	753.0	2311.9	531.0	17,182.5	20,491.2	3.41	4.07
1991-2	8684.3	6198.8	809.5	2443.4	621.6	18,757.6	22,593.8	3.24	3.90
1992-3	9477.3	7178.1	907.1	2700.0	690.5	20,953.0	25,030.3	3.17	3.79
1993-4	10,821.8	7768.6	1017.2	3103.6	701.9	23,413.1	28,279.7	3.04	3.68
1994-5	12,638.9	9049.5	1189.3	3525.3	827.1	27,230.1	32,606.2	3.02	3.62
1995-6	15,217.8	10,344.1	1290.3	3871.3	783.3	31,506.8	38,178.1	2.99	3.61
1996-7	17,850.5	11,735.8	1450.0	4287.9	1031.2	36,355.4	43,896.5	2.97	3.59
1997-8	21,078.8	13,107.6	1685.2	5047.1	1408.2	42,326.9	51,930.6	3.10	3.79
1998-9	24,456.2	15,112.4	2130.5	6771.2	1747.8	50,218.1	60,856.5	3.14	3.81

Year	Intrasectoral allocation (%)					
	Elementary	Secondary	Technical	Higher	Others	Total exp. on edu. from Edu. Dept.
1990-1	46.3	32.2	4.4	13.9	3.1	100.0
1991-2	46.3	33.0	4.3	13.1	3.3	100.0
1992-3	45.2	34.3	4.3	12.9	3.3	100.0
1993-4	46.2	33.2	4.3	13.3	3.0	100.0
1994-5	46.4	33.2	4.4	13.0	3.1	100.0
1995-6	48.3	32.8	4.1	12.3	2.5	100.0
1996-7	49.1	32.3	4.0	11.8	2.8	100.0
1997-8*	49.8	30.9	4.0	11.9	3.3	100.0
1998-9@	48.7	30.1	4.2	13.5	3.5	100.0

Notes: * Revised estimates.
@Budget estimates.
Source: Tilak (2001) taken from 'Analysis of Budget Expenditure on Education' (various years), MHRD, New Delhi.

TABLE 6.4
Social Sector Expenditure (Social services + Rural Dev) by Centre

	As percentage of		percapita 93-4 prices		As percentage of		Percapita 93-4 prices
	GDP	Agg. exp (rev+cap)			GDP	Agg. exp (rev+cap)	
1980-1	0.84	5.48	48	1992-3	1.28	8.62	119
1981-2	0.80	5.56	49	1993-4	1.49	10.46	144
1982-3	0.89	5.62	56	1994-5	1.48	9.35	147
1983-4	1.04	6.73	70	1995-6	1.54	10.23	162
1984-5	1.24	7.33	85	1996-7	1.55	10.55	176
1985-6	1.27	7.13	93	1997-8	1.60	10.49	190
1986-7	1.52	7.93	115	1998-9	1.68	10.48	212
1987-8	1.63	8.48	127	1999-2000	1.60	10.42	213
1988-9	1.51	8.03	127	2000-1	1.41	9.11	187
1989-90	1.55	8.18	137	2001-2	1.59	10.05	218
Trend of growth rate per annum				2002-3(R)		10.76	247
				Trend of growth rate per annum			
(1980-1—1989-90)	8.93	5.41	14.12	(1992-3—2002-3)	1.34	0.82	6.34

Source: Budget Documents, GOI.

this shift in favour of elementary education was due to the introduction of nutrition programmes and the District Primary Education Programme (DPEP). The shift towards elementary education led to a decline in the shares of secondary, university and higher, technical, and adult education.

(2) The intraallocations for health and family welfare show that there was a sharp increase in the share of reproduction and child health from around 5 per cent in 1992–3 to 15 per cent in the late 1990s.

(3) In the case of rural development, the share of rural wage employment programmes declined drastically since the mid-1990s. In 2002–3, however, the share increased again.[5] The share for rural housing and other programmes increased in the 1990s. In the case of the latter, there was a twelve-fold increase between 1999–2000 and 2000–1, as a result of the introduction of the rural roads scheme, known as the Prime Minister's Gram Samrudhi Yojana (PMGSY).

External Aid for the Social Sector

Over time, the contribution of external aid to social sector expenditure has increased. The main donors/lenders include international organizations such as World Bank, several organs of the UN, and the British Department for International Development (DFID). We do not have sufficient information to examine the importance of this contribution in all the major heads of the social sector, but we have information on sectoral spending on children, as shown.

TABLE 6.5
Intrasectoral Allocation (%) in Education, Health, and Rural Development:
Central Government Expenditure 1992–3 to 2002–3

	1992–3	1993–4	1994–5	1995–6	1996–7	1997–8	1998–9	1999–2000	2000–1	2001–2	2002–3
Education											
Education sector	100.0	100.0	100.0	100.0	100.0	100.0	100.0	100.0	100.0	100.0	100.0
Elementary	18.6	20.2	20.5	39.6	42.0	48.1	42.9	39.0	37.8	44.3	41.7
Secondary	25.0	25.6	24.1	19.9	19.0	15.0	15.5	14.4	14.3	15.3	13.6
University and higher	28.0	24.9	25.6	19.9	19.5	20.2	25.1	29.6	31.0	20.5	19.4
Adult	6.3	7.8	8.5	4.7	3.1	1.8	1.3	1.1	1.3	2.2	2.4
Technical	18.7	18.3	18.6	14.0	14.5	13.0	13.6	14.1	13.5	15.4	15.0
Others	3.4	3.2	2.7	1.9	1.9	1.9	1.6	1.8	2.1	2.3	8.0
Health and family welfare											
Health and family welfare	100.0	100.0	100.0	100.0	100.0	100.0	100.0	100.0	100.0	100.0	100.0
Public health	16.6	16.6	18.0	17.7	19.7	18.9	16.4	14.1	14.4	12.6	11.5
Medical education	13.6	12.4	12.3	12.2	12.3	13.1	15.2	13.1	13.6	12.5	11.7
Rural family welfare	17.2	15.8	13.2	13.7	12.4	13.9	15.3	21.4	15.8	15.5	25.0
Maternal and child heath	5.4	6.0	6.3	11.0	11.9	13.6	15.3	13.6	15.4	16.6	14.6
Other services and supplies	21.1	26.2	28.5	23.1	19.5	17.6	16.5	17.9	19.7	20.7	12.2
Others	26.1	23.0	21.7	22.3	24.2	22.9	21.3	19.7	21.0	22.5	25.2
Rural development											
Rural development	100.0	100.0	100.0	100.0	100.0	100.0	100.0	100.0	100.0	100.0	100.0
Water supply and sanitation	13.3	13.6	13.2	14.1	14.7	16.7	17.7	19.3	16.0	14.0	11.0
Special programmes	13.8	14.5	12.9	10.7	10.6	10.4	9.6	12.1	9.9	9.8	8.8
Social sector and welfare	–	–	–	6.6	7.0	5.8	6.8	7.6	6.2	4.9	0.0
Rural wage employment prog.	70.5	68.9	70.8	57.3	44.5	46.0	42.8	39.8	23.7	31.1	51.6
Other rural development prog.*	1.0	1.0	1.2	4.0	6.4	5.8	5.3	1.9	23.2	20.3	13.6
Housing	0.1	0.2	0.3	5.9	15.2	13.6	16.2	17.7	12.6	13.4	8.4
Others	1.3	1.8	1.6	1.4	1.6	1.7	1.6	1.6	8.2	6.7	6.6

Note: (1) All the data in this table refer to revised estimates; (2) Others in health and family welfare refer to central government health schemes, hospitals and dispensaries, urban family welfare. Maternal and child health was replaced by reproductive and child health in 1998–9; (3) Special programmes for rural development refer to IRDP, TRYSEM, DPAP, Desert Area development programme etc. Rural wage employment programmes are JRY and EAS. Other rural development programmes refer to DWCRA, rural roads, million wells scheme and training.
Source: Vol. II, Budget Papers, GOI.

---

[5] This increase was the result of the massive Food-for-Work programme initiated as drought relief and to get rid of the huge food stocks held by the GOI.

Table 6.6 shows that the share of external aid in sectoral spending on children in the Union budget has increased from 0.5 per cent in 1990–1 to around

29 per cent in 1997–8. On an average, for the 1990s, out of every 100 rupees spent on children around 20 rupees came from external aid.[6] The share of external aid is the highest for children in the health sector. More than 50 per cent of child health expenditure came from external sources.

TABLE 6.6
Share of External Aid in Sectoral Spending on Children (Union Budget) (%)

Year	Health	Child development	Education	Total
1990–1	–	–	1.4	0.5
1991–2	32.2	16.5	2.5	13.4
1992–3	53.3	13.4	4.9	17.1
1993–4	50.6	16.7	10.3	22.7
1994–5	53.2	13.1	20.6	26.2
1995–6	40.6	12.4	19.6	21.7
1996–7	33.6	21.6	13.6	19.5
1997–8	56.3	13.0	26.9	28.6
1998–9	79.0	9.9	22.5	25.3
1999–2000	63.6	15.0	25.0	25.9
Average	51.4	14.6	16.4	20.1

Source: Haq (2001).

TRENDS IN EXPENDITURE BY THE STATES

As mentioned above, the main responsibility for social sector expenditure lies with the states. Earlier studies by Prabhu (1997), UNDP (1997) and Chelliah and Sudarshan (1999) have shown that social sector expenditure, either taken as a proportion of GSDP or as a proportion of aggregate expenditure, started to decline for the majority of the states since the mid-1980s and that this trend continued in the early 1990s. Our data confirm this trend for the entire decade of the 1990s.

Table 6.7 shows trend growth rates per annum of the average level of social sector expenditure for all states during the pre- and post-reform periods. The trend growth of real per capita expenditure for the social sector declined from around 9 per cent in the 1980s to around 5 per cent in the 1990s (col. 7). The same trends can be seen for the growth rates of social sector expenditure as percentage of total expenditure and as percentage of GDP. The only items that did relative well in the 1992–2002 period come under the 'total others' category, and include housing and urban development, labour and employment, welfare, and the welfare of the SC/ST. If we compare columns 7 and 8, we see that in the 1980s and 1990s, the performance of the states had been worse than that of the centre.

There are very few states that have been able to increase their social sector expenditure as percentage of GSDP. In terms of real per capita expenditure, however, the expenditure often increased in the 1990s. Table 6.8 shows the interstate differences in per capita expenditure on the social sector. The per capita expenditure is very low in Uttar Pradesh, Bihar, and Orissa and relatively high in Goa, Gujarat, Kerala, and Tamil Nadu. Table 6.9 shows the trends in the 1990s. In Table 6.9, the states are clustered according to their per capita SDP, and divided into three categories: rich, middle, and poor. The rich states did slightly better in education. The middle-income states performed better in health, and the poorer states did best in rural development. The intragroup variation is, however, considerable, which makes it difficult to draw group-wise conclusions. Uttar Pradesh, for instance, has done much worse in education, health, and social services than other poor states. In the case of rural development, all except six states recorded a decline in the index in 1999–2000 as compared to that of 1990–1.

TABLE 6.7
Trend Growth Rates of Social Sector Expenditure of All States (% per annum)

	Education, sports, art, and culture, etc.	Health and family welfare	Water supply and sanitation	Total others	Social services	Rural development	Social sector (services and rural development) states	Social sector centre
	(1)	(2)	(3)	(4)	(5)	(6)	(7)	(8)
Per capita real expenditure (at 1993–4 prices) on social sector								
1980-1—1989-90	7.65	0.18	7.27	6.09	6.95	–1.25	9.27	14.12
1992-3—2002-3	5.91	4.50	6.13	7.41	6.06	1.21	5.44	6.34
Expenditure (revenue + capital) on social sector as % of GDP								
1980-1—1989-90	2.80	–4.34	2.10	1.31	2.13	–6.01	4.34	8.93
1992-3—2002-3	1.59	–0.03	1.78	2.53	1.57	–4.15	0.85	1.34
Expenditure (revenue + capital) on social sector as % of total expenditure								
1980-1—1989-90	0.94	–6.07	1.82	–0.52	0.28	–6.26	2.46	5.41
1992-3—2002-3	–0.05	–1.38	0.16	1.37	0.10	–4.48	–0.48	0.82

Source: Calculated from the data given in Appendix Tables A1 to A3.

[6] For more information see Haq (2001).

TABLE 6.8
Per capita Expenditure in Social Services and Rural Development at Current Prices (in Rs): 1999–2000, 2000–1

States	Social services		Social services and rural development	
	1999–2000	2000–1(R)	1999–2000	2000–1(R)
Andhra Pradesh	1008	1093	1150	1298
Bihar	777	731	996	883
Goa	3502	4170	3591	4255
Gujarat	1384	1914	1498	2072
Haryana	1176	1325	1235	1390
Karnataka	1129	1262	1215	1390
Kerala	1355	1469	1631	1812
Madhya Pradesh	1051	1007	1180	1176
Maharashtra	1198	1427	1261	1491
Orissa	1120	918	1261	1040
Punjab	1156	1640	1175	1721
Rajasthan	1077	1231	1148	1313
Tamil Nadu	1288	1431	1379	1570
Uttar Pradesh	547	645	667	806
West Bengal	1061	1120	1155	1243
All states	1009	1128	1127	1271

Source: RBI Bulletins.

COMPARISONS WITH OTHER COUNTRIES AND INTERNATIONAL NORMS

Table 6.10 compares India with: (a) South Asia generally, (b) East Asian countries, and (c) all developing countries. It is clear that the total public expenditure as proportion of GDP is much higher in India as compared to the averages of the other groups. However, the share of public expenditure allocated to social services is much lower in India than in East Asian countries and all developing countries. The share of education in public expenditure is also lower than in East Asian countries (but much higher than in South Asia generally). In the case of health, India's public expenditure allocation is low, even when compared to that of other South Asian countries. The data for India in Table 6.10 are from 1992–3, but a similar picture emerges from Table 6.11, which is based on the 2003 Human Development Report. Education expenditure (taken as a percentage of GDP or as a percentage of overall public expenditure) was lower in India than in Malaysia and Thailand. Health expenditure is also very low in India as compared to the other countries listed in Table 6.11. On the other hand, private expenditure on health is higher in India than many other countries.

TABLE 6.9
Index of Per capita Real Expenditure on Social Services and Rural Development (at 1993–4 prices) at State Level

	Education, sport, art and culture			medical, health and family welfare			Social services			Rural development		
	1990–1	1995–6	1999–2000	1990–1	1995–6	1999–2000	1990–1	1995–6	1999–2000	1990–1	1995–6	1999–2000
Goa	100	94	149	100	86	116	100	94	139	100	58	96
Gujarat	100	113	157	100	102	159	100	106	173	100	71	88
Haryana	100	107	155	100	103	136	100	135	146	100	55	71
Maharashtra	100	117	177	100	100	118	100	116	152	100	137	51
Punjab	100	97	151	100	85	141	100	100	131	100	95	75
Rich												
Sub-total	100	111	165	100	98	133	100	113	153	100	108	65
Andhra Pradesh	100	96	148	100	104	159	100	124	158	100	70	101
Karnataka	100	119	165	100	115	173	100	120	166	100	73	78
Kerala	100	106	155	100	109	151	100	105	152	100	90	321
Tamil Nadu	100	99	157	100	106	143	100	103	144	100	58	79
West Bengal	100	80	158	100	76	124	100	81	155	100	86	88
Middle												
Sub-total	100	98	156	100	99	146	100	105	154	100	73	107
Bihar	100	101	179	100	126	165	100	103	169	100	81	290
Madhya Pradesh	100	111	174	100	108	171	100	114	179	100	126	108
Orissa	100	115	186	100	106	137	100	120	203	100	56	116
Rajasthan	100	111	152	100	119	139	100	117	149	100	79	67
Uttar Pradesh	100	89	116	100	87	85	100	90	110	100	46	88
Poor												
Sub-total	100	101	150	100	105	126	100	104	148	100	70	121
Total	100	103	157	100	101	136	100	107	153	100	79	104

Source: Estimates based on data from RBI Bulletins.

TABLE 6.10
Composition of Public Expenditure in India and Developing Countries

Major heads	India (1992–3)	All south Asian countries (1985–90)	All east Asian countries (1985–9)	All developing countries (1990)
Total expenditure—GDP ratio	27.9	21.3	22.5	20.8
Gen. adm. and pub. order	11.6	17.2	17.3	15.3
Defence	11.7	12.0	10.9	1.0
Economic services	29.8	30.6	30.6	21.1
Education	13.5	9.0	20.5	13.6
Health and family welfare	2.9	4.2	7.0	5.9
Housing and community services	4.6	5.4	2.2	2.7
Other social services	3.9	7.9	3.8	9.1
Total social services	25.3	26.5	33.5	31.3
Other expenditure	21.6	13.7	7.5	21.3
Total expenditure	100.0	100.0	100.0	100.0

Source: M. G. Rao (1995) quoted in Mundle and Rao (1997).

TABLE 6.11
Public Expenditure on Education and Health: International Comparisons

Countries	Education			Health		HDI rank
	As % of GNP 1998–2000	As % of total govt. exp. 1998–2000	Primary and secondary as % of all education	Public exp. as % of GDP 2000	Private exp. as % of GDP 2000	
India	4.1	12.7	79.9	0.9	4.0	127
Bangladesh	2.5	15.7	89.7	1.5	2.6	139
China	2.1	12.8	69.6	2.0	3.4	104
Egypt	3.7	–	–	1.8	2.3	120
Korea	3.8	17.4	78.5	2.6	3.3	30
Malaysia	6.2	26.7	66.2	1.8	1.6	58
Sri Lanka	3.1	–	84.3	1.4	1.7	99
Thailand	5.4	31.0	63.1	2.1	1.6	74
Sweden	7.8	13.4	67.3	6.2	1.8	3
Canada	5.5	–	62.2	6.5	2.5	8
United States	4.8	12.3	–	5.8	7.3	7
UK	4.5	11.4	79.9	5.9	1.4	13

Source: UNDP, Human Development Report (2003).

In order to facilitate cross-country comparisons and monitoring of social sector expenditure over time, the UNDP has proposed the following four ratios (UNDP 1991):

• The Public Expenditure Ratio: The percentage of national income that goes into public expenditure. The recommendation is to keep this ratio around 25 per cent.

• The Social Allocation Ratio: The percentage of public expenditure earmarked for social services. This ratio, according to the UNDP, should be more than 40 per cent.

• The Social Priority Ratio: The percentage of social expenditure devoted to human priority concerns. This ratio has to be more than 50 per cent.

• The Human Expenditure Ratio: The percentage of national income devoted to human priority concerns. This ratio is the product of the above three ratios and the UNDP recommends that it should be about 5 per cent.

Table 6.12 gives these ratios for India in the late 1980s and the late 1990s. It is clear that there had been some progress in the 1990s, but the ratios are still far removed from the UNDP norms.

TABLE 6.12
Social Sector Ratios

	UNDP norm	late 1980s	1998–9
Public expenditure ratio	25	37*	25
Social allocation ratio	40	20	27
Social priority ratio	50	34	40
Human expenditure ratio	5	2.5	2.8

Note: Social priority ratio was taken as the share of social sector allocation to elementary education, water and sanitation, public health, maternal and child health, and child nutrition.
* This is much higher than our calculation, and it may be that there is a difference in the methodologies used by the two sources.

EFFECTIVENESS OF SOCIAL SECTOR EXPENDITURE

The discussion above on social sector expenditure suggests that the expenditure is too low and should be stepped up. This, no doubt, is true. But apart from that, there are major problems in the utilization of the funds. There are three different issues that require attention, namely, (1) underspending—allocated funds are either not released or not fully utilized, and (2) the quality of expenditure—the neglect of infrastructural investments and (3) the ineffective use, or even misuse, of funds.

Underutilization of Funds

An important phenomenon of social sector expenditure is underspending of the allocated resources. Underspending hardly occurs in non-Plan expenditure, but it does occur in most years in most sectors in the Plan. Labour and employment is a big underspending sector, but the other sectors also underspend most of the years (Dev and Mooij 2002a, Table 14).

The problem is even worse when one looks at mid-year utilization rates. This has been done in a study by Rajaraman (2001a and b). The study focuses on some major schemes of the Ministry of Rural Development for the year 2000–1. The utilization rates of these funds, for most of the schemes, were less than 50 per cent of the funds allocated for the first six months. In other words, in the first six months, less than 25 per cent of the annual allocation was used. The utilization rate of the two major employment schemes (the Employment Assurance Scheme and Jawahar Gram Samridhi Yojana (JGSY), the successor of Jawahar Rozgar Yojana (JRY) was 42 per cent (of 50 per cent). This, according to Rajaraman, is especially surprising, 'since the first six months of the fiscal year from April encompass the agricultural slack season, when the demand for rural employment should be at its peak' (Rajaraman 2001a, p. 20). The utilization rates at the end of the year are, however, much higher 'suggesting hasty, wasteful utilization in the second half of the fiscal year' (Rajaraman 2001a, p. 20). Underutilization of funds seems to be more in the poorer states. 'A simple regression shows a statistically significant rise in the mean mid-year utilization rate of 4 per cent for every increase in the SDP of Rs 1000 per capita. The worse-off states are also less efficient in using JGSY funds' (Rajaraman 2001b). So although these schemes are meant to alleviate poverty, the poor states make less efficient use of them than the better-off states.

Several reasons may explain this underutilization. First, new schemes bring new guidelines and require new procedures. It takes time before the state governments or local bodies are fully aware of them and are able to fulfil the criteria. Second, for some schemes, the central government gives a grant that has to be complemented by matching funds from the states. If these matching funds are not available, the grants for the Centrally Sponsored Schemes will not be given. Third, there can be a deliberately created or unintentional delay in the central bureaucracy, with spillover effects for the following year's allocation (which is partly based on spending figures of the previous year). Fourth, some schemes presuppose the availability of local infrastructure, such as rural PHCs. If this infrastructure does not exist, schemes make no sense and funds are not allocated. Some central government schemes are also not relevant in each and every state. Fifth, there may be other forms of institutional disability or disinterest. State governments may not be able to get their act together and design a plan (for instance, for a rural road) and, therefore, can not receive the money. It may also be that low priority is given by some state governments to implement the schemes. This can be the case, for instance, when the states are ruled by a party that does not participate in the central government. It may also be that there is hidden or open opposition (Dev and Mooij 2002b).

Quality of Expenditure

One of the problems with social sector expenditure is the high share of revenue expenditure in overall expenditure. Revenue expenditure consists mainly of salaries, while capital expenditure refers to physical infrastructure (schools, hospitals, medical technology, etc.). Table 6.13 shows the upward trend of the revenue share. By the late 1990s, more than 95 per cent of overall social sector expenditure was revenue expenditure. This suggests a neglect of basic social sector infrastructure—something that is confirmed in, for instance, the Public Report on Basic Education (PROBE) report that reports of dilapidated schools, absence of toilets, lack of blackboards and other teaching equipment, etc. It might well be that the demotivating effects of the absence or poor condition of basic infrastructure on teachers, doctors, and others is as much as the demotivating effect of low salaries.

TABLE 6.13
Composition of Social Sector Expenditure

Year	Composition of social sector expenditure	
	Revenue	Capital
1986–7	91.05	8.95
1987–8	93.40	6.60
1988–9	94.07	5.93
1989–90	94.95	5.05
1990–1	95.09	4.91
1991–2	94.92	5.08
1992–3	95.21	4.79
1993–4	95.63	4.37
1994–5	94.70	5.30
1995–6	95.36	4.64
1996–7	95.31	4.69
1997–8	95.47	4.53
1998–9	95.20	4.80
1999–2000	95.50	4.50
2000–1	94.87	5.13
2001–2(R)	93.75	6.25
2002–3(B)	93.39	6.61

The neglect of infrastructure is surprising in view of the widespread preference of policy-makers to spend on infrastructure, rather than on salaries. In an earlier study (Dev and Mooij 2002b), we found that both bureaucrats and technocrats in the government prefer concrete targets. Spending on physical infrastructure gives concrete results, while the results of revenue expenditure are not or much less measurable. Even when there is corruption in capital investments, at the end of the day, there is a road, a hospital, or a power station. Nevertheless, despite this preference, the trend in the 1990s in the other direction: revenue expenditure going up and capital expenditure is going down.

Misuse and (In) Effective Use of Funds

There is no doubt that a substantial proportion of the money meant for general social development purposes or targeted anti-poverty interventions is misused. This is even acknowledged by the Government of India (GOI) itself. The mid-term appraisal of the Ninth Five-Year Plan is very critical about the implementation of many schemes. In fact, the sixth chapter (on poverty alleviation programmes) reads as a long list of various kinds of failures of the government to implement the schemes properly (GOI 2000). The Approach Paper to the Tenth Five-Year Plan states that there are serious deficiencies in the capability to design viable schemes and in the delivery system on the ground, and these can be 'regarded broadly as due to poor governance'. (GOI 2001, p. 48). On the other hand, there are also examples of states that have made considerable progress, sometimes even with limited funds.

EXPERIENCES OF SOME STATES

Kerala is often mentioned as an example of a state that has been able to achieve spectacular improvements in terms of basic needs and standards of living. The differences in success rates between Kerala and other states seem to lie more in the quality of educational and health facilities and the efficiency with which they are used than in a substantially higher allocation of resources.

Some people have attributed Kerala's success to historical reasons.[7] There is some truth in this argument, but it may also be noted that at the time that the State of Kerala was formed, the Malabar region was very much behind Travancore and Cochin in terms of its social development. Nevertheless, by the 1980s, the Malabar region had caught up with the other regions. It was primarily well-directed state action that was responsible for this improvement. Apart from this, public participation and local leadership have also played an important role. Social movements like caste-based reform movements (for example, the Izhava movement), missionary activities, and left movements have helped in raising human development and social security for the poor. Women have also played an active role in raising the levels of social development in the state.

Another positive example is Tamil Nadu, which has been a pioneer in the implementation of nutrition schemes and protective social security measures. There are two important state-sponsored special nutrition programmes in Tamil Nadu, namely, the Chief Minister's Nutrition Meal Programme (CMNMP) and the Tamil Nadu Integrated Nutrition Project (TNIP). The first programme, which is considered the largest feeding programme in the world, has increased the nutritional intake of many school-going children. The TNIP experience has showed that a limited package of health-linked nutrition interventions can be successful and that it does not need to be very costly.

Apart from Kerala and Tamil Nadu, some other states have also taken important initiatives. We can refer to the Employment Guarantee Scheme in Maharashtra, primary education in Himachal Pradesh and Madhya Pradesh, public distribution in Andhra Pradesh, and land reform in West Bengal. By contrast, the less developed

---

[7] See Ramachandran (1997) for a discussion of this argument.

states like Bihar and Uttar Pradesh seem to be characterized by apathy, rather than concerted public action. This may well be related to rather extreme forms of social inequality. As Dreze and Gazdar (1997, p. 106) remark in the context of Uttar Pradesh, 'the high concentration of power and privileges deriving from the combined effects of inequalities based on class, caste, and gender has made for an environment that is extremely hostile to change and broad based political participation'.

How to Improve Effectiveness in Social Sector Policy Implementation

A number of measures have been suggested to address recurrent problems of poor implementation and lack of political will. The most important of these measures are briefly discussed here. All these are, in a way, strategies to make the policy process more participatory and increase effective demand—in the political sense—for better government performance.

Decentralization

Among the important new legislations introduced in the 1990s are the 73rd and 74th Amendment to the Constitution, devolving power from the state government to rural and urban elected bodies. In order to empower and include women, there are provisions for reserving seats for women in the panchayats. The 73rd Amendment lists 29 subjects for devolution. These include some key social services, such as sanitation, health, and primary education, which are of immediate relevance to social development.

Decentralization has been advocated for several reasons. First, it is thought that decentralization could improve governance. Reducing the distance between those who plan and those who are supposed to benefit would help in raising accountability. Second, decentralization would enhance political participation and, therefore, deepen democracy. Third, decentralization would help to improve the quality and suitability of services, as programmes could become more needs-based when designed by the target group or by people who are in close contact with them, rather than by a state-level bureaucracy.

Based on these arguments, one would expect that decentralization would contribute to social development generally, and to poverty alleviation in particular. Mahal, Srivastava, and Sanan (2000) have tried to test whether decentralization in the area of health and education has, indeed, led to improved outcomes in rural India. Their conclusion is that 'indicators of democratization and public participation, such as frequency of elections, presence of non-governmental organizations, parent-teacher associations, and indicator variables for decentralized states generally have the expected positive effects, although these are not always statistically indistinguishable from zero'. The database used in this study was the 1994 survey by the NCAER, so the study captured interstate variation in decentralization, and not so much the impact of the 1992 Amendment to the Constitution.

In general, most scholars of decentralization in India emphasize that there are potential benefits for the poor, but that decentralization can also provide the rural rich with an additional arena in which they can assert their power (Mathew and Nayak 1996). In his review of the literature, Johnson (2003) states that 'studies of decentralization have consistently highlighted the fact that the 73rd Amendment and earlier attempts at decentralization have failed to prevent a local (and primarily landed) elite from controlling local *panchayats*. Micro-level studies have shown that *gram sabha* often fail to fulfil their role as deliberative bodies or as mechanism for accountability. (…) Even when there are reservations to ensure that marginal groups have a place in the *panchayat* system, there is evidence to suggest that these formal institutions have been usurped by more informal patterns of domination and power. Reservations for women, for instance, are notoriously prone to corruption by male relatives (…). Similar patterns have been observed among [Scheduled Castes and Scheduled Tribes], whose economic well being is dependent on the patronage of local elites'. Moreover, in actual practice, decentralization has sometimes taken place only with regard to the functions the state governments were no longer willing to perform. Decentralization can become a means of shedding government responsibilities, rather than of increasing meaningful participation. Experiences elsewhere have further shown that effective service delivery at the local level sometimes requires a strong central government that stimulates and fosters a culture of accountability between local officials and the poor (Moore and Putzel 2000, Tendler 1997). Altogether these observations suggest that, while decentralization may sometimes be helpful in increasing people's participation in policy implementation and may sometimes enhance the quality of service provision, there is no a priori reason to assume that it will always do so. In fact, it is an empirical—and very important-question as to which modes of decentralization, under which conditions, have led to what kind of effects on policy implementation and social development levels. Much more detailed research is necessary to shed light on this question.

Access to information

One way of increasing the accountability of panchayats, other local bodies, and the government delivery system in general, is the right to information. This right was first demanded by the people of Rajasthan. This struggle was initiated by the Mazdoor Kisan Shakti Sangathan, a people's organization working in central Rajasthan. The struggle, which began to gain momentum in 1994 through the organization of four public hearings stressing the need for transparency and a social audit of development expenditure, has subsequently spread to other parts of Rajasthan, and a variety of people and organizations have become involved. In recent years, the idea has also spread to some other states, and some state governments have introduced 'Right to Information' legislation.

NGOs and public–private partnerships

Community-based organizations (CBOs) and (NGOs) can play an important role in creating an environment for social mobilization and for sustainable human development. The main objective of social mobilization is to induce the poor or otherwise excluded categories of people to organize themselves, so that their voices become louder and can have more impact. This is absolutely necessary. Several decades of poor implementation have shown that it is not sufficient to rely on the government alone to implement social development policies. There has to be an effective demand from the potential beneficiaries as well, in order to force the government to do a better job. To a certain extent, the state can play a role in creating this demand, by providing full openness about what it intends to do, and also by designing policies in such a way that they may contribute to social mobilization and/or participation in policy making. This requires a different set of parameters in the policy design process. Rather than desired *outcomes* in the conventional sense—decreasing poverty rates, increasing literacy, etc.—planners and policy-makers should also plan for increased voice, knowledge, and inclusion through a strategic design of the policy *process*. The challenge is to (re)design government programmes in such a way that the process becomes more participatory, there is more scope for collective action, and there is a better chance for the creation of effective countervailing power (Moore and Putzel 2000).

An increasingly popular idea, especially in circles of international donors, is that NGOs, CBOs, and governments should work more closely together. The 2004 World Development Report on 'making services work for poor people' is partly dedicated to this theme of 'co-production' or 'public–private partnerships'. The rationale behind the idea is simple and appealing. Most states suffer from bureaucratization, corruption etc. On the other hand, civil society organizations are sometimes amateurish. Their activities lack sustainability and are sometimes of poor quality. Partnerships, it is argued by its advocates, can help in overcoming the weaknesses of both. Some successful examples exist, in India—for instance, the women's self-help groups in Andhra Pradesh, or health-focused NGOs through which the government implements its AIDS campaigns. On the other hand, critics have pointed out that, in actual practice, there are often a number of difficulties.[8] State bureaucracies and NGOs are usually characterized by different organizational cultures, and there may be a great deal of suspicion on both sides. Moreover, successful partnerships require strong NGOs or CBOs that are able to cooperate with the government on an equal basis. Partnerships can easily result in rift within the NGO-CBO world, as some organizations are selected while others are excluded. By reinforcing certain activities of NGOs and CBOs, partnerships are also likely to undermine their other activities which may be equally important but which are not funded, supported, or appreciated by the partner-government. Therefore, those within the government who advocate the idea of partnerships, as well as concerned social scientists, must first address the question about the conditions under which partnerships may work effectively, and without compromising the potential of the NGOs and the CBOs to challenge the government from the position of an outsider.

By Way of Conclusion

To conclude this chapter, a number of observations may be made. First, overall (centre and states taken together) anti-poverty and social development expenditure increased in the reform era in terms of per capita expenditure. As percentage of GDP and aggregate government expenditure, the picture is mixed. The question that immediately arises is whether the expenditure levels should be considered as high or low. The answer to this question depends on the yardstick, of course, but we can nevertheless conclude that the expenditure on the social sector is low, as compared with (a) the proportion of GDP India used to spend on the social sector in the late 1980s, (b) some other developing countries, and certainly with East Asian countries, and (c) the norms/rationales that are developed by the UNDP for comparing and monitoring social sector expenditure at the country level.

Second, the centre has done much better than the states. For both the centre and the states the trend growth rates in social sector spending was higher in the 1980s than in the 1990s. The trend growth rates for the centre are higher than the rates for the states. Altogether this means that the share of the states in overall (combined centre and states) social sector expenditure continues to

---

[8] See, for instance, Manor (2002)

come down. This is a worrisome development. It may indicate a declining commitment to social development on the part of the states. In the area of health it goes together with a shift in the emphasis from the normal (public) health services to vertical disease-related programmes.

Third, education expenditure from all departments declined as percentage of GDP from around 4.1 per cent in 1990–1 to 3.8 per cent in 1998–9. This is mainly due to a decline in expenditure at the state level. Within education, there is a shift towards expenditure on elementary education at the central level. There is no such trend at the state level. A further disaggregation shows that this increase is to a large extent (but not completely) related to the introduction and expansion of the midday meal scheme. Within the expenditure for health, there has been a shift towards mother and child related activities.

Fourth, there is an urgent need for stepping up social sector expenditure. At the same time, given the characteristics of the budget-making process (Mooij and Dev 2004), it is very unlikely that this is going to happen in the near future. A substantial increase in the allocation for the social sector is only likely to happen when something changes in the budget-making process. In that respect, movements towards decentralized planning and increasing awareness among the public about budgets are to be welcomed. They can play a very important role in involving a wider group of people in the budget-making process and, thereby, in changing the policy bias and the content of the allocation decisions.

Finally, there is an obvious need for a better utilization of the allocated money. As mentioned earlier, underutilization of funds, poor implementation, neglect of infrastructure, misuse of funds, and corruption are openly acknowledged in various policy documents. We have briefly discussed three strategies that are sometimes believed to improve effectiveness of policy implementation, but have also stressed that, unfortunately, there are no magic bullets. There is, however, a challenging research agenda. There are important questions regarding the conditions under which particular forms of decentralization or partnerships produce the desired results. There are equally relevant questions about how particular designs of policies could promote social mobilization or other forms of public action. Such studies are necessary as strategic inputs in the process of policy formulation, so that policy-makers can start planning not only for desired outcomes, but also for more public demand and a more inclusive policy process.

References

Chelliah, R. J. and R. Sudarshan (1999), *Income Poverty and Beyond: Human Development in India*, Social Science Press, New Delhi.

Dev, S. Mahendra and Jos Mooij (2002a), 'Social sector expenditures in the 1990s. An analysis of central and state budgets', *Economic and Political Weekly*, Vol. 37, No. 9, pp. 853–66.

———— (2002b), 'Social Sector Expenditures and Budgeting: An Analysis of Patterns and the Budget making process in India in the 1990s', Working Paper No. 43, Centre for Economic and Social Studies, Hyderabad.

Dreze, Jean and Amartya Sen (eds) (1997), *Indian Development: Selected Regional Perspectives*, Oxford University Press, New Delhi.

———— (1995), *Economic Development and Social Opportunities*, Oxford University Press, New Delhi.

Dreze, Jean and Haris Gazdar (1997), 'Uttar Pradesh: the burden of inertia', in Jean Dreze and Amartya Sen (eds), *Indian Development: Selected Regional Perspectives*, Oxford University Press, New Delhi, pp. 33–128.

Government of India (2001), *Approach Paper to the Tenth Five Year Plan (2002–2007)*, Planning Commission, Government of India, New Delhi.

———— (2000), *Mid-Term Appraisal of Ninth 5-Year Plan, 1997–2002*, Planning Commission, Government of India, New Delhi.

HAQ (2001), *India's Children and the Union Budget*, published by HAQ, Centre for Child Rights, Supported by Save the Children, New Delhi.

Johnson, Craig (2003), 'Decentralization in India: Poverty, Politics and *Panchayats*', ODI Working Paper No. 199, Overseas Development Institute, London.

Mahal, Ajay, Vivek Srivastava, and Deepak Sanan (2000), 'Decentralization and Public Sector Delivery of Health and Education Services: The Indian Experience', ZEF Discussion Paper No. 20, Centre for Development Research, Bonn.

Manor, James (2002), 'Partnerships between Governments and Civil Society for Service Delivery in Less Developed Countries: Cause for Concern', Background Paper for DFID–World Bank workshop in support of the 2004 World Development Report, Eynsham Hall, Oxfordshire, 4–5 November 2002.

Mathew, George and Ramesh C. Nayak (1996), 'Panchayats at work. What it means for the oppressed', *Economic and Political Weekly*, Vol. 31, No. 27, pp. 1765–71.

Mooij, J. and S. Mahendra Dev (2004), 'Social Sector Priorities: An Analysis of Budgets and Expenditures in India in the 1990', *Development Policy Review*, Vol. 22, No. 1, pp. 97–120, Overseas Development Institute.

Moore, Mick and James Putzel (2000), 'Thinking Strategically about Politics and Poverty', IDS Working Paper No. 101, Institute of Development Studies, Sussex.

Mundle, S. and M. G. Rao (1997), 'Public Expenditure in India:

Trends and Issues', in S. Mundle (ed.), *Public Finance: Policy Issues for India*, Oxford University Press, New Delhi.

Prabhu, Seeta (2001), *Economic Reform and Social Sector Development. A Study of Two Indian States*, Sage, New Delhi.

——— (1997), 'Social Sector Expenditures in India: Trends and Implications', Background Paper for UNDP.

PROBE Team (1999), *Public Report on Basic Education in India*, Oxford University Press, New Delhi.

Rajaraman, Indira (2001a), 'Growth-Accelerating Fiscal Devolution to the Third Tier', paper presented at the Conference on Fiscal Policies to Accelerate Economic Growth, organized by the World Bank, 21–2 May 2001, New Delhi (www.fiscalconf.org).

——— (2001b), 'Expenditure Reform', *The Economic Times*, 10 May 2001.

Ramachandran, V. K. (1997), 'On Kerala's Development Achievements', in Dreze and Sen (eds), *Indian Development: Selected Regional Perspectives*, Oxford University Press, New Delhi.

Saxena, N. C. and John Farrington (2002), 'Trends and Prospects for Poverty Reduction in Rural India: Context and Options', paper presented at Rural Livelihood Futures Workshop, 17–19 October 2002, New Delhi.

Tendler, Judith (1997), *Good Government in the Tropics*, John Hopkins University Press, Baltimore and London.

Tilak, J. B. G. (2001), 'Public Subsidies in the Education Sector in India', paper presented at the Conference on Fiscal Policies to Accelerate Economic Growth, organized by the World Bank, 21–2 May 2001, New Delhi (www.fiscalconf.org).

UNDP (1997), *India: Road to Human Development*, New Delhi Office, June 1997.

Table 6.A1
All State Social Sector Expenditures as per cent of GDP

	Edu, sports, art & cul etc.	Health & fam. wel	Water supply sanitation	Total others	Social services	Rural develop	Social sector
1980–1	2.19	1.12	0.00	1.08	4.39	0.00	4.39
1981–2	2.16	1.16	0.00	1.04	4.36	0.00	4.36
1982–3	2.34	1.24	0.00	1.22	4.79	0.00	4.79
1983–4	2.31	1.30	0.00	1.16	4.77	0.00	4.77
1984–5	2.40	1.30	0.00	1.19	4.89	0.00	4.89
1985–6	2.49	1.01	0.31	1.26	5.08	0.80	5.87
1986–7	2.53	0.88	0.49	1.30	5.20	0.93	6.13
1987–8	2.58	0.91	0.49	1.32	5.30	0.93	6.23
1988–9	2.64	0.87	0.43	1.21	5.15	0.88	6.03
1989–90	2.85	0.85	0.37	1.11	5.18	0.60	5.78
1990–1	2.78	0.85	0.35	1.16	5.14	0.84	5.98
1991–2	2.66	0.82	0.36	1.18	5.01	0.84	5.85
1992–3	2.61	0.79	0.35	1.08	4.84	0.87	5.72
1993–4	2.55	0.81	0.36	1.02	4.74	0.86	5.61
1994–5	2.52	0.76	0.38	1.01	4.67	0.70	5.37
1995–6	2.47	0.74	0.34	1.18	4.73	0.57	5.30
1996–7	2.45	0.72	0.34	1.11	4.63	0.58	5.21
1997–8	2.48	0.74	0.37	1.12	4.71	0.58	5.29
1998–9	2.66	0.76	0.40	1.13	4.95	0.62	5.57
1999–2000	2.92	0.78	0.37	1.13	5.21	0.57	5.78
2000–1	2.89	0.77	0.41	1.21	5.28	0.54	5.82
2001–2	2.84	0.80	0.42	1.42	5.48	0.63	6.11

Table 6.A2
All States Social Sector Expenditure as per cent of Total Expenditure

	Edu, sports, art & cul etc.	Health & fam. wel	Water supply sanitation	Total others	Social services	Rural develop	Social sector
1980–1	17.48	8.93	0.00	8.60	35.01	0.00	35.01
1981–2	17.64	9.43	0.00	8.46	35.53	0.00	35.53
1982–3	18.37	9.72	0.00	9.59	37.68	0.00	37.68
1983–4	18.03	10.13	0.00	9.10	37.25	0.00	37.25
1984–5	17.74	9.56	0.00	8.81	36.12	0.00	36.12
1985–6	18.13	7.33	2.29	9.18	36.92	5.81	42.73
1986–7	17.76	6.19	3.42	9.14	36.51	6.55	43.06
1987–8	17.66	6.26	3.33	9.04	36.29	6.34	42.64
1988–9	18.73	6.21	3.03	8.62	36.59	6.27	42.86
1989–90	20.29	6.08	2.66	7.91	36.94	4.30	41.24
1990–1	19.52	5.95	2.46	8.14	36.07	5.91	41.99
1991–2	18.03	5.54	2.43	8.01	34.00	5.70	39.71
1992–3	18.31	5.54	2.47	7.58	33.90	6.13	40.03
1993–4	17.98	5.70	2.52	7.21	33.41	6.09	39.57
1994–5	17.47	5.31	2.64	7.00	32.42	4.88	37.30
1995–6	17.96	5.41	2.47	8.55	34.39	4.14	38.53
1996–7	18.00	5.27	2.52	8.16	33.94	4.26	38.20
1997–8	18.00	5.38	2.72	8.16	34.26	4.18	38.44
1998–9	19.04	5.45	2.86	8.10	35.45	4.45	39.91
1999–2000	19.67	5.26	2.52	7.61	35.06	3.87	38.93
2000–1	18.68	5.00	2.64	7.85	34.17	3.51	37.68
2001–2	17.63	4.94	2.57	8.82	33.97	3.89	37.86
2002–3	16.86	4.77	2.43	8.53	32.60	3.97	36.56

TABLE 6.A3
All States Per Capita Real Expenditure (at 1993–4 prices) on Social Sector

	Edu, sports, art & cul etc.	Health & fam. wel	Water supply sanitation	Total others	Social services	Rural develop	Social sector
1980–1	126	64	0	62	252	0	252
1981–2	130	70	0	63	263	0	263
1982–3	147	78	0	77	301	0	301
1983–4	154	86	0	78	318	0	318
1984–5	165	89	0	82	335	0	335
1985–6	181	73	23	92	369	58	427
1986–7	190	66	37	98	391	70	461
1987–8	200	71	38	102	410	72	482
1988–9	221	73	36	102	432	74	506
1989–90	251	75	33	98	456	53	509
1990–1	254	77	32	106	469	77	546
1991–2	240	74	32	107	454	76	530
1992–3	242	73	33	100	447	81	528
1993–4	245	78	34	98	455	83	539
1994–5	248	75	37	99	460	69	529
1995–6	260	78	36	124	497	60	557
1996–7	278	81	39	126	525	66	591
1997–8	294	88	44	133	559	68	627
1998–9	334	96	50	142	622	78	700
1999–2000	386	103	50	149	688	76	764
2000–1	378	101	53	159	691	71	762
2001–2	387	109	57	194	746	85	831
2002–3	378	107	55	191	731	89	820

7 India's Patent Policy and Political Economy of Development

Anitha Ramanna[1]

> Instead of 'publish or perish', our new slogan is 'patent, publish, and prosper'.... We must patent every new innovation before publishing.... We lost out because we did not patent.
> —R. A. Mashelkar, Director General, CSIR, India

India's policy on patents is currently undergoing a shift that reflects changes not only in the corporate sector, but also within major public sector research institutions in India. The Indian Council for Scientific and Industrial Research (CSIR), the coordinating body for over 40 scientific institutes in India, played a key role in setting the framework for patent reforms in the country. India's Patent Act of 1970 had established that India granted only process and not product patents in pharmaceuticals. India amended this provision with the Patent Amendment Acts of 1999 and 2002 by enabling the filing of patent applications on pharmaceutical products. This amendment to India's Patent Law emerged after enormous opposition to reform by some NGOs and some domestic private sector firms. The pharmaceutical companies in India who benefited from India's 1970 Patent Act opposed the reform, while NGOs protested against the implications of patents on the price of medicines and seeds, on biodiversity, and on local communities. The CSIR's stance was important in leading to a turnaround in the opposition to patent reform in India that arose from these groups.

The CSIR and other public sector research institutions in India adopted a proactive role on patents, unlike the opposition to some aspects of liberalization found among the public sector taken as a whole.[2] According to one study of the reform in various countries, 'Frequently, the most vociferous opposition to change in policy comes not from interest groups, legislators, or voters, but from ministers and bureaucrats within the government or even from the executive himself' (Haggard and Webb 1994). In India's case, Kohli (1990) points out that, 'Opposition to the reform came from organized working class in the public sector'. In the evidence of public sector opposition to some aspects of liberalization, what factors explain the reasons for public sector research institutions to promote patent reform? What does this revision in strategy and the role of public sector scientific institutes mean for India's development policy agenda? This chapter focuses on India's patent policy shifts, and the changing role of public sector research institutions within this framework, to evaluate its implications for setting of development priorities in India.

India recently revised its long standing Patent Act of 1970 with amendments in 1999 and 2002. These changes represent a shift in India's policy of restricting the scope, term, and subject matter of patentability. The major explanation forwarded for India's policy change is that of external pressure arising out of India's signing the TRIPs (Trade Related Intellectual Property Rights Agreement) of the World Trade Organization (WTO). TRIPs stipulated that India must revise its patent laws, and trade

---

[1] Anitha Ramanna is a lecturer with the department of politics and public administration, University of Pune. E-mail: anithar@unipune.ernet.in. The author would like to thank Kirit Parikh and Veena Mishra for their comments and Rijo John for providing useful research assistance. The author bears sole responsibility for any errors.

[2] In this study, 'public sector' essentially focuses on public sector research institutions.

threats from the USA were a major factor in promoting the change.[3] It is not so widely acknowledged, however, that the change in the interests of the domestic actors has also played an important role in leading to the new policy. Currently, a strong pro-patent lobby exists in India which points out that greater patent protection would lead to an increase in foreign direct investment (FDI), transfer of technology, and R&D by foreign companies, and would enable domestic actors to become more innovative and acquire patents. This new constituency supporting reform arose not only from the domestic private sector or the MNCs, but also from important public sector research institutions in India. One of the leading proponents of this reform was the CSIR. This leads us to some of the basic questions surrounding the interests and role of the public sector in the post-liberalization scenario. This chapter attempts to address some of these issues within the patent policy changes taking shape in India.

Economic Costs and Benefits of Patents

Intellectual Property Rights (IPRs) are limited property rights over information resources and come in various forms including patents, copyrights, trademarks, etc. Patents are a form of IPRs that protect industrial inventions and grant the inventor the right to exclude others from making, using, or selling his/her invention for a limited period. Patents, in economic terms, can be seen as a trade-off. A legal monopoly is granted to the inventor in exchange for the disclosure of the invention and the gains from investing. It is argued that without IPRs, the inventor would not have an incentive to invest in the creation of information or to disclose the invention. This arises mainly due to what is known as the 'free-rider' problem where each individual wants others to supply the product in the hope of free-riding the latter (Panagariya 1995). Information is a public good and has the characteristic of non-exclusion, that is, once a good has been supplied, individuals can access it free of charge (Panagariya 1995). Due to the free-rider problem, there may be underinvestment in developing useful products. Patents are a means to solve the free-rider problem by providing the inventor with a legal right to his invention for a specified period and ensuring that others cannot copy his/her invention. It is claimed that patents lead to greater R & D, investment, and innovation.

Since a patent involves granting a monopoly right to the inventor, there are economic costs associated with IPRs. These include:

[3] Analysts have drawn linkages between the threat of US special 301 law against India and India's charge of stance on patents in GATT. See, Krishna Iyer et al. (1996).

(1) impact on price. If an inventor has a patent on a new drug he may restrict the production of the drug to make monopoly profits. The price will exceed the marginal cost of production and the drug will be undersupplied relative to the optimum level (Panagariya 1995);

(2) rent-seeking activities such as the race for patents whereby inventors pursue the discovery of a product simultaneously (Panagariya 1995);

(3) costs of enforcement and protection; and

(4) distortion. This may lead to the diversion of resources from important aspects of research to more patentable areas.

Patent System in India

India's patent system is based on the Patent Act of 1970. The major features of the Indian Patent Act of 1970 are (adapted from Vedaraman 1977):

(1) Patentability of inventions relating to substances intended for use as food, drug, medicines, or substances produced by chemical process will be limited to claims for the methods or processes of manufacture only;

(2) Compulsory licences and licence of rights can be granted. Compulsory licences enabling another party to work the patent can be applied for any time after the expiry of three years from the date of sealing of the patent. In the area of food, drug, medicine, or chemicals, after the expiry of three years from the date of patent grant, they shall be endorsed with the word 'License of Right'. This will enable any interested person to be entitled to work such patents as a matter of right;

(3) Certain types of inventions will not be patentable. They included:

(a) an invention which is frivolous or which claims anything obviously contrary to establish natural laws;

(b) an invention, the primary or intended use of which would be contrary to law or morality or injurious to public health;

(c) the mere discovery of a scientific principle or the formulation of an abstract theory;

(d) the mere discovery of any new property or new use for a known substance or of the mere use of a known process, machine, or apparatus unless such known process results in a new product or employs at least one new reactant;

(e) a substance obtained by a mere admixture resulting only in aggregation of the properties of the compounds thereof or a process for producing such substance;

(f) the mere arrangement or re-arrangement or duplication of known devices each functioning independently of one another in a known way;

(g) a method or process of testing applicable during the process of manufacture for rendering the machine, apparatus, or other equipment more efficient or for the improvement or control of manufacture;

(h) a method of agriculture or horticulture; and

(i) any process for the medicinal, surgical, curative, prophylactic or other treatment of human beings; or any process for a similar treatment of animals or plants to render them free of disease or to increase their economic value or that of their products'.

(4) Term of patent will be 14 years from the date of patenting, that is, the date of filing the complete specification. In the case of inventions in the field of food, drug, or medicine, the term will be seven years from the date of filing or five years from the date of sealing, whichever is shorter.

The Patent Act of 1970 was amended in 1999 and 2002 resulting in changes in some of these provisions. The Controller General of Patents, Designs, and Trademarks under the Department of Industrial Development, Ministry of Industry, is the administrative authority on patents in India. Patent Offices are located in New Delhi, Mumbai, and Chennai with the head office being based in Kolkata. The patent application must be filed in the appropriate Patent Office and the process consists of several stages. The inventor must first ensure that his/her invention meets the criteria of novelty and non-obviousness and conduct a search to establish the state of knowledge relating to the invention (known as prior art). The inventor then files a patent application with provisional specification before any public disclosure of the invention (Ganguli 1998). The Patent Act of 1970 laid down the following procedures in relation to patent applications and some of these provisions may be modified with the Amendments to the Patent Act in 1999 and 2002. The provisional specification contains the broad aspects of the patentable invention and the inventor has 12 months (extendable to 15 months with a fee) to file a complete specification (Ganguli 1998). The patent application should contain the title, the inventor's name and address, the abstract, and a text defining the claims made. The text may also contain tables, drawings, etc. to support the claims. A technical examination of the application is conducted by the Patent Office and, if accepted, it is published in the Gazette of India, which is published weekly from New Delhi (Ganguli 1998). Interested parties who consider that the patent has been wrongfully granted can oppose the patent within four months from the date of advertisement of the acceptance of the complete specification. If no opposition is filed, the patent is granted and the inventor must file for the sealing of the patent no later than six months from the date of advertisement of the acceptance of the complete specification. The patent is then granted and the inventor must pay annual renewal fees to keep the patent in force.

INDIA'S PATENT POLICY SHIFT

India established its Patent Act in 1970 after detailed study and forethought to the role of patents in the overall development agenda. The history of patents in India actually dates back to 1856, but policy-makers turned their attention seriously towards patents only immediately after independence. Two expert committees were established in independent India to study patents and provide suggestions on the type of patent system that India should implement. The Patent Enquiry Committee (1948–50) and the Ayyangar Committee (1957–9) suggested that a patent system that focused on access to resources at lower prices would be beneficial to India. This was in tune with the S&T mission of developing indigenous technology and fostering R&D activities in areas of national significance. The Patent Act of 1970, the current legislation on patents in India, was based on the recommendations of these committees. The main aim in India was to ensure that patents should not lead to monopoly by foreign companies or to high prices for medicines and food items. India sought to ensure this in its Patent Act by granting only process and not product patents in food, pharmaceutical, and chemical fields, restricting the term of patents, and formulating an elaborate system of licences to ensure that patents are worked in India. In tune with this policy, India refused to join the main international treaty on patents—the Paris Convention—as it stipulated higher standards of patent protection.

The statement by Indira Gandhi at the World Health Assembly in 1982 that, 'The idea of a better-ordered world is one in which medical discoveries will be free of patents and there will be no profiteering from life and death' (quoted in Lanjow 1997), symbolized India's stance on patents. In India, patents were seen more as a tool for economic development. Industrialized nations conceive of patents as a fundamental right comparable to the right of physical property, whereas developing nations view it 'fundamentally as an economic policy question' (Gradbow and Richards 1988). From the perspective of developed countries, intellectual property is a private right that should be protected as any other tangible property, but for developing nations, intellectual property is a public good that should be used to promote economic development (Stewart 1993).

India's philosophy on patents underwent a revision with the Patent Amendment Acts of 1999 and 2002. India also joined the Paris Convention and the Patent Cooperation Treaty in 1998. The amendments led to revisions in India's policy on granting only process and not product patents in pharmaceutical and agro-chemical fields, increasing the term of patents to 20 years as demanded by TRIPs, and restricting the system of licences found in India's Patent Act. Table 7.1 outlines the major changes resulting from the amendments.

various aspects of TRIPs. India was one of the most vocal opponents of TRIPs and demonstrated enormous resistance to patent reform. The puzzle then is why did India adopt reforms on patents?

Two perspectives in international relations theory—neo-realism and neo-liberalism—offer different explanations for policy change (Sell 1995). While neo-realism focuses on compliance of weak states with more powerful ones as a reason for policy change, neo-liberalism focuses more on the redefinition of interests to explain change. A neo-realist-based assessment of India's policy shift would focus on the role of bilateral and multilateral

TABLE 7.1
Major Changes to India's Patent Law

India's Patent Act of 1970	Amendments to Patent Act, 1999 and 2002
Only process and not product patents allowed on medicines, food, agro-chemicals	Applications allowed for product patents in medicines, food, agro-chemicals and Exclusive Marketing Rights introduced
Term of patents 14 years; 5–7 in chemicals, drugs	Term of patents 20 years
Compulsory licensing and licence of right (these provisions allow governments to issue licences to allow other companies to make a patented product or use a patented process without the consent of the patent owner under certain circumstances)	No licences of right; Compulsory licensing allowed but more restricted
Government allowed to use patented invention to prevent scarcity and included 'right to sell goods' Government had to notify the patentee of use 'unless it appears to the Government that it would be contrary to the public interest to do so' Royalty payment not to exceed 4 per cent of price	Right of government restricted to 'right to sell on non-commercial basis' Government must notify patentee of use 'except in the case of national emergency or other circumstances of extreme emergency or for non-commercial use' Not more than adequate renumeration taking into account economic value of patent

Source: Indian Patent Act 1970, Patent (Amendment) Act 2002, Patent (Amendment) Act 1999, Chaudhuri (2002), Cullet (2002).

Provisions were also included to protect the Indian systems of medicine and to protect public health. The amendments essentially pave the way for full product patents in pharmaceuticals and agro-chemicals, which must be granted according to TRIPs, from 2005.

EXPLAINING INDIA'S PATENT POLICY REFORMS

Evaluating the reasons for India's policy revision is important in providing the background for the role of the public sector in the reform process. Understanding that reform took place in India not only due to coercion, but also due to shifts in the interests of the actors—including the public sector research institutions—enables us to evaluate more clearly how strategy changes within these institutions will affect the development agenda. It is interesting to explore the reasons for India's patent reforms when there existed a strong domestic constituency that favoured India's Patent Act. This lobby consisted of both powerful domestic companies who benefited from India's policy and NGOs who opposed

trade threats utilized by the USA against India to coerce India to change its patent laws. The use of Special 301 trade legislation by the USA against India and the multilateral trade pressure under the WTO would be analysed as the factors responsible for policy change. Neo-liberal accounts would look into the changing nature of interests within India and the possible benefits that India now perceives from revising its patent system. While not denying the role of external trade pressure, this chapter points out that policy change took place only with the change in the interests of the important actors. It is difficult to clearly state whether policy change takes place due to coercion or from the ability of actors to redefine their interests. As pointed out by Sell (1995) '...the distinction between power and learning is hardly black and white'. In India's case, while the threat of trade sanctions both bilaterally and within the WTO was important, the changing mindsets of the actors was also significant. The ability of Indian innovators, particularly in the field of IT, to amass fortunes must have reverberated through to other scientists who could also envision monetary gains and ways to be globally competitive from intellectual property. Rather than trying to decipher the relationship between trade pressure and shifting interests, it is more important for us to recognize that both the factors were significant in leading to policy change. Analysing the role of the rise of this pro-patent lobby also enables us to have a more nuanced understanding of the nature of changes shaping development policy.

Opposition to Patent Reform

The TRIPs Agreement was concluded in 1994 as a result of the Uruguay Round Negotiations. In order to comply with TRIPs and join the WTO by 1994–5, India was required to establish legislation that would allow for applications for agro-chemical and pharmaceutical product patents and grant EMRs (exclusive marketing rights),[4] though India was given time till 2005 to actually grant product patents. In spite of this requirement and trade pressure by the USA, India could not pass a legislation to revise its laws due to domestic opposition. The government issued an ordinance in 1994 to comply with TRIPs requirements (an ordinance does not require immediate assent by the legislature but has to be passed in six months). However, when the government attempted to introduce a legislation to put the ordinance into effect, it failed to get it passed in the Upper House of the Parliament. Two important lobbies, namely pharmaceutical companies and NGOs, played a role in blocking reform and, from 1994 to 1998, they were able to prevent a change in India's patent law.

Pharmaceutical companies benefited from India's Patent Act and, therefore, voiced strong opposition to reform. Through the provisions provided in the Patent Act and other measures, the pharmaceutical industry in India grew from just a handful of MNC players to today's 16,000 licensed pharmaceutical companies (Smith 2000). As pointed out by one analyst, the structure of the Indian Patent Act has enabled India to achieve self-sufficiency in the production of bulk drugs, and the prices of most drugs in India are lower than in other countries (Alam 1996). Thus when pressure arose for reform, the domestic industry in India began to mobilize to counter India's policy shift in global negotiations on IPRs. Pharmaceutical companies and other interested parties established an organization to lobby the government against changing patent laws. In 1988, the National Working Group on Patent Laws was established in India as a lobby (Alam 1996). Composed of experts from science, law, and health industries, the lobby was supported by certain industry groups and was influential at the government level in fostering resistance against change. The National Working Group mobilized a lobby within the Parliament known as the Forum of Parliamentarians (a group of legislators from various parties) that played a crucial role in defeating the bill introduced to amend India's Patent Act.

A second powerful lobby opposing reform came from NGOs who focused on the bio-piracy issue, turning it into a prominent argument against reforming patent laws in India. Bio-piracy refers to the utilization of traditional knowledge or resources by industrialized nations to create profitable products without compensation. NGOs effectively raised public opinion in India against patent reforms by pointing out that IPR laws enable companies to acquire patents based on local resources and knowledge, but that these resources are taken freely without any recognition of the contributions of farmers and local communities. Their campaign was launched not only in India, but also globally, with the *neem* issue. Neem is a common tree in India that has a variety of pesticidal, medicinal, and other uses. W. R. Grace, a company based in the USA, acquired a patent in 1992 covering the method of extracting the active ingredient in neem and stabilizing it for longer shelf life in the US Patent Office. In 1995 over 200 organizations led by various activists including Vandana Shiva (a prominent activist in India against IPRs) and the leader of a farmers' lobby in India filed a petition in the United States Patent and Trademark Office (USPTO) requesting the withdrawal of the patent (*Science* 1995). This petition was dismissed but led to an enormous public outburst both in India and in other countries on the implications of patents on traditional knowledge/genetic resources. It enabled the NGOs to effectively turn around the accusation by MNCs against Indian 'piracy' by claiming that the real pirates were the MNCs themselves.

Rise of Actors that Promoted Reform

A domestic policy shift, along with multilateral trade pressure, led to revisions in India's patent laws in 1998–9. Multilateral trade pressure was placed on India through the Dispute Settlement Body of the WTO. The USA filed a case with the WTO for India's failure to implement TRIPs and the WTO ruled that India must reform its laws by April 1999. The patent amendment bill allowing for EMRs for drugs and agro-chemical products—similar to the one which had been proposed in 1995 and had been defeated—was passed by the Parliament in March 1999. The WTO ruling that India must

---

[4] A transition to product patents that gives the firm the exclusive right to sell the product for five years.

comply with TRIPs by April 1999 did play an important role in the timing of the legislation and the initiation of policy change by the ruling party, but the emergence of new lobbies was important in securing the policy change.

The pro-patent lobby that arose in India was composed of various actors. One of these groups consisted of political parties. With the initiation of economic liberalization in 1991, sections of the Congress Party began favouring changes in patent laws. The BJP, after coming to power in 1998, abandoned its opposition to patent reform and adopted a pro-patent position. Although opposition to reform existed within both the parties, the BJP and the Congress eventually ensured the dominance of the groups within their parties and the affiliations that favoured change on patents (*Economic Times* 1998, *Deccan Herald* 1999). A second group, closely related to this pro-reform element within political parties was the rise of a more 'modern' and professionally managed segment of industry in India. The gradual emergence of a technologically more advanced segment among industrial companies was an important factor in promoting economic liberalization in India (Pedersen 2000). In tune with this pro-reform policy, during the 1990s, important industry bodies such as the Confederation of Indian Industry (CII) and the Federation of Indian Chambers of Commerce and Industry (FICCI) began to advocate the need for greater patent protection in India. A component of this change within industry bodies arose from some domestic firms who prospered under the existing patent structure, but came to visualize significant avenues for profit from the new patent regime. Dr Reddy's Laboratories, which has been preparing for the change in patent policy since 1984, believes that it has a competitive edge in new drug discovery which will lead to its growth under the revised policy (Smith 2000). Interviews with several Indian and MNC subsidiary firms and two industry associations conducted by Lanjouw revealed a shift in the debate on patents in India around 1997–8. Comparing with the situation that had existed just a year before, she notes, 'No one any longer expressed doubt that India would, in fact, be in compliance with WTO intellectual property requirements when deadlines were reached…', and that, 'recent interviews indicated that there was an entirely new debate underway in the country on whether India should voluntarily skip the end of the period under EMR and go straight for product patents' (Lanjow 2001). A third section arose from within the NGOs that took an alternative view of patents from that of the existing groups, thus paving the way for changes in India. These organizations made the case that measures could be devised to prevent bio-piracy while reforming patent laws. These NGOs promoted the view that traditional knowledge keepers and barefoot innovators should benefit from their efforts and that opposing reform would have denied them rewards. They suggested steps such as the requirement for the disclosure of the origin of the material in patent applications, documentation of traditional knowledge, and registration of the innovations of communities as ways to promote India's skills in local scientific knowledge while conforming with global IPR regimes. Organizations like the Society for Research and Initiatives for Sustainable Technologies and Institutions (Sristi) run by Anil Gupta and the Foundation for Revitalization of Local Health Traditions (FRLHT) influenced by Madhav Gadgil took different positions from that of the NGOs that opposed patents. Anil Gupta, for example, in one of his publications, makes the case that 'there is a genuine case for reforms of patent regime' and what is needed is a system requiring full disclosure regarding the origin of patents based on local knowledge or resources involving prior informed consent and benefit sharing (Gupta 1999). The rise of this pro-patent lobby required the articulation of a strategy to protect traditional knowledge in order to ensure patent reform. Changes in outlook towards patent protection in high technology fields could not have taken place in India if they were not accompanied by measures to protect traditional knowledge. The CSIR played an important part in framing the outline of a new strategy.

Public Sector Research Institutions and Patent Policy Shift

The CSIR, with its chain of 40 laboratories, played a crucial role in creating an atmosphere that supported patent reform in India. In January 1999, Atal Behari Vajpayee, who was then the prime minister, stated, 'I compliment CSIR for creating an intellectual climate supportive of the early passage of the bill to amend the Patents Act' (quoted in Kanavi 1999). The CSIR's role in promoting policy change occurred both through promoting a shift from publishing to patenting in research institutions and through the formulation of a strategy to counter the bio-piracy threat.

Promoting Patent Activity

Tracing the CSIR's role in promoting patent activity takes us back to the CSIR's current director, Mashelkar's, tenure as director of the National Chemical Laboratory (NCL) of which he became director in 1989 (Jolly 2001). At this time NCL did not have a single patent, and publications rather than patents brought recognition. Mashelkar initiated a change by convincing his colleagues at NCL that, while the output of the laboratory in terms of science was excellent, it had not staked its claim in technology markets with patents (*Business India* 1999). Mashelkar advised his colleagues to scan patent databases before they started a research project, and file a patent before publishing the results of their research (Kanavi 1999). 'He replaced the old adage in science 'publish and perish' with a new slogan 'patent, publish, and prosper' and tom-tommed it constantly and today it has caught on all over CSIR' (Kanavi 1999). The CSIR laboratories began increasing their patent filings after 1998–9 coinciding with the shift in the CSIR policy that required the laboratories to earn a significant portion of their budgets through research sponsored by industries (Ganguli 1998). Between 1992–7 the CSIR filed 920 patents in India and 120 abroad, filing 110 applications abroad in 1998–9 (Jolly 2001, Kanavi 1999).

The CSIR played the key role, but it is clear that other public sector research institutions also began to focus on patenting. The Department of Biotechnology established a Patent Facilitating Cell in July 1999, 'to create awareness and understanding about Intellectual Property Rights (IPRs) among scientists and researchers, by arranging workshops, seminars, conferences, etc. at all levels and for introducing patent information as a vital input in the process of formulation of R&D programmes in biotechnology and providing patenting facilities to biotechnologists in the country, for filing Indian and foreign patents on a continuous basis' (http:/dbtindia.nic.in/). The Indian Council of Medical Research (ICMR) has also created an IPR cell. The Indian Council of Agricultural Research (ICAR) established an Intellectual Property Section that began functioning in 1998 (ICAR 2001). The shift in thinking is clear from the framing of a manual on patent applications by the ICAR. Its prior policy agenda and recent change on patents is evident from the following introduction to the manual:

> The council has served as the lighthouse for free exchange of genetic material and technology with the rest of the world, respecting the global interdependence for food and agriculture… No doubt, the national agriculture has advanced in terms of technology and practices but the mind set for protection and commercialization of technology was hardly there. However, with the emerging intellectual property rights regimes under new and upcoming legislations, in conformity with the global developments and inter-governmental agreements, there is an urgent need to understand and analyse the situation to suitably change our attitude towards protecting the intellectual property developed in the ICAR and SAU+ systems for not only commercial gains but also to support further research and development in agriculture. It is the duty of all ICAR scientists and technical officers to make best efforts to compete and excel in their respective areas so as to bring credits to their own names and that of the Council. They should also give importance to systematic protection of the intellectual property developed by them during the entire period of their service whether in the ICAR laboratories/fields or in collaboration with other partners having the ICAR funded projects' (ICAR 2001).

DEFEATING THE BIO-PIRACY ARGUMENT AGAINST PATENT REFORM

The second role played by the CSIR was to legally challenge a patent in the USA on turmeric, thereby creating a means to defeat the bio-piracy argument against reforming patent laws. India's ability to defeat a patent that was the source of debate on bio-piracy led to new thinking that enabled a more pro-patent view. In 1995 a patent was granted in the USA on the process of using turmeric as a healing agent. Turmeric or *haldi* is a plant with medicinal properties that grows abundantly in India and which is routinely used to help wounds heal faster. When this patent came to light in India, the government responded quickly to ensure that the criticism it had received on the neem case did not emerge again. The CSIR gathered documents to prove that knowledge of the wound healing properties of turmeric had been documented in India. It was pointed out that as far back as in 1953 the wound healing properties of turmeric were reported in the Journal of the Indian Medical Association by scientists who had tested it in King George's Medical College in India (*The Times of India* 1996). The CSIR challenged the patent in the USPTO in 1996 and was able to get the patent revoked in 1997. This case was touted as a victory for India and as evidence of the fact that India could legally oppose such patents and there was nothing to fear in terms of patents exploiting traditional knowledge. The CSIR claimed, 'This success story strongly sends signals that if patent cases are fought on well-argued and well-supported techno-legal grounds, then there is nothing to fear about protecting our traditional knowledge base.'[5] The case also led to the opinion that India must document its resources because only written evidence will hold up in American courts and the fact that the CSIR could present written evidence on the turmeric case enabled it to win. Kanavi (1999) writes, 'At one stroke the turmeric case showed that the IPR system works if backed by proper documentation…India's knowledge base, be it traditional or modern, requires protection too. At once Mashelkar became a swashbuckling national hero who "rescued haldi from Western biopirates".' A key factor that influenced the turnaround on patent reform was the CSIR's victory in the turmeric case (Kanavi 1999).

+ SAU = State Agricultural University

[5] 'Why CSIR Won the Battle of Haldi: The Text of the Indian Council of Scientific Research Statement Describing the Facts behind the Case', www.rediff.com/news/aug/27haldi.htm

Building Coalitions for Reform

Haggard and Webb (1994, p. 16) assert, 'A critical aspect of political management of policy reform therefore involves encouraging the reorganization of interests: expanding the representation and weight of interest groups that benefit from the reforms and either marginalizing or compensating the losers.' Public sector research institutions are involved in creating this coalition for reform on patents both directly by involving NGOs and indirectly by promoting a culture of patents within the scientific community.

Public sector research institutions are involved in building coalitions with NGOs on the issue of bio-piracy and protection of traditional knowledge. The acceptance of patent reform came about due to India's ability to get a patent on turmeric revoked by producing documented evidence. Once it was clear that India's traditional base could be protected through documentation and protection of traditional knowledge, the government devised a strategy involving the actors who had already begun such activities. With support from the Department of Science and Technology, the National Innovation Foundation (NIF) was established in Ahmedabad in 2000 to register grassroots innovations. The NIF was established '...with the main goal of providing institutional support in scouting, spawning, sustaining and scaling up grassroots green innovations and helping their transition to self supporting activities' (http://www.nifindia.org/about.html). The chairperson of the board is R. A. Mashelkar, and the Department of Biotechnology and the ICAR are also involved. This initiative involves the NGO Sristi whose president, Anil Gupta, is the executive chairperson of the NIF. Sristi was one of the NGOs that was involved in advocating a strategy that promotes both greater patent rights and documentation and protection of genetic resources/traditional knowledge. A significant aspect of forging networks that promoted patent reform involved the inclusion of NGOs in the government's strategy of protecting traditional knowledge in India. The CSIR is also involved in building linkages internationally to promote the protection of traditional knowledge. In 1998 India was elected the first chairperson of the standing committee that was established by World Intellectual Property Organization (WIPO) on IT in relation to IPRs (*The Hindu* 1998). Mashelkar served as India's representative on this body.

A second aspect of forging links was through promoting the patent culture not only within public sector research institutions, but with scientists both inside and outside industry. Entrepreneurs like Parvinder Singh and Anji Reddy point clearly to Mashelkar's role in this regard. 'In fact one of his greatest contributions to CSIR is to inculcate the culture of patenting. Many years before we filed patents from our research foundation, it was NCL which was at the forefront of filing process patents licencing to big multinationals like Akzo. He was a kind of inspiration for me and always used to say that we should stand in the forefront in technology and file patents in developed countries. To that extent, I must admit that he has not only inspired scientists in CSIR to create wealth by harnessing intellectual property, but was also an inspiration for all of us in the industry,' says Reddy. 'He has increased the awareness in the Indian scientific community towards patent-worthy innovation...,' adds Singh.

Public Sector Research Institutions and Patent Activity

The patent activity of many public sector research institutions in India has increased in recent years. For decades, public sector institutions in India have focused on building indigenous capabilities and disseminating it cheaply to industry rather than patenting inventions and exercising ownership rights. This accounted for a low level of patents acquired by public sector research institutions. Patents granted from 1972–94 show that a majority of patents in India were awarded to transnational companies and about 80 per cent of the patents went to foreigners (Ganguli 1998). Even among the domestic actors, the private sector had a greater share than the public sector (Mani 1997).

The CSIR, the Department of Biotechnology (DBT), and the ICAR are some of the public sector research institutions that have begun filing patent applications both in India and abroad. Figure 7.1 represents a steady increase in the patent applications filed in India by the CSIR.

Table 7.2 shows that the CSIR has also increased its success rate in terms of number of patents granted and filed.

The CSIR has also increased its patent filings in the USA. By November 2002, CSIR laboratories had acquired a hundred patents in the USA.

The DBT's Patent Facilitating Cell has facilitated filing more than 100 Indian and international patent applications out of which more than 10 patents have been granted (http://dbtindia.nic.in/). According to its 2002–3 Annual Report, 15 patent applications have been received out of which 13 have been recommended for filing, taking the total number of patents supported by the DBT to 112. Tables 7.3 and 7.4 show some of the recent patent applications filed by the DBT in India and the patents granted.

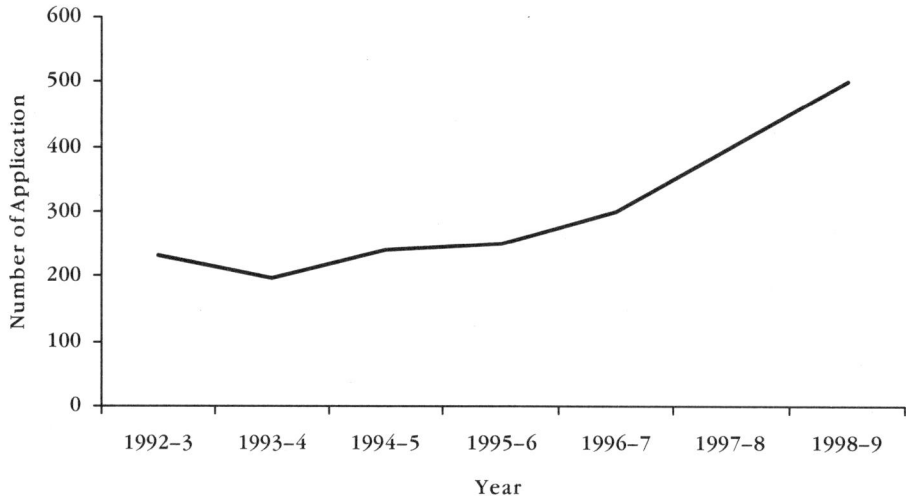

Figure 7.1: Patent Applications Filed in India by the CSIR
Source: Adapted from Vijay K. Jolly, 'CSIR Profiting from R&D' in Ghosal et al. *World Class in India: A Case of Companies in Transformation,* Penguin, India, p. 302.

TABLE 7.2
Patenting Record of the CSIR in India 1990-1 to 1998-9

Year	Filed	Granted	Success rate (%)
1990-1	202	55	27.23
1991-2	230	66	28.70
1992-3	232	38	16.38
1993-4	198	80	40.40
1994-5	241	104	43.15
1995-6	260	106	40.77
1996-7	209	92	44.02
1997-8	264	155	58.71
1998-9	310	134	43.23

Source: Adapted from Mani, S. (2002) *Government, Innovation and Technology Policy: An International Comparative Analysis,* UNU, Tokyo, p. 246.

Patenting activity under the ICAR is handled centrally and a total of 31 patent applications received from scientists were examined centrally and those found complete were filed at the Patent Office, Delhi (DARE/ICAR 2001-2). In terms of institute-wise filing of patent applications, IARI topped with nine applications, followed by NDRI with four, IVRI and ILRI with two each, CMFPRI, CTRI, NIRJAFT, and NCIPM with one each (DARE/ICAR 2001-2). Table 7.5 lists some of the recent patent applications by ICAR.

PUBLIC SECTOR RESEARCH INSTITUTIONS AND DEVELOPMENT STRATEGY

The appropriate role of the public sector institutions in the post-liberalization scenario is a topic of debate among both the supporters and opponents of liberalization. The crucial position of public sector research institutions in India in promoting and creating the climate for patent reform provides some insights into the way we approach the issue of defining public sector functioning. Clearly, delineating the proper boundaries of public sector operations requires some understanding of how we define the interests of the public sector. Some studies assume that since the government in a 'traditional' framework does not exist for its own sake but rather performs functions 'determined' by its citizens, the objective function of governments is the maximization of the utility of its citizens or the maximization of social welfare (Ott 2002). Niskanen introduced the idea that one needs to incorporate the objective function of bureaucrats along with that of the public sector and argued that bureaucrats seek to maximize power (Ott 2002). Public choice theories have pointed out that understanding the behaviour of private agents, whether seeking political influence or as rent seekers, is fundamental to the evolution of public sector outcomes (Ott 2002).

In the case of patents, one may have expected the public sector research institutions to protest against change. Public sector research institutions were engaged in reverse engineering and, in this sense, benefited from the earlier process patent regime. In addition, they may have feared competition from the private sector, particularly when they had adopted a policy of freely transferring their materials and research output to the private sector. These factors could have led the public sector institutions to attempt to prevent revision of India's patent laws. Yet, the reverse occurred. As the study has shown, public sector research institutions paved the way

TABLE 7.3
Department of Biotechnology
Patent Applications Filed in India According To TIFAC Database, 1995–2002

Filing date	Applicant	Title of application
7/14/1995	DoBT Ministry of Science	A Process for the chemical modification of enzymes
10/5/1995	Centre for Biochemical Technology (CSIR) and DoBT	Process of preparing transfer vectors pcbt1 to pcbt4 for the purpose of expressing proteins for commercial use
10/29/1996	The Secretary DoBT New Delhi	A process for the preparation of highly monodispersed polymeric Nanoparticles
9/15/1997	Registrar Osmania University and Secretary DoBT	Process for producing myceliuj of streptomuces clavuligerus with active cephamycin C along with fermented components mixed with animal feed for veterinary application
2/26/1998	Council of Scientific & Industrial Research and DoBT	A process for the preparation of a non-toxinogenic oral vaccine for Cholera
6/18/1998	CPIMCO; PF Scientific and Industrial Research DoBT and Department of Science and Technology	A process for the preparation of a ceramide from placental extract. Useful as an inducer of melanin in eukaryotic system
6/18/1998	Council of Scientific and Industrial Research, DoBT and DST	A process for the preparation of prottzoan cell-protein suspension. Useful as an immunomodulator for enhancement of host defense
6/25/1998	Bose Institute & DoBT	Development of a microbial based arsenic assay kit
11/17/1998	University of Delhi and The Secretary DoBT	An enzymatic method for preparation of bread
3/31/1999	The Secretary DoBT and University of Delhi	A process for the preparation of highly monodispersed polymeric hydrophilic nanoparticles
5/20/1999	The Secretary DoBT India	Highly monodispersed polymeric hydrophillc manoparticles
6/10/1999	The Secretary, DoBT Tata Energy Research Institute	A biofertilizer and to a process for the preparation threof
3/31/2000	Council of Scientific & Industrial Research and DoBT	An improved process for the preparation of stable phycocyanin
5/3/2001	The Secretary DoBT India	An oligonucleotide primers for detection of whitespot syndrome virus WSSV affecting shrimp polymerase chain reaction PCR method
7/12/2001	The Secretary DoBT New Delhi	A microbial control agent for mosquito vectors of human diseases
11/8/2001	The Secretary DoBT New Delhi	Sequences of a portion of the genome of whitespot syndrome virus (WSSV) affecting shrimp
11/13/2001	The Secretary DoBT and University of Nagpur	A method for determination of biopotency a lethal dose titre 50 (LDT 50) of live antaghonist against pathogen
11/13/2001	University of Delhi South Campus Department of Biotechnology	A non-aggregating derivative of HIV 124 for haemagglutination based rapid detection of antibodies to HIV in whole blood
12/13/2001	Ranbaxy laboratories DoBT	A fermentor
12/13/2001	Ranbaxy laboratories DoBT	Stable topical formulation of clarithromycin and method for the treatment of acne
12/14/2001	The Secretary DoBT New Delhi	A fermentor
1/18/2002	The Secretary DoBT and Other	A process for the isolation of flanking sequences and a kit therefor

Source: Calculated from TIFAC, 1998 updated 2002, Database on Patent Applications Filed in India

TABLE 7.4
DBT Patents Granted so far

Inventor	Title of Invention
Asis Datta, SLS, JNU	Seed storage protein with nutritionally balanced amino composition. (3 US Patents)
Rup Lal, Department of Zoology, University of Delhi	A Process for development of cloning vectors. (2 Patents, Europe, USA)
Debi P. Sarkar, Delhi University South Campus	1. A targeted drug delivery carrier (1 Patent, USA) 2. A Process for Producing a targeted gene for drug delivery carrier(1 Patent, USA)
A. N. Maitra, Deptt. Of Chemistry University of Delhi	Particles of below 109 mm highly mono-disposed drug loaded…medical systems (1 Patent, USA)
Padma Sridhar, Department of Microbiology Osmania University Hyderabad	1. Process of producing Cephamycin-C by Solid state formation 2. Process for continuous production of Cephamycin-C by fermation. 3. Process of producing Cephamycin-C by submerged batch fermentation (3 Patents India)
Rekha Hari Das, CBT, Mall Road, Near Jubilee Hall	Process for Preparing transfer vector PCTB1 to PCTB4 for the purpose of expressing proteins for commercial use (1 Patent India)

Source: http://dbtindia.nic.in/aboutdbt/overviewmain.html.

for patent reform in India. The roots of its view towards patents can be traced back to its perceived need for adaptation to liberalization. The need for a change in the CSIR had begun to be felt in the 1980s itself and after the initiation of liberalization in 1991, it was clear that these laboratories could not just absorb and adapt foreign technologies to the Indian environment, but that it had to become an equal player in the global marketplace for new technologies (Jolly 2001). Before the issue of patent reform came to the forefront in India, these institutions had already begun making changes in their strategy. This laid the foundation for public sector research institutions like the CSIR to envisage gains from promoting rather than opposing reform. Under the liberalization scenario, it was clear that there would be a cutting back of funds for the public sector. Patents, in one sense, were perceived as a means for earning revenue as old sources of funding were being reduced. According to the CSIR's Vision document for 2001, published in 1996, one of the goals of the Institute is to realize 10 per cent of operational expenditure from intellectual property licencing (Jolly 2001). This points to the fact that interests and their articulation are not fixed, but are subject to interpretation. Public sector institutions could have defined their interests in terms of opposition to patent reform and built coalitions with actors who advocated resistance to change. The fact that these institutions shifted their interests and no longer believed that reverse engineering was in the best strategy was strongly shaped by how the interests of the public sector were defined. Assigning to the public sector the objective function of maximization of social welfare could have lead us to predict either strategy. What is significant here is that ideas and interpretations strongly influence the way the public sector defines its interests. In attempting to analyse the public sector functioning in the post-liberalization scenario, we must take into account the fact that interpretation of strategy objectives is an important factor in determining outcomes. This is also influenced by the role of other actors.

The position of NGOs was important in determining the behaviour of the public sector research institutions on the issue of patents. The ability of NGOs to effectively build public opinion against patents due to biopiracy meant that any move towards reform had to focus on the protection of traditional knowledge. The CSIR and other institutions understood that promoting patent activity would not be adequate and that measures had to be evolved to ensure that patents on indigenous innovations such as turmeric would not be granted in the USA. The point made by the NGOs that a strategy that promotes both patent rights and documentation and protection of genetic resources/traditional knowledge would be effective for India, enabled a policy shift. The public sector could forge links with these NGOs to ensure that the reforms on patents could take place without having to face the criticism that traditional knowledge was not being protected. Public sector strategy was shaped by the positions of these actors.

The redefinition of public sector goals is diminishing the divide between the public and private sectors. Reinike notes, 'the unbundling of the political and economic geography brought about by globalization has created a structural imbalance, and possibly even a disjuncture, between the public and private spheres of society' (quoted in Ott 2002). As the public sector

TABLE 7.5
Indian Council of Agricultural Research
Patent Applications According to TIFAC Database, 1995–2002

Date of filing	Applicant	Title of application
2/9/1996	ICAR, New Delhi	A process for extracting starch from cassava tuber
5/8/1996	ICAR	Mangrove microbial consortium for bioremediation of marine oil spill
6/20/1996	ICAR, New Delhi	Lac scrapping machine
9/30/1996	Indian Veterinary Research Institute & ICAR	Indigenous drug formulation against skin diseases of animals
10/9/1996	ICAR Krishi Bhavan	Immunostick elisa kit for equines herpes virus-1 disease forecasting
11/6/1996	ICAR unit	Slow-release lac based pesticidal formulation for control of cockroach (bigermanica)
8/8/1997	ICAR, New Delhi	A polymeric composition
8/8/1997	ICAR, New Delhi	A process for the preparation of plastic films
8/8/1997	ICAR , New Delhi	A process for the preparation of plastic films
8/18/1997	ICAR	A process for determination of maturity of cotton fibres
9/1/1997	ICAR	A method of producing improved jute based bulked yarn for Manufacturing diversified product including apparers
1/15/1998	ICAR	Method of producing mushroom by utilizing biogas waste slurry with straw for improved mushroom cultivation
11/12/1998	The Director General ICAR	A process for the preparaton of powdered azadirachtin a rich concentrate from neem
2/11/1999	Director, Indian Agricultural Research Institute	Pusa neem -me coated urea
4/4/2001	ICAR Krishi Bhawan, New Delhi	Environmentally sound process for improvement in or relating to soil fertility and rice productivity
4/4/2001	ICAR Krishi Bhawan, New Delhi	A process for the preparation of mosquito larvicidal formulations Based on rabdosia melissoides ingredients
4/4/2001	ICAR Krishi Bhawan, New Delhi	Improvement in or relating to cultivation of azotobacter by Fermentation for sustainable agriculture
4/4/2001	ICAR Krishi Bhawan, New Delhi	Bacterial fortified mushroom spawn for oyster mushroom pleurotus SP cultivation
4/4/2001	ICAR Krishi Bhawan, New Delhi	On shore marine pearl culture
4/4/2001	ICAR Krishi Bhawan, New Delhi	Palmyrah fibre separator
4/4/2001	ICAR Krishi Bhawan, New Delhi	Additives for improved photostability of azadirachtin a
4/4/2001	ICAR Krishi bhawan, New Delhi	Improvements in or relating to the preparation of powdered azadir
4/12/2001	ICAR, New Delhi	Indigenously developed cost effective and patent aluminum hydroxide gel concentrated oil adjuvanted vaccine for foot and mouth disease
4/12/2001	ICAR, New Delhi	Groundnut pod grader
4/12/2001	ICAR, New Delhi	Development of live attenuated homologous vaccine from a peste des petits ruminats PPR virus strain of Asian origin
5/15/2001	ICAR, New Delhi	Process of making instant makhana kheer mix
12/31/2001	ICAR, New Delhi	Process for the industrial manufacture of instant kheer mix
12/31/2001	ICAR, New Delhi	Development of Whymango beverage
12/31/2001	ICAR, New Delhi	Process for low-fat tomato-whey soup
1/11/2002	ICAR, New Delhi	Degumming of ramie gibre with recovery of degraded gum

Source: Calculated from TIFAC, 1998 updated 2002, Database on Patent Applications Filed in India.

institutions take on a greater commercial orientation, they become internally competitive and may also become competitors with the private sector. This competitive atmosphere may rectify one of the crucial reasons why public sector research institutions were thought to have failed in India (Katrak 1998). Parikh (1981) notes that the failure of CSIR laboratories to perform better than they have, even on their own terms, may be explained by the lack of competition.

While competition may increase efficiency, another failure pointed out by Parikh (1981) is that of the lack of a proper perspective as to what is socially relevant, and appropriate research on this remains to be addressed. As one research manager of the CSIR notes, 'We have always been torn between our mission of working on problems unique to India and doing good science to come up with internationally needed technologies in a competitive way.... The Vision expects us to strike a balance between the two, but how should one do that?' There are also issues raised about the direction of research. One of the CSIR institutes, the CDRI, is revising its decades of research focusing on control of parasitic diseases and family planning and turning towards areas that have greater international market potential—raising questions about its mission (Jolly 2001). While celebrating NCL's golden jubilee earlier this year several senior scientists who have retired from the CSIR—like B. D. Tilak, L. K. Doraiswamy, and A. V. Rama Rao—expressed the fear that NCL might become 'a lab on rent' for MNCs (Kanavi 1999). Operational difficulties in maintaining an efficient system for evaluating patent applications is also a factor that may affect research interests. A liberal patent regime in the USA has led to problems with processing patent applications.

Concerns are also being expressed internationally regarding the impact of IPR on science and public sector research. The Royal Society of the UK (2003), in a recent study, notes, 'A desire by funders or research workers in the Science Base to obtain IPRs may also affect the direction of publicly funded research, encouraging short-term, applied research that has merit but is usually better done in industry if a vibrant industrial base exists. The longer-term work on which industry relies may be displaced or partially reduced.' They also recommend that, 'the encouragement and funding of research in universities and PSREs (Public Sector Research Enterprises) depend on quality rather than its potential to generate IPRs' (The royal Society 2003). While noting that the two may be linked, the report also points out that even a small percentage change in the direction and efficiency of research, potentially caused by a shift toward acquisition of IPRs, is large in real terms (The royal Society 2003). Byerlee (2000), focusing specifically on agricultural biotechnology, points out that due to various types of market failures, the public sector will have to play an important role in serving resource-poor farmers, at least in the initial stages. He notes that public research is often crucial to reduce the cost of entry for private firms and that once a competitive private sector is operating, the public sector can redirect those resources towards farmers and environments that are not being targeted by the private sector.

There is a definite need to evolve a balance between promoting patentable innovations and directing research to correct for market failures. Where the twin objectives coincide, the task is easy, but the difficulties arise when certain areas of research that are important but not patentable are not pursued. It is clear that public sector institutions must adapt to India's shift in development strategy and the earlier focus on adaptation and imitation are no longer as relevant. The technology statement of 1983 outlined India's earlier approach of emphasizing development of indigenous technology, and efficient absorption and adaptation of imported technology appropriate to national priorities and resources (Byerlee 2000). The recent Science and Technology Policy of 2003 points to a new path and states, 'The development of skills and competence to manage IPR and leveraging its influence will be given a major thrust. This is an area calling for significant technological insights and legal expertise and will be handled differently from the present, and with high priority' (TIFAC 2003).

The evolution of patent reform in India due to a revision in the interests of domestic actors (as opposed to occurring only because of external pressure) indicates that there is a fundamental, rather than a cosmetic or short-term, shift in development strategy on patents. That the public sector research institutions chose to join and help consolidate the pro-patent lobby reveals that development priorities within these institutions are shifting towards a new twin objective of promoting patents and protecting traditional knowledge. The stance that public sector institutions will adopt towards the reform process is influenced by the interpretation of interests and the role of other actors including NGOs. It is clear that on certain aspects of liberalization, public sector institutions may take the lead in promoting change, and may be crucial for promoting and consolidating reform. In formulating India's strategy for development, it is important to analyse the shifting priorities of the public sector research institutions towards intellectual property, taking into account the factors that shape the ways by which these institutions are redefining their interests.

References

Alam, Ghayar (1996), *Impact of the Proposed Changes in IPR on India's Pharmaceutical Industry*, Center for Technology Studies, New Delhi, December.

Byerlee, Derek and Ken Fischer (2000), 'Accessing Modern Science: Policy and Institutional Options for Agricultural Biotechnology in Developing Countries', AKIS Discussion Paper, 3 November.

Chaudhuri, Sudip (2002), 'TRIPs Agreement and Amendment of Patents Act in India', *Economic and Political Weekly*, 10 August, pp. 3354-60.

DARE/ICAR (2001), Annual Report, 2001-2.

Deccan Herald (1999), 'BJP Eases Stand on Swadeshi Plant, Backs Government Policy', 5 January.

Economic Times (1998), 'Parties undecided on Patents Bill', 21 December and 'Congress Support to Ensure Passage of Patents Bill', 23 December.

Gupta, Anil (1999), 'Rewarding Creativity for conserving diversity in third world: Can IPR regime Serve the Needs of Contemporary and Traditional Knowledge Experts and Communities in the Third World?', http://csf.Colorado.edu/sristi/papers/cottier.html.

Gadbow, Michael and Timothy Richards (1988), 'Intellectual Property Rights. Global Consensus, Global Conflict?', Westview Press, Colorado.

Ganguli, Prabuddha (1998), *Gearing Up for Patents: The Indian Scenario*, Universities Press, Hyderabad.

Government of India (2002), The Patent (Amendment) Act, 2002.

——— (1999), The Patent (Amendment) Act, 1999.

Haggard, Stephen and Steven Webb (eds) (1994), *Voting for Reform: Democracy, Political Liberalization and Economic Adjustment*, World Bank, Washington, D.C., p. 13.

ICAR (2001), *ICAR Guidelines for filing patent applications*, ICAR, New Delhi. (Compiled under the guidance of Mangala Rai, Deputy Director General, (Crop Science), by Sudhir Kochhar, Assistant Director General, (IPR), Acting Charge and Principal Scientist (Plant Breeding), Crop Science Division, ICAR, Krishi Bhavan, New Delhi).

Jolly, Vijay (2001), 'CSIR: Profiting from R&D', in Sumantra Ghosal et al., *World Class in India: A Casebook of Companies in Transformation*, Penguin Books, New Delhi.

Kanavi, Shivanand (1999), 'Catalyst for Change', *Business India*, 28 June-11 July, pp. 50-7.

Katrak, Homi (1998), 'Economic Analyses of Industrial Research Institutes in Developing Countries: the Indian Experience', *Research Policy*, Vol. 27, Issue 4, pp. 337-47.

Kohli, Atul (1990), 'Economic Liberalization in India', in John Waterbury and Ezra Suleiman (eds), *The Political Economy of Public Sector Reform and Privatization*, Westview Press, Colorado.

Krishna, Iyer (1996), Chinnappa O Reddy, D. A. Desai, Rajinder Sachar People's Commission on GATT: On the Constitutional Implications of the Final Act Embodying the Results of the Uruguay Round of Multilateral Trade Negotiations, Centre for the Study of Global Trade System and Development, New Delhi.

Lanjow, Jean (1997), 'The Introduction of Pharmaceutical Product Patents in India: Heartless Exploitation of the Poor and Suffering?', Economic Growth Center, Yale University, 26 August.

Mani, Sunil (1999), 'Public Innovation Policies and Developing Countries: In a Phase of Economic Liberalization', UNU/INTECH Discussion Paper.

——— (1997), 'Government Intervention in Industrial R&D, Some Lessons From the International Experience For India', Working Paper No. 281, Centre for Development Studies, August.

Nayar, Baldev Raj (1990), *The Political Economy of India's Public Sector Policy and Performance*, Popular Prakasan, Mumbai.

——— (1989), *India's Mixed Economy: The Role of Ideology and Interests in Its Development*, Popular Prakasan, Mumbai.

Ott, Altiat F. (2002), *The Public Sector in the Global Economy: From Driver's Seat to the Back Seat*, Edward Elgar Publishers, UK.

Panagariya, Arvind (1996), 'Some Economic Aspects of TRIPs', Paper prepared for presentation at the Conference on Law and Economics Interface, 11-13 January, New Delhi.

Parikh, Kirit (1981), 'Building Technological Capability for Self Reliance', *Technology in Society*, Vol. 3, pp. 423-31.

Pederson, Jorgen Dige (2000), 'Explaining Economic Liberalization in India: State and Society Perspectives', *World Development*, Vol. 28, No. 2, pp. 265-82.

Philippe, Cullet (2001), *Patents Bill, TRIPs and Right to Health*, EPW Commentary, 27 October.

Science (1995), 'Patents on Native Technology Challenged', Vol. 269, Washington, D.C., 15 September, p. 1506.

Sell, S. K. (1995), 'Intellectual Property Protection and Antitrust in the Developing World: Crisis, Coercion, and Choice', *International Organization*, Vol. 49, No. 2, pp. 315-49.

Smith, Sean Eric (2000), 'Opening Up to the World: India's Pharmaceutical Companies Prepare for 2005', Asia/Pacific Research Center, Stanford University, May.

Stewart, P. Terence (ed.) (1993), *The GATT Uruguay Round: A Negotiating History 1986-1992*, Vol. 2, Commentary, Netherlands.

The Hindu (1998), 'India Elected Chairperson of Panel on IPRs, 15 July.

TIFAC (2003), IPR Bulletin, January, http://www.tifac.org.in/do/pfc/pub/jan03.pdf.

——— (1998), Database on Patent Applications Filed in India, updated 2002.

Times of India (1996), 5 July.

The Royal Society (2003), *Keeping Science Open: The Effects of Intellectual Property Policy on the Conduct of Science*, April, The Royal Society, London, UK.

Vedaraman, S. (1997), 'New Indian Patents Law', *International Review of Industrial and Copyright Law*, Vol. 3, No. 1, Munich, pp. 39-54.

8 New Technologies for India's Development

Jayan Jose Thomas[1]

It is widely believed that knowledge is going to be the principal driver of development and growth of this planet in the coming years. New technologies, especially digital and genetic technologies, offer immense opportunities for development. This chapter discusses the opportunities and challenges to India in this emerging era of knowledge-based development.

Information and communication technologies (ICTs) and biotechnology have made rapid strides in recent years. There has been huge reduction in costs and massive increases in power of both computing and communications. It is predicted that computing power doubles itself every 18–24 months, and communications power does so every six months. Between 1970 and the end of the 1990s, the cost per mega hertz (MHz) of computing power has fallen from US$ 760 to 17 cents and that of a megabyte of storage from US$ 5257 to 17 cents, while that of transmitting a trillion bits of information from US$ 150,000 to 12 cents.[2] In 1953, deoxyribonucleic acid (DNA), which provides the genetic code that determines the characteristics of any organism, was discovered. Subsequent years have witnessed great advances in genetic science and biotechnology (UNDP 2001).

It is quite possible that these new technologies might transform the future economic and societal landscape. Consider the impact of some of the earlier technologies in advancing development. For example, the impact of immunization and antibiotics in raising life expectancy at birth in Latin American and East Asian countries, or the important role of plant breeding, better-yielding seeds and fertilizers in improving agricultural productivity and ensuring food security in many developing countries. The emerging technological advances will produce more influential outcomes. Through their cheap and rapid access to information ICTs can dramatically enhance the capabilities for acquiring knowledge. They cut across geographical, political, and social barriers and, in this way, aid participation and empowerment of isolated societies. Opportunities for income growth and employment generation are vastly increased by ICTs, either directly by the ICT industry itself, or indirectly by the productivity enhancing effect of ICTs in conventional economic activities. Biotechnology promises great advances in the fields of medicine and agriculture. It can, for example, help in the cure of diseases like malaria and AIDS and speed up agricultural growth (UNDP 2001, ch. 2).

India has a lot to gain from the new technologies. At the same time, it faces great hurdles in the way of realizing these gains. India's highly talented technical manpower has produced world-class innovators and entrepreneurs in the new technologies. At the same time, vast sections of its population still survive under high levels of illiteracy, problems of social exclusion, and with medieval technologies. It is a challenge for public policy in India to foster economic growth aided by the new technologies. A greater challenge for public policy, however, is to reach modern technologies to a large number of people who are at present excluded from its benefits. Otherwise, these people will fall behind in the evolving social and economic conditions. The aim of this chapter is to bring out the many dimensions of this challenge.

---

[1] The author is grateful to Kirit Parikh for useful suggestions and to Madhura Swaminathan and V. K. Ramachandran for encouragement and suggestions on an earlier version of this study.

[2] All these figures have been quoted from Chandrasekhar and Ghosh (2001).

OPPORTUNITIES FROM NEW TECHNOLOGIES

India's Successes in Knowledge-based Economic Activities

Software Industry

From the 1990s, India's software industry has been growing at an average annual rate of approximately 50 per cent—a rate three times plus faster than the growth of the country's whole economy (both the growth rates at current prices). Although starting from a low base, the growth of India's software industry has indeed been phenomenal. In fact, India's software industry has been doubling itself every two years between 1992–3 and 2001–2 (Figure 8.1).

jobs in India by 2008 (GOI 2001a, pp. 35–6; GOI 2001b, pp. 1–7, 15) (Tables 8.1 and 8.2).

India's recent successes in the software industry is largely due to its vast pool of English-speaking engineers, who earn much less than their counterparts in developed countries (20 per cent of the US wage levels). The quality of their service is high. In the initial years of the boom in software production in India, most of the work by Indian IT firms was in the form of 'body shopping', that is, Indian engineers travelling on temporary visas to the client's site in foreign countries to do simple software jobs like fixing the 'Y2K' (year 2000) problem. Of late, foreign companies have been outsourcing software jobs

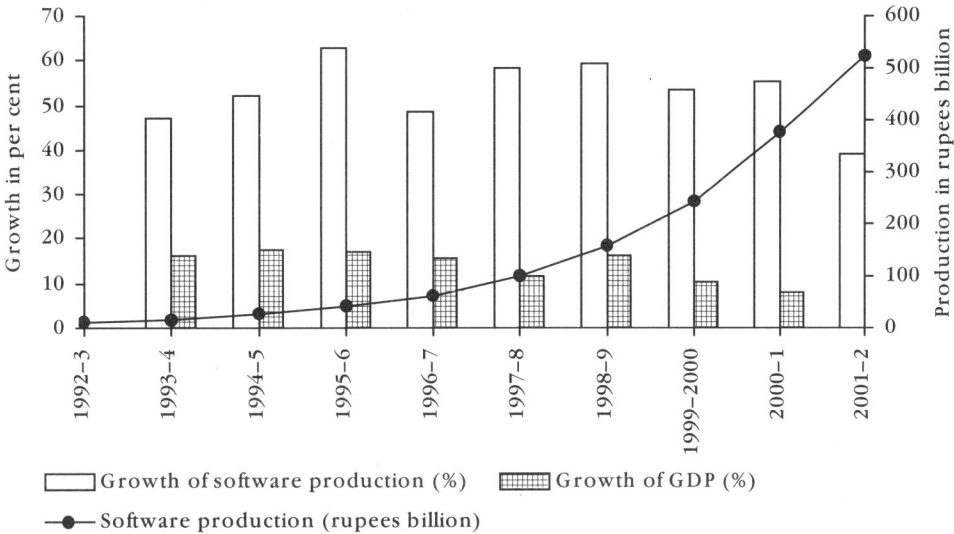

Figure 8.1: Annual Rates of Growth of Software Production and GDP (both at current prices) in India, 1992–3 to 2001–2
Sources: GOI (2001b) Table 1B, p.7 and EPW Research Foundation (2002) Table 1.B, p. 28.

Exports have been a major source of growth for India's software industry from the 1990s onwards. In 2000–1, exports of software products and services from the country reached US$ 6.2 billion—that was 76 per cent of India's total software production, 14 per cent of its total exports, and 2 per cent of the global software exports in that year. The software industry accounts for approximately 2 per cent of India's GDP today, and employed 180,000 people in 1998.[3] By 2008, it is estimated that production in India's IT industry—including software and ITES—will expand to US$ 87 billion, accounting for 7.7 per cent of the country's estimated GDP in that year. By 2008, exports by India's IT industry is expected to reach US$ 50 billion, which will account for 35 per cent of India's total exports and 6 per cent of the total global IT exports. It is also estimated that the IT industry will generate 2.2 million

TABLE 8.1
Production of IT Products and Services in India: Projections for the year 2008

	Total production		Exports	
	Billion US$	Billion rupees	Billion US$	Billion rupees
IT services	38.5	1732.5	23	1035
Software products	19.5	877.5	8	360
IT enabled services	19	855	15	675
E-business	10	450	4	180
Total-IT	87	3915	50	2250
Total-IT as % share of the total for India's economy*		7.7%		35%

Notes: * Total IT production as % share of the country's total GDP, and total IT exports as % share of the country's total exports. All projections for 2008. Total Production = Exports + Production for the domestic market.
Source: Projections made by National Task Force on IT and Software development, and NASSCOM–McKinsey Study Report, cited in GOI (2001a), p. 121 and p. 15.

---

[3] The figure for employment in India's software industry is taken from UNDP (2001), Box 2.5, p. 37.

TABLE 8.2
Employment Generation in India by IT Sector, Projections for 2008

(in million numbers)

	Employment generation as per:	
	MIT study	NASSCOM–Mc kinsey study
Software products	0.20	–
IT services	0.57	–
Jobs in hard core IT	0.77	1.1
E-business	0.33	–
IT enabled services	1.26	–
IT related jobs	1.59	1.1
Total jobs in IT, 2008	2.36	2.2
Total organized sector employment, India, 1999–2000	28.06	
Total number of job seekers on the live registers of employment exchanges, India, 1999–2000	41.34	

Notes: MIT is Ministry of Information Technology, GOI.

Sources: 10th Plan study team on Human Resources Development, MIT (http://www.mit.gov.in/Studyteam.ppt); RBI (2001), Table 10.

to Indian IT firms—these jobs being executed in India itself. In 1996–7, 90 per cent of the total exports by Indian IT firms were accounted for by on-site services. In 2000–1, the share of on-site services in total software exports fell to 56 per cent, with jobs executed in India accounting for the remaining 44 per cent (GOI 2001b, p. 7). After 2001, despite the worldwide slowdown in demand for IT, revenues of Indian IT firms have not fallen much, as foreign companies have stepped up outsourcing their software jobs to India to save costs.

Today Indian software professionals have created a brand image for themselves in the global market. Indian IT firms supply software to more than half of the FORTUNE 500 companies. Reports suggest that Indian IT firms like Infosys, Wipro, Tata Consultancy Services (TCS), and Satyam have focused on climbing up the value chain—from being providers of high-quality IT services to IT consultants—and on becoming one of the global IT giants (*The Economist* 2001c, GOI 2001b, p. 4; Paul 2002). Bangalore, where many of the IT firms are located, has been rated 11th among the 46 top global hubs of innovation identified by the *Wired* magazine. Hyderabad is soon expected to join this select group (UNDP 2001, p. 38).

Indian engineers have been migrating to the USA in large numbers from the early 1970s to work in high-tech companies there (in the USA, domestic supply has been inadequate to meet the demand for technically qualified professionals, and professionals from India have come to fill in this gap). It is estimated that 40 per cent of the 81,000 visas approved in the USA between October 1999 and February 2000 went to Indian citizens, most of them engineering professionals (UNDP 2001). Indian engineers, particularly those from the Indian Institutes of Technology (IITs) have typically been highly talented, thanks to the high quality of education they receive and the filtering they pass through to enter these institutes.

Over the years, India's immigrant engineers have evolved from accomplished technical professionals to high-technology innovators and entrepreneurs. During the last 10 years, the roughly 200,000 strong Indian population in the Silicon Valley—the nerve centre of the global IT industry—has emerged as the most successful immigrant community in the USA. Many of the successful first-generation entrepreneurs have been promoting newer ventures by Indians in the USA and in India (Warner 2000). The highly influential diaspora of Indian technologists have played a key role in bringing high-technology investments to Bangalore, Hyderabad, and other Indian cities. Venture capital, which is used for financing small, technology-based start-ups, has boomed in India in recent years—from an investment of only US$ 3 million in 1995 to US$ 342 million in 2000. Venture capital investments in India in 2000 was higher than the venture capital investments in China (US$ 84 million) and South Korea (US$ 65 million) in that year.[4]

Information Technology Enabled Services (ITES)

Newer opportunities for growth based on ICTs are emerging today. In recent years, firms in western countries have been outsourcing their business operations to India. ITES or 'teleworking' has grown so phenomenally in the

---

[4] In current US dollars. From *Thomson Financial Data Services 2001* cited in UNDP (2001), Table 2.4, p. 38.

country in recent years that India is predicted to be a 'back office to the world', and clerical activities in the developed world are expected to move to India just as manufacturing activities had moved to China and East Asian countries earlier (*The Economist* 2001b). Business operations outsourced by foreign companies include data entry, data conversion, and direct telephonic interaction with customers. Call centres and centres for medical transcription have come up in several Indian cities. India's English-speaking population, that numbers 30–50 million (almost as large as the population of a medium-sized country), and whose labour costs are low by western standards, is the major attraction for firms in the developed world. It is estimated that a typical bank in a western country can outsource 17–24 per cent of its cost base, and, thereby, reduce its cost–income ratio by 6–9 per cent and also double its profits (*The Economist* 2001b, Paul 2002).Outsourcing of business activities to India, however, has led to considerable job losses and strong public reaction in the USA and European countries (Box 8.1).

Box 8.1

The Outcry Against Outsourcing

Outsourcing of business operations to India and other developing countries has raised strong waves of public protest in the USA and Europe. in the USA, the Democratic Party has unleashed a strong campaign against the George Bush administration for its failure to prevent job losses. Trade unions in Europe have been expressing alarm over the shift of jobs to India.

Outsourcing—global corporations shifting their operations to locations of cheaper wage rates—is not a new phenomenon. In the 1980s and 1990s, a large number of manufacturing sector jobs in the USA and European countries have moved to East Asian and Latin American countries. Today, with the faster and efficient communication facilities made possible with the ICTs, companies have begun outsourcing service sector jobs too. The most attractive location for outsourcing of service sector jobs is India, which has a large English-speaking workforce.

What is the basic reason behind the strong public reaction in the USA and Europe against outsourcing of jobs to India? Forrester Research predicted in late 2002 that 3.3 million service sector jobs in the USA will move to cheaper wage locations by 2015, about 500,000 of these jobs in computer software and services. In USA, this threat of job losses in the service sector comes in the wake of a long period of gloom in that country's job market. America has reportedly lost 3 million jobs in the manufacturing sector over the past 3½ years. While the George Bush administration had promised to create 5.5 million jobs in the 18-month period from July 2003 to December 2004, only 2,960,000 new jobs—or just 5 per cent of the administration's projection—have been added in the first seven months of this period. To the workers in the USA and Europe, the threat from outsourcing is not just limited to jobs like call centre operation that require only low skills; there are increasing signs of job losses even to high skilled workers like financial analysts, management consultants, and researchers.

Irrespective of job losses, many economists including Gregory Mankiw, Chairman of the White House Council of Economic Advisers, and Jagdish Bhagwati, argue that outsourcing will be more beneficial to the USA than to India (or the country to which jobs are outsourced) in the long run. They argue that, to the USA, outsourcing leads to a reduction of production costs, increase in productivity, and, ultimately, cheaper products and services for their citizens. Companies in the USA can devote a larger share of their resources for innovation and development of new products and services. Also, more jobs and more incomes in India will aid the growth of exports from the USA to India. According to a study by the consulting firm, McKinsey, every US$ 1 previously spent in the USA and now outsourced to India creates a global impact of US$ 1.47. Of this, while the USA receives US$ 1.14 as benefits, only 33 cents reaches India as new wages, extra profits, and extra taxes.

As workers and political parties in the USA and Europe debate the pros and cons of outsourcing, what are India's concerns in this respect? First, India is the country that has gained the most from outsourcing of service sector jobs. Naturally, the ongoing protests in the USA and Europe against job losses have considerable implications for India. Secondly, although outsourcing has opened up an entirely new range of job opportunities to Indians, not everything is bright on the Indian side. The employees in India's call centres—the major scene of business process outsourcing—complain of long, monotonous hours of work in the night, and, not infrequently, of abusive conversations from callers. Many of them also suffer from identity crisis as they speak and work with an American name. Lastly, there is no guarantee that India will continue to enjoy the status of being the favourite destination for outsourcing of service-sector jobs. Countries like Philippines, Romania, Israel and also China are strongly competing with India to secure a part of the global outsourcing market.

Sources: Bhagwati (2004), Finch (2004), Lohr (2004), Porter (2004), and Ramesh (2004).

Knowledge-based Activities Enabled by ICTs

Very recent trends indicate that India is becoming a favoured destination for outsourcing of very advanced knowledge-based activities. Foreign companies have set up over 100 R&D centres in some of the Indian cities (prominently in Bangalore, Hyderabad, Gurgaon, and Pune)—more than 70 of these centres having come up in the last five years. These centres employ the large pool of technical and scientific professionals available in India. Interestingly, investments in R&D centres by foreign firms are not only in the area of software, where India has made a name for herself in the last decade, but also in IT hardware, engineering, automobiles, chemicals, food, pharmaceuticals, and telecommunications (Dubey 2003). Global opportunities await knowledge workers of India who are equipped with the tools of ICTs and they may operate from India. For instance, there are opportunities for animation experts in Mumbai to work for a Hollywood movie. There are opportunities for Indian lawyers operating in various Indian cities to give legal advice to firms in different parts of the world (*The Economist* 2001b).

Public Investment in Research and Education, and Successes in Knowledge-Economy

The roots of India's successes today in knowledge-economy lie in the large public investment in scientific research and higher education in the post-independence period in the country. India has a reasonably successful programme of scientific research, notably in areas like space and nuclear sciences. In 1999–2000, there were 236 universities for higher education, and under these universities, 11,865 colleges offering degrees in diverse subjects.[5] In 2000–1, 8 million students had enrolled in the country for degree courses. Among them 0.53 million students had enrolled for degrees in engineering, 0.26 million students in medicine, and 1.57 million students in various science streams. There were also 45,000 students registered for doctoral degrees in that year.[6] The UNDP reported that India has the seventh largest number of scientists and engineers in the world (UNDP 2001, p. 38).

The Need to Go Much Farther

It is important to note, however, that there is no reason to be complacent about India's recent successes in knowledge-economy. While India spent heavily on higher education and harvested rich benefits, primary or basic education has been greatly neglected in the country. This has resulted in wide disparities in educational achievements, along with other forms of inequalities that already existed between the different sections of the country's population. Today 72 per cent of India's population live in rural areas, 29 per cent are below the poverty line, and 34.6 per cent are illiterates.[7] It is pertinent to note that Andhra Pradesh, which sends large numbers of software professionals to the USA every year and whose capital city, Hyderabad, is an emerging knowledge centre, also has a high incidence of starvation deaths, distress migration of landless agricultural labourers, and suicides among handloom textile workers.[8]

The 2.2 million jobs that India's IT sector promises to generate by 2008 is still not large enough given that there are, at present, 41.3 million job seekers on the live registers of the country's employment exchanges (Table 8.2). Of course, the high paying IT jobs will lead to an increase in demand for consumption goods, and this, in turn, will generate substantially large number of jobs in the tertiary sector. But until new jobs are created in the primary and secondary sectors, there will be no lasting solution to the problem of unemployment that the country faces today.

Two points emerge from the above discussion. First, despite the fast growth of the knowledge economy-driven service sector in recent years, the importance of the agriculture and industrial sectors remain crucial. Second, for new technologies to make noticeable improvement in the lives of India's millions, their impact has to go beyond the well-educated urban dwellers, and reach, directly or indirectly, the large numbers of poor and illiterate people.

Information and Communication Technologies for Development of Marginalized Sections of Society

Some of the ongoing experiments in various Indian states show that it is indeed possible to use ICTs for the development of rural areas and the disadvantaged sections of society.

---

[5] See Department of Education, Ministry of Human Resources Development cited in GOI (2001c).

[6] See provisional results from *Annual Report 2000–01*, University Grants Commission, and *Report of the National Statistical Commission, Volume II*, August 2001, both cited in www.indiastat.com.

[7] Poverty data for the year 1993–4, measured by head-count ratio, from Drèze and Sen (2002), Table A.3. Date on literacy rates and rural–urban population from Census of India (2001) (www.censusindia.net).

[8] Software professionals from Andhra Pradesh accounted for 23 per cent of all Indian software professionals working in the USA in 1998, according to Ramachandraiah (2003). Large numbers of small farmers and landless agricultural workers in several parts of the Telangana region of Andhra Pradesh migrate to Mumbai and major towns in Maharashtra in search of jobs (Sainath 2003). Krishnakumar (2001) writes on the distressful living conditions of weavers in Andhra Pradesh.

Innovations in IT can enhance the effectiveness in the delivery of health services, particularly in rural and remote locations, and in locations affected by natural disasters like earthquakes. In this respect, the emerging area of telemedicine—medical advice and delivery of medical services through satellites—offers great prospects (Chandrasekhar and Ghosh 2001). One example of the use of ICTs in the delivery of health services is the case of health care workers in Rajasthan. These workers use personal digital assistants to reduce the time spent in paperwork, to improve health counselling and to aid the collection of accurate demographic and health data (Reddy and Graves 2000). Tools of ICTs such as multimedia are effectively used in education, particularly in programmes to impart functional literacy among working adults. A project of this nature is reported to be going on in 80 locations in Andhra Pradesh (Patel 2002).

The role of ICTs in improving productivity in manufacturing and service sector activities in the formal sector is too well known. With applications like enterprize resources planning (ERP), ICTs reduce lead times in many business functions, ensure quality standards and timely delivery of raw materials by suppliers, and increase customer–industry interaction. In a similar manner, ICTs can vastly improve efficiency and effectiveness in agriculture and traditional industries. With the tools of ICTs, a small leather manufacturing unit in a remote town in India can keep itself up-to-date with the latest advancements in leather manufacturing technology, and can also sell its products to, for instance, a European customer through the Internet.

As a result of a project coordinated by the M. S. Swaminathan Research Foundation (MSSRF), small and medium farmers in some villages in Pondicherry use ICTs for obtaining information on market prices for their agricultural products. Fishing communities in these villages obtain from the Internet weather information and satellite images of fish shoal locations (Dugger 2000). To cite another such example, sugarcane farmers in 54 villages in the Warana region in southern Maharashtra use a central IT network to obtain information on the ideal time for planting and harvesting of crops, market rates for their agricultural products, and also information on payments made by sugar factories (Vijayaditya 2000).

The processes of interaction between citizens and the administration can be speeded up by the use of ICTs in governance (e-governance). For instance, ICTs can speed up the issue of government certificates to citizens, and facilitate the sending of e-mail complaints by citizens to the administration. Experiments in e-governance are going on in many parts of the country. They include the Gyandoot project, which electronically network 15 *gramapanchayats* (administrative units at the local level) comprising 25–30 villages and approximately half a million people in the Dhar district of Madhya Pradesh, and computerization of land registration in Andhra Pradesh, which earlier was a cumbersome process involving several government offices, private agents, and a voluminous generation of documents. They also include electronic networking of various levels of administrative units, including the creation of a citizens database in 23 districts of Andhra Pradesh, and electronic networking of 1215 local bodies in Kerala.[9]

In many ways, ICTs can be sources of empowerment to the poor and to those sections of the population which are traditionally excluded from development, including women. Avenues for communication with the outside world are opened up by the ICTs—much more than the newspapers, the radio, or the television. In this way, they are powerful tools for breaking the barriers to participation in democratic decision-making (UNDP 2001). For instance, a campaign for the developmental needs of an isolated hilly region—from where it would be difficult for conventional methods of protest, like staging a rally, to catch public attention—can be effectively led through e-mail. The increased incomes achieved with the aid of ICTs are another important source of empowerment. It is because of this reason that ICT projects in rural Pondicherry give particular emphasis to assetless poor and to women.[10] In Kerala, women from households below the poverty line have organized themselves into neighbourhood groups (*Kudumbashree* self- help groups) and set up IT-based units, undertaking jobs such as data entry and desktop publishing (Krishnakumar 2002).

Through ICTs fair wages to workers and fair prices to producers may be ensured. Among coir workers in Mararikkulam in Kerala, a proposed IT network with comprehensive information of all workers and coir enterprizes, along with vigilant intervention by local self-governments, is expected to ensure fair wages and decent working conditions.[11] Using mobile phones, fishermen in Kerala keep themselves informed, while at sea, of fish prices—which fluctuate throughout the day and between the various landing spots—and manage to get higher prices than what they used to get earlier by selling their catch to middlemen (*The Economist* 2001a).

[9] See <http://gyandoot.nic.in> on the Gyandoot project; Satyanarayana (2000) on computerization of land registration in Andhra Pradesh; Kumar (2000) and <http://www.ap-it.com> on the e-governance projects in Andhra Pradesh; and <http://www.keralaitmission.org/> and Unnikrishnan et al. (2002) on the e-governance projects in Kerala.

[10] See <http://www.mssrf.org/index.html> for more details.

[11] T. M. Thomas Isaac, an academic and a member of the Kerala State Legislative Assembly, in personal communication, 23 January 2003.

Benefits from Biotechnology

Biotechnology is today capable of producing new varieties of crops that are more resistant to pests and pathogens, can produce output on a large scale, and have higher nutritional value. Biotechnology has great applications in the development of bio-fertilizers and bio-pesticides, in integrated nutrient management, in development of aquatic resources, in enhancing the yield of livestock, in pollution control, and in clearing large river systems (Sharma 1999). According to Swaminathan (1999), large numbers of India's small farms will benefit greatly from 'precision agriculture'—which involves 'the use of right inputs at the right time and in the right way'—enabled by biotechnology.

The ongoing research in biotechnology aims to develop vaccines for diseases such as AIDS-HIV, TB, malaria, and hepatitis. It also aims to develop new drugs and pharmaceuticals that are expected to provide low cost and efficient health care services to the millions of poor people in India (Sharma 1999, Swaminathan 1999).

CHALLENGES TO TECHNOLOGY-AIDED GROWTH

There are important challenges to accelerating India's development with the aid of new technologies. These challenges range from poor physical infrastructure to the iniquitous nature of India's social structure.

Physical Infrastructure for Diffusion of ICTs

India is far behind most countries with respect to the physical infrastructure for the spread of digital technologies. This is particularly true of the country's rural areas. In 1999, the number of telephone mainlines per 1000 population was 27 in India, compared with 438 in South Korea and 682 in the USA. The number of Internet subscribers per 1000 population was 0.1 in India, compared with 7.2 in Brazil and 179.1 in the USA in that year. In the same year, the cost of a 3-minute local call in India was 50 per cent higher than that in South Korea, China, and Japan. As a proportion of the average household income, costs of telephone or Internet access will be several times higher in India than in the latter set of countries, given the much lower per capita incomes in India (Table 8.3).

Telecommunications

India's telecommunications sector has been passing through important reforms from the 1990s. Following the national telecom policy of 1994 (NTP 94), the private sector was allowed entry into basic and value added telecom services, including cellular and paging services. The Telecom Regulatory Authority of India (TRAI) was formed in 1996. A new national telecom policy was announced in India in 1999 (NTP 99) to keep pace with the changes in technology and market structure that occurred after NTP 94. As per NTP 99, private Internet Service Providers (ISPs) have been allowed to set up international gateways based on satellite or submarine cable, so that they can hire bandwidth directly from foreign satellites and provide bandwidth from their gateways to other ISPs.[12] Also, as per the new policy, national long-distance telecom services have been opened up for private sector participation from 2000. International long-distance telecom services have been similarly opened up from 2002. Internet telephony, which is cheaper than the usual voice telephony, has been introduced in the country in 2002 (Jain 2001, Sikdar 2002).

TABLE 8.3
Diffusion of ICTs, India and Selected Countries

Country	Telephone mainlines per 1000 people 1999	Cellular mobile per 1000 people 1999	Internet subscriptions per 1000 people 2000	Cost of a three-minute local call PPP US$ 1999	Waiting list for mainlines per 1000 people 1999
India	27	2	0.1	0.09	4
South Korea	438	500	4.8	0.06	0
Japan	558	449	49	0.06	0
China	86	34	0.1	0.06	0
Brazil	149	89	7.2	–	–
USA	682	312	179.1	–	0

Notes: There are variations in the figures for Internet subscriptions in India per 1000 people, as reported in this table and in Table 8.4. The figures are from different sources.
Source: UNDP (2001), Table A2.4.

---

[12] For national telecom policies in 1994 and 1999, see Department of Telecommunications, Ministry of Communications and Information Technology, GOI in <http://www.dotindia.com/ntp/ntpindex.htm>

There has been a perceptible improvement in the telecom infrastructure in the country in the 1990s, the period of reforms in the telecom sector. The number of direct exchange telephone lines (DELs) (including cellular phones) in the country increased from 5 million in 1990–1 to 9.8 million in 1994–5, 28.5 million in 1999–2000 and 45 million in 2001–2—thus an average annual increase of 22 per cent during this 11-year period. Telephone density, or the number of telephone lines per 1000 population grew at a very slow rate from 0.5 in 1950–1 to 4.0 in 1980–1 and 10.8 in 1994–5. Telephone density grew at much faster rates after that and reached 26.6 in 1999–2000 and 50 in March 2003 (Table 8.4).[13] Charges for national long distance telephone calls were reduced by more than 60 per cent, and airtime charges in cellular phone calls were brought down by a factor of eight after 1994 (Sikdar 2002). There had also been significant modernization of the telecom network in the country during this period. By February 2002, 89.1 per cent of the total 493,317 km of telecom transmission network in the country had been digitalized—57.1 per cent of the digitalization was through optical fibres.[14]

new telephone connections, although NTP 99 had declared as one of its policy objective that telephones would be made available on demand by 2002 (Table 8.4). It is also important to note that the expansion of DELs in recent years has been unequally spread across different sections of the country's population. In March 2002, 16 per cent of all DELs in India were cellular phone lines, subscribed by people many of whom already hold a landline. At the same time, public call offices (PCOs), which are centres of mass access to the telecom network, accounted for only 3 per cent of the total number of DELs in the country (Chandrasekhar 2003).

There exist large variations in telephone density across the different Indian states. In 2003, telephone density (mainlines per 1000 people) varied from 268.5 in Delhi to 13.2 in Bihar. Telephone density in India's rural areas was 14.9 and telephone density in the country's urban areas was 151.6 at that point in time (Table 8.5). In March 2002, when the population in rural areas accounted for more than 70 per cent of India's total population, the number of DELs in rural areas formed only 23.5 per cent of the total number of DELs in the

TABLE 8.4
Growth of Telecommunication Network and Internet in India, over the Years

Year	Direct exchange telephone lines* in 000s	Waiting list for telephones in 000s	Telephone mainlines per 1000 people	Internet subscriptions in millions	Internet users in millions	Internet subscriptions per 1000 people
1991–2	5810	2290	7.9	–	–	–
1995–6	11,978	2277	13.0	0.002	0.01	0.002
1996–7	14,882	2894	15.5	0.05	0.25	0.054
1997–8	18,684	2706	18.4	0.09	0.45	0.095
1998–9	22,813	1983	22.0	0.14	0.7	0.145
1999–2000	28,537	3681	26.6	0.28	1.4	0.285
2000–1	36,279	2917	35.6	0.9	2.8	0.903
2001–2	44,968	1687	–	2.3	7	2.272
2002	–	–	42.9	4.5	13.5	4.379
2003	–	–	50.0	10	30	9.508

Notes: *includes cellular phones and phones provided by private basic operators. In figures for telephones, 2002 and 2003 refer to 31 March of the corresponding year. In figures for Internet subscriptions 1995–6 refer to 31 August 1995, 2003 to 31 December 2003, and other years to 31 March of the beginning year. Figures for Internet subscriptions from 2001–2 are projections.
Sources: Data on telephones from Annual Report, Ministry of Communications and Information, GOI, various years; on Internet from Mahanagar Telecom Nigam Limited (MTNL), cited in www.indiastat.com.

However, a lot remains to be achieved with respect to telecom infrastructure in the country. In 2001–2, there were 1687,000 applications in the waiting list for

[13] Press Information Bureau, and Lok Sabha unstarred question No. 1561, dated 13 March 2002 cited in www.indiastat.com.
[14] See Bharat Sanchar Nigam Limited (BSNL), cited in www.indiastat.com.

country (Chandrasekhar 2003). It had been declared in the NTP 94 that all Indian villages would be connected with the telecom network by 1997. However, in January 2002, only 410,757 villages out of a total 607,491—or 68 per cent of the total—were provided with village public telephones (VPTs) (Sikdar 2002).

The failure in expanding telephone network to rural areas raises some important questions with respect to

TABLE 8.5
Variations in Diffusion of Technologies Across Indian States

State	Electricity connection (per 100 households) 1998–9	Telephone mainlines (per 1000 people) 2003*			Internet subscriptions (per 1000 people) 2002**
		Urban	Rural	Total	
Andhra Pradesh	74.4	164.5	20.3	55.6	3.4
Assam	26.4	115.4	5	19.4	0.6
Bihar	18.2	93	4.8	13.2	0.1
Delhi	97.7	301.8	–	268.5	59.1
Gujarat	84.3	178.1	24.8	74.4	3.4
Haryana	89.1	164.6	23.2	60.6	0.8
Himachal Pradesh	97.2	396.3	54.3	84	0.6
Jammu and Kashmir	90.1	83.4	5.2	24.8	0.4
Karnataka	80.9	158.4	23.7	64.5	5.6
Kerala	71.8	237	78.5	111.3	3.6
Madhya Pradesh	68.1	101.5	5.6	28.8	0.9
Maharashtra	82.1	192.7	21.6	89.9	10.8
Orissa	33.8	113.3	8.7	22.2	0.5
Punjab	95.5	256.6	46	116	3.3
Rajasthan	64.4	113.4	12.5	34	2.2
Tamil Nadu	78.8	152	21.2	78.2	6.0
Uttar Pradesh	36.6	88.2	5.6	21.3	0.6
West Bengal	36.7	115.3	8.9	37.2	2.0
North-east	–	91.7	8.8	27	0.9
India	60.1	151.6	14.9	50	3.8

Notes: * figures for 31 March; ** figures for 30 September.
There are variations in the figures for Internet subscriptions in India per 1000 people, as reported in this table and in Table 8.4. The figures are from different sources.
Sources: Data on Internet subscriptions from the Ministry of Telecommunication, GOI; on telephone mainlines from Press Information Bureau, GOI, cited in www.indiastat.com; and on electricity connection from IIPS (2000), Table 2.12.

India's telecom reforms so far. Private-sector licensees for telecom services have not honoured their commitments as regards the supply of VPTs. Private-sector licensees provided only 906 VPTs by April 2002. This was less than 1 per cent of the target of 97,806 VPTs which they were committed to provide by that point in time.[15] At the same time, it was the public-sector telecom operator, Bharat Sanchar Nigam Limited (BSNL), that connected more than 400,000 villages to the telecom network. It is argued that private-sector telecom operators have been targeting the thin strata of upper-income consumers, who ensure higher rates of profits. There is no doubt that, under the present circumstances, any weakening of public sector telecom units like BSNL will only delay the spread of rural telephony. It is also argued that the recent trends in telecom tariffs towards increases in basic access and local charges, though with a reduction in long distance subscriber trunk dialling (STD) rates, will make the telecom network further out of reach to marginal sections of India's population (Purkayastha 2002).

The Internet

The number of Internet subscriptions and users in India has increased remarkably in recent years. The number of Internet subscriptions was 0.002 million in 1995, 0.28 million in March 1999, 4.5 million in March 2002, and 10 million in December 2003. The estimated number of Internet users (assuming that more than one user access the Internet from one Internet subscription) was 0.01 million in 1995, 1.4 million in March 1999, 13.5 million in March 2002, and 30 million in December 2003 (Table 8.4). Despite such rapid increases, the estimated number of Internet subscribers and users in India in 2003 were, respectively, less than 1.5 per cent and 5 per cent of the country's adult population of 680.6 million.

[15] Rajya Sabha unstarred question No. 4549, dated 9 May 2002 cited in www.indiastat.com.

As in telephony, there are major variations in the spread of Internet across different sections of the country's population. Internet users are heavily concentrated in urban areas. According to the National Readership Survey in 2002, the eight major metros in the country accounted for 48.6 per cent of all Internet users in India. Towns with a population of 0.1–0.5 million and with a population of less than 0.1 million, accounted for, respectively, 18.8 per cent and 11.0 per cent of the total number of Internet users (Chandrasekhar 2003). There are also significant interstate variations in the spread of the Internet. In September 2002, the number of Internet subscriptions among 1000 people ranged from 59.1 in Delhi to 0.1 in Bihar (Table 8.5).

An important barrier to the effective use of the Internet in India is the limited availability of bandwidth. Bandwidth is a measure of how much information can be carried over a wired or wireless communications link during a given period of time. According to estimations by the International Telecommunications Union, bandwidth available for connectivity to the Internet in India was 1475 megabits per second (Mbps) in 2001. The corresponding figures were 2639 Mbps for Singapore, 5432 Mbps for South Korea, 6308 Mbps for Hong Kong, and 7598 Mbps for China (Chandrasekhar 2003). Given that there were 3 million Internet subscribers and approximately 9 million Internet users in India in 2003, bandwidth available to each individual user in India was 100 bits per second. At the same time, the ideal bandwidth required at the individual user level is 5–8 kilobits per second. As a consequence of such low level of bandwidth availability, information access through the Internet is very slow in India. This is a serious constraint to development of all types of applications enabled by the Internet. For fast and efficient information access, it is estimated that India requires a bandwidth of approximately 20 Gbps (or 20,000 Mbps) today and 300 Gbps by 2005 (GOI 2001b).

The spread of the Internet to rural areas in India is limited by many other problems as well. Today, much of the content available on the Internet is in the English language. For effective use of the Internet in rural areas, it is important that content is created in the Indian languages. Such content should be created in the Internet that will meet the information needs of the people in rural areas—including, for example, information on grain prices, price and availability of farm inputs like fertilizers, and also information on public schemes for rural welfare. The high cost of telecom access is another factor that restricts the spread of the communication network to people in rural areas. Today, the monthly cost of a telephone connection in India is approximately Rs 800 per month, an amount that is unaffordable for most rural households in the country (Jhunjhunwala 2001).

Challenges in Reaping the Benefits from Biotechnology

The world over, R&D in biotechnology is today dominated by the private sector—in fact, by a few large MNCs. This has important implications for the prospects of development aided by biotechnology in India.

Research and development efforts in biotechnology by the MNCs are focused more on the interests of large farmers in richer countries, not on the interests of small, poor farmers in countries like India.[16] For instance, research programmes by MNCs place greater emphasis on the improvement of crop quality—a concern for consumers in richer countries, than on increasing drought tolerance or enhancing the yield of crops—which can help to ensure food security in poor countries (Scoones 2002). There are fears that the nature of ongoing R&D in biotechnology might increase genetic homogeneity and produce an adverse impact on biodiversity (Swaminathan 1999). It may be noted here that concerns have been raised in India in recent years on the import of genetically modified 'terminator seeds', which yield seeds that do not germinate again; this will compel the farmers to buy seeds from the seed companies in every new season, contrary to the age-old Indian practice of saving a portion of the harvest to provide seeds for the next sowing season (Krishnakumar 1998). There are also concerns that, with the expansion of proprietary sciences and large biotech firms, traditional communities, who are the primary preservers of genetic resources and traditional knowledge, will be denied their share of the benefits from such resources and knowledge (Swaminathan 1999).

THE URGENT NEED TO CREATE NEW TECHNOLOGIES

For widespread use of the new technologies as a tool for development, India should move ahead from being exporters of low-value adding software services to creators of new technologies, including ICTs and biotechnology.

Research on ICTs in India should primarily focus on the domestic market for new technologies. The domestic market for ICTs in India is vast yet untapped. Information and Communication Technologies have been developed largely in western countries, where consumers have high paying capacities and firms have lesser incentives to

---

[16] India has 106 million small farm holdings, 75 per cent of them with a size of 1 hectare or less (see Swaminathan 1999).

invest in cheaper technologies (Jhunjhunwala 2001). Therefore, there is huge potential in India for the development of technologies that are more affordable and appropriate to the needs of India's domestic consumers. These include technologies like Simputer, wireless in local loop (WLL), voice over Internet protocol (VoIP), and Ka-band satellite communications.

Similarly, there is a need to enhance domestic research in biotechnology addressing India's problems and concerns, including food security.

To meet the challenges from the emerging knowledge-economy, it is important that domestic investment in R&D in India is stepped up. Per capita expenditure (in all areas of research) on R&D in India is much lower than per capita expenditure on R&D in countries like Japan and South Korea. Scientists and engineers working in R&D per 100,000 people and patents granted per million people are also significantly lower in India (Table 8.6). Public sector units in India invest about 5–6 per cent of their turnover in R&D. Investment in R&D by private sector units in the country is even lower (GOI 2001b, p. 144). Expenditure on R&D as a proportion of India's GNP increased from 0.58 per cent in 1980–1 to approximately 0.91 per cent by the end of the 1980s, but declined thereafter to 0.71 per cent in 1995–6—the proportion marginally increased after 1995–6. The annual rates of growth of central government expenditure on R&D were, in general, lower in the 1990s than in the 1980s (Figure 8.2).

TABLE 8.6
Investment and Achievements in the Creation of New Technologies, India and Selected Countries

Country	Per capita R&D expenditure 1996 in US dollars	Scientists and engineers in R&D 1987–97 per 100,000 people	Patents granted to residents 1998 per million people
India	3.1*	149	0.201
South Korea	290.5	2193	779
Japan	1001.84	4909	994
Brazil	36.19	168	2
USA	720	3676	289

Notes: * figures for 1998.
Sources: per capita R&D expenditure from Research and Development Statistics 2000–1, Ministry of Science and Technology, GOI, cited in www.indiastat.com; others cited in UNDP (2001), pp. 48–55.

HUMAN DEVELOPMENT AND DIFFUSION OF NEW TECHNOLOGIES

The greatest challenge that India faces today in development aided by the new technologies is in overcoming the varying forms of restrictions on freedom among several sections of the country's population. These relate to income poverty, undernourishment, illiteracy, as well as to social exclusion based on caste and gender. Under the prevalence of such backward societal conditions, the

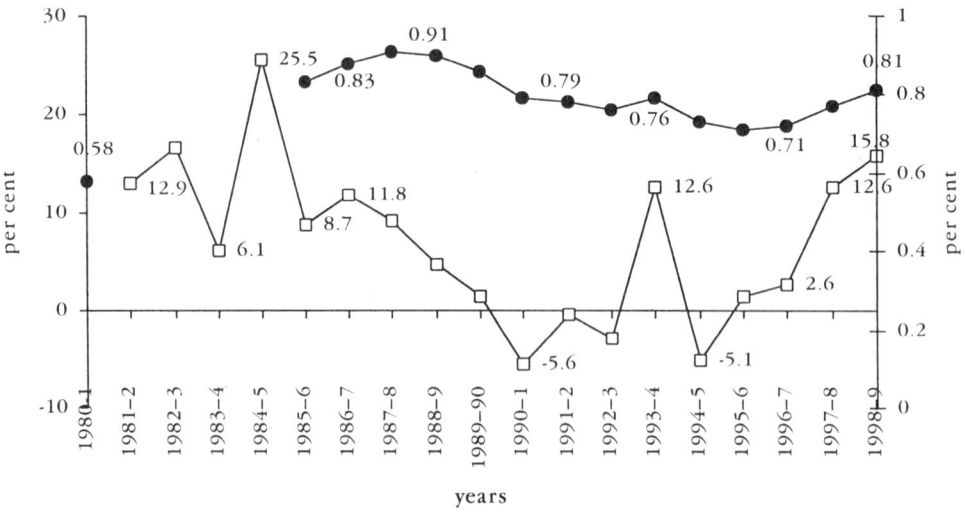

Figure 8.2: Annual Rates of Growth of Central Government Expenditure on R&D, and National Expenditure on R&D as Proportion of GNP: India, 1980–1 to 1998–9 (in per cent)
Notes: Central government R&D expenditure at constant 1993–4 prices; national R&D expenditure and GNP in current prices.
Source: Research and Development Statistics, various issues, Ministry of Science and Technology, GOI, cited in www.indiastat.com.

new technologies might even aggravate inequalities in India—between people in urban and rural areas, between the educated and the illiterates, and between those who possess some form of entitlements and those who do not. Diffusion of new technologies will be very difficult among persons who do not know how to read or write. It will also be difficult when the worst forms of social exclusion are rampant, as, for example, when a person belonging to the scheduled castes is barred from using a village community Internet server.

An important reason for the continuance of backward social conditions in India is the failure of the Indian state in imparting basic education to its citizens. In 1999, adult male literacy rate in India was 72 per cent, compared with 91 per cent in China and 99 per cent in South Korea (Drèze and Sen 2002, Table A.1). In 2000, the average years of schooling (for persons aged 15 years and above) in India was 5.1 years; the corresponding figures were 6.4 years in China and 10.8 years in South Korea (UNDP 2001, Table A2.1). Literacy rates were low in India even among the younger sections of the population. In 1998-9, 32 per cent of India's females in the age group of 15-19 years could not read or write (Table 8.7).

There exist large variations in educational achievements between different Indian states, between rural and urban areas of the country, between males and females, and between members of different castes. Educational achievements are low in rural areas, among females, among members of socially disadvantaged castes, and in the states of Bihar, Madhya Pradesh, Orissa, Rajasthan, and Uttar Pradesh. According to the census of 2001, female literacy rate varied from 35 per cent in Bihar to 88 per cent in Kerala (Table 8.7). According to the census of 1991, the literacy rate was below 5 per cent among rural SC women and below 1 per cent among ST women in some districts of Rajasthan (Drèze and Sen 2002, pp. 146-7).

The state of school education in India today is far from adequate. India has still not achieved the goal of providing free universal primary education although, according to one of the directive principles of the Indian constitution, this goal was to have been achieved by 1960. School attendance is very low in several parts of the country. A sizeable proportion of students who are officially enrolled in schools do not move up to complete the upper-primary level (or 8th grade) of education

TABLE 8.7
Indicators for Educational Achievements across Indian States

States	Literacy rate, age 7+, 2001 (%)		Literacy rate, age 15-19, 1998-9 (%)		Proportion of never-enrolled children in 10-12 age group, rural areas, 1992-3, (%)		Proportion of persons aged 15-19 who have attained 8th grade in school, 1992-3 (%)	
	Female	Male	Female	Male	Female	Male	Female	Male
Andhra Pradesh	51	71	64	80	43	23	33	52
Assam	56	72	73	82	25	19	37	47
Bihar	35	62	49	73	63	32	26	52
Gujarat	59	81	73	88	25	9	43	58
Haryana	56	79	83	92	19	5	38	56
Himachal Pradesh	68	86	95	97	7	3	51	63
Jammu and Kashmir	42	66	63	85	19[a]	4[a]	46[a]	62[a]
Karnataka	57	76	72	82	35	19	36	55
Kerala	88	94	98	99	1	1	77	73
Madhya Pradesh	51	77	62	85	42	21	25	47
Maharashtra	68	86	82	91	26	21	49	67
Orissa	51	76	69	87	34	9	30	50
Punjab	64	76	86	89	21	18	57	57
Rajasthan	44	76	51	86	60	12	19	47
Tamil Nadu	65	82	82	94	14	19	45	59
Uttar Pradesh	44	71	58	84	50	7	30	55
West Bengal	60	78	72	84	29	20	28	39
India	54	76	68	84	40	25	36	54

Notes: [a] Jammu region only.
Sources: GOI (2001d), IIPS (2000), and other sources cited in Drèze and Sen (2002), Table A.3.

(Table 8.7). Elementary education in several parts of India are characterized by overcrowded classrooms, lack of teaching aids, absence of classroom activity, poor teaching standards, and a high rate of students repeating the same class. Public expenditure on education as a proportion of SDP has declined in the 1990s in a majority of Indian states (Drèze and Sen 2002, pp. 146–72).

COMPLEMENTARITIES BETWEEN POLICY INTERVENTIONS FOR ECONOMIC GROWTH AND DIFFUSION OF NEW TECHNOLOGIES

New technologies can be very effective tools in the revival of economic opportunities in the primary and secondary sectors in the rural and urban areas. At the same time, they cannot be a replacement for public policy measures for income growth and redistribution, particularly so given the existing social and economic conditions in India. The stimulus to income growth in agriculture and traditional industries offered by the new technologies cannot, for instance, substitute investment in irrigation, financial assistance for SSIs, and land reforms.

An example may be given here in support of the above argument. Exquisite varieties of textile products, particularly handloom textile products, are produced in several parts of India. There exist immense opportunities today, given the tools provided by ICTs, for marketing these products in foreign countries. Despite such opportunities, traditional handloom and power-loom workers in many regions in India have been facing joblessness and starvation. There have been suicides too. Problems faced by handloom and power-loom workers in Andhra Pradesh, for instance, include rise in power tariffs and yarn prices, and absence of government support that hindered modernization (Krishnakumar 2001). It is clear that until strong policy measures to support the textile industry are implemented, the opportunities offered by new technologies will be of little help.

In summary, we can say that new technologies, especially ICTs and biotechnology, promise great opportunities for India's development. From the 1990s, there has been a surge in export of software services from the country. This was driven largely by the relatively low wage levels of India's English-speaking technical professionals. In fact, in recent years, there has been a significant increase in outsourcing of all kinds of knowledge-based activities to India from firms in developed countries. No doubt, India's recent successes with the new technologies, particularly with the ICTs, have been truly impressive. These successes owe greatly to public investment in scientific research and higher education in the post-independence period.

Despite these successes, there is still a long way to go before the new technologies make their impact felt across wider sections of India's population, a large proportion of them illiterate, poor, and residing in rural areas.

New technologies can indeed make an impact on the development of the people in the rural areas and the marginalized sections of the Indian society. Efficiency in the delivery of health services and aid in programmes to impart literacy among adults can be enhanced by ICTs. They can be efficient tools in agriculture and traditional industries. E-governance can speed up the processes of interaction between citizens and the administration. Information and communication technology can also be a source of empowerment to the disadvantaged sections of society. Biotechnology can ensure low-cost and efficient health care to India's population, and can come up with agricultural techniques suited for small farmers in the country.

There are, however, important hurdles in India in the way of reaping such opportunities promised by the new technologies. While penetration of telephones is very low in the country, that of the Internet is even lower. There exist wide regional variations in the country in the spread of the telecommunications network. Rural areas lag far behind urban areas with respect to the physical infrastructure for telecommunications network. Limited availability of bandwidth and the near non-availability of content in the Indian languages are among the important constraints to the effective use of the Internet in India's rural areas.

There is an urgent need to step up India's domestic investment in R&D in the new technologies. The focus of research in India should be on developing technologies that are appropriate to the country's requirements and address the country's concerns.

The most difficult hurdle to development aided by the new technologies in India is the high level of illiteracy and social inequalities that continue to prevail in the country. The Indian state has not been committed enough in ensuring the basic education of the country's population. Public policy in India should urgently realize that the benefits from investment in primary education are ever so great in this emerging era of knowledge-based growth, and the costs of under-investment are ever so high.

Public policy in India must also realize that the new technologies can only be very efficient tools for development. They cannot replace the much needed policy interventions in income growth and distribution.

REFERENCES

Bhagwati, Jagdish (2004), 'Why Your Job Isn't Moving to Bangalore', *New York Times*, 15 February.

Bhatnagar, Subhash and Robert Schware (eds) (2000), 'Information and Communication Technology', in *Development: Cases from India*, Sage Publications, New Delhi.

Chandrasekhar, C. P. (2003), 'The Diffusion of Information Technology: The Indian Experience', *Social Scientist*, Vol. 31, Nos 7-8, July-August.

Chandrasekhar, C. P. and Jayati Ghosh (2001), 'Information and Communication Technologies and Health in Low Income Countries: The Potential and the Constraints', *Bulletin of the World Health Organization*, Vol. 79, Issue 9.

Drèze, Jean and Amartya Sen (2002), *India: Development and Participation*, Oxford University Press, New Delhi.

Dubey, Rajeev (2003), 'India as a Global R&D Hub', *Business World*, Vol. 22, Issue 38, 11-17 February, New Delhi.

Dugger, W. Celia (2000), 'Connecting Rural India to the World', *New York Times*, 28 May.

EPW Research Foundation (2002), *National Accounts Statistics of India 1950-51 to 2000-01*, EPW Research Foundation, Mumbai.

Finch, Julia (2003), 'In India, it's Service with a Compulsory Smile', *The Guardian*, 17 November.

GOI (2001a), *India as Knowledge Superpower: Strategy for Transformation*, Task Force Report, Planning Commission, New Delhi.

—— (2001b), *Report of the Working Group on Information Technology for Formulation of the Tenth Five Year Plan*, Ministry of Information Technology, New Delhi.

—— (2001c), *Statistical Abstract India 2001*, Central Statistical Organization, Ministry of Statistics and Programme Implementation, New Delhi.

—— (2001d), 'Provisional Population Totals', Census of India 2001, Series 1 (India), Paper 1 of 2001, Office of the Registrar General, New Delhi.

International Institute of Population Sciences (IIPS) (2000), *National Family Health Survey (NFHS-2) 1998-99: India*, IIPS, Mumbai.

Jain, Rekha (2001), 'A Review of the Indian Telecom Sector' in 3iNetwork.

Jhunjhunwala, Ashok (2001), 'Looking Beyond NTP 99', in 3iNetwork.

Krishnakumar, Asha (2001), 'Weavers in Distress', *Frontline*, Vol. 18, Issue 8, 14-27 April.

—— (1998), 'Terminator of Food Security', *Frontline*, Vol. 15, Issue 21, 10-23 October.

Krishnakumar, R. (2002), 'Women on the Move', *Frontline*, Vol. 19, Issue 12, 8-21 June.

Kumar, Asok (2000), 'Computerization of *Mandal* Revenue Offices in Andhra Pradesh: Integrated Certificate Application', in S. Bhatnagar and R. Schware (eds) *Development: Cases from India*, Sage Publications, New Delhi.

Lohr, Steve (2004), 'Many New Causes for Old Problem of Jobs Lost Abroad', *New York Times*, 15 February.

Mansell, Robin and Uta Wehn (eds) (1998), *Knowledge Societies: Information Technology for Sustainable Development*, United Nations Commission on Science and Technology for Development, Oxford University Press, New York.

3i Network (2001), *India Infrastructure Report 2001*, Oxford University Press, New Delhi.

Patel, Ila (2002), 'Information and Communication Technology and Distance Adult Literacy Education in India', Working Paper No. 166, Institute of Rural Management, Anand, Gujarat.

Paul, Anthony (2002), 'Can India Catch Up?', *Fortune*, Friday, 19 April.

Purkayastha, Prabir (2002), 'Skimming the cream', *Frontline*, Vol. 19, Issue 2, 19 January-1 February.

Porter, Eduardo (2004), 'The Bright Side of Sending Jobs Overseas', *New York Times*, 15 February.

Ramachandraiah (2003), 'Information Technology and Social Development', *Economic and Political Weekly*, 22-9 March, pp. 1192-7.

Ramesh, Randeep (2004), 'Cheap Phone Services Come at a Price', *The Guardian*, 6 February.

Reddy, Naresh Kumar and Mike Graves (2000), 'Electronic Support for Rural Healthcare Workers', in S. Bhatnagar and R. Schware (eds), *Development: Cases from India*, Sage Publications, New Delhi.

RBI (2001), *Handbook of Statistics on Indian Economy*, RBI, Mumbai.

Sainath, P. (2003) 'The bus to Mumbai', *The Hindu*, 15 June.

Satyanarayana, J. (2000), 'Computer-aided Registration of Deeds and Stamp Duties' in S. Bhatnagar and R. Schware (eds), *Development: Cases from India*, Sage Publications, New Delhi.

Scoones, Ian (2002), 'Biotech Science, Biotech Business: Current Challenges and Future Prospects', *Economic and Political Weekly*, 6 July, Vol. 37, Issue 27, pp. 2725-33.

Sharma, Manju (1999), 'India: Biotechnology Research and Development', Consultative Group on International Agricultural Research (CGIAR)/US National Academy of Sciences (NAS) Biotechnology Conference, 21-2 October.

Sikdar, Tapan (2002), Address at OECD (Organization of Economic Cooperation and Development) Global Conference on Telecommunications Policy for the Digital Economy, Dubai, 22 January.

Swaminathan, M. S. (1999), 'Genetic Engineering and Food, Ecological and Livelihood Security in Predominantly Agricultural Developing Countries', Consultative Group on International Agricultural Research (CGIAR)/US National Academy of Sciences (NAS) Biotechnology Conference, The World Bank, Washington, D.C., 21-2 October.

The Economist (2001a), 'Mobile Phones in India: Another Kind of Network', 3 March.

—— (2001b), 'Outsourcing to India: Back office to the World', 5 May.

—— (2001c), 'Islands of Quality', 2 June.

United Nations Development Programme (UNDP) (2001), *Human Development Report 2001: Making New*

Technologies Work for Human Development, Oxford University Press, New York.

Unnikrishnan, P. V., M. Sureshkumar, and Anvar Sadath (2002), 'Information Communication Technology (ICT) for People—a Human Centred Approach to Grassroots Level Empowerment', in the Seminar on *Decentralization, Sustainable Development and Social Security*, Panchayats of Aryad and Kanjikkuzhy Blocks, Kerala, 11 May.

Vijayaditya, N. (2000), 'A Wired Village: The Warana Experiment', in S. Bhatnagar and R. Schware (eds) *Development: Cases from India*, Sage Publications, New Delhi.

Warner, Melanie (2000), 'The Indians Of Silicon Valley', *Fortune*, 15 May.

World Bank (1999), *World Development Report 1998–99: Knowledge for Development*, Oxford University Press, Oxford and New York.

Hybrid Rice
The Indian Experience and Comparison with the Rest of Asia

Aldas Janaiah

The technological progress in agriculture has had three important effects on the economy throughout the development path. First, it improved the overall food supply while real prices declined and thus improved consumer welfare. Second, it made it possible to produce more output with relatively less labour and thus facilitated the development of the non-agricultural sector. Third, the surpluses generated through increased farm production are re-invested in the development of the non-agricultural sectors and on improved human capital. Several earlier studies have empirically illustrated that growth in the agricultural sector has economy-wide effects (Hayami et al. 1978, Hazel and Ramasamy 1991, Hayami 1999). Thus technological change in agriculture serves the rest of the economy through the necessary adjustments in land, labour, and capital markets over the development path. Although the share of the agricultural sector in the overall economy goes down through the development process, it supports the overall economy through backward and forward linkages. Thus, over the period, the role of technological change is much stronger as more and more output is to be produced from less and less land and labour to augment growth of the non-agricultural sector.

Technological progress and infrastructure, especially irrigation, are the important factors that contributed significantly to achieving rapid growth in the agricultural sector, particularly rice production, in developing countries such as India. This, in turn, had a positive effect on poverty reduction over the past 35 years (Pingali et al. 1997, Pingali and Hossain 1999). Several studies in the past also indicated a strong negative association between rural poverty and growth of the agricultural sector, especially food-grain production (Ahluwalia 1978, Ghosh 1996, Desai and Namboodri 1998, Pradhan et al. 1998, Batia 1999). Further, accelerated growth in the farm sector in the 1970s and 1980s led to significant improvements in the rural non-farm sector, thus achieving significant poverty reduction in India through a 'trickledown' mechanism. The power of this mechanism on poverty reduction, however, has been weakening as the non-farm sector is growing significantly over the period.

Therefore, modern rice technology and reliable irrigation are crucial inputs for improving the rice sector, and thereby, reducing rural poverty in India, especially in the rice-producing regions. The adoption of MVs of rice coupled with irrigation expansion has had a significant impact on poverty reduction in India. Poverty ratios are lower in states where there was higher adoption rate of MVs and irrigation coverage, for example, Punjab, Haryana, Andhra Pradesh, and Tamil Nadu. Thus, increases in rice supply through the green revolution era significantly brought down real prices of rice, reducing poverty in India from about 56 per cent in 1973 to 36 per cent during 1997 (Janaiah et al. 2000).

Rice Production in Asia and India

Asia's rice production increased at 2.4 per cent per year during 1968–2002, keeping pace with population growth and the income growth induced change in per capita food consumption. However, it slowed down from 2.6 per cent during 1968–80 to 1.4 per cent during the 1990s. Over four-fifths of the increase in rice production was due to increases in yields, made possible through the gradual replacement of traditional varieties with MVs developed in rice research stations, supported by public investment for the expansion of irrigation infrastructure (Barker and Herdt 1985, David and Otsuka 1994, Pingali et al. 1997). The downward trend in the real price of rice (adjusted for inflation) observed in many Asian countries from the late 1970s to the mid-1990s contributed to poverty reduction by empowering the rural landless and the urban labour class to acquire more food from the market (Hossain and Pingali 1999).[1]

The impressive growth in rice production over the last three and a half decades has generated a sense of complacency regarding Asia's ability to meet the growing demand for staple food. However, the 1990s witnessed a significant deceleration in the growth of rice yield in Asia to less than 1 per cent per year, whereas it had grown at the rate of 2.3 per cent per year during the green revolution period of 1968–90 (Table 9.1). The growth in rice production in South and South-East Asia slackened considerably in the 1990s, mostly due to substantial slowing down in the growth of yield. In East Asia—which had been ahead of the rest of Asia in experiencing the green revolution—area planted to rice significantly declined at the rate of about 1 per cent per year in the 1990s. Major East Asian countries such as China, Japan, and South Korea had covered nearly 100 per cent rice area with irrigation supply and with MVs by as early as the 1970s. Thus, rice yields have already reached more than 6 tonne per hectare in East Asian countries, which have released considerable areas of rice land to meet the demand for growing non-rice crops without affecting rice supplies. The issue is whether Asia will be able to sustain favourable food balances and further improve food security for low-income households in low-income countries in the twenty-first century.

In view of recent changes in yield trends of rice, the sense of complacency in the demand-supply balance has begun to disappear since the early 1990s when it was observed that yield advances in rice drastically slowed down for the irrigated rice systems in Asia including India (Pingali et al. 1997, Janaiah and Hossain 2003). In many countries across Asia, except in Nepal, Vietnam, Japan, and Bangladesh (Table 9.1) growth in rice yield was slower in the 1990s than in the 1980s. In fact, rice production growth was lower than population growth in many Asian countries, reversing the upward trend in the per capita availability of rice from domestic production.

TABLE 9.1
Changes in Growth of Rice Yield in Major Countries in Asia, 1968–90 and 1991–2002

Country	Growth in rice yield (%/year)		% rice area irrigated, 1998	% rice area under modern varieties, 1998	Paddy yield (t/ha), 2001
	1968–90	1991–2002			
Japan	0.44	1.11	100	100	6.63
South Korea	1.84	1.24	98	100	7.08
China	3.04	0.97	99	98	6.26
Sri Lanka	2.11	1.68	72	96	3.83
Philippines	3.37	0.60	70	96	3.14
Indonesia	3.36	−0.06	78	84	4.23
Vietnam	2.27	2.69	85	92	4.15
Bangladesh	1.88	2.85	42	65	3.58
India	2.22	1.30	50	76	3.08
Nepal	0.63	2.31	49	74	3.17
Myanmar	3.57	1.30	30	76	3.42
Thailand	0.57	2.21	20	30	2.72
Asia	2.29	0.98	57*	80*	4.03

Note: * Computed using the available by-country data in Asia.
Source: FAOSTAT 2003.

---

[1] A detailed study on 'Impact of Rice Research in Asia', was conducted at IRRI, Philippines during the mid-1990s. For more details, please refer 'Rice Research, Technological Progress and Impact on Productivity and Poverty: An Overview', in Pingali and Hossain (eds), *Impact of Rice Research*, International Rice Research Institute, Los Banos, Philippines and Thailand Development Research Institute, Bangkok.

The real prices of rice, which were declining until the mid-1990s across Asia, have started reversing their trend since the mid-1990s, posing a serious threat to Asia's ability to sustain its food security.

In India, the rice output growth was 2.6 per cent per year during 1966–2002 with the highest rate of growth (4 per cent per year) achieved during the 1980s. Yield improvements in rice—especially in the intensive rice systems (green revolution belts)—were major sources of a strong output growth in India. However, the intensive rice-growing states (irrigated eco-system) of Andhra Pradesh, Tamil Nadu, Punjab, and Haryana, which performed significantly in terms of yield improvements until the 1980s, witnessed either a plateau or negative yield growth during the 1990s (Figure 9.1 and Table 9.2).

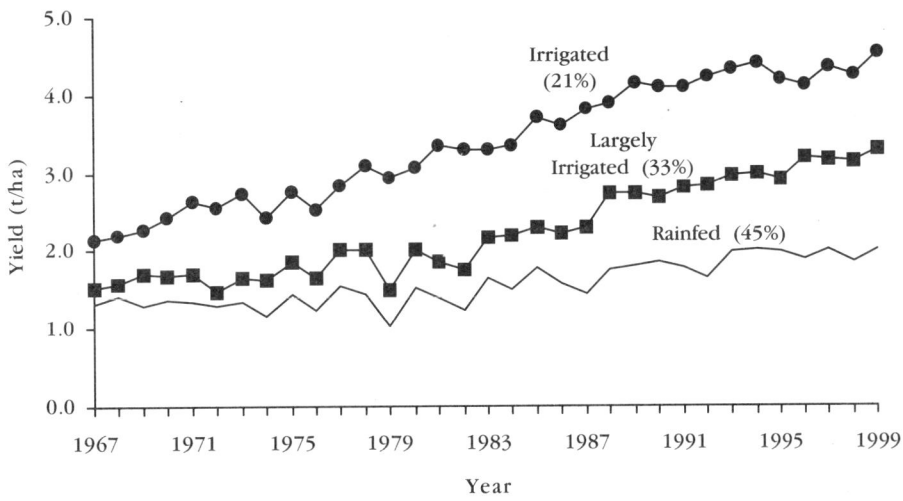

Ecosystem	Average yield (t/ha)			Growth rate (%/yr)	
	1967–9	1984–6	1995–7	1967–85	1985–97
Irrigated	2.21	3.56	4.23	2.7	1.4
Largely irrigated	1.59	2.23	3.10	1.8	2.9
Rainfed	1.33	1.61	1.96	0.8	1.9

Note: Figures in parentheses above line graphs indicate percentage of total rice area.

Figure 9.1: Trends in rice yield for irrigated and rainfed ecosystems, India, 1967–99

TABLE 9.2
Compound Growth Rates of Yield for Rice
in Major States of India

(%/year)

Crop/State	Irrigated area (%) 1998–9	1971–80	1981–90	1991–2000	1971–2000
Andhra Pradesh	96	2.37	1.96	1.74	1.99
Tamil Nadu	94	0.11	5.79	1.36	2.40
Karnataka	71	1.48	0.39	1.32	1.27
Punjab	99	4.14	0.72	0.12	1.56
Uttar Pradesh	65	1.30	5.66	1.97	3.94
Assam	23	−0.03	1.69	1.42	1.52
Bihar[a]	41	−0.20	5.02	5.23	1.80
Madhya Pradesh[a]	23	−1.72	3.45	−3.82	1.50
Orissa[a]	38	1.19	4.10	−2.88	1.71
West Bengal[a]	26	1.70	6.20	1.37	2.73
India	50	1.65	3.51	1.10	2.30

Note: [a] Huge yield fluctuations were observed for these eastern Indian states, which resulted in abnormal variations in yield growth rates.
Source: Directorate of Economics and Statistics, Ministry of Agriculture, GOI.

Hybrid Rice: Viewed as an Innovative Technology

The policy-makers and research managers in tropical Asia, including India, considered hybrid rice as a readily available technology to improve the rice sector by reversing the declining trend of productivity growth under irrigated environments and, thereby, sustaining food security in the long run. Further, China's miraculous success in the popularization of hybrid rice technology—that contributed substantially to rice development in that country in the late 1970s and the 1980s—motivated some countries in tropical Asia to invest more resources for hybrid rice R&D in the 1990s.

Several international agencies like UNDP, FAO, ADB, the International Rice Research Institute, etc. generously supported hybrid rice R&D in order to improve the rice sector in tropical Asia in the early 1990s. India received nearly US$ 8 million of financial support from all these external donors between 1990 and 2001 for various activities under the hybrid rice programme, initiated in 1989 at the Directorate of Rice Research, Hyderabad (Janaiah 2002). In addition to external funding, both central government—through the ICAR—and state governments have invested huge capital and human resources for the development and making available of suitable hybrid rice technology to the Indian farmers.

The private sector participated in hybrid rice research and seed production in a big way in India during the early 1990s, expecting a huge seed business and a guaranteed seed market in view of rice being a widely cultivated crop in the country and the farmer not being able to keep hybrid seed from his own harvest. Out of about 130 private seed companies (including small companies) engaged in rice seed business across the country, 15 relatively large companies such as Pioneer Hybrid International Biogene (PHI Biogene), Maharashtra Hybrid Seeds Company (MAHYCO), Indo-American Seeds Co., ProAgros Seed Co. (Hybrid Rice International-HRI Pvt. Ltd.), Vickey Seeds, Nath Seeds, etc. participated in the hybrid rice seed production and distribution in the early 1990s. A few big seed companies such as PHI Biogene, MAHYCO, and HRI have also been actively engaged in hybrid rice research with close collaboration with national and international research institutions in the public sector.

The hybrid rice R&D programme over the past one decade resulted in the development and release of about 20 rice hybrid varieties for farmers in India as well as in some other Asian countries in the tropics. It was expected that the hybrid rice technology would bring another revolutionary improvement in the rice sector. However, it was reported, based on early experiences, that many farmers who grew hybrid rice initially for one or two seasons had started dropping out from hybrid rice cultivation in India (Janaiah 1995, 2000) and in Bangladesh (Hussain et al. 2001). Therefore, the rate of hybrid rice adoption by the farmers is too limited and scattered in these countries—except in Vietnam which has similar socio-economic, institutional, and agro-ecological features as China.

The slow pace of hybrid rice adoption raised serious concern as to whether the currently available hybrid rice technology could make the desired impact on rice economy in the Asian countries, including India. If hybrid rice was a 'grand success' story in China—as frequently cited by the scientists for continuing hybrid rice research outside China—why have the farmers of the Asian tropics not readily accepted the present hybrid rice technology? What is wrong with the hybrid rice programme outside China, although the basic science of hybrid rice remained the same? Are there any non-technological factors (like socio-economic and political factors) responsible for the miraculous success of this technology in China?

There is no empirical evidence from farm-level experiences as to 'why farm-level adoption of hybrid rice has been slow outside China. This chapter addresses these issues based on the overall findings of various case studies of the farmers' experiences with the adoption of hybrid rice varieties carried out by the author over the past 10 years.[2] This chapter provides some insights into why hybrid rice technology has not made the desired impact on the rice sector in the tropics and suggests a few alternatives for the improvement of the rice sector with special reference to the Indian context.

Insights from the Farm Level Experiences in India

Nature and Extent of Adoption

The Indian story on the nature and extent of hybrid rice adoption by the farmers is very interesting.[3] Before any

---

[2] The author has carried out various case studies on hybrid rice adoption issues at the Directorate of Rice Research, Hyderabad (1993–5 and 1997–8). A multi-country project was also initiated during 2000–01 at the International Rice Research Institute, Philippines in close collaboration with various national agricultural research systems for selected countries. This study covered four sites in South Asia (Bangladesh, and Andhra Pradesh, Karnataka and Tamil Nadu in India), and two sites in Southeast Asia (The Philippines and Viet Nam) during the period 2000–2002. The reports of various case studies were completed after the author joined IGIDR. For more details, please refer Janaiah (2002) and Janaiah and Hossain (2003).

[3] For more details, refer Janaiah (2002).

country had even thought about hybrid rice, Indian scientists had reported on the possibility of developing hybrids in rice at the Central Rice Research Institute, Cuttack, in the early 1950s (Sampath and Mohanty 1954). However, inspired by the Chinese success, systematic research efforts on hybrid rice were initiated only in the early 1990s to develop suitable rice hybrids for reversing the current yield trend in the irrigated systems. Later on, favourable environments in eastern India, especially the *Boro* rice lands, were targeted for expansion of hybrid rice cultivation during 1994–5, when it was realized that the current hybrids were not suited to the coastal rice lands of south India and the intensive rice–wheat belts of north India (DRR 1997, Rao et al. 1998).

After four years of rigorous research efforts in India (1989–93), the first rice hybrid was released in Andhra Pradesh in the 1993–4 *rabi* season. Subsequently, as many as 20 rice hybrids were released by both the public sector research institutions and the private sector (seed companies) in other states such as Karnataka, Tamil Nadu, West Bengal, Orissa, Maharashtra, and Uttar Pradesh between 1994 and 2001. Indian farmers were very enthusiastic about hybrid rice cultivation during the first couple of years after the release of the first two rice hybrids during the 1993–4 dry season. It was estimated, based on seed sale data, that the area under rice hybrids expanded from 5200 hectares in 1994 to 34,000 hectares by 1996. However, many farmers started dropping out from hybrid rice cultivation, in spite of the subsidy provided on hybrid rice seeds by some state governments during the mid-1990s.

In many regions, hybrid rice was noted to have spread from one location to another without continuous adoption in any location because of the private sector moving hybrid seed from one region to another, to explore the market. These hybrids were not grown continuously in the same region/state. For instance, about 3.0 tonnes of hybrid rice seed of one private hybrid seed company was sold in the Nizamabad district of Andhra Pradesh during 1995 (year of introduction). The seed sale of this hybrid dropped to 1.5 tonnes in 1996 and it was less than 1.0 tonne in 1997 in the same district. A large quantity of seed of the same rice hybrid was marketed in West Bengal during 1995–6, but seed sale was reduced in subsequent years. Later, during 1997–8, the same private company introduced seeds of the same rice hybrid on a large scale in Orissa with the government's subsidy on hybrid seeds. But the poor performance of this hybrid disappointed the farmers and policy-makers. This later became a political issue in the State Assembly because of heavy crop losses incurred as a result of indiscriminate introduction of hybrids in the rainfed lowland ecosystems of the state by the government—with subsidies provided through the private sector. Surprisingly, the same Indian seed company exported about 450 tonnes of seeds of the same rice hybrid with a different name to Bangladesh in 1999, where the experience of the farmers was similar to that of the farmers in Orissa (Hussain et al. 2001).

Although India released hybrid rice much earlier and there has been a concerted effort from both the public and private sectors to disseminate the hybrid rice technology, India could not make much headway in diffusing the technology to the farmers. Thus the adoption rate of hybrid rice in India is too meagre, that is, less than 0.3 per cent of total rice area even 7–8 years after the release of the first rice hybrid. The situation on hybrid rice adoption was reported as being nearly the same in other tropical countries in Asia as in India, except Vietnam (Janaiah and Hossain 2003).

Yield and Profitability Gains

As in the case of any other technology the adoption of hybrid rice in a market economy is basically an economic decision of the farmers. The profitability of the technology compared to any other existing activity that competes for the same resources is the ultimate factor that would determine farmers' decision in the reallocation of rice land from existing varieties to hybrids. The extent of profitability gains is a more important consideration for the commercial farmers in the irrigated rice environment than for the subsistence farmers in the rainfed environments whose activity choice is much more limited.

Any new technology in crop production can generate an additional profit margin over the existing technology through three basic means: (a) change in yield, (b) change in the price of the product, and (c) change in the cost of production. Here we decompose the change in profitability on account of these three factors. The estimates based on farm-level studies during 1993–5, 1997–8 and 2000–1 can be reviewed from Table 9.3 for India.

The findings of various studies as summarized in Table 9.3 show that the hybrid rice varieties are indeed superior to the existing inbred rice varieties with regard to yield. The yield gains over inbred rice varieties are on average 12 to 16 per cent. The results are relatively robust as shown by the almost similar results over a number of years. However, the hybrid rice grain is of inferior quality, so they command lower price in the market compared to the inbred varieties that farmers currently grow. So in terms of gross returns per unit of land (yield valued at market prices) the gains are relatively low. For India the price of hybrid rice grain in the market was about 9 and 11 per cent lower in 1995

TABLE 9.3
Comparative Cost–Return Profile for the Cultivation of Hybrid and
Inbred Rice Varieties Over the Period in India.

(in US$ per ha)

Cost/Return	1993–5			1997–8			2000–1		
	HR	IR	% Diff.	HR	IR	% Diff.	HR	IR	% Diff.
Grain yield (tonns/ha)	6.31	5.63	12.1	6.91	5.91	16	6.8	6.0	13.3
Market price (US$/tonne)	98	107	–8.5	105	117	–11	119	128	–7.0
Gross return[a]	676	665	1.7	758	739	2.6	845	869	–2.8
Total costs[b]	295	263	12.1	283	239	19	377	320	17.8
Net profit	381	402	–5.2	475	500	–5.0	468	549	–14.8

Notes: HR-Hybrid rice; IR-Inbred rice varieties (conventional modern varieties)
[a] Gross return also includes straw value (byproduct value)
[b] Includes imputed cost of seeds when it is subsidized.
For better comparison with other countries, all values were converted into US dollars using official exchange rates as follows:
IUS$ = Rs 32.0 (average of 1993–5) ; IUS$ = Rs 40.0 (average of 1997–8)
IUS$ = Rs 47.0 (average of 2000–1).
Source: Janaiah and Hossain (2003).

and 1998, respectively, and 7 per cent lower in 2001, indicating marginal improvement in grain quality in the newly released varieties. In India, rice straw is an important component of the product since it is used as livestock feed and as material for the thatching of houses. It appears from the surveys that the value of straw is also lower for hybrid rice compared to that of the existing varieties. Taken together, the gross value of production was about 3 per cent lower for hybrid rice compared to that of the inbred ones (Table 9.3).

About 18–19 per cent of higher input costs were registered for hybrid rice cultivation—mainly for hybrid seed cost—as compared to the existing inbred varieties. Although seed requirement per hectare for hybrid rice is only one-third of the seed used for the existing inbred varieties, the price of hybrid rice seed was about Rs 100–120 per kg in India, which was 8–15 times costlier than the seed of inbred varieties. This further contributes to the lower profitability of hybrid rice. The net profit in the cultivation of hybrids was about 5 per cent lower in 1997–8 and 15 per cent lower in 2001 (Table 9.3). This explains why the adoption of hybrid rice has so far been very slow and lingering in India as well as in other countries.

Comparison with the Chinese Experience

It may be noted here that the level of yield gains, and the difference in the output price and the production cost for hybrid rice cultivation in India—as discussed above—are relatively comparable with results reported from the Chinese experience in the farmers' fields.

The Chinese hybrid rice programme was initiated in Hunan Province in 1964. The first rice hybrid with a marked yield potential was developed in 1974 and released to the farmers in 1976 after on-farm testing across the regions. Hybrid rice had about a 15 per cent yield advantage over the best inbred varieties in China, but suffered from lower output price due to poor grain quality. Thus hybrid rice production was not more profitable than the popular inbred varieties (He et al. 1987). It was also reported that rice hybrids were more susceptible to insect pests and diseases (Lin 1991). When rice hybrids were experimented in the farmers' fields in the USA and Japan during the 1980s, inspired by the Chinese success, almost similar problems were reported that led to the discarding of hybrid rice in these countries (Virmani 1993). What is disquieting here is how hybrid rice was widely adopted in China despite all these constraints? It was hypothesized that the nature of political economy of China in the 1970s and 1980s was a primary factor for the large-scale adoption of hybrid rice in that country (Barker and Herdt 1985). Later on it was reported that political pressure from the government was the major factor that contributed to the rapid adoption of hybrid rice in China, especially during the initial stage—pre-reform period (Lin 1991). Often farmers were instructed to plant varieties that the government considered good for the country and the local government agencies/communes ensured that the farmers implemented the decision. It was not unusual in China, when it was a centrally planned economy, to promote certain technologies without considering relative profitability. Government agencies produced hybrid rice seeds and supplied them for free to farmers, supported with subsidies on fertilizers and plant protection chemicals (Lin 1991). The Chinese objective of promoting hybrid rice with direct policy intervention was to increase the domestic rice production to feed rural and urban masses, as well as to feed the livestock—rice is the major feed for livestock in China. As supply of hybrid seed and the procurement of the final produce were in the hands of the state, poor grain quality and higher hybrid seed cost were not constraints to large-scale adoption of this technology in China. In addition to the distinct political set up, other socio-economic factors also favoured the rapid adoption of hybrid rice in China.

Almost 100 per cent rice area is under irrigation and transplantation of rice seedlings is a common practice in about 97 per cent of the rice area in this country. Further, the average size of an operational land holding is very small in China where rice production at the household level is mainly for family consumption as food and feed. Availability of labour is not a limiting factor in rural China for adopting a labour-intensive technology like hybrid rice which, in fact, helped to increase labour earnings of small and marginal households. Therefore, it was the nature of the political economy and other socio-economic factors that were behind the rapid diffusion of hybrid rice in China, not the inherent economic superiority of hybrid rice over the existing inbred varieties. It may be mentioned here that in the 1990s after the introduction of liberalized food production and distribution system the expansion of the area under hybrid rice has halted, and in some of the prosperous south-eastern provinces the area has been declining (Figure 9.2). Area planted to hybrid rice was about 58 per cent in the early 1990s, which declined to about 40 per cent by the year 2001 (Janaiah et al. 2002). With the onset of economic liberalization, farmers and rice consumers in China have started expressing their own preferences. Quality enhancement, therefore, has become the primary breeding objective for hybrid rice research in China to improve the price competitiveness.

Can the Chinese model of hybrid rice promotion be replicated in toto in other Asian countries whose socio-economic conditions under a democratic social system with free operation of the market forces are different from that of China? The answer is a straightforward 'no' (for more details, refer Janaiah et al. 2002). Nevertheless, China is ahead of many Asian countries in the development and use of new frontiers of rice technology, and other countries can learn lessons from these experiences.

It is quite often argued that India is far behind China in terms of paddy yields. China's paddy yields (about 6.2 tonnes per hectare) are nearly double that of India (3 tonnes per hectare). However, it is important to recognize some differences in production environments of rice between China and India. In China, almost 100 per cent rice area is irrigated while it is only about 50 per cent in India. Therefore, the average national yield—which includes about 50 per cent of very low-yielding rainfed areas—of paddy in India is low. In fact, average paddy yields of irrigated areas (Figure 9.1), such as in Andhra Pradesh and Punjab, are almost similar to China's yield figure. Further, average fertilizer use per hectare in China was about 250 kg of plant nutrients, whereas in India, plant nutrient use was only 100 kg per hectare. Thus, the difference in the average yield of paddy between India and China is largely due to variation in production environments and fertilizer uses, not due to technological superiority.

Comparison with Other Tropical Countries in Asia

Many other countries in the Asian tropics initiated hybrid rice R&D in the early 1990s, except Bangladesh,

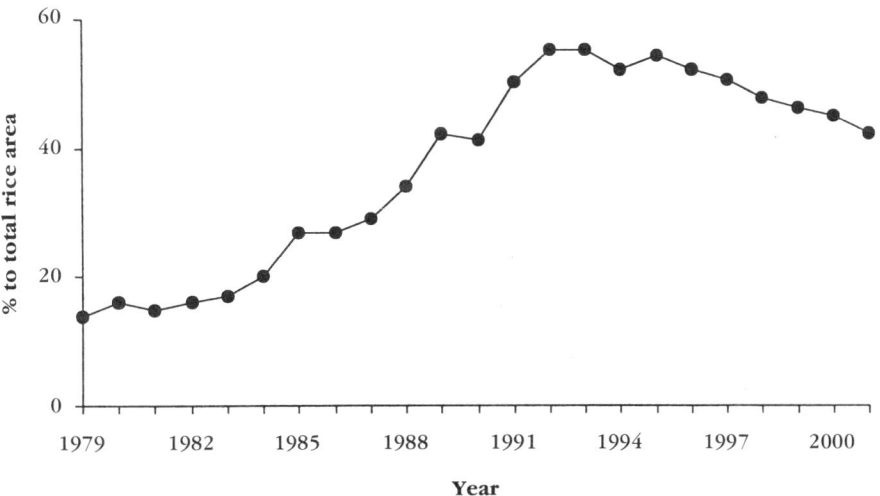

Figure 9.2: Trend in the adoption of hybrid rice in China

which started it in the mid-1990s. However, as in India, other Asian countries in the tropics with the exception of Vietnam, have not made any appreciable progress in the diffusion of hybrid rice technology to the farmers. Most of the farmers who grew hybrid rice in countries such as The Philippines, Bangladesh, and Vietnam were provided with hybrid rice seeds either at subsidized cost under different hybrid rice promotion programmes by the respective governments or by seed agencies for on-farm demonstrations (Janaiah and Hossain 2003).

In Bangladesh, majority of the farmers who grew during 1999 were supplied with hybrid seeds either through micro-credit programmes of NGOs or the Department of Agricultural Extension. The Government of Bangladesh permitted four private seed companies to import 2200 metric tonnes of hybrid rice seeds for the 1998–9 Boro (dry) to cover up the shortage of rice seeds after the devastating floods in the 1998 *Aman* (monsoon) season. It is estimated from the seed sales data that about 24,000 hectares of area was planted with the hybrid rice in the 1999 Boro season. The Bangladesh Rural Advancement Committee (BRAC), the largest NGO, was involved in the commercialization programme of hybrid rice seeds during 1999. However, it was reported that hybrids were introduced in Bangladesh without a clear deployment strategy and without scientific evaluation of the new rice hybrids under farm conditions before importing their seeds. As hybrids did not out-perform other varieties during 1999, farmers have dropped out from continuing hybrid rice during subsequent seasons in Bangladesh (Hussain et al. 2001).

Although hybrid rice R&D had been initiated long ago in The Philippines—both by the public and the private sectors—its adoption by the Filipino farmers is still very limited due to the lack of availability of acceptable hybrid seeds. The total area planted for commercial cultivation of hybrid rice during the 2000 wet season was only 2096 hectares, mostly located in Region 2 and Region 11, while the targeted area was 25,000 hectares, and 150,000 hectares for 2001 and 2002, respectively (Malabanan 2001). The Philippines government initiated a national hybrid rice promotion programme in 1998. The programme's goal is to attain self-sufficiency in the rice sector by promoting hybrid rice technology. At present, the adoption of hybrid rice has been largely due to the vigorous efforts of the Department of Agriculture and the Philippines Rice Research Institute under the special programme, which includes procuring and free distributing of hybrid seeds to the farmers through the technology demonstration farms, and through the 'plant-now-pay-later' and the 50 per cent price subsidy schemes. Farmers who bought hybrid rice seeds on their own (voluntary adopters) were almost absent until 2001, although rice hybrid had been released as early as in 1994. Lack of demand from rice farmers owing to the poor grain quality of the currently available rice hybrids seems to be the principal reason for the non-expansion of the hybrid rice seed industry by the private sector despite appreciable yield gains of hybrid rice over the inbred varieties during the dry season.

Vietnam is the only country in the humid tropics of Asia where the rate of hybrid rice adoption has been growing in its northern and central regions, which have closely similar agro-ecological, political, socio-economic, and institutional features as south China where hybrid rice was popularized in the 1970s and the 1980s. Although Vietnam is a rice surplus country, its northern region is a rice deficit area by about 1.0–1.5 million tones. Thus, in 1992, the government launched a hybrid rice production programme to achieve self-sufficiency in food at the provincial level for the remote and mountainous regions and for provinces with small average sized farms in north and central Vietnam. It is expected that the rice deficit region of north Vietnam can reduce its dependency on the rice surplus southern region through the promotion of hybrid rice in northern Vietnam (Nguyen et al. 1995, Janaiah et al. 2002). Thus the government made a serious commitment for the promotion of hybrid rice in these regions by strengthening R&D efforts and the public and private sector partnership in seed production in the 1990s. Moreover, farmers' cooperatives and communes still play an important role in farmers' decision on farm operations in the north and central regions unlike in the southern region. Since the government has committed itself to the promotion of hybrid rice in the north region, these cooperatives and communes implemented the government decision at the local level, like in China in the 1970s and the 1980s. Most of the farmers were provided with hybrid seeds at subsidized costs either by the government's agency or by the private seed companies under the special promotion programme in Vietnam. By 2002, about 500,000 hectares of rice area was planted to hybrid rice covering 24 provinces out of the total of 61 provinces in Vietnam.

It is important to note that the farm size of households had a significantly negative relation with the rate of hybrid rice adoption in Bangladesh and Vietnam. This indicates that it is the subsistence farmers who are adopting the technology more than the commercial farmers. Presumably, the technology is more attractive to smaller farmers because the higher yield through hybrid rice enables them to produce more food for the family from the small piece of land holding. Since they produce essentially for the family the level of profits is not a factor that influences the decision of which rice seed variety to adopt. Also, since these farmers have low opportunity costs for labour the cost of producing the additional output on the farm is lower than that of the cost acquisition from the market when the size of the farm is not large enough to meet the food needs of the family (Janaiah and Hossain 2003). However, the high cost of hybrid rice seed is a constraint for the small and marginal farmers to adopt this technology. Further, irrigation was also reported to be positively associated with hybrid rice adoption. It indicates the risk aversive behaviour of farmers. Since the cost of hybrid rice cultivation is higher farmers would like to ensure that the crop is not lost due to lack of water control at times of drought (Janaiah and Hossain 2003).

As summarized in Table 9.4, the yield of hybrid rice was higher than the inbreds only for Vietnam, but lower for The Philippines for the wet season—a major rice growing season. However, the yield gains were about 14 per cent, 17 per cent, and 21 per cent, respectively, for the dry season for Bangladesh, The Philippines, and Vietnam.

However, it was reported that the hybrid rice grain was of inferior quality and this got reflected in the increasing difference in the prices of hybrid and inbred varieties. In Bangladesh and Vietnam the hybrid rice faced a lower price in the market but the price difference between hybrids and inbreds was relatively smaller compared to that in India. One reason could be the use in these countries of hybrid varieties of inferior quality imported from China. In The Philippines the same price was assumed for both varieties for the evaluation of profitability gains, because the market was yet to evaluate the quality of the hybrid grains owing to only limited amounts of hybrid coming into the market. The Filipino hybrid was relatively sticky compared to the most popular variety, IR64. Although stickiness is considered to be a sign of inferior quality by south Asian consumers, many Filipinos prefer sticky rice, so this characteristic may not depress the market price significantly, if cooking and keeping qualities are ensured. Overall the gains in net profit for hybrids seem to be appreciable except in The Philippines where it is negative during the wet season (Table 9.4). The profitability gains in hybrid rice cultivation were about 9 per cent and 14 per cent higher for Bangladesh and The Philippines, respectively, during the dry season. But for the wet season the net profit for hybrid rice cultivation was lower for The

TABLE 9.4
Comparative Cost-Return Profile for the Cultivation of Hybrid and Inbred Rice Varieties in Bangladesh, the Philippines, and Vietnam

(in US$ per ha.)

Cost/Return	Bangladesh 1999 Boro			Philippines 2000-1			Vietnam 2000-1		
	HR	IR	% Diff.	HR	IR	% Diff.	HR	IR	% Diff.
Wet season									
Grain yield (tonnes)				5.2	4.9	6.0	6.07	4.99	22
Market price (US$/tonne)				144.4	144.4	–	118.0	123.7	–5.0
Gross return[a]				754	712	6.0	720.3	621.7	16.0
Total costs[b]				411	332	24.0	478.8	443.4	8.0
Net profit				343	380	–10.0	214.5	151.3	42.0
Dry season									
Grain yield (tonnes/ha)	6.44	5.63	14.4	5.9	5.1	17	6.33	5.25	21
Market price (US$/tonne)	126	122	3.0	162.8	162.8	–	124.4	128.4	–3.0
Gross return[a]	853	735	16.2	969	829	17	788.9	676.4	17
Total costs[b]	469	382	22.6	445	370	20	522.6	482.4	8
Net profit	384	353	9.0	524	459	14.0	266.3	194.0	37.0

Notes: HR-Hybrid rice; IR-Inbred rice varieties (conventional modern varieties)
[a] Gross return also includes straw value (byproduct value)
[b] Includes imputed cost of seeds when it is subsidized.
For better comparison among countries, all values were converted into US dollars using official exchange rates as follows:
IUS$ = Bangladeshi Taka 50.0 (average of 1999);
IUS$ = Filipino Pesos 50.0 (average of 2000-1);
IUS$ = Vietnamese Dongs 14,400 (average of 2000-01).
Source: Janaiah and Hossain (2003).

Philippines (Table 9.6) due to lower yield gains.[4] Only in Vietnam, hybrid rice cultivation was of substantially higher profitability compared to the cultivation of inbred rice because of huge subsidies on seeds and fertilizers. However, poor cooking and keeping quality, high seed costs, and other technical constraints remained the same in these countries as it did in India.

Farmers' Perception

In general, most of the sample farmers in all earlier studies reported that hybrid rice had a higher-yielding potential. However, most of them expressed the opinion that hybrid rice had a poor grain quality in terms of cooking and keeping qualities. Farmers in India reported that there was no consumer demand for hybrid rice due to its poor grain quality. The same opinion had been reported by earlier studies based on the farmers' perception during on-farm verification of rice hybrids (1992–3 and 1993–4) that the poor grain quality of the tested rice hybrids would constrain large-scale adoption of this technology in India (Janaiah et al. 1993, Janaiah 1995). Despite a few constraints, some sample farmers—mostly small and marginal farmers in eastern India—expressed their willingness to continue hybrid rice cultivation. Reasons reported by these farmers for continuing hybrid rice cultivation are: (a) higher yields and (b) expecting new hybrids with better quality in the future (Janaiah and Hossain 2003).

Many farmers reported that lack of consumer acceptance of hybrid rice grain because of its poor cooking, eating, and keeping qualities leading to lower market price (especially in India), lower head-rice recovery due to more broken rice after milling, leading to higher costs of rice seed, and formation of sterile grains in the productive tillers were serious constraints that led to the discontinuance of hybrid rice cultivation.

SOME POLICY ISSUES

In recent debates on hybrid rice it has been argued that the lack of policy support is a major factor for the non-adoption of hybrid rice in India. Therefore, it is essential to analyse whether any policy support attract the adoption of the current hybrid rice technology. A few policy options were assessed with regard to their possible impact to minimize some of the currently encountered constraints to large-scale adoption of hybrid rice.

[4] The pest and disease infestations are more serious in the wet season than in the dry season for rice cultivation. As hybrid rice was more susceptible to pests and diseases as compared to the inbred varieties, yield gains were also low for hybrid rice during the wet season.

Subsidy on Hybrid Seed: Is it Enough?

One of the easily available policy options, visible to many policy-makers, for the promotion of any new variety or technology in any crop is subsidizing the seed supply at the initial stage. The same option was also contemplated to promote hybrid rice in some states such as Orissa, West Bengal, and Karnataka. However, farmers in Orissa also expressed unwillingness to continue hybrid rice cultivation despite the 50 per cent subsidy on hybrid seeds. As reported in Table 9.5, subsidy on hybrid seeds alone would not add much extra value to hybrid rice production. Since seed cost accounts for a small fraction of the cost of rice production, the possible impact of subsidy on hybrid seeds alone on hybrid rice promotion would be rather meagre.

TABLE 9.5
Sensitivity analysis on how much subsidy is required for hybrid seed for commercial cultivators of hybrid rice in India
(Rs ha^{-1})

Cost/Return	Alternate scenarios		
	25% subsidy	50% subsidy	75% subsidy
Amount of subsidy on hybrid seed	379	758	1136
Net seed cost	1136	757	379
Total input cost	10,952	10,573	10,195
Net returns to hybrid rice	19,368	19,747	20,125
Net returns to inbred rice	19,999	19,999	19,999
Relative profitability of hybrid rice over inbred rice	−631	−252	126
% relative profitability of hybrid over inbred	−3.2	−1.3	0.6

Source: Janaiah (2002).

Support Output Price: Is Special Incentive Price for Hybrid Rice Feasible?

Another very important and powerful policy instrument to boost technology adoption is incentive output price, and assured market for farm products as experienced during the green revolution era. Unlike in China, in India market forces determine the output price based on grain quality and consumer demand especially in the case of food grains. One option being considered here is whether the government can take the initiative in setting the same market price for hybrid and inbred rice grain as was done in China. In a country such as India, it is very difficult to do so. However, assuming that output price is the same for the hybrid and the existing inbred varieties, the farmer would find hybrid rice production more profitable by about 12 per cent for the current level of yield gains (16 per cent) (Table 9.6). Another possible option—although that has a remote

TABLE 9.6
Sensitivity Analysis on How Much Market Price is Required for Hybrid Rice Grain in India

(Rs ha^{-1})

Cost/Return	Existing price without subsidy on seed	If market price is the same for both hybrid and inbred grains		
		Without seed subsidy	25% seed subsidy	50% seed subsidy
Total input cost				
Hybrid	11,331	11,331	10,952	10,573
Inbred	9563	9563	9563	9563
Gross return				
Hybrid	30,320	33,797	33,797	33,797
Inbred	29,562	29,562	29,562	29,562
Net return				
Hybrid	18,989	22,466	22,845	23,224
Inbred	19,999	19,999	19,999	19,999
Relative profitability of hybrid over inbred	−1010	2467	2846	3225
% relative profitability of hybrid over inbred	−5.1	12.3	14.2	16.1

Source: Janaiah (2002).

possibility with limited scope—is for the government to procure hybrid rice grain in certain areas at the support price fixed for fine varieties; the same may be utilized after parboiling for a PDS. Quality-related constraints could be minimized to a certain extent by parboiling, as experienced in a few locations in Andhra Pradesh and West Bengal (Janaiah 1999). Similarly, the procured hybrid rice grain can be harnessed in rice-based industries for alternative uses. However, such procurement may not be feasible on a large scale, unless consumer demand is improved.

Reorient Research Policy on Hybrid Rice

Since the initiation of hybrid rice research in the early 1990s, it has become largely a 'sole show' of plant breeders—who were mainly drawn from conventional rice improvement programmes. At the moment, the involvement of biotechnologists, molecular geneticists, crop management specialists, plant protection specialists, and social scientists is too limited in the ongoing hybrid rice research in India. As a matter of policy, it is essential to involve all of them through multi-disciplinary approach to achieve the overall goal of having a successful hybrid rice programme in India in view of the country's food security.

Policy on Seed Price: Is it Necessary?

Some seed growers mention the low procurement price paid by private seed agencies. The difference between the price paid by the seed companies to seed growers (Rs 35 per kg) and the control of marketing margin on the seed trade make the price of hybrid seed exorbitant (Rs 100–120 per kg). Therefore, the private seed sector should be enticed to reduce the selling price of the seed and also to pay a higher procurement price to seed growers. Protection of the seed growers' interest through policy intervention may not be either desirable or feasible in the long run. If the market for hybrid seeds expands through wider adoption of hybrid rice, the marketing margin will come down as traders benefit from the economies of scale and the competition among them.

CONCLUSIONS

In conclusion, we can say that hybrid rice had shown a higher yielding potential by 12–16 per cent under farmers' fields in India. Yield gains of hybrid rice were associated with additional production costs. In India, lower market price for hybrid rice grain due to poor grain quality was reported, which resulted in negative relative profitability for hybrid rice farmers. This implies that there was not much improvement in the technology over the period in India. This explains why hybrid rice adoption at farm-level is very slow and lingering across regions/states within India without continued adoption in any region/state over the period.

It was the nature of the political economy and other socio-economic factors that were behind the rapid diffusion of hybrid rice in China, not the inherent economic superiority of hybrid rice over the existing inbred varieties. It may be mentioned here that in the 1990s after the introduction of a liberalized food production and distribution system the expansion of the area under hybrid rice was halted, and in some of the prosperous south-eastern provinces the area continues to decline. Area planted with hybrid rice was about 58 per cent in the early 1990s, but decreased to about 40 per cent by the year 2001.

Vietnam is the only country in tropical Asia where hybrid rice adoption has been growing. It appears that Vietnam's success in hybrid rice is due to the use of Chinese hybrid rice seeds, as well as serious government commitment for a vigorous seed production programme in the public and private sectors. Moreover, farmers' cooperatives and communes in north Vietnam still play an important role in farmers' decision on farm operations as they did in China.

The presently available hybrid rice technology cannot help reverse the decelerating trend in rice productivity growth in the Asian tropics, unless new hybrids with improved grain quality which are acceptable by both farmers and consumers are made available. Although huge capital and human resources—largely diverted from conventional rice improvement programmes that brought in the green revolution in India—were invested in hybrid rice R&D in India over the past 10–12 years, it has not made any difference in the rice sector. The opportunity costs of those resources are enormous. Thus a few viable alternatives and strategies may be considered for the improvement of the rice sector in the Indian context.

In addition to hybrid rice seeds, there are many other viable and simple options available to increase rice yields by 15–20 per cent. For instance, regular replacement of quality seeds of the existing high yielding varieties of rice by the farmers can increase yields by 17–22 per cent without much extra investment (Pal et al. 2000, Hossain et al. 2001). Similarly, timely completion of certain farm operations such as transplanting, weeding, harvesting, etc. with the introduction of labour-saving devices can avoid the increasingly growing labour-shortage in the irrigated region and ultimately improve crop yields. Thus, R&D should focus more on development and popularization of such farmer-friendly methods besides pursuing knowledge-intensive approaches like hybrid rice.

In view of the increasing demand for high quality grain, especially in the irrigated rice systems where farming is highly commercialized, higher yield potential alone does not induce farmers to adopt any variety as has been shown by the hybrid rice experience. It is the profitability gains from production and marketing of a new variety or hybrid that would motivate commercial farmers to replace existing varieties with the new ones in India unlike in China where the choice of the individual farmer to produce what he wants is limited. Therefore, future research on rice improvement in general and hybrid rice in particular should focus on breeding for high value varieties. Further, farmer-realizable yield potential of any new variety/hybrid ought to be increased substantially unlike for hybrid rice with only 12–15 per cent higher potential. Future R&D should also focus on developing pest and disease resistant varieties/hybrids. Since hybrid rice is management-intensive technology (Janaiah 2000), improved complementary crop management methods are needed to exploit the full potential of improved varieties and hybrid rice. Rice hybrids suitable for direct seeding should also be developed in view of the growing labour shortage in the irrigated rice systems.

Many public sector R&D institutions in tropical Asia, including India, have already invested huge resources for hybrid rice development and use. Future research in the public sector, however, may be confined mainly to the development of new parental lines with improved grain quality. As the private sector is going to be the main beneficiary among all key players of hybrid rice R&D, private seed companies should participate actively not only in hybrid seed production and marketing, but also in applied research such as for the refinement of seed production technologies and development of new location—specific hybrids using parental lines from public sector institutions—as experienced for other hybrid crops such as maize, sorghum, sunflower, etc.

References

Ahluwalia, M. S. (2000), 'Economic Performance of States in the Post-Reform Period', *Economic and Political Weekly*, Vol. 35, pp. 1637–47, 6 May 2000.

———— (1978), 'Poverty and Agricultural Performance in India', *Journal of Development Studies*, Vol. 14, pp. 298–323.

Barker, R. and R. W. Herdt (1985), '*The Rice Economy of Asia*', Resources for the Future, Washington, D.C.

Batia, M. S. (1999), 'Rural Infrastructure and Growth in Agriculture', *Economic and Political Weekly*, Vol. 34, pp. A.43–A.68, 27 March 1999.

David, C. C. and K. Otsuka (1994), '*Modern Rice Technology and Income Distribution in Asia*', Lynne Reiner Publishers Inc., Boulder, Colorado.

Desai, B. M. and N. V. Namboodri (1998), 'Policy Strategy and Instruments for Alleviating Rural Poverty', *Economic and Political Weekly*, Vol. 33, pp. 2669–74, 10 October 1998.

Directorate of Rice Research (DRR) (1997), *Development and Use of Hybrid Rice Technology in India- Project Report*, DRR, Hyderabad.

Ghosh, M. (1996), 'Agricultural Development and Rural Poverty in India', *Indian Journal of Agricultural Economics*, Vol. 51, pp. 374–80.

Hayami, Y., M. Kikuchi, P. F. Moya, L. M. Bambo, and E. B. Marciano (1978), *Anatomy of a Peasant Economy: A Rice Village in the Philippines*, IRRI, Los Banos, The Philippines.

Hayami, Y. (1999), *Development Economics*, Oxford University Press, New York, USA.
Hazel, P. and C. Ramasamy (1991), *Green Revolution Reconsidered: Impacts of High-Yielding Varieties in Southern India*, John Hopkins Publishers, Baltimore, UK.
He Guiting, X. Zhu, and J. C. Flinn (1987), 'A Comparative Study of Economic Efficiency of Hybrid and Conventional Rice Production in Jiangsu Province', *Oryza*, Vol. 24, pp. 285–96.
Hossain, M. and P. L. Pingali (1999), 'Rice Research, Technological Progress and Impact on Productivity and Poverty: An Overview', in P. L. Pingali and M. Hossain (eds), *Impact of Rice Research*, International Rice Research Institute, Los Banos, The Philippines and Thailand Development Research Institute, Bangkok, pp. 1–26.
Husain, Muazzam, M. Hossain, and A. Janaiah (2001), 'Hybrid Rice Adoption in Bangladesh: A socio-economic Assessment of Farmers', Experiences', *monograph No. 18*, BRAC, Dhaka and IRRI, The Philippines.
Janaiah, Aldas (2002), 'Hybrid Rice for Indian Farmers: Myths and Realities', *Economic and Political Weekly*, Vol. 37, No. 42, pp. 4319–28.
——— (2000), 'Economic Impact of Crop Management on Productivity and Profitability of Hybrid and Inbred Rice in India: Evidences from a Farm-Level Study', *The Indian Journal of Agricultural Sciences*, Vol. 70, No. 2.
——— (1999), 'Rice Hybrids: Can Indian Farmers and Consumers Accept Them?', *Farmer and Parliament*, Vol. 36, No. 6, pp. 15–17.
——— (1995), 'Economic Assessment of Hybrid Rice Potential in India: An Ex-ante Study', Ph.D thesis (unpublished), Institute of Agricultural Sciences, Banaras Hindu University, Varanasi.
Janaiah, Aldas, A. G. Agarwal, and M. Hossain (2000), 'Poverty and Income Distribution in the Irrigated and Rainfed Ecosystems: Insights from Village Studies in Chhattisgarh, India', *Economic and Political Weekly*, Vol. 35, No. 52.
Janaiah, Aldas, M. Hossain, and M. Hussain (2002), 'Hybrid Rice for Tomorrow's Food Security: Can the Chinese Miracle Be Replicated in Other Countries?', *Outlook on Agriculture*, Vol. 31, No. 1, pp. 27–37.
Janaiah, Aldas and M. Hossain (2003), 'Can Hybrid Rice Technology Help Productivity Growth in Asian Tropics? Farmers' Experiences', *Economic and Political Weekly*, Vol. 38, No. 25, pp. 2492–2501, 21 June.
Lin, J. Y. (1994), 'Impact of Hybrid Rice on Input Demand and Productivity', *Agricultural Economics*, Vol. 10, pp. 153–64.
——— (1991), 'The household responsibility system reform and adoption of hybrid rice in China', *Journal of Development Economics*, Vol. 36, pp. 353–72.
Malabanan, F. (2001), 'Presentation Material for Briefing on National Hybrid Rice Commercialization Targets', Philippines Rice Research Institute (PhilRice), Nueva Ecija, The Philippines.
Nguyen, V. L., V. S. Nguyen, and S. S. Virmani (1995), 'Current Status and Future Outlook on Hybrid Rice in Vietnam', in Denning Glenn and Xuan VT (eds), Vietnam and IRRI: A Partnership in Rice Research. International Rice Research Institute, Los Banos, Philippines.
Pal, S., R. Tripp, and A. Janaiah (2000), 'Public-Private Interface and Information Flow in the Rice Seed System of Andhra Pradesh, India', Policy paper 12, National Centre for Agricultural Economics and Policy Research (NCAP), New Delhi, India.
Pingali, P. L., M. Hossain and R. V. Gerpacio (1997), '*Asian Rice Bowls: the Returning Crisis?*' Oxon: CAB International, Wallingford, oxford.
Pingali, P. L. and M. Hossain (eds) (1999), *Impact of Rice Research in Asia*, International Rice Research Institute, The Philippines.
Pradhan, K. B., P. K. Roy, M. R. Sailaja, and S. Venkataraman (2000), 'Rural-Urban Disparities: Income Distribution, Expenditure Pattern and Social Sector', *Economic and Political Weekly*, Vol. 35, pp. 2527–39, 15 July 2000.
Rao, N. G. P., Ambika Singh, V. Sivasubramanian, K. S. Murthy, A. N. Mukhopadhyay, and C. C. Abraham (1998), 'Rice Research and Production in India: Present Status and a Future Perspective', *Quinquennial Review Report*, Directorate of Rice Research, Hyderabad.
Sampath, S. and H. K. Mohanty (1954), 'Cytology of Semi Sterile Rice Hybrid', *Current Science*, Vol. 23, pp. 182–3.
Virmani, S. S. (1993), 'Global Status of Hybrid Rice Research and Development', in *Hybrid Rice Food Security in India (edited by R. Barwale, 1993)*, Macmillan India Limited, Madras, India, pp. 3–21.

10 Trade Facilitation

Nirmal Sengupta • Moana Bhagabati[1]

Trade liberalization can effectively promote development by allowing the optimal allocation of resources in an economy. Liberalization in trade encompasses more than tariff reduction measures. Within this context, trade facilitation measures are an essential part of libralization as they accelerate trade flows and also support a country's domestic trade regulatory process. As tariff levels have declined through successive GATT/WTO rounds, and global supply chains have come to dominate production patterns, growing attention has been directed to the cost factors that are important for international competitiveness, in particular those incurred in connection with trade formalities and procedures. Much attention has been paid to transaction costs, which are considered alongside tariffs and non-tariff measures as constraints on international trade. An import/export transaction involves a series of processes which translate into costs, both in time and money. This adds to the cost of doing business and ultimately affects a country's growth rates in international trade. In many cases, the losses that businesses suffer at the borders are estimated to exceed the cost of tariffs. Trade transaction costs differ from country to country, depending not only on the characteristics of the traded goods and on factors such as the size and type of businesses but also on the efficiency and integrity of interacting businesses and administrations.

The term 'trade facilitation' is used for a set of tasks designed to reduce the transaction cost incurred in trade. The United Nations Conference on Trade and Development (UNCTAD) estimates[2] that an average customs transaction involves 20–30 different parties, 40 documents, 200 data elements (30 of which are repeated at least 30 times) and the re-keying of 60–70 per cent of all data at least once. In the near future, after full implementation of the Uruguay Round Agreements, the tariff rates will be nominal leading to increase in relative importance of transaction costs. In recent years, therefore, trade facilitation is gaining importance in international trade. International trade in goods involves more procedures and regulations than domestic trade, leading to higher transaction cost for the former. But trade facilitation is important even for domestic trade.

By its narrowest definition, trade facilitation deals only with the logistics of moving goods through ports or more efficiently moving documentation associated with cross-border trade. A broader definition includes the environment in which trade transactions take place—transparency and professionalism of customs and regulatory environments, as well as harmonization of standards and conformance to international or regional regulations. Since improvements in cross-border trade often involve improvements in 'domestic' policies and institutional structures, the definition of trade facilitation has been broadened further. Finally, in the light of the rapid integration of technology into trade facilitation, particularly through the dimension of networked IT, the definition has come to embody a technological imperative as well. It naturally follows, then, that capacity-building efforts can also be considered as part of the trade facilitation effort. The UN agencies, the World Bank, the EU, Asia Pacific Economic Cooperation

---

[1] The authors acknowledge valuable help extended by several individuals, officials, and organizations. The views expressed in this chapter are those of the authors and not of their institutes or the government. Special mention is made of contributions by Rachna Ganatra who has assisted us throughout the project.

[2] Briefing note issued before Doha Ministerial Conference (WTO website—Ministerial Conferences).

(APEC), Organization For Economic Cooperation and Development (OECD), Commonwealth Secretariat, and the International Trade Centre (ITC) use definitions with different scopes (Wilson et al. 2002b, Satpathy 2002). The exhaustive UN/CEFACT (United Nations Centre For Trade Facilitation and Electronic Business) and UNCTAD-compiled Compendium of Trade Facilitation Recommendations lists 237 recommendations conveniently grouped under nine heads. Different fora deal with some but not all these recommendations. Nineteen of the 237 recommendations listed in this Compendium are already subject to WTO discipline. Still, the question of definition of trade facilitation is a highly debated issue in WTO.

formation of a high powered committee under the revenue secretary to go into the problems of transaction costs and to suggest measures/steps to reduce such costs on India's exports. The committee made its recommendations in 1999, many of which have been pursued since then. Recently, the Task Force on Indirect Taxes (Kelkar Committee) indicated the importance of the subject; and its report outlined the basic reforms in customs procedures and trade facilitation. In his budget speech 2003-4, the finance minister recommended trade facilitation measures not only for customs but also for excise. The Medium Term Export Strategy announced by the GOI in January 2002 in the Export and Import (EXIM) Policy 2002-7, and the modified EXIM Policy for

---

Box 10.1

The WTO

The WTO is the only global international organization dealing with the rules of trade between nations. Created by the Uruguay Round negotiations (1986–94) the WTO was established on the 1 January 1995 at Geneva. Its current membership is 146 countries (as on 4 April 2003). The topmost decision-making body of the WTO is the Ministerial Conference, which has to meet at least every two years. It brings together all members of the WTO, and can take decisions on all matters under any of the multilateral trade agreements. Ministerial Conferences were held at Singapore (1996), Geneva (1998), Seattle (1999), Doha (2001), and Cancún (10–14 September 2003).

The four new issues that were proposed for inclusion in the WTO Agreements at the first Ministerial Conference at Singapore, namely, trade and investment, competition policy, transparency in government procurement, and trade facilitation, are known as the Singapore Issues. The Cancún Ministerial Conference could not come to a satisfactory conclusion due to disagreements over the Singapore Issues.

The Singapore Ministerial Declaration defined[3] it as: the simplification of trade procedures in order to assess the scope for WTO rules in this area. It was different from the definition of trade facilitation used in the Doha Ministerial Declaration:[4] ...further expediting the movement, release and clearance of goods, including goods in transit. Trade facilitation, one may note, is one of the four Singapore Issues brought into the WTO agenda.

Trade Facilitation in India

Trade facilitation programmes in India were not undertaken in response to the WTO agenda. India has voluntarily embarked on Trade Facilitation from its felt needs and priorities and depending on available resources. In a Vision Document published by the Central Board of Excise and Customs (CBEC) in 1998, trade facilitation was given the same thrust as realizing revenue and combating duty evasion. In his budget speech for 1999–2000 the Union finance minister announced the

2003–4 have set broad policy directions for facilitating trade and for reducing transaction time and costs.

The number of international conventions[5] a country is party to can, to a certain extent, ascertain the extent of its commitment to trade facilitation. India has a commendable position in this matter. Next to the European countries, India is in the league of countries such as the USA, Canada, or Korea that have accepted most trade facilitation instruments. India's commitments to trade facilitation instruments are better than some of the countries known in the WTO as the 'Friends of Trade Facilitation'[6], for example, Japan, Singapore, Hong Kong China, Chile, Colombia, Costa Rica, and Paraguay.

About 95 per cent of India's foreign trade by weight/volume and about 70 per cent by value involve transportation by sea. As much as 60 per cent of the total freight traffic of India moves on roads. For obtaining

---

[3] Paragraph 21 of the Singapore Declaration.
[4] Paragraph 27 of the Doha Declaration.
[5] As listed in (a) Compendium of Trade Facilitation Recommendations, UN (2001) and (b) Trade Facilitation: Background Note: (Revision), -G/C/W/132/Rev.1; 29 March 1999, Council for Trade in Goods, WTO.
[6] Also known as the Colorado Group.

customs clearance, goods for import or export are brought to the customs stations and kept at customs areas for clearance by the customs authorities. Customs stations include customs ports, inland container depots (ICDs), customs airports, and land customs stations (LCSs). India has a coastline of approximately 6000 kms with 12 major ports and 145 minor ports. It has a very long border with its neighbouring countries with more than 100 LCSs. The Airports Authority of India (AAI) maintains five international cargo terminals in Delhi, Mumbai, Kolkata, Chennai, and Thiruvananthapuram. In addition, there are six other airports granted international airport status (as on June 2000), namely, Amritsar, Ahmedabad, Goa, Guwahati, Hyderabad, and Bangalore. There are eight customs airports in the country—Calicut, Coimbatore, Tiruchirapalli, Jaipur, Agra, Lucknow, Varanasi, and Patna—for clearing import-export cargo. The AAI handles export cargo on behalf of over 55 operating airlines.

The container system for the movement of general cargo was introduced late in India, but has shown a steady increase. Over 160 ICDs and container freight stations (CFSs) have been set up outside the ports and in their hinterland to give the exporters and importers easier access to cargo clearance. The multimodal transport and door-to-door movement of goods under the responsibility of a single transport operator—multimodal transport operator (MTO)—is in operation in India with around 200 MTOs. India is one of the few developing countries that have standards imposed on MTOs by the government. The GOI enacted the Multimodal Transportation of Goods Act 1993, based on the UNCTAD/ICC (The International Chamber of Commerce) rules. The Directorate General of Shipping, Mumbai regulates the multimodal transport governed by the Act.

Data and Documentation

On an average, documents required for importing or exporting one consignment in/out of India includes:[7]

Type of documents	29
No. of copies	118
No. of signatures	256
Manpower required	7
Cost of procedures	10 per cent of consignment value

The following documents are expected to be submitted by an importer/exporter for the clearance of goods through customs.[8]

[7] An UN ESCAP estimate.
[8] Customs Law Manual, 2002-3, pp. 1.14.

For Import	For Export
1. Bill of entry	1. Shipping bill
2. Invoice and packing list	2. Invoice and packing list
3. Import licence where necessary	3. Export licence/quota certificate where necessary; PAN (permanent account number)-based business identification number (BIN)
4. Country of origin certificate where preferential rate is claimed	4. Export inspection agency's certificate where necessary
5. Insurance memo/policy	5. G.R.I form/S.D.F declaration under electronic data interchange (EDI) system
6. Bill of lading or delivery order	6. A.R.E—1/2 forms on central excise

The present format of the Shipping Bill, evolved in 1991, is the only notable success in simplification of customs procedures. It is already a common document used by various departments, such as the customs, the RBI, and the port trust. Prior to this, numerous declarations were required to be signed by the importer/exporter, in addition to the specific legal provisions, for certifying and validating the information provided. A new form for obtaining entry inwards was introduced in 1995, designed according to the IMO-FAL Convention. A host of enclosures were sought with these forms—a practice having its origin in other statutes such as the Merchant Shipping Act, 1880. However, in keeping with the said Convention, the CBEC has issued instructions dispensing with the submission of various documents.

Several other attempts were made to simplify this system of documents, but few have been pursued further. In 1991, along with the modified Shipping Bill, a UN aligned documentation was evolved for several commercial documents such as invoice, proforma invoice, packing list, inspection certificate, shipping order, etc. which was left to voluntary adoption and, therefore, did not become extensive. The United Nations Economic and Social Commission for Asia and the Pacific (UN ESCAP) started a project[9] for this, with little consequence. The Sunder Committee looked into the feasibility of evolving a single transport document, and suggested that the Multimodal Transport (MMT) document may be used for this purpose. But implementing this suggestion requires the acceptance of this document by several agencies, including banks and insurance; and no initiative has been taken as yet. On the import side, the Sunder

[9] In May 1999, the UN ESCAP, with the financial support of the Government of Japan initiated the Project on the Alignment of Trade Documents and Procedures of India, Nepal, and Pakistan.

Committee recommended evolving a Single Administrative Document (SAD) along the lines of the European Commission (EC), again without any positive impact.

Some other procedures such as for the trans-shipment of imported cargo from the gateway ports to other ports/ICDs/CFSs have been simplified. For issuance of permission for trans-shipment from a gateway port, a single window system has been introduced, where applications for trans-shipment are processed expeditiously with the use of computers. The drawback payment system has been re-engineered to provide for direct disbursement of the amount into the exporters' bank accounts after the goods have been exported. All central as well as state public sector undertakings and custodians of ICDs/CFSs, have been exempted from the requirement of bank guarantee for undertaking trans-shipment of imported cargo from the gateway ports of ICDs/CFSs.

Electronic Facilities

To reduce the paperwork for the clearance of import/export goods, the government has introduced a system of EDI. Automation leads to quicker clearances, standardization of procedures, reduced discretion, less interface, and faster decision-making, all of which greatly benefit trade and industry. At the same time, compliance issues are not neglected and, in fact, there is far greater control, though unobtrusive—which is desirable. However, a successful automation programme rests upon committed administrative support backed by significant financial investment (Kelkar Report 2002).

India joined the EDI movement in 1992, when it became a member of the Asia Pacific Council for Facilitation of Procedures and Practices for Administration, Commerce and Transport (AFACT, earlier Asia EDIFACT Board). The apex body, the EC/EDI Council of India, is gradually laying down a policy framework. National standards for EDI implementation, commercial transactions and bar coding have been announced. The Information Technology Act was adopted in 2000. The Act provides legal recognition for transactions carried out by means of EDI and other means of electronic communication.

There are three systems which form the major components of custom automation and EDI:

(i) The Indian Customs EDI System (ICES). These are now operational at 23 major customs locations handling nearly 75 per cent of India's international trade in terms of import and export consignments. ICES has two aspects:

(a) Internal automation of the customs house for a comprehensive, paperless, fully automated customs clearance system that makes the functioning of customs clearance transparent.

(b) Online, real-time electronic interface with the trade, transport, and regulatory agencies concerned with customs clearance of import and export cargo.

ICES is designed to exchange/transact customs clearance electronically using EDI. A large number of documents that trade, transport, and regulatory agencies (collectively called trading partners) are required to submit/receive in the process of live customs clearance are now being processed online.

(ii) The Message Exchange Servers (MES): These are computers installed in the customs houses alongside the ICES computers and play as intermediate stations holding incoming and outgoing messages.

(iii) ICEGATE (Indian Customs and Central Excise Electronic Commerce/Electronic Data Interchange Gateway) and ICENET (Indian Customs and Central Excise Network): ICENET is a network of all the 23 ICES locations, the CBEC, the Directorate of Valuation, the National Informatics Centre (NIC), and the Directorate General of Revenue Intelligence (DGRI).

An infrastructure project, ICEGATE fulfils the department's EC/EDI and data communication requirements. Through this facility the department would be able to offer a host of services including electronic filing of the bills of entry (import goods declaration) and shipping bills (export goods declaration) and related electronic messages between customs and the trade using a choice of communication facilities including the communication protocols commonly used on the Internet. The airlines and shipping agents can file manifests on the Internet file using this facility. Besides, data will flow between customs and the various regulatory and licensing agencies such as the Directorate General of Foreign Trade (DGFT), the RBI, the Apparel Export Promotion Council (AEPC), the Textile Export Promotion Council (TEXPROCIL), and the Directorate General of Commercial Intelligence and Statistics (DGCI&S). The National Import database (NIDB) is also being serviced through ICEGATE. All electronic documents/messages being handled by ICEGATE would be processed at the customs' end by the ICES. To ensure that all links and equipment are functioning properly to sustain the services on the gateway, a certain software called the Enterprize Management Systems has been installed to centrally manage the facility. The system provides for helpdesk facility. To ensure secure filing, it is proposed to use digital signatures on bills of entry and other documents/messages to be handled on the gateway. For this purpose, a Certificate Authority is being set up for issuance of digital signature certificates. Table 10.1 shows the customs' EDI trading partners.[10]

TABLE 10.1
The Customs' EDI Trading Partners

EDI trading partner	Nature of information exchanged through EDI
Importers/Exporters/Customs house agents	Bills of Entry/Shipping bills and related messages
Airlines/Shipping agents	Manifests and cargo logistics messages
Custodians (AAI/Port Authorities/CONCOR)	Cargo logistics messages
Banks	Financial messages—duty drawback disbursal and customs duty payment
AEPC/TEXPROCIL	Export quota information
DGFT	Licence, shipping bills, and IE code data
RBI	Forex. Remmittance data
DGCI&S	Trade statistics
Directorate of valuation	Valuation data

The gateway project has emerged from the necessity to enable remote filing of customs declarations by the importers and exporters from their offices and to enable EDI with the trading partners. Under this system, the custom house agent (CHA) or the importer lodges the import document called the bill of entry by using service centres. The appraising officers of customs assess the document online and their approval is communicated electronically to the CHA/importer. The system provides for clarification of doubts through an exchange of queries and replies between customs and trade. Thereafter, the import duty can be paid at the designated banks that are linked to customs on EDI. The only interface between customs and the import trade is at the time of collection of goods.

By establishing the gateway, the customs will be able to facilitate:

• Filing of import and export declarations online over the Internet to any of the 23 major customs locations and obtain online clearance.

• The international cargo carriers can file the customs cargo reports or manifests electronically.

• Regulatory agencies such as the DGFT, the RBI and the export quota agencies can exchange online information with the major custom houses.

EDI has been introduced at almost all the major ports and air cargo complexes. The software required for the EDI operation has been developed by the NIC and the EDI customs service centres are manned by CMC Ltd. However, this is at variance with the United Nations Electronic Data Interchange for Administration, Commerce, and Transport (EDIFACT) and is not able to send or receive EDIFACT messages. A serious problem is that the measures taken in India are not always in harmony with international systems. Every port was left to develop its own system. They chose the EDIFACT standards. As a consequence, at present, the EDI cannot operate between customs and ports. Traders are required to establish necessary infrastructure to send the same message in two different formats for ports and customs. They are not ready to make such investments, in absence of any visible benefits, when ports and customs are yet to be linked.

Computerization in India started spontaneously through independent initiatives by departments and agencies. The efforts made at present are largely standalone using different systems and not always in accordance with international documentation and data formats. The effectiveness of the EDI system depends on the connectivity between all the players—ports, airports, customs, the DGFT, the RBI, steamer agents, shippers—ultimately reaching railways, road transport, banks, insurance and so on. The Customs Gateway Project is seen as the panacea to all problems. Until its full implementation, the traders have to make extra effort for entering the data. Transaction cost has indeed gone up as a consequence of partial implementation of EDI. Even the claim that about 80 per cent of India's international trade is covered by the 23 automated customs stations is suspect. In most stations only a part of the data has been computerized, leaving ample room for unscrupulous parties to take advantage of loopholes. It is not clear what policy directives have been issued by the government, although the details are required to be finalized after meetings and discussions. Future plans, policies, goals, timeframe, EDI architecture and practice, or quality of service and certification criteria could not be traced. The current EDI system lacks documented architectural framework in keeping with international standards. Lack of knowledge of standards is a major drawback. There is a complete lack of EDI expertise to manage a comprehen-

[10] CBEC website, http://www.icegate.gov.in/ICES.html

sive solution. However, there is excellent IT expertise to build the system and individually, the EDI set-up appears to be operating well within the respective agencies. However, the systems do not connect well or extend.

In an example of the operation of EDI, the Chennai Port Trust (ChPT) is moving towards facilitating paperless transaction for port users with plans to introduce an electronic facility to access all information at the ports including vessel arrival and berthing. Users can also book workers, hire equipment and other marine services. In the second phase, the ChPT will include electronic payment whereby port users can make all port-related payments online. At the Air Cargo Complex, Delhi, the ICES also provides for the filing of the declarations, that is, bills of entry and shipping bills electronically from the premises of the importer/exporter or his agent through the Remote EDI System. This facility does away with the requirement of the importer/CHA of having to come to the custom house for filing a declaration. In locations other than the Air Cargo Complex, Delhi, the importers and exporters have to use the service centre facilities till the Gateway Project gets implemented. Remote filing has been standardized and made universal. Tele-enquiry systems have been introduced at major custom houses for automated information regarding status of import and export consignments. The facility for filing the import and export documents over the Internet is also expected to be introduced shortly. Touch screen kiosks have been installed in some custom houses.

Transparency

All the rules and notifications are available real time on the DGFT website and 75 per cent of the licence applications are being filed and processed online. The CBEC website has gone online in August 2000. However, both these websites carry only a fraction of the necessary information. Given the present facilities, the comprehensive notification on customs procedure, ruling, or guideline of general application that is needed for international trade is not difficult to meet; but a systematic effort is lacking.

In the past few years, a number of steps have been taken to simplify the tariff structure. Some of these measures are: (i) reduction in the number of slabs of duty rates, (ii) reduction in the number of exemption notifications, and (iii) uniformity in rates of duty in chapters. These measures have considerably reduced disputes in classification and delays in customs clearance. The simplification in tariff structure has, in turn, simplified the customs clearance procedures to a great extent. A new commodity classification for imports and exports has been adopted by the DGFT and will also be adopted by the CBEC and the DGCI&S. The common classification to be used by the DGFT and the CBEC will eliminate the classification disputes and, hence, reduce transaction cost and time.

Customs and central excise procedures are being changed rather frequently. Invariably, the procedures are framed in consultation with the field officers and there is no apparent involvement of the trade and industry (Kelkar Committee Report 2002). Informal prior consultation goes on before the budget and other policy announcements. The Kelkar Committee recommended constituting a Standing Committee on Procedures. New procedures come into effect from the date they are brought to the notice of field formations. Each instruction contains a direction to the field formations to issue suitable public notices/trade notices to inform the trade. Not only does this catch the trade by surprise but it may also happen that a procedure had been in force but had not been complied with for the reason that the trade may not have been aware of it. Invariably, such situations also lead to compliance issuance and disputes. Also, the departmental systems personnel are unable to modify their software, if required (Kelkar Committee Report 2002).

The judicial and administrative systems in India, in general, are complete with review and appeal procedures. Provisions for Advance Rulings exist in the Customs Act, and also in the Finance Bill, 1999. Procedures and organizational set-up for advance rulings may be developed in due course. As per the revised Kyoto Convention, an adjudication order is to be issued by the customs within the period specified in the national legislation. The Indian Customs Act has since been amended with a provision that the adjudication order is to be issued by the proper officer within a period of one year in cases involving collusion, wilful misstatement or suppression of facts, and within six months in other cases. These are yet to be effective.

Appeals against any decisions regarding valuation and procedures taken by the customs authorities is examined by the commissioner (appeals) within three months of communication from customs. Judicial appeals to the Customs, Excise, and Service Tax Appellate Tribunal (CESTAT)[11] may be made within three months of communication from customs. However, it is not possible for the commissioner (appeals) to decide all appeals within the three-month period, due to shortage of staff and infrastructure support, and given the fact that the tribunal receives appeals on matters other than valuation and classification. It is claimed that the number of

---

[11] Earlier known as Customs Excise and Gold Control Appellate Tribunal (CEGAT).

appeals made to the Appellate Tribunal on customs matters and decisions taken on appeals for this period have come down though there is still a long way to go.[12] The regular appellate machinery broadly works under the following mechanism:

There are four tiers of officials: assistant commissioners → deputy commissioners → joint commissioners → commissioners;
↓
The first round of appeals to the commissioner (appeals);
↓
Majority of cases to be decided by the commissioner;
↓
Appeals against the commissioners' order to go to CESTAT;
↓
A percentage of cases to go to the high court;
↓
and, a finally, the Supreme Court to arbitrate the cases which move up.

Alternate to this system is the Settlement Commission which was set up in 1998 to deal with tax and trade-related disputes and offences. The Commission, inter alia, has the power to grant immunity from prosecution and full or partial, immunity, from infliction of fine, penalty, and interest provided the assessee makes a true and full declaration of his duty liability. It is a forum for self-surrender and seeking relief and not a forum for challenging legality of assessment orders.

The EXIM Policy (1999–2000) proposed the appointment of an ombudsman at Mumbai. For attending to problems at gateway ports and airports, no regular system exists. The Sunder Committee recommended the appointment of a high level functionary for mediation.

Dwell Time Reduction

Special attention is given to the speedy handling of cargo for reducing its dwell time. The objective is to reduce dwell time of exports to 12 hours, and of imports to 24 hours to conform with internationally accepted norms. An EXIM Bank sample survey of select firms followed by an update (EXIM 2003), show the perceptions of Indian exporters about the importance of transaction costs in different industries, expressed as percentage of export revenues. The two studies show that very remarkable improvements have been brought about in dwell time reduction, in just five years, between 1998 and 2003. Infrastructure relating to cargo handling—like satellite freight cities with MMT, cargo terminals, cold storage, automatic storage and retrieval systems, mechanized transportation of cargo, computerization and automation, etc.—is being set up. Exporters can now stuff their cargo at the CFS approved by the customs authority. These CFSs have also been given the authority of acting as the custodians of the cargo, where customs examination facilities are available. Likewise, importers can take their import boxes for destuffing, and take charge of their cargo. This reduces the dwell time for import/export boxes at the port of entry/exit.

The procedure for movement of goods in coastal vessels has been simplified considerably. To allow the trader to take clearance of cargo at their nearest port, a scheme has been introduced to allow the imported cargo to be unloaded at a gateway port to be taken to another port in a coastal vessel. The formalities for customs clearance are undertaken at such other ports. Similarly, export cargo after clearance at a port may be taken to another port in a coastal vessel for loading on to an outbound vessel. In such cases, duty drawback is paid immediately after export has been allowed at the originating port without waiting for the proof of export from the gateway port. For better capacity utilization of such coastal vessels and to reduce the freight cost, the government has allowed the carriage of domestic cargo along with import/export cargo. Also, to increase the competitiveness among various modes of transport, it has allowed movement of export cargo from one port to another by rail. A procedure for the carriage of export cargo from ICDs/CFSs/factories to gateway ports/airports by trucks has also been introduced for faster movement of cargo.

To develop Indian ports as consolidation hub ports, the government has allowed consolidation of LCL cargoes at Indian ports. The facility allows shipping lines to take the containers stuffed with LCL export cargo, irrespective of destination, from ICD/CFS to a gateway port, where these are opened and reworked with cargoes received from different ICDs/CFSs. After such re-working, cargoes are stuffed in containers destinationwise. Similarly, LCL import cargo brought from different destinations at any gateway port is allowed to be re-worked and consolidated to stuff containers ICD-wise. The facility of re-working of containers at gateway ports has immensely benefited the exporters and importers by way of saving in freight charges, reduction in transit time, and better handling and safer delivery of cargoes.

Exporters are allowed to get their goods stuffed in containers in their factories in the presence of officers from the customs or central excise. Such factory stuffed containers are not subject to further examination at the gateway ports. Until very recently, the exporters were required to take permission from the concerned department each time they wanted to avail of the facility.

---

[12] Pending matters are in the range of 10 or 20 thousands.

In some of the field formations, permission was being given for a fixed period ranging from three to six months. To avoid procedural hassles involved in renewal of permission for factory stuffing, the government has recently introduced a system of one-time permission, to be valid forever unless withdrawn by the customs in case of the exporter's involvement in irregular activities.

Regulations have been framed to allow import and export through the courier mode. The customs clearance facility for items imported and exported through courier mode is presently available at Delhi, Chennai, Kolkata, Mumbai, Ahmedabad, Jaipur, Bangalore, and Hyderabad airports and at land customs stations at Petrapole and at Gojadanga in West Bengal. As soon as goods arrive, these are cleared by customs on the fulfilment of simple formalities by the courier companies. The importer/exporter or his representation need not come to the customs for taking clearance.

It is claimed that approximately 80 per cent of daily air cargo shipments are assessed on the same day by the customs (subject to the condition that all the required documentation is complete). The AAI has launched 'Operation Instant Cargo' which envisages decongesting of the Import Cargo Terminals by disposing of all unclaimed/uncleared cargo in consultation with the customs. To allow expeditious clearance of import/export goods, the government has introduced two-shift working, extended working hours for customs at the air cargo complexes and allowed work on holidays. The EDI system that enables ships to inform the port authorities about their cargo arrangements so that the port authorities can prepare for a speedy unloading of vessels, together with linkage to customs to enable cargo clearance in advance, has not, however, been established in all the major ports.

Faster Clearance and Risk Analysis

Modern best practice calls for a systems approach that relies on self-compliance (through the maintenance of business records by taxpayers), risk analysis and management (development of profiles of risky transactions), and supported by periodic post audits of records. This approach reduces delays for legitimate transactions while allowing full scrutiny of high-risk transactions. In this background, systemic changes were recommended by the Kelkar Committee.

As a measure of trade facilitation and to reduce the transaction cost of exports, the government has reduced the scale of examination for export goods considerably and also simplified the procedure for examination of such cargo. For a long time now, books, periodicals, newspapers, and lifesaving drugs are being allowed clearance on a fast track mode, that is to say, these goods are cleared instantaneously without any procedural delays.

Perishables, commercial samples, and exhibition goods are also cleared on observance of simple formalities. The government has also introduced a Fast Track Clearance Scheme under which certain categories of importers have been allowed to pay duty and clear the imported goods on the basis of self-assessment of duty. A facility for obtaining faster clearance through the green channel is available to select importers, especially those who have a good track record. In view of the fact that the examination norms for export cargo have been lowered significantly, a little higher percentage of examination has been prescribed for export consignments sent to sensitive places.

The government has constituted a Project Team to work on the customs re-engineering exclusively. The Project Team is working on several projects to simplify and modernize customs procedures such as: Accelerated Customs Clearance Procedure (ACCP), post-clearance audit, and risk management strategy. ACCP will be based on self-assessment principle available to all eligible importers and exporters subject to fulfilment of certain conditions. The goods cleared under the ACCP will be subject to post-clearance audit. With respect to importers not eligible for the ACCP, the existing assessment process will continue. However, even in these cases, there shall be no concurrent audit and they too will be subject to post-audit. For hazardous goods, there are special procedures like a 'cooling off' period of 24 hours, insisted upon at the airports.

At present, the initial audit of the assessments is done through the mechanism of concurrent audit. In line with best international practices, the Project Team is working on a project for introduction of post-clearance audit. The CBEC recently introduced a new self-assessment scheme called the Accelerated Clearance of Import and Export Scheme (ACS). The importer will determine the 8-digit custom classification, claim the relevant exemption benefit, declare the correct value as loaded in the invoice and the EDI system will calculate the duty based on such declaration. Physical inspection of imported goods will be done by using risk assessment and management techniques on a computer-based system, and not on the order of customs examining staff. The existing system of concurrent audit of import documents will be replaced by post-clearance audit. The scheme would apply to those importers/exporters operating for the past two years from a particular customs station, who have filed at least 25 bills of entry during the preceding year at that station, and against whom no proceedings have been initiated under Customs, Central Excise/Foreign Exchange Management Act (FEMA), etc. Initially, the scheme would be operated on a pilot basis at Air Customs (import/export) at Sahar, ICD Tughlakabad in New Delhi, and Chennai Sea Customs (import/export).

A post-clearance audit, to be conducted through desk audit, commodity-based audit, and field audit—either individually or in combination—is being introduced by the GOI. The scheme will be launched through a few pilot projects. The feedback from the pilot projects will be taken as the basis for designing the whole process. This is because considerable ground will have to be covered and a great deal of details spelt out for implementing the post-clearance audit. The experiences of many European countries show that it takes a decade or more for the system to take firm root. Recently, a systems appraisal procedure has been introduced by the customs department, but very few have come forward to avail of this opportunity.

India has already reduced the percentage of check on consignment to about 2 per cent. At present, the various customs formations have been informally using the technique of risk analysis that can be observed from the existing procedures. The department relies upon the experience of its officers to evaluate the risk towards revenue while processing the information provided by the importer. The officers evaluate the risk by taking into account factors such as the country of origin, nature of transaction, current domestic prices, background of the importer, etc. A codified risk management module has been tested recently for import consignments at ICD Tughlakabad. The computerized module assesses import consignments through 21 risk factors and analyses 11,640 items, identifying sensitive consignments and indicating the rest for immediate release. Since there is a tendency to draw parallels, we note, risk assessment in this area has no similarity to that of the Sanitary and Phyto-sanitary Measures (SPS) Agreement. Under Article 3.3 of the SPS Agreement of the WTO, countries may set their own level of protection. But it is mandatory to notify such country standards in advance to enable traders to comply with them. However, if this procedure is followed and the customs department discloses its risk assessment parameters it might direct smuggling through 'low-risk lines'.

Many of these reforms have not made much impact because of some serious bottlenecks. For example, customs-cleared containers are not allowed to be moved from one port to another—even in case of disruption of the scheduled arrival of a vessel—without following the 'back to town' procedure. Many of the export consignments require clearance/certification from designated export inspection agencies. The respective agencies are located at different places and some of them are far away from the port/airport and ICD/CFS. As a result, exporters have to spend considerable time and effort in obtaining these certificates. Moreover, departments and agencies dealing with the clearance of import/export cargo have different holidays and limited working hours.

Very few of exporters and importers are able to avail of the facilities of self-sealing of export containers by exporters with good records and the fast track scheme for customs clearance. Customs officials rarely accept self-sealing of export containers because they feel that there are numerous export incentive schemes providing immense scope of frauds leading to loss of revenue. For similar reasons, very few cases are allowed under the fast track scheme for customs clearance. The developed countries have succeeded not because of low tariff rates or absence of export incentives but because of complementary mechanisms like the post-clearance audit. For various reasons the development of such practices is slow. One reason is the absence of excise audit without which post-clearance audit is not possible. In the absence of a common identification number for scrutiny, audit of this nature is impossible. Without a common identification the databases available at different departments cannot be accessed. Recently, a high level decision was taken to use the PAN (Permanent Account Number) for the purpose of a unique identification number. But this is applicable only for the income-tax payers.

Owing to much higher rate of tariffs, customs-related malpractice is high in the developing countries and there is a greater incidence of smuggling, undervaluation, misclassification as well as importation of substandard and counterfeit/pirated goods. It is argued that security of revenue demands greater control and vigilance since goods get diverted en route within the transit country itself without payment of duty. According to Finger and Schuler (1999), where the tariffs are high and accounting expertise and access to electronic information limited, shifting to a risk-based valuation system that depends on in-depth examination of a sample (15 or 20 per cent) of shipments might increase (rather than decrease) the number of shipments on which importers attempt to under-invoice. Traders might view the change as giving them a better, not worse, chance to get away with under-invoicing. However, these arguments seem to be based on imperfect understanding of the suggested procedures. Risk analysis is conducted with the sole purpose of paying greater attention to high risk shipments instead of dividing the resources equally. If high risk areas are correctly identified in the risk analysis method adopted, the approach will increase the intensity of scrutiny of such areas leading to a consequent reduction in chances of getting away with under-invoicing. In effect, it allows greater control and vigilance where needed and, therefore, it is not likely to have an adverse effect on security of revenue. But there are genuine problems in some other spheres, which may limit the ability of the customs officials to deal with deliberately under- or over-valued imports.

Financial Matters

In India, the major ports are placed in Serial 27 under the Union List of the Constitution, and are administered under the Major Port Trusts Act (MPTA), 1963 by the GOI. Other ports are placed in Serial 31 of the Concurrent List of the Constitution and are administered under the India Ports Act, 1908. The other Acts applicable in the port sector are the Merchant Shipping Act 1958, and the Dock Workers (safety, health, and welfare) Act 1986. In 1997, the GOI allowed the major ports to set up joint ventures with foreign ports, minor ports, or private companies. For modernization, the government took the decision that all new ports would be set up as companies under the Indian Companies Act and the existing port trusts would also be gradually corporatized and set up as companies, eventually leading to their privatization. Once the private sector was allowed entry into the major ports to provide services often in competition with the port trusts, there was a demand from the private sector for an independent regulator to set port tariffs. In 1996 the Tariff Authority for Major Ports (TAMP) was established. All the powers of the government pertaining to transaction of business, appointment of staff, and guidelines for regulations on tariff are now vested with TAMP. An attempt has been made by TAMP to introduce transparency and promote participation of interested parties, but it has no jurisdiction over the minor/private ports (Sunder and Sarkar 1999).

After its formation, the TAMP became an authority for fixing tariffs. But it had no other regulatory functions or powers. All the conservancy powers in ports and all other regulatory functions in regard to safety, etc. were vested in the port trust. With private investment coming in, some of the port trusts have been arguing that there is no need for TAMP and what is required at best is a tribunal to hear complaints, if any, against port tariffs. A recent proposal is to convert TAMP into an appellate tribunal and restore powers to the major port trusts to fix and revise tariffs. This, in effect, would leave the tariff-setting mechanism to market forces. In this scenario, major port trusts and private operators at major ports would be free to fix and revise their own tariffs with an appellate body at the helm to take care of user grievances. While the rates approved by the TAMP would be the tariff for the major port trusts, it would only act as a ceiling for the private operators beyond which they cannot charge. However, this may not ensure a fair, simple, and transparent system of tariffs. Ideally, competition should ensure that the charges levied are reasonable and that the quality of service is satisfactory. However, competition is lacking in most areas. Many private service providers are monopoly operators. On many occasions traders have to pay extra for inefficiencies even if the payment is to be at approved rates. Services received may not be commensurate with the charges. Many agents such as the steamer agents, freight forwarders, air cargo agents, stevedores, MTOs, etc. often charge very high rates for nominal services. Agents of foreign MTOs, who are registered neither with the Directorate General of Shipping nor with the customs, often collect very high sums of money for delivery of goods without rendering additional service.

Unless competition develops, the situation will not improve. Till then, regulation may be another way for keeping the fees and charges at reasonable levels. Indeed, TAMP was constituted with this purpose. But each port has its own tariff schedule and scales and also the accounting procedures are different. Without uniformity and common accounting procedures amongst ports, TAMP cannot hope to move towards fixing uniform principles for tariffs.

Foreign manufacturers are required to observe certain provisions of the Bureau of Indian Standards (BIS) Act. The Act also specifies liabilities for the violation of certain provisions. In order to meet the statutory provisions, it has been considered necessary to make some person legally liable, under a certification scheme, for non-adherence to such statutory provisions. For purposes of registration and licence application formalities, the foreign exporter must have a liaison office or a commercial subsidiary in India. He cannot have recourse to an agent (importer, distributor). Indeed, the licence application must be submitted through a subsidiary or through the Indian office of the foreign company. In addition, the exporter must provide proof of authorization from the Indian authorities to open such an office in India. Finally, the foreign manufacturer undertakes not to relocate his office within Indian territory without authorization from the BIS. However, in order to simplify the matter further, while keeping the provision for liabilities intact, the issue of permitting appointment of an Indian agent located in India (who would accept the liabilities under the Act on behalf of the foreign manufacturer through an agreement/undertaking) is being considered.

The financial agencies related to export and import play the primary role in safeguarding receipt and payment of funds; banking institutions have also been playing an active role in creating export capability among Indian companies. These agencies are involved at all stages of the export–import business cycle—import of technology, export product development, export production, export marketing, pre-shipment, post-shipment, and overseas investment. However, in the current scenario a paradoxical situation exists. While RBI rules permits the banks to finance Indian exporters dollar credit at London Interbank Offer Rate (LIBOR)+0.75 basis, banks could make LIBOR+3 percentage points from others, so they prefer to lend to others than to exporters.

The 'International Standard Banking Practice' for the examination of documents under documentary credits has been approved by the ICC. In India, training programmes have been undertaken to sensitize bankers about Uniform Customs and Practices for Documentary Credits (UCP) and e-UCP and their use in overcoming the problems of discrepancies on paper and in the electronic media. Though voluntary, UCP rules are observed in countless number of transactions everyday and have become a part of the fabric of international trade. A supplement to the UCP covering electronic presentations has been developed by the ICC, but the market expectation is that paper documents would be in circulation for a considerable time to come. The uptake of electronic means of document delivery would depend on their ability to be able to communicate electronic data on a common platform. The readiness of banks and companies to move to such an environment would depend upon a number of factors including the requirement to move away from the letter of credit concept, with its excessive terms and conditions, that we have today, to the one which would provide for simple data messaging service to achieve compliance.

Transit with Neighbouring Countries

India is a natural hub for several of its neighbours. Except The Maldives and Sri Lanka, the other neighbouring countries share long land borders with India. Indian administrative procedures affect intraregional trade in many ways. For instance, for trans-shipment to a third country, Indian customs clearance has to be obtained before re-export. Formalities in re-export of courier consignments intended for third countries delay shipments to inland consignees and stifle trade with neighbouring SAARC (South Asian Association for Regional Cooperation) countries. Thus reduction of procedural complexities will benefit both India and its neighbours. India has taken a number of steps towards forging free trade agreements with its neighbouring countries, but with different degrees of success. As such there is a thriving cross-border trade, often through informal channels.

The goal of forging a South Asian Free Trade Area (SAFTA) Treaty has not yet been achieved. SAARC has also begun work on harmonizing quality and measurement standards which will facilitate intraregional trade flows. Trade between neighbours in the SAARC region are facilitated by bilateral agreements. India has bilateral trade agreements with Nepal and Bhutan, giving substantial market access to products originating from these countries and a free trade agreement (FTA) with Sri Lanka under which duty concessions are being exchanged on a bilateral basis. This existing FTA will soon be replaced by the Comprehensive Economic Partnership Agreement (CEPA). Since 1996, India has accorded the Most Favoured Nation (MFN) status to Pakistan; but the latter is yet to reciprocate, flouting its WTO obligation. India–Myanmar official meetings at different levels have addressed issues such as border management, promotion of trade and travel through land route, etc. India has spent Rs 1000 million (US$ 22 million) in building a 160-km Tamu–Kelewa border highway, located in Myanmar's north-western border area, forming an important link from the India–Myanmar border to central Myanmar and the commercial and cultural centre of Mandalay. Recently, the foreign ministers of Myanmar, India, and Thailand held a meeting in Yangon on transport linkage of the three nations and agreed to build a 1448-km highway from Moreh in India to Mae Sot in Thailand through Myanmar's central city of Bagan. This transport link will provide more facilities for India's 'look-east' policy.

Nepal is landlocked, and most of its trade has to transit through India. Indo-Nepal trade is free and Nepal has much lower tariffs on imports of third country goods than India. The Indo-Nepal Treaty on Trade and Transit is very favourable for this landlocked country. Nepalese goods are allowed preferential entry into India on meeting a minimum material content requirement (value addition norm) defined under the Treaty. India tried to remove this norm and for some time all the products manufactured in Nepal were made eligible for duty free exports to India. But that led to flooding of Chinese made goods through Nepal. In later renewals of the Treaty the provisions relating to value addition and certificate of origin, etc. have been incorporated. Imports are now allowed on the basis of a certificate of origin issued by the agency designated by the Government of Nepal in the format prescribed. The Treaty provides for consultation in the event of problems of excessive imports. The scope of railway transit facility to Nepal is limited because of physical constraints. However, recently, India and Nepal have signed an agreement to set up the first ever rail link between the two countries. A Railway Agreement for the operation of the multimillion dollar inland container depot (ICD) in Birgunj, bordering India, clears the plying of cargo trains between the two countries. In 1998, the World Bank financed construction of three ICDs at Birgunj. With the construction of a 5.4 km rail extension from Raxaul these ICDs will have a direct rail connection to the seaports. It is estimated that Nepal will save US$ 16 million in transport cost annually as a result of the ICDs.

Nepal's international trade as well as bilateral trade with India is expected to increase manifold after the ICDs come into operation. This will reduce the transport cost of raw materials imported by Nepal from a third country by 30–40 per cent. To facilitate traffic between landlocked Nepal and a third country, a transit traffic agreement between the governments of Nepal, India, and Bangladesh was concluded in 1997. The transit traffic could move by road from Nepal to Bangladesh through India and avail a second port facility at Chittagong. Initially, the agreement was for six months but has been extended time and again.

India has agreements with Bhutan and Nepal that allow trucks to move across the border, though not inland. Indian trucks/vehicles are allowed free entry into Nepal whereas Nepalese trucks/transport vehicles are not provided similar facilities in India. The Federation of Nepalese Chambers of Commerce and Industry (FNCCI) has been advocating free entry to India for Nepal-registered transport vehicles.

India shares broad gauge railways with Pakistan and Bangladesh—a historical legacy. India has bilateral rail interchange agreements with these two neighbours. But the conditions are stringent and the performance poor.

The India–Bangladesh Protocol on Inland Transit & Trade has a framework, which may facilitate movement of cargo to the north-eastern states. Under the new Protocol Kolkata, Haldia, Pandu, and Karimganj on the Indian side and Narayanganj, Sirajganj, Khulna, and Mongla on the Bangladesh side have been designated as ports of call. The Protocol also provides for steps to ensure equal sharing of intercountry and transit cargo by the ships of the two countries to and from ports of call/customs stations including extended places for loading and unloading. Both sides also agreed upon the restoration of multimodal communication links between the two countries which should go a long way in providing the infrastructure necessary to enable economic interaction between India and Bangladesh attain its true potential. Both sides also focused on the need to provide a framework for border trade. A proposal for the transshipment of Indian goods across Bangladesh by Bangladesh carriers is under active consideration by the Government of Bangladesh.

Customs and cross-border procedures are complex. Access for transit cargo to or from north-east India through Bangladesh may reduce distance by about 60 per cent but this road route is not open under the current trade protocol. No foreign vehicle is allowed on Bangladesh roads. The procedural requirements are that the cargo is transferred from Indian to Bangladeshi trucks and back to Indian trucks. Also there are considerable delays for cross-border processing at the borders.

A procedure has been established to allow exporters to take clearance of export cargo meant for Nepal and Bangladesh at any of the ICDs and then take the cargo in sealed containers to these countries by rail/road through Land Customs Stations (LCSs). At the LCSs, the customs officers check the seal of the containers and allow export. The facility helps in reducing congestion at the LCSs. As already mentioned, the facility of import and export by courier mode was earlier available through international airports only. To facilitate Indo-Bangladesh trade, this facility has been extended at LCSs at Petrapole and Gojadanga at the Indo-Bangladesh border.

Even though the SAARC countries have begun to liberalize trade, failure to address logistic inefficiencies not only compromises the extent and depth of other reforms, but also risks loss in market share. Excessive dwell times at the borders are common. For instance, at the India–Bangladesh border at Gede-Darsana, the average dwell time is of the order of two days. Benapole is the principal land port for border-crossing between India and Bangladesh. There is often acute congestion here with lines of up to 1500 trucks and waiting time of one to five days. The average wagon cycle time between Lahore (Pakistan) and Amritsar (India) is as much as 5–6 days. In contrast, between the Islamic Republic of Iran and Turkey, which also share a common track gauge, the average border dwell time is about two hours. The India–Pakistan bilateral rail interchange agreement requires both sides to achieve a zero balance in their exchange of wagons at the end of every ten-day accounting period—a complex and inefficient exercise. Operational inefficiencies exist in the cross-border exchange of wagons between India and Bangladesh also. Though India has agreements with Bhutan and Nepal that allow trucks to move across the border, their movements within the country are restricted.

There is a proposal for the construction of a 2600 km pipeline (1600 km from Iran to Sindh province in Pakistan and 1000 km on to India) to transfer gas from Iran to India through Pakistan. Pakistan hopes to receive around US$ 600 million as transit fee annually from the pipeline and is, therefore, keen on the project. A pipeline for transferring gas from Iran to India will certainly be in India's interest. Both Iran and Pakistan are interested. But India is hesitant for legitimate reasons. Among other proposals is one for the construction of a trans-Afghan pipeline that will carry gas from Turkmenistan to Afghanistan and Pakistan and, possibly, include India at a later stage.

Infrastructure and Capacity Constraints

Simplification of import and export procedures, reduction of data and documentation requirements, publication of information, consultation, non-discriminatory treatment, and excellent scope of review and appeal would not serve any purpose without the requisite capacity to meet the obligations. India faces severe capacity constraints.

Following liberalization and the opening up of the economy in the early 1990s, there has been a significant increase in India's maritime trade. In this short time, considerable improvements of containerization of general cargo, berthing capacity, etc. have been brought about at major ports. But there are still large gaps between what is needed and what is in existence. Most major ports were originally designed to handle specific categories of cargo, and have not been able to adjust to the newer categories. There are, thus, several berths for traditional cargo, which are under-utilized and fewer for new cargo which are over-utilized? The equipment available is obsolete and poorly maintained. The major ports of India deal with traffic much in excess of capacity. As a result, in India, ships have to wait for berths instead of berths having to wait for ships. The average vessel turnaround time at Indian ports in 2000 varied from 37–50 hours to 145 hours as compared to the international benchmark of 24 hours and less than 12 hours in Singapore in the same year. However, in the period 2001–2 to 2002–3, the all-India average for vessel turnaround time has improved from 3.02 days to 2.6 days. Chennai, which got privatized in 2001, showed the greatest improvement. Turnaround time at the port fell by 39 per cent from 4.1 days in 2001–2 to 2.5 days in 2002–3 (Figures calculated from Indian Ports Association [IPA] data 2003. Indian ports have one of the lowest rates of productivity in handling cargo (World Bank 2002a). The manpower productivity at the Jawaharlal Nehru Port Trust (JNPT)—India's most modern container terminal—is 330 TEU (Twenty-foot Equivalent Units)/person as compared to 2303 TEU/person in Singapore port. While efficiency has since improved, productivity of Indian ports is still below international standards. In many ports shore facilities cannot be fully utilized and operations are adversely affected as the rail and road connections do not have capacity matching with port throughput. Surface transport connections to the hinterland are inadequate.

Few large liner ships are willing to call at Indian ports, as they cannot afford the long waiting time. Indian container cargo is trans-shipped at Colombo, Dubai, or Singapore resulting in additional costs and transit time. As a consequence, an Indian exporter, with rare exception, is not in a position to avail of the 'fixed-day-of-the-week' services offered by the liner industry at a time when manufacturing and trading companies abroad are increasingly selling and buying on 'just-in-time' basis.

Most Indian exporters are, therefore, operating on the basis of substantial buffer stocks, except probably a few who operate on 'just-in-time' basis. Substantial buffer stocks make Indian exporters less competitive. It has been estimated that the annual incidence of these factors such as demurrage charges, trans-shipment costs, pre-berthing delays and vessel turn-around time could be as high as US$ 1.5 billion per annum (Sunder 2000). These costs have to be borne ultimately by the end users, raising the cost of India's exports in international markets and the prices of imports for the Indian economy. The government recognizes that additional port capacity to cope with the increasing traffic cannot be met without the help of massive private investment. Accordingly, policy guidelines were issued in 1997 to enable the major ports to set up joint ventures with foreign ports, minor ports, or private companies. The major Port Trust Act was amended to give effect to the guidelines issued in 1996 and 1997.

The proposed Rs 100,000 crore Sagar Mala Project is set to give a facelift to the maritime sector with two new major ports and 50 minor ports coming up along the Indian coastline. This ambitious project encompasses plans ranging from port modernization and infrastructure upgradation to developments in the shipping sector and inland water transportation. Some of the features of the project include—integrated development of Cochin and JNPT, developing a hub port at Chennai, capital dredging, port connectivity, setting up five new Single Point Moorings (SPMs) used for transportation of liquid cargo such as petroleum, two container terminals at Mumbai, liquefied natural gas jetty and a coal berth at Ennore, a container terminal at Kandla, etc. Other policy measures include treating the charges paid by the private port operators to the respective port trusts as deemed exports under the Export Promotion Capital Good Scheme. This would enable private operators of container or the berth terminals to claim duty concession on import of equipment under the duty drawback scheme.

The government is planning to establish vessel traffic service (VTS) on the west and east coasts at a cost of Rs 785 crore. One such system is coming up at the Gulf of Kachchh and another is being planned at the Gulf of Khambat. Besides these, there are plans for five more VTS on either side of the peninsula in the next 10 years. VTS is a combination of radar, direction finder, satellite positioning system, and various other sensors for effective control of traffic in waterways. Other systems being planned for improving navigation facilities include monitoring of lighthouses through remote control and automation systems requiring an expenditure of Rs 140 crore. The setting up of an automatic identification system is also being planned to ensure collision free and safe navigation.

International cargo at five major international airports, six newly declared international airports, and at domestic airports increased by 13.4 per cent, 54.2 per cent, and 48.7 per cent, respectively, in the period April to January 2002–3 vis-à-vis April to January 2001–2. There has been a rise of 16.6 per cent in the total international cargo handled by the AAI during this period. The total cargo traffic handled in January 2003 has increased by 15.5 per cent as compared to January 2002, with international cargo traffic increasing by 14.2 per cent (AAI website:www.airportsindia.org.in/aaiabout.htm).

The importance of air transportation of cargo has grown rapidly in recent years in India's foreign trade. But the infrastructure necessary has not grown in tandem. All the international airports in India have shortage of space in their air cargo complexes resulting in severe congestion, often making storage of goods on the tarmac unavoidable. Also, the limitations of space make it difficult to allocate spaces to other operators to facilitate competition. For courier services new and separate fully equipped courier terminals are required. State-of-the-art equipments for quick inspection of sealed containers are very costly and India cannot afford to purchase the adequate numbers.

The national highway system suffers from capacity constraints and inadequacies. The government has embarked upon an ambitious project to upgrade the existing national highway infrastructure. A programme for 4/6 laning of national highways under the NHDP comprising the Golden Quadrilateral connecting the four metros of Delhi, Mumbai, Chennai and Kolkata and the North–South, East–West Corridors connecting Srinagar to Kanniyakumari and Silchar to Porbandar, respectively, has been formulated. An ambitious project called Pradhan Mantri Gram Sadak Yojana was launched in December 2000 with the annual allocation of Rs 25 billion to improve road transport links in rural areas.

A special economic zone (SEZ) scheme has been introduced in the EXIM policy from 2000 to provide an internationally competitive environment for export production. The SEZs in the public, private, and joint sectors or in the state government domain are marked by certain features. These include duty-free enclaves, with no licence requirements for imports; exemption from customs duty on import of capital goods, raw materials, spares, etc.; 100 per cent FDI in the manufacturing sector; no routine customs examination of export/import cargo; in-house customs clearance; support services such as banking, post offices, clearing agents in zone complexes, etc.

Along India's long border with neighbouring countries, the infrastructure for storage and movement of goods and vehicular traffic is highly inadequate. Even basic facilities like post offices, banks, vehicle parking, hotels, etc. are not available at all places. Customs organizational set-up along the border is barely enough to cope with the present volumes. The condition of roads leading to border stations are chaotic due to road traffic congestioins and local law and order problems. From land border stations samples have to be brought over a long distance, for example, the import of food articles from Myanmar involves testing of the items in laboratories located in Kolkata. Laboratories for testing of samples are a serious bottleneck in both import and export cargo. Moreover, the ICDs/CFSs in the hinterlands often do not function well because of lack of requisite equipment and facilities.

Trade facilitation includes a whole set of procedures for clearance of goods starting from the time of arrival at ports to deporting to warehouses. To make this process effective all personnel associated with trade, namely, licensing authorities, customs officials, inspectors, scientists manning testing and quality control laboratories, banking and insurance staff, are required to be present at each of the trading points. This involves enormous time and effort. Besides, the Sunder Committee observed that the staff of department/agencies at the grassroot level are not always aware of the extant provisions of policy, law and procedures. The shortfall in personnel and information levels contribute to the delay in trade.

The number or knowledge base of the personnel are not the only factors. The Sunder Committee also observed that a very large number of problems relating to delays are attributable to tardy procedures, excessive documentation, and narrow sectoral perception of the respective departments/organizations (The Sunder Committee Report 1999). But many of these are also the result of a lack of positive approach and service orientation on the part of officers and staff. Thus, training inputs for officers working in the hinterland require special attention. Prohibitive infrastructure cost is not the only reason why EDI is not being developed at a quicker pace. Many operational modernization projects have not been extended for a long time even after successful experimentation at one or two places. The Sunder Committee thought it important and essential to evolve a holistic approach to deal with the needs and difficulties of the trade. The Kelkar Committee was even more emphatic about the requirement of a change in mindset away from controls rigidly administered, towards a more liberal policy environment in line with international standards. However, it also observed that some effort has been made, for example, the CBEC has suo moto taken up the exercise of evolving modern and efficient procedures, reflecting the changed mindset.

Much has been said about the necessity of changing the mindset of government personnel. But little has been said about a matching requirement in private parties, traders, operators, and business executives. Fiddling with government rules is almost a cultural practice. Unless this mindset is changed, a regime based on trust—suggested so strongly by the Kelkar Committee—can only be misused.

Legal changes are needed to make many facilitation measures effective. The Customs Act 1962 provides for advance filing of the bill of entry only for vessels and not for aircrafts. In most countries, the multimodal transport document (MTD) includes air transport. A major lacuna in the Indian legislation is it excludes air transport so the trade is restricted to sending containers only through rail, road, and sea. Also, Indian Railways have not taken any initiative in tying up with transport companies or shipping lines. This will require amendments in the Railways Act. Most Indian banks still do not recognize the MTD as a single document valid for all modes of transport. An RBI notification is required permitting domestic banks to treat MTD as a negotiable instrument. No major domestic insurance company is willing to offer insurance cover, a value addition for the customers. On the other hand, some foreign insurance firms have agents in India and give insurance cover for cargo sent through MMT.

Trade facilitation measures in some areas may be offset by an increase in trade restrictive measures in some other areas. In the trading world non-tariff barriers (NTBs) are increasing rapidly. In the EC, some 75 per cent of the value of intra-EU trade in goods is subject to mandatory technical regulations. An estimated 60 per cent or more of exports to the USA are subject to mandatory health, safety, and related trade registration system (TRS) (Messerlin and Zarrouk 1999). While developed countries are critical of the complex and slow customs procedures of developing countries, the latter are increasingly worried about the imposition of ever-expanding technical regulations and standards by the former. Delays in clearance for NTBs like SPS lead to an increase in the transaction value. This increase in transaction value is writing off the effect of even the decrease in tariffs brought about by the WTO. Since we are discussing the trade facilitation measures within India in this chapter, the fact that Indian exports suffer on this account at the borders of the developed countries remains out of our purview. However, the trend is worth our attention. Until now India does not impose many NTBs on imports into the country. But things may change in future along the lines of the USA, the EU, and other developed countries.

Conclusions

We may conclude that the tangible benefit of trade facilitation is a reduction in trade transaction costs. Trade transaction costs consist of the following: (a) direct costs such as those directly related to formalities, and costs incurred for trade-related services; and (b) indirect costs incurred due to procedural delays, lost business opportunity, and lack of predictability. An EXIM Bank study (1998) estimated that firms perceived avoidable transaction costs in different sectors.[13] These worked out to an average of 10.78 per cent of export revenue in 1998. The estimates may provide some idea of the type of benefits available from trade facilitation activities. However, this is an underestimate of the benefits.

The EXIM Bank study includes transaction costs due to procedural delays like untimely clearance at customs, complex bureaucratic regulations, avoidable harassment faced by firms, problems with licences, banks, transportation, etc. But there are other heads which were not covered by this study. Factors such as multiple documentation requirements, lacunae in the existing system of automation (EDI), bottlenecks in implementation of reform measures including lack of efficiency among personnel, infrastructure and capacity constraints also add to transaction costs. Moreover, indirect costs such as loss due to (a) lack of predictability and (b) lost business opportunity were not included in the estimates. Taneja and Pohit's (2002) study, for example, shows the high level of illegal trade between Nepal and India much of which is due to high transaction cost in official trade.

The EXIM Bank re-survey in 2003 shows that reforms in the five years after 1998 could eliminate, on an average, 60 per cent of avoidable transaction costs identified in the earlier survey. These estimates refer to transaction costs for exports leaving India. Exports incur transaction costs at the destination country as well, for which no estimate is presently available. Nor do we have any figures for the avoidable transaction cost of imports into India.

To be competitive in the international market, the export product must match, if not better, the competition in terms of pricing and quality. Also, the exporter must have an incentive to enter the highly uncertain export market. Trade facilitation, along with infrastructure, financing, income tax relief, etc. helps attain these

---

[13] This was not the estimate of transaction costs. The survey conducted inquired about the impediments and the costs arising therefrom.

objectives. In the import sector, trade facilitation makes imported items cheaper. It follows that domestic reforms must match with foreign trade. Otherwise domestic traders will be at a disadvantage while global trade is privileged. The Kelkar Committee had very correctly put equal stress on trade facilitation on both the fronts—domestic and international trade.

Trade facilitation, it is argued, is an instrument for promoting Small and Medium-Sized Enterprizes (SMEs). Various reasons have been cited (OECD 2002, Hellqvist 2003a, b). Excessive regulation curtails private sector participation and competition, thereby stifling entrepreneurship and private investment. Lack of predictability entails significant disadvantages for SMEs and enterprizes in developing countries. When the necessary information on applicable regulations is not readily available, trade operators have to spend additional resources to obtain that information. Enterprizes operating in a non-transparent business environment, as is often the case in developing countries, would need to spend more resources or time to obtain regulatory and market information. To this they frequently have to add expenses for bribes, penalties, and administrative or judicial appeals. As these additional expenses do not usually vary according to the value of goods or the volume of sales, they drive the operational costs quite high and put SMEs in a weaker position than larger enterprizes.

When trade formalities are extensive and complex, trade operators require more manpower. Trade formalities might require spending significant time in internal transactions. This could result in disproportionately high compliance costs, since manpower costs are composed of unit wages multiplied by working hours. Quite often such services are outsourced. But outsourcing of such intermediate services is more costly than in-house services.

Lengthy processing time affects not only the opportunity costs but also the capital standing of firms, since capital bears interest and frozen capital compromises further business opportunities. Therefore, the interest required for the time until receipt of payment reduces the exporter's capital standing. Similarly, the interest requirements for the time until the receipt of shipping documents reduces the importer's capital standing. For operators such as SMEs, whose capital reserves are thin, lengthy processing constitute a prohibitive trade barrier. These factors can deter SMEs and enterprizes in developing countries from seeking to expand in international markets. This may be one of the reasons why the bulk of exports today are made by a small number of large firms.

References

Asian Institute of Transport Development (1999), workshop on 'International Conventions on Land Transport Facilitation', organized by the Asian Institute of Transport Development from 19–21 May 1999, New Delhi.

Department of Administrative Reforms and Public Grievances (1996), 'Study of Procedural Aspect of Export-Cargo Clearance by Customs Department of Indira Gandhi Airport', GOI, New Delhi, http://persmin.nic.in/arpg/PGP-AIRPORT.htm.

Department of Commerce (Economic Division) (2002), 'Report of the Committee on Informal Cross Border Trade', Ministry of Commerce and Industry, GOI.

EXIM Bank of India (2003), 'Transaction Costs of Indian Exports: A Review', Working Paper No.4, EXIM Bank of India.

——— (2002), '20th Annual Report 2001-2'.

Finger, J. M. and P. Schuler (1999), 'Implementation of Uruguay Round Commitments: The Development Challenge', Policy Research Working Paper No. 2215, World Bank, (Internet).

Finger, J. Michael (2000), 'The WTO's Special Burden on Less Developed Countries', *Cato Journal*, Vol. 19, No. 3, Cato Institute.

Government of India (2003), 'Union Budget 2003-4', budget speech.

Hellqvist, Marcus (2003a), 'Trade Facilitation: Impact and Potential Gains', Swedish National Board of Trade.

——— (2003b), 'Trade Facilitation from a Developing Country Perspective', Swedish National Board of Trade.

Jain, R. K. (2004), *Customs Law Manual*, 23rd edition, Centax Publications, New Delhi.

Kelkar, V. (2002), 'Final Report on Indirect Taxes', New Delhi.

Messerlin, A. Patrick and Jamel Zarrouk (1999), 'Trade Facilitation: Technical Regulations and Customs Procedures', WTO-World Bank Conference on Developing Countries' in a Millennium Round, 20-1 September 1999, WTO Secretariat, Geneva.

Ministry of Commerce (1999), 'Report of The Expert Committee on an Integrated Approach to the Movement of Goods in International Trade', GOI.

OECD (2002), 'Costs And Benefits of Trade Facilitation', A. Kleitz, Trade Directorate.

——— (2002), 'Business Benefits of Trade Facilitation', T. Matsudaira, supervised by Anthony Kleitz, Working Party of the Trade Committee.

Rege, V. (2002a), 'Points Made on Selected Issues in the Case Studies on Trade Facilitation: Synthesis Document', Workshop organized by the Commonwealth Secretariat on Trade Facilitation, 26-8 September 2002.

——— (2002b), 'Comments on the Proposals Tabled by Delegations in the WTO Discussions for Clarification of GATT Articles X and VIII', Workshop organized by the Commonwealth Secretariat on Trade Facilitation, 26-8 September 2002.

Satpathy, C. (2002), 'Trade Facilitation: A Singapore Issue Knocking at WTO's Door', *Economic and Political Weekly*, Vol. 37, No. 17, pp. 1587–90.

Sundar, S. (2000), 'Port Restructuring in India', in *Second SAFIR Core Training Course on Infrastructure Regulation and Reform* (Sri Lanka, 4–15 December 2000) Tata Energy Research Institute, New Delhi. http://www.teriin.org/division/regdiv/docs/ft22.pdf.

Sundar, S. and S. K. Sarkar (1999), 'Background Paper on the Port Sector', in L. Srivastava and S. K. Sarkar (eds), *Transition to a Liberalized Environment: Experiences and Issues in Regulation*, pp. 255–62, Tata Energy Research Institute, New Delhi, http://www.teriin.org/division/regdiv/docs/ft03.pdf.

Taneja, N. and S. Pohit (2002), 'Characteristics of India's Informal and Formal Trading with Nepal: A Comparative Analysis', *Indian Economic Review*, Vol. XXXVII, No. 1, pp. 69–89.

UN/CEFACT (2001), 'Compendium of Trade Facilitation Recommendations', United Nations (Internet).

UN Economic Commission for Europe (2002), 'Trade Facilitation—An Introduction to the Basic Concepts and Benefits'. www.unece.org/trade/forums/forum02/docs/02tfbroch.pdf.

Varde, V. et al. (2002), 'Study of Process Re-Engineering at Mumbai Port' (mimeo), Agricultural Finance Corporation Limited, Mumbai.

——— (2001), 'Dwell Time Study of Import-Export Cargo' (mimeo), Agricultural Finance Corporation Ltd, Mumbai.

Verwaal, E. and B. Donkers (2001), 'Customs-Related Transaction Costs, Firm Size and International Trade Intensity', ERIM Report Series, ERS-2001-13-MKT, Erasmus Research Institute of Management, The Netherlands, http://www.eur.nl/WebDOC/doc/erim/erimrs20010226105731.pdf.

World Bank (2002a), 'India's Transport Sector—The Challenges Ahead', Vols 1 & 2, http://www.worldbank.org.in/sar/sa.nsf/6062ad876fb8c066852567d7005d648a/6fcfc02e809feb0c85256beb00440cde?OpenDocument.

——— (2002b), 'Trade Facilitation and Economic Development: Measuring the Impact' (mimeo), J. S. Wilson et. al.

——— (2002c), 'Trade Facilitation: A Development Perspective in the Asia Pacific Region', World Bank & Asia Pacific Economic Cooperation, J. S. Wilson et al., http://econ.worldbank.org/files 20929_APEC_TF_Report_Final.pdf.

11 The New Basel Capital Accord
Rationale, Design, and Tentative Implications for India

D. M. Nachane • Partha Ray • Saibal Ghosh

The structure and operations of banks in India, have been evolving rapidly during the last two decades. With the revolution in IT and an associated increase in competition at both the national and international levels, the major financial intermediaries have become global in geographical coverage and universal in their financial functions, encompassing banking, securities, and insurance.

This increasing competition combined with difficult financial conditions in the early 1980s, put downward pressure on banks' profit margins and capital ratios (measured as the ratio of capital to total assets) in both developed and developing countries. Commercial banks' concerns about international competitiveness compelled the regulatory community to respond with an international agreement, which was the genesis of the Basel Capital Adequacy Risk-related Ratio Agreement of 1988.

The question is : why do banks need to hold capital? Two reasons have generally been advanced. First, bank capital helps to prevent bank failure, which arises in case the bank cannot satisfy its obligations to pay the depositors and other creditors. Second, the amount of capital affects returns for the owners (equity holders) of the bank. Following Mishkin and Eakins (2003), we examine each of these in turn.

As regards the first issue, let us consider a simple numerical example. Consider two banks—one with capital to asset ratio of 10 per cent (high capital bank) and another with capital to asset ratio of 4 per cent (low capital bank), and let the hypothetical balance sheets of the two banks be as given below (with all figures in Rs crore):

High capital bank		Low capital bank	
Assets	Liabilities	Assets	Liabilities
Reserves 10	Deposits 90	Reserves 10	Deposits 96
Loans 90	Capital 10	Loans 90	Capital 4

Suppose both banks make some loans, only to discover subsequently that Rs 5 crore of their loans have become worthless. When these bad loans are written off (valued at zero), the total value of assets declines by Rs 5 crore, and so bank capital, which equals total assets minus liabilities, also declines by Rs 5 crore. The balance sheets of the two banks thus become:

High capital bank		Low capital bank	
Assets	Liabilities	Assets	Liabilities
Reserves 10	Deposits 90	Reserves 10	Deposits 96
Loans 85	Capital 5	Loans 85	Capital −1

The high capital bank is able to take the Rs 5 crore loss in its stride, because its initial cushion would imply that it still has a positive net worth (bank capital) of 5 after the loss. The low capital bank, on the other hand, has a negative net worth after the loss; in other words, it turns insolvent. Capital, therefore, acts as a cushion to lessen the chance of the bank turning insolvent.

Second, it is commonly agreed that a basic measure of bank profitability is the return on assets (RoA): it indicates how much profits are generated on average for each unit of asset.[1] However, what the bank's owners

---

[1] RoA = Net profit after taxes/Total assets; RoE = Net profit after taxes/Equity capital; EM = Total assets/Equity capital.

(equity holders) care most about is the bank's earning capacity on its equity investment. The information is provided by the other basic measure of bank profitability: return on equity (RoE). A direct relationship runs between RoA (which measures how efficiently a bank is being run) and RoE (which measures how well the owners are doing on their investment). This relationship is determined by the equity multiplier (EM), which defines the amount of assets per unit of equity capital. In other words, the EM traces the interlinkage between RoA and RoE.[2] Linking to the earlier example, the high capital bank initially has Rs 100 crore of assets and Rs 10 crore of equity, which gives an EM of 10 (=Rs 100 crore/Rs 10 crore). The low capital bank, by contrast, has only Rs 4 crore of equity, so its equity multiplier is higher, equalling 25 (=Rs 100 crore/Rs 4 crore). Suppose that both these banks have been equally well run, so that they both have the same RoAs of 1 per cent. The RoE for the high capital bank equals (1 per cent*10) = 10 per cent; while RoE for the low capital bank equals (1 per cent*25) = 25 per cent. In other words, the equity holders of the low capital bank are better placed than those of their high capital counterparts. This would mean that, given the RoAs, the lower the bank capital, the higher the return for the owners of the bank.

The above discussion suggests that bank capital imposes benefits as well as costs on banks. Bank capital benefits owners of a bank in the sense that it makes their investment safer by reducing the likelihood of bankruptcy. On the other hand, bank capital is costly, because the higher it is, the lower will be the return on bank equity for a given RoA. In determining the amount of bank capital, managers would need to factor in this trade-off—the increased safety that comes with higher capital (the benefit) and the lower RoE that comes with higher capital (the cost). It often happens, however, that because of both moral hazard and the principal–agent problems, banks may be induced to hold less bank capital than optimal. To override this contingency, it is customary for national regulatory authorities to impose minimum capital requirements on banks. The emergence of the EC provided a fillip to the harmonization of financial practices (including bank capital requirements), and it was but natural that this process of harmonization should gradually take on an international aspect.

It is in this context that the Basel Capital Accord of 1988 of the Bank for International Settlements (BIS 1988) is an event of paramount importance to the banking world. It was the outcome of a long-drawn-out initiative to strive for greater international uniformity in prudential capital standards for banks' credit risks. The objectives of the Accord were not only to strengthen the international banking system, but also to promote convergence of national capital standards, thereby ironing out competitive inequalities among banks across countries.

The 1988 Basel Agreement was not a legal document. It was designed to apply to internationally active banks of member countries of the Basel Committee on Banking Supervision (BCBS) of the BIS at Basel, Switzerland, but the details of its implementation were left to national discretion. The reasons for the primarily G-10-centric structure of the institution of the 1988 Accord are not far to seek.[3] First, over 80 per cent of global banking assets rest with banks incorporated in these countries. Therefore, the focus of banking systems in these countries was a priority agenda. Second, with state-of-the-art IT being used by banks in these countries, it was believed that a proactive approach to banking supervision in these countries would necessarily stave off any failures and also address the dangers of contagion stemming therefrom. While these facts might have had a fair degree of credibility in the autarkic world of the 1980s, the inference may not be as valid in the globalized world of today. Moreover, the way in which the minimum capital adequacy ratio of 8 per cent was incorporated in regulatory regimes varied across countries, and several applied more stringent standards. The impact of the 1988 Accord rapidly spilt beyond the original G-10 countries and, by 1999, it formed part of the regime of prudential regulation not only for internationally active, but also for domestic banking systems in more than 100 countries (BIS 1999). The major success of these regulatory standards was to raise the capital levels in banking systems, especially in G-10 countries. As observed by Jackson et al. (1999), the average ratio of capital to risk-weighted assets of major banks in the G-10 countries increased from 9.3 per cent in 1988 to 11.2 per cent in 1996.

From the very beginning, the 1988 Accord was subject to criticism, which was hardly surprising in view of the fact that the Accord had to accommodate banking practices and regulatory regimes in countries with varied legal systems, business norms, and prevalent institutional structures. Criticisms were mainly directed at its failure to make adequate allowance for the degree of reduction in risk exposure achievable through diversification and

---

[2] To see this, note that RoE = Net profit after taxes/Equity capital = (Net profit after taxes/Total asset)*(Total asset/Equity capital) = RoA*EM.

[3] G-10 comprises Belgium, Canada, France, Germany, Italy, Japan, The Netherlands, Sweden, The UK, and the USA; the group was subsequently extended to incorporate Luxembourg, Switzerland and, more recently, Spain.

at its arbitrary and non-discriminatory calibration of certain credit risks. Illustratively, a credit to a blue-chip corporate was treated in the same fashion as a loan to a lesser-known financial company. The uniform weight attributed in almost all circumstances to private borrowers (regardless of their creditworthiness) was considered an incentive to regulatory arbitrage, under which banks were tempted to exploit the opportunities afforded by the Accord's classification of risk exposure to increase their holding of high-yielding, but also high-risk assets for a given level of regulatory capital. However, recurring crises over the past two decades in both the developed and developing world have provided graphic evidence of the fact that, given the globalization and univeralization of banking operations, the onset of banking crises can impact the banking systems in both the home and host countries in equal measure through contagion effects. Since banking crises are difficult to predict and can have devastating effects on the macroeconomy, proactive supervision of banks in developed economies, while necessary, is not sufficient to prevent failures. Thus, with both international and domestic banking systems coming increasingly under the same regulatory umbrella and the growing interest in adoption of international standards being shown by the non-G-10 countries, the distinction between 'internationally active' versus 'domestic' banks on the one hand, and 'sophisticated' versus 'less sophisticated' banks on the other, tends to have a more limited relevance than it did in the past (Narain and Ghosh 2003).

In view of these factors, the Basel Committee proposed a New Capital Adequacy Framework (hereafter referred to as the 'Basel II') in June 1999 incorporating three major elements or 'pillars': (a) minimum capital requirements, based on weights intended to be more closely aligned to economic risks than the 1988 Accord; (b) supervisory review, which set basic standards for bank supervision to minimize regulatory arbitrage; and, (c) market discipline, which envisages greater levels of disclosure and standards of transparency by the banking system. Ever since its publication, the Basel II has generated intense debate among policy-makers and academia alike. Various questions have been raised in this connection. Does the Basel II discriminate against developing countries? Will the Accord engender a reduction in the flow of resources to emerging markets? Considering the fact that a number of economies, including India, are envisaging implementing the Basel II, these are questions of topical relevance.

It is in this context, viewed in the light of the historical backdrop of the 1988 Accord, that this chapter focuses on the Basel II—its objective, the obstacles, and the concerns expressed about it.

REGULATION OF BANKS

There are three key types of market failure in banking, namely, those relating to externalities, information asymmetry, and monopoly (Goodhart 1998). The most obvious type of potential externality in banking relates to the risk of contagious runs, when failure of one bank leads to heightened risk of failure by others. The possibility of runs, even for sound and solvent banks, arises basically from their function of 'maturity transformation': offering savers alternate forms of deposits according to their liquidity preferences, while providing borrowers with loans of desired maturities. As regards information asymmetry, if it is difficult or costly for the purchasers of a financial service to obtain sufficient information on the quality of the service in question, they may be vulnerable to exploitation by financial intermediaries. Such phenomena are of particular importance to retail users of banking and other such financial services, because clients are often seeking advice or safekeeping for a sizeable proportion of their wealth, contracts are often one-off and involve a commitment over time.

In regard to financial regulation, however, there is a slight change in emphasis in the objectives of regulation in the sense that the focus is on maintaining systemic stability and protecting the interests of the customer. Maintaining systemic stability is important because the social costs of financial distress are high in the form of the contagion effect. A wholesale customer, such as a corporate or large net worth individual, should be in a position to have the capacity and resources to make informed choices. But a retail customer, such as a small saver or a small borrower, cannot incur the cost of getting information, acquire or employ skills to analyse, have large enough volumes to learn from experience, a big enough portfolios to spread risks, and as such will be unequal in relation to the financial intermediary. Above all, economies of scale are likely in monitoring of information on a collective basis. In brief, the why of financial regulation needs to be considered essentially in the light of the primary objectives, namely, maintaining systemic stability and protecting the interests of the retail customer; and implicitly, other objectives will have to be secondary.

There has been significant debate on whether banks are special, and should be treated as such. The rapid development of capital markets, increasing importance of non-bank sources of financial intermediation and the emergence of 'one-stop financial services' have led to the erosion of importance as well as uniqueness of banks as financial institutions. There are, however, three major reasons advanced for treating them as special.

First, they are participants in the payments system and, hence, are the backbone of the financial system. The systemic risks of any one bank being affected either on account of its banking operations or on account of non-banking operations are high. Second, the banks contract for liquid deposits to acquire illiquid assets and, hence, are vulnerable to liquidity crises. This would underline the need for a lender of last resort. Third, the banks are the major service providers for retail customers and are, therefore, on a separate footing in terms of consumer protection, especially since the customers of a bank are typically risk-averse. In other words, while retaining incentive for banks to be always solvent, there is constructive ambiguity in extending liquidity by the lender of last resort. Thus banks, particularly those with access to payments system, are generally treated as a separate class in a regulatory framework—particularly in developing countries.

Regulation policy needs to recognize and admit that the mere fact of regulation does not guarantee that there will be no risk of failure or insolvency of a regulated unit. There is always the danger that people perceive that the mere act of an entity being regulated provides a guarantee from the regulator that it is risk-free to transact business with the unit. The risks arise due to several problems, mainly related to lack of information. First, it is difficult to precisely assess even for the regulator how good the internal controls in a regulated entity are on an on-going basis. More importantly, there is no way for a perfect and continuous assessment of adherence to the external rules imposed by the regulator.

Regulation may be institution-based or function-based or even product- or market-oriented. In other words, a regulator may regulate banks, though banks may involve themselves in other activities such as being an intermediary in capital markets. Alternatively, the capital market regulator may regulate all activities relating to public issue or trading in securities whether those functions are performed by banks or non-banks. Similarly, all institutions which take public deposits may be regulated by one regulator. Yet another approach is to consider regulation in terms of markets, say government securities, or money market or forex. In India, for instance, capital markets and insurance activities were regulated by the Ministry of Finance till the Securities Exchange Board of India (SEBI) and the Insurance Regulatory and Development Authority (IRDA) were set up recently; while Development Financial Institutions (DFIs) have recently begun to be regulated/supervised by the RBI. While most banks are regulated by the RBI, some are under the dual control of the government and the RBI. The Department of Company Affairs (DCA) regulates deposit-taking activities of corporates other than banks and non-banking financial companies registered under the Companies Act, but not those which are registered under separate statutes.

THE NEW BASEL ACCORD: GENESIS AND MAJOR FEATURES

A Brief Historical Backdrop

The 1988 Accord reflected a consensus of the member countries of BIS as to the proportions in which various suitable financial instruments could be permitted to be part of the banks' capital base. It is perceived that a bank should maintain a certain amount of capital (numerator)—depending on the risk of its asset portfolio (denominator)—to cover for the risks of failure. Three basic categories of capital could be purported to serve these purposes: debt capital, equity capital, and hybrid capital (which combines features of equity and debt). There existed wide divergence in market and regulatory practices among Basel member countries regarding which instruments could be considered for possible inclusion in the three basic forms of capital. Accordingly, the solution adopted for the 1988 Accord involved distinguishing between two tiers: tier I (comprising equity shares, disclosed reserves and capital reserves) and tier II (comprising less pure forms of capital like hybrid debt instruments, sub-ordinated debt,[4] and undisclosed reserves); furthermore, tier II (or 'supplementary') capital in the aggregate was limited to a maximum of 100 per cent of tier I capital (Box 11.1). The pattern of risk weights on assets was accordingly specified, linking the capital position of banks to its risk-weighted assets. The ratio, thus arrived, was not to fall below 8 per cent.

The 1988 Accord was subject to amendments intended to refine and extend its treatment of banks' exposure to credit risk and the list of eligible instruments for inclusion in capital. For example, the 1996 Amendment to the Capital Accord to Incorporate Market Risks accommodates two alternative ways of measuring minimum levels of capital for market risks: one based on banks' own internal risk-measurement models and the other on a standardized methodology under which capital requirements are estimated separately for different categories of market risk and then summed to give an overall capital charge.

As the reform of banking regulation became an important policy agenda of developing and transition economies (a tendency given impetus by the East Asian financial crisis), the appropriateness of the Basel standards to such economies became a subject of debate. Inter alia, the question was raised as to whether economies vulnerable

---
[4] Capital with maturity not below 5 years.

> **Box 11.1**
> **Capital Adequacy**
>
> Capital adequacy is the aggregate of Tier-I and Tier-II capital, of which the latter is not to exceed 100 per cent of the former. In the Indian context, the following items form part of Tier-I and Tier-II capital.
>
> Tier-I: (a) Paid-up capital, (b) Disclosed free reserves, (c) Capital reserves representing the surplus arising out of sale proceeds of assets, (d) Reserves (excluding revaluation reserves) less (i) losses, including accumulated losses, (ii) Equity investments in subsidiaries and (iii) Intangible assets.
>
> Tier-II: (a) Undisclosed reserves, (b) Cumulative perpetual preference shares, (c) Revaluation reserves (at a discount of 55 per cent), (d) Hybrid debt capital instruments, (e) General provision/general loan loss reserves (subject to a ceiling of 1.25 per cent of risk-weighted assets), (f) sub-ordinated debt, and (g) investment fluctuation reserve.
>
> How do we calculate a bank's Tier-I and Tier-II capital? Consider the following hypothetical balance sheet of a representative XYZ bank:
>
> | Assets | Amount | Liabilities | |
> |---|---|---|---|
> | Cash in hand and balances with RBI | 10 | Equity capital | 10 |
> | Call money | 5 | Sub-ordinated debt | 5 |
> | Investments | 30 | Deposits | 65 |
> | Loans | 50 | Borrowings | 5 |
> | Fixed assets | 5 | Other liabilities | 15 |
> | Total | 100 | Total | 100 |
>
> Under the BIS-weighting norms as adopted to the Indian context, cash and balances receive zero risk weight, investments receive zero risk weight,[a] call money receive 20 per cent risk weight, and loans and fixed assets have 100 per cent risk weight. Therefore, the total risk weighted assets of the XYZ bank would work out to be:
>
> RWA = 0% x (10 + 30) + 20% x 5 + 100% x (50 + 5) = 56
> Tier 1 capital: 10/56 = 17.9%
> Tier 2 capital: 5/56 = 8.9%
> BIS capital ratio = Tier 1 + Tier 2 = 17.9% + 8.9% = 26.8%
>
> However, the picture is much more complicated than these simple calculations suggest. For instance, suppose the bank has off-balance sheet items (for example, financial guarantees) on its books. In that case, the amount of such guarantees would have to be multiplied by a credit conversion factor to arrive at an on-balance sheet equivalent and further multiplied by the appropriate risk weight and added to the on-balance sheet risk-weighted assets to arrive at the total risk-weighted assets.
>
> [a] Since 1999–2000, investments have been subjected to a market risk of 2.5 per cent. We ignore market risk considerations from the analysis.

to macroeconomic shocks and with fragile financial sectors necessitated a more stringent standard than the 8 per cent ratio. At the same time, financial sector stability assessment came to dominate the policy agenda of international agencies with the health of the banking sector and the overall capital position becoming a matter of prime focus. The 'Core Principles for Effective Banking Supervision' (BIS 1997) emphasized the need for banking supervisors to set minimum capital requirements for banks in order to adequately reflect the risks undertaken by banks and simultaneously the need to define the components of capital, bearing in mind banks' ability to absorb losses. While such developments were underway, it was increasingly realized that in addition to credit risk (which was the preponderant focus of the 1988 Accord), the growing complexity of banking operations and the move towards a market-driven financial sector in the aftermath of financial liberalization across large parts of the globe (Williamson and Mahar 1998) brought to the fore other forms of risks, such as liquidity risk (risk of default arising from cash flow mismatches), market risks (risk arising from adverse movements in market variables, such as interest rate), and operational risks (risks arising from failure of systems and controls).

New Basel Accord

The proposals in the BIS document, A New Capital Adequacy Framework, originated in the aftermath of the turbulence in financial markets which followed the Russian government's forced restructuring of its own short-term debt and its moratorium on the servicing of a wide range of private sector external obligations in August 1998 and the rescue operation of the Long-Term Hedge Fund, which followed in the autumn (Fleming 1999).

The objectives of the Basel II, as enunciated by the BIS are five-fold: (a) promoting safety and soundness of the financial system; (b) enhancing competitive equality; (c) a comprehensive approach to addressing risks; (d) greater sensitivity to the degree of risk involved in banks' activities; and (e) focus on internationally active banks, with the capability of being applicable to banks with varying levels of complexity and sophistication (BIS 2001).

The Basel II rests on three pillars: (a) minimum capital requirement, (b) supervisory review process, and (c) market discipline. In other words, the inherent idea has been to introduce greater risk sensitivity by supplementing the present quantitative standards by introducing two additional pillars (Pillars 2 and 3), thereby providing a more balanced approach to the capital assessment process (Table 11.1).[5] We will delve into each of the three pillars separately.

TABLE 11.1
Proposed New Accord versus 1988 Accord: Salient Features

The 1988 accord	The proposed mew accord
Focus on a single risk measure	Emphasis on banks' own internal methodologies; two additional pillars: Pillar 2 (supervisory review of capital adequacy) and Pillar 3 (market discipline)
One-size-fits-all approach	Flexibility; menu of approaches to ascertain capital requirements
Broad-brush structure	Greater risk sensitivity
Focus on credit risk alone	In addition to credit risk, emphasis provided on market risk and operational risk

Source: Compiled from BIS (1988) and BIS (1999).

Minimum Capital Requirements

Much of the concern about Basel II comes from the first pillar of minimum capital requirements. As per the January 2001 Consultative Paper (BIS 2001), banks can choose from the following three evolutionary variants to measure the risks, namely, (a) a basic standardized model (modified version of the existing approach), (b) an IRB foundation model, and (c) an advanced IRB model. While the basic standardized model is based on the ratings of the external rating agencies like Moody's or Standard and Poor's, a basic requirement for the foundation or advanced IRB model is to develop the bank's own internal rating system. It may be noted that depending on which model is chosen the capital requirement will vary. This has important implications for the emerging market economies.

Furthermore, as far as the minimum capital requirement of a bank is concerned, it needs to be noted that the Basel II makes a distinction between credit risk, market risk, and operational risk, so that,

Regulatory Total Capital = Credit Risk Capital Requirement + Market Risk Capital Requirement + Operational Risk Capital Requirement

The definition of capital in the Basel II has been retained unchanged from that of the original Accord.

What are the methods of calculations of the above three kinds of risks? At the risk of oversimplification, Table 11.2 summarizes the basic approaches to ascertaining minimum capital requirements.

TABLE 11.2
Variants of Risk Calculation in Basel II

	Credit Risk	Market Risk	Operational Risk
Standardized	Standardized	Standardized	Basic indicator
Advanced	Foundation IRB Advanced IRB	Internal (e.g. Risk Metrics, historical or Monte Carlo simulation)	Advanced measurement

Source: Compiled from BIS (2001).

What is the importance of these types of risks in the portfolio of a typical commercial bank? Hammes and Shapiro (2001), following McKinsey's analysis on actual capital risk allocation (as opposed to regulatory capital) of a typical commercial/investment bank, report that credit risk constitute of the majority share in the banks' portfolio (Figure 11.1).[6]

Note that, in calculating the capital ratio, the total risk weighted assets (or the denominator) will be calculated as follows:

Total Risk Weighted Assets = 12.5 * [Market Risk Capital Requirement + Operational Risk Capital Requirement] + Sum of Risk Weighted Assets compiled for Credit Risk.[7, 8]

---

[5] See BIS (2001), RBI (2001), and Saunders and Allen (2002) for a discussion of the three new pillars of the new Basel Accord.

[6] The November 2001 modifications to the Basel II reduce the share of operational risks to 12 per cent.

[7] Note that 12.5 is the reciprocal of the minimum capital ratio of 8 per cent.

[8] See Saunders and Allen (2002) for details on credit risk measurement under the Basel II.

Figure 11.1: Risk Decomposition of a Typical Commercial/Investment Bank
Source: Hammes and Shapiro (2001).

The Standardized Model for Calculating Credit Risk

Much of the discussion stimulated by the Basel II has focused on its standardized approach to the risk weighting of different elements among the assets of banking books. This is because of the proposed reliance on external credit assessment institutions in delineating risk weights. The calibration of sovereign risk weights is considerably finer than that of the 1988 Accord; with the highest risk weight allowed being 150 per cent, instead of 100 per cent as in the 1988 Accord.

The Basel II puts forward two alternative options for the risk-weighting of banks. The first would be linked to the weighting attributed to the country in which the bank is incorporated. The weight attributed to the bank would be one category less favourable than that applying to the country (Table 11.3; option 1). However, there would be a ceiling of 100 per cent on the weights for exposures to banks of all but the lowest rated countries, for which the ceiling would be 150 per cent. The second option would involve recourse to external agencies own ratings of banks. Under this option, claims on banks with a rating of AA- or better would be assigned the lowest risk weight, which increases gradually as the sovereign rating of the country declines. Under this option (unlike the first), inter-bank claims would also be differentiated by their maturity, but the benchmark for such differentiation has been tightened from a residual maturity of up to one year (in the 1988 Accord) to an original maturity of up to six months (in the Basel II).

The weights in the new framework also provide for differentiation in the case of non-financial corporates to recognize variations in their credit quality. Illustratively, a weight of 20 per cent is attributed to entities with credit rating of AA- or better (subject to the proviso that no corporate should receive a weight lower than that of its country of incorporation); corporates with rating below B- would be assigned 150 per cent risk weight. Other changes in the standardized approach concern the weights for off-balance sheet items and treatment of securitized assets.

The IRB Approach

The IRB framework for corporates, sovereign, and bank exposures builds on current best practice in credit risk measurement and management. While the standardized approach is, in principle, close to the existing arrangement, under the IRB approach, banks will be allowed to use their internal estimates of borrowers' creditworthiness, subject to supervisory validation.[9] Under the IRB approach, banks will be required to classify banking book exposures into the six broad classes of assets which underlie different credit risk characteristics, namely, (a) corporate, (b) bank, (c) sovereign, (d) retail, (e) project finance, and (f) equity. For the first three

TABLE 11.3
Risk-weights of Basel II: Exemplified with Standard and Poor's Rating

	Claim	AAA to AA-	A+ to A-	BBB+ to BBB-	BB+ to B-	Below B-	Unrated
Sovereign		0	20	50	100	150	100
Banks	Option 1[a]	20	50	100	100	150	100
	Option 2[b]	20	50	50	100	150	50[c]
Corporates		20	100	100	100	150	100

Notes: a—risk weighting based on risk weighting of sovereign in which the bank is incorporated.
b—risk weighting based on the assessment of the individual bank.
c—claims of a short original maturity less than six months on banks with a rating above BB+ would receive a weighting that is one category more favourable than the usual risk weight on the bank's claims subject to a floor of 20 per cent or the level of the risk weight applying to its country of incorporation.
Source: BIS (2001).

---

[9] There are, however, some differences between the existing approach and the standardized approach proposed in the New Basel Accord. Under the standardized approach the risk-weights have been enlarged to encompass exposures to a broad group of borrowers with reference to rating provided by the rating agencies so as to take care of greater risk differentiation.

types of exposures, the committee has developed both foundation and advanced methodologies for the estimation of risk components (there is no distinction between foundation and advanced methodologies in the retail framework). For corporate, bank, sovereign, and retail risks, there is a specific set of risk weights. For each of these classifications, exposure risk weights are derived from a specific continuous function of risk weighted assets and is defined as the product of risk weight of transaction and a measure of exposure.

The basic structure of the IRB approach is as follows. A bank's internal measures of credit risk are based on an assessment of borrower and transaction risk. Most banks have an internal rating grade assigned to a borrower, and estimate an implicit probability of default (PD) associated with the borrower in each of these internal grades. Besides, banks not only measure the likelihood of a default but also estimate the extent of loss in case of a default. This will depend on two elements: (a) loss given that the borrower defaults (LGD), expressed as a percentage of exposure, and (b) exposure at default (EAD), providing the bank's exposure to the borrower at the time of default. The risk weights (RW) under the IRB are expressed as a single continuous function of the PD and LGD, so that risk-weighted assets (RWA) will be written as, RW(PD,LGD) * EAD.

Foundation IRB Approach

The calculation of total RWA under the IRB approach is a two-step process. First, taking into account for each instrument its PD and LGD (and also maturity, wherever applicable), the first step for the bank would be to calculate a baseline level of RWA by summing the individual exposures after multiplying by their respective IRB risk weights. Second, the banks' total RWA for non-retail exposure classes is calculated by adding to this baseline level an adjustment for the degree of single borrower risk concentration within non-retail exposure classes. As this adjustment factor may be positive or negative, the total RWA could go up or down after the adjustment. The LGD values in this case are set by supervisory rules.

Advanced IRB Approach

In the advanced approach, the banks can estimate the LGD of an exposure, subject to meeting additional, more rigorous minimum requirements for LGD estimation. In this approach, the range of eligible collateral is not restricted. However, banks would be required to consider the risks which the restrictions in the foundation approach are designed to address. Accordingly, the additional minimum requirements are considerably more rigorous than those required of banks using foundation

methodologies. Mention may be made in this context that VaR models are part of the internal models approach for measuring market risk in the Basel II. Basically, a VaR estimate is simply an appropriate percentile of the bank's portfolio loss distribution. For any given bank portfolio, one can calculate a loss distribution, showing the probability of various amounts of loss. The 99 per cent VaR, for example, is the loss magnitude, which will be exceeded only with 1 per cent probability. Stated otherwise, 'the 99 per cent VaR of a bank portfolio is Rs X' means that one can assert with 99 per cent confidence that the bank's losses from this portfolio will be less than Rs X.

In addition, the new Basel accord provides a menu of approaches towards measurement of operational risk. Three such approaches have been proposed: basic indicator approach, standardized approach, and the advanced measurement approach. Under the first approach, operational risk capital allocation is based on a single indicator (gross income) as a proxy for operational risk exposure. Under the second approach, banks' activities are divided into eight business lines (corporate finance, trading and sales, retail banking, commercial banking, payment and settlement, agency services, asset management, and retail brokerage). The capital charge for each business line is calculated by multiplying gross income by a factor (denoted as beta) assigned to that business line. Under the third approach, the regulatory capital requirement will equal the risk measure generated by the bank's internal operational risk measurement using both qualitative and quantitative criteria. The qualitative criteria include independent operational risk management function, active involvement of the board of directors/senior management in the overseeing of the operational risk management process, regular reporting of operational risk exposure and loss experience and documentation of risk management system. The quantitative criteria include the demonstrated ability of the bank to capture potentially severe 'tail' loss events, and sufficient 'granularity' in risk measurement systems to capture the major drivers of operational risk. In addition, the process of operational risk measurement would also need to include four key elements: track of internal loss data, use of relevant external data, scenario analysis to evaluate exposure to high severity events and finally, capturing key business environment and internal control factors that can change the operational risk profile of the bank. In other words, these approaches are gradually increasing in sophistication and have built-in incentives to encourage banks to continuously improve their risk management and measurement capabilities and undertake more accurate assessment of regulatory capital.

Supervisory Review Process

The second pillar of the new Basel Accord focuses on improving the supervisory review process and views the role of supervisory review as a critical complement to capital requirement and market discipline. It emphasizes that, despite improving the risk sensitivity of the minimum capital requirements, supervisors need to take a comprehensive view on how banks handle their risk management and internal capital allocation process. Subject to shortcomings in these, supervisors could require higher than the minimum capital target from a given institution.

The discussion is concerned primarily with the application of the following four principles: (a) supervisors expect banks to operate above the minimum regulatory capital ratios and should be able to require banks to hold capital in excess of the minimum; (b) a bank should have a process for assessing its overall capital adequacy in relation to its risk profile, as well as a strategy for maintaining its capital levels; (c) supervisors should review and evaluate a bank's internal capital adequacy assessment and strategy, as well as its compliance with regulatory capital ratios; and (d) supervisors should seek to intervene at an early stage to prevent capital from falling below prudent levels.

Market Discipline

The potential of market discipline to reinforce capital regulation depends on the disclosure of reliable and timely information with a view to enabling banks' counterparties to make well-founded risk assessments. In a recent discussion paper, the BIS has elaborated the recommendations of the Basel II concerning the nature of information which should be disclosed under this pillar (BIS 2000). These include (i) the structure and components of bank capital, (ii) the terms and main features of its capital instruments, (iii) the accounting policies used in the valuation of assets and liabilities and for provisioning and income recognition, (iv) qualitative and quantitative information about its risk exposures and its strategies for risk management, (v) its capital ratio and other data related to its capital adequacy on a consolidated basis, and (vi) a breakdown of its risk exposures. The information needs to be supplemented by an analysis of factors affecting the banks' capital position. Moreover, banks are encouraged to disclose ways in which they allocate capital among their different activities. The disclosures envisaged under this pillar need to be made on a semi-annual basis.

The Third Consultative Document

In the light of the comments received on the second consultative paper, the BIS issued the Third Consultative Document (CP3) in April 2003. As compared to the Second Consultative Document, the salient differences in the revised document pertain to, among others, applicability of advanced and foundation IRB approaches for commercial real estate lending, an alternative approach to operational risk and lowering of risk weights on lending that is fully secured by mortgages on residential property. The salient new features contained in the Third Consultative Document are detailed in Box 11.2.

The Plan for Transition to the New Accord

Subsequent to the release of the Third Consultative Document, BIS conducted the Quantitative Impact Study (QIS 3) in October 2002, which focused on the proposed minimum capital requirements under Pillar 1 of the Basel II. The results of the exercise, pertaining to more than 350 banks in 43 countries, were released in May 2003. The findings indicated some increases in capital requirements, relative to current levels for all the country groupings.[10] While the reported increases in capital requirements were 'small' in the foundation IRB approach, there were 'reductions in capital requirements compared with those under the current Accord' under the advanced IRB approach (BIS 2003). The BIS also published a document delineating the timeframe for migrating to the Basel II (Table 11.4).

POSSIBLE IMPLICATIONS FOR EMERGING MARKET ECONOMIES

Against the backdrop of the aforesaid discussion, the present section dwells on the issue of the likely impact of the Basel II on developing and/or emerging markets.[11]

One of the main arguments about the effect of the Basel II on the developing and/or emerging market economies rests on the postulate that the bulk of the borrowers in these countries fall under the speculative grade. In particular, it has been argued that speculative-grade borrowers will suffer from a dramatic rise in debt costs and from the heightened cyclicality of the global bank credit expected as a result of the Basel II (Reisen 2001). If the 'internal ratings-based' approach suggested is implemented, then there will be a substantial rise in risk weights. By contrast, the 'standardized' approach, which links risk weights to ratings by eligible external credit assessment institutions, would leave banks' regulatory capital charges, risk-adjusted returns and, hence, required spreads largely unchanged (except for the very

---

[10] Comprising G-10, the EU and others.
[11] See Ray (2001) and Ward (2002) for a discussion on the issues relating to implications of the Basel Accord for the developing countries.

> ### Box 11.2
> ### Major Features of the Third Consultative Document (2003)
>
> *Pillar 1: Minimum Capital Requirements*
>
> - At national discretion, banks will be able to risk weight all corporate claims at 100 per cent without regard to external ratings.
> - New section on the treatment of past due loans (other than mortgages). Risk weights 150 per cent or 100 per cent dependent on whether specific provisions cover more or less than 20 per cent of outstanding loans.
> - A credit conversion factor of 100 per cent will be applied to the lending of banks' securities or the posting of securities as collateral by banks, including repo.
> - Backtesting requirements for use of VaR are set out.
> - PD floor of 0.03 per cent introduced for retail PD.
> - At national discretion, a bank can use an Alternative Standardized Approach (footnote 91 of BIS 2003). For the retail and commercial banking business lines, the regulators are proposing an index other than Gross Income.
>
> *Pillar 2: Supervisory Review Process*
>
> - New Section identifying important issues that banks and supervisors should particularly focus on, including a number of key issues, which are 'not directly addressed under Pillar 1' as well as 'important assessments that supervisors should make to ensure the proper functioning of certain aspects of Pillar 1'.
> - A bank should ensure that it has sufficient capital to meet Pillar 1 requirements and the results of Pillar 1 stress tests.
> - Supervisors to assess banks' application of the reference definition of default and its impact on capital requirements.
> - Supervisors may increase the capital required to prevent 'cherry picking' where the poorer quality assets and most of the credit risk of the underlying exposures remains with the bank.
>
> *Pillar 3: Market Discipline*
>
> - The table of requirements has been amended in respect of the disclosures required.
> - The Committee observed that considerable efforts have been made to ensure that the disclosure requirements of Basel II focus on capital adequacy, and do not conflict with broader accounting disclosure standards with which banks need to comply.
>
> *Source:* BIS (2003a), April.

TABLE 11.4
Timetable for Implementing Basel II

Date	Action point
October 2002	Basel committee, in conjunction with national supervisors, launched quantitative impact survey (QIS 3) with a view to enable banks to conduct (within 20 December 2002) a concrete and comprehensive assessment of how the committee's proposals would affect their particular firm.
Second quarter 2003	In light of responses received from QIS 3, the Committee will assess whether adjustments would be required in the proposed aggregate level of regulatory capital in the banking system and the updated version of the proposals would be released for public comment.
Fourth quarter 2003	Finalization of the new capital accord.
2004–6	Adaptation and development of necessary systems and procedures by banks and supervisors so as to bring them in conformity with the new capital accord. The banks adopting internal rating based (IRB) approach and advanced measurement approach (AMA) will be required to conduct parallel calculations with the current Basel Accord for one year prior to implementation.
End 2006	Implementation of New Capital Accord.

Source: BIS (2002), July.

lowest rating notches). Thus, to the extent it increases the capital requirement of the banks, Basel II might have adverse repercussions on the credit portfolios of the banking sector.[12]

From a developing country perspective, the OECD/non-OECD distinction in risk-weights in Basel I is somewhat arbitrary and provides a distorting incentive for developing countries to seek OECD membership (Griffith-Jones and Spratt 2001). Most importantly, the lower (20 per cent) risk-weights attached to short-term loans for emerging markets created a bias in their favour; on the other hand, credit to non-OECD banks with over one year maturity was discouraged by a far higher (100 per cent) risk weight. The removal of the OECD/non-OECD distinction under Basel II is likely to have negative consequences for lowly-rated OECD countries. Countries like Mexico may find that the conditions attached to loans more closely reflect their actual rating rather than the fact of their OECD membership. Conversely, highly rated non-OECD countries (such as Chile) are likely to benefit from more favourable terms. Thus, the alterations to the current treatment of maturity should remove some of the incentives towards short-term lending to banks rated below AA-. Consequently, it might lengthen the aggregate maturity of such lending. Overall, however, as a result of Basel II capital requirements could align better with actual risk. This could benefit the highly rated sovereigns, banks, and corporates regardless of OECD membership.

One of the major critiques of the new Basel Accord is perhaps the adoption of the IRB system. Two allegations are made in particular. First, that the application of IRB is costly and discriminates against the smaller banks and, second, that it will exacerbate cyclical fluctuations. Let us take up each of these aspects separately.[13]

Theoretical models have demonstrated that if the bank is capital constrained, then Basel II will intensify the difference in bank lending rates and in bank loans between corporate borrowers with different probabilities of default (Chen 2002) or make the entire banking system worse off, if all of them attempt to raise capital simultaneously from the capital market (Hellmann et al. 2000). This is especially so in case such markets are not sufficiently deep and liquid (as is often the case in developing economies).

[12] It has also been argued that the Basel II will raise the volatility of private capital flows to speculative-grade developing countries and, hence, their vulnerability to currency crises (Griffith-Jones and Spratt 2001).

[13] It needs to be recognized that some of these issues have been addressed in the Third Consultative Document, released by BIS in April 2003.

Discrimination against the Smaller Banks

A major impact of the New Accord could be an increase in the quantity of loans to borrowers rated above BBB and a fall in loans to borrowers rated below BBB (Griffith-Jones and Spratt 2001). Given that the majority of the former kind of borrowers are likely to be in the developed world, one major impact on the developing world will be a reduction in overall levels of lending from internationally active banks. What lending does occur is, therefore, likely to be concentrated in highly rated sovereigns, corporates, and banks. In fact, as pointed out in Jackson (2001), for any bank, the effect of the internal ratings approach on required capital will depend on the risk profile of its particular book—high risk books will demand more capital than allotted currently and low risk books will demand less. Table 11.5 compares the capital requirements under the current accord, the standard approach, and the IRB foundation for senior unsecured corporate borrowers. The lower the rating the higher is the increase in capital requirement under the IRB foundation approach vis-à-vis current capital levels.

TABLE 11.5
Capital Requirements for Unsecured Corporate Borrowers

Ratings	Probability of default (PD) (%)	Current capital	Standard approach	IRB foundation
AAA*	0.03	8.0	1.6	1.13
AA*	0.03	8.0	1.6	1.13
A	0.03	8.0	4.0	1.13
BBB	0.20	8.0	8.0	3.61
BB	1.40	8.0	8.0	12.35
B	6.60	8.0	12.0	30.96
CCC	15.00	8.0	12.0	47.04

Note: * Floor PD is set at 0.03.
Source: Jackson (2001).

Pro-cyclicality

One of the most significant charges levelled against the new proposals is that they will exacerbate pro-cyclicality in their lending since the substantially increased provisions which can result from deteriorations in loan quality in cyclical downturns can lead to greater restrictiveness regarding new lending (European Central Bank 2001, Ghosh and Nachane 2003). In the case of an economic downswing if capital requirement becomes a constraint, then the bank may shrink its credit disbursement in an excessive way. Thus it may exacerbate the recession/economic slowdown via the Fisherian debt–deflation spiral.[14] Another important potential source of more pro-cyclical bank lending which might result from the New Accord is the reliance on credit rating agencies in setting risk weights under the standardized approach to credit risk. This is one of the reservations expressed about reliance on credit rating agencies. Others concern the limited coverage of the ratings of existing agencies, the difficulty in establishing guidelines that would assure high quality of rating agencies and the closely related problem of incentives provided by Basel II for the proliferation of new agencies and the likelihood of use of unsolicited credit ratings.

Furthermore, when the risk-profiles of the lenders are assessed on the basis of an internal rating, the elements of pro-cyclicality are going to be higher still. In fact, Danielsson et al. (2001) has interpreted this pro-cyclicality of regulation as an inherent conflict between regulation and macroeconomic stabilization.[15]

Such elements of pro-cyclicity are inherent even in the existing accord. There is however, the fear that greater risk sensitivity under the new Basel accord will aggravate this tendency. The drive for risk weights to more accurately reflect PD is inherently pro-cyclical in that, during an upturn, average PD will fall—and thus incentives to lend will increase. Conversely, during a downturn, average PD will increase and, as a consequence, a credit crunch may develop with all but the most highly rated borrowers facing difficulty in attracting funds. The Basel Committee has recognized this concern, but argued that it would be outweighed by the benefits of a risk-sensitive capital framework. The findings of the Quantitative Impact Survey 3 seem to validate this point.

Impact on International Capital Flows

A basic aim of Basel II is to ensure that the regulatory capital of the international banks should be in alignment with the credit quality of their loan portfolio. Thus, for lending to low quality borrowers capital charges are likely to be higher. This had led some commentators to argue that the resultant risk sensitivity would lead to a curtailment of supply of capital to emerging economies.

There are two channels through which Basel II could affect the supply of capital to the emerging markets: (a) cross-border flows to such markets, and (b) credit flows within such markets. As far as the cross-border flows are concerned, because of the withering away of the distinction between OECD and non-OECD countries, it is clear that the requirement for regulatory capital for loans to low-rated OECD countries (like Turkey) would rise (Hayes and Saporta 2002). Similarly, the average regulatory minimum for low credit quality countries is also likely to go up. If such additional regulatory requirement imposes a capital constraint higher than the economic capital of the banks, then the credit flows to the emerging markets could be adversely affected. As far as the credit flows within emerging markets are concerned, if most of the banks of the emerging markets adopt the standardized approach, it would be unaffected.

How far do these conjectures get translated in terms of calculations of credit risk? While both Reisen (2001) and Griffith-Jones and Spratt (2001) predict dramatic increases in spreads for the low-rated countries, Weder and Wedow (2002) see such increases in spreads as rather low. Using the November (2001) version of the Basel II, and the Standard and Poor rating as of December 2001, the capital requirement for India is found to be unaltered at 8 per cent under both Basel I and Basel II (standardized approach). The requirement under the IRB approach (using a one year PD) was, in fact, found to be lower at 6.15 per cent! While the scenario for India is found to be reasonably bright, for countries like Venezuela or Russia the difference in the capital requirement between the standardized approach and the IRB approach is rather large (Table 11.6).

While this may not have any immediate concern for India, it is a fact that the credit flows do become more sensitive to the external credit ratings. It is in this context, that the comment of the RBI about the undesirability of unsolicited external credit agencies needs to be taken all the more seriously, so that international capital flows via the banking channels are not subjected to the vagaries of international rating arbitrage. As observed in the Third Consultative Document of the BIS (2003), external credit assessment institutions need to satisfy the six criteria of objectivity, independence, transparency, disclosure, resources, and credibility in order to be recognized for assigning ratings by types of claims or by jurisdiction.

REACTIONS FROM THE DEVELOPING COUNTRIES

Generic Concerns

Basel II has evoked diverse reactions from various groups of economies. A number of views have emerged in this

---

[14] Ed Crooks, the economic editor of the *Financial Times*, puts it succinctly, '…the effect of the capital requirements could be to encourage banks to lend more in the good times and discourage them from lending in hard times. That in turn could mean that economic cycles are more severe: the peaks of the booms will be higher, because credit is easy, and the troughs of the busts lower, because no one can borrow' (*Financial Times*, 17 January 2001).

[15] To quote, 'regulation not only renders bank crisis more likely but could also destabilize the economy as a whole by exaggerating fluctuation' (p. 15). Similar concerns have been expressed by Altman and Saunders (2001).

TABLE 11.6
Capital Requirements By Emerging Market

(per cent)

Country	Rating S&P 7 December 2001	Basel I capital requirement	Basel II capital requirement (standardized)	Basel II capital requirement (IRB approach)
Singapore	AAA	8	0	0
Hong Kong	A+	8	1.6	0
Chile	A−	8	1.6	0
Czech Rep	A−	0	1.6	0
Estonia	A−	8	1.6	0
Hungary	A−	0	1.6	0
Korea	BBB+	0	4	2.24
Poland	BBB+	0	4	2.24
Latvia	BBB	8	4	2.07
Malaysia	BBB	8	4	2.07
Lithuania	BBB−	8	4	5.3
South Africa	BBB−	8	4	5.3
Thailand	BBB−	8	4	5.3
Mexico	BBB−	0	4	5.3
Philippines	BB+	8	8	6.62
India	BB	8	8	6.15
Colombia	BB	8	8	6.15
Brazil	BB−	8	8	11.09
Peru	BB−	8	8	11.09
Russia	B+	8	8	12.63
Romania	B	8	8	16.39
Venezuela	B	8	8	16.39
Pakistan	B−	8	8	22.97
Turkey	B−	0	8	22.97
Ecuador	CCC+	8	12	29.11
Indonesia	CCC	8	12	29.11
Argentina	SD	–	–	–

Source: Weder and Wedow (2002).

context. A view which is widespread among developing countries has been that the regulatory regime for bank capital should be able to make a contribution to the stability of capital flows. One of the major proposals along these lines is that supervisors in major countries should vary the capital requirements on banks' international lending in response to changes in the risks of different borrowers. A widespread concern among developing countries is that if the announcements of agencies simply parallel changes in market sentiment then developing countries could be affected adversely. The outcome could even be worse in the sense that recourse to ratings for setting risk weights for capital standards might magnify the instability of bank lending. Another point of major concern to developing countries is regarding the coverage of ratings of the major agencies. In India, for example, in early 1999, out of 9640 borrowers enjoying fund-based working capital facilities from banks, only 300 had been rated by any of the major agencies (Raghavan 2001). In this context, the present section takes a look at select reactions from various quarters to Basel II.

Several comments emphasize that Basel II would considerably increase the complexity of responsibilities for both supervisors and banks and would impose substantial additional costs. This has led to the suggestion that Basel II provide for a more gradual phasing of its implementation than presently envisaged. In particular, attention has been drawn to the special problems occasioned by the implementation of the IRB approach, and the greater difficulties in this respect of banks not belonging to the category of 'internationally active'.

There is also widespread recognition of the advantages to banks of the IRB approach, but this is combined with the belief that its introduction would generally be more difficult in developing countries than their developed counterparts, owing to weaker managerial and supervisory capacity and limited availability of historical data in the former. The suggestion has thus been made that there should be a relaxation of the requirement that a banking group using the 'foundation' IRB approach for some exposures be required to adopt it across all exposure classes and across all significant business units (groups, subsidiaries, and branches) within a reasonably short period. Instead, it has been proposed that national supervisors should be allowed to adopt a more selective application of the 'foundation' approach'—segments not covered being subject to the standardized approach.

Many comments have been critical of the aggregation in Basel II of expected and unexpected losses as well as of the way in which part of, but typically not all, loan-loss provisions are included in the regulatory capital. This reflects a preference for treating expected losses as a cost of doing business to be covered by provisions (amount set aside to cover default on loans), while requiring capital for unexpected losses. Several points have been raised in this area. For example, the eligibility of only part of the provisions for inclusion in regulatory capital could act as a disincentive to banks to carry adequate provisions; and the lack of guidelines in Basel II on provisioning could blur the process of attributing provisions to prospective future loan losses with the result that some of the banks' credit risks may be covered both by regulatory capital and by provisions not recognized as being part of such capital (so-called 'double counting'). Concerns about the treatment of expected and unexpected losses are accompanied by the need for clearer guidelines on the subject as also for national supervisory discretion regarding their application.

International bodies like the World Bank in their comments have raised two sets of concern for the application of the new Basel accord for developing economies. First, it has been pointed out that the application of the IRB system could turn out to be extremely difficult for a number of developing countries. In particular, 'even G-10 supervisors may find it difficult to verify the accuracy of a bank's internal rating system, let alone most supervisors in developing and emerging economies. As the determination of the adequate level of capital is expected to include some form of banks' judgment subject to supervisor's review, the risk of distortions is even increased' (World Bank 2001). Second, a risk sensitive framework, that might trigger volatility within the banking system, may have some adverse consequences on capital inflows. However, if the banks adopt a forward-looking approach, the risks of such potential volatility could be minimal.

The comments by leading rating agencies like Moody's Investors Services also stressed the possibility of the disadvantage that the smaller banks might face due to adherence to Basel II. Many of the smaller banks—savings, cooperative, and specialized—would find it more difficult to diversify their activities towards 'fee—generating business'; in fact, too much of such diversification could even be harmful. The Moody's go one step further and note categorically that, 'It is unlikely that many of these banks will have the financial resources, intellectual capital, skills and large-scale commitment that their larger competitors have to build performing sophisticated systems to allocate regulatory capital optimally for both credit and operational risk' (p. 3).

Specific Concerns

The proposed approach to capital requirements for operational risk under the New Accord has been the concern of a large number of countries. Their major focus has been the Basic Indicator Approach, regarded as the framework likely to be employed by most developing countries. The capital charges which would result from application of this approach are criticized as being too high and not adequately reflective of the lesser complexity of banking operations (and thus, lower operational risk) in developing countries. The point has also been stressed that gross income to which the capital charge would be proportional under the basic indicator approach is frequently not closely correlated with operational risk in a simple way (if at all). There have also been criticisms of the proposed floor for the capital charge in the most sophisticated approach to operational risk, the Internal Measurement Approach: this, it has been argued, would be a disincentive to its adoption and more generally, to improved risk management in this area. Other observations made concerning operational risk are the need to allow for insurance cover as well as possible recourse to an alternative approach, which would put greater reliance on enhanced supervision and on locally set rules for capital charges, owing to the difficulty of making generally applicable measurements to operational risk and to the close links between the problems of controlling operational and other kinds of banking risks.

Another recurring subject in the comments of developing countries involves disclosure and select definitional issues. The reservations as to enhanced disclosure focus on two issues: (a) the way in which financial markets in developing countries would absorb and respond to greater disclosure and (b) competitive effects. Regarding the first issue, skepticism has been expressed about the capacity of market participants to interpret the increased information resulting from enhanced disclosure. Regarding the second issue, there is concern that the rules of Basel II for disclosure of proprietary information could impinge unfavourably on a bank's competitive position.

Several comments have been directed at the estimation of capital requirements for equity exposures. Of special interest in the context of restructuring of banks' balance sheets after the recent Asian financial crises has been the attention drawn by Thailand to possible consequences of the rule that minority-owned, non-controlling equity investments should be deducted from capital (or in certain cases, be subject to consolidation on a pro rata basis). Such equity investments in countries which have recently experienced financial crises may constitute an exceptionally high proportion of banks' exposures owing to recourse to debt-for-equity swaps as part of debt restructuring, but are not intended to be long-term holdings. Since the rule in the Basel II may lead to further depletion of banks' already low capital, the suggestion has been made that such equity exposures be attributed lower risk weights (than under the standardized or IRB approach).

Attention has also been drawn to the sharp rise in risk weights for borrowers with probabilities of defaults above a certain threshold: a rise that is capable of leading to levels of capital for exposures to borrowers of below investment grade substantially higher than under the standardized approach. This is regarded as counterproductive with regard to Basel II's objective of promoting banks adoption of the IRB approach. On the one hand, banks with large concentrations of low-rated borrowers would have an incentive to use the standardized approach to keep down capital requirements and, on the other hand, low-rated borrowers would have an incentive to become clients of banks using the standardized (as opposed to the IRB) approach. This inconsistency between the risk weights of the two approaches is one of the several opportunities for regulatory arbitrage which would result from the Basel II, and is widely regarded as likely to be especially important in many developing economies where most borrowers have relatively high probabilities of defaults and low ratings.

Commentators have expressed the view that the rules in Basel II for the recognition and valuation of collateral in the form of commercial real property would be too restrictive. Attention has been drawn to the fact that commercial real estate tends to be an important source of collateral in developing rather than developed countries, owing to the underdeveloped state of financial markets in the former and thus, the lesser availability of financial instruments suitable for this purpose. It has, therefore, been proposed (subject to appropriate 'haircuts' to allow for the volatility in vlaue of such property) that commercial real estate should be recognized as allowable collateral alongside eligible financial instruments under the standardized approach. Moreover, several countries have objected to the attribution of a risk weight of 150 per cent on the unsecured portion of loans overdue for more than 90 days (net of specific provisions), preferring a less severe approach, better reflecting the real risk of such exposures, which would impose an exceptionally high risk weight only on loans overdue for a significantly longer period.

India's Reactions

The RBI, in its comments on the Second Consultative Document, pointed out that Basel II would involve a shift in direct supervisory focus away to the implementation issues, and that banks and the supervisors would be required to invest large resources in upgrading their technology and human resources to meet the minimum standards.[16] It came down forcefully on the increasing reliance on external rating agencies in the regulatory process on the ground that such a move would undermine the initiative of banks in enhancing their risk management policies and practices and internal control systems. It categorically stated that:

The minimum standards set even for the Internal Rating Based (IRB) foundation approach are complex and beyond the reach of many banks. Further, while the Basel Committee desires neither to produce a net increase nor a net decrease in minimum regulatory capital, it is felt that the current proposals are going to result in significant increase in the capital charge for banks, especially in emerging markets. The emerging markets with their low technical skills, structural rigidities and less robust legal system, etc. would face serious implementation challenges. The RBI, therefore, feels that the spirit of flexibility, universal applicability and discretion to national supervisors, consistent with the macro economic conditions specific to emerging markets ought to be preserved while finalizing the New Accord (RBI 2001; p. 2).

While the RBI agreed with the view that the focus of Basel II might be primarily on internationally active banks, it contended that, after a period of time, all 'significant' banks would be expected to adhere to it. It was, however, pointed out that the standardized approach

---

[16] Reddy (2001) has observed that, in the medium term perspective, the main challenge for banks would be to subscribe to Basel II. Given that the New Accord is likely to be more complex and more binding, it would warrant early preparatory work by both the RBI and the banks.

might not suit the needs of the smaller banks.[17] As a consequence, it suggested a simplified standardized approach for those banks that are not internationally active. Under this approach, standardized risk weights in the range of 0 per cent to 150 per cent on the basis of internal ratings of banks, could be assigned, subject to the mapping of such ratings with the benchmark PD estimated by the supervisor on the basis of pooled data from select banks.[18] The RBI recognized that even this simplified approach is likely to be more extensive and complex than the 1988 Accord and, hence, the New Accord may be applied in phases.

A basic point of difference between the Basel II and the RBI lies in the relative role of supervisors vis-à-vis external rating agencies. The RBI in its comment categorically reiterated that the External Credit Assessment Institutions should not be assigned the direct responsibility for risk assessment of banking book assets. This was primarily to avoid the contagion effect in the eventuality of a financial crisis and the proprietary information that domestic rating agencies have regarding their domestic clients. Furthermore, the RBI pointed out that unsolicited ratings by external agencies are generally superficial, and could lead to a potential trade-off between competition and quality in the rating industry. Consequently, it favoured the view that preferential risk weights should be assigned only on the basis of solicited ratings.

In a similar spirit, the RBI pointed out that the risk weighting of the banks should be de-linked from the credit rating of the sovereign in which these banks are incorporated. After all, country risk and firm-specific risks could be independent. A related issue is the assigning of weights to sovereign claims. The RBI felt that the national supervisors should be given some discretion to assign lower risk weight in specific cases.

The RBI proposed that while internationally active banks may be required to follow the IRB approach, a simplified standardized approach may be evolved for other banks, whereby standardized risk weights in the range of 20 per cent to 150 per cent could be assigned on the basis of internal ratings of banks.

As far as the IRB approach is concerned, it was argued that the minimum standards set for the same are complex and beyond the reach of many banks. Instead, it suggested that a simplified standardized approach might be evolved and applied to banks that are not internationally active. These banks may be allowed to use internal ratings for assigning preferential risk weights on certain types of exposures after validation of the internal ratings systems by national supervisors. In particular, it noted that the line of demarcation between the six broad classes of exposures (corporate, sovereigns, banks, retail, project finance, and equity) could often be quite indistinct. Therefore, without recognizing the institutional framework and geographical spreads such segregation could pose serious implementation problems. Furthermore, the RBI felt that national supervisors might have discretion and flexibility in defining the exposure classes, that is, corporate, retail, sovereign, project finance, etc.

Some recent developments in the run-up to Basel II deserve mention in this context. Subsequent to the publication of the compliance status with Basel Core Principles, the RBI has taken several steps to implement certain important components of the Basel II. Illustratively, the Risk-Based Supervision (RBS) process was put into effect from April 2003. With a view to assisting banks in setting up an appropriate risk management framework, guidelines on credit risk management, market risk management, and risk-based internal audit were issued. In response to requests made by banks, the Risk Profile Template (RPT) for use in commercial banks was forwarded to them. Side by side, guidelines on country risk management and provisioning have been issued to banks. These guidelines require banks to formulate appropriate, well-documented, and clearly defined Country Risk Management (CRM) policies, with the approval of the respective boards and address the issues of identifying, measuring, monitoring, and controlling country exposure risks. In tandem with these developments, the third pillar of Basel II is being bolstered by broadening the range of disclosures that banks have to disclose as part of 'Notes on Accounts' to their balance sheet.

The RBI has recently come out with its comments on the Third Consultative Paper (RBI 2003b). The salient

---

[17] In this context, the views of the RBI are comparable to that expressed by Lawrence H. Meyer, member of the board of governors of the Federal Reserve System that 'it is not at all obvious that the proposed standardized approach fits the needs of smaller banking organization engaged primarily in traditional banking activities, but I question whether the added implementation burdens are cost-effective for traditional banking organizations, especially since neither the current nor the proposed capital frameworks yet address what is perhaps the most critical risk factor for smaller banks—geographic and sectoral concentrations of credit risk' (Meyer 2001).

[18] As a precursor, the RBI pointed out that internal rating systems of banks need to be substantially upgraded and strengthened, keeping in view the best practices and the standards prescribed by the Basel Committee for the IRB approach. As far as the ambit of 'internationally active banks' is concerned, the RBI defined these as banks with cross-border business exceeding 20 or 25 per cent of their total business (RBI 2003b). 'Significant banks', on the other hand, have been defined as those banks with complex structures and whose share in the total assets of the domestic banking system exceeds 1 per cent.

features of the observations of the RBI can be summarized as under:

(a) Prescribing a material limit (10 per cent of total capital) up to which cross-holdings of capital and other regulatory investments can be permitted.

(b) Rating of only those ECAIs should be eligible for use in assigning preferential risk weights which disclose publicly their risk scores, rating process, and procedure and are recognized by national supervisors.

(c) De-linking the risk-weighting of banks from the credit ratings of sovereigns in which they are incorporated.

(d) Discretion and flexibility to national supervisors to define the exposure classes, such as corporate, retail, sovereign, and project finance.

(e) Strong case for revisiting the risk weights assigned to sovereign exposures when the exposures are aggregated as a portfolio which enjoy the benefits of diversification.

The RBI emphasized the need to take into account the structural characteristics of different economies in the process of implementing Basel II. Furthermore, the RBI favoured domestic rating agencies in the work relating to assessment because of their up-to-date access to domestic conditions, proprietary information, and legal and regulatory framework (RBI 2002).[19]

Therefore, while discussions on Basel II continues, it needs to be recognized that, unless suitably modified, the adoption of Basel II in its present form would possibly result in a significant increase in the capital charge for banks, especially in emerging markets. Besides, Basel II could enhance the minimum regulatory capital, especially for banks in the developing economies, due to a number of reasons, namely, (a) withdrawal of uniform risk weight of 0 per cent on all sovereign claims (OECD and non-OECD), (b) explicit capital charge, or (c) imposition of higher risk weights on claims on certain high-risk exposures like venture capital or private equity.

Emerging Scenario

Bank capital is intended to reduce the probability of default of debt of a banking firm. In principle, all categories of banking risk that can lead to such losses needs to be covered by capital, and any of them, if left unattended, are capable of eroding the capital base of the institution. Those concerned with the management of banks are inevitably confronted with the interrelationships among different categories of banking risks. Banks' internal controls reflect awareness of this and are designed to deal with the problems which these interlinkages pose. Recent periods of financial turbulence have brought forth the connections between different categories of banking risks, in particular, between credit and market risks. These connections have been highlighted in academic as well as policy publications.

Not surprisingly, the efforts of major banks to upgrade their risk management function in response to the increased complexities of banking business are characterized by an increasingly integrated approach to risk management. While there are certain essentials that still need to be tackled as far as the robustness of these new methods and their ability to predict financial vulnerability are concerned, one might envision further improvements in this area in the near future. Moreover, in various forms, these methods are likely to spread from the larger, more sophisticated institutions to the less-complex rungs of the industry.

The increasingly heterogeneous banking sector with which the BIS is concerned is a source of growing difficulty for global standard-setting, since the objectives of the BIS include a reasonable measure of regulatory uniformity for the institutions covered and thus the reduction in differing competitive advantages accruing from differences in national regulatory regimes. Efforts at harmonization of banking regulation and supervision have, therefore, been rendered overtly complex by the diverse range of practices in loan classification and provisioning, differences in the legal and institutional frameworks and the varied accounting standards and fiscal regimes to which banks are subject to in different countries. One basic duality is the broad division of the international banking system into those banks, which have been following such standards (and, thus, conform to 'international best practice') and those that have only recently begun aspiring towards such standards. This duality has, in its wake, led to the call for development of differential standards for sophisticated and less sophisticated banks, for internationally active and domestically active banks and, as a corollary, to banks in developed and developing/emerging/transition economies. Mention may be made that the forerunner of banking standards—the 1988 Accord—made a distinction between internationally active banks and other banks, while Basel II speaks, in addition, of a class of sophisticated banks to which international standards could be applicable (Narain and Ghosh 2003).

---

[19] India is also participating in the Quantitative Impact Study (QIS 3) being conducted by the Basel Committee to assess the impact of the Basel II. The RBI has since constituted a group of seven banks (three public sector banks, two new private banks, and two old private banks) that have begun participating in the exercise (RBI 2002).

Second, the progressive shift in the nature of banking supervision sway from the reliance on relatively simple rules and procedures is placing greater demand on supervisors and, in particular, on quantitative skills. The trend is already widespread and likely to gain momentum in the near future. While not all countries will be affected uniformly by these changes, emerging markets with developing banking sectors are likely to be significantly affected, as supervisory skills begin to command a premium. This might engender a migration of supervisory resources to places where it receives the highest remuneration.

Third, in licensing foreign banks, countries need to take account of their capacity to supervise the activities the banks are permitted to engage in. This is, however, easier said than done. The impact of the WTO-GATT arrangements is likely to lead to greater opening of financial markets to foreign competition, with a concomitant effect on the banking sector as well. Large financial conglomerates, with highly skilled personnel and technology orientation, are capable of producing highly competitive types of banking, which domestic banking systems might find hard to replicate. A crisis involving such banks can often engender contagion effects with adverse ramifications for the entire economy. To some extent, supervisors can rely on their counterparts in the country of the bank's parent institution, but there are limits to which such reliance is feasible (Goodhart et al. 1998). Moreover, in situations of banking crisis where infusion of capital to local institutions from foreign banking groups is regarded as essential to restructuring, countries can often be left in a weak bargaining position regarding the licensing of the activities which new entrants are permitted to undertake. With the passage of time, one might expect to witness a convergence in banking practices with supervisory standards, which can help attenuate these difficulties, but there is no gainsaying the fact that the process can, at best, be gradual.

Does this mean that banks from developing countries are likely to be put at a further competitive disadvantage vis-à-vis large, internationally active banks from the industrialized world? Several commentators have been skeptical of the efficacy of Basel II to strengthen banks in emerging countries (Rojas-Suarez 2001, Ward 2002). Their argument is based on the premise that such countries can be divided into two groups according to their capacity to enforce regulatory capital: (a) those with inappropriate accounting standards and reporting systems and (b) those with a high concentration of asset ownership, that allows a degree of manoeuverability for market-based financing. Under such circumstances, capital ratios cease to play their desired role since there exists no capital markets to validate the 'real' value of capital, as distinct from its accounting value. However, it seems fair to say that an answer to this question at the present juncture can, at best, be tentative. First, the existing proposals of the new Basel accord are still in the process of being actually implemented. Different countries might face different constraints in implementing them. Second, and more fundamentally, in so far as the proposals are applicable to internationally active banks and to the extent such banks are less dominant in developing country markets, developing countries and emerging markets are possibly likely to be less affected by Basel II.

What are the implications for India as far as the application of Basel II is concerned? The New Accord, when implemented, is likely to have significant implications for the banking system as a whole. Besides requiring increased capital, it attaches urgency to the development of efficient and comprehensive internal systems for assessment and management of risks, setting up and adhering to adequate internal exposure limits, and improving internal control generally. The guidelines for risk management and asset liability management provided by the RBI serve as a useful foundation for building more sophisticated control systems. The feedback received from a few banks indicates the need for substantial upgradation of existing management information systems, risk management practices, and technical skills. Capital allocation is also expected to be more risk sensitive and, therefore, banks and financial institutions will have to plan in advance so that there are no disruptions in the capital structure. Further sophistication in risk management and control mechanisms will have to evolve as experience with preferential risk-weighting and sensitivity to external ratings is accumulated. A key requirement when the New Accord, after further modification, becomes operational is that of high quality human resources to cope with and adapt to the new environment. Enhancing technical skills and abilities to handle new technologies and new risks, exploiting information flows to factor them in, and developing foresight in anticipating changing risk–return relationships will become essential.

One can do no better than to quote from Jalan (2002) about India's stance regarding Basel II:

The Reserve Bank…has supported flexibility, discretion to national supervisors and a phased approach in implementing the (New Basel) Accord. The Accord could initially apply to internationally active—banks with over 15 per cent of their business in cross-border transactions, as proposed by the Reserve Bank—and significant banks whose domestic market share exceeds 1 per cent—with a simplified standardized approach to be evolved for other banks. Material limits on cross-holdings of capital and eschewing of direct responsibility on external credit rating agencies in the assessment of bank assets have also been proposed by the Reserve Bank. It has also expressed its preference for external credit rating agencies that publicly disclose risk scores, rating processes and methodologies.

REFERENCES

Altman, I. Edward and Anthony Saunders (2001), 'An Analysis and Critique of the BIS Proposal on Capital Adequacy and Ratings', *Journal of Banking and Finance*, Vol. 25, No. 1, pp. 25-46.

Bank for International Settlements (2003a), *The New Basel Capital Accord*, BIS, Basel, April.

────── (2003b), *Quantitative Impact Study (QIS): Overview of QIS Documents*, BIS, Basel, May.

────── (2002), 'Basel Committee Reaches Agreement on New Capital Accord Issues', BIS, Basel, July.

────── (2001), *Consultative Document—Overview of the New Basel Capital Accord*, BIS, Basel.

────── (2000), *A New Capital Adequacy Framework: Pillar 3 Market Discipline*, BIS, Basel, January.

────── (1999), 'Capital Requirements and Bank Behaviour: The Impact of the Basel Accord', BIS Working Paper No. 1, BIS, Basel.

────── (1997), *Core Principles for Effective Banking Supervision*, BIS, Basel.

────── (1988), *International Convergence of Capital Measurement and Capital Standards*, BIS, Basel.

Caprio, Gerard and Patrick Honohan (1999), 'Restoring Banking Stability: Beyond Supervised Capital Requirements', *Journal of Economic Perspectives*, Vol. 4, No. 1, pp. 43-64.

Chen, John-ren (2002), 'Basel Accord and Macroeconomic Activity', at www.uibk.ac.

Danielsson, Jon, Paul Embretchs, Charles Goodhart, Con Keating, Felix Muennich, Olivier Renault, and Hyun Song Shin (2001), 'An Academic Response to Basel II', *Financial Markets Group*, Special Paper No. 130, London School of Economics, UK.

European Central Bank (2001), 'The New Basel Capital Accord: Comments', (www.bis.org).

Financial Times (2001), 'Basel makes Life Tougher on Regulators of Credit Risk', 17 January.

Fleming, Stephen (1999), 'Disarming Bank Credit Risk', *Institutional Investor*, August.

Goodhart, Charles (1998), 'Some Regulatory Concerns', in C. Goodhart (ed.), *The Emerging Framework of Financial Regulation*, Central Banking Publications, London.

Goodhart, Charles, Philip Hartmann, David Llewellyn, Liliana Rojas-Suarez and Susan Weisbrod (1998), *Financial Regulation: Why, How and Where Now?*, Routledge, London and New York.

Ghosh, Saibal and Dilip M. Nachane (2003), 'Are Basel Capital Standards Pro-cyclical: Some Empirical Evidence from India', *Economic and Political Weekly*, Special Issue in Money, Banking, and Finance, January.

Ghosh, Saibal, Dilip M. Nachane, Aditya Narain, and Satyananda Sahoo (2003), 'Capital Requirements and Bank Behaviour: An Empirical Analysis of Indian Public Sector Banks', *Journal of International Development*, Vol. 15, No. 2, pp. 18-29.

Griffith-Jones, Stephany and Stephen Spratt (2001), 'Will the proposed New Basel Accord have a net negative effect on developing countries?', mimeo, University of Sussex.

Hammes, Wolfgang and Mark Shapiro (2001), 'The Implications of the New Capital Adequacy Rules for Portfolio Management of Credit Assets', *Journal of Banking and Finance*, Vol. 25, No. 1, pp. 97-114.

Hayes, Simon and Victoria Saporta (2002), 'The Impact of Supply of Capital to Emerging Market Economies', *Financial Stability Review*, Bank of England, UK.

Hellmann, Thomas, Kevin Murdock, and Joseph E. Stiglitz (2000), 'Liberalization, Moral Hazard in Banking and Prudential Regulation: Are Capital Requirements Enough?', *American Economic Review*, Vol. 90, No. 3, pp. 147-65.

Jackson, Patricia, Craig Furfine, H. Groenveld, Diana Hancock, David Jones, William Perraudin, Lawrence Radecki, and Masao Yoneyama (1999), 'Capital Requirements and Bank Behaviour: The Impact of the Basel Accord', Working Paper No. 1, Basel Committee on Banking Supervision, Basel, Switzerland.

Jackson, Patricia (2001), 'Bank Capital Standards: The New Basel Accord', *Bank of England Quarterly Review*, pp. 55-63, spring.

Jalan, Bimal (2002), 'Indian Banking and Finance: Managing New Challenges', *RBI Bulletin*, February.

Mayer, Lawrence (2001), 'The New Basel Accord: Challenges for Banks and their Supervisors', remarks at the Risk Management Association's Conference on Capital Management, Washington, D.C., May.

Moody's Investors Service (2001), 'The New Basel Capital Accord', *Global Credit Research*, January.

Mishkin, S. Fredric and S. G. Eakins (2003), *Financial Markets+Institutions*, Addison Wesley, Boston.

Nachane, Dilip M. (1999), 'Capital Adequacy Ratios: An Agnostic Viewpoint', *Economic and Political Weekly*, special nos 3 and 4 on Money, Banking and Finance, January.

Nachane, M. Dilip, Aditya Narain, Saibal Ghosh, and Satyananda Sahoo (2001), 'Bank Response to Capital Requirements: Theory and Indian Evidence', *Economic and Political Weekly*, special issue on Money, Banking and Finance, pp. 329-35.

Narain, Aditya and Saibal Ghosh (2003), 'Evolving International Supervisory Framework', *Economic and Political Weekly*, Vol. 38, No. 44, pp. 74-81.

Raghavan, C. (2001), 'New Basel Capital Draft faces continuing Concerns', *North-South Development Monitor* <available at www. twnside. sg>.

Ray, Partha (2001), 'The New Basel Capital Accord: Possible

Implications for Developing Countries', paper presented at the Bank Economists' Conference, Kolkata.

Reddy, Y. Venugopal (2001), 'Financial Sector Reforms: An Update', www.bis.org/review/r010328.

Reisen, H. (2001), 'Will New Accord Contribute to Convergence in International Capital Flows', OECD Development Centre, Paris.

Reserve Bank of India (2003a), *Report on Currency and Finance*, RBI, Mumbai.

——— (2003b), 'Comments of the Reserve Bank of India on the Third Consultative Document of the New Basel Capital Accord', RBI, Mumbai.

——— (2002), *Report on Trend and Progress of Banking in India*, RBI, Mumbai.

——— (2001), *Comment of the Reserve Bank of India on the New Basel Capital Accord*, RBI, Mumbai.

——— (various years), *Annual Report* RBI, Mumbai.

——— (various years), *Statistical Tables Relating to Banks in India*, RBI, Mumbai.

Rojas-Suarez, Liliana (2001), 'Can International Capital Standards Strengthen Banks in Emerging Markets', Institute for International Economics, October, IIE: Washington, D.C.

Salas, Vincent and Jesus Saurina (2002), 'Credit Risk in Two Institutional Settings: Spanish Savings and Commercial Banks', *Journal of Financial Services Research*, Vol. 22, No. 4, pp. 203–24.

Saunders, Anthony and Linda Allen (2002), 'A Survey of Cyclical Effects in Credit Risk Measurement Models', BIS Working Papers No. 126, BIS, Basel.

Ward, Jonathan (2002), 'The New Basel Capital Accord and its Implications for Developing Countries', University of Cambridge, Working Paper No. 4, Cambridge, UK.

Weder, Beatrice and Michael Wedow (2002), 'Will New Accord Affect International Capital Flows to Emerging Markets ?', OECD Technical Papers No. 199, OECD: Paris.

Williamson, John and Molly Mahar (1998), 'A Survey of Financial Liberalization', *Princeton Essays in International Finance No. 211*, Princeton, New Jersey.

World Bank (2001), 'Comments on the Basel Committee's New Capital Framework', www.bis.org.

12 Puzzles in Indian Performance Deficits without Disasters

Ashima Goyal[1]

Risk aversion and adverse expectations resulted in the absence of a vigorous investment boom explaining the uneven growth and the slowdown of the Indian economy after the mid-1990s. The chapter examines two alternative explanations for this. Did the high fiscal deficit raise interest rates, risk and crowd out private investment or were shocks and the absence of compensating policy responsible? We start by examining broad macroeconomic parameters, and the relationship between the three sectors—agriculture, industry, and services, in order to establish if there has been a change in the trend rate of growth or if shocks are responsible for the ups and downs. Each section of this chapter brings out an anomaly or puzzle. Puzzles offer an opportunity to learn, and suggest ways in which standard paradigms must be stretched in order to understand events, and design policy. The puzzles are either deviations from a theoretical benchmark or just outcomes that are difficult to explain.

Our conclusion is that more than the fiscal deficit, the belief in its disastrous consequences, was a disaster. Since domestic plus foreign savings together exceeded investment and compensated for government borrowing the fiscal deficit did not put pressure on Indian interest rates. Rather, foreign inflows led to rising foreign exchange reserves and the current account deficit shrank as imports stagnated. It cannot be that the fiscal deficit absorbed too much of savings when savings were unutilized. The policy choices that impounded foreign savings must be held responsible.

There is an argument that higher growth cannot occur unless deep second generation reforms take place. The analysis in this chapter suggests an incremental position, counter to the argument: macropolicies can stimulate growth, make it easier to undertake deep reform, and the latter can reinforce growth, allowing it to reach potential. Some evidence comes from the success of the stable softening interest rate regime, and rise in infrastructure spending, in stimulating higher industrial growth in 2003 and lowering the fiscal deficit (to 4.8 per cent) for the first time in many years.

Lower interest rates have encouraged housing construction and consumer expenditure, which, along with road building, has helped industry. The demand for good infrastructure rises in an economy that is opening out and facing export opportunities. India's political parties have realized that delivering this can now win more votes than the earlier narrowly targeted subsidies. Thus the BJP coined a successful new slogan 'Bijli–Sadak–Pani' for the state elections. The structure of the argument discussed in this chapter and the main conclusions are summarized in Box 12.1.

Trend or Shocks

Over the period 1997–2003 the average real GDP growth rate was 5.3 per cent per annum compared to 7.4 in the three preceding years. So we get our first puzzle.

P1: Is the new trend rate of growth of the economy around 5 per cent or is it above 7 per cent?

To begin addressing this question we will first examine whether there has been a fall in the trend rate of growth, or if the decline in performance was due to shocks.

---

[1] The autor would like to thank R. R. Radhakrishna for encouragment me to write on this topic; Kirit Parikh, Raghbendra Jha, and an anonymous OUP referee for valuable comments; Ankita Aggarwal, Arvind Kumar Jha, Ayan Kumar Pujari, Ishita Chatterjee, Sucharita Sinha, and Vidya Balakrishna for research assistance; and T. S. Ananthi for help in word processing.

192 INDIA DEVELOPMENT REPORT

> **Box 12.1**
>
> **The Structure of the Argument and the Main Conclusions**
>
> Our thesis that macro policies can stimulate growth, making it easier to undertake deep reform, and that the latter can reinforce growth, allowing it to reach potential, is supported by the growth stimulus following the stable softening interest rate regime, the rise in infrastructure spending, and from a systematic examination of the causes of the uneven growth and the slowdown of the Indian economy after the mid-1990s.
>
> The results of simulations with a dynamic model suggest that the economy was ready to move to higher trend rates of growth by the end of the twentieth century, but shocks delayed the higher growth phase. Although excess demand was absent, the fall in inflation was due more to a fall in costs and improvements in productivity. Therefore, a revival in demand need not be inflationary.
>
> Moreover, nominal interest and exchange rates have shown much larger relative variation in the reform period and correlations of private investment with nominal interest rates are high and negative. A steep rise in nominal interest rates reduces the net worth of firms and raises risk aversion. High and fluctuating nominal rates may have added to shocks and their endogenous amplification, coordinated expectations to low growth paths, and thus reduced private investment. In the 1990s, short-term nominal interest rates were raised in periods of expected depreciation of the currency, and affected long-term rates with a lag that is reducing. Reducing volatility in nominal exchange rates was achieved initially at too great a cost in terms of monetary tightening and adverse expectations. The second factor raising uncertainty was that exposing manufacture to international competition was delayed too long.
>
> Indian nominal interest rates fell smoothly especially since 2001, despite high government deficits, and aggressive sterilization, showing the leeway that existed to reduce interest rates. But inflation fell even faster so that real interest rates remained high, even as growth still did not recover. Arbitrage gaps and continuing poor absorption are part of the reason for the huge accumulation of forex reserves after January 2002.
>
> Despite widespread reforms higher risk aversion also affected the financial system, so that it could not fully contribute to diversify risk, improve credit availability to industry, and intermediate savings effectively for investment. The share of industry in annual non-food gross bank credit fell drastically over the period, while stock markets suffered from a series of scams and the absence of the small investor.
>
> The key to using inflows more productively are mechanisms that lower risk and uncertainty facing firms and households. The improvement in macroeconomic policy has begun to yield results. Robust business expectations and a fall in risk aversion of firms and financial institutions, as net worth rose with the fall in nominal interest rates, offer a window of opportunity. A fall in nominal interest rate helps even if real interest rates do not follow fully. The boom in share markets can be used to attract retail investors back by offering PSU shares at attractive prices, while leveraging the improvement in microstructure and regulation. Improving credit delivery to small enterprizes, stimulating activity, lowering import tariffs, smoothing interest rates close to international rates, keeping exchange rates competitive, and encouraging hedging of exchange risk will absorb reserves and bring us closer to our potential growth. The focus should be on reducing the revenue deficit while infrastructure spending is maintained. If interest rates are low and tax revenues rise with activity the revenue deficit will improve, thus reducing the fiscal deficit. The rise in real interest rates and fall in growth rates were responsible for its stubborn rise over the past few years, just as reverse trends have allowed the fiscal deficit to fall for the first time in years.

Table 12.1 shows the fluctuations in growth—aggregate as well as sectoral—the secular fall in inflation, and in interest rates.

Table 12.2 documents the range of shocks that hit the economy after the mid-1990s. But they were absorbed without a major slump. It is a sign of a mature economy that asymmetric or sectoral shocks do not have aggregate effects. Since we are still not fully mature the shocks were able to lower growth rates below potential, although the intensity of their effects has been falling, especially after 2000 (Box 12.2).

'Diversity plus shocks' is a useful framework for interpreting India's performance.[2] The hypothesis is that increasing diversity has helped us grow despite repeated shocks over 1995–2002. One sector covered for shocks affecting another; openness and the size of the country both increased its diversity. Openness can be a source of shocks itself, but it is also a source of diversity. Even so, better policy could have moderated the shocks.

[2] The term was first used in comments of a discussion on NCAER's Mid-year Review of the Indian Economy 2002–3 (Vohra (ed.) 2003, Goyal (2002)).

TABLE 12.1
Price and Output Trends (per cent per year)

	Growth rate of real GDP at factor cost				Wholesale Price Index (average basis)					Govt. securities interest	Profit share
	Real GDP at factor cost	Agriculture and allied	Industry	Services	All commodities Inflation	Manufacturing (weight 63.75)	Fuel, power, light, lubs (wt. 14.2)	Primary articles (wt. 22)	Food articles (wt. 15.4)		
1990-1	5.6	4.6	7.4	5.6	10.3	8.4	12.3	13	11.9	11.41	0.538
1991-2	1.3	-1.1	-1	5.7	13.7	11.3	13.2	18.1	20.2	11.78	0.553
1992-3	5.1	5.4	4.3	5.4	10.1	10.9	14.1	7.4	12.4	12.46	0.567
1993-4	5.9	3.9	5.6	7.7	8.4	7.8	15.5	6.9	4.9	12.63	0.579
1994-5	7.3	5.3	10.3	7.1	12.5	12.2	8.9	15.7	12.7	11.9	0.589
1995-6	7.3	-0.3	12.3	10.5	8.1	8.6	5.1	8.3	8.4	13.75	0.596
1996-7	7.8	8.8	7.7	7.2	4.6	2.1	10.4	8.4	12.4	13.69	0.601
1997-8	4.8	-1.5	3.8	9.8	4.4	2.9	13.8	2.7	3	12.01	0.602
1998-9	6.5	5.9	3.8	8.4	5.9	4.4	3.2	12	12.7	11.86	0.601
1999-2000	6.1	0.6	5.0	10.1	3.3	2.7	9	1.1	3.8	11.77	0.598
2000-1P	4.4	-0.4	6.5	5.7	7.2	3.3	28.5	2.9	3	10.95	
2001-2Q	5.6	5.7	3.2	6.5	3.6	1.8	9.0	3.6	3.4	9.44	
2002-3R	4.3	-3.2	5.7	7.1	3.4	2.8	5.6	3.4	1.7	7.34	

Notes: 1. Inflation rates are calculated from the index numbers of wholesale prices, on an average basis—Base 1993-4 = 100.
2. P, Q, R: Provisional, quick, and revised estimates from the CSO, source RBI, Annual Report (2003), and Economic Survey (2002-3).
3. Profit share calculated as a weighted average of formal and informal sector data on wages and productivity from NSS (47-55th Rounds), see NSSO (2001).
Source: Calculated from RBI (2003).

Counter-cyclical macro policy can be used to neutralize temporary shocks, but it has not really been practised in India. The fall in public investment and fluctuations in private investment are one factor that has prevented us from reaching our full growth potential. Monetary policy has also been periodically tightened to defend the exchange rate. Business has been waiting for stability in order to begin investing, and the government could have done more to provide it. Even so, business has begun to believe in the future—after waiting so long in fear of a collapse that did not come. Our model (Box 12.2) shows that the economy was ready to shift to a higher growth trend in 1999-2000, industrial growth had also revived (Table 12.1), but a number of shocks hit the economy from 1999 (Table 12.2), including a temporary monetary tightening in July 2000.

Growth estimate for 2003-4 is 8.1 per cent, since all three sectors did well. Exports began to rise even when the global slowdown was not fully reversed because firms had been restructuring, raising firm level efficiency and competitiveness, and turning to global markets when domestic demand was insufficient. This is especially evident in the sunrise sectors. The pick-up in global demand will benefit industry. The view that Indian manufacturing would collapse under competition was too hasty. The production and import of capital goods has also perked up—a sign that the excess capacity built in the mid-1990s has been absorbed, and investment may rise.

Agricultural exports have not done as well as expected and fluctuations have occurred, but fruits and vegetables exports seem to have been consistently growing. These have good employment potential. Private investment in agriculture rose in the 1990s, after a fall in the 1980s. Agriculture's good performance in 2001-2, after two preceding lean years, and the 9 per cent growth in 2003-4, counters those who saw structural problems, and doubted if agriculture would grow rapidly again unless these were removed. This is not to deny that major reforms are required in agriculture.

Services have consistently done well. But there is a view that the boom in services is temporary, due to the Fifth Pay Commission bonanza (Acharya 2002). But banking and financial services are the part of services whose share has increased the most comparing the 1980s to the 1990s, while the share of public administration remains the same. Therefore, there are long-term changes in services, due to these new growth sectors.

Other structural factors are favourable. There is a sharp improvement in the literacy rate, which is now above 65 per cent. The poverty ratio has also fallen, narrowing the gap from East Asia in these basic

TABLE 12.2
Shocks hitting the Economy after the mid-1990s

Incidents	Date	Details
Exchange rate volatility	October 1995–March 1996	Sharp extended rise in interest rates and short-lived credit squeeze
Asian currency crisis	1997	Hightened fear of volatility in currency markets and of capital flight
India's bomb	11 May 1998	India conducts three nuclear explosions at its Pokhran nuclear test-site. These include a fission-device, a low-yield device, and a thermonuclear device.
	13 May 1998	India conducts tests of two sub-kiloton nuclear devices at Pokhran
Sanction	13 May 1998	President Bill Clinton reported to Congress that he had imposed sanctions on India under Section 102 of the Arms Export Control Act, otherwise known as the Glenn Amendment.
Earthquake	29 March 1999	Chamoli UP
War	31 May 1999–28 June 1999	Kargil war
Cyclone	18–19 October 1999	Orissa, Andhra Pradesh, and West Bengal
Global price shock	October 2000	Oil price hike
US recession	Last quarter 2000–First quarter 2001	Triggers global slowdown
Stock prices fall	Early 2001	Dotcom burst
Scam	March 2001	SEBI restrains Anand Rathi from trading
Earthquake	26 January 2001	Gujarat earthquake
Scam	13 March 2001	Tehelka.com tapes released
Scam	30 March 2001	Madhavpura Mercantile Cooperative Bank in trouble
Enron dispute	May 2001	Work stops at Dabhol
Financial crisis	May 2001	Software slowdown
Scam	May 2001	Home trade CEO held for fraud
Scam	August 2001	Arvind Johari, promoter of Lucknow-based Cyberspace Infosys Ltd (CIL), held on the charge of misappropriating Rs 32.08 crores from Unit Trust of India (UTI),
International terrorism	11 September 2001	WTC bombing In New York
War	November 2001	Afghan war
Terrorism in India	13 December 2001	Bombing at the Parliament
Price shocks	7 February 2002	Gold prices zoom to 5-year high
Riot	27 February to 16 March 2002	Riots in Gujarat after Godhra Incident
Tension	June 2002	Indo-Pak tension at the border
Monsoon failure	June 2002	
Scam	July 2002	Worldcom scandal
War	March 2003	Iraq war
Epidemic	3 April 2003	SARS hits Asia
Strike	3 April 2003	Truckers' strike

Source: Various newsportals and *The Economic Times*, 28 April 2003.

attributes of human capital. Demographic changes also favour India. The proportion in the age group 20–59 years has been at 35 per cent for the past two decades. An Asian Development Bank (ADB) study estimates that it will increase to about 47 per cent by 2010. This is the most productive age group—if they are equipped with skills and jobs—and countries with a higher share of population in this group have done well.

The endogenous growth literature finds that on starting modern growth, countries grow at rates similar to industrial country growth rates. But when they reach a critical threshold,[3] even if the country is far behind the current industrial leader, it grows rapidly. Reasons

[3] Prescott identifies this as around 10 per cent of the 1985 US per capita income level. In purchasing power parity terms China reached this threshold in 1992, India in 1999 (Goyal 2001a).

BOX 12.2

Modelling India's Openness to the Rest of the World

A general equilibrium model with optimizing risk-averse firms yields insights on the effect of Indian reforms on consumption and investment decisions and, therefore, on changes in the CAD over time. In the model, high investment may lead to instability but choice of a mark-up (which decides the profit share) restores stability and maximize expected profits for the risk-averse representative firm. The model is reduced to two dynamic simultaneous differential equations—one based on goods market clearing (whereby savings are equated to investment), and the other giving the firm's pricing decision. The model is calibrated using Indian macroeconomic time series from the 1960s onwards. Foreign inflows, which affect S, I, and close the gap between them, play a major part. The discipline comes from the necessity of reproducing the historical series. The latter gives endogenous estimates of the parameters. Changes in savings and investment coefficients imply a change in the output growth rate. Large shocks and endogenous responses can imply a switch from a high to a low growth path. A coordinated switch of business expectations magnifies the effects of the shocks. This makes the model relevant to our debate—trend versus shocks. Work on extending the model for the current period is going on, but some preliminary results are reported. Table 12.3 reports changes in some key coefficients of the model.

TABLE 12.3
Percentage Changes in the Parameters of the Model in One Simulation Period Compared to the Previous One

Simulation periods	Savings parameter	Private investment parameter	Public investment parameter	Competitiveness parameter
1975/6–84/5	11.66	24.03	40.00	0.00
1985/6–90/1	–42.42	–26.52	–14.29	7.83
1991/2–92/3	37.06	–1.76	–16.67	15.79
1993/4–95/6	14.81	64.24	0.00	0.00
1996/7–98/9	–15.58	–20.56	0.00	0.00
1999/2000–2000–2	25.00	27.74	4.00	0.00

Note: Positive values in the last column indicate that competitiveness fell or profit shares rose.

Points to note are:

• Calibrated parameters values were stable for much longer periods before the 1990s. More frequent parameter changes in the 1990s indicate the presence of shocks large enough to affect trends. The pre-1990s break periods were also all associated with changes in the degree of openness and foreign inflows (for example, remittances in the 1970s), suggesting the usefulness of the dynamic CA approach and foreign savings in understanding Indian economic performance.

• The decline and stagnancy in public investment, with a minor reversal towards the end of the twentieth century; the large fluctuations in both domestic savings and investment in the reform period.

• Private investment rises when expected future output and productivity rise. Savings should fall if consumption is smoothed under these conditions of a credible rise in future incomes. But the rise in consumption in a developing country would be moderated by the lack of access to credit, and the precautionary motive for savings. Therefore, despite the availability of foreign savings, domestic savings and investment would be positively correlated (they do move together, that is, there is a positive correlation of 0.6).

• The best conditions for growth occur when rise in calibrated investment parameters exceeds that in savings. Such conditions were there during the growth burst in the mid-1990s and during the end of the twentieth century. If growth continued to falter in the twenty-first century the reason may lie in the concentrated series of external shocks and financial scams that hit the economy in this period (Table 12.2). Increasing ability of the economy to absorb shocks implied that growth remained positive, the changes in parameters and the endogenous magnification of shocks were reduced.

The model was initially calibrated for the pre-reform period ending in 1984–5. In the first extension to the post-reform period (Goyal 1999) data to calculate historical profit shares for the non-agricultural sector was not available. Assuming that the reforms would lead to a rise in competitiveness, a fall in the competitiveness parameter was built in, which implied decreasing profit shares. Total profits could

> still rise if capacity utilization rose. Recent survey data from the NSSO (2001)[a] allowed a calculation of the profit shares. It was a surprise to find that these had actually risen in the 1990s and were just beginning to fall in 1998–9. Therefore, in the new simulations, the estimated competitiveness parameter was raised. This implied a fall in competitiveness or rising profit shares (Table 12.3).
>
> Perhaps productivity had improved in the reform period, but competitiveness had not. Since the manufacturing slowdown had continued over 1997–2002, there were many reports that Indian manufacturing was dying from the threat of the Chinese dragon. But its reversal in 2003 was characterized by Indian companies that had restructured, improved quality, and become fit for global competition (Ninan 2003). The simulations suggest that the problem was not too much competition but too little. Continued high duties as well as the blanket depreciation protected Indian industry, and only as the deadline for reduction in duties approached and quantitative trade restrictions were removed in 2000, did Indian manufacturing wake up and show what it could do. Faster duty reduction may have brought about this desirable outcome earlier.
>
> [a] I am grateful to Jeemol Unni for sending me this data and to Arvind Kumar Jha who did the calculations.

for such a fast catching-up process are openness to new technology and more efficient forms of organization. At the threshold level there is sufficient critical mass; networks of markets and associations are dense, so that transaction costs fall. Tacit hands-on learning and quality can rise rapidly. Moreover, ICT, in which India has developed some expertise, helps in the rapid spread of best practices, and can improve transparency and governance. ICT allows independence and networking to go together. New decentralized yet efficient forms of organization become feasible. The perception that India produces poor quality is changing as Indians learn from, benchmark, and compete with the best in the world.

Therefore, our answer to the first puzzle is that shocks lowered the rate of growth below trend, the economy is showing greater resilience to shocks, but support is required from counter-cyclical policy.

Another indication that the economy has been performing below potential is the absence of excess demand pressures. There has been a decline in the inflation rates in this period (Table 12.1). This brings us to our second puzzle.

P2: Is the fall in inflation due to low demand or is it due to a fall in costs, and improvements in productivity?

Among components of demand, broad money growth had been flat in the 1990s. The fiscal deficit is large but, since the government spends more on non-tradables, this fact, together with and foreign inflows, should have raised non-tradable prices, and appreciated the real exchange rate. Yet the latter has largely depreciated. Among cost push factors, in the late 1990s, food prices were steady (Table 12.1), since they approached falling world prices and buffer stocks were large. Table 12.1 shows the inflation peak in 2001–2 coinciding with the rise in oil prices. Table 12.1 and Figure 12.1 show industry's falling contribution to inflation, which indicates a rise in industrial productivity since the weight

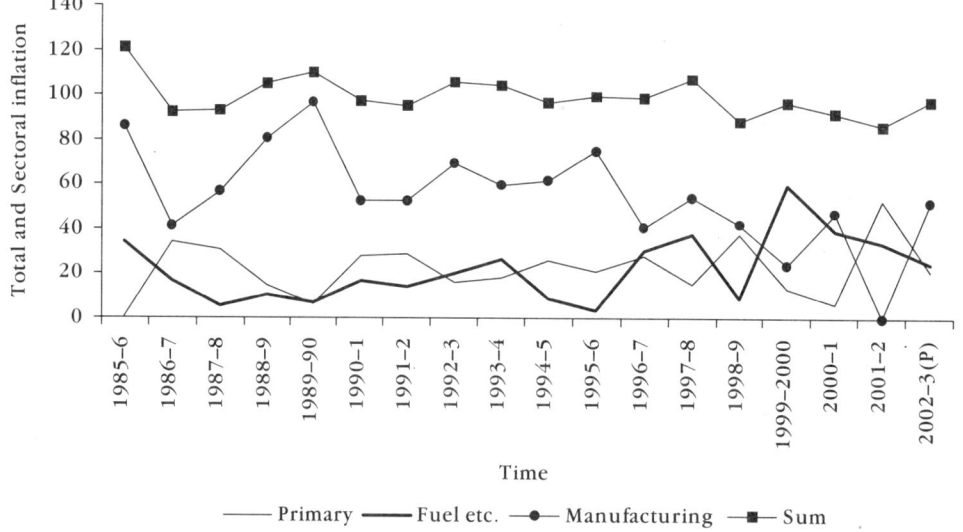

Figure 12.1: Sector-wise contribution to inflation

of manufacturing in wholesale price index (WPI) has risen from about 50 to 64 in the current series with base 1993-4. The sensitivity of industrial inflation to agricultural inflation is further evidence of cost-push factors affecting inflation. Our tentative answer to the second puzzle is that excess demand was absent, but supply side factors were important—implying that inflation could continue to be low even if demand rises. With higher growth, more activity will shift to better technology and more efficient processes; costs will continue to fall. As these trends are understood, and low inflation rates persist, inflationary expectations will also fall.

In 1998-9 the decision not to tighten monetary policy when inflation peaked with certain food prices, turned out to be correct as inflation fell (Jalan 2000). Similarly, inflation fell again as the oil shock wore out, without a sharp tightening in monetary policy, both in 2000-1 (Table 12.1), and in early 2003-4.

We have seen some of the beneficial effects of openness. These are examined systematically below.

Openness and the Current Account

A key post-reform feature was the availability of foreign capital to boost domestic savings and make higher investment possible. With more access to international capital markets it was possible for investment to exceed domestic savings. Of course, foreign inflows contribute through technology spillovers and improvements in efficiency, apart from boosting resources for investment.

Using foreign savings requires a temporary[4] widening of the current account deficit (CAD) of the balance of payments. But this has not happened. On the contrary, the current account (CA) moved into surplus for the first time in 2001-2, partly because of the large inflow of invisibles from exports of services.

P3: Why have foreign inflows lead to a shrinking CAD and rising foreign exchange reserves rather than contributing to a rise in investment?

This is the central puzzle facing the economy and we will keep returning to it. In order to address it, we first need to develop the rudiments of the determinants of the CA. The CA is defined as the acquisition of foreign assets by domestic residents minus foreign residents' acquisition of domestic assets. If this is positive the CA is in surplus. The basic macroeconomic identity, that income must equal expenditure, implies that the current account surplus (CAS) must equal both net exports of goods and services, and also gross national saving (GNS) minus investment (I). GNS is calculated by subtracting consumption from GNP. That is, from gross domestic product GDP with income payments sent abroad subtracted from it. The popular conception of CAS is identified with the net exports of goods and services.

Modern theory brings out the underlying determinants of CAS in the forward-looking decisions of consumers and firms.[5] The latter's investment decisions depend on the discounted present value of future profits (or Tobin's q), so that expectations of the future are important. Consumers seek to smooth income over time, if capital markets permit it. Savings fluctuate to smooth consumption and, therefore, absorb temporary shocks to income. Any permanent positive income shock should result in a rise in smoothed consumption while, with any temporary shock, savings will also adjust in order to maintain smoothed consumption levels.

It is also a tautology that a CAD must equal the capital account (comprising all types of capital inflows) minus any rise in foreign exchange reserves. The latter are the balancing component and are affected by the monetary and exchange rate policy being followed—both directly and indirectly—through the effect of these policies on investment and consumption. Investment is the most volatile component of expenditure and expectations of the future can be particularly volatile in a reforming economy. The major shift in perspective that the intertemporal approach to the balance of payment (BOP) brings is that it makes clear that the CA depends on macro policies affecting GNS and I, and not on trade policies.

Thus in Table 12.4 the trade balance and net invisibles add to the CA which, in turn, must equal capital inflows (the capital account) plus monetary adjustments including changes in reserves. Table 12.4 shows the steady rise in non-debt creating foreign investments such as Foreign Direct Investment (FDI), Foreign Portfolio Investment (FPI), and also debt creating inflows such as non-resident Indian (NRI) balances. The latter are more volatile. Ever since 1991-2 the CAS has been larger than the CAD, thus adding to the reserves.

In a developing country with incomplete capital markets, without full capital account convertibility, or access to world capital markets, forward looking decisions will be severely constrained. Intertemporal optimization theory can give only a rough benchmark, but still

---

[4] The period can be shorter under a vigorous export boom. For example, China ran a deficit in the 1980s but a substantial surplus thereafter.

[5] Sachs (1981) first worked out this theory, in the context of the large CA deficits that some nations ran in order to smooth consumption, after the oil shocks. The theory is surveyed in Obstfeld and Rogoff (1995). They were instrumental in developing it further.

TABLE 12.4
Items in India's BOP as a percentage of GDP

	Trade balance	Net invisibles	Current account	Capital account	Reserves, inc−, dec+	Estimated FDI	FPI	NRI deposit inflows
1990–1	−3.0	−0.1	−3.1	2.3	0.4	0.1	0.0	0.7
1991–2	−1.0	0.7	−0.3	1.5	−1.4	0.1	0.0	0.2
1992–3	2.3	0.6	−1.7	1.6	−0.3	0.2	0.1	0.9
1993–4	−1.5	1.1	−0.4	3.5	−3.2	0.4	1.3	0.4
1994–5	−2.8	1.8	−1.0	2.8	−1.4	0.7	1.2	0.3
1995–6	−3.2	1.6	−1.7	1.3	0.8	1.0	0.8	0.3
1996–7	−3.8	2.7	−1.2	3.0	−1.5	1.2	0.9	0.9
1997–8	−3.8	2.4	−1.4	2.5	−0.9	1.4	0.4	0.5
1998–9	−3.2	2.2	−1.0	2.0	−1.0	1.0	0.0	0.2
1999–2000	−4.0	2.9	−1.0	2.5	−1.4	0.8	0.7	0.3
2000–1	−3.1	2.6	−0.5	1.9	−1.3	0.9	0.6	0.5
2001–2	−2.6	2.9	0.3	2.2	−2.5	1.3	0.4	0.6
Mean 94/95–01/02 (Rs crs)						17741.57	10441.75	7687.38
Std dev 94/95–01/02						5947.12	3978.58	3717.61
Coeff. of variation 94/95–01/02						0.34	0.38	0.48

Note: Using the percentage increase in the revised RBI (30 June 2003) figures for FDI of the last two years FDI is estimated by scaling up FDI reported by the factor (1+0.66).
Source: Calculations based on data in RBI (2003).

it can help explain a more open India's CA. In the 1950s and the 1960s there were some aid inflows but foreign inflows into the economy really started with the influx of remittances from the mid-1970s.

Heightened uncertainty under reform implies that the precautionary motive for savings dominates. But if reform is credible and successful, it is associated with a positive productivity shock. This should raise investment financed by foreign inflows that come in to take advantage of the higher productivity. Since future incomes are expected to be higher, current consumption will also rise to higher smoothed levels. Box 12.2 briefly outlines a model that makes possible an analysis of the effects of openness on investment and savings behaviour. It shows that both savings and investment are affected, and in times of high growth both rise together, with the rise in investment exceeding that in savings. Openness makes the latter feasible.

This section suggests that the central issues to answer P3 are risk aversion and adverse expectations resulting in the absence of a vigorous investment boom. The key to using inflows more productively would seem to be mechanisms that lower risk and uncertainty. Before addressing this, we turn to the role of the government deficit. Did it contribute to adverse expectations or crowd out private investment?

THE TWIN DEFICITS

In an open economy, a fiscal deficit should spread to a current account deficit but it has not. The absence of these twin deficits leads us to the fourth puzzle: Why has the large fiscal deficit not led to a rise in the current account deficit?

On introducing government, a static derivation from macroeconomic identities gives the CAD as the excess of I over S plus the excess of government expenditure over taxes. So as government expenditure exceeds taxes, unless I falls or S rises, the CAD will widen. Under simplifying assumptions of low holding of international wealth by domestic residents, a one good economy, and a rate of discount equal to the international interest rate, the theory of the dynamic CA gives the following equation (Obstfeld and Rogoff 1995):

$$CA_t = (Y_t - \bar{Y}_t) - (G_t - \bar{G}_t) - (I_t - \bar{I}_t) \quad \text{(Equation 12.1)}$$

Bars over the variables denote average values. Thus when government expenditure (G) is above its average level the CA should go into deficit (become negative) as citizens borrow abroad to smooth their consumption during the period of higher than average government expenditure. But if the increase in government expenditure is regarded as permanent, smoothed consumption should fall.

Under credible reform and a permanent productivity shock both C and I would rise and S may rise or fall depending on the size of the productivity shock and the degree of incompleteness of markets. In the India of the 1990s the adjustments in S and I (Box 12.2) dominated the rise in G. Moreover, the rise in government spending took the form of subsidies and transfers to households, which in the reform environment may have been regarded as temporary. In order to smooth consumption over time, savings should rise if subsidies are regarded as temporary. Savings did rise in some periods, and investment did not rise as much as it could have, suggesting risk aversion and poor credibility of reform.

Apart from the distinction between temporary and permanent shocks, changes in taxes and subsidies, it is necessary to move beyond the one-good assumption and bring in the presence of non-traded goods to understand the absence of the twin deficits (Baxter 1995). Since traded goods dominate in I a rise in I would have required a widening of the CAD. But I was low, and government spending was high, but it falls more on non-tradables. All these arguments explain P4.

P5: Did the high fiscal deficit raise interest rates and crowd out private investment?

P5 is a very common assertion. But since sufficient domestic and foreign savings were available in the economy to compensate for government borrowing the latter was not the reason for higher Indian interest rates. G did not directly crowd out private I. Moreover, the forward looking optimization approach implies that to the extent agents foresee the implications of government spending, and compensate for it, fiscal deficits have no effect on interest rates. Government expenditure on non-tradables and foreign inflows should have raised non-tradable prices, but inflation fell. This again points to the absence of excess demand in the economy. It is not surprising that the fiscal deficit did not cause a disaster.

The arguments in Box 12.3 suggest that a reduction in real interest rates and a rise in growth is the best way to reduce government deficits and it was the converse movements in these two variables that were responsible for rising fiscal deficits in the late 1990s. Indian interest rates have fallen, especially since 2000, despite high government deficits, and aggressive sterilization, showing the leeway that existed to reduce interest rates.

Box 12.3

What is the Government's Primary Deficit?

Since there are many problems in data and definitions and these also affect measured values of deficits, we obtain a simple aggregate measure of the primary deficit (PD), which helps to bring out the contribution of changing real interest and growth rates. The public debt income ratio $b = B/PY$, where B nominal debt is divided by nominal GDP (at market prices to the base 1993–4, denoted by PY). Public debt increases in any year by nominal interest payments on debt plus the primary deficit PDPY, where PD is the ratio of the primary deficit to nominal income. PDPY is defined as the non-interest budget deficit, while the fiscal deficit includes interest payments and is the total government borrowing requirement, or excess of expenditure over taxes.

Simple algebraic manipulations using the definition of B, of PD, and that the real interest rate (r) equals the nominal interest rate (i) minus inflation, imply that the change in b equals $b(r-g) + PD$, where g is the growth rate of real GDP. The relationship is intuitive since it says that the public debt ratio will rise with the PD, the real interest rate paid on past debt, and fall with the rate of growth of GDP, which is its denominator.[a]

This relationship gives a simple way to calculate the PD ratio as the change in b minus $b(r-g)$. We calculate this ratio for two estimates of r. One derives i from actual government interest payments iB divided by B, and the second uses annual weighted average data on the interest rate on government securities (RBI 2003). Inflation calculated from the GDP deflator is then subtracted from both estimates of i, in order to get r. The two calculated series are graphed, together with the Gross PD reported in government budget documents, in Figure 12.2. Points to note are:

- The Gross PD lies approximately between the two calculated series until before 2001–2, after which it is considerably higher than both. It needs to be investigated why the reported figure fails this simple consistency check.

Perhaps Figure 12.3 can provide part of the answer. This graphs rb (with both the calculated real interest rates) and gb as percentages of the Gross Fiscal Deficit ratio (GFD). The first gives the contribution of real interest payments towards raising the GFD, and the second gives the contribution of the growth rate towards lowering it. The change in b already includes, and partly arises from PD. Therefore, br, which raises the PD, has to be subtracted from the change in b, and bg, which reduces the PD, has to be added to the change in b, in order to estimate the PD from the change in b. Interest payments recorded in the budget document are lower than those calculated from weighted average interest the government pays, accounting for the ordering of our two r series. It is in 2000–1 that the effects of rising real interest rates (in both the calculated series) in raising the GFD decisively overtake

[a] See Dornbusch and Fischer (1998), chapter 19, Appendix, pp. 595–6, for this simple derivation.

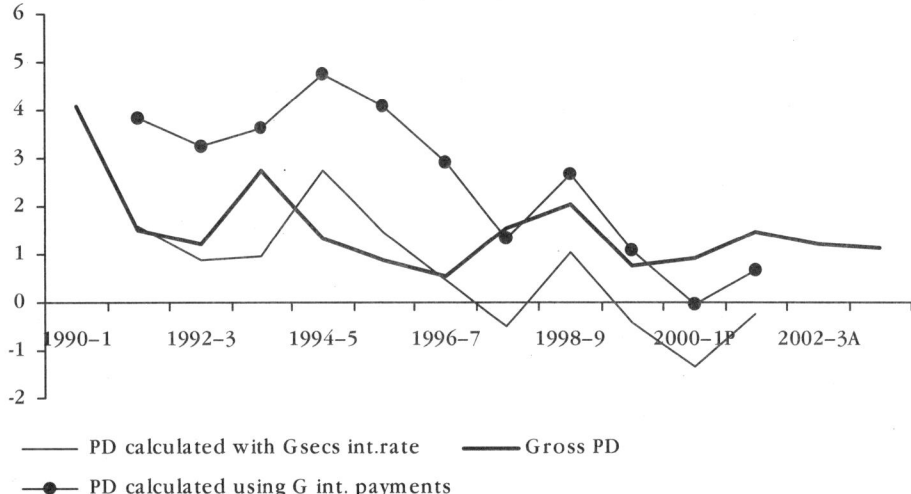

Figure 12.2: Is the primary deficit as large as it seems?

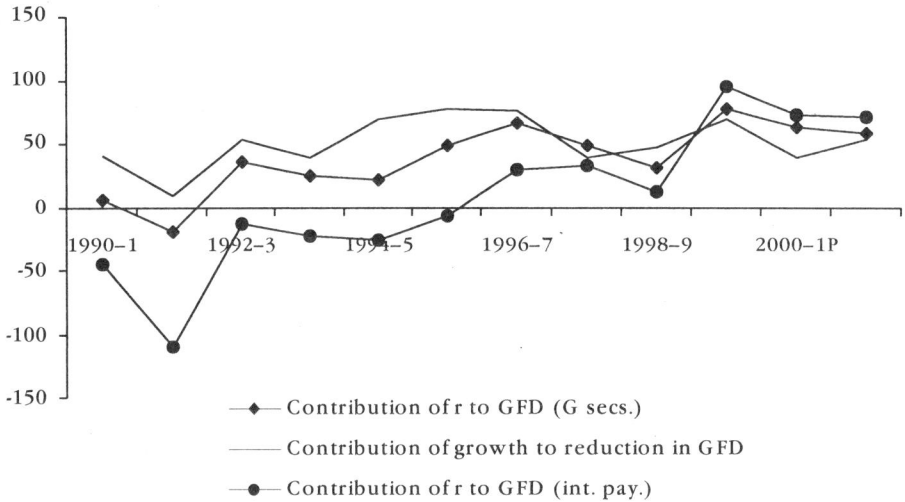

Figure 12.3: Contribution of growth and real interest rates to the fiscal deficit

the contribution of growth towards lowering it. Therefore, the negative adjustment in our calculation rises from that year. The PD has to be lower than that reported by the government to be consistent with the recorded change in government debt. Therefore, the following puzzle arises:

P6: If the government actually paid out any of the two calculated interest series, the change in debt should have been much higher.

If the PD, as reported, is correct, then the government must be paying less interest on its debt than either of our two interest series. Perhaps some of the government interest payments are to its own departments and, therefore, do not add to its debt. In order to answer P6, how much interest the government actually pays out needs to be investigated more fully.

Other points to note are:

- Although nominal interest rates on government securities have been falling steadily (Table 12.1), the real interest rates have risen sharply over 1998–2002, as inflation fell, and their average is above 6 per cent. During the same period average growth was 5.6 per cent. Thus in this period the rise in r and fall in g explain the rising GFD. This point is brought home even more starkly with the implicit r calculated from actual government interest payments. This was negative earlier, became positive in 1996–7, and averaged 4.43 over 1999–2002. While everyone was emphasizing the benefit to the government of falling nominal i in this period, the government was actually paying the highest real interests in the decade!

> - Earlier the government acquired cheap credit in the repressed financial system but its borrowings are much more expensive now. This is reflected in a debt ratio which fell to a low of 0.49 in 1996–7 (coinciding with peak growth rates) but rose after that, more rapidly in the last few years, reaching 0.6 in 2001–2. PD calculated with government securities interest rate lies below that calculated with interest payments, and lies above the other in contributions to GFD. This suggests the government is still using some cheap credit options.
> - The main culprits for the rise in b are rising r and falling g, not current government profligacy in high PDs. Moreover, the tax ratio has fallen although expenditure has been contained. But in a regime of more variable interest rates active management of government borrowing can reduce its interest costs.
> - It follows that lowering r and raising g will help to substantially improve the GFD.
> - A small primary surplus and $g > r$ will make the government debt sustainable. It is easy to see this using the figures from the vote on account 2004. The PD ratio was 0.3, $r = 6$, $g = 8$. Our formula implies that in the steady-state when b is not changing, $b = PD/g\text{-}r = 1.5$ per cent. Contrast this with the current b of above 60 per cent! Improved growth can easily reverse outcomes.

INVESTMENT FLUCTUATIONS

Since investment fluctuations have been traced as the primary explanation for P3, and it has been established that these were not due to crowding out by government borrowing, we want to look for other factors affecting these. One way of finding these factors is a comparison across decades.

P7: What caused the uneven behaviour of investment in the post-reform period?

Summary statistics for the 1980s and the 1990s[6] (Table 12.5) show the qualitative changes that have taken place between the two decades. Public sector investment has been trending downwards in the 1990s. It was around 10 per cent as a ratio to GDP in the late 1980s and had fallen to 6 per cent by the end of the decade. Was this decay compensated by a rise in private investment? The average decadal share of investment in GDP went up from 12.06 in the 1980s to 15.33 in the post-1990 period, partially compensating for the fall in the corresponding public investment share from 9.98 to 7.59. But since private investment was already at around 14 per cent in the last years of the 1980s, the rise in the 1990s has not been that much. And there have been much more fluctuations. The standard deviation of the decadal ratio has gone up from 1.39 to 1.53 (1.6 for the period 1990–1 to 1998–9). The standard deviation and coefficient of variation of public investment was also higher in the reform period.

TABLE 12.5
Averages and Deviations from Average

Variable	Annual average		Standard deviation		Coefficient of variation	
	1980–1 to 1989–90	1990–1 to 2000–1	1980–1 to 1989–90	1990–1 to 2000–1	1980–1 to 1989–90	1990–1 to 2000–1
Private investment as percentage of GDP	12.06	15.33	1.39	1.53	0.11	0.1
Public investment as percentage of GDP	9.98	7.59	0.78	1.04	0.08	0.14
GDP annual growth (1993–4 to 2002–3)	6.55	5.97	1.74	1.3	0.27	0.22
Call money rate (%)	9.46	11.13	1.01	4.29	0.12	0.39
IDBI PLR (%)	14.0	15.32	0	2.07	0	0.14
Real IDBI PLR (%)	6.03	7.65	3.69	2.65	0.62	0.35
% Re-depreciation	7.6	9.6	5.8	10.23	0.76	1.07

Note: PLR is the prime lending rate.
Source: Calculated with data from RBI (2003).

---

[6] Similar statistics were presented in Goyal (2000) although in those calculations the data for the 1990s were available only until 1998–9. Since the latter years were smoother the fluctuations were even more pronounced in the earlier calculations. Moreover, the data used now consistently have 1993–4 as the base year; the base earlier was 1980–1.

What has caused these fluctuations? The fall and fluctuation in public investment was first due to ideology, and continues due to lack of resources with the government. But what affected private investment? Two variables, whose fluctuations have influenced macro-economic outcomes in the past, are agricultural output and oil prices. But the variation in both of these was lower in the 1990s compared to the 1980s. Therefore, they cannot serve as the explanation. And correlations of current and lagged private investment with agricultural rates of growth are indeed lower in the 1990s compared to the 1980s. Correlations measure the extent to which variables move together and whether they move in the same (positive) or opposite (negative) direction.

The factors that have shown much larger relative variation in the reform period are nominal interest and exchange rates. Since nominal interest rates were rigid in the 1980s, variation in real interest rates was entirely due to that in inflation. This variation was larger in the 1980s, since nominal interest rates were not free to respond to expected or past inflation. Industry is concerned with purchasing power of the goods it produces. Therefore, real, and not nominal, interest rates should influence investment. If interest rates rise, investment should fall, so that the correlations are expected to be negative.

Correlations of private investment with the lagged nominal call money rate and the nominal and real prime lending rate of the Industrial Development Bank of India (IDBI) are shown in Table 12.6. They throw up a puzzle.

TABLE 12.6
Correlations among private investment (PI), interest, exchange, and inflation rates

	1980–1 to 1989–90	1990–1 to 2000–1
PI, lagged CMR	0.43	–0.48
PI, lagged IDBI PLR	0	–0.32
PI, IDBI PLR	0	–0.17
PI, real IDBI PLR	0.33	0.43
PI, lagged real IDBI PLR	–0.1	–0.15
PI, inflation	–0.34	–0.45
PI, Re-depreciation	0.39	–0.36
CMR, Re-depreciation	–	0.67
Nominal IDBI PLR, Re-depreciation	–	0.63
Real IDBI PLR, lagged CMR	–	0.14
Real IDBI PLR, inflation	–	–0.78
Nominal PLR, inflation	–	0.60

Note: PLR is the prime lending rate, CMR is the call money rate.
Source: Calculated with data from RBI (2003).

P8: In the post-reform period, correlations of private investment with nominal interest rates are high and are negative.

P8 suggests a possible answer for P7 in the effect of nominal interest rates on investment, but P8 is itself a puzzle. P8 can be explained if a steep rise in nominal interest rates raises uncertainty and reduces the net worth of firms. Under asymmetric information and the inability to fully diversify risk, a fall in the net worth would reduce activity. Stiglitz and Weiss (2003) argue that nominal interest rates often outperform real interest rates if both are included in an investment regression, for these reasons. High nominal rates may have added to shocks and their endogenous amplification, coordinated expectations to low growth paths and, thus, reduced private investment. In the 1990s, short-term nominal interest rates were raised in periods of expected depreciation of the currency, and affected long-term rates with a lag that is reducing. The correlation of both the nominal interest rates with rupee depreciation is above 0.6.

Real interest rates are positively correlated with investment because with rigidities in nominal rates, real interest rates rise when inflation falls, and inflation is negatively correlated with investment. The latter correlation is further support for cost-push being the dominant cause of Indian inflation.

Our results are preliminary since bi-variate correlations do not necessarily imply causality. But they do suggest that excessive interest rate volatility may have harmed investment. Monetary authorities may have done better with an exchange rate policy that would have reduced the necessity to resort to frequent monetary tightening.

MONETARY POLICY, THE TERM STRUCTURE OF INTEREST RATES, AND EXPECTATIONS

Monetary policy is committed to a soft interest rate regime and, especially since 2001, after the implementation of the liquidity adjustment facility (LAF), domestic short-term interest rates drifted downward steadily. This spread to long-term rates and flattened the yield curve by 2003. The bank rate was reduced from 11 per cent to the current 6 per cent over a period of five years.

But the other prime aim of monetary policy has been to prevent volatility in the exchange rate. Bi-annual policy statements carried stern warnings that interest rates could be reversed whenever necessary depending on the evolving situation or adverse external circumstances. In practice reversals were carried out only to defend the exchange rate.[7] The last such episode occurred under pressure on the rupee, from mid-May to early August 2000, when the rupee depreciated by about

---
[7] The severe credit squeeze that followed the first episode of exchange rate volatility in 1995–6 helped trigger off the sustained slowdown (Goyal 1997).

3 per cent against the dollar, together with a net outflow by foreign institutional investors (FIIs). The RBI reversed direction drastically in July. The bank rate, the CRR, and short-term repo rates were all increased.

There is a trade-off between variability of nominal exchange and interest rates. Although the RBI wants to be free to raise nominal interest rates sharply anytime to quell excess volatility in exchange rates; it could make it clear that such a rise, if at all it occurs, will hold only for a very short time, which is sufficient to contain speculative activity against the exchange rate.

Sudden sharp changes in interest rates disturb financial markets too much. Greenspan, for example, cuts the nominal interest rate only 25–50 basis points at a time. The advantage of smoothing, or successive cuts in the same direction, is that markets internalize future cuts, the expected real interest rates fall, and stimulatory effects of lower interest rates are realized even before the rates themselves fall. Thus taking markets into confidence helps monetary policy achieve its purpose.[8] In the Annual Monetary Policy Statement for the year 2002–3 (Jalan 2002) a warning was given of a possible future 50 basis point cut, and this did help nudge the longer-term interest rates downwards. The statements rightly warn that most countries make frequent changes in response to events, and this should be expected here also. But other countries adjust monetary policy to suit internal requirements. Since our interest rates have been too vulnerable to exchange rate fears, policy was unable to remove self-fulfilling pessimism that has the economy performing below its potential.

Current international research is supporting managed exchange rate regimes compared to the earlier emphasis on floating or currency boards. To that extent, the RBI's 'middling' regime is validated. A middling regime is not like an exchange rate target and gives some flexibility to achieve other targets. The RBI's interventions did successfully quell excess volatility but they led to a steady accumulation of reserves and to the one-way movement of the rupee. More genuine two-way movements in exchange rates would develop the forex market and give the RBI more freedom to tailor interest rates to domestic needs. If low managed exchange rate volatility makes smoother interest rates more feasible it would be better for markets and activity. It is easy to hedge small exchange rate movements, and interest rates have a much wider impact. Markets see what the RBI does, not only what it says, so the softened tone, together with the absence of a reversal since 2000, has contributed to expectations of lower interest rates and an upswing in activity.

The RBI is open to ideas and welcomes the debate on exchange rate regimes. There is, however, a genuine fear of excess volatility in shallow Indian forex markets (Jalan 2003). But the RBI has such large reserves and clout in the market, that any intervention by it would be respected as a credible signal of future movement.

P9: What explains the huge accumulation of forex reserves of above US$ 30 billion in 18 months over January 2002 to August 2003?

The answer to P9 is partly that arbitrage occurred at different points of the interest rate spectrum, and aggressive sterilization maintained positive interest gaps, thus attracting more inflows, but reducing the stimulus to activity that would have absorbed some of the inflows. Even the LAF was used largely for absorbing liquidity.

Movements in Indian interest rates continue to be uneven with banking spreads, prime lending rates (PLRs) and savings deposit rates resisting downward movement. In an open economy the gap between Indian and foreign interest rates also affects foreign inflows and, if rigidities prevent the gap from closing, it further encourages the accumulation of reserves. But the size of the gap, its resistance to policy and its effect on arbitrage vary at different points on the interest rate spectrum. If domestic short interest rates exceed international rates (Box 12.4), arbitrage occurs at the short end of the interest rate spectrum. It is possible to make money by borrowing dollars, selling them spot for rupees, lending the rupees, and then selling the proceeds in the forward market for dollars. At the longer end, two major sources of arbitrage are corporates borrowing abroad, and NRI's depositing money in India.[9]

Despite the downward drift in the call money rate, ever since the US recession international interest rates fell faster—so the gap between domestic and international rates rose. Since the end of 2001, the excess of our annual call money rates over those of the USA, at plus 4 per cent, was back to 1998 levels. In October 2001 the average gap in monthly rates became double its average value over the past year. It is probably not a coincidence that in 2001–2 the increase in forex reserves as a percentage of GDP doubled to 2.5 compared to 1.3 in the previous year. Since forward premiums also fell in early 2004, the interest gap minus the forward premium became positive for the first time. Transaction costs and other barriers have been falling. Therefore, there were

---

[8] Some of these arguments were made in a series of articles on monetary policy, largely in *The Economic Times*. They are available at http://economictimes.indiatimes.com/search.cms and at www.igidr.ac.in/~ashima. The point on interest smoothing was first made in Goyal (2001b).

[9] These arguments were first made in Goyal (2003).

Box 12.4
Arbitrage at the short end

Arbitrage implies two relationships that must hold in forex markets. Covered interest parity (CIP) implies that the forward premium (fp) on any currency must equal the interest gap between the two currencies. Thus fp = i-i*, where both refer to the same time period. If i > fp+i*, riskless profit can be made by borrowing the foreign currency at i*, buying the domestic currency spot, investing it at i, and then selling in the forward market. There is a band determined by transaction costs, and profit opportunities lie outside this band. In Figure 12.4, the i-i*-fp graph, for one-month rates, lies close to the X-axis. This normally lay below the axis since the *fp* was large. Since actual depreciation was less than the *fp* sellers of dollar forwards made money. From March 2003 the curve has been consistently above the x-axis because the *fp* fell and world interest rates were softer than domestic. Since transaction costs were also falling there were opportunities for riskless arbitrage, although the latter were limited by quantitative restrictions that were increased. Moreover, arbitrage occurs only for *i*, *i**, and *fp* involved in actual dealer transactions—not the average values reported in Figure 12.4 or in Table 12.7.

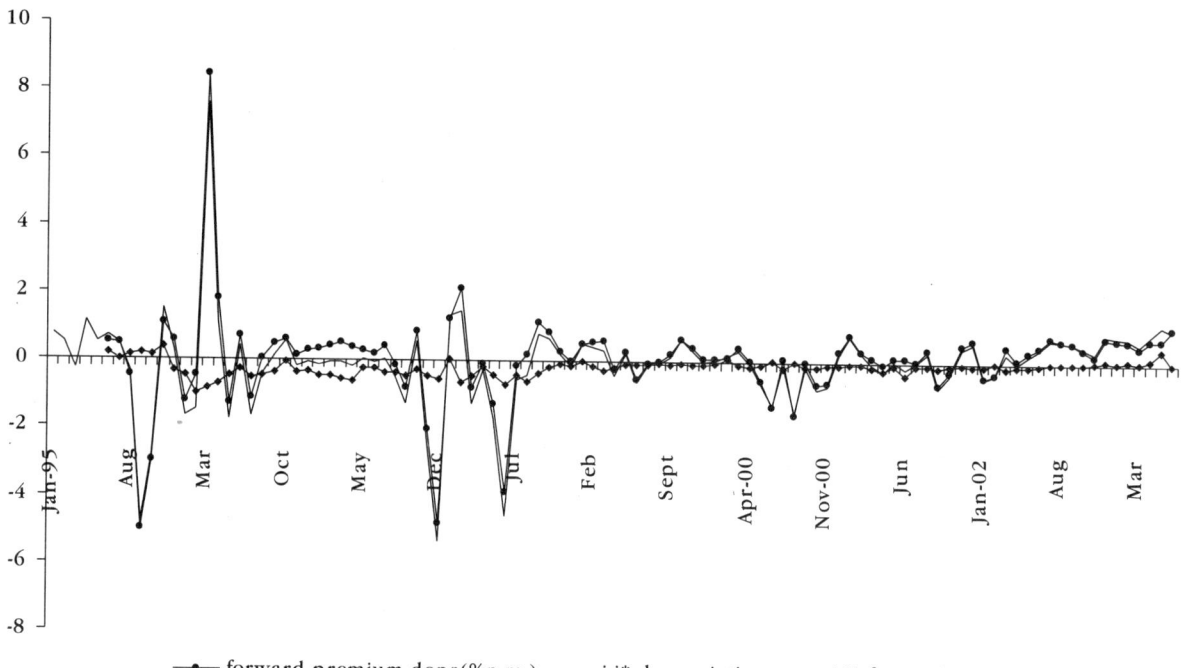

Figure 12.4: The risk premium in Indian currency markets

Table 12.7
Arbitrage in Currency Markets

Year	Re-depreciation (d)	Forward premium (fp)	i–i*	p–p*	Risk premium (rp) fp–d	i–i*–d	i–i*–fp
1995	3.35	9.236	9.73	8.08	5.88	6.38	0.498
1996	9.27	12.140	5.98	1.56	2.87	–3.29	–6.156
1997	2.48	5.047	–0.17	2.28	2.57	–2.65	–5.217
1998	13.62	8.333	4.13	4.21	–5.29	–9.49	–4.201
1999	4.35	4.965	3.89	1.32	0.61	–0.47	–1.078
2000	4.38	3.755	3.03	2.84	–0.62	–1.35	–0.726
2001	5.00	4.803	3.41	2.37	–0.20	–1.59	–1.396
2002	3.01	4.716	4.48	0.87	1.70	1.46	–0.238
2003	–2.47	2.672	4.36	1.15	5.14	6.83	1.686

Notes: 1. i—Indian call money rate, i*—US federal funds rate, p—Indian WPI, p*—US CPI.
2. All variables are in percentage changes per annum.
Source: Calculated from RBI (2003) and Federal Reserve Bank of New York, http://www.newyorkfed.org/http://minneapolisfed.org/research/data/us/calc/hist1913.cfm

> If prices fully reflect market information so that no trader can earn excess returns from speculation uncovered interest parity (UIP) must hold. That is, expected depreciation (ed) must equal the interest gap, ed = i-i*, again for the same time horizon. UIP implies that the opportunity cost of holding the two currencies is equal. Assuming CIP, UIP implies fp = ed, since the i-i* term cancels out.
>
> But market efficiency is actually a joint hypothesis of rational expectations and risk neutrality of market participants. If a risk premium is allowed for, then it becomes a joint hypothesis of equilibrium returns including a risk premium (rp), and rational expectations. Including rp, UIP is written as, ed +rp = i-i*. Now if CIP holds, UIP implies, fp-ed = rp. Assuming depreciation equals its expected value, ed, Figure 12.4 graphs both fp-d, and i-i*-d, giving two estimates of rp. To the extent expectations are not rational, or lack of full capital account convertibility puts restrictions on transactions, the estimates measure something apart from a pure risk premium. The graph shows that the two rp series are very close. It also shows the decline in the volatility of rp over the years. This reduction in risk and volatility has been a major success for monetary policy.
>
> In Table 12.7, at the one-year frequency, the two estimates of rp are not that close because even more averaging is involved. But the Table 12.7 clearly shows that the gap under CIP is higher than it has been since 1998, suggesting arbitrage opportunities and explaining the rise in quantitative restrictions imposed by the RBI. It shows the reduction in volatility and amount of depreciation, and the appreciation in 2003. The fp was steadily falling and so was i, but since the fall in i* was even higher, i-i* rose above its 1998 level. The annual rp in 2003 was as high as it had been in 1995. If rp was constant then UIP together with a positive interest differential implies an expected future depreciation, which is equally dangerous and raises risk.
>
> Depreciation had largely exceeded the gap in domestic and foreign inflation, p-p*, so that the rupee remained competitive, but if appreciation continues, overvaluation becomes a possibility.

probably some opportunities for riskless arbitrage at the short end. Even if some interest rates are resistant the RBI can affect short rates through indirect market-based instruments that have become more sophisticated.

At the longer end, blue-chip firms can access cheap loans abroad. A fixed or appreciating currency, domestic interest rates that exceeded international ones, implying large short-term foreign borrowing by domestic entities, was the recipe for the Asian currency crisis. In 2003, the RBI was forced to put a ceiling of US$ 100 million on the amount that firms could borrow abroad.

Second, NRI's can hold money in Indian banks either in foreign currency deposits (FCNR (B)), or in rupee NR (E) deposits. In the first option banks bear the exchange risk, in the second, the NRIs do. Since the rupee was appreciating in 2003, there were huge inflows into NR (E) deposits. FCNR (B) deposit interest rates were subject to a ceiling of global rates, but for NR (E), on 10 July, the Bank of India (BOI) was offering the same interest rate (of 5 per cent for less than 3 years and 5.25 for 3 to 5 years) as on domestic deposits. An NRI could earn much more compared to very low US rates, as well as gain from rupee appreciation. Lower deposit rates reduce costs for banks, but one bank will not cut rates unless others do, competition affects other services offered. On 17 July the RBI imposed an interest ceiling, 250 basis points above the LIBOR/SWAP rates for US dollars of the corresponding maturity, on NR (E) deposits. Pensioners deserve to be protected but NRIs should be content with the interest rates close to those available in their country of residence. At a time of foreign exchange scarcity these deposits met a social objective. In today's time of glut a large interest differential cannot be justified. Table 12.4 shows that NRI deposits had the highest coefficient of variation compared to FPI, and FDI. One of the most desirable components of foreign investment, FDI, does not require a large interest gap. Indeed, insofar as lower domestic interest rates stimulate profitability this attracts more FDI.

Reducing domestic interest closer to the foreign one is a more effective way of reducing arbitrage and reserve accumulation, compared to clumsy quantitative restrictions that impede the working of markets. It will also serve to stimulate investment and thus absorb foreign inflows productively.

Credit and Finance

We have examined the effect of volatility in interest rates and in expectations. Although the cost of credit fell, with a fluctuating trend, what happened to its quantity, and other aspects of quality? Was the financial sector able to successfully intermediate household savings and diversify risk for its participants?

Table 12.8 clearly shows the substitution of foreign assets for credit to the government in the RBI's portfolio, and the slight rise in commercial bank's credit to the government as a result. But priority credit to the small-scale sector fell only marginally, and non-food credit has actually risen. Moreover, since large companies are able to access cheap credit abroad there is probably no fall in aggregate credit availability. There is, however, some change in its composition.

Non-performing assets (NPAs) have fallen, and successful voluntary retirement schemes (VRS) together with the securitization bill have lowered costs for banks. Profits have improved, but spreads between deposit and lending rates remain high and banks continue to neglect the credit needs of small firms.

P10: Why has the share of bank loans going to industry fallen?

Table 12.10 shows that the share of industry in annual non-food gross bank credit has been falling drastically over the period, while the share of other sectors has almost doubled. Prominent among these other sectors are housing and personal loans, reflecting the boom in retail banking. Old customers are being squeezed because of new more profitable avenues. The uncertainty and slowdown in industry may have made banks more cautious. It also reduced the demand for loans. Under restructuring and improvements in efficiency many firms is to make information intensive local finance available and to remove reservations so that these industries can restructure and become profitable in their own right.

Equally serious, in this period, has been the failure of equity markets. Table 12.8 records the fall in market capitalization and new capital issues since the mid-1990s. The rise in non-transparent private placements, together with the collapse in equity, implied a dangerous rise in leverage and sensitivity to a rise in interest rates in India's corporate sector. Table 12.9 captures the reflections of these changes on the household's savings choices, with a drastic fall in shares and debentures, linked to the fall in the Bombay (Brihanmumbai) Stock Exchange (BSE) index of stock prices.

P11: What explains the sustained slump in stock markets?

Part of the reason was the succession of scams in the financial sector, documented in Table 12.2. Adverse

TABLE 12.8
Indicators of Credit and Financial Markets as % of GDP

	Net bank credit to government	Net RBI credit to central government	Foreign currency assets	Market capital -ization of BSE	Priority credit going to small-scale industries	Gross bank non-food credit	Resource mobilization in private placements	New capital issues—non-govt. public ltd. cos.
1990–1	24.7	15.3	0.8	16.0	3.0	20.0	0.0	0.8
1991–2	24.2	14.1	2.2	49.5	2.8	18.6		0.9
1992–3	23.5	12.9	2.7	25.1	2.7	18.8		2.6
1993–4	23.7	11.3	5.5	42.8	2.6	17.0		2.2
1994–5	22.0	9.8	6.5	43.0	2.7	18.2		2.6
1995–6	21.7	10.0	4.9	44.3	2.7	18.7	1.1	1.3
1996–7	21.1	8.8	5.9	33.9	2.6	18.4	1.1	0.8
1997–8	21.7	8.8	6.7	36.8	2.9	18.9	2.0	0.2
1998–9	22.2	8.4	7.2	31.3	2.8	18.7	2.9	0.3
1999–2000	22.8	7.2	7.9	47.1	2.7	19.4	3.2	0.3
2000–1	24.3	7.0	8.8	27.2	2.7	20.4	3.2	0.2
2001–2	25.5	6.2	10.8	26.7	2.5	21.0	2.8	0.2

Source: Calculated from RBI (2003).

had become cash-rich and reduced their need for loans. Since their best customers could raise loans abroad,[10] banks may have been reluctant to take on the high-risk ones remaining. They were now accountable to markets, and had to make provision for high-risk loans. These new trends are impacting credit outstandings more slowly, but small-scale priority sector industries are the major sufferers since they cannot access foreign markets. The answer

[10] Goyal and Dash (2000) show that in the presence of a large interest differential, low risk firms raise money abroad, and since high-risk firms are left, banks find it more difficult to reduce loan rates of interest.

TABLE 12.9
Household Savings Choices

Percentage distribution over	2000–1	1998–9	1994–5
Deposits	44.3	39.2	45.5
Shares and debentures	2.7	3.6	11.9
Small savings (claims on government)	11.6	12.8	9.0
Insurance funds	12.8	11.2	7.8
Provident and pension funds	20.7	22.1	14.7
BSE sensitive index (% changeover past year)	–22	–13.6	37.13

Source: RBI Annual Report 2001–2.

TABLE 12.10
Credit to Selected Sectors as a Percentage of Non-food Gross Bank Credit

	Outstandings in March		Variations during						
	2002	2000	2001–2	2000–1	1999–2000	1998–9	1997–8	1996–7	1995–6
SSI (priority sector)	11.85	13.8	2.23	5.9	6.63	13.3	20.78	13.85	11.37
Medium, large industry	35.7	39.2	17.7	28.72	33.4	34.72	39.27	32.57	49.2
Non-priority sectors apart from industry and trade—	23.76	21.17	38.52	27.58	26.63	22.89	16.41	26.81	19.50
of which: Housing,	4.63	3.76	11.58	3.78	5.37	6.28	–	–	–
Personal loans	4.85	4.11	9.96	4.9	6.25	5.77	–	–	–

Note: SSI is small-scale industry.
Source: RBI Annual Reports, various issues. Data relate to about 50 Scheduled Commercial Banks, which account for about 90–5 per cent of bank credit.

expectations and the continuing industrial slowdown contributed to this situation. Stock indices reflect expectations of future performance, although they do tend to overreact. The thorough reforms in regulation and modernization in market microstructure did reduce transaction costs, but were unable to overcome the negative aspects, partly because of a neglect of the small investor. For example, the fee structure in paperless trading made it very expensive for the small player to dematerialize shares and enter the market. Although regulatory rules were now of international standards their implementation was not adequate to win the confidence of the investor.

In 2003, there was a robust broad-based revival with the recovery in industry, as softening nominal interest rates and government spending on roads compensated for continuing shocks. Stock indices rose, the Maruti initial public offering (IPO) was a big success and many more IPO's are slated to follow. In December, Indraprastha Gas IPO gave a reward of 150 per cent premium over the issue price to subscribers. It is instructive that one reason for the success of the Maruti IPO was that a large part was reserved for the household sector. Savers are more willing now to return to equity and share more risk, as interest rates have fallen sufficiently to lower returns from debt and deposits. It is necessary to provide them with an adequate array of instruments offering a combination of risk and return. Consumers should be able to choose from a spectrum of low return-low risk to high return–high risk assets.

As households become ready to share more risk, firms and banks have become willing to undertake more risk. The steady fall in nominal interest rates has raised the net worth of both banks and firms, reducing risk aversion. There are huge cash reserves with firms, and banks have reduced NPAs with large treasury profits. Although firms have begun to invest, they still do not need large bank loans. Banks can target households and small firms with innovative instruments, credit delivery mechanisms, and lower PLRs. At last the real and financial sectors may be ready to work in tandem, under watchful regulators, to yield steady and robust growth.

Conclusions

In summary, we can say that part of the fall below potential growth was caused by the repeated shocks the economy faced, but the level of diversity has reached a point such that the shocks can be absorbed with less damage. The results of simulations with a dynamic model suggest that the economy was ready to move to higher trend rates of growth by the end of the twentieth century, but shocks delayed the higher growth phase. Government policies smoothed some shocks, such as supply-side inflation pressures, but they multiplied others and macropolicies were not sufficiently counter-cyclical.

Although the fiscal deficit is pointed out most often as the source of problems, we find it did not cause crowding out or excess demand pressures, since growth was below potential, and domestic savings rose, while investment did not rise to match the resources available. Other government polices could have played a greater role in smoothing the uncertainties that reduced investment. Reducing volatility in nominal exchange rates was achieved initially at too great a cost in terms of monetary tightening and adverse expectations. Exposing manufacture to international competition was delayed too long.

The softening and smoothing of nominal interest rates helped contribute to the revival, as did government spending on infrastructure. The softening was helped by the fall in international interest rates, but Indian rates did not follow fully and some rigidities remain, which are partly responsible for the accumulation of reserves. A fall in nominal interest rate can have a beneficial effect even if real interest rates do not follow fully. Because we are below potential growth, the reserves are best absorbed by stimulating activity, lowering import tariffs, smoothing interest rates close to international rates, and keeping exchange rates competitive. Lower tariffs will raise imports and make Indian industry even more competitive, and are a good alternative for rupee appreciation which can harm exports. The focus should be on reducing the revenue deficit while infrastructure spending is maintained. If interest rates are low and tax revenues rise with activity the revenue deficit will improve. Robust business expectations and a fall in risk aversion of firms and financial institutions, as net worth rose with the fall in interest rates, offer a window of opportunity. In a more open economy behaviour changes and policy has to evolve, in order to keep pace.

References

Acharya, S. (2002), 'Macroeconomic Management in the Nineties', *Economic and Political Weekly*, 20 April, pp. 1515–38.

Baxter, M. (1995), 'International Trade and Business Cycles', chapter 35 in G. M. Grossman and K. Rogoff (ed.), *Handbook of International Economics, Vol. III*, Amsterdam, North-Holland.

Dornbusch, R. and S. Fischer (1998), *Macroeconomics*, 6th edition, Tata-McGraw Hill, New York.

Goyal, A. (2003), 'Arbitrage and the Interest Rate Spectrum', *The Economic Times*, 12 August.

——— (2002), 'A Decade of Diversity and Shocks', *The Economic Times*, 5 November.

——— (2001a), 'Reasoned Optimism', *The Economic Times*, 19 June.

——— (2001b), 'Beyond Money Illusion', *The Economic Times*, 20 November.

——— (2000), 'Why Has Investment Fluctuated in the 90s?', *The Economic Times*, 2 November.

——— (1999), *Developing Economy Macroeconomics: Fresh Perspectives*, Allied Publishers, New Delhi.

——— (1997), 'Inflation, Exchange and Interest Rates; A Macroeconomic "Rashomon"', in Kirit S. Parikh (ed.) *India Development Report 1997*, Indira Gandhi Institute of Development Research, Mumbai and Oxford University Press, New Delhi.

Goyal, A. and S. K. Dash (2000), 'Real and Financial Sector Interaction under Liberalization in an Open Developing Economy', *Meteoreconomica*, Vol. 15, No. 3, pp. 257–83.

Jalan, B. (2003), 'Exchange Rate Management: An Emerging Consensus?', keynote address at the 14th National Assembly of Forex Association of India, Mumbai, 14 August.

——— (2002), 'Monetary and Credit Policy for the Year 2002–2003', statement by Bimal Jalan, Governor, Reserve Bank of India, April, available at www.cpolicy.rbi.in.

——— (2000), 'Mid-Term Review of Macroeconomic and Monetary Developments in 2000-1', statement by Bimal Jalan, Governor, Reserve Bank of India, April, available at www.cpolicy.rbi.in.

Ninan, T. N. (2003), Manufacturing will be Tomorrow's Star, 11 January, http://www.rediff.com/money/2003/jan/11guest.htm.

NSSO (2001), Employment and Unemployment Situation, Part II, 55th Round, July 1999–2000, May.

Obstfeld, M. and K. Rogoff (1995), 'The Intertemporal Approach to the Current Account', chapter 34 in G. M. Grossman and K. Rogoff (ed.), *Handbook of International Economics*, Vol. III, Amsterdam, North-Holland.

Reserve Bank of India (2003), *Handbook of Statistics on the Indian Economy*, RBI, Mumbai.

RBI, *Report on Currency and Finance*, and *Annual Report* and *Handbook of Economic Statistics*, various issues, RBI, Mumbai.

Sachs, J. D. (1981), 'The Current Account and Macroeconomic Adjustment in the 1970s', Brookings Papers on Economic Activity 1, 201–68.

Stiglitz, J. and B. Greenwald (2003), *Towards a New Paradigm in Monetary Economics*, The Raffaele Mattioli Lecture Series, Cambridge University Press, Cambridge.

Vohra, N. N. (ed.), (2003), *Mid-year Review of the Indian Economy 2002–2003*, by Suman Bery and NCAER, Shipra and India International Centre, New Delhi.

13 Urban Transportation Trends, Alternatives, and Policy Issues

Sudhakar Yedla[1]

The number of motorized vehicles in Indian cities has outgrown the number of people. This trend is predominant in mega cities owing to high economic growth and urbanization. However, road infrastructure has not developed commensurately to support the high growth in vehicle stock. As a result, congestion, air and noise pollution, travel time, and accident rates have increased while fuel efficiency has gone down. Increased dependence on personalized motor vehicles is apparent from their rising stock in metropolitan cities. Various policy initiatives taken by the GOI have succeeded to some extent in controlling urban air pollution in some cities. However, the ever-rising vehicular stocks, the lack of any integrated clean-fuel policy, lag in application of economic tools to control the traffic growth, and the resulting pollution keep the situation at the same level as before. Delhi, the leading metropolitan city, is among the most polluted in the world. It is experiencing very high levels of air pollution, mostly coming from urban transportation. Though air quality in Delhi has been improving, a most alarming fact is that many class II cities like Hyderabad, Kanpur, and Varanasi are closely following trends similar to what Delhi followed in the early 1990s.

This chapter presents the trends in urban transportation development and various policy options executed so far to control the growth in transportation and environmental emissions. Various potential technological, management, and policy measures taken up to achieve sustainable transportation in Indian urban centres are discussed along with various barriers to their implementation and alternative options.

Efficient systems of transportation make key contributions to economic growth, competitiveness, and cohesion. Addressing the issue of urban transportation is a complex exercise and any effort to achieve sustainable transportation needs to go by a holistic view of diverse aspects of travel demand, vehicular growth pattern, emissions, auto technologies, traffic management, and efficient land use pattern and auto fuel quality on the one hand, and the absorptive capacity and acceptability on the other. To make an attempt to arrive at a solution from any of these dimensions in isolation would not be successful in achieving sustainability as most of these are essentially interlinked. In this chapter we present the trends and facts under each module of this integrated component of urban transportation.

Growth of Vehicular Stock

All metropolitan cities (cities with more than a million population) have been facing consistent rise in vehicular stock and growth in demand for travel. Travel demands are very high in the case of mega cities, namely, Chennai, Delhi, Kolkata, and Mumbai. Delhi stands out among these cities with a total vehicular population equal to the vehicular stock in the other three metros, that is, Chennai, Kolkata, and Mumbai, put together. Rapid expansion of city boundaries and increased number of suburbs to cater for migrating populations could be the reason for such growth. Table 13.1 presents the growth rates of vehicular stock in all major cities in India from 1985 to 2002. It is interesting to observe that the class I cities, other than the five mega cities, are competing with the mega metropolitan cities.

---

[1] The report on auto fuel policy and reports of the research projects funded by SIDA at IGIDR (2002) and TERI (1997) along with other major policy documents have been referred to in the preparation of this chapter. Use of data and tables from these reports is duly acknowledged.

TABLE 13.1
Annual Growth Rates of Motor Vehicles (Cars, Taxis, Buses, Trucks,
Three Wheelers, and Two Wheelers) in Major Indian Cities from 1985 to 2002 (%)

City/District	1985–90	1990–5	1995–2002	Population (2001)
Greater Mumbai UA	9.05	5.87	11.14	16,368,084
Kolkata UA	19.44	24.89	9.53	13,216,546
Delhi state	18.93	9.71	6.57	12,791,458
Chennai UA	29.27	11.05	10.49	6,424,624
Bangalore district	17.84	9.11	14.43	5,686,844
Hyderabad	26.96	13.66	9.76	5,533,640
Ahmedabad district	16.39	10.76	10.76	4,519,278
Pune district	14.35	14.13	11.95	3,755,525
Surat district	20.87	9.18	11.42	2,433,787
Jaipur district	17.24	11.97	10.79	2,324,319
Lucknow district	5.39	5.48	6.93	2,266,933
Nagpur district	24.4	8.94	11.22	2,122,965
Patna district	20.77	10.23	13.51	1,707,429
Indore district	16.98	10.14	12.95	1,639,044
Vadodara district	26.37	14.28	13.83	1,492,398
Bhopal district	6.02	8.84	5.96	1,454,830
Ludhiana district	23.71	9.52	15.95	1,395,053
Visakhapatnam district	13.66	14.32	15.32	1,329,472
Varanasi district	16.72	10.33	9.96	1,211,749
Nashik district	23.46	10.38	11.75	1,152,048
Jabalpur district	21.31	8.25	14.05	1,117,200
Faridabad district	38.86	36.82	1.57	1,054,981

Note: UA—urban agglomeration.
Source: Urban statistics (1997); GOI (1996 and 1997).

Cities like Pune, Jaipur, Jabalpur, and Surat have experienced tremendous growth in vehicular stock over the last 17 years and are catching up with the mega cities. Hyderabad, Ahmedabad, and Bangalore are already among the mega cities with respect to vehicular stock. Hyderabad has climbed from the sixth position to the fourth position in vehicular stock whereas Surat reached the nineth position from the thirteenth position. Given the fact that unlike other mega cities, no concrete measures/efforts are on to check the travel growth or pollution in these cities, very soon they could reach alarming levels of traffic and resulting environmental emission. Figure 13.1 presents the increase in vehicular stock in different cities from 1985 to 2002.

Among the total vehicular stock, personalized modes of transport are dominating in almost all cities. Table 13.2 presents the mode-wise break up of vehicular stock in different cities for the year 2002. Delhi roads are predominantly occupied by two-wheelers whereas in the case of Mumbai cars dominate. Lack of proper/efficient public transportation in Delhi could be the reason for the rapid growth of the two-wheeler population over time. However, it is an interesting observation that their growth rate has started declining in very recent times. The rate of registration of two-wheelers came down to around 50,000 per annum by 2002 although earlier they were being registered at a rate of around 0.1 million per annum. Considering that old two-wheelers above a certain age get phased out, in Delhi the total number of two-wheelers plying may actually be reducing (GOI 2002). In contrast, the trend observed in the other cities indicates fast growth. The number of two-wheelers as percentage of total registered vehicles is considerably high among the small and industrialized cities like Pune, Surat, and Kanpur. Figure 13.2 presents the percentage share of each travel mode in various cities of India in the year 2002. City/public transport in small cities is fairly low compared to mega cities like Delhi and Mumbai. This could be due to the fact that the distance travelled to reach the workplace is considerably shorter in smaller cities than it is in mega cities like Delhi and Mumbai. Further, this could be attributed to the fact that these mega cities have undergone proper planning and development of public transport so as to cater to the impending travel needs of the population whereas the class II cities are still adopting an add-on approach.

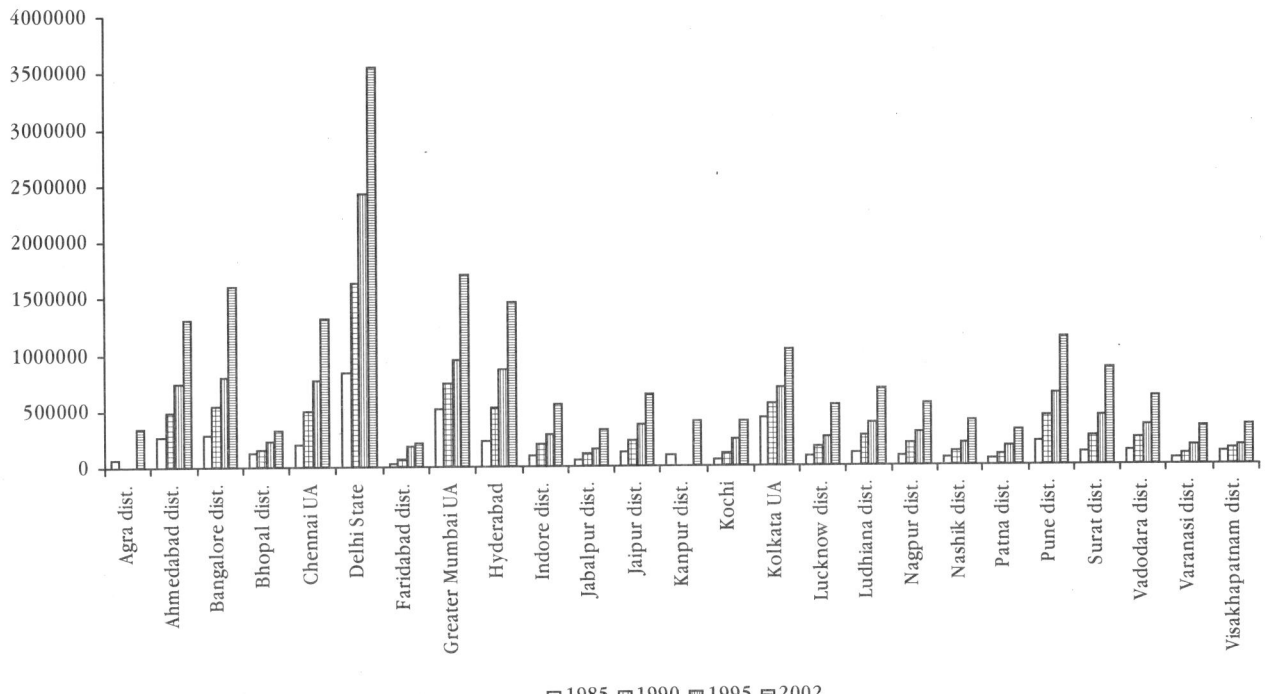

Figure 13.1: Pattern of vehicular stock in different cities from 1985 to 2002

TABLE 13.2
Total Registered Motor Vehicles in Major Cities of India in the Year 2002

City/District	Two-wheelers	Autos/Tempos	Cars/Cabs	Buses	Goods carriers	Tractors and others	Total
Agra	267,272	8541	23,584	1303	9368	29,385	339,453
Ahmedabad district	932,991	68,064	168,833	22,106	46,138	67,137	1,305,269
Bangalore district	1183,752	64,520	259,001	10,077	49,037	30,171	1,596,558
Bhopal district	263,737	12,586	30,835	2898	5500	13,255	328,811
Chennai UA	988,630	44,771	250,080	4541	31,459	6202	1,325,683
Delhi state	2265,955	86,985	989,522	47,578	161,650	NA	3,551,690
Faridabad district	99,983	8738	23,265	1183	69,249	6563	208,981
Greater Mumbai UA	787,527	212,862	547,224	20,718	124,718	8215	1,701,264
Hyderabad	1153,681	73,785	177,012	5318	50,050	7118	1,466,964
Indore district	425,114	11,993	47,542	12,751	28,250	24,743	550,393
Jabalpur district	280,567	2184	12,205	4232	10,812	9888	319,888
Jaipur district	480,570	9669	62,231	14,963	51,606	21,691	640,730
Kanpur district	323,699	4648	46,024	1464	18,064	4729	398,628
Kochi	253,745	27,572	71,825	10,048	37,245	2703	403,138
Kolkata UA	467,756	27,003	380,079	28,923	105,687	28,003	1,037,451
Lucknow district	438,897	7768	63,192	3096	11,731	14,096	538,780
Ludhiana district	527,444	13,824	79,327	1367	18,216	45,780	685,958
Nagpur district	464,831	15,293	42,626	3235	23,057	5066	554,108
Nashik district	270,198	22,981	41,781	1281	33,105	23,833	393,179
Patna district	195,894	28,776	46,394	8089	26,010	8381	313,544
Pune district	851,746	71,238	130,289	10,000	58,550	18,211	1,140,034
Surat district	696,418	38,275	76,456	1399	41,529	14,949	869,026
Vadodara district	455,501	22,052	59,623	1478	36,144	31,177	605,975
Varanasi district	285,068	7391	22,322	1989	5837	22,648	345,255
Visakhapatnam district	298,693	12,851	27,525	1123	10,474	4002	354,668

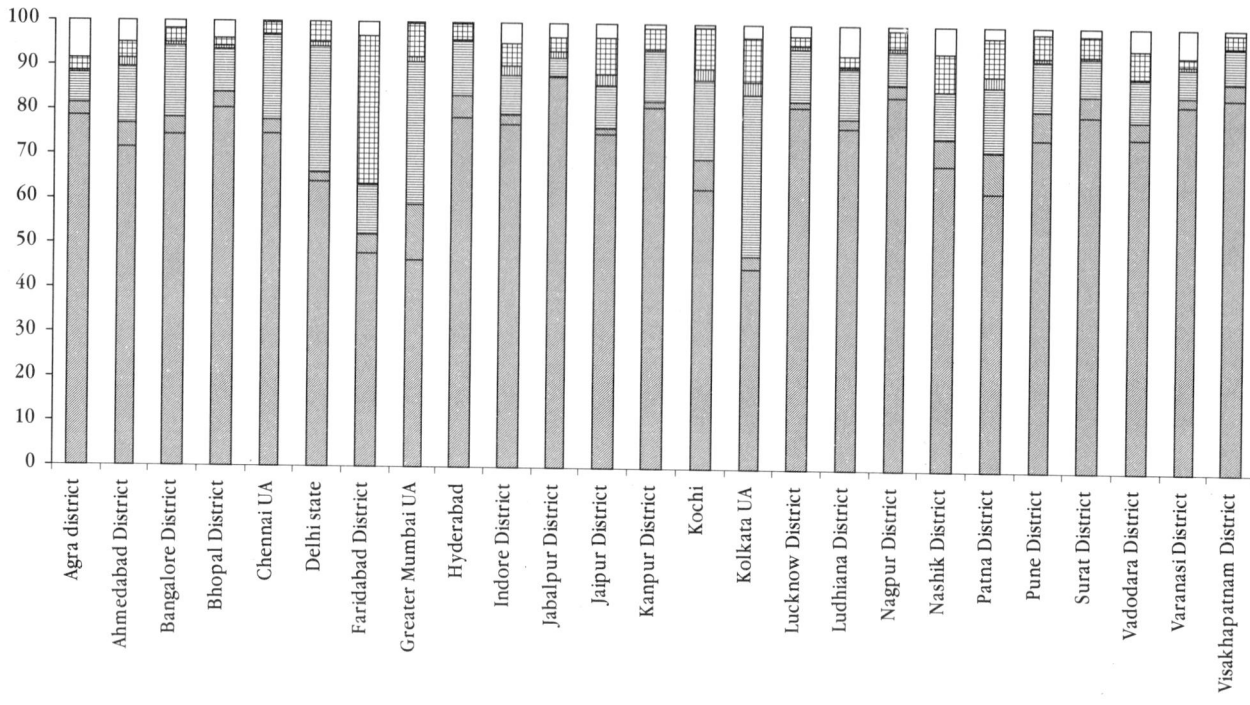

Figure 13.2: Percentage share of travel modes in different cities in the year 2002

The number of vehicles like tractors is considerable except in the case of mega cities like Delhi, Mumbai, and Chennai. The share of public transport like buses and autorickshaws is high in the case of mega cities compared to the rest. Hyderabad is showing alarming trends of growth in two-wheeler population which is a dangerous indication of worsening ambient air quality in that city. Two-wheeler population in Hyderabad was 76 per cent of the total vehicular stock whereas in the case of Delhi it was only 63 per cent in the year 2002. Two more cities following similar trends are Kanpur (81 per cent) and Pune (74 per cent).

PROJECTION OF VEHICULAR STOCK

Increased economic activity and urbanization trends tend to raise the vehicular population and a study carried out at IGIDR (IGIDR 2002) estimates that a three-fold increase in total vehicles is expected in Delhi by the year 2020 under the existing economic growth conditions (5.6 per cent annual GDP growth rate). The same study estimated that Mumbai vehicular stock would experience a four-fold rise in vehicular stock by 2020 under the existing economic growth levels (6.6 per cent annual GDP growth rate). Tables 13.3 and 13.4 present the estimated segregated mode-wise vehicular stock for Delhi and Mumbai, respectively, for the period of 1998–2020. Econometric models were used to predict the total vehicular stock and spreadsheet model to predict the model split.

Mumbai, traditionally, is a 'public transport' city with a major share of its travel demand being catered for by the local train network and the feeder services. It is expected to continue to rely on public transport system

TABLE 13.3
Projected Vehicular Stock in Delhi

Year	2-W	3-W	Taxis	Car	Bus	Total passenger vehicles	LCV	HCV	Total goods vehicle
2005	2,148,900	70,700	9,300	1,103,400	19,500	3,351,800	95,500	61,100	156,600
2010	3,130,600	123,700	14,900	1,292,500	26,400	4,588,000	135,700	73,100	208,800
2015	4,170,100	169,800	17,800	1,695,200	27,800	6,080,600	168,900	90,900	259,800
2020	5,782,400	214,300	22,400	2,454,400	39,300	8,512,800	222,100	119,600	341,700

Source: IGIDR 2002.

TABLE 13.4
Projected Vehicular Stock in Mumbai

Year	2-W	3-W	Taxis	Car	Bus	Total passenger vehicles	LCV	HCV	Total goods vehicle
2005	451,000	91,600	25,100	267,900	12,800	848,400	17,000	10,400	27,400
2010	668,900	104,100	35,600	342,300	16,700	1,167,600	24,800	14,000	38,800
2015	1,087,900	148,300	33,800	476,800	20,000	1,766,700	37,200	20,900	58,100
2020	1,534,200	210,400	44,700	623,100	27,300	2,439,700	51,100	28,700	79,800

Source: IGIDR 2002.

for the next 20 years whereas Delhi is set to experience further bulging of roads in spite of the fact that the Metro would start sharing a part of travel demand in the next 20 years. Affordability in terms of number of vehicles per thousand population is expected to be higher in Mumbai than in Delhi. Mumbai is expected to experience uniform trends of growth in all modes of transport whereas in Delhi the growth is going to be predominant in personal modes of transport with a slight fall in the share of public transport (IGIDR 2001).

Vehicles Registered vis-à-vis Vehicles on Road

The records of the motor vehicle registering authorities show the cumulative number of vehicles registered within their jurisdiction, right from the inception of The Motor Vehicles Act, 1939. Therefore, the number of registered vehicles entered in the vehicle registration records is not the total number of vehicles in use, or plying on roads. The number of vehicles actually plying on roads is considerably lower than the numbers shown in the vehicle registration records. Considering that the on-road 3-wheelers over 12 years of age and other vehicles over 17 years of age are negligible, the number of on-road vehicles up to 31 March 2002 are considered to be actually contributing to the problems. The estimated number of on-road vehicles is given in Table 13.5.

It has been the practice to consider the total number of registered vehicles in order to determine the trend of

TABLE 13.5
On-road Vehicles in Different Cities as a Percentage of Registered Vehicles (2002)

Urban agglomeration/district	2-Wheelers	3-wheelers	Cars/cabs	Total*
Agra district	82.28	74.30	78.96	79.46
Ahmedabad district	83.65	59.40	81.11	79.23
Bangalore U&R districts	83.51	90.00	77.23	82.30
Bhopal district	63.75	47.70	46.45	61.88
Chennai UA	87.65	87.54	77.80	84.97
Delhi state	74.45	57.48	83.20	76.12
Faridabad district	98.24	111.89	110.60	90.00
Greater Mumbai UA	78.75	80.36	56.84	69.54
Hyderabad & RR districts	86.67	90.79	79.59	85.29
Indore district	82.96	41.76	81.84	81.06
Jabalpur district	84.75	72.94	61.65	82.70
Jaipur district	84.07	53.41	79.80	80.65
Kanpur district	77.80	52.41	80.95	76.24
Kochi	90.10	74.43	75.39	85.91
Kolkata UA	65.68	73.71	5.32	58.17
Lucknow district	86.10	54.66	101.44	85.63
Ludhiana district	84.61	67.32	89.72	82.23
Nagpur district	84.96	60.80	77.66	82.74
Nashik district	86.72	67.43	75.97	82.23
Patna district	83.44	38.76	86.83	79.53
Pune district	83.05	65.45	80.76	80.42
Surat district	88.74	68.75	88.25	86.57
Vadodara district	81.40	32.86	82.63	77.90
Varanasi district	83.44	38.76	86.83	82.85
Visakhapatnam district	68.54	69.61	74.35	69.00

Note: * total includes the commercial and other vehicles.

vehicular growth and the resulting emissions. However, as Table 13.5 explains, the actual vehicles contributing to the pollution generation is substantially low. Kolkata is on top with only 60 per cent of the registered vehicles actually plying on roads. This could be a reason for the better air quality that Kolkata has been enjoying in comparison to other mega cities like Delhi. In Delhi the difference between the registered vehicles and on-road vehicles is about 24 per cent. Hyderabad has the least difference in registered and on-road vehicles. This could be due to the fact that in this city the trends in vehicular stock have started to rise very recently. Mumbai had slightly higher difference compared to Delhi. Figure 13.3 presents the difference in registered vehicles and on-road vehicles in mega cities, namely, Delhi, Mumbai, Kolkata, Chennai, Bangalore, and Hyderabad.

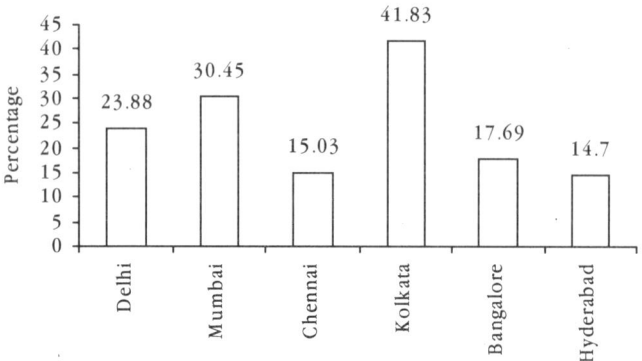

Figure 13.3: Percentage difference in registered vehicles and on-road vehicles

Travel Demand Projection

Different modes of vehicles have different occupancy rate (TERI 1997). Hence, the effectiveness of any transportation mode is measured in terms of the passenger kilometers (pkm)/tonne kilometer (tkm) served by the respective mode. Two-wheelers have very poor occupancy (1.5 persons per vehicle) against buses (37 persons per vehicle). Passenger kilometers catered by buses is much higher than any other mode and, hence, they cover the major share of the travel demand in many cities. Due to the high occupancy rate, the emission per pkm is very low in the case of buses as compared to cars and two-wheelers. This makes the bus not only an effective transport mode but also environmentally efficient.

Passenger travel demand—an indicator of travel demand—is expected to grow by leaps and bounds in the case of mega cities like Delhi and Mumbai during the coming years. In a study carried out at IGIDR, employing econometrics and spreadsheet models, the total passenger travel demand in Delhi was estimated to increase from 73 billion pkms in 1997 to 253 billion pkms in 2020, registering an annual growth rate of 5.3 per cent. Freight travel demand is expected to increase from 2.63 billion tkms to 7.18 billion tkms in 2020 (IGIDR 2002). Total passenger travel demand for Mumbai is expected to grow from 32 billion pkms in 1998 to 137 billion pkms by 2020 with an annual growth of 6.8 per cent, which is higher than Delhi's growth rate. freight travel demand is estimated to rise from 0.36 billion tkms to 1.37 billion tkms during the same time period. A better strategy to handle this growth is not just providing infrastructure to support the increasing stock of vehicles, but taking measures to control the number of vehicles without compromising on the travel needs. This necessitates an improved public transport system. Table 13.6 presents the segregated mode-wise estimated vehicle kilometers of travel in the year 2010 for different cities (reproduced from the Auto Fuel Policy Expert Committee Report).

TABLE 13.6
Estimated Vehicle Kilometers of Travel in 2010 for All Major Cities (million)

Vehicle type	Delhi		Mumbai	Kolkata	Chennai	Bangalore	Hyderabad
	Without metro	With metro					
Cars/Jeeps	521.82	496.97	163.20	109.26	94.69	123.12	89.02
Taxis	6.59	6.59	40.88	42.31	6.52	4.05	3.36
Two-wheelers	494.15	352.96	106.91	75.17	164.98	231.63	163.26
Autos—CNG	78.23	78.23	0.00	0.00	0.00	0.00	0.00
Auto—petrol	24.33	24.33	84.52	34.68	49.34	86.94	52.92
LCVs	45.38	45.38	16.17	8.68	10.15	11.42	10.65
HCVs	23.47	23.47	17.72	8.57	9.05	8.21	17.67
Buses—CNG	27.45	26.33	0.00	0.00	0.00	0.00	0.00
Buses—diesel	8.85	8.85	17.41	29.06	9.40	14.83	17.38
Total	1230.27	1063.11	446.81	307.73	344.13	480.20	354.26

Source: GOI 2002.

In the future, introduction of high capacity systems like Mass Rapid Transit System (MRTS) and Light Rail Transport (LRT) in Delhi and some other cities may be a reality. As such the impact of projected vehicle-kilometers with the Metro system is presented in Table 13.6. The Metro system in Delhi is expected to reduce the vehicle-kilometers travelled. In other cities the increased travel demand, leading to increased vehicle-kilometers, will consume more fuel and generate more pollution. Therefore, to minimize the pollution loads in the cities of the future, technological options will have to be explored in terms of improved automobile engines and fuels and also efficient public transport in lieu of personal transport.

Trends in Environmental Emissions and Ambient Air Quality

Growing vehicular stock results in increased environmental emission. The transport sector contributes a major share of environmental pollution (around 70 per cent). Carbon monoxide (CO) is the major pollutant coming from the transport sector, contributing almost 90 per cent of the total emission. Hydrocarbons (HC) are next to CO. It is indeed interesting to observe that the contribution of the transport sector to the particulate pollution is as less as 3–5 per cent. Most of the suspended particulate matter (SPM) is due to the re-suspension of dust. Pollutant emission levels have gone up substantially owing to the fast growth in vehicular stock. In Delhi, about 420 metric tonnes of CO are emitted with almost 1400 metric tonnes of total pollution everyday. Daily emissions of various pollutants from the transport sector are presented in Figure 13.4. With Delhi standing high, Hyderabad is catching up with Bangalore at a very fast rate.

In fact, it is observed that the growing trend of emissions is due to the fact that the vehicles are used for an extended lifetime without proper maintenance. Ill-maintained vehicles tend to emit more pollutants than others. Improper inspection and maintenance (I&M), use of poor quality fuels, poor road conditions, and increased congestion add to emissions. At present, in Delhi, owing to initiatives from various sectors, some of the above mentioned factors are showing improvement. As a result, Delhi is experiencing improved air quality. This should set a trend for the other cities.

Ambient Air Quality in Different Cities

The Central Pollution Control Board (CPCB) has been assigned various functions under the Air Act, 1981 to plan a nationwide programme for the prevention, control, and abatement of air pollutants. Accordingly, the National Air Quality Monitoring Programme (NAMP) was initiated in 1984–5 at the national level, and had been steadily expanded and, at present, comprises 290 monitoring stations covering 90 cities in 24 states and five union territories. The NAMP network is operated with the involvement of various agencies, that is, the State Pollution Control Boards (SPCBs), the CPCB headquarters and zonal offices, pollution control committees, research institutes, universities, and colleges.

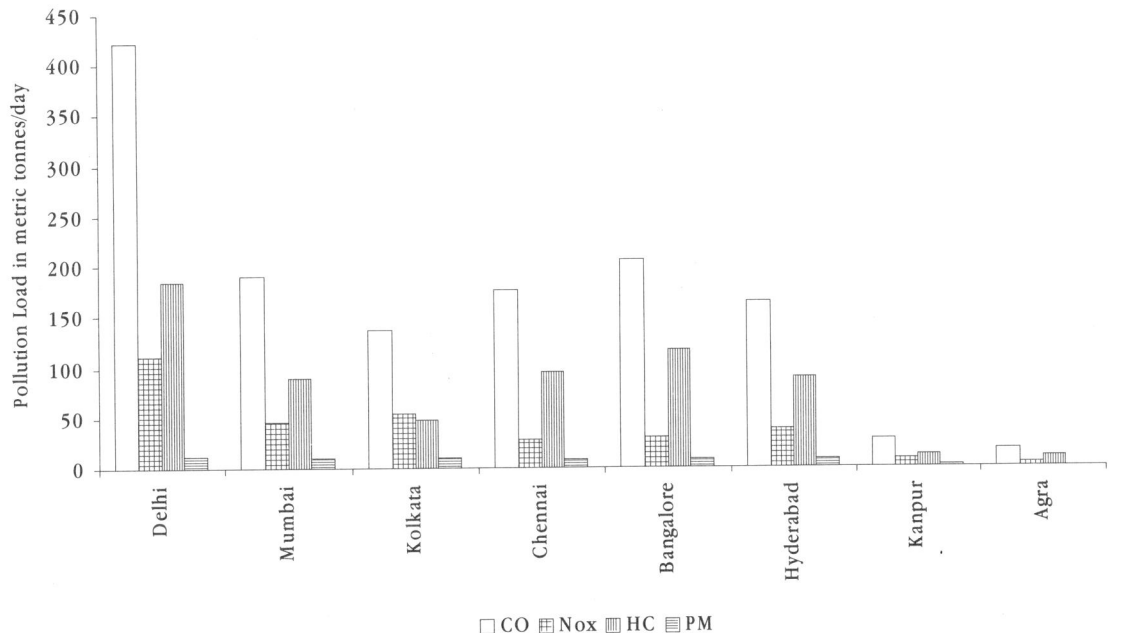

Figure 13.4: Pollutant load from transport sector in different cities in India (2002)

216 INDIA DEVELOPMENT REPORT

The air quality parameters regularly monitored nationwide are SPM (8 hourly for 24 hours), sulphur dioxide (SO2), and nitrogen oxide (NOx) (4 hourly for 24 hours), while additional parameters like CO, polycyclic aromatic hydrocarbons (PAH), ozone, respirable suspended particulate matter (RSPM), benzene, and trace metals are additionally monitored in Delhi and some other cities, but not in all the cities. As per CPCB, the published air quality data statistics are more indicative than absolute due to certain systemic limitations.

The most common air quality indicator is SPM, which exceeds the permissible level in many cities. Levels of SPM in different cities across the country from 1995 to 2001 are presented in Figure 13.5. Another important air quality indicator is NOx whose dynamics are presented in Figure 13.6. The variation in air quality is a mixed scenario as some cities follow a rising trend with others experiencing an improvement. Kolkata, Bangalore, and Pune are experiencing rise in NOx over time. Delhi showed a steady fall after initial rise.

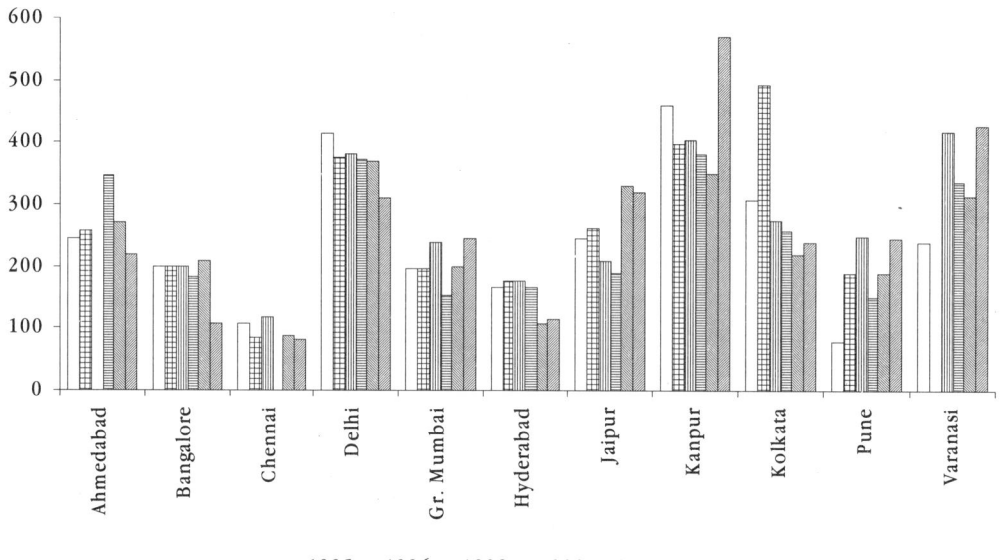

Figure 13.5: Changes in SPM concentration over the period 1995–2001

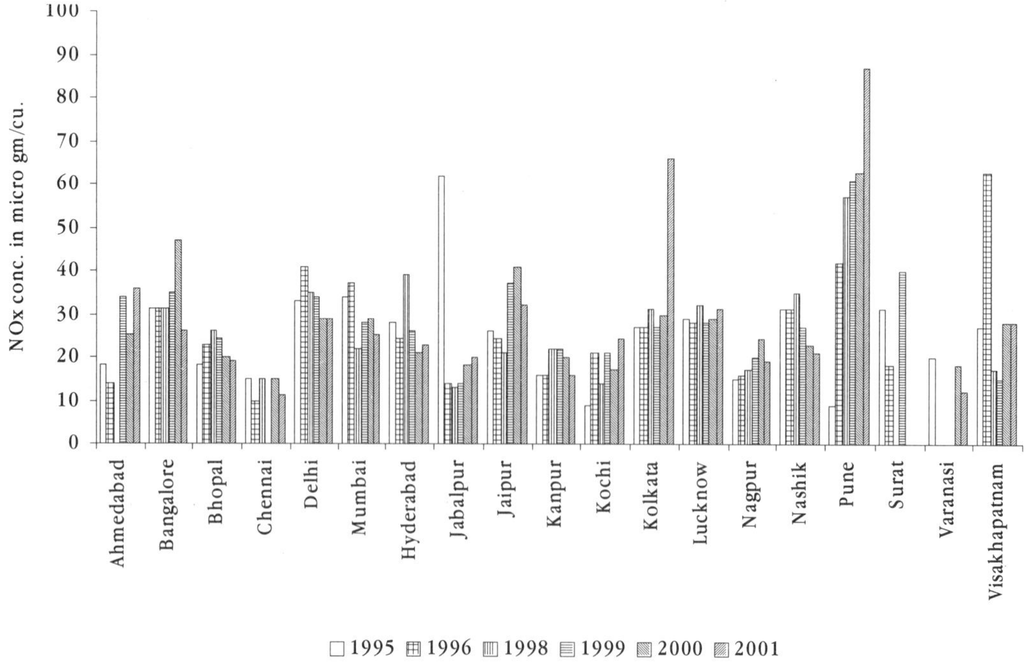

Figure 13.6: Changes in NOx concentration over the period 1995–2001
Source: CPCB National Ambient Air Quality Monitoring Series (NAAQMS/8, 10, 15, 21).

Share of the Transport Sector

Air pollution comes from various natural sources as well as anthropogenic sources. For certain pollutants like CO and HC the major source has been anthropogenic while for others like SPM the sources of pollution are natural ones. Even among anthropogenic sources of pollution, various sectors influence different pollutant levels in a different way. For instance, the transport sector contributes most of the CO emission. The industrial sector contributes most of the SO_2. Table 13.7 presents a summary of the share of various pollutants from different sectors. This depends on the location, activity, and prevailing meteorological conditions. As can be observed from Table 13.7, the share of the various sectors for various pollutants differs between Delhi and Mumbai.

TABLE 13.7
Share of Air Pollution from Different Sectors

Pollutants	Sector contributing to pollution	Percentage contribution	
		Delhi	Mumbai
CO	Transport	76–90	92
	Industrial	37–13	8
	Domestic and others	10–16.3	0
Nox	Transport	66–74	60
	Industrial	13–29	40
	Domestic and others	1–2	0
SO_2	Transport	5–12	2–4
	Industrial	84–95	82–98
	Domestic and others	0–4	0–16
PM	Transport	3–22	0–16
	Industrial	74–16	34–96
	Domestic and others	2–4	53–56

Note: adopted from the expert committee report on auto fuels.

Is the Pollution Coming Exclusively from the City Vehicles?

Another important aspect of urban transportation is garaging. All vehicles plying on a city's roads are not from within the city. There is a significant inflow of vehicles into the cities and vehicles passing through them. In a study carried out by the Central Road Research Institute (CRRI), Delhi, based on the fuelling pattern and their garaging character, it was observed that a majority of commercial vehicles (trucks) filling fuel in the city fuel stations are garaged (housed) outside the city. This fact particularly influences the transportation planning and the emission estimation. Table 13.8 presents the details of garaging status by vehicle type in different cities.

In almost all cities commercial vehicles constitute a major share of the vehicles garaging outside the city. It is interesting to observe that this fraction is almost two times in the case of Delhi. Given the fact that commercial vehicles are more polluting and these are 'unaccounted part' of the stock, Delhi landed up experiencing more pollution than the estimated levels. Among personal vehicles all cities have similar character except in the case of Hyderabad where the inflow of cars and two-wheelers is considerably high. This could be due to the fact that Hyderabad does not have suburbs. As a result people stay in neighbouring places and commute to the city for daily needs. This could be the reason for this abnormal behaviour regarding the garaging status. Hence, it is essential to account for this 'non-resident' vehicle stock in the estimation of emission, infrastructure development, and also transportation planning.

TECHNOLOGICAL AND MANAGEMENT ALTERNATIVES

Natural Gas Vehicles

The use of gaseous fuels, that is, CNG and LPG for automotive applications has been undertaken in different parts of the world. Commercialization activities of natural gas vehicles (NGVs) have taken place for varying reasons in different countries since their initial

TABLE 13.8
Garaging Status of Vehicle Type in Different Cities

Vehicle type	Garaging status (%)											
	Delhi		Mumbai		Kolkata		Chennai		Bangalore		Hyderabad	
	Inside city	Outside city	Inside city	Outside city	Inside city	Outside city	Inside city	Outside city	Inside city	Outside city	Inside city	Outside city
Cars	90.42	9.58	92.11	7.89	95.26	4.74	84.00	16.00	97.83	2.17	75.72	24.28
2-Wheelers	92.20	7.80	95.30	4.70	82.56	17.44	95.40	4.60	96.93	3.07	80.46	19.54
Autos	98.56	1.44	96.33	3.67	86.13	13.87	92.40	7.60	96.79	3.21	86.04	13.96
Buses	83.08	16.92	100.0	0.00	87.83	12.17	70.70	29.30	77.78	22.22	79.31	20.69
LCVs	73.53	26.47	94.46	5.54	83.65	16.35	66.00	34.00	83.76	16.24	53.53	46.47
HCVs	30.51	69.49	88.45	11.55	67.56	32.44	66.30	33.70	68.29	31.71	50.10	49.90
MCVs	35.62	64.38	70.31	29.69	66.66	33.34	71.70	28.30	50.00	50.00	65.85	34.15

introduction in Italy in the mid-1930s. In India, they were introduced during the 1990s. Table 13.9 presents the list of countries where the number of NGVs is high.

TABLE 13.9
Natural Gas Vehicles (NGVs) in the World (2001–2)

Country	NGVs
Argentina	721,830
Italy	380,000
Pakistan	265,000
Brazil	232,973
USA	102,430
India	95,150

Source: NGV statistic (2002).

When Italy began to use CNG as a fuel for transport in the beginning of the Second World War it became the first country in the world to do so. This was mainly owing to its desire to become self-sufficient in fuels. Italy had remained the leader in the NGV market—only recently outpaced by Argentina—and exported vehicle conversion systems and compressor station equipment to the Middle East, South America, China, and India, to name a few countries. European NGV activities outside Italy started only after the advent of the European Union Natural Gas Vehicle Association (UNGVA) in 1994. In other EU countries like Germany, though pipeline infrastructure for gas distribution exists, NGV markets are in the initial stages of development. In the USA, NGVs had their initiation in 1969 at the South California Gas Company and now the Los Angeles Metropolitan Transport Authority has a fleet of above 2600 buses out of which 800 are NGVs. All around the world, application of NG is predominant in buses though it has been used for cars as well. Table 13.10 presents the details of CNG-driven buses in different parts of the world. Delhi enjoys the distinction of having the highest share of CNG-driven buses in the world with 51.5 per cent of its fleet running on CNG followed by Los Angeles with 30.5 per cent.

Vehicles using CNG are proved to be economically viable in many countries. In a study carried out at IGIDR in the year 2001, it was found that CNG technology with discount rate of 10 per cent outperforms the conventional technology. Details are presented in Table 13.11. In another study carried out by the Tata Energy Research Institute (TERI), the ratio of present net value of cars using CNG over cars using conventional fuel was found to be less than unity and the options of CNG is a financially attractive proposition even with a very high discount rate of 15 per cent with assumed life of cars being 15 years or more.

TABLE 13.10
CNG City Buses in Different Cities Around the World (2000)

City	Total buses	CNG buses	% of CNG buses
Los Angeles	2638	795	30.1
New York	5675	358	6.3
New Jersey	3094	55	1.8
Toronto	1500	125	8.3
Berlin	1700	10	0.6
Paris	4000	53	1.3
Rome	2383	40	1.7
Madrid	1000	15	1.5
Athens	1500	40	2.7
Sydney	3900	254	6.5
Brisbane	1100	12	1.1
Melbourne	1400	24	1.7
Shanghai	18,500	330	1.8
Beijing	10,000	1640	16.4
Seoul	8200	880	10.7
Delhi	12,000	6175	51.5

Source: NGV statistics (2002).

TABLE 13.11
Cost Comparison of Conventional Vehicles vis-à-vis CNG Vehicles in Delhi

Alternative	Life cycle operating cost* (Rs pkm)**
Conventional three-wheelers (autos)	1.18
CNG three-wheelers (autos)	0.65
Conventional cars	2.45
CNG cars	1.92
Conventional buses	0.07
CNG buses	0.074

Notes: * LCC includes the capital cost, fuel cost, operation and maintenance cost, etc.
** discount rate—10%; year of estimate—2001.

However, lack of elaborate pipeline grid is a major barrier in many countries due to which the NG economics becomes unfavourable and promoting NGVs is tough, despite subsidies. In India, due to its vastness, NGVs can be commercially viable only in the cities where natural gas pipelines exist or will be laid in future. Cost of establishing fresh gas grids is quite high and for that reason alone it may not be feasible to dispense with CNG for automotive purposes in most cities in the near future. Currently, vehicles run on CNG are prominent in major metropolitan cities like Delhi and Mumbai only. Improvement in the ambient air in Delhi is attributed to the conversion of the entire bus fleet to CNG. Accounting for the external benefits from the clean environment might even favour the development of new pipeline grids in other potential polluting cities like Hyderabad and Bangalore.

LPG Technology

Major countries using LPG as automobile fuels are Italy, The Netherlands, Poland, the USA, Canada, Mexico, Australia, New Zealand, Algeria, Turkey, Iran, South Korea, and Japan. Italy heads the list with 1.2 million vehicles running on LPG. China is the most recent entry on the list with 50,000 LPG vehicles in 1999.

In India, LPG is the main domestic fuel in urban areas. The indigenous availability of LPG is expected to fall much short of the household demand alone. For LPG to be competitive as an auto fuel, India would need government support in the form of substantially lower taxation. Further, in the cases of both CNG and LPG, refilling and retrofitting are highly technology intensive and need expertize in handling. Safety issues are another major concern. Availability of infrastructure for distribution is a major barrier for their implementation. As CNG pipelines do not exist in most other cities, only major metros like Delhi and Mumbai are using CNG at present. Figure 13.7 presents the difference in pricing for various auto fuels in Delhi and Pune.

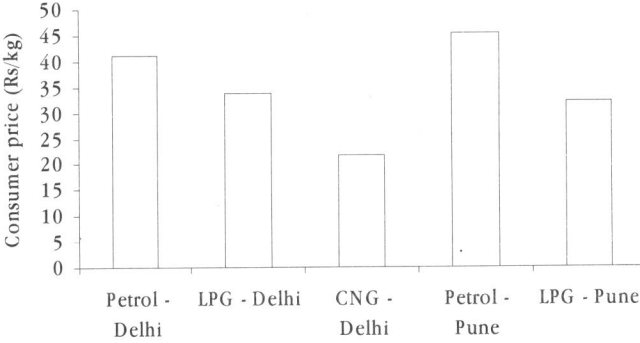

Figure 13.7: Consumer price of various auto fuels in Indian cities (2000–2 average prices)

Electric Vehicles

An electric vehicle (EV) is operated by an electric motor, which draws electricity from a battery bank. Different types of batteries for EVs and other applications are being developed for better performance. Storage batteries store a fixed amount of chemical energy. The batteries can be recharged when the electro-chemically active materials in these batteries have been used up. Most of the EVs at present use rechargeable lead acid batteries. Because of availability and low price, lead acid batteries are more widely used than other batteries. The electric vehicles should match with comparable petrol or diesel-driven vehicles in terms of performance, reliability, durability, and cost. Therefore, the manufacturers should develop these types of EVs. Reliability, cost, and useful life of the batteries used in EVs are important. The useful life can be expressed in terms of number of cycles and in calendar periods. For the battery to be economical it should have a minimum 1000 full cycles, meaning that the battery can be fully charged and discharged at least 1000 times before its capacity goes below 80 per cent of its rating. If we go by the calendar period, the battery should last at least five years.

In India, efforts towards EVs have begun with the Mashelkar Committee (2000), on high energy density batteries for EVs, set up by the Ministry of Non-conventional Energy Sources (MNES), which came out with certain recommendations for accelerated commercialization of EVs in India (GOI 2002). Now, a number of EVs are already plying on the roads. A 16-sealed electrically-operated bus had been developed and commercialized by Bharat Heavy Electricals Limited (BHEL) more than a decade ago. Three-wheeler EVs are also commercially available in the country. Scooter India Limited has developed and demonstrated electric three-wheelers, which are now in the advanced stage of commercialization. Other major players for electric three-wheelers include Mahindra Eco Mobiles, which has come up with a three-wheeler EV called Bijli. Bajaj Auto and Eicher (Basu 2001) are also entering the three-wheeler EV market. Ashok Leyland has developed a hybrid EV. Passenger EVs are also available commercially in the country. Reva, Bangalore has developed battery-operated passenger cars. With further technical performance improvement, cost reduction, and increasing awareness, EVs are expected to find greater acceptance and market penetration. The main targeted users of EVs would be public transport systems, urban services industries, service sectors, and the government at the central and state levels. Extensive research is on to improve battery performance and achieve lightweight cells. The government has been extending its support to many such efforts with the help of various premier technological institutions in the country. Exide Industries Ltd at Kolkata and other manufacturers are producing lead acid traction batteries for EV applications. Lucas TVS Ltd is also entering the EV area (Nair 2001).

In a financial viability study carried out by TERI (1997), it was found that the ratio of the present net value of battery-operated three-wheelers (autos) to that of conventional three-wheelers (autos) is less than unity for a discount rate of 6 per cent with a life of nine years. But the higher discount rates proved this technology uneconomical even at a higher life cycle of vehicles. In a study carried out at IGIDR it was found that battery-operated autos are more feasible that conventional autos in terms of life cycle operating cost (LCC). In spite of the higher initial investment, the life cycle operating cost of battery-operated vehicle (BOV) was Rs 0.63/pkm whereas that of a conventional auto was Rs 1.18/pkm. The discount rate assumed was 10 per cent and a life span of nine years. For this option to penetrate further subsidies on initial investments is essential.

Hybrid Electric Vehicles (HEVs) use the engine of a conventional vehicle in combination with an electric motor powered by traction batteries and/or fuel cells. This combination helps in achieving both the energy and environmental goals. The deployment of a large number of this type of vehicles would help us in terms of environmental benefits, reduction of oil consumption, and reduction in emissions. In HEVs propulsion, energy is available from more than one source of energy. The three configurations of the HEV are series hybrid system, parallel hybrid system, and split hybrid system. A number of automobile manufacturers like Toyota, Honda, and Daimler Chrysler have started production of HEVs at different experimental levels. However, penetration depends on the market demand.

Table 13.12 presents the cost comparison of various auto technologies in India. It clearly demonstrates that BOVs perform well under subsidies. The CNG technology proved to be doing better than that of the BOV. However, due consideration to the environmental benefits would favour BOVs.

TABLE 13.12
Comparison of Various Auto Technologies in India

Fuel type	Cost/km (Rs)	O & M (Rs)	Mileage (km/ltr)	Total cost/ km (Rs)
Petrol	1.96	1.43	14	3.39
Diesel	0.58	0.80	20	1.38
CNG*				1.17
BOV	1.64	0.32	16 kWh/ 90kms	1.96
50% concession on power tariff and concession on custom duty for battery	1.03	0.32	16 kWh/90kms	1.35

Note: * LCC of CNG 3-wheelers was taken from IGIDR (2002) where 10 per cent discount rate and nine years of life span are assumed.

Fuel Cells

Fuel cells produce electricity, employing reaction between hydrogen and oxygen gases, electro-chemically. Fuel cells are efficient, environmentally benign, compact, modular, and reliable for power generation. Different types of fuel cells currently under development are the Protons Exchange Membrane Fuel Cells (PEMFCs), Phosphoric Acid Fuel Cells (PAFCs), Molten Carbonate Fuel Cells (MCFCs), Solid Oxide Fuel Cells (SOFCs), Direct Methanol Fuel Cells (DMFCs) and Alkaline Fuel Cells (AFCs).

Fuel cells operate on hydrogen gas and oxygen from air. Hydrogen gas can be obtained from a variety of fuels. Fuel cell power plants can be operated with overall system efficiencies of about 45 to 60 per cent or even higher. They offer high efficiency and low emission even at part/load and in small sizes. Because of high fuel utilization efficiencies, fuel cells help in carbon dioxide (CO_2) emission reductions. Owing to noiseless operation, fuel cells can be installed in densely populated areas as well.

Fuel cells can be used for stationary/portable power generation and automotive applications. High conversion efficiency, extremely low or no emissions, noiseless operation, high current density, and compactness are some of the advantages which make fuel cells an ideal power option for automobile application. The use of fuel cells has been demonstrated in transport applications. For regular operation of fuel cell electric vehicles, refuelling infrastructure needs to be created. A number of firms such as Ballard Power Systems, Plug Power, Fuel Cell Energy, International Fuel Cells Corporation, Energy Partners, H-Power, Honeywell, Northwest Power Systems, Toyota, Siemens and others have been targeting fuel cell markets for transportation.

In India, several agencies, and principally MNES, have supported projects on different types of fuel cell technology. Small PAFC stacks have been developed and tested by BHEL.

Hydrogen Energy

Hydrogen is receiving worldwide attention as a clean fuel and efficient energy storage medium for automobiles. Hydrogen can replace or supplement oil used in road transportation.

Hydrogen production technologies can be classified as fossil fuel based and renewable resource based. Hydrogen gas is being produced on a commercial scale by steam reformation and thermal cracking of natural gas or partial oxidation of naphtha, conventional electrolysis, and coal gasification. In India, hydrogen is produced from steam reforming/thermal cracking of natural gas, partial oxidation of naphtha, and from conventional electrolysis of water.

Hydrogen from water and solar energy can be produced through several ways. The cost of production of pure hydrogen from the electrolysis of water using photovoltaic device needs to be reduced substantially, before it becomes economically viable. Storage, transportation, and delivery are of great importance as it involves considerable hazard. In India, as part of a R&D

project, a photo bio-reactor for producing hydrogen from distillery waste treatment was installed at Nillikuppam in Tamilnadu. Research and development projects were also taken up for the production of hydrogen using solar energy and water through photo electro-chemical/photo catalytic methods. It will take a while to get this technology into the market.

Bio-fuels

Bio-fuel is an efficient, environment friendly, 100 per cent natural energy alternative to petroleum fuels (TERI 1999). In view of its potential for being produced from several agricultural sources and because of its low emission characteristics, bio-fuel has been receiving a great deal of attention in recent years as a substitute to petroleum fuels. Ethanol and bio-diesel are the two bio-fuels which are being looked upon as the potential fuels for surface transportation.

Ethanol, which is used mainly as a raw material for chemical industries, in medicines, and for potable purposes, is being increasingly looked upon as a potential fuel for powering automobiles. This can be obtained through the processes of fermentation and distillation of molasses—a by-product of the sugar industry. Other possible raw materials are cassava, corn, rice straw, and potato. The government has already taken the initiative to blend 5 per cent ethanol in petrol on a commercial scale in a phased manner. Further R&D work on the use of ethanol in diesel fuel has also been taken up.

The terms 'bio-diesel' refers to the neat ethyl easters of vegetable oils. Presently pure 100 per cent or neat ethyl esters of rapeseed, soyabean, sunflower, talon, and other fats and oils are used as diesel fuel without any substantial modification to the existing design of the engine. Bio-fuel is an ideal synergistic partner for oxidation catalytic converter and reduces CO_2 emissions by 78 per cent when compared to conventional diesel fuel (TERI 2002). Bio-diesel is produced from wild crops grown on wasteland. According to the Economic Survey, GOI, out of the cultivable land area, about 175 million hectare are classified as waste and degraded land. Therefore, there is a good potential to tap this resource (GOI 2002).

Inspection and Maintenance and Certification System

Vehicle inspection is a tool employed to ensure that vehicles meet applicable exhaust emission standards under normal operating conditions. Two different types of inspections are commonly performed:

• Periodic inspection in which the vehicle is inspected at an approved testing station at regular fixed time interval (that is, every 3/6 months).

• Spot inspection performed on a random basis by pulling vehicles off the road for on-site inspection ('roadside inspection').

If testing determines that the vehicle is exceeding the emission requirements, the vehicle owner is required to perform the necessary corrective actions within a prescribed time period. Fines or withholding registration tags are normally employed to ensure that the vehicle owner carries out the necessary corrective action. Any I&M programme requires a considerable amount of investment not only to set up the facilities but also for the tests.

Retrofitting of Emission Control Devices

Even after enforcing a thorough and reliable I&M programme for in-use vehicles, the emission level of the vehicles cannot go below the levels for which the vehicle has been designed. The successful implementation of a retrofit programme for reducing emissions would depend on necessary engine modification, if any, in conjunction with the retrofitting of emission control devices, which have adequate durability. There should be a sustainable and widespread availability of the required quality of fuel. Active participation of various regional transport authorities, vehicle manufacturers, and fleet operators is essential to make this process effective.

Traffic Management and Construction of Bypasses

Traffic management has great potential to control traffic growth and resulting environmental emissions. For effective traffic management the following points are considered:

• Installation of traffic control devices at intersections;

• Optimization of signal cycle timings and synchronization of traffic signals;

• Different cycle timings for different periods;

• Provision of adequate road geometric and flyovers, and free left turns;

• Increased build-up of mass transport systems;

• Diversion of vehicles to less crowded routes and closing streets at peak times selectively;

• Segregating fast moving and slow moving traffic by means of designated lanes;

• Physical restraint of traffic by closing roads, providing one way systems, etc.;

• Restrictions on personalized low occupancy vehicle use on specified days/times/roads;

• Incentives to share a car and, conversely, prohibiting single passenger personalized vehicles at peak times on congested roads;

• Congestion charges on crowded roads, and parking charges that vary with vehicle type and time of day and location.

Barriers to the Alternative Options

It is important to keep in mind that virtually all major technological options to reduce environmental emissions depend on economic, institutional, and political factors like energy prices, government support for the new technological alternatives, environmental policies, availability of land and other resources, consumer preferences, etc. (Deluchi 1993). Komor et al. (1993) describe the barriers to transportation energy efficiency improvements as technical (like availability of high-efficiency technology, information, R&D, etc.), financial/economic (currency exchange rate, energy pricing, international energy prices, etc.), and institutional (poor integration between modes, disconnection between owners and operators, poor service by mass transport, etc.). A set of possible barriers to the implementation of energy efficiency alternative options in the transport sector are listed below under separate categories.

Technical Barriers

• Availability of efficient technologies, skilled manpower and accessories;

• Availability of infrastructure like road network: some technologies perform well at a higher speed, which may not be possible due to congested road, network, etc. Similarly, some technologies depend on high quality fuel, and cannot operate because of poor fuel quality;

• Less reliable alternative technologies;

• Inadequate R&D of efficient technologies in the transport sector.

Economic and Financial Barriers

• Higher capital cost;

• Higher fuel/operational cost;

• Energy efficiency of secondary interest to the potential users; they might prefer bigger cars with accessories like air conditioning, etc. Hence, adequate pricing policy would be required.

Institutional/Administrative Barriers

• Multiplicity of authorities, from which the Asian cities suffer quite often;

• Poor land use planning that prevents the establishment of efficient transportation corridors for mass transportation and encourage low-density development resulting in increased personal transport;

• Poor service (in terms of frequency, comfort, etc.) of mass transport.

Informational Barriers

Individual consumers often lack adequate information about the alternative options. For instance, many people are not aware that regular I&M of vehicles, pollution checking, etc. would lead to substantial reduction of fuel consumption. The cognitive skills also act as a barrier at times. Even if all relevant information is available to the users, individual users may, in some cases, be unable to make proper use of the information. This may be so because of the users' lack of cognitive skills—the absorption and interpretation of factual information and use of that information in decision-making.

Other Barriers

These include individual barriers, political barriers, and others. For example, individual preference is a major issue. Due to various reasons, every individual prefers personal transport which are more energy intensive and environment unfriendly. They would not accept alternative options unless these are easily accessible, less or equal time consuming (as their personal mode), and comfortable. Political issues can also be a crucial constraint for implementation of a mitigation option.

In a research study undertaken at IGIDR (2002) to identify and rank the barriers using multi-criteria analysis with the help of various actor groups, it was observed that lack of infrastructure has been ranked as the most important barrier to the implementation of alternative transportation options like CNG-driven cars and three-wheelers and BOVs, followed by the barrier of additional cost. This emphasizes the need for the development of policies supporting an elaborate network of CNG filling stations/battery recharge stations and support from financial institutions to realize the change.

POLICY INITIATIVE AND MEASURES

Standards for controlling emission levels of new vehicles were incorporated into the Motor Vehicles Act, 1989 only as late as in 1991, enforcing some quality control on the automobile industry. The mass emission standards refer to gram of pollutant emitted per kilometer travelled by the vehicles during mass emission tests conducted under specified driving conditions, are notified by the Ministry of Surface Transport and enforced by the State Transport Department.

The existing BIS started incorporating emission parameters for fuel during the same period. But in both cases, the standards were set according to the terms and conditions dictated by the industry. Both the regulatory authorities and the manufacturers pleaded incapacity to make any drastic improvements, and so the standards they followed were far too lax compared to those elsewhere in the world. In 1996, the government came up with mass emission standards for vehicles, which are stricter than earlier. Other measures during 1994–6, are use of unleaded petrol and fitting of catalytic converters in the car. Fitting catalytic converters to cars have reduced emissions of CO. Now EURO II and EURO III norms also have been enforced.

Poor maintenance of vehicles adversely affects their emission efficiency. The role of maintenance in combating vehicular pollution was reflected in government policy for the first time in 1989, which made the certificate of fitness as mandatory for registration of public vehicles, commercial vehicles, and personal vehicles older than 15 years. The 1990 vehicular emission rules required all motor vehicles to comply with the laid down exhaust emission standards. The Delhi State Transport Department issues Pollution Under Control (PUC) certificates to vehicles. Vehicles owners are required to check the emissions level of their vehicles every three months and obtain a PUC certificate. Vehicles failing to meet the standards are required to rectify the fault and obtain the certificate. The State Transport Authority fines vehicles not possessing a PUC certificate.

This is a step towards minimizing vehicular pollution by regular checks. This system, however, has come under severe public criticism due to the existing lacunae in the issue of certificates and the discrepancies in pollution readings from one station to another. For example, though it is necessary for all vehicles to have a valid PUC at all times, according to statistics maintained by the transport department, the percentage of vehicles with valid PUC was highest at 23 per cent in 1997 since the introduction of this legislation. There is a provision to levy a monetary fine of Rs 1000 on motorists who fail to abide by the law. However, enforcement of the law is poor. For instance, since the introduction of the law in 1991, vehicles fined, as a per cent of those without PUC was highest at 1.07 in 1997. Statistics maintained by the Automobile Association of Upper India reveals that more than 50 per cent of vehicles in Delhi in May 1995, failed to comply with the prescribed standards. What is more alarming is that nearly 44 per cent of the new vehicles checked were found to be not in compliance with the standards. This shows that the regulation for PUC certificates, despite being a potentially powerful instrument in controlling pollution from vehicles, has had only limited impact on vehicular pollution. However, it has created a lot of awareness among citizens about environmental pollution.

The failure of the administration to enforce environmental regulations, has led to judicial interventions. The Supreme Court has come up with several guidelines in the last few years. The Court has urged the government to accept the emissions standards EURO I, II, III, etc. for the vehicles as adopted by the ECs. In the last few years, the Supreme Court issued a number of directives aiming at environmental emission control (Box 13.1).

Two of the major initiatives towards emission control are enforcement of unleaded petrol first in mega cities and then in the entire country, and low sulphur diesel. These initiatives, implemented by 1 April 2000 and 1999, respectively, have had a visible impact on deteriorating environmental quality, especially in Delhi.

Box 13.1

Directives of the Supreme Court aiming at Environmental Emission Control

- Elimination of leaded petrol from NCT of Delhi by 1 September 1998;
- Phasing out of all commercial vehicles which are more than 15 years old by 2 October 1998;
- From 1 June 1999, Euro I norm made effective for all private vehicles;
- No 8-year old buses to ply except on CNG and other clean fuels by 1 April 2000;
- Entire city bus fleet to be steadily converted to single fuel mode on CNG by 31 March 2001;
- Replacement of all pre-1990 auto and taxis with new vehicles running on clean fuels by 31 March 2000;
- From 1 April 2000, no vehicles to be registered in the National Capital Region (NCR), unless it conforms to EURO II norms;
- Supply of diesel with 0.05 per cent sulphur content in the NCR from May 2002;
- Supply of petrol with 1 per cent benzene content in the NCR from 31 October 2001;
- Supply of only pre-mix petrol in filling stations to two stroke engines by 31 December 1998;
- Ban on registering two stroke vehicles from July 2000;
- All in-use vehicles with two stroke engines to be fitted with catalytic converter.

Source: CPCB (1999).

Unleaded Petrol

The specification of lead in Indian petrol used to be 0.56 gm/L max. in 1994. Lead has been phased out from petrol during the last six years in India. From 1 February 2000 only unleaded petrol is produced and sold in the entire country. In the developed countries, lead phasing out was spread over a period of 10 to 20 years. China and many other countries in the Asia Pacific region and in Europe, South America, and Africa have not phased out lead as yet.

Reduction of Sulphur Content

The sulphur content in diesel has been reduced by 75 per cent from 1.0 per cent max. in 1996 to 0.25 per cent max. in the entire country in a period of four years from 1 April 1996 to 1 January 2000. The government had approved setting up of nine Diesel Hydro Desulphurization (DHDS) plants in nine refineries for reducing the diesel sulphur content from 1.0 per cent max. to 0.25 per cent max. at a total cost of Rs 5568.31 crore in June 1997. This has enabled supply of diesel with 0.25 per cent max. sulphur in the entire country from 1 January 2000. Further, in the four metropolitan towns, sulphur content in diesel has been reduced by 95 per cent to 0.05 per cent max. The entire unleaded petrol and low sulphur programme is presented in Box 13.2.

With the implementation of such initiatives, some results have been visible. For instance, about 3000 taxis and 9000 three-wheelers, which are old, have been scrapped so far. Oil companies have already started supplying petrol and diesel with less than 0.05 per cent sulphur content from 1 April 2000. They had already begun supplying lead free petrol. Reduction in vehicular emission load and improvement in ambient air quality is apparent in Delhi.

In another demonstration of legal institutions taking initiatives for improvement of environment, Mumbai High Court set up a Committee on December 1999, headed by the Transport Commissioner to examine the entire matter and to come with future directions. Salient features of the same are given in the box below.

This chapter has discussed patterns of growth of urban transport in India, various alternatives available, respective barriers for their implementation and various policy initiatives taken so far to control the environmental emissions in urban centres. It has been noticed that the vehicular stock is increasing in all urban centres with class II cities trying to outpace mega cities. Personalized transport is found to be growing much faster and leading the share in almost all cities. The share of public transport is higher in bigger cities than in smaller ones. That is a major cause of concern. Class II cities like Hyderabad and Ahmedabad are fast catching up with the mega cities with respect to the vehicular stock as well as pollution. In the projection of travel demand, Mumbai is expected to face higher growth than Delhi. There is a considerable difference between the registered vehicles and on-road vehicles with Kolkata having a difference as high as 70 per cent. Hence, it was suggested that on-road vehicles rather than registered vehicles be considered for traffic management plans and emission control strategies. Garaging was noted to be another major issue affecting transport planning in urban centres. About 70 per cent of commercial vehicles filling fuel in fuel stations in Delhi were found to be garaging outside the city. In the case of Hyderabad, the two-wheelers garaging outside were found to be very high (around 25 per cent). This essentially leads to an under-estimation of pollution, since these vehicles plying on city roads are not considered in the calculation as they are registered elsewhere.

Box 13.2
Gasoline Lead Phase-out Programme in India

Phase	Date	Type	Area
Phase I	June 1994	Low leaded (0.15 g/l)	Cities of Delhi, Mumbai, Kolkata and Chennai
Phase II	1.4.1995	Unleaded (0.013g/l)	
Phase III	1.1.1997	Low leaded (0.15g/l)	Entire country
Phase IV	1.9.1998	Ban on leaded fuel	NCT of Delhi
Phase V	31.12.1998	Unleaded (0.013g/l)	All capitals of states/UT, and other major cities
Phase VI	1.1.1999	Unleaded only	NCR
Phase VII	1.4.2000	Unleaded	Entire country

Diesel Sulphur phase-out Programme in India

Phase	Date	Type	Area
Phase I	April 1996	Low sulphur (0.5 %)	Four metros and Taj Trapezium
Phase II	August 1997	Low sulphur (0.25%)	Delhi and Taj Trapezium
Phase III	April 1998	Low sulphur (0.25%)	Metro cities
Phase IV	April 1999	Low sulphur (0.25%)	Entire country

Source: CPCB (1999).

> Box 13.3
> **Recommendations Made by the Committee Constituted by the Mumbai High Court**
>
> - The sulfur content in the entire diesel to be supplied in Mumbai city at all the petrol pumps should be reduced to 0.05 per cent by 1 October 2000. It should be further reduced to 0.035 per cent by 1 April 2003 and to 0.005 per cent by 1 April 2005.
> - The benzene content in all the petrol supplied in Mumbai city at all the petrol pumps should be reduced from the present level of 3 per cent to less than 1 per cent by 1 October 2000.
> - With effect from 1 May 2000, all new buses to be purchased by BEST, should be CNG operated until EURO II compliant engines become available in these new vehicles. BEST may exercise an option either to have CNG operated buses or EURO II or higher version diesel engine buses in such a manner that by 1 April 2005 at least 1000 buses are operated on CNG.
> - Engines of all the existing BEST buses, which are not even EURO I compliant must be changed to EURO II compliant engines by 1 October 2002.
> - With effect from 1 January 2001, all taxis above the age of 15 years must be converted to CNG or any other clean fuel. Further, with effect from 1 January 2002, all diesel taxis above the age of 8 years should be converted to clean fuel.
> - With effect from 1 January 2001, all 3-wheelers above the age of 10 years should be converted on CNG or any other clean fuel. Further with effect from 1 January 2002, all 3-wheelers above the age of 8 years should run on clean fuel.
> - The present permissible limit of 4.5 per cent CO emission in respect of 2- and 3-wheelers should be reduced to 3 per cent with effect from 1 October 2000 for Mumbai city to bring it at par with the CO emission level of 4-wheelers.
> - All heavy commercial vehicles as well as light good vehicles to be registered in the Mumbai Metropolitan Region from 1 April 2000 must be EURO II compliant.
> - With effect from 1 January 2001, all 2-wheelers registered in Mumbai Metropolitan Region and which are more than 15 years old shall be scrapped and their registration deemed to have been cancelled.
> - With effect from 1 January 2001, all 3-wheelers registered in Mumbai Metropolitan Region and which are more than 10 years old shall be scrapped unless converted to clean fuel.
> - With effect from 1 January 2001, all transport vehicles other than 3-wheelers and BEST buses over the age of 15 years shall be scrapped unless converted to clean fuel.
> - All two stroke 2- and 3-wheeler in-use vehicles in Mumbai should be fitted with Catalytic converter by 1 July 2001.
> - All petrol driven vehicles registered in Mumbai prior to 1 April 1995 should fit catalytic converter by 1 July 2001.
> - All catalytic converters supplied by the manufacturers for 2-wheeler will carry a warranty of effective working of the catalytic converter over a distance of 30,000 km.

A similar problem is noticed with traffic that could be bypassed. Trends in ambient air quality were analysed and it was found that some cities like Delhi have been experiencing improved air quality because of certain initiatives taken over the last few years. However, class II cities like Hyderabad have been experiencing rising environmental emissions. Share of urban transportation in atmospheric pollution was presented. It was observed that the transport sector contributes most of the CO and a major share of the HC and NOx. It contributes very little to SPM. This chapter discussed various alternative options in urban transportation aiming at the control of emission and improvement in energy efficiency. Alternative fuels, like CNG, LPG, bio-fuels, EVs, fuel cells, hydrogen energy, I&M, retrofitting to control emissions from the in-use vehicles, and traffic management measures were discussed in detail for their merits and demerits and their present status in India. Further, all possible barriers to these alternative options/measures were presented categorically. Lack of infrastructure and additional costs were found to be major barriers for CNG implementation. All policy initiatives taken so far in India for the betterment of transportation and control of environmental emissions were presented in detail. Improving the state of urban transportation needs an integrated approach with various issues, like fuels, technology, adaptability, social costs, policy solutions, and institutional arrangement being addressed.

References

Basu, T. (2001), 'Indian Zero Emission Transportation Programme—A driving force for change', proceedings of International Symposium and Exposition on Automotive Electronics and Alternate Energy Vehicles, 23–5 November 2001, IIT, Kanpur, pp. 107–18.

BMRDA (1995), Draft regional plan for Bombay Metropolitan Region 1996–2011.

CPCB (2000), Transport fuel quality for the year 2000, CPCB, New Delhi.

——— (1999), *Parivesh*, Vol. 6, No. 1, Central Pollution Control Board, Ministry of Environment and Forests, GOI, New Delhi.

Deluchi, M. A. (1993), 'Greenhouse Gas Emissions from the Use of New Fuels for Transportation and Electricity in the Developing World', *Transportation Research*—A, 27A (3), pp. 187–91.

GOI (2002), Report of the expert committee on Auto Fuel Policy, Government of India.

——— (2000), Report of Mashelkar's Committee on Development of High Energy Batteries for Electric Vehicles, Ministry of Non-conventional Energy Sources, GOI.

——— (1997), The Gazette of India: Extraordinary, Part II, Section 3, G.S.R No. 493(E), Ministry of Surface Transport, GOI, New Delhi.

——— (1996), The Gazette of India: Extraordinary, Part II, Section 3, G.S.R No. 163(E), Ministry of Surface Transport, GOI, New Delhi.

——— (1990), The Gazette of India: Extraordinary, Part II, Section 3, G.S.R. No. 54(E), Ministry or Environment and Forests, GOI, New Delhi.

IGIDR (2002), Report on 'Analysis of Barriers for the Alternative Transportation Options in Delhi and Mumbai', under the project of Analysis of Technological Alternatives for Mitigation of GHG Emissions from Urban Transport Sector in Selected Asian Cities, IGIDR, Mumbai.

——— (2001), 'Techno-economic assessment of alternative options in urban transport sector for Delhi and Mumbai', under the project of Analysis of Technological Alternatives for Mitigation of GHG Emissions from Urban Transport Sector in Selected Asian Cities, IGIDR, Mumbai.

Komor, P., S. F. Baldwin, and J. Dunkerley (1993), 'Technologies for Improving Transportation and Energy Efficiency in the Developing World',

Nair, K. R. A. (2001), 'Side Mounted Starter-Generator for Small Size Passenger Cars', proceedings of International Symposium and Exposition on Automotive Electronics and Alternate Energy Vehicles, 23–5 November 2001, IIT, Kanpur, pp. 170–6.

NGV Statistics (2002), International Association for Natural Gas Vehicles, New Zealand.

Ramanathan, R. (2000), Link between population and number of vehicles: Evidence from Indian cities, *Cities*, Vol. 17, No. 4, pp. 263–9.

Tata Energy Research Institute (1999), *Energy Data Directory and Year Book 1998-9*. TERI, New Delhi.

——— (1997), Environmental Aspects of Energy Use in Large Indian Metropolis, Vol. I, New Delhi.

Transportation Research—A, 27A (5), pp: 359–372.

Urban Statistics (1997), Ministry Surface Transport, Government of India.

World Bank (1997), Urban Air Quality Management Strategy in Asia, Greater Mumbai Report, World Bank Technical Paper No. 381, World Bank, Washington, D.C.

WS (1994), Comprehensive Transport Plan for Bombay Metropolitan Region, WS Atkins International in association with Kirloskar Consultants Ltd and Operations Research Group.

A Statistical Profile of India's Development

TABLE I(1)
Key National Accounts Aggregates at 1993-4 Prices

(Rupees, crore)

Year	GDP at factor cost		Net factor income from abroad	GNP at factor cost (2+3)		Consumption of fixed capital	NNP at factor cost (4-5)	NDP at factor cost (2-5)	Indirect taxes less subsidies		GDP at market prices (2+8)		NDP at market prices (7+8)		GNP at market prices (4+8)		NNP at market prices (6+8)	
(1)	(2)		(3)	(4)		(5)	(6)	(7)	(8)		(9)		(10)		(11)		(12)	
1950-1	140,466		-554	139,912		7544	132,367	132,921	8037		148,503		140,958		147,949		140,404	
1951-2	143,745	2.3	-346	143,399	2.5	7848	135,551	135,897	9234	14.9	152,979	3.0	145,131	3.0	152,633	3.2	144,785	3.1
1952-3	147,824	2.8	-281	147,544	2.9	8165	139,379	139,660	9136	-1.1	156,960	2.6	148,796	2.5	156,680	2.7	148,515	2.6
1953-4	156,822	6.1	-232	156,590	6.1	8431	148,159	148,391	9803	7.3	166,625	6.2	158,194	6.3	166,393	6.2	157,962	6.4
1954-5	163,479	4.2	-354	163,126	4.2	8942	154,184	154,537	11,266	14.9	174,745	4.9	165,803	4.8	174,392	4.8	165,450	4.7
1955-6	167,667	2.6	-132	167,535	2.7	9534	158,001	158,133	12,863	14.2	180,530	3.3	170,996	3.1	180,398	3.4	170,864	3.3
1956-7	177,211	5.7	-205	177,006	5.7	10,213	166,793	166,998	13,367	3.9	190,578	5.6	180,365	5.5	190,373	5.5	180,160	5.4
1957-8	175,068	-1.2	-312	174,756	-1.3	10,854	163,902	164,214	14,892	11.4	189,960	-0.3	179,106	-0.7	189,648	-0.4	178,794	-0.8
1958-9	188,354	7.6	-429	187,925	7.5	11,442	176,483	176,913	15,604	4.8	203,958	7.4	192,517	7.5	203,529	7.3	192,087	7.4
1959-60	192,476	2.2	-759	191,717	2.0	12,125	179,592	180,351	16,932	8.5	209,408	2.7	197,283	2.5	208,649	2.5	196,524	2.3
1960-1	206,103	7.1	-907	205,196	7.0	12,961	192,235	193,142	14,457	-14.6	220,560	5.3	207,599	5.2	219,653	5.3	206,692	5.2
1961-2	212,499	3.1	-1212	211,287	3.0	13,773	197,514	198,726	16,422	13.6	228,921	3.8	215,148	3.6	227,709	3.7	213,936	3.5
1962-3	216,994	2.1	-1393	215,601	2.0	14,705	200,895	202,289	18,840	14.7	235,834	3.0	221,129	2.8	234,441	3.0	219,735	2.7
1963-4	227,980	5.1	-1403	226,577	5.1	15,631	210,946	212,349	22,228	18.0	250,208	6.1	234,577	6.1	248,805	6.1	233,174	6.1
1964-5	245,270	7.6	-1798	243,472	7.5	16,832	226,640	228,438	23,551	6.0	268,821	7.4	251,989	7.6	267,023	7.3	250,191	7.3
1965-6	236,306	-3.7	-1912	234,394	-3.7	18,150	216,244	218,156	25,723	9.2	262,029	-2.5	243,879	-3.2	260,117	-2.6	241,967	-3.3
1966-7	238,710	1.0	-1864	236,846	1.0	19,420	217,427	219,291	22,876	-11.1	261,586	-0.2	242,167	-0.7	259,722	-0.2	240,303	-0.7
1967-8	258,137	8.1	-2293	255,843	8.0	20,425	235,418	237,712	23,834	4.2	281,971	7.8	261,546	8.0	279,677	7.7	259,252	7.9
1968-9	264,873	2.6	-2186	262,687	2.7	21,453	241,234	243,420	26,886	12.8	291,759	3.5	270,306	3.3	289,573	3.5	268,120	3.4
1969-70	282,134	6.5	-2342	279,791	6.5	22,432	257,359	259,702	28,713	6.8	310,847	6.5	288,415	6.7	308,504	6.5	286,072	6.7
1970-1	296,278	5.0	-2345	293,933	5.1	23,336	270,597	272,942	30,647	6.7	326,925	5.2	303,589	5.3	324,580	5.2	301,244	5.3
1971-2	299,269	1.0	-2581	296,688	0.9	24,436	272,252	274,833	33,247	8.5	332,516	1.7	308,080	1.5	329,935	1.6	305,499	1.4
1972-3	298,316	-0.3	-2564	295,752	-0.3	25,691	270,061	272,625	32,278	-2.9	330,594	-0.6	304,903	-1.0	328,030	-0.6	302,339	-1.0
1973-4	311,894	4.6	-1944	309,950	4.8	26,888	283,061	285,005	29,156	-9.7	341,050	3.2	314,161	3.0	339,106	3.4	312,217	3.3
1974-5	315,514	1.2	-1005	314,509	1.5	28,092	286,417	287,422	29,587	1.5	345,101	1.2	317,009	0.9	344,096	1.5	316,004	1.2
1975-6	343,924	9.0	-751	343,173	9.1	29,530	313,643	314,395	32,807	10.9	376,731	9.2	347,202	9.5	375,980	9.3	346,450	9.6
1976-7	348,223	1.2	-693	347,530	1.3	31,173	316,358	317,050	34,940	6.5	383,163	1.7	351,990	1.4	382,470	1.7	351,298	1.4
1977-8	374,235	7.5	-771	373,464	7.5	32,713	340,751	341,522	36,638	4.9	410,873	7.2	378,160	7.4	410,102	7.2	377,389	7.4
1978-9	394,828	5.5	-493	394,335	5.6	34,603	359,732	360,225	39,609	8.1	434,437	5.7	399,834	5.7	433,944	5.8	399,341	5.8

(contd.)

TABLE I(1): (contd.)

(1)	(2)		(3)	(4)	(5)	(6)	(7)	(8)		(9)	(10)	(11)	(12)	
1979-80	374,291	-5.2	349	374,640	-5.0	36,515	337,775	-6.2	37,372	-5.6	411,663	-5.2	375,147	-6.2	412,012	-5.1	375,496	-6.0
1980-1	401,128	7.2	842	401,970	7.3	38,553	362,575	7.3	38,073	1.9	439,201	6.7	400,648	6.8	440,043	6.8	401,490	6.9
1981-2	425,073	6.0	95	425,168	5.8	40,776	384,392	6.0	42,066	10.5	467,139	6.4	426,363	6.4	467,234	6.2	426,458	6.2
1982-3	438,079	3.1	-1503	436,577	2.7	43,303	393,274	2.7	46,138	9.7	484,217	3.7	440,915	3.4	482,715	3.3	439,412	3.0
1983-4	471,742	7.7	-2449	469,293	7.5	46,028	423,265	7.8	46,749	1.3	518,491	7.1	472,463	7.2	516,042	6.9	470,014	7.0
1984-5	492,077	4.3	-2871	489,206	4.2	49,087	440,119	4.1	47,797	2.2	539,874	4.1	490,787	3.9	537,003	4.1	487,916	3.8
1985-6	513,990	4.5	-2930	511,058	4.5	51,873	459,187	4.3	56,277	17.7	570,267	5.6	518,394	5.6	567,338	5.6	515,464	5.6
1986-7	536,257	4.3	-4235	532,021	4.1	54,863	477,158	4.2	61,593	9.4	597,850	4.8	542,986	4.7	593,614	4.6	538,751	4.5
1987-8	556,778	3.8	-5369	551,409	3.6	58,097	493,312	3.6	66,593	8.1	623,371	4.3	565,274	4.1	618,002	4.1	559,905	3.9
1988-9	615,098	10.5	-7891	607,207	10.1	61,635	545,572	11.0	69,734	4.7	684,832	9.9	623,197	10.2	676,941	9.5	615,306	9.9
1989-90	656,331	6.7	-8223	648,108	6.7	65,591	582,518	6.7	72,621	4.1	728,952	6.4	663,362	6.4	720,729	6.5	655,139	6.5
1990-1	692,871	5.6	-9201	683,670	5.5	69,465	614,206	5.5	78,424	8.0	771,295	5.8	701,831	5.8	762,094	5.7	692,630	5.7
1991-2	701,863	1.3	-10720	691,143	1.1	73,771	617,372	0.8	76,426	-2.5	778,289	0.9	704,518	0.4	767,569	0.7	693,798	0.2
1992-3	737,792	5.1	-11417	726,375	5.1	78,193	648,182	5.0	81,526	6.7	819,318	5.3	741,125	5.2	807,901	5.3	729,708	5.2
1993-4	781,345	5.9	-12080	769,265	5.9	83,353	685,912	5.8	77,875	-4.5	859,220	4.9	775,867	4.7	847,140	4.9	763,787	4.7
1994-5	838,031	7.3	-13215	824,816	7.2	90,458	734,358	7.1	85,318	9.6	923,349	7.5	832,891	7.3	910,134	7.4	819,676	7.3
1995-6	899,563	7.3	-12602	886,961	7.5	99,152	787,809	7.8	94,383	10.6	993,946	7.6	894,794	7.4	981,344	7.8	882,192	7.6
1996-7	970,083	7.8	-10723	959,360	8.2	107,275	852,085	8.2	97,362	3.2	1,067,445	7.4	960,170	7.3	1,056,722	7.7	949,447	7.6
1997-8	1,016,594	4.8	-10649	1,005,945	4.9	114,860	891,085	4.6	98,653	1.3	1,115,247	4.5	1,000,387	4.2	1,104,598	4.5	989,738	4.2
1998-9	1,082,748	6.5	-11974	1,070,774	6.4	122,193	948,581	6.5	99,273	0.6	1,182,021	6.0	1,059,828	5.9	1,170,047	5.9	1,047,854	5.9
1999-00	1,148,442	6.1	-11602	1,136,840	6.2	129,071	1,007,769	6.1	117,916	18.8	1,266,358	7.1	1,137,287	7.3	1,254,756	7.2	1,125,685	7.4
2000-1	1,198,685	4.4	-12439	1,186,246	4.3	136,069	1,050,177	4.2	117,655	-0.2	1,316,340	3.9	1,180,271	3.8	1,303,901	3.9	1,167,832	3.7
2001-2@	1,267,833	5.8	-8004	1,259,829	6.2	142,547	1,117,282	5.9	116,178	-1.3	1,384,011	5.1	1,241,464	5.2	1,376,007	5.5	1,233,460	5.6
2002-3$	1,318,321	4.0	-11510	1,306,811	3.7	150,097	1,156,714	3.8	129,274	11.3	1,447,595	4.6	1,297,498	4.5	1,436,085	4.4	1,285,988	4.3
2003-4*	1,424,507	8.1	-11510	1,412,997	8.1	159,265	1,253,732	8.3	135,504	4.8	1,560,011	7.8	1,400,746	7.8	1,548,501	8.0	1,389,236	8.0

(contd.)

TABLE I(1) (contd.)
Key National Accounts Aggregates at 1993-4 Prices

(Rupees, crore)

Year	GDP at factor cost Public sector	Per cent of GDP	GDP at factor cost Private sector	Per cent of GDP	Private final consumption expenditure in domestic market (PFCE)		Government final consumption expenditure (GFCE)		Gross domestic capital formation (adjusted)		Net domestic capital formation (adjusted)		Per capita GNP at factor Cost (in Rupees)***		Per capita NNP at factor cost ***		Population (million)***
(1)	(13)	(14)	(15)	(16)	(17)		(18)		(19)		(20)		(21)		(22)		(23)
1950–1	–	–	–	–	128,612		9067		20,755		13,211		3897		3687		359
1951–2	–	–	–	–	136,787	6.4	9161	1.0	26,579	28.1	18,731	41.8	3929	0.8	3714	0.7	365 1.7
1952–3	–	–	–	–	142,307	4.0	9172	0.1	19,554	–26.4	11,389	–39.2	3966	1.0	3747	0.9	372 1.9
1953–4	–	–	–	–	150,862	6.0	9287	1.3	20,993	7.4	12,562	10.3	4132	4.2	3909	4.3	379 1.9
1954–5	–	–	–	–	155,811	3.3	9341	0.6	22,661	7.9	13,719	9.2	4226	2.3	3994	2.2	386 1.8
1955–6	–	–	–	–	157,301	1.0	9600	2.8	30,552	34.8	21,018	53.2	4263	0.9	4020	0.7	393 1.8
1956–7	–	–	–	–	164,259	4.4	10,268	7.0	39,364	28.8	29,150	38.7	4414	3.5	4159	3.5	401 2.0
1957–8	–	–	–	–	161,014	–2.0	11,563	12.6	37,667	–4.3	26,813	–8.0	4273	–3.2	4007	–3.7	409 2.0
1958–9	–	–	–	–	175,796	9.2	11,973	3.5	32,760	–13.0	21,319	–20.5	4496	5.2	4222	5.4	418 2.2
1959–60	–	–	–	–	177,795	1.1	12,188	1.8	34,404	5.0	22,279	4.5	4500	0.1	4216	–0.1	426 1.9
1960–1	18,555	9.0	187,548	91.0	187,909	5.7	12,846	5.4	40,941	19.0	27,981	25.6	4728	5.1	4429	5.1	434 1.9
1961–2	20,763	9.8	191,736	90.2	191,112	1.7	13,757	7.1	38,502	–6.0	24,730	–11.6	4759	0.6	4449	0.4	444 2.3
1962–3	24,234	11.2	192,760	88.8	193,602	1.3	16,693	21.3	43,775	13.7	29,070	17.6	4749	–0.2	4425	–0.5	454 2.3
1963–4	26,607	11.7	201,373	88.3	200,804	3.7	20,822	24.7	45,962	5.0	30,330	4.3	4883	2.8	4546	2.7	464 2.2
1964–5	28,969	11.8	216,301	88.2	212,800	6.0	21,482	3.2	50,839	10.6	34,006	12.1	5137	5.2	4781	5.2	474 2.2
1965–6	31,717	13.4	204,589	86.6	212,988	0.1	23,458	9.2	57,911	13.9	39,762	16.9	4833	–5.9	4459	–6.8	485 2.3
1966–7	33,697	14.1	205,013	85.9	215,756	1.3	23,725	1.1	60,052	3.7	40,632	2.2	4785	–1.0	4392	–1.5	495 2.1
1967–8	35,916	13.9	222,221	86.1	227,962	5.7	24,180	1.9	56,137	–6.5	35,712	–12.1	5056	5.7	4653	5.9	506 2.2
1968–9	38,928	14.7	225,945	85.3	233,950	2.6	25,473	5.3	54,839	–2.3	33,386	–6.5	5071	0.3	4657	0.1	518 2.4
1969–70	42,032	14.9	240,102	85.1	242,640	3.7	27,888	9.5	62,355	13.7	39,923	19.6	5289	4.3	4865	4.5	529 2.1
1970–1	45,805	15.5	250,473	84.5	250,880	3.4	30,453	9.2	64,638	3.7	41,302	3.5	5433	2.7	5002	2.8	541 2.3
1971–2	48,516	16.2	250,753	83.8	255,761	1.9	33,663	10.5	66,704	3.2	42,268	2.3	5355	–1.4	4914	–1.7	554 2.4
1972–3	51,631	17.3	246,685	82.7	257,475	0.7	33,761	0.3	65,287	–2.1	39,596	–6.3	5216	–2.6	4763	–3.1	567 2.3
1973–4	56,891	18.2	255,003	81.8	263,793	2.5	33,372	–1.2	77,055	18.0	50,167	26.7	5344	2.5	4880	2.5	580 2.3
1974–5	58,184	18.4	257,330	81.6	263,594	–0.1	31,862	–4.5	68,649	–10.9	40,557	–19.2	5304	–0.8	4830	–1.0	593 2.2
1975–6	63,313	18.4	280,611	81.6	278,563	5.7	35,170	10.4	71,655	4.4	42,126	3.9	5654	6.6	5167	7.0	607 2.4
1976–7	69,958	20.1	278,265	79.9	284,118	2.0	37,873	7.7	80,238	12.0	49,065	16.5	5605	–0.9	5103	–1.2	620 2.1

(contd.)

TABLE I(1) (contd.)

(1)	(13)	(14)	(15)	(16)	(17)		(18)		(19)		(20)		(21)		(22)		(23)	
1977-8	73,525	19.6	300,710	80.4	307,285	8.2	39,011	3.0	90,648	13.0	57,934	18.1	5891	5.1	5375	5.3	634	2.3
1978-9	78,888	20.0	315,940	80.0	326,066	6.1	41,862	7.3	105,080	15.9	70,477	21.6	6085	3.3	5551	3.3	648	2.2
1979-80	82,283	22.0	292,008	78.0	318,753	-2.2	44,482	6.3	92,895	-11.6	56,379	-20.0	5642	-7.3	5092	-8.3	664	2.5
1980-1	88,719	22.1	312,409	77.9	347,443	9.0	46,581	4.7	99,719	7.3	61,166	8.5	5920	4.9	5352	5.1	679	2.3
1981-2	93,206	21.9	331,867	78.1	362,552	4.3	48,675	4.5	100,425	0.7	59,649	-2.5	6144	3.8	5555	3.8	692	1.9
1982-3	102,535	23.4	335,544	76.6	366,178	1.0	53,280	9.5	100,271	-0.2	56,968	-4.5	6166	0.4	5555	0.0	708	2.3
1983-4	109,445	23.2	362,297	76.8	394,599	7.8	55,605	4.4	103,784	3.5	57,756	1.4	6491	5.3	5854	5.4	723	2.1
1984-5	117,738	23.9	374,339	76.1	405,973	2.9	59,620	7.2	112,567	8.5	63,480	9.9	6620	2.0	5956	1.7	739	2.2
1985-6	127,845	24.9	386,145	75.1	422,916	4.2	66,255	11.1	123,113	9.4	71,240	12.2	6769	2.3	6082	2.1	755	2.2
1986-7	138,862	25.9	397,395	74.1	436,262	3.2	72,802	9.9	123,552	0.4	68,689	-3.6	6900	1.9	6189	1.8	771	2.1
1987-8	147,945	26.6	408,833	73.4	451,215	3.4	78,698	8.1	142,152	15.1	84,055	22.4	6998	1.4	6260	1.2	788	2.2
1988-9	158,483	25.8	456,615	74.2	479,378	6.2	82,775	5.2	160,762	13.1	99,127	17.9	7543	7.8	6777	8.3	805	2.2
1989-90	171,575	26.1	484,756	73.9	503,167	5.0	86,659	4.7	172,046	7.0	106,455	7.4	7885	4.5	7087	4.6	822	2.1
1990-1	176,720	25.5	516,151	74.5	525,641	4.5	89,601	3.4	195,650	13.7	126,185	18.5	8149	3.3	7321	3.3	839	2.1
1991-2	187,758	26.8	514,105	73.2	536,980	2.2	89,008	-0.7	171,553	-12.3	97,782	-22.5	8074	-0.9	7212	-1.5	856	2.0
1992-3	192,708	26.1	545,084	73.9	550,828	2.6	91,795	3.1	187,478	9.3	109,285	11.8	8330	3.2	7433	3.1	872	1.9
1993-4	202,512	25.9	578,833	74.1	574,772	4.3	97,725	6.5	198,412	5.8	115,059	5.3	8624	3.5	7690	3.4	892	2.3
1994-5	216,995	25.9	621,036	74.1	601,481	4.6	98,935	1.2	243,882	22.9	153,424	33.3	9064	5.1	8070	4.9	910	2.0
1995-6	230,061	25.6	669,502	74.4	638,938	6.2	106,881	8.0	271,015	11.1	171,863	12.0	9558	5.4	8489	5.2	928	2.0
1996-7	240,452	24.8	729,631	75.2	689,566	7.9	111,640	4.5	268,435	-1.0	161,160	-6.2	10,141	6.1	9007	6.1	946	1.9
1997-8	269,001	26.5	747,593	73.5	707,285	2.6	123,978	11.1	289,058	7.7	174,198	8.1	10,435	2.9	9244	2.6	964	1.9
1998-9	288,939	26.7	793,809	73.3	752,440	6.4	139,963	12.9	290,971	0.7	168,778	-3.1	10,893	4.4	9650	4.4	983	2.0
1999-00	305,160	26.6	843,282	73.4	797,653	6.0	158,432	13.2	350,159	20.3	221,088	31.0	11,357	4.3	10,068	4.3	1001	1.8
2000-1	309,766	25.8	888,919	74.2	818,636	2.6	159,338	0.6	345,209	-1.4	209,140	-5.4	11,641	2.5	10,306	2.4	1019	1.8
2001-2@	334,341	26.4	931,088	73.4	866,736	5.9	164,037	2.9	346,907	0.5	204,360	-2.3	12,149	4.4	10,774	4.5	1037	1.8
2002-3$	-	-	-	-	897,243	3.5	169,069	3.1	373,399	7.6	223,302	9.3	12,387	2.0	10,964	1.8	1055	1.7
2003-4*	-	-	-	-	-	-	-	-	-	-	-	-	13,169	6.3	11,684	6.6	1073	1.7

Notes: *, ** Based on mid-financial year (as on October 1 each year) population as given by the CSO.
@ Provisional Estimates
$ Quick Estimates
* Advance Estimates
- information not available
Figures in italics denote percentage changes over previous years.

Source: Central Statistical Organisation (CSO): *National Accounts Statistics*, various issues.

TABLE I(2)
Gross and Net Domestic Savings by Type of Institutions (at Current Prices)

(Rupees, crore)

Year	GDP at current market prices	NDP at current market prices	Domestic savings						Household sector savings						Private corporate sector savings						Public sector savings					
			GDS		CFC**		NDS		Gross		CFC**		Net		Gross		CFC**		Net		Gross		CFC**		Net	
			(4)		(5)		(6)		(7)		(8)		(9)		(10)		(11)		(12)		(13)		(14)		(15)	
(1)	(2)	(3)																								
1950-1	9934	9570	887	8.9	364	3.7	523	5.5	612	6.2	256	2.6	356	3.7	93	0.9	45	0.5	48	0.5	182	1.8	63	0.6	119	1.2
1951-2	10,566	10,155	985	9.3	411	3.9	574	5.7	583	5.5	285	2.7	298	2.9	136	1.3	52	0.5	84	0.8	266	2.5	74	0.7	192	1.9
1952-3	10,366	9924	861	8.3	442	4.3	419	4.2	637	6.1	305	2.9	332	3.3	64	0.6	55	0.5	9	0.1	160	1.5	82	0.8	78	0.8
1953-4	11,282	10,818	888	7.9	465	4.1	423	3.9	655	5.8	321	2.8	334	3.1	90	0.8	56	0.5	34	0.3	143	1.3	88	0.8	55	0.5
1954-5	10,678	10,167	1005	9.4	511	4.8	494	4.9	719	6.7	354	3.3	365	3.6	118	1.1	64	0.6	54	0.5	168	1.6	93	0.9	75	0.7
1955-6	10,873	10,327	1370	12.6	546	5.0	824	8.0	1046	9.6	371	3.4	675	6.5	134	1.2	72	0.7	62	0.6	190	1.7	103	1.0	87	0.8
1956-7	12,951	12,340	1584	12.2	611	4.7	973	7.9	1178	9.1	408	3.2	770	6.2	155	1.2	80	0.6	75	0.6	251	1.9	123	1.0	128	1.0
1957-8	13,349	12,687	1384	10.4	661	5.0	723	5.7	997	7.5	430	3.2	567	4.5	121	0.9	88	0.7	33	0.3	266	2.0	142	1.1	124	1.0
1958-9	14,874	14,102	1407	9.5	772	5.2	635	4.5	1016	6.8	514	3.5	502	3.6	140	0.9	99	0.7	41	0.3	251	1.7	159	1.1	92	0.7
1959-60	15,675	14,832	1748	11.2	843	5.4	905	6.1	1301	8.3	544	3.5	757	5.1	185	1.2	113	0.7	72	0.5	262	1.7	186	1.2	76	0.5
1960-1	17,167	16,223	1989	11.6	944	5.5	1045	6.4	1254	7.3	592	3.4	662	4.1	281	1.6	136	0.8	145	0.9	454	2.6	217	1.3	237	1.5
1961-2	18,196	17,138	2127	11.7	1058	5.8	1069	6.2	1281	7.0	634	3.5	647	3.8	320	1.8	172	0.9	148	0.9	526	2.9	252	1.4	274	1.6
1962-3	19,566	18,401	2479	12.7	1164	5.9	1315	7.1	1533	7.8	673	3.4	860	4.7	344	1.8	198	1.0	146	0.8	602	3.1	293	1.5	309	1.7
1963-4	22,482	21,169	2763	12.3	1313	5.8	1450	6.8	1618	7.2	725	3.2	893	4.2	394	1.8	245	1.1	149	0.7	751	3.3	343	1.5	408	1.9
1964-5	26,220	24,743	3129	11.9	1477	5.6	1652	6.7	1875	7.2	776	3.0	1099	4.4	389	1.5	286	1.1	103	0.4	865	3.3	415	1.6	450	1.8
1965-6	27,668	25,998	3870	14.0	1671	6.0	2199	8.5	2602	9.4	872	3.2	1730	6.7	405	1.5	304	1.1	101	0.4	863	3.1	495	1.8	368	1.4
1966-7	31,305	29,330	4375	14.0	1975	6.3	2400	8.2	3223	10.3	1039	3.3	2184	7.4	424	1.4	348	1.1	76	0.3	728	2.3	587	1.9	141	0.5
1967-8	36,649	34,427	4355	11.9	2222	6.1	2133	6.2	3210	8.8	1174	3.2	2036	5.9	410	1.1	369	1.0	41	0.1	735	2.0	679	1.9	56	0.2
1968-9	38,823	36,407	4721	12.2	2416	6.2	2305	6.3	3349	8.6	1267	3.3	2082	5.7	439	1.1	394	1.0	45	0.1	933	2.4	755	1.9	178	0.5
1969-70	42,750	40,072	6104	14.3	2678	6.3	3426	8.5	4440	10.4	1428	3.3	3012	7.5	549	1.3	413	1.0	136	0.3	1115	2.6	837	2.0	278	0.7
1970-1	45,677	42,707	6649	14.6	2970	6.5	3679	8.6	4634	10.1	1521	3.3	3113	7.3	672	1.5	462	1.0	210	0.5	1343	2.9	988	2.2	355	0.8
1971-2	48,932	45,640	7367	15.1	3292	6.7	4075	8.9	5219	10.7	1658	3.4	3561	7.8	769	1.6	502	1.0	267	0.6	1379	2.8	1133	2.3	246	0.5
1972-3	53,947	50,226	7872	14.6	3721	6.9	4151	8.3	5624	10.4	1845	3.4	3779	7.5	806	1.5	564	1.0	242	0.5	1442	2.7	1312	2.4	130	0.3
1973-4	65,613	61,274	10,999	16.8	4339	6.6	6660	10.9	7985	12.2	2096	3.2	5889	9.6	1083	1.7	656	1.0	427	0.7	1931	2.9	1588	2.4	343	0.6
1974-5	77,479	71,919	12,380	16.0	5560	7.2	6820	9.5	8080	10.4	2634	3.4	5446	7.6	1465	1.9	876	1.1	589	0.8	2835	3.7	2049	2.6	786	1.1
1975-6	83,269	76,820	14,346	17.2	6449	7.7	7897	10.3	9743	11.7	2980	3.6	6763	8.8	1083	1.3	1053	1.3	30	0.0	3520	4.2	2416	2.9	1104	1.4
1976-7	89,739	82,833	17,408	19.4	6907	7.7	10,501	12.7	11,849	13.2	3180	3.5	8669	10.5	1181	1.3	1068	1.2	113	0.1	4378	4.9	2659	3.0	1719	2.1
1977-8	101,597	94,100	20,142	19.8	7497	7.4	12,645	13.4	14,354	14.1	3405	3.4	10,949	11.6	1413	1.4	1083	1.1	330	0.4	4375	4.3	3009	3.0	1366	1.5
1978-9	110,133	101,560	23,676	21.5	8573	7.8	15,103	14.9	17,015	15.4	3903	3.5	13,112	12.9	1652	1.5	1203	1.1	449	0.4	5009	4.5	3467	3.1	1542	1.5

(contd.)

TABLE I(2) contd.

(1)	(2)	(3)	(4)	(5)	(6)	(7)	(8)	(9)	(10)	(11)	(12)	(13)	(14)	(15)
1979-80	120,841	110,392	24,314	20.1 10,449	8.6 13,865	12.6 16,690	13.8 4748	3.9 11,942	10.8 2398	2.0 1457	1.2 941	0.9 5226	4.3 4244	3.5 982	0.9
1980-1	143,764	131,477	27,136	18.9 12,288	8.5 14,848	11.3 19,868	13.8 5579	3.9 14,289	10.9 2339	1.6 1717	1.2 622	0.5 4929	3.4 4992	3.5 -63	0.0
1981-2	168,600	153,892	31,355	18.6 14,708	8.7 16,647	10.8 21,225	12.6 6709	4.0 14,516	9.4 2560	1.5 2022	1.2 538	0.3 7570	4.5 5977	3.5 1593	1.0
1982-3	188,262	171,087	34,368	18.3 17,175	9.1 17,193	10.0 23,216	12.3 7690	4.1 15,526	9.1 2980	1.6 2364	1.3 616	0.4 8172	4.3 7121	3.8 1051	0.6
1983-4	219,496	199,931	38,587	17.6 19,565	8.9 19,022	9.5 28,165	12.8 8531	3.9 19,634	9.8 3254	1.5 2811	1.3 443	0.2 7168	3.3 8222	3.7 -1054	-0.5
1984-5	245,515	223,028	46,063	18.8 22,487	9.2 23,576	10.6 35,067	14.3 9650	3.9 25,417	11.4 4040	1.6 3231	1.3 809	0.4 6956	2.8 9606	3.9 -2650	-1.2
1985-6	277,991	251,274	54,167	19.5 26,717	9.6 27,450	10.9 39,795	14.3 11,109	4.0 28,686	11.4 5426	2.0 3976	1.4 1450	0.6 8946	3.2 11,632	4.2 -2686	-1.1
1986-7	311,177	280,788	58,951	18.9 30,389	9.8 28,562	10.2 45072	14.5 12,327	4.0 32,745	11.7 5336	1.7 4675	1.5 661	0.2 8543	2.7 13,388	4.3 -4845	-1.7
1987-8	354,343	320,369	72,908	20.6 33,974	9.6 38934	12.2 59,157	16.7 13,665	3.9 45,492	14.2 5932	1.7 5052	1.4 880	0.3 7819	2.2 15,257	4.3 -7438	-2.3
1988-9	421,567	381,874	87,913	20.9 39,693	9.4 48,220	12.6 70,657	16.8 15,607	3.7 55,050	14.4 8486	2.0 6130	1.5 2356	0.6 8770	2.1 17,955	4.3 -9185	-2.4
1989-90	486,179	439,619	106,979	22.0 46,560	9.6 60,419	13.7 86,955	17.9 17,813	3.7 69,142	15.7 11,845	2.4 7401	1.5 4444	1.0 8179	1.7 21,346	4.4 -13,167	-3.0
1990-1	568,674	515,410	131,340	23.1 53,264	9.4 78,076	15.1 109,897	19.3 20,092	3.5 89,805	17.4 15,164	2.7 8861	1.6 6303	1.2 6279	1.1 24,311	4.3 -18,032	-3.5
1991-2	653,117	588,715	143,908	22.0 64,402	9.9 79,506	13.5 110,736	17.0 23,356	3.6 87,380	14.8 20,304	1.8 8727	1.5 12,868	1.5 12,868	2.0 29,470	4.5 -16,602	-2.8
1992-3	748,367	673,855	162,906	21.8 74,512	10.0 88,394	13.1 131,073	17.5 26,170	3.5 104,903	15.6 19,968	2.7 2,714,451	1.9 5517	0.8 11,865	1.6 33,891	4.5 -22,026	-3.3
1993-4	859,220	775,867	193,621	22.5 83,353	9.7 110,268	14.2 158,310	18.4 28,941	3.4 129,369	16.7 29,866	3.5 3,517,028	2.0 12,838	1.7 5445	0.6 37,384	4.4 -31,939	-4.1
1994-5	1,012,770	914,776	251,463	24.8 97,994	9.7 153,469	16.8 199,358	19.7 33,933	3.4 165,425	18.1 35,260	3.5 3,520,628	2.0 14,632	1.6 16,845	1.7 43,433	4.3 -26,588	-2.9
1995-6	1,188,012	1,070,086	298,195	25.1 117,926	9.9 180,269	16.8 215,588	18.1 41,929	3.5 173,659	16.2 58,542	3.4 4,926,059	2.2 32,483	3.0 24,065	2.0 49,938	4.2 -25,873	-2.4
1996-7	1,368,208	1,231,705	317,261	23.2 136,503	10.0 180,758	14.7 233,252	17.0 47,552	3.5 185,700	15.1 61,092	4.5 4,532,381	2.4 28,711	2.3 22,917	1.7 56,570	4.1 -33,653	-2.7
1997-8	1,522,547	1,370,550	352,178	23.1 151,997	10.0 200,181	14.6 268,437	17.6 52,437	3.4 216,000	15.8 63,486	4.2 4,237,826	2.5 25,660	1.9 20,255	1.4 61,734	4.1 -41,479	-3.0
1998-9	1,740,985	1,572,919	374,931	21.5 168,066	9.7 206,865	13.2 327,074	18.8 57,251	3.3 269,823	17.2 65,026	3.9 3,743,583	2.5 21,443	1.4 -17,169	-1.0 67,232	3.9 -84,401	-5.4
1999-00	1,936,925	1,754,566	466,640	24.1 182,359	9.4 284,281	16.2 402,360	20.8 61,814	3.2 340,546	19.4 84,329	4.3 4,448,674	2.5 35,655	2.0 -20,049	-1.0 71,871	3.7 -91,920	-5.2
2000-1	2,104,298	1,906,442	491,761	23.4 197,856	9.4 293,905	15.4 453,641	21.6 66,064	3.1 387,577	20.3 86,142	4.1 4,155,485	2.6 30,657	1.6 -48,022	-2.3 76,307	3.6 -124,329	-6.5
2001-2@	2,282,143	2,064,389	535,185	23.5 217,754	9.5 317,431	15.4 519,040	22.7 77,177	3.4 441,863	21.4 78,849	4.2 3,558,097	2.5 20,752	1.0 -62,704	-2.7 82,480	3.6 -145,184	-7.0
2002-3$	2,469,564	2,234,521	597,697	24.2 235,043	9.5 362,654	16.2 559,258	22.6 84,600	3.4 474,658	21.2 84,169	4.1 3,462,739	2.5 21,430	1.0 -45,730	-1.9 87,704	3.6 -133,434	-6.0

Notes: * Advance Estimates.
** This has been worked out from the estimated value of capital stock and the expected age of various types of assets.
@ Provisional Estimates
$ Quick Estimates.
Figures in italics are as percentages to GDP at current market prices except those for net savings in cols(6), (9), (12) and (15) which are as percentages to NDP at current market prices.
Source: Central Statistical Organisation (CSO): *National Accounts Statistics*, various issues.

TABLE I(3)
Gross Capital Formation by Type of Institutions at Current Prices

Year	Gross capital formation (GCF)							Gross domestic savings	Net foreign capital inflow	Finances for gross capital formation (6+7)	Errors and omissions (8−2)**	GCF adjusted (2+9)		Consumption of fixed capital (CFC)	Net capital formation (NCF)		NCF adjusted		Price deflators (1993-4=100)	
	Aggregate (3+4+5)		Public sector		Private corporate sector		Household sector													GDCF (unadjusted)	GDP at market prices
(1)	(2)		(3)		(4)		(5)		(6)	(7)	(8)	(9)	(10)		(11)	(12)		(13)		(14)	(15)
1950-1	1044	10.5	276	2.8	218	2.2	550	5.5	887	−21	866	−178	866	8.7	364	680	7.1	502	5.2	4.1	6.7
1951-2	1146	10.8	321	3.0	256	2.4	569	5.4	985	183	1168	22	1168	11.1	411	735	7.2	757	7.5	4.4	6.9
1952-3	917	8.8	274	2.6	78	0.8	565	5.4	861	−34	827	−90	827	8.0	442	475	4.8	385	3.9	4.2	6.6
1953-4	833	7.4	311	2.8	9	0.1	513	4.5	888	−13	875	42	875	7.8	465	368	3.4	410	3.8	4.2	6.8
1954-5	1063	10.0	477	4.5	149	1.4	437	4.1	1005	16	1021	−42	1021	9.6	511	552	5.4	510	5.0	4.5	6.1
1955-6	1361	12.5	522	4.8	222	2.0	517	5.7	1370	39	1409	48	1409	13.0	546	815	7.9	863	8.4	4.6	6.0
1956-7	1881	14.5	691	5.3	345	2.7	845	6.5	1584	360	1944	63	1944	15.0	611	1270	10.3	1333	10.8	4.9	6.8
1957-8	1959	14.7	859	6.4	394	3.0	706	5.3	1384	473	1857	−102	1857	13.9	662	1297	10.2	1195	9.4	4.9	7.0
1958-9	1740	11.7	844	5.7	242	1.6	654	4.4	1407	376	1783	43	1783	12.0	772	968	6.9	1011	7.2	5.4	7.3
1959-60	2103	13.4	932	5.9	303	1.9	868	5.5	1748	231	1979	−124	1979	12.6	843	1260	8.5	1136	7.7	5.7	7.5
1960-1	2516	14.7	1178	6.9	540	3.1	798	4.6	1989	481	2470	−46	2470	14.4	944	1572	9.7	1526	9.4	6.0	7.8
1961-2	2723	15.0	1187	6.5	744	4.1	792	4.4	2127	345	2472	−251	2472	13.6	1058	1665	9.7	1414	8.3	6.4	7.9
1962-3	3063	15.7	1490	7.6	539	2.8	1034	5.3	2479	440	2919	−144	2919	14.9	1164	1899	10.3	1755	9.5	6.7	8.3
1963-4	3477	15.5	1733	7.7	869	3.9	875	3.9	2763	440	3203	−274	3203	14.2	1313	2164	10.2	1890	8.9	7.0	9.0
1964-5	4074	15.5	2007	7.7	906	3.5	1161	4.4	3129	600	3729	−345	3729	14.2	1477	2597	10.5	2252	9.1	7.3	9.8
1965-6	4517	16.3	2282	8.2	705	2.5	1530	5.5	3870	599	4469	−48	4469	16.2	1671	2846	10.9	2798	10.8	7.7	10.6
1966-7	5193	16.6	2209	7.1	625	2.0	2359	7.5	4375	923	5298	105	5298	16.9	1975	3218	11.0	3323	11.3	8.8	12.0
1967-8	5580	15.2	2415	6.6	820	2.2	2345	6.4	4355	837	5192	−388	5192	14.2	2222	3358	9.8	2970	8.6	9.2	13.0
1968-9	5582	14.4	2259	5.8	769	2.0	2554	6.6	4721	416	5137	−445	5137	13.2	2416	3166	8.7	2721	7.5	9.4	13.3
1969-70	6557	15.3	2361	5.5	675	1.6	3521	8.2	6104	241	6345	−212	6345	14.8	2678	3879	9.7	3667	9.2	10.2	13.8
1970-1	7227	15.8	2919	6.4	1045	2.3	3263	7.1	6649	394	7043	−184	7043	15.4	2970	4257	10.0	4073	9.5	10.9	14.0
1971-2	8283	16.9	3415	7.0	1204	2.5	3564	7.5	7367	478	7845	−438	7845	16.0	3292	4991	10.9	4553	10.0	11.7	14.7
1972-3	8721	16.2	3875	7.2	1350	2.5	3496	6.5	7872	297	8169	−552	8169	15.1	3721	5000	10.0	4448	8.9	12.5	16.3
1973-4	10,928	16.7	4904	7.5	1651	2.5	4373	6.7	10,999	392	11,391	463	11,391	17.4	4339	6589	10.8	7052	11.5	14.8	19.2
1974-5	14,192	18.3	5753	7.4	2733	3.5	5706	7.4	12,380	653	13,033	−1159	13,033	16.8	5560	8632	12.0	7473	10.4	18.9	22.5
1975-6	15,800	19.0	7806	9.4	2169	2.6	5825	7.0	14,346	−117	14,229	−1571	14,229	17.1	6449	9351	12.2	7780	10.1	19.8	22.1
1976-7	17,144	19.1	8822	9.8	1325	1.5	6997	7.8	17,408	−1309	16,099	−1045	16,099	17.9	6907	10,237	12.4	9192	11.1	20.1	23.4

(contd.)

TABLE I(3) contd.

(1)	(2)		(3)		(4)		(5)		(6)	(7)	(8)	(9)	(10)		(11)	(12)		(13)		(14)	(15)
1977-8	18,979	18.7	8101	8.0	2377	2.3	8501	8.4	20,142	-1465	18,677	-302	18,677	18.4	7497	11,482	12.2	11,180	11.9	20.6	24.7
1978-9	22,810	20.7	10,165	9.2	2288	2.1	10,357	9.4	23,676	128	23,804	994	23,804	21.6	8573	14,237	14.0	15,231	15.0	22.7	25.4
1979-80	25,824	21.4	12,137	10.0	3078	2.5	10,609	8.8	24,314	580	24,894	-930	24,894	20.6	10,449	15,375	13.9	14,445	13.1	26.8	29.4
1980-1	26,868	18.7	12,105	8.4	3505	2.4	11,258	7.8	27,136	2094	29,230	2362	29,230	20.3	12,288	14,580	11.1	16,942	12.9	29.3	32.7
1981-2	37,783	22.4	16,986	10.1	9186	5.4	11,611	6.9	31,355	2611	33,966	-3817	33,966	20.1	14,708	23,075	15.0	19,258	12.5	33.7	36.1
1982-3	40,786	21.7	20,139	10.7	10,170	5.4	10,477	5.6	34,368	2566	36,934	-3852	36,934	19.6	17,175	23,611	13.8	19,759	11.5	36.8	38.9
1983-4	43,196	19.7	21,265	9.7	7060	3.2	14,871	6.8	38,587	2517	41,104	-2092	41,104	18.7	19,565	23,631	11.8	21,539	10.8	39.6	42.3
1984-5	53,026	21.6	25,600	10.4	10,238	4.2	17,188	7.0	46,063	3292	49,355	-3671	49,355	20.1	22,487	30,539	13.7	26,868	12.0	43.8	45.5
1985-6	65,803	23.7	29,990	10.8	14,556	5.2	21,257	7.6	54,167	6234	60,401	-5402	60,401	21.7	26,717	39,086	15.6	33,684	13.4	49.0	48.7
1986-7	72,203	23.2	34,772	11.2	15,695	5.0	21,736	7.0	58,951	6355	65,306	-6897	65,306	21.0	30,389	41,814	14.9	34,917	12.4	52.9	52.0
1987-8	78,357	22.1	33,757	9.5	12,263	3.5	32,337	9.1	72,908	6825	79,733	1376	79,733	22.5	33,974	44,383	13.9	45,759	14.3	56.1	56.8
1988-9	99,876	23.7	40,136	9.5	16,266	3.9	43,474	10.3	87,913	12,304	100,217	341	100,217	23.8	39,693	60,183	15.8	60,524	15.8	62.3	61.6
1989-90	115,035	23.7	46,405	9.5	19,673	4.0	48,957	10.1	106,979	12,279	119,258	4223	119,258	24.5	46,560	68,475	15.6	72,698	16.5	69.3	66.7
1990-1	136,854	24.1	53,099	9.3	23,498	4.1	60,257	10.6	131,340	18,196	149,536	12,682	149,536	26.3	53,264	83,590	16.2	96,272	18.7	76.4	73.7
1991-2	143,260	21.9	57,633	8.8	36,992	5.7	48,635	7.4	143,908	3377	147,285	4025	147,285	22.6	64,402	78,858	13.4	82,883	14.1	85.9	83.9
1992-3	178,019	23.8	63,997	8.6	48,316	6.5	65,706	8.8	162,906	13,816	176,722	-1297	176,722	23.6	74,512	103,507	15.4	102,210	15.2	94.3	91.3
1993-4	182,619	21.3	70,834	8.2	48,213	5.6	63,572	7.4	193,621	4791	198,412	15,793	198,412	23.1	83,353	99,266	12.8	115,059	14.8	100.0	100.0
1994-5	236,784	23.4	88,206	8.7	69,953	6.9	78,625	7.8	251,463	11,893	263,356	26,572	263,356	26.0	97,994	138,790	15.2	165,362	18.1	108.0	109.7
1995-6	315,179	26.5	90,977	7.7	113,781	9.6	110,422	9.3	298,747	20,780	319,527	4348	319,527	26.9	117,926	197,253	18.4	201,601	18.8	117.9	119.5
1996-7	297,862	21.8	96,187	7.0	110,084	8.0	91,591	6.7	317,261	17,738	334,999	37,137	334,999	24.5	136,503	161,359	13.1	198,496	16.1	124.8	128.2
1997-8	343,712	22.6	100,653	6.6	121,399	8.0	121,660	8.0	352,178	22,302	374,480	30,768	374,480	24.6	151,997	191,715	14.0	222,483	16.2	129.5	136.5
1998-9	372,209	21.4	114,545	6.6	111,208	6.4	146,456	8.4	374,931	18,090	393,021	20,812	393,021	22.6	168,066	204,143	13.0	224,955	14.3	135.1	147.3
1999-00	458,262	23.7	134,484	6.9	125,120	6.5	198,658	10.3	466,640	21,988	488,628	30,366	488,628	25.2	182,359	275,903	15.7	306,269	17.5	139.6	153.0
2000-1	473,621	22.5	134,025	6.4	103,796	4.9	235,800	11.2	491,761	12,977	504,738	31,117	504,738	24.0	197,856	275,765	14.5	306,882	16.1	146.2	159.9
2001-2@	509,060	22.3	133,003	5.8	111,321	4.9	264,736	11.6	535,185	-7268	527,917	18,857	527,917	23.1	217,754	291,306	14.1	310,163	15.0	152.2	164.9
2002-3$	563,816	22.8	140,386	5.7	118,579	4.8	304,851	12.3	597,697	-22,664	575,033	11,217	575,033	23.3	235,043	328,773	14.7	339,990	15.2	154.0	170.6
2003-4*	–	–	–	–	–	–	–	–	–	–	–	–	–	–	–	–	–	–	–	–	176.6

Notes: @ Provisional Estimates
$ Quick Estimates
* Advance Estimates
** (Domestic Savings + Net Capital Inflow—Domestic Capital Formation)
Figures in italics are as percentage to GDP at current market prices, except for net capital formation in cols (12) and (13) which are as percentages to NDP at current market prices.

Source: Central Statistical Organisation (CSO): *National Accounts Statistics*, various issues.

TABLE I(4)

Net Capital Stock by Type of Institutions and Capital-Output Ratios

Amounts in rupees crore

Year (As on March 31)	Net capital stock				Net fixed capital stock				Inventory			Fiscal year	Average capital-output ratio (ACOR)							Incremental capital-output (ICOR)	
		Public sector	Private sector			Public sector	Private sector			Public sector	Private sector		Net capital stock to Output *			Net Fixed Capital Stock to Output*			ND-CF to output	NFCF to output $
	Total (3+4)			Household sector	Total (7+8)			Household sector	Total (11+12)			Household sector		Total	Public sector	Private sector	Total	Public sector	Private sector		
(1)	(2)	(3)	(4)	(5)	(6)	(7)	(8)	(9)	(10)	(11)	(12)	(13)	(14)	(15)	(16)	(17)	(18)	(19)	(20)	(21)	(22)
					At 1993-4 prices											At 1993-4 prices					
1981	1,231,085	512,169	718,916	612,928	1,121,610	471,861	649,749	577,767	109,475	40,308	69,167	35,161	1980-1	–	–	–	–	–	–	–	–	–
1982	1,312,238	545,386	766,852	642,779	1,188,209	500,219	687,990	606,093	124,029	45,167	78,862	36,686	1981-2	3.31	5.7	2.55	3.01	5.21	2.30	2.14	2.10
1983	1,379,366	580,645	798,721	656,008	1,244,576	532,944	711,632	617,431	134,790	47,701	87,089	38,577	1982-3	3.41	5.5	2.68	3.08	5.04	2.39	3.28	2.61
1984	1,433,963	613,846	820,117	668,652	1,295,600	565,457	730,143	627,167	138,363	48,389	89,974	41,485	1983-4	3.30	5.5	2.56	2.98	5.02	2.28	6.45	5.43
1985	1,496,083	650,509	845,574	680,021	1,347,822	598,708	749,114	635,736	148,261	51,801	96,460	44,285	1984-5	3.31	5.4	2.56	2.98	4.94	2.27	2.04	1.91
1986	1,568,302	687,969	880,333	694,032	1,402,628	632,494	770,134	645,308	165,674	55,475	110,199	48,724	1985-6	3.32	5.2	2.58	2.98	4.82	2.27	4.16	3.57
1987	1,640,960	729,394	911,566	705,716	1,462,759	672,294	790,465	652,300	178,201	57,100	121,101	53,416	1986-7	3.33	5.1	2.62	2.98	4.70	2.28	4.30	3.44
1988	1,699,672	702,288	937,384	719,174	1,517,223	707,803	809,420	662,039	182,449	54,485	127,964	57,135	1987-8	3.35	4.8	2.64	2.99	4.66	2.28	4.24	3.59
1989	1,771,459	798,155	973,304	739,929	1,575,554	744,439	831,115	674,199	195,905	53,716	142,189	65,730	1988-9	3.14	4.7	2.42	2.79	4.58	2.08	4.72	4.47
1990	1,839,659	834,418	1,005,241	754,625	1,634,309	778,117	856,192	687,930	205,350	56,301	149,049	66,695	1989-90	3.06	4.8	2.36	2.72	4.44	2.01	1.80	1.55
1991	1,918,761	872,496	1,046,265	777,430	1,704,760	813,524	891,236	707,661	214,001	58,972	155,029	69,769	1990-1	3.01	4.8	2.30	2.68	4.50	1.96	2.69	2.45
1992	1,995,190	904,901	1,090,289	792,377	1,781,854	848,542	933,312	722,573	213,336	56,359	156,977	69,804	1991-2	3.12	4.7	2.43	2.78	4.43	2.07	3.36	3.09
1993	2,077,675	936,973	1,140,702	807,065	1,853,469	877,739	975,730	735,804	224,206	59,234	164,972	71,261	1992-3	3.09	4.8	2.39	2.76	4.48	2.04	19.87	20.01
1994	2,144,285	970,452	1,173,833	808,478	1,921,762	909,237	1,012,525	737,706	222,523	61,215	161,308	70,772	1993-4	3.02	5.8	2.17	2.70	5.41	1.87	3.51	3.17
1995	2,283,999	1,011,406	1,272,593	861,463	2,048,289	950,773	1,097,516	786,379	235,710	60,633	175,077	75,084	1994-5	2.96	5.6	2.14	2.66	5.25	1.85	3.00	2.63
1996	2,470,063	1,045,338	1,424,725	938,056	2,212,699	985,081	1,227,618	854,650	257,364	60,257	197,107	83,406	1995-6	2.97	5.5	2.20	2.66	5.14	1.90	3.09	2.33
1997	2,611,101	1,075,323	1,535,778	983,904	2,365,943	1,013,446	1,352,497	907,745	245,158	61,877	183,281	76,159	1996-7	2.94	5.4	2.22	2.65	5.06	1.94	3.25	2.77
1998	2,754,003	1,103,351	1,650,652	1,029,843	2,498,316	1,038,500	1,459,816	946,589	255,687	64,851	190,836	83,254	1997-8	2.97	4.9	2.35	2.70	4.57	2.08	2.58	2.28
1999	2,878,178	1,135,160	1,743,018	1,067,948	2,623,861	1,068,576	1,555,285	985,633	254,317	66,584	187,733	82,315	1998-9	2.93	4.6	2.36	2.67	4.34	2.10	4.48	3.60
2000	3,017,238	1,175,841	1,841,397	1,108,153	2,737,349	1,099,229	1,638,120	1,021,470	279,889	76,612	203,277	86,683	1999-00	2.89	4.5	2.35	2.63	4.20	2.10	2.87	2.63
2001	3,136,697	1,210,543	1,926,154	1,158,253	2,847,281	1,129,826	1,717,455	1,068,498	289,416	80,717	208,699	89,755	2000-1	2.90	4.6	2.35	2.63	4.27	2.09	3.76	2.95
2002	3,244,490	1,248,956	1,995,534	1,193,627	2,943,486	1,162,483	1,781,003	1,101,477	301,004	86,473	214,531	92,150	2001-2	2.84	–	–	2.57	–	–	4.84	4.12
																				3.26	2.97

(contd.)

TABLE I(4) contd.

(1)	(2)	(3)	(4)	(5)	(6)	(7)	(8)	(9)	(10)	(11)	(12)	(13)	(14)	(15)	(16)	(17)	(18)	(19)	(20)	(21)	(22)
					At current prices											At current prices					
1981	351,395	146,629	204,766	167,777	310,669	131,043	179,626	155,538	40,726	15,586	25,140	12,239	1980–1	–	–	–	–	–	–	0.87	0.74
1982	431,181	176,163	255,018	206,678	381,653	157,436	224,217	192,966	49,528	18,727	30,801	13,712	1981–2	2.85	6.38	2.05	2.52	5.70	1.80	0.99	0.89
1983	509,014	208,603	300,411	240,552	452,612	188,002	264,610	225,388	56,402	20,601	35,801	15,164	1982–3	3.09	6.27	2.28	2.74	5.63	2.01	1.32	1.27
1984	582,900	240,272	342,628	274,984	520,828	218,097	302,731	257,327	62,072	22,175	39,897	17,657	1983–4	3.05	6.29	2.24	2.72	5.69	1.98	0.81	0.82
1985	669,406	279,996	389,410	309,836	597,918	254,689	343,229	289,447	71,488	25,307	46,181	20,389	1984–5	3.13	6.29	2.30	2.79	5.71	2.03	1.27	1.21
1986	777,279	333,360	443,919	347,659	693,136	304,679	388,457	323,763	84,143	28,681	55,462	23,896	1985–6	3.25	6.29	2.39	2.90	5.74	2.10	1.49	1.35
1987	886,426	381,767	504,659	391,916	791,770	350,925	440,845	364,289	94,656	30,842	63,814	27,627	1986–7	3.36	6.21	2.49	3.00	5.69	2.18	1.39	1.40
1988	993,908	431,337	562,571	435,781	890,329	399,979	490,350	404,162	103,579	31,358	72,221	31,619	1987–8	3.33	6.12	2.48	2.98	5.65	2.16	1.34	1.23
1989	1,127,961	495,583	632,378	482,372	1,005,150	461,908	543,242	441,403	122,811	33,675	89,136	40,969	1988–9	3.13	5.87	2.30	2.80	5.46	1.99	1.07	0.91
1990	1,286,196	576,172	710,024	533,239	1,144,039	537,748	606,291	486,433	142,157	38,424	103,733	46,806	1989–90	3.08	5.89	2.23	2.75	5.50	1.91	1.38	1.18
1991	1,457,212	653,192	804,020	598,616	1,296,299	609,291	687,008	545,606	160,913	43,901	117,012	53,010	1990–1	3.00	5.91	2.14	2.67	5.51	1.83	1.45	1.16
1992	1,711,605	772,374	939,231	681,228	1,534,234	725,219	809,015	624,143	177,371	47,155	130,216	57,085	1991–2	3.02	5.74	2.18	2.70	5.37	1.87	1.24	1.19
1993	1,944,754	880,457	1,064,297	747,259	1,737,747	825,616	912,131	681,975	207,007	54,841	152,166	65,284	1992–3	3.05	5.84	2.19	2.73	5.48	1.88	1.38	1.26
1994	2,144,285	970,452	1,173,833	808,478	1,921,762	909,237	1,012,525	737,706	222,523	61,215	161,308	70,772	1993–4	2.93	5.60	2.10	2.62	5.25	1.81	1.16	1.02
1995	2,479,822	1,109,118	1,370,704	926,943	2,222,611	1,041,958	1,180,653	848,783	257,211	67,160	190,051	78,160	1994–5	2.82	5.44	2.03	2.53	5.11	1.75	1.37	1.03
1996	2,998,698	1,270,492	1,728,206	1,159,654	2,696,837	1,199,172	1,497,665	1,067,742	301,861	71,320	230,541	91,912	1995–6	2.87	5.40	2.11	2.57	5.09	1.82	1.48	1.26
1997	3,384,845	1,426,154	1,958,691	1,290,942	3,086,238	1,350,268	1,735,970	1,201,887	298,607	75,886	222,721	89,055	1996–7	2.88	5.60	2.13	2.61	5.29	1.87	1.31	1.16
1998	3,745,028	1,563,424	2,181,604	1,420,215	3,422,806	1,481,724	1,941,082	1,317,796	322,222	81,700	240,522	102,419	1997–8	2.88	5.14	2.19	2.63	4.87	1.94	1.70	1.36
1999	4,125,124	1,714,274	2,410,850	1,551,295	3,794,555	1,626,912	2,167,643	1,449,121	330,569	87,362	243,207	102,174	1998–9	2.75	4.83	2.11	2.52	4.58	1.88	1.17	1.07
2000	4,507,095	1,851,659	2,655,436	1,704,478	4,119,239	1,747,838	2,371,401	1,581,303	387,856	103,821	284,035	123,175	1999–00	2.73	4.73	2.11	2.51	4.48	1.89	2.05	1.60
2001	4,821,350	1,963,023	2,858,327	1,810,734	4,402,554	1,846,400	2,556,154	1,678,669	418,796	116,623	302,173	132,065	2000–1	2.71	4.87	2.08	2.48	4.59	1.86	2.19	1.87
2002	5,243,262	2,121,436	3,121,436	1,985,034	4,795,862	1,991,896	2,803,966	1,845,909	447,400	129,540	317,860	139,125	2001–2	2.69	–	–	2.46	–	–	2.02	1.84

Notes: * Average of beginning and year-end capital stock as ratio of the year's Net Domestic Product (NDP) at factor cost for respective sectors
$ Based on increase in NDP at factor cost
– data are not available.

Source: Central Statistical Organisation (CSO): *National Accounts Statistics,* various issues.

TABLE II(1)
Production Trends in Major Agricultural Crops

(Million tonnes)

Year	Rice	Wheat	Coarse cereals	Total cereals	Pulses	Total food-grains	Total# oil-seeds	Cotton (Lint)@	Jute and mesta*	Tobacco	Sugar-cane	Tea $ (in million kgs)	Coffee
(1)	(2)	(3)	(4)	(5)	(6)	(7)	(8)	(9)	(10)	(11)	(12)	(13)	(14)
1950–1	20.58	6.46	15.38	42.42	8.41	50.83	5.16	3.04	3.31	0.26	57.05	–	–
1951–2	21.30	6.18	16.09	43.57	8.42	51.99	5.03	3.28	4.72	0.21	61.63	–	–
1952–3	22.90	7.50	19.61	50.01	9.19	59.20	4.73	3.34	5.32	0.25	51.00	–	–
1953–4	28.21	8.02	22.97	59.20	10.62	69.82	5.37	4.13	3.77	0.27	44.41	–	–
1954–5	25.22	9.04	22.82	57.08	10.95	68.03	6.40	4.45	3.86	0.26	58.74	–	–
1955–6	27.56	8.76	19.49	55.81	11.04	66.85	5.73	4.18	5.39	0.30	60.54	–	–
1956–7	29.04	9.40	19.87	58.31	11.55	69.86	6.36	4.92	5.81	0.31	69.05	–	–
1957–8	25.53	7.99	21.23	54.75	9.56	64.31	6.35	4.96	5.33	0.24	71.16	–	–
1958–9	30.85	9.96	23.18	63.99	13.15	77.14	7.30	4.88	6.91	0.32	73.36	–	–
1959–60	31.68	10.32	22.87	64.87	11.80	76.67	6.56	3.68	5.69	0.29	77.82	–	–
1960–1	34.58	11.00	23.74	69.32	12.70	82.02	6.98	5.60	5.26	0.31	110.00	–	–
1961–2	35.66	12.07	23.22	70.95	11.76	82.71	7.28	4.85	8.24	0.34	103.97	–	–
1962–3	33.21	10.78	24.63	68.62	11.53	80.15	7.39	5.54	7.19	0.34	91.91	–	–
1963–4	37.00	9.85	23.72	70.57	10.07	80.64	7.13	5.75	7.98	0.36	104.23	–	–
1964–5	39.31	12.26	25.37	76.94	12.42	89.36	8.56	6.01	7.66	0.36	121.91	–	–
1965–6	30.59	10.40	21.42	62.41	9.94	72.35	6.40	4.85	5.78	0.29	123.99	–	–
1966–7	30.44	11.39	24.05	65.88	8.35	74.23	6.43	5.27	6.58	0.35	92.83	–	–
1967–8	37.61	16.54	28.80	82.95	12.10	95.05	8.30	5.78	7.59	0.37	95.50	–	–
1968–9	39.76	18.65	25.18	83.59	10.42	94.01	6.85	5.45	3.84	0.36	124.68	–	–
1969–70	40.43	20.09	27.29	87.81	11.69	99.50	7.73	5.56	6.79	0.34	135.02	–	–
1970–1	42.22	23.83	30.55	96.61	11.82	108.42	9.63	4.76	6.19	0.36	126.37	419.00	110.20
1971–2	43.07	26.41	24.60	94.07	11.09	105.17	9.08	6.95	6.84	0.42	113.57	435.00	68.90
1972–3	39.24	24.74	23.14	87.12	9.91	97.03	7.14	5.74	6.09	0.37	124.87	456.00	91.10
1973–4	44.05	21.78	28.83	94.66	10.01	104.67	9.39	6.31	7.68	0.46	140.81	472.00	86.40
1974–5	39.58	24.10	26.13	89.81	10.02	99.83	9.15	7.16	5.83	0.36	144.29	489.00	92.50
1975–6	48.74	28.84	30.41	108.00	13.04	121.03	10.61	5.95	5.91	0.35	140.60	487.00	84.00
1976–7	41.92	29.01	28.88	99.81	11.36	111.17	8.43	5.84	7.10	0.42	153.01	512.00	102.20
1977–8	52.67	31.75	30.02	114.43	11.97	126.41	9.66	7.24	7.15	0.49	176.97	556.00	125.10
1978–9	53.77	35.51	30.44	119.72	12.18	131.90	10.10	7.96	8.33	0.45	151.66	564.00	110.50
1979–80	42.33	31.83	26.97	101.13	8.57	109.70	8.74	7.65	7.96	0.44	128.83	544.00	149.80
1980–1	53.63	36.31	29.02	118.96	10.63	129.59	9.37	7.01	8.16	0.48	154.25	569.60	118.60
1981–2	53.25	37.45	31.09	121.79	11.51	133.30	12.08	7.88	8.37	0.52	186.36	560.40	150.00
1982–3	47.12	42.79	27.75	117.66	11.86	129.52	10.00	7.53	7.17	0.58	189.51	560.70	130.00
1983–4	60.10	45.48	33.90	139.49	12.89	152.37	12.69	6.39	7.72	0.49	174.08	581.50	105.00
1984–5	58.34	44.07	31.17	133.58	11.96	145.54	12.95	8.51	7.79	0.49	170.32	639.90	195.10
1985–6	63.83	47.05	26.20	137.08	13.36	150.44	10.83	8.73	12.65	0.44	170.65	656.20	122.30
1986–7	60.56	44.32	26.83	131.71	11.71	143.42	11.27	6.91	8.62	0.46	186.09	624.60	192.30
1987–8	56.86	46.17	26.36	129.39	10.96	140.35	12.65	6.38	6.78	0.37	196.74	674.30	123.00
1988–9	70.49	54.11	31.47	156.07	13.85	169.92	18.03	8.74	7.86	0.49	203.04	701.10	215.00
1989–90	73.57	49.85	34.76	158.18	12.86	171.04	16.92	11.42	8.29	0.55	225.57	684.10	118.00
1990–1	74.29	55.14	32.70	162.13	14.26	176.39	18.61	9.84	9.23	0.56	241.05	720.34	170.00
1991–2	74.68	55.69	25.99	156.36	12.02	168.38	18.60	9.71	10.29	0.58	254.00	754.19	208.00

(contd.)

TABLE II(1) contd.

(1)	(2)	(3)	(4)	(5)	(6)	(7)	(8)	(9)	(10)	(11)	(12)	(13)	(14)
1992–3	72.86	57.21	36.59	166.66	12.82	179.48	20.11	11.40	8.59	0.60	228.03	703.93	169.40
1993–4	80.30	59.84	30.82	170.95	13.30	184.26	21.50	10.74	8.43	0.56	229.66	760.83	208.00
1994–5	81.81	65.77	29.88	177.46	14.04	191.50	21.34	11.89	9.08	0.57	275.54	752.90	180.00
1995–6	76.98	62.10	29.03	168.11	12.31	180.42	22.11	12.86	8.81	0.54	281.10	756.02	223.00
1996–7	81.74	69.35	34.10	185.19	14.24	199.44	24.38	14.23	11.13	0.62	277.56	780.14	205.00
1997–8	82.53	66.35	30.40	179.29	12.98	192.26	21.32	10.85	11.02	0.64	279.54	837.64	228.30
1998–9	86.08	71.29	31.34	188.71	14.91	203.61	24.75	12.29	9.81	0.74	288.72	854.78	265.00
1999–00	89.68	76.37	30.33	196.38	13.42	209.80	20.72	11.53	10.56	0.52	299.32	835.35	292.00
2000–1	87.70	69.68	31.08	188.46	11.08	199.54	18.44	9.52	10.56	0.49	295.96	848.36	301.00
2001–2	93.08	71.81	33.94	198.84	13.23	212.02	20.80	10.09	11.64		300.10	847.25	306.00
2002–3A	72.66	65.10	25.29	171.30	11.14	174.19	15.06	8.72	11.30		281.58	–	280.00
Decadal Growth Rates in Per Cent per Annum													
1950–1 to 1959–60	4.46	5.17	3.66	4.27	4.10	4.25	4.10	4.30	5.73	2.63	4.35	–	–
1960–1 to 1969–70	1.19	6.81	1.51	2.34	–1.28	1.86	0.29	0.30	–2.18	0.82	1.82	–	–
1970–1 to 1979–80	1.90	4.31	1.12	2.34	–0.39	2.07	0.73	3.68	2.59	2.08	2.55	3.32	5.01
1980–1 to 1989–90	3.61	3.57	0.35	2.85	1.49	2.74	5.45	2.80	0.14	–1.04	2.71	2.69	2.17
1990–1 to 2000–1	1.94	3.10	0.00	2.00	–0.37	1.84	1.03	0.86	1.76	–0.11	2.57	1.87	5.49

Notes: A: Advance Estimates (Fourth)
* Production in million bales of 180 kg. each.
# Total of nine oilseeds.
@ Production in million bales of 170 kg. each.
$ January to December.
Source: RBI (2003): *Handbook of Statistics on the Indian Economy 2002–3.*

TABLE II(2)
Trends in Yields of Major Crops

(kg per hectare)

Year	Rice	Wheat	Coarse cereals	Total cereals	Pulses	Total food-grains	Total# oil-seeds	Cotton	Jute and mesta	Tobacco	Sugar-cane	Tea	Coffee
(1)	(2)	(3)	(4)	(5)	(6)	(7)	(8)	(9)	(10)	(11)	(12)	(13)	(14)
1950-1	668	663	408	542	441	522	481	88	1043	731	33422	–	–
1951-2	714	653	414	557	448	536	430	85	1074	723	31786	–	–
1952-3	764	763	462	607	463	580	424	89	1028	675	29495	–	–
1953-4	902	750	506	678	489	640	488	100	992	737	31497	–	–
1954-5	820	803	520	664	500	631	511	100	1021	737	36303	–	–
1955-6	874	708	449	639	476	605	474	88	1038	739	32779	–	–
1956-7	900	695	473	664	495	629	509	104	977	728	33683	–	–
1957-8	790	682	495	630	424	587	502	105	944	669	34325	–	–
1958-9	930	789	519	707	541	672	561	104	1130	836	37658	–	–
1959-60	937	772	522	713	475	662	470	86	1049	716	36414	–	–
1960-1	1013	851	528	753	539	710	507	125	1049	766	45549	–	–
1961-2	1028	890	519	763	485	706	493	103	1104	811	42349	–	–
1962-3	931	793	556	733	475	680	482	122	1041	842	40996	–	–
1963-4	1033	730	540	757	416	687	481	119	1130	817	46353	–	–
1964-5	1078	913	514	817	520	757	561	122	1136	876	46838	–	–
1965-6	862	827	483	676	438	629	419	104	936	778	43717	–	–
1966-7	863	887	533	707	377	644	428	114	1058	834	40336	–	–
1967-8	1032	1103	608	840	534	783	530	123	1137	871	40665	–	–
1968-9	1076	1169	545	843	490	781	473	122	855	821	49236	–	–
1969-70	1073	1208	578	865	531	805	522	122	1120	770	49121	–	–
1970-1	1123	1307	665	949	524	872	579	106	1032	810	48322	1182	816
1971-2	1141	1380	564	936	501	858	526	151	1107	914	47511	1221	499
1972-3	1070	1271	548	886	474	813	452	127	1104	837	50933	1271	620
1973-4	1151	1172	623	918	427	827	555	142	1188	1001	51163	1311	554
1974-5	1045	1338	606	907	455	824	529	161	1068	954	49855	1353	593
1975-6	1235	1410	694	1041	533	944	627	138	1164	950	50903	1341	488
1976-7	1089	1387	689	985	494	894	512	144	1173	969	53383	1407	544
1977-8	1308	1480	710	1100	510	991	563	157	1108	979	56160	1519	652
1978-9	1328	1568	721	1136	515	1022	570	167	1186	1109	49114	1528	564
1979-80	1074	1436	652	982	385	876	516	160	1177	1031	49358	1455	749
1980-1	1336	1630	695	1142	473	1023	532	152	1130	1065	57844	1491	565
1981-2	1308	1691	733	1157	483	1032	639	166	1311	1172	58359	1461	691
1982-3	1231	1816	685	1150	519	1035	563	163	1265	1157	56441	1422	573
1983-4	1457	1843	813	1296	548	1162	679	141	1320	1120	55978	1468	453
1984-5	1417	1870	795	1285	526	1149	684	196	1242	1113	57673	1606	830
1985-6	1552	2046	664	1323	547	1175	570	197	1524	1111	59889	1641	507
1986-7	1471	1916	675	1266	506	1128	605	169	1454	1187	60444	1508	791
1987-8	1465	2002	721	1315	515	1173	629	168	1274	1155	60006	1628	508
1988-9	1689	2244	814	1493	598	1331	824	202	1540	1307	60992	1693	878
1989-90	1745	2121	922	1530	549	1349	742	252	1646	1335	65612	1652	478
1990-1	1740	2281	900	1571	578	1380	771	225	1634	1353	65395	1727	627
1991-2	1751	2394	778	1574	533	1382	719	216	1662	1369	66069	1800	746

(contd.)

TABLE II(2) contd.

(1)	(2)	(3)	(4)	(5)	(6)	(7)	(8)	(9)	(10)	(11)	(12)	(13)	(14)
1992–3	1744	2327	1063	1654	573	1457	797	257	1658	1425	63843	1664	582
1993–4	1888	2380	939	1701	598	1501	799	249	1713	1463	67120	1796	712
1994–5	1911	2559	929	1760	610	1546	843	257	1760	1486	71254	1767	614
1995–6	1797	2483	940	1703	552	1491	851	242	1712	1356	67787	1770	731
1996–7	1882	2679	1072	1831	635	1614	926	265	1818	1444	66496	1809	675
1997–8	1900	2485	986	1775	567	1552	816	208	1792	1394	71134	1865	746
1998–9	1921	2590	1068	1856	634	1627	944	224	1722	1451	71203	1995	805
1999–00	1986	2778	1034	1926	635	1704	853	225	1836	1211	70935	1840	858
2000–1	1961	2708	1027	1871	544	1648	810	190	1867	1704	68577	–	869
2001–2	2086	2770	1142	1983	609	1739	897	189	1996	–	68154	–	861
Decadal Growth Rates in Per Cent per Annum													
1950–1 to 1959–60	3.15	1.09	2.33	2.59	0.93	2.26	1.55	1.24	–0.03	0.46	1.72		
1960–1 to 1969–70	0.36	4.46	0.91	1.36	0.03	1.32	–0.12	0.44	–0.70	0.15	0.73		
1970–1 to 1979–80	1.02	1.87	2.00	1.90	–0.98	1.60	0.33	3.30	1.06	2.58	0.64	2.79	0.05
1980–1 to 1989–90	3.19	3.11	1.70	3.11	1.58	2.97	2.95	4.09	3.11	1.81	1.23	1.67	0.45
1990–1 to 2000–1	1.34	1.82	2.14	2.16	1.28	2.16	2.07	–0.41	1.12	–0.50	1.05	1.15	2.83

Notes: # For nine Oilseeds out of eleven in all.
– means not available
Source: RBI (2003): *Handbook of Statistics on the Indian Economy 2002–3.*

TABLE II(3)
Structural Changes in Indian Industry and Decadal Growth

Sector group	Weight as per index numbers					Growth rates per cent per annum			
	1956 =100	1960 =100	1970 =100	1980–1 =100	1993–4 =100	1970–1 to 1979–80	1980–1 to 1990–1	1990–1 to 1993–4	1993–4 to 2002–3
Mining and quarrying	7.47	9.72	9.69	11.5	10.47	4.6	7.6	1.4	3.0
Manufacturing	88.85	84.91	81.08	77.1	79.36	4.7	7.7	2.4	6.7
Electricity	3.68	5.37	9.23	11.4	10.17	4.2	9.1	6.8	5.7
General index	100.00	100.00	100.00	100.00	100.00	7.6	7.9	2.9	6.3
Use-based category									
Basic goods	22.33	25.11	32.28	39.42	35.51	6.0	7.9	5.8	5.0
Capital goods	4.71	11.76	15.25	16.43	9.69	5.6	11.3	–3.9	6.6
Intermediate goods	24.59	25.88	20.95	20.51	26.44	3.5	6.3	4.9	7.4
Consumer goods	48.37	37.25	31.52	23.65	28.36	3.4	6.5	2.2	6.6
Consumer durables	2.21	5.68	3.41	2.55	5.12	4.6	14.8	0.7	10.4
Consumer non-durables	46.16	31.57	28.11	21.10	23.25	3.3	5.1	2.6	5.5

Note: Growth indicates compound growth rate in index numbers of industrial production for groups and general index calculated for the specified period using the semi-log model lnY = a + bt, where, t = time, Y = index value and the compound growth is obtained by taking antilog of 'b', deducting one from it and multiplying it with 100.
Source: EPWRF (2002): *Annual Survey of Industries 1973–4 to 1997–8: A Data Base on the Industrial Sector in India*, EPW Research Foundation, Mumbai.

TABLE II(4)

Index of Industrial Production with Major Groups and Sub-groups

1993-4 = 100

Major groups	Weight	Annual average growth		2002-3	2001-2	2000-1	1999-2000	1998-9	1997-8	1996-7	1995-6	1994-5
		1993-4 to 2002-3	1980-1 to 1992-3									
(1)	(2)	(3)	(4)	(5)	(6)	(7)	(8)	(9)	(10)	(11)	(12)	(13)
General index	100.0	6.6	6.8	176.7 (5.8)	167.0 (2.6)	162.7 (5.2)	154.7 (6.5)	145.2 (4.1)	139.5 (6.7)	130.8 (6.1)	123.3 (13.0)	109.1 (9.1)
Mining and quarrying	10.47	3.9	7.0 183.1	139.6 (5.8)	131.9 (0.4)	131.4 (3.7)	126.7 (1.0)	125.4 (-1.7)	126.4 (6.9)	118.2 (-1.9)	120.5 (9.7)	109.8 (9.8)
Manufacturing	79.36	7.0	6.5	172.7 (6.0)	167.9 (2.9)	159.4 (5.3)	148.8 (7.1)	142.5 (4.4)	133.6 (6.7)	124.5 (7.3)	109.1 (14.1)	(9.1)
Electricity	10.17	5.7	8.6	164.3 (3.2)	159.2 (3.1)	154.4 (4.0)	148.5 (7.3)	138.4 (6.5)	130.0 (6.6)	122 (4.0)	117.3 (8.1)	108.5
Use-based classification												
Basic goods industries	35.57	5.4	7.3	159.8 (4.8)	152.5 (2.4)	148.9 (3.9)	143.3 (5.5)	135.8 (1.6)	133.6 (6.9)	125 (3.0)	121.4 (10.8)	109.6 (9.6)
Capital goods industries	9.26	6.7	8.8	177.3 (10.4)	160.6 (-3.4)	166.2 (1.8)	163.3 (6.9)	152.7 (12.6)	135.6 (5.8)	128.2 (11.5)	115 (5.3)	109.2 (9.2)
Intermediate goods industries	26.51	7.3	5.2	187.0 (3.8)	180.1 (1.5)	177.4 (4.7)	169.5 (8.8)	155.8 (6.1)	146.8 (8.0)	135.9 (8.1)	125.7 (19.4)	105.3 (5.3)
Consumer goods industries	28.66	7.3	5.8	187.7 (7.2)	175.1 (6.0)	165.2 (8.0)	153 (5.7)	144.8 (2.2)	141.7 (5.5)	134.3 (6.2)	126.5 (12.8)	112.1 (12.1)
a. Consumer durables	5.37	10.4	10.6	237.4 (-6.4)	253.7 (11.5)	227.6 (14.5)	198.7 (14.1)	174.1 (5.6)	164.9 (7.8)	152.9 (4.6)	146.2 (25.8)	116.2 (16.2)
b. Consumer non-durables	23.30	6.6	5.1	176.3 (12.3)	157 (4.1)	150.8 (5.8)	142.5 (3.2)	138.1 (1.2)	136.5 (4.8)	130.2 (6.6)	122.1 (9.8)	111.2 (11.2)
Groupwise (2-digit level)												
20-1 food products	90.83	6.2	5.0	168.2 (10.6)	152.0 (-1.6)	154.5 (10.1)	140.3 (4.2)	134.7 (0.7)	133.8 (-0.4)	134.3 (3.5)	129.8 (6.7)	121.6 (21.6)
22 Beverages, Tobacco and related products	23.82	12.6	1.4	286.1 (27.3)	224.8 (12.2)	200.4 (4.3)	192.1 (7.6)	178.5 (12.9)	158.1 (19.4)	132.4 (13.5)	116.7 (13.3)	103 (3.0)
23 Cotton Textiles	55.18	2.4	3.7	121.5 (-2.4)	124.5 (-2.2)	127.3 (2.9)	123.7 (6.7)	115.9 (-7.7)	125.6 (2.4)	122.7 (12.1)	109.5 (10.5)	99.1 (-0.9)
24 Wool, silk and man-made fibre textiles	22.58	9.7	-0.6	226.7 (3.8)	218.5 (4.4)	209.3 (5.8)	197.8 (11.9)	176.8 (2.8)	172 (18.5)	145.1 (10.5)	131.3 (14.7)	114.5 (14.5)
25 Jute and other vegetable fibre textiles (except cotton)	5.9	1.1	-0.3	108 (8.4)	99.6 (-5.8)	105.8 (0.8)	105 (-0.9)	106 (-7.3)	114.3 (16.9)	97.8 (-4.5)	102.4 (7.7)	95.1 (-4.9)

(contd.)

TABLE II(4) contd.

(1)	(2)	(3)	(4)	(5)	(6)	(7)	(8)	(9)	(10)	(11)	(12)	(13)
26 Textile Products (including wearing apparel)	25.37	8.1	7.4	192.2 (15.6)	166.3 (2.4)	162.4 (4.0)	156.1 (2.0)	153.1 (-3.5)	158.7 (8.5)	146.3 (9.4)	133.7 (35.7)	98.5 (-1.5)
27 Wood and wood products and fixtures	27.01	-2.2	6.6	76.3 (-17.8)	92.8 (-11.0)	104.3 (2.9)	101.4 (-16.2)	121 (-5.8)	128.5 (-2.6)	131.9 (7.1)	123.2 (24.1)	99.3 (-0.7)
28 Paper & paper products and printing, publishing & allied Industries	26.52	6.9	6.2	178.4 (5.6)	169.0 (3.0)	164 (-9.1)	180.5 (6.3)	169.8 (16.0)	146.4 (6.9)	136.9 (9.1)	125.5 (15.6)	108.6 (8.6)
29 Leather and leather & fur products	11.39	5.2	4.9	153.4 (-2.9)	158.0 (5.4)	150 (10.7)	135.5 (13.8)	119.1 (8.1)	110.2 (2.2)	107.8 (9.4)	98.5 (13.7)	86.6 (-13.4)
30 Basic chemicals & chemical products (except products of petroleum & coal)	140.02	7.6	9.0	192.4 (4.0)	185.0 (4.8)	176.6 (7.3)	164.6 (10.0)	149.7 (6.6)	140.4 (14.4)	122.7 (4.8)	117.1 (11.2)	105.3 (5.3)
31 Rubber, plastic, petroleum and coal products	57.28	6.7	6.6 (4.9)	178.7 (11.1)	170.4 (11.8)	153.4 (-1.1)	137.2 (11.3)	138.7 (5.2)	124.6 (2.0)	118.4 (7.8)	116.1 (7.7)	107.7
32 Non-metallic mineral products	43.97	10.1	4.6	231.8 (5.0)	220.7 (1.2)	218.2 (-1.2)	220.8 (24.4)	177.5 (8.3)	163.9 (13.4)	144.5 (7.9)	133.9 (23.6)	108.3 (8.3)
33 Basic metal and alloy industries	74.53	6.2	2.1	170.3 (9.2)	156.0 (4.3)	149.6 (1.8)	146.9 (5.0)	139.9 (-2.5)	143.5 (2.6)	139.8 (6.7)	131 (15.8)	113.1 (13.1)
34 Metal products and parts, except machinery and equipment	28.1	5.1	5.2	151.7 (6.4)	142.6 (-10.1)	158.5 (15.0)	137.8 (-1.2)	139.5 (17.0)	119.2 (7.9)	110.5 (9.7)	100.7 (-4.6)	105.6 (5.6)
35-36 Machinery and equipment other than transport equipment	95.65	8.3	15.0	201.9 (1.8)	198.3 (1.3)	195.8 (7.3)	182.5 (17.7)	155 (1.5)	152.7 (5.8)	144.3 (5.0)	137.4 (18.7)	115.8 (15.8)
37 Transport equipment and parts	39.84	10.1	6.0	233.6 (14.9)	203.3 (6.8)	190.3 (-2.0)	194.1 (5.7)	183.6 (20.1)	152.9 (2.5)	149.1 (12.5)	132.5 (17.4)	112.9 (12.9)
38 Other manufacturing industries	25.59	7.0	11.5	172.4 (-0.5)	173.2 (8.9)	159.1 (11.6)	142.5 (-16.0)	169.7 (1.0)	168 (-1.3)	170.2 (24.7)	136.5 (25.8)	108.5 (8.5)

(contd.)

TABLE II(4)
Index of Industrial Production with Major Groups and Sub-groups

	Weight	1993-4	1992-3	1991-2	1990-1	1989-90	1988-9	1987-8	1986-7	1985-6	1984-5	1983-4	1982-3	1981-2
		(14)	(15)	(16)	(17)	(18)	(19)	(20)	(21)	(22)	(23)	(24)	(25)	(26)
General index	100.00	232.0	218.9	213.9	212.6	196.4	180.9	166.4	155.1	142.1	130.7	120.4	112.8	109.3
	(6.0)	(2.3)	(0.6)	(8.2)	(8.6)	(8.7)	(7.3)	(9.1)	(8.7)	(8.6)	(6.7)	(3.2)	(9.3)	
Mining and quarrying	11.46	231.5	223.7	222.5	221.2	211.6	199.1	184.6	177.9	167.5	160.9	147.8	132.3	117.7
	(3.5)	(0.5)	(0.6)	(4.5)	(6.3)	(7.9)	(3.8)	(6.2)	(4.1)	(8.9)	(11.7)	(12.4)	(17.7)	
Manufacturing	77.11	223.5	210.7	206.2	207.8	190.7	175.6	161.5	149.7	136.9	124.8	115.6	109.4	107.9
	(6.1)	(2.2)	(-0.8)	(9.0)	(8.6)	(8.7)	(7.9)	(9.3)	(9.7)	(8.0)	(5.7)	(1.4)	(7.9)	
Electricity	11.43	290.0	269.9	257.0	236.8	219.7	198.2	181.0	168.1	152.4	140.4	125.4	116.5	110.2
	(7.4)	(5.0)	(8.5)	(7.8)	(10.8)	(9.5)	(7.7)	(10.3)	(8.5)	(12.0)	(7.6)	(5.7)	(10.2)	
Use-based Classification														
Basic goods industries	39.42	254.9	232.9	226.9	213.1	199.4	189.2	172.2	163	149.2	139.7	125.7	118.7	110.9
	(9.5)	(2.6)	(6.5)	(6.9)	(5.4)	(9.9)	(5.6)	(9.2)	(6.8)	(11.1)	(5.9)	(7.0)	(10.9)	
Capital goods industries	16.43	255.4	266.4	266.8	291.6	251.5	206.4	192.8	166.3	140.7	127.2	123.5	110.6	106.7
	(-4.1)	(-0.1)	(-8.5)	(15.9)	(21.9)	(7.1)	(15.9)	(18.2)	(10.6)	(3.0)	(11.7)	(3.7)	(6.7)	
Intermediate goods industries	20.51	203.9	182.6	173.2	176.8	168.9	161.9	148.3	141.5	135.5	126.1	114.9	104.6	103.7
	(11.7)	(5.4)	(-2.1)	(4.7)	(-4.3)	(9.2)	(4.8)	(4.4)	(7.5)	(9.7)	(9.8)	(0.9)	(3.7)	
Consumer goods industries	23.65	202.0	194.2	190.8	189	177	166.2	156.6	147.1	137.3	122	113.8	112	113.8
	(4.0)	(1.8)	(1.0)	(6.8)	(6.5)	(6.1)	(6.5)	(7.1)	(12.5)	(7.2)	(1.6)	(-1.6)	(13.8)	
a. Consumer durables	2.55	369.4	318.1	320.5	359.6	324.9	317.3	260.1	241.2	202.8	170.8	140.5	121	110.9
	(16.1)	(-0.8)	(-10.9)	(10.7)	(2.4)	(22.0)	(7.8)	(18.9)	(18.7)	(21.6)	(16.1)	(9.1)	(10.9)	
b. Consumer non-durables	21.10	181.7	179.3	175.1	168.4	159.2	148	144.1	135.7	129.4	116.1	110.5	110.9	114.1
	(1.4)	(2.4)	(4.0)	(5.8)	(7.6)	(2.7)	(6.2)	(4.9)	(11.5)	(5.1)	(-0.4)	(-2.8)	(11.4)	
Groupwise (2-digit level)														
20-21 Food products	5.33	160.0	175.3	178	169.8	150.9	148.5	139	133.2	125.6	119.1	121.1	129.5	113.5
	(-8.7)	(-1.5)	(4.8)	(12.5)	(1.6)	(6.8)	(4.4)	(6.1)	(5.5)	(-1.7)	(-6.5)	(14.1)	(13.5)	
22 Beverages, tobacco and tobacco products	1.57	137.8	113.7	107.3	104.8	103	92.1	84.9	98.5	112.1	111.7	104.5	107.8	104.3
	(21.2)	(6.0)	(2.4)	(1.7)	(11.8)	(8.5)	(-13.8)	(-12.1)	(0.4)	(6.9)	(-3.1)	(-3.4)	(-4.3)	
23 Cotton textiles	12.31	160.5	150.1	139	126.8	112.3	107.8	111.2	112.5	110.4	102.2	100.2	89.4	99.7
	(6.9)	(8.0)	(9.6)	(12.9)	(4.2)	(-3.1)	(-1.2)	(1.9)	(8.0)	(2.0)	(12.1)	(-10.3)	(-0.3)	
25 Jute, hemp and mesta textiles	2.00	103.2	87	90.8	101.2	97	101.9	91	101.1	97.3	99.4	78.2	92.9	95.7
	(18.6)	(-4.2)	(-10.3)	(-4.3)	(-4.8)	(12.0)	(-10.0)	(3.9)	(-2.1)	(27.1)	(-15.8)	(-2.9)	(-4.3)	
26 Other textiles (incl. wearing apparel other than footwear	0.82	73.4	75.8	97.2	103.2	151.7	134.2	91.7	87.1	112.8	95.6	92.1	99.3	96.7
	(-3.2)	(-22.0)	(-5.8)	(-32.0)	(3.0)	(46.3)	(5.4)	(-22.8)	(18.0)	(3.8)	(-7.3)	(2.7)	(-3.3)	
27 Wood and wood products furnitures and fixtures	0.45	199.3	190.5	185	197.2	176	171.7	161.7	246.1	223.2	216.5	167.5	153	153.2
	(4.6)	(3.0)	(-6.2)	(12.1)	(2.5)	(6.2)	(-34.5)	(10.3)	(3.1)	(29.3)	(9.5)	(-0.1)	(53.2)	
28 Paper and paper products and printing and publishing and allied industries	3.24	224.8	210.9	203	198	181.5	171.6	166.3	163.2	148.5	131.9	109.3	105.5	108.3
	(6.6)	(3.9)	(2.6)	(9.0)	(5.8)	(3.2)	(1.9)	(9.9)	(12.6)	(20.7)	(3.6)	(-2.6)	(8.3)	

(contd.)

TABLE II(4) contd.

	(14)	(15)	(16)	(17)	(18)	(19)	(20)	(21)	(22)	(23)	(24)	(25)	(26)	
29 Leather and leather prod.	0.49 (8.8)	204.3 (3.5)	187.7 (−6.7)	181.3 (3.2)	194.3 (6.2)	188.3 (−4.4)	177.4 (4.4)	185.5 (5.0)	177.7 (21.1)	169.2 (20.1)	139.7 (16.3)	116.3 (−21.9)	100 (28.1)	128.1
30 Rubber, plastic, petroleum and coal products	4.00	176.4 (1.0)	174.6 (1.5)	172 (−1.1)	174 (0.3)	173.5 (3.1)	168.3 (8.5)	155.1 (3.7)	149.6 (−2.2)	153 (3.9)	147.2 (8.2)	136.1 (14.4)	119 (−0.2)	119.2 (19.2)
31 Chemicals and chemical products except products of petroleum and coal	12.51	297.9 (7.6)	276.9 (6.0)	261.2 (2.8)	254.1 (2.6)	247.6 (6.1)	233.4 (16.1)	200.9 (14.5)	175.5 (13.7)	154.3 (8)	142.9 (9.1)	131 (8.1)	121.2 (3.7)	116.9 (16.9)
32 Non-metallic mineral products	3.00	218.5 (4.5)	209 (1.8)	205.2 (6.2)	193.1 (1.7)	189.9 (2.8)	184.6 (16.8)	158.1 (−1.4)	160.3 (1.9)	157.3 (13.7)	138.4 (13.3)	122.2 (17.8)	103.7 (−2.8)	106.7 (6.7)
33 Basic metal and alloys products	9.80	224.2 (33.1)	168.5 (0.4)	167.8 (5.7)	158.8 (10.5)	143.7 (−0.8)	144.9 (6.9)	135.6 (7.0)	126.8 (8.4)	117 (9.0)	107.3 (12.8)	95.1 (−8.7)	104.2 (4.2)	100 (0.0)
34 Metal products and parts except machinery and transport equipment	2.29	126.5 (1.6)	124.6 (−6.4)	133.1 (−7.0)	143.1 (0.4)	142.6 (6.8)	133.5 (3.0)	129.6 (4.1)	124.5 (8.5)	114.7 (9.2)	105.0 (19.2)	88.1 (−2.0)	89.9 (−5.0)	94.6 (−5.4)
35 Machinery, machine tools and parts except electrical machinery	6.24	189.2 (4.4)	181.1 (−1.2)	183.3 (−1.9)	186.9 (8.6)	172 (6.7)	161.2 (15.8)	139.2 (−1.8)	141.8 (8.9)	130.2 (2.0)	127.6 (6.7)	119.6 (6.8)	112 (0.8)	111.1 (11.1)
36 Electrical machinery apparatus, appliances and supplies and parts	5.78	460.1 (−4.9)	483.6 (−2.0)	493.7 (−12.4)	563.6 (22.7)	459.2 (32.7)	346 (3.2)	335.2 (31.6)	254.7 (27.0)	200.6 (34.8)	148.8 (4.0)	143.1 (23.5)	115.9 (11.5)	103.9 (3.9)
37 Transport equipment and parts	6.39	211.2 (5.3)	200.6 (5.0)	191.1 (−0.7)	192.5 (6.3)	181.1 (5.7)	171.3 (12.8)	151.9 (4.8)	144.9 (6.7)	135.8 (3.2)	131.6 (6.6)	123.4 (10.9)	111.3 (3.0)	108.1 (8.1)
38 Other manufacturing industries	0.91	267.0 (−5.1)	281.3 (4.2)	269.9 (−16.1)	321.8 (−3.5)	333.3 (8.8)	306.3 (12.5)	272.1 (15.6)	235.4 (54.2)	152.7 (24.2)	122.9 (17.5)	104.6 (−32.5)	155 (3.9)	149.2 (49.2)

Notes: Figures in brackets indicate percentage changes over previous year; average annual growth rates are simple arithmatic averages of annual percentage changes.
Source: Central Statistical Organisation, Government of India, Ministry of Planning and Programme Implementation (www.mospi.ni.in/t2.htm).

TABLE III(1)
Budgetary Position of Government of India

(Rupees crore)

Budget Heads	2004-5 Budget	2003-4 Revised	2003-4 Budget	2002-3 Actuals	2001-2 Actuals	2000-1 Actuals	1999-00 Actuals	1998-9 Actuals	1997-8 Actuals	1996-7 Actuals	1995-6 Actuals	1994-5 Actuals	1993-4 Actuals	1992-3 Actuals	1991-2 Actuals
(1)	(2)	(3)	(4)	(5)	(10)	(12)	(13)	(14)	(15)	(16)	(17)	(18)	(20)	(21)	(22)
(1) Revenue Receipts	290,882	263,027	253,935	231,748	201,449	192,624	181,513	149,485	133,901	126,279	110,130	91,083	75,453	74,128	66,031
(a) Tax Revenue (net to centre)	220,132	187,539	184,169	159,425	133,662	136,916	128,271	104,652	95,672	93,701	81,939	67,454	53,449	54,044	50,069
(b) Non-Tax Revenue	70,750	75,488	69,766	72,323	67,787	55,708	53,242	44,833	38,229	32,578	28,191	23,629	22,004	20,084	15,962
(2) Capital Receipts	166,552	211,228	184,860	168,648	161,004	132,987	116,571	130,064	99,077	61,544	58,338	68,695	55,440	36,178	38,528
(a) Non-Debt Capital Receipts	30,100	660,752	31,223	37,342	20,049	14,171	11,855	16,507	9230	7920	6867	11,423	6143	8317	9059
of which:															
(a.1) Recovery of loans	14,100	646,252	18,023	34,191	16,403	12,046	10,131	10,633	8318	7540	6505	6345	6191	6356	6021
(a.2) Other Receipts	16,000	14,500	13,200	3151	3646	2125	1723	5874	912	455	1397	5607	-48	1961	3038
of which:															
(ai) Disinvestment of equity of PSEs	16,000	14,500	13,200	3151	3646	2125	1724	5874	912	380	362	5078	-48	1961	3038
(b) Borrowing and Other Liability	136,452	132,103	153,637	131,306	140,955	118,816	104,717	113,557	89,847	53,624	51,471	57,272	49,297	27862	29,469
(3) Total Receipts	457,434	474,255	438,795	400,396	362,453	325,611	298,084	279,549	232,963	187,823	168,468	159,778	130,893	110,306	104,559
(4) Non-Plan Expenditure	322,363	352,748	317,821	288,942	261,259	242,942	221,902	212,547	172,976	147,473	131,901	113,361	98,191	85,958	80453
(a) On Revenue Account	295,359	284,801	289,384	268,074	239,954	226,782	202,309	176,900	145,161	127,298	110,839	93,847	83,545	72,925	67,217
of which:															
(a.1) Interest payment	129,500	124,555	123,223	117,804	107,460	99,314	90,249	77,882	65,637	59,478	50,045	44,060	36,741	31,075	26,596
(b) On Capital Account	27,004	679,473	28,437	208,681	21,305	16,160	19,593	35,648	27,815	20,175	21,062	19,514	15,453	13,033	13,234
(5) Plan Expenditure	135,071	121,507	120,974	111,455	101,194	82,669	76,182	66,818	59,077	53,534	46,374	47,378	43,662	36,660	30,961
(a) On Revenue Account	85,383	78,086	76,843	71,554	61,657	51,076	46,800	40,519	35,174	31,635	29,021	28,265	24,848	19,777	15,074
(b) On Capital Account	49,688	43,421	44,131	39,901	39,537	31,593	29,382	26,299	23,903	21,899	17,353	19,113	18,814	16,883	15,887
(6) Total Expenditure (4+5)	457,434 [14.7]	474,255 [16.9]	438,795 [15.7]	400,396 [16.2]	362,453 [15.8]	325,611 [15.5]	298,084 [15.2]	279,365 [12.8]	232,053 [15.2]	201,007 [14.7]	178,275 [15.0]	160,739 [15.9]	141,853 [16.5]	122,618 [16.4]	111,414 [17.1]
(7) Revenue Deficit (1-4.a-5.a)	89,860 [2.9]	99,860 [3.6]	112,292 [4.1]	107,879 [4.4]	100,162 [4.3]	85234 [4.1]	67,596 [3.5]	67,934 [3.9]	46,449 [3.1]	32,654 [2.4]	29,730 [2.5]	31,029 [3.1]	32,716 [3.8]	18,574 [2.5]	16,261 [2.5]
(8) Fiscal Deficit (1+2a-6)	136,452 [4.4]	132,103 [4.8]	153,637 [5.6]	131,306* [5.4]	140,955* [6.1]	118,816 [5.6]	104,717 [5.4]	113,373 [6.4]	88,937 [5.8]	66,733 [4.9]	60,243 [5.1]	57,704 [5.7]	60,257 [7.0]	40,171 [5.4]	36,325 [5.6]
(9) Primary Deficit (8-4a1)	6952 [0.2]	7548 [0.3]	30,414 [1.1]	13,502 [0.6]	33,495 [1.5]	19,502 [0.9]	14,468 [0.7]	35,491 [2.0]	23,300 [1.5]	7255 [0.5]	10,198 [0.9]	13,643 [1.3]	23,562 [2.7]	9136 [1.2]	9729 [1.5]

Notes: * Based on provisional Actuals for 2002-3 and 2001-2.
Figures in brackets represent percentages to GDP at current market prices.
Source: "Union Government Accounts at a Glance", Controller General of Accounts (GOI) (www.cga.nic.in) and Central Government Budget Document Various Issues.

Table III(2)
Consolidated Budgetary Position of State Governments at a Glance

(Rs crore)

Year	Revenue account				Capital account@				Aggregate		Overall surplus(+)/ deficit (−)	Gross fiscal deficit (GFD)	Revenue deficit (RD)	RD as per cent to aggregate disbursements	GFD as per cent to aggregate disbursements
	Receipts	Expenditures	Surplus(+)/ deficit (−)	Receipts	Disbursements	Surplus(+)/ deficit (−)	Receipts	Disbursements	Receipts	Disbursements					
(1)	(2)	(3)	(4)	(5)	(6)	(7)	(8)	(9)			(10)	(11)	(12)	(13)	(14)
1980-1	16,294 (11.3)	14,808 (10.3)	1486	5473 (3.8)	7856 (5.5)	−2383	21,767 (15.1)	22,664 (15.8)			−897	3713 (2.6)	−1486 (−1.0)	−6.6	16.4
1981-2	18,455 (10.9)	17,075 (10.1)	1380	5695 (3.4)	8095 (4.8)	−2400	24,150 (14.3)	25,170 (14.9)			−1020	4062 (2.4)	−1379 (−0.8)	−5.5	16.1
1982-3	21,125 (11.2)	20,238 (10.7)	887	6796 (3.6)	8504 (4.5)	−1708	27,921 (14.8)	28,742 (15.3)			−821	4986 (2.6)	−888 (−0.5)	−3.1	17.3
1983-4	24,014 (10.9)	23,803 (10.8)	211	8966 (4.1)	9737 (4.4)	−771	32,980 (15.0)	33,540 (15.3)			−560	6359 (2.9)	−210 (−0.1)	−0.6	19.0
1984-5	27,425 (11.2)	28,349 (11.5)	−924	10,993 (4.5)	11,508 (4.7)	−515	38,418 (15.6)	39,857 (16.2)			−1439	8199 (3.3)	923 (0.4)	2.3	20.6
1985-6	33,424 (12.0)	32,770 (11.8)	654	13,131 (4.7)	12,097 (4.4)	1034	46,555 (16.7)	44,867 (16.1)			1688	7521 (2.7)	−654 (−0.2)	−1.5	16.8
1986-7	38,226 (12.3)	38,057 (12.2)	169	12,892 (4.1)	13,729 (4.4)	−837	51,118 (16.4)	51,786 (16.6)			−668	9269 (3.0)	−170 (−0.1)	−0.3	17.9
1987-8	44,000 (12.4)	45,088 (12.7)	−1088	15,806 (4.5)	14,783 (4.2)	1023	59,806 (16.9)	59,871 (16.9)			−65	11,219 (3.2)	1088 (0.3)	1.8	18.7
1988-9	50,421 (12.0)	52,228 (12.4)	−1807	17,037 (4.0)	14,850 (3.5)	2187	67,458 (16.0)	67,078 (15.9)			380	11,672 (2.8)	1807 (0.4)	2.7	17.4
1989-90	56,535 (11.6)	60,217 (12.4)	−3682	20,086 (4.1)	16,565 (3.4)	3521	76,621 (15.8)	76,782 (15.8)			−161	15,433 (3.2)	3682 (0.8)	4.8	20.1
1990-1	66,467 (11.7)	71,776 (12.6)	−5309	24,693 (4.3)	19,312 (3.4)	5381	91,160 (16.0)	91,088 (16.0)			72	18,787 (3.3)	5309 (0.9)	5.8	20.6
1991-2	80,535 (12.3)	86,186 (13.2)	−5651	27,238 (4.2)	21,743 (3.3)	5495	107,773 (16.5)	107,929 (16.5)			−156	18,900 (2.9)	5651 (0.9)	5.2	17.5
1992-3	91,090 (12.2)	96,205 (12.9)	−5115	30,073 (4.0)	23,129 (3.1)	6944	121,163 (16.2)	119,334 (15.9)			1829	20,891 (2.8)	5114 (0.7)	4.3	17.5
1993-4	105,564 (12.3)	109,376 (12.7)	−3812	28,623 (3.3)	25,272 (2.9)	3351	134,187 (15.6)	134,648 (15.7)			−461	20,596 (2.4)	3813 (0.4)	2.8	15.3
1994-5	122,284 (12.1)	128,440 (12.7)	−6156	43,738 (4.3)	33,114 (3.3)	10,624	166,022 (16.4)	161,554 (16.0)			4468	27,697 (2.7)	6156 (0.6)	3.8	17.1
1995-6	136,803 (11.5)	145,004 (12.2)	−8201	43,630 (3.7)	32,580 (2.7)	11,050	180,433 (15.2)	177,584 (14.9)			2849	31,426 (2.6)	8201 (0.7)	4.6	17.7
1996-7	152,836 (11.2)	168,950 (12.3)	−16,114	42,891 (3.1)	33,819 (2.5)	9072	195,727 (14.3)	202,769 (14.8)			−7042	37,251 (2.7)	16,114 (1.2)	7.9	18.4
1997-8	170,301 (11.2)	186,634 (12.3)	−16,333	59,937 (3.9)	41,501 (2.7)	18,436	230,238 (15.1)	228,135 (15.0)			2103	44,200 (2.9)	16,333 (1.1)	7.2	19.4
1998-9	176,448 (10.0)	220,090 (12.5)	−43,642	86,393 (4.9)	46,271 (2.6)	40,122	262,841 (14.9)	266,361 (15.1)			−3520	74,254 (4.2)	43,642 (2.5)	16.4	27.9
1999-00	207,201 (10.6)	260,998 (13.3)	−53,797	103,575 (5.3)	52,891 (2.7)	50,684	310,776 (15.9)	313,889 (16.0)			−3113	91,480 (4.7)	53,797 (2.7)	17.1	29.1
2000-1	237,953 (11.4)	291,522 (14.0)	−53,569	111,591 (5.3)	55,677 (2.7)	55,914	349,544 (16.7)	347,198 (16.6)			2346	89,532 (4.3)	53,569 (2.6)	15.4	25.8
2001-2RE	270,901 (11.9)	331,440 (14.5)	−60,539	123,532 (5.4)	70,131 (3.1)	53,401	394,433 (17.3)	401,571 (17.6)			−7138	106,595 (4.7)	60,540 (2.7)	15.1	26.5
2001-2	255,599 (11.2)	314,833 (13.8)	−59,233	124,507 (5.5)	62,722 (2.7)	61,786	380,107 (16.7)	377,555 (16.5)			2552	95,986 (4.2)	59,233 (2.6)	15.7	25.4
2002-3BE	306,845 (12.4)	355,159 (14.4)	−48,314	118,811 (4.8)	75,683 (3.1)	43,129	425,656 (17.2)	430,842 (17.4)			−5186	102,882 (4.2)	48,314 (2.0)	11.2	23.9
2002-3RE	293,873 (11.9)	355,175 (14.4)	−61,302	143,419 (5.8)	87,434 (3.5)	55,985	437,292 (17.7)	442,609 (17.9)			−5317	116,730 (4.7)	61,302 (2.5)	13.9	26.4
2003-4BE	332,919 (12.1)	381,927 (13.9)	−49,008	136,527 (5.0)	94,112 (3.4)	42,415	469,446 (17.0)	476,039 (17.3)			−6593	108,861 (4.0)	49,008 (1.8)	10.3	22.9

Notes: @ Excluding (i) Ways and means advances (WMA) from the RBI and (ii) purchases/sales of securities from cash balance investment account;these serve as financing items for overall deficit (see cols. 12 and 13).
(1) Figures in brackets represent percentage to GDP at current market prices.
(2) In column 12 & 13 negative sign represents surplus.
(3) Overall surplus or deficit shown in col. 10 represents conventional deficit, that is, the difference between aggregate disbursements and aggregate receipts without any adjustments except for entries difference elating to temporary financing items mentioned above
(4) The above aggregate disbursements and aggregate receipts are adjusted somewhat for deriving the figures of gross fiscal deficit (GFD). Thus, GFD is the difference between aggregate disbursements net of debt repayments and recovery of loans and total receipts consisting of revenue receipts and non-debt capital receipts (i.e., in practice, only disinvestment proceeds).

Source: With a view to maintaining consistency in the series, this table is prepared from *RBI's Handbook of Statistics on the Indian Economy*, 2002–3 and earlier issues.

TABLE IV(1)
Select Aggregates—Scheduled Commercial Banks (Outstandings and Growth Rates)

(Rupees crore)

Year	Aggregate deposits (3+4)		Demand deposits		Time deposits		Investments in govt. securities	Investments in other approved securities	Investments (5+6)		Bank credit (9+10)	Food credit	Non-food credit		Cash in hand	Balances with RBI	Borrowings from RBI	Investment to deposit ratio	Non-food credit to deposit ratio
																		in per cent	
(1)	(2)		(3)		(4)		(5)	(6)	(7)		(8)	(9)	(10)		(11)	(12)	(13)	(14)	(15)
1970-1	5906		2626		3280		1362	410	1772		4684	214	4469		167	197	368	30.0	75.7
1971-2	7106	(20.3)	3127	(19.1)	3979	(21.3)	1650	540	2190	(23.6)	5263	345	4918	(10.0)	181	267	208	30.8	69.2
1972-3	8643	(21.6)	3794	(21.3)	4849	(21.9)	2161	736	2897	(32.3)	6115	340	5775	(17.4)	221	279	139	33.5	66.8
1973-4	10,139	(17.3)	4336	(14.3)	5803	(19.7)	2362	924	3286	(13.4)	7399	367	7032	(21.8)	246	610	409	32.4	69.4
1974-5	11,827	(16.6)	4963	(14.5)	6865	(18.3)	2826	1089	3915	(19.1)	8762	613	8149	(15.9)	296	612	473	33.1	68.9
1975-6	14,155	(19.7)	5817	(17.2)	8338	(21.5)	3283	1324	4607	(17.7)	10,877	1521	9356	(14.8)	305	608	798	32.5	66.1
1976-7	17,566	(24.1)	6943	(19.4)	10,623	(27.4)	3930	1606	5536	(20.2)	13,173	2191	10,982	(17.4)	354	1146	967	31.5	62.5
1977-8	22,211	(26.4)	4872	(−29.8)	17,340	(63.2)	5907	1990	7897	(42.6)	14,939	1984	12,955	(18.0)	469	1674	331	35.6	58.3
1978-9	27,016	(21.6)	5826	(19.6)	21,190	(22.2)	6622	2488	9109	(15.3)	17,795	2210	15,585	(20.3)	557	2634	546	33.7	57.7
1979-80	31,759	(17.6)	6643	(14.0)	25,116	(18.5)	7444	3181	10,624	(16.6)	21,537	2100	19,437	(24.7)	616	3634	739	33.5	61.2
1980-1	37,988	(19.6)	7798	(17.4)	30,190	(20.2)	9219	3967	13,186	(24.1)	25,371	1759	23,612	(21.5)	766	4092	589	34.7	62.2
1981-2	43,733	(15.1)	8383	(7.5)	35,350	(17.1)	10,157	4984	15,141	(14.8)	29,682	2127	27,555	(16.7)	788	4883	831	34.6	63.0
1982-3	51,358	(17.4)	9984	(19.1)	41,374	(17.0)	12,078	6257	18,334	(21.1)	35,493	2965	32,528	(18.0)	878	5208	815	35.7	63.3
1983-4	60,596	(18.0)	11,312	(13.3)	49,284	(19.1)	13,473	7772	21,246	(15.9)	41,294	4022	37,272	(14.6)	928	7783	1336	35.1	61.5
1984-5	72,244	(19.2)	14,132	(24.9)	58,113	(17.9)	18,697	9441	28,138	(32.4)	48,953	5665	43,287	(16.1)	1044	6884	1558	38.9	59.9
1985-6	85,404	(18.2)	15,612	(10.5)	69,792	(20.1)	19,045	11,509	30,553	(8.6)	56,067	5535	50,533	(16.7)	1127	11,053	954	35.8	59.2
1986-7	102,724	(20.3)	19,227	(23.2)	83,496	(19.6)	24,847	13,735	38,582	(26.3)	63,308	5104	58,204	(15.2)	1174	14,381	1293	37.6	56.7
1987-8	118,045	(14.9)	20,247	(5.3)	97,798	(17.1)	30,517	15,987	46,504	(20.5)	70,536	2190	68,346	(17.4)	1306	17,656	1753	39.4	57.9
1988-9	140,150	(18.7)	23,342	(15.3)	116,808	(19.4)	35,815	18,847	54,662	(17.5)	84,719	769	83,950	(22.8)	1444	21,376	3527	39.0	59.9
1989-90	166,959	(19.1)	28,856	(23.6)	138,103	(18.2)	42,292	22,078	64,369	(17.8)	101,453	2006	99,446	(18.5)	1649	23,463	2399	38.6	59.6
1990-1	192,541	(15.3)	33,192	(15.0)	159,349	(15.4)	49,998	25,067	75,065	(16.6)	116,301	4506	111,795	(12.4)	1804	23,861	3468	39.0	58.1
1991-2	230,758	(19.8)	45,088	(35.8)	185,670	(16.5)	62,727	27,469	90,196	(20.2)	125,592	4670	120,922	(8.2)	2008	34,179	577	39.1	52.4
1992-3	268,572	(16.4)	46,461	(3.0)	222,111	(19.6)	75,945	29,711	105,656	(17.1)	151,982	6743	145,239	(20.1)	2293	28,535	1619	39.3	54.1
1993-4	315,132	(17.3)	56,572	(21.8)	258,560	(16.4)	101,202	31,321	132,523	(25.4)	164,418	10,907	153,510	(5.7)	2283	47,760	1813	42.1	48.7
1994-5	386,859	(22.8)	76,903	(35.9)	309,956	(19.9)	117,685	31,568	149,253	(12.6)	211,560	12,275	199,286	(29.8)	2972	60,029	7415	38.6	51.5
1995-6	433,819	(12.1)	80,614	(4.8)	353,205	(14.0)	132,227	32,555	164,782	(10.4)	254,015	9791	244,224	(22.5)	3113	50,667	4847	38.0	56.3
1996-7	505,599	(16.5)	90,610	(12.4)	414,989	(17.5)	158,890	31,624	190,514	(15.6)	278,401	7597	270,805	(10.9)	3347	49,848	560	37.7	53.6
1997-8	598,485	(18.4)	102,513	(13.1)	495,972	(19.5)	186,957	31,748	218,705	(14.8)	324,079	12,485	311,594	(15.1)	3608	57,698	395	36.5	52.1
1998-9	714,025	(19.3)	117,423	(14.5)	596,602	(20.3)	223,217	31,377	254,595	(16.4)	368,837	16,816	352,021	(13.0)	4362	63,548	2894	35.7	49.3
1999-00	813,345	(13.9)	127,366	(8.5)	685,978	(15.0)	278,456	30,488	308,944	(21.3)	435,958	25,691	410,267	(16.5)	5330	57,419	6491	38.0	50.4
2000-1	962,618	(18.4)	142,552	(11.9)	820,066	(19.5)	340,035	30,125	370,159	(19.8)	511,434	39,991	471,443	(14.9)	5658	59,544	3896	38.5	49.0
2001-2	1,103,360	(14.6)	153,048	(7.4)	950,312	(15.9)	411,176	27,093	438,269	(18.4)	589,723	53,978	535,745	(13.6)	6245	62,402	3616	39.7	48.6
2002-3	1,280,853	(16.1)	170,290	(11.3)	1,110,564	(16.9)	523,417	24,129	547,546	(24.9)	729,215	49,479	679,736	(26.9)	7567	58,335	79	42.7	53.1

Notes: Figures in brackets are percentage variations over the previous year.
Data pertain to last Friday of March up to 1984-85 and last reporting Friday of March thereafter. Data include merger effects of ICICI with ICICI Bank Ltd.

Source: *Handbook of Statistics of Indian Economy* (RBI) and *Reserve Bank of India Weekly Supplement to Bulletin*.

TABLE IV(2)
Components of Money Stock (Outstandings and Growth Rates)

(Rupees crore)

Year	Currency in circulation	Cash with banks	Currency with the public (2–3)	'Other' deposits with the RBI	Bankers' deposits with the RBI	Demand deposits	Time deposits	Reserve money (M0) (2+5+6)		Narrow money (M1) (4+5+7)		Broad money (M3) (10+8)	
1970–1	4557	186	4371	60	205	2943	3646	4822		7374		11020	
1971–2	5006	205	4801	80	296	3442	4370	5382	(11.6)	8323	(12.9)	12693	(15.2)
1972–3	5680	242	5438	58	295	4204	5313	6033	(12.1)	9700	(16.5)	15013	(18.3)
1973–4	6595	274	6321	53	625	4826	6424	7273	(20.6)	11200	(15.5)	17624	(17.4)
1974–5	6701	354	6347	75	828	5553	7574	7604	(4.6)	11975	(6.9)	19549	(10.9)
1975–6	7053	348	6705	77	678	6543	9155	7808	(2.7)	13325	(11.3)	22480	(15.0)
1976–7	8288	415	7873	121	1389	8030	11757	9798	(25.5)	16024	(20.3)	27781	(23.6)
1977–8	9152	521	8631	70	1719	5687	18518	10941	(11.7)	14388	–(10.2)	32906	(18.4)
1978–9	10835	604	10231	166	3081	6895	22820	14082	(28.7)	17292	(20.2)	40112	(21.9)
1979–80	12382	728	11654	391	3800	7955	27226	16573	(17.7)	20000	(15.7)	47226	(17.7)
1980–1	14307	881	13426	411	4734	9587	32350	19452	(17.4)	23424	(17.1)	55774	(18.1)
1981–2	15411	937	14474	168	5419	10295	37815	20998	(7.9)	24937	(6.5)	62752	(12.5)
1982–3	17639	980	16659	186	5285	11690	44649	23110	(10.1)	28535	(14.4)	73184	(16.6)
1983–4	20643	1040	19603	291	8060	13504	53127	28994	(25.5)	33398	(17.0)	86525	(18.2)
1984–5	23875	1203	22672	595	10746	16648	63018	35216	(21.5)	39915	(19.5)	102933	(19.0)
1985–6	26524	1465	25059	289	11352	18747	75299	38165	(8.4)	44095	(10.5)	119394	(16.0)
1986–7	29913	1531	28382	309	14586	22825	90116	44808	(17.4)	51516	(16.8)	141632	(18.6)
1987–8	35122	1563	33559	397	17970	24599	105720	53489	(19.4)	58555	(13.7)	164275	(16.0)
1988–9	40119	1790	38329	694	22145	27763	126707	62958	(17.7)	66786	(14.1)	193493	(17.8)
1989–90	48286	1986	46300	598	28707	34162	149890	77591	(23.2)	81060	(21.4)	230950	(19.4)
1990–1	55282	2234	53048	674	31823	39170	172936	87779	(13.1)	92892	(14.6)	265828	(15.1)
1991–2	63738	2640	61098	885	34882	52423	202643	99505	(13.4)	114406	(23.2)	317049	(19.3)
1992–3	71326	3053	68273	1313	38140	54480	239950	110779	(11.3)	124066	(8.4)	364016	(14.8)
1993–4	85396	3095	82301	2525	50751	65952	280306	138672	(25.2)	150778	(21.5)	431084	(18.4)
1994–5	104681	4000	100681	3383	61218	88193	335338	169283	(22.1)	192257	(27.5)	527596	(22.4)
1995–6	122569	4311	118258	3344	68544	93233	384356	194457	(14.9)	214835	(11.7)	599191	(13.6)
1996–7	137217	5130	132087	3194	59574	105334	455397	199985	(2.8)	240615	(12.0)	696012	(16.2)
1997–8	151056	5477	145579	3541	71806	118725	553488	226402	(13.2)	267844	(11.3)	821332	(18.0)
1998–9	175846	6902	168944	3736	79703	136388	671892	259286	(14.5)	309068	(15.4)	980960	(19.4)
1999–00	197061	7979	189082	3034	80460	149681	782378	280555	(8.2)	341796	(10.6)	1124174	(14.6)
2000–1	218205	8654	209550	3630	81477	166270	933771	303311	(8.1)	379450	(11.0)	1313220	(16.8)
2001–2	250974	10179	240794	2850	84147	179199	1075512	337970	(11.4)	422843	(11.4)	1498355	(14.1)
2002–3 P	282473	11490	270983	3242	83346	198602	1252396	369061	(9.2)	472827	(11.8)	1725222	(15.1)

Note: P—Provisional.
Figures in brackets are percentage variations over the previous year.
Source: Handbook of Statistics on the Indian Economy (RBI) and *RBI Monthly Bulletin.*

TABLE V(1)
Business Growth of Capital Market Segment of National Stock Exchange (NSE)

Month/Year	No. of companies listed*	No. of companies permitted to trade $	No. of companies available for trading*@	No. of trading days	No. of companies traded	No. of trades (million)	Traded quantity (million)	Turnover (Rs crore)	Average daily turnover (Rs crore)	Average trade size (Rs)	Demat securities traded (million)	Demat turnover (Rs crore)	Market capitalisation (Rs crore)*
(1)	(2)	(3)	(4)	(5)	(6)	(7)	(8)	(9)	(10)	(11)	(12)	(13)	(14)
2003-04													
Dec-03	897	23	779	22	754	38	7175	110373	5017	29112	7175	110373	1167029
Nov-03	891	23	777	20	738	31	5672	92886	4644	30304	5672	92886	979541
Oct-03	887	26	776	23	728	36	7177	115595	5026	32315	7177	115595	926748
Sep-03	883	27	774	22	761	35	7185	103346	4698	29527	7185	103346	863481
August.03	873	35	775	20	752	32	8455	85346	4267	26485	8455	85346	836651
July.03	865	44	774	23	755	32	6491	78877	3429	24672	6491	78877	719145
June.03	853	52	769	21	744	27	5190	61585	2932	23029	5190	61585	678550
May.03	847	61	769	21	743	25	4400	54690	2604	21889	4400	54690	612030
Apr.03	830	78	771	20	749	21	3145	48971	2449	23649	3145	48971	530630
2002-03	818	107	788	271	899	240	36407	617988	2280	25776	36405	617984	537133
Mar.03	818	107	788	20	762	18	2492	43159	2158	24378	2492	43159	537133
Feb 03	818	107	788	19	760	19	2868	48289	2542	25273	2868	48289	581985
Jan 03	814	112	789	23	763	24	3634	64762	2816	27054	3634	64762	572277
Dec 02	809	116	788	21	762	22	3302	61973	2951	28236	3302	61973	672862
Nov 02	805	118	788	19	767	17	2363	51352	2703	29354	2363	51352	645388
Oct 02	803	119	803	21	770	20	2646	51902	2472	25806	2646	51902	606788
Sep 02	801	161	840	20	806	18	2558	46499	2325	25177	2558	46499	599603
Aug 02	799	161	839	21	806	19	2600	46113	2196	24090	2600	46113	632618
July 02	799	163	841	23	820	21	3682	51398	2235	24311	3682	51398	608643
June 02	799	170	848	20	825	19	3852	44241	2212	23378	3852	44241	659991
May 02	798	172	863	22	821	22	3530	54979	2499	25384	3530	54978	631609
Apr 02	800	173	865	22	843	20	2880	53320	2424	26512	2878	53316	649551
2000-01	785	320	1029	251	1201	168	32954	1339510	5337	86980	30722	1264337	657847
1999-00	720	479	1152	254	–	98	24270	839052	3303	85244	15377	711706	1020426
1998-99	648	609	1254	251	–	55	16533	414474	1651	75954	854	23818	491175
1997-98	612	745	1357	244	–	38	13569	370193	1520	97054	–	–	481503
1996-97	550	934	1484	250	–	26	13556	295403	1176	112086	–	–	419367
1995-96	422	847	1269	246	–	7	3991	67287	276	101505	–	–	401459
Nov 94–Mar 95	135	543	678	102	–	0.3	139	1805	17	56310	–	–	363350

Notes: * At the end of the period.
@ Excludes suspended securities.
$ Permitted to trade are those securities not listed in the NSE.
Source: NSE News (Various issues).

TABLE V(2)
Trade and Settlement Statistics of Bombay Stock Exchange (BSE)

Month/Year	No. of companies listed*	No. of trading days	No. of trades (thousand)	Total shares traded (crore)	Total turnover (Rs crore)	Total average daily turnover (Rs crore)	Market capitalization (estimated) (Rs crore)	Total deliveries		Per cent of total turnover	
								No. of shares (crore)	Value (Rs crore)	Shares delivered	Value delivered
2003-04											
Dec. 03	5644	22	23286.00	473.38	54815.54	2491.62	1273361.02	226.3	16697.35	0.41	30.46
Nov. 03	5641	20	17564.00	328.69	45029.19	2251.46	1065853.17	100.04	11052.43	0.22	24.55
Oct. 03	5639	23	18943.62	363.11	52630.54	2288.28	1000494	100.64	12221.86	51.3	43.0
Sep. 03	5639	22	18036.87	364.49	44697.72	2031.71	933087	115.95	11022.21	31.8	24.7
Aug. 03	5635	20	18096.16	455.74	36334.28	1816.71	905193	171.2	10096.31	37.6	27.8
July. 03	5643	23	17267.26	357.67	32975.70	1433.73	775996	144.47	9670.94	40.4	29.3
June. 03	5641	21	13884.51	264.91	24932.90	1187.28	734389	104.89	7105.82	39.6	28.5
May. 03	5645	21	11836.30	216.52	22510.44	1071.93	660982	87.33	6077.43	40.3	27.0
Apr. 03	5647	20	9620.86	141.42	20822.58	1041.13	572526	46.69	4364.90	33.0	21.0
2002-03	5699	251	141308.3	2213.79	314073.19	15003.6	7224800.6	719.47	61258.27	32.5	19.5
Mar. 03	5650	20	8506.01	126.65	20264.72	1013.24	572197	46.06	4477.65	36.4	22.1
Feb 03	5647	19	9533.26	143.33	23460.94	1234.79	619873	44.48	4871.31	31.0	20.8
Jan 03	5651	23	13019.39	193.72	30898.12	1343.4	611472	60.78	5836.29	31.4	18.9
Dec 02	5650	21	12310.55	187.03	30581.59	1456.27	628197	58.94	5429.94	31.5	17.8
Nov 02	5649	19	9624.89	136.21	25981.39	1367.44	601289	37.67	4117.74	27.7	15.8
Oct 02	5654	21	11366.17	158.32	27640.94	1316.24	563750	38.80	4210.90	24.5	15.2
Sep 02	5711	20	10611.05	156.01	24410.09	1220.50	570273	51.19	3946.65	32.8	16.2
Aug 02	5710	21	11504.65	156.23	23779.66	1132.36	605303	42.98	4153.19	27.5	17.5
July 02	5711	23	14486.62	283.75	26723.67	1161.90	584042	98.37	5999.87	34.7	22.5
June 02	5786	20	12916.45	271.33	23319.78	1165.99	637753	99.38	5466.25	36.6	23.4
May 02	5784	22	13928.73	217.93	28137.79	1278.99	605065	74.25	5940.46	34.1	21.1
Apr 02	5784	22	13500.5	183.28	28874.50	1312.48	625587	66.57	6808.02	36.3	23.6
2001-02	5874	247	127721.6	1821.66	307292.36	14941.14	6531012	576.43	55729.2	31.6	18.1
Mar 02	5782	19	11233.25	160.09	25719.04	1353.63	612224	58.72	5043.59	36.7	5.4
Feb 02	5798	20	12146.85	183.16	28571.56	1428.58	596716	59.48	5608.1	32.5	8.3
Jan 02	5796	23	14381.72	210.02	39169.00	1703.00	544397	52.33	5988.26	24.9	15.3
Dec 01	5795	19	12046.83	192.54	30032.96	1580.68	532328	53.42	4256.67	27.7	14.2
Nov 01	5791	20	10726.64	167.47	24401.66	1220.08	535724	56.58	4349.21	33.8	17.8
Oct 01	5805	21	9979.54	122.2	21921.52	1043.88	481851	34.02	3471.46	27.8	15.8
Sep 01	5939	20	9521.36	109.65	21593.16	1079.66	456263	33.02	3400.26	30.1	15.7
Aug 01	5938	21	7908.33	102.38	17444.06	830.67	523036	28.87	3149.8	28.2	18.1
Jul 01	5962	22	7799.33	99.27	17244.03	783.82	531576	37.81	3829.85	38.1	22.2
Jun 01	5962	21	10478.11	154.04	25450.84	1211.94	553230	53.96	5284.09	35.0	20.8
May 01	5961	22	11964.11	181.2	31868.3	1448.56	595938	48.76	5048.51	26.9	15.8
Apr 01	5961	19	9535.48	139.64	23876.23	1256.64	567729	59.46	6299.4	42.6	26.4
2000-01	5914	251	27622887	2563.98	1000031.5	47775.42	8500290	866.56	166900.4	33.80	16.7
Mar 01	5955	21	12201	223.52	45170.27	2150.97	571553	98.97	11954.67	44.3	26.5
Feb 01	5953	20	14057	378.41	101427.1	5071.36	716173	101.16	16129.76	26.7	15.9
Jan 01	5951	22	16582	337.48	114848.66	5220.39	736631	95.58	16655.46	28.3	14.5
Dec 00	5937	20	14402728	279.58	99198.69	4959.93	691162	78.96	13530.08	28.2	13.6
Nov 00	5929	22	13104852	237.08	86971.37	3953.24	699230	72.43	13127.69	30.6	15.1
Oct 00	5917	21	10850	173.36	76304.31	3633.54	653437	62.85	11590.66	36.3	15.2
Sep 00	5910	20	12945.47	211.84	114432.28	5721.61	692657	64.34	15556.01	30.4	13.6
Aug 00	5897	22	11547.9	179.62	92562.8	4207.4	766642	61.44	13953.76	34.2	15.1
Jul 00	5890	21	11141.87	149.84	80345.88	3825.99	720884	54.87	13667.28	36.6	17.0
Jun 00	5886	22	11091.09	156.09	86277.36	3921.7	793230	59.19	14045.92	37.9	16.3
May 00	5876	22	8986.89	125.27	57891.38	2631.43	702777	63.10	13249.82	50.4	22.9
Apr 00	5868	18	5903.89	111.89	44601.44	2477.86	755914	53.67	13439.25	48.0	30.1

Source: The BSE Stock Exchange Review (Mumbai) (Various issues).

TABLE V(3)
Growth of Derivatives Segment in National Stock Exchange (NSE)

Month/Year	No. of trading days	Index futures		Stock futures		Interest rate futures		Index Options				Stock Options				Total		Average daily turnover (Rs crore)
								Call		Put		Call		Put				
		Number of contracts traded	Turnover (Rs crore)	Number of contracts traded	Turnover (Rs crore)	Number of contracts traded	Turnover (Rs crore)	Number of contracts traded	Notional turnover (Rs crore)	Number of contracts traded	Notional turnover (Rs crore)	Number of contracts traded	Notional turnover (Rs crore)	Number of contracts traded	Notional turnover (Rs crore)	Number of contracts traded	Turnover (Rs crore)	
(1)	(2)	(3)	(4)	(5)	(6)	(7)	(8)	(9)	(10)	(11)	(12)	(13)	(14)	(15)	(16)	(17)	(18)	(19)
2003–4																		
Dec-03	22	1,875,468	65578	3,334,468	150,933	0	0	87,683	3100	68,394	2355	294,596	14,095	63,426	3046	5,724,035	238,907	10,859
Nov-03	20	1,557,909	49486	2,761,725	122,463	0	0	71,696	2314	48,281	1534	269,032	13,314	61,295	3061	4,769,938	192,171	9609
Oct-03	23	1,866,407	56435	3,469,563	146,377	0	0	89,794	2761	60,330	1812	405,706	18,558	97,405	4420	5,989,205	230,365	10,016
Sep-03	22	1,676,358	45861	3,122,432	113,874	0	0	110,014	3088	69,920	1925	401,660	16,379	101,555	4025	5,481,939	185,151	8416
August 03	20	990,731	24988	2,620,897	91,287	50	10	96,875	2476	54,649	1361	434,526	16,027	116,370	4219	4,314,098	140,362	7018
July 03	23	641,002	14743	2,282,426	70,515	963	19	87,149	2040	50,669	1163	495,853	16,180	162,501	5190	3,720,563	109,850	4776
June 03	21	439,151	9348	1,694,505	46,505	9768	182	55,874	1207	34,895	735	383,603	11,303	132,498	3739	2,750,294	73,017	3477
May 03	21	325,784	6283	1,354,581	32,752	–	–	53,198	1039	30,109	578	332,529	8861	155,849	3911	2,252,050	53,423	2544
Apr 03	20	362,157	6934	1,291,493	29,749	–	–	54,890	1091	31,107	616	297,270	7471	168,533	4098	2,205,470	50,020	2501
2002–03	251	2126,763	43952	1,0676,843	286,532	–	–	269,674	5670	172,567	3578	2,456,501	69,644	1,066,561	30,489	16,768,909	439,855	1752
Mar 03	20	325,299	6624	1,138,980	29,770	–	–	53,788	1117	35,739	740	255,658	7163	140,540	3919	1,950,004	49,332	2467
Feb 03	19	237,803	5040	1,198,564	32,445	–	–	26,501	571	17,681	375	268,156	7644	114,512	3319	1,863,217	49,395	2600
Jan 03	23	258,955	5557	1,304,122	38,299	–	–	26,376	577	16,805	364	322,876	10,174	132,021	4179	2,061,155	59,140	2572
Dec 02	21	277,403	5958	1,217,873	35,532	–	–	30,216	660	19,973	427	309,573	9552	111,756	3491	1,966,839	55,620	2649
Nov 02	19	175,567	3500	970,251	25,463	–	–	25,413	509	17,191	336	261,600	7106	104,529	2922	1,554,551	39,836	2097
Oct 02	21	164,934	3145	856,930	21,213	–	–	23,628	459	13,910	267	214,027	5595	104,659	2761	1,378,088	33,441	1592
Sep 02	20	144,303	2836	700,051	17,501	–	–	16,578	332	12,543	251	151,291	4016	80,038	2205	1,104,804	27,140	1357
Aug 02	21	152,375	2978	726,310	17,881	–	–	15,967	318	10,124	200	147,646	3837	65,630	1725	1,118,052	26,983	1283
July 02	23	122,663	2513	789,290	21,205	–	–	16,637	350	7688	162	154,089	4341	65,530	1837	1,155,897	30,407	1322
June 02	20	99,514	2123	616,461	16,178	–	–	10,272	223	7805	166	123,493	3325	48,919	1317	906,464	23,332	1167
May 02	22	94,312	2022	605,284	15,981	–	–	13,070	294	7719	169	126,867	3490	57,984	1643	905,236	23,600	1073
Apr 02	22	73,635	1656	552,727	15,065	–	–	11,183	260	5389	122	121,225	3400	40,443	1170	804,602	21,674	985

Notes: In NSE Index Futures, Stock futures, Index Options and Stock Options were introduced in June 2000, November 2001, June 2001and July 2001 respectively.
Notional Turnover = (Strike price + Premium)
* Quantity.

Source: *NSE News (Various issues)* (–) Means the period when Derivative trade was not operational.

TABLE V(4)
Growth of Derivatives Segment in Bombay Stock Exchange (BSE)

Month/Year	No. of trading days	Sensex futures series		Sensex options series		Stock options		Stock futures		Total		Average daily turnover (Rs crore)
		Number of contracts	Notional value of contracts (Rs crore)	Number of contracts	Notional value of contracts (Rs crore)	Number of contracts	Notional value of contracts (Rs crore)	Number of contracts	Notional value of contracts (Rs crore)	Number of contracts	Notional value of contracts (Rs crore)	
2003-04												
Nov-03	20	18137	449.63	0	0	15	1.45	13185	477.62	31337	928.70	46.44
Oct-03	23	17704	419.56	0	0	25	2.72	12939	435.1	30668	857.38	37.28
Sep-03	22	18850	407.88	0	0.00	69	1.50	15355	441.48	34274	850.86	38.68
Aug-03	20	15085	302.54	0	0.00	3	0.08	8546	206.34	23634	508.96	25.45
July. 03	23	2747	50.80	0	0.00	185	3.40	1786	48.90	4718	103.10	4.48
June. 03	21	35	0.58	0	0.00	123	2.54	265	6.08	423	9.20	0.44
May. 03	21	542	8.13	1	0.03	185	4.33	427	10.46	1155	22.95	1.09
Apr. 03	20	4221	64.77	0	0.00	80	1.80	979	20.77	5280	87.34	4.37
2002-03	251	111324	1810.99	70	1.98	801	21.17	25839	644.21	138034	2478.36	9.87
Mar. 03	20	41147	650.68	41	1.30	330	10.37	2130	55.87	43648	718.22	35.91
Feb 03	19	35869	589.42	1	0.03	230	5.68	3413	89.70	39513	684.84	36.04
Jan 03	23	32824	546.57	0	0.00	9	0.27	3637	100.26	36470	647.10	28.13
Dec 02	21	0	0.00	0	0.00	20	0.45	591	15.51	611	15.96	0.76
Nov 02	19	0	0.00	0	0.00	7	0.10	539	13.15	546	13.25	0.70
Oct 02	21	0	0.00	0	0.00	7	0.15	611	13.85	618	14.00	0.67
Sep 02	20	6	0.09	0	0.00	91	1.99	813	18.10	910	20.18	1.01
Aug 02	21	1	0.02	0	0.00	22	0.46	2036	43.93	2059	44.41	2.11
July 02	23	54	0.89	0	0.00	19	0.40	3210	77.38	3283	78.67	3.42
June 02	20	752	12.31	0	0.00	18	0.43	3780	90.27	4550	103.01	5.15
May 02	22	608	9.90	1	0.04	14	0.32	4124	104.70	4747	114.96	5.23
Apr 02	22	63	1.11	27	0.61	34	0.55	955	21.49	1079	23.76	1.08

Notes: (–) Means the period when Derivative trade was not operational.
In BSE Sensex futures, Sensex options, Stock options and Stock futures were introduced in April 2001, June 2001, July 2001 and November 2001 respectively.
Notional Turnover = (Strike price + Premium) * Quantity.
Source : BSE Market Data (Various issues) (Mumbai).

TABLE VI(1)
Wholesale Price Index: Point-to-Point and Average Annual Variation

Year	Point-to-Point				Average			
	All commodities	Annual change (per cent)	Food index	Annual change (per cent)	All commodities	Annual change (per cent)	Food index	Annual change (per cent)
(1)	(2)	(3)	(4)	(5)	(6)	(7)	(8)	(9)
	Base Year August 1939 = 100							
1950-1	449.6	–	414.1	–	409.7	–	416.4	–
1951-2	378.2	-15.9	339.3	-18.1	434.6	6.1	398.3	-4.3
1952-3	385.0	1.8	362.6	6.9	380.6	-12.4	351.3	-11.8
	Base Year 1952-3 = 100							
1953-4	103.1	3.1	104.2	4.2	101.2	1.2	100.1	0.1
1954-5	90.8	-11.9	80.8	-22.5	89.6	-11.5	82.1	-18.0
1955-6	101.4	11.7	99.0	22.5	92.5	3.2	86.3	5.1
1956-7	109.3	7.8	110.0	11.1	105.3	13.8	102.3	18.5
1957-8	106.1	-2.9	103.4	-6.0	108.4	2.9	106.4	4.0
1958-9	112.1	5.7	112.7	9.0	112.9	4.2	115.2	8.3
1959-60	118.6	5.8	116.5	3.4	117.1	3.7	119.3	3.6
1960-1	126.2	6.4	116.9	0.3	124.9	6.7	120.0	0.6
1961-2	122.9	-2.6	118.4	1.3	125.1	0.2	120.1	0.1
1962-3	127.3	3.6	123.5	4.3	127.9	2.2	126.1	5.0
1963-4	139.0	9.2	141.0	14.2	135.3	5.8	136.3	8.1
1964-5	151.0	8.6	153.7	9.0	152.7	12.9	159.9	17.3
1965-6	174.0	15.2	175.3	14.1	165.1	8.1	168.8	5.6
1966-7	202.7	16.5	217.6	24.1	191.2	15.8	199.8	18.4
1967-8	200.6	-1.0	204.0	-6.3	212.6	11.2	242.0	21.1
1968-9	165.1	-17.7	182.0	-10.8	210.2	-1.1	231.0	-4.5
	Base Year 1961-2 = 100							
1962-3	104.9	4.9	105.0	5.0	103.8	3.8	105.0	5.0
1963-4	113.3	8.0	120.0	14.3	110.2	6.2	113.9	8.5
1964-5	122.3	7.9	132.0	10.0	122.3	11.0	133.1	16.9
1965-6	137.5	12.4	150.0	13.6	131.6	7.6	145.0	8.9
1966-7	158.9	15.6	188.0	25.3	149.9	13.9	171.0	17.9
1967-8	160.3	0.9	194.0	3.2	167.3	11.6	208.0	21.6
1968-9	165.1	3.0	186.0	-4.1	165.4	-1.1	197.0	-5.3
1969-70	175.7	6.4	200.0	7.5	171.6	3.7	197.0	0.0
1970-1	180.6	2.8	200.0	0.0	181.1	5.5	204.0	3.6
1971-2	192.3	6.4	216.0	8.0	188.4	4.0	210.0	2.9
1972-3	220.0	14.5	253.0	17.1	207.1	9.9	240.0	14.3
1973-4	283.3	28.8	321.0	26.9	254.0	22.6	322.0	34.2
1974-5	309.1	9.1	358.0	11.5	313.0	23.2	364.0	13.0
	Base Year 1970-1 = 100							
1971-2	108.2	8.2	109.8	9.8	105.6	5.6	106.3	6.3
1972-3	121.5	12.3	126.8	15.5	116.2	10.0	123.0	15.8
1973-4	158.0	30.0	154.9	22.2	139.7	20.2	147.5	19.9
1974-5	173.9	10.1	172.2	11.2	174.9	25.2	176.6	19.7
1975-6	162.6	-6.5	145.7	-15.4	173.0	-1.1	169.3	-4.2
1976-7	182.1	12.0	171.2	17.5	176.6	2.1	165.5	-2.2
1977-8	182.8	0.4	168.3	-1.7	185.8	5.2	177.1	7.0
1978-9	191.1	4.5	168.8	0.3	185.8	0.0	167.4	-5.5

(contd.)

TABLE VI(1) contd.

Year	Point-to-Point				Average			
	All commodities	Annual change (per cent)	Food index	Annual change (per cent)	All commodities	Annual change (per cent)	Food index	Annual change (per cent)
(1)	(2)	(3)	(4)	(5)	(6)	(7)	(8)	(9)
1979–80	232.0	21.4	206.9	22.6	217.6	17.1	195.6	16.9
1980–1	270.7	16.7	247.3	19.5	257.3	18.2	239.2	22.3
1981–2	277.1	2.4	239.0	-3.4	281.3	9.3	254.8	6.5
1982–3	295.3	6.6	258.1	8.0	288.7	2.6	252.3	-1.0
1983–4	321.7	8.9	286.3	10.9	316.0	9.5	288.0	14.1
1984–5	346.3	7.6	304.7	6.5	338.4	7.1	305.3	6.0
1985–6	359.3	3.8	326.6	7.2	357.8	5.7	326.5	6.9
1986–7	378.2	5.3	348.4	6.7	376.8	5.3	352.0	7.8
1987–8	418.4	10.6	385.8	10.7	405.4	7.6	381.0	8.2
1988–9	NA	–	–	–	435.3	7.4	411.5	8.0
				Base Year 1981–2=100				
1982–3	107.2	7.2	109.6	9.6	104.9	4.9	106.8	6.8
1983–4	114.8	7.1	118.8	8.4	112.8	7.5	119.8	12.2
1984–5	121.2	5.6	123.4	3.8	120.1	6.5	125.2	4.5
1985–6	127.4	5.1	130.0	5.4	125.4	4.4	127.9	2.2
1986–7	134.2	5.3	138.8	6.8	132.7	5.8	140.9	10.2
1987–8	148.5	10.7	158.4	14.1	143.6	8.2	153.5	8.9
1988–9	156.9	5.7	164.8	4.0	154.3	7.5	166.3	8.3
1989–90	171.1	9.1	174.1	5.6	165.7	7.4	174.1	4.7
1990–1	191.8	12.1	203.6	17.0	182.7	10.3	193.6	11.2
1991–2	217.8	13.6	238.4	17.1	207.8	13.7	228.8	18.2
1992–3	233.1	7.0	259.8	9.0	228.6	10.0	253.7	10.9
1993–4	258.3	10.8	269.7	3.8	247.8	8.4	270.5	6.6
1994–5	285.2	10.4	303.3	12.5	274.7	10.9	297.2	9.9
1995–6	299.5	5.0	326.6	7.7	295.8	7.7	314.7	5.9
1996–7	320.1	6.9	365.8	12.0	314.6	6.4	346.4	10.1
1997–8	337.1	5.3	389.7	6.5	329.8	4.8	363.4	4.9
1998–9	353.3	4.8	417.5	7.1	352.4	6.9	405.4	11.6
				Base Year 1993–4=100				
1994–5	117.1	17.1	114.2	14.2	112.8	12.8	115.3	15.3
1995–6	122.2	4.4	121.4	6.3	121.6	7.8	122.8	6.5
1996–7	128.8	5.4	134.6	10.8	127.3	4.7	132.4	7.8
1997–8	134.6	4.5	141.0	4.8	132.8	4.3	137.8	4.1
1998–9	141.7	5.3	154.0	9.2	140.8	6.0	154.2	11.9
1999–00	150.9	6.5	160.3	4.1	145.3	3.2	155.7	1.0
2000–1	159.2	5.5	158.1	-1.3	155.7	7.2	156.7	0.6
2001–2	161.8	1.6	163.3	3.3	161.3	3.6	163.2	4.1
2002–3	171.6	6.1	168.8	3.4	166.8	3.4	167.9	2.9

Source: Various issues of Economic Survey, Govt. of India & RBI Bulletin.

TABLE VI(2)
Cost of Living Indices
(A) Consumer Price Index for Industrial Workers: Point-to-Point and Average Annual Variation

| Year | Point-to-Point ||||||||||||
| | 1949=100 |||| 1960=100 |||| 1982=100 ||||
	Total index	Annual change (per cent)	Food index	Annual change (per cent)	Total index	Annual change (per cent)	Food index	Annual change (per cent)	Total index	Annual change (per cent)	Food index	Annual change (per cent)
(1)	(2)	(3)	(4)	(5)	(6)	(7)	(8)	(9)	(10)	(11)	(12)	(13)
1950-1	103.0	3.0	–	–	–	–	–	–	–	–	–	–
1951-2	98.0	-4.9	–	–	–	–	–	–	–	–	–	–
1952-3	104.0	6.1	105.0	–	–	–	–	–	–	–	–	–
1953-4	101.0	-2.9	101.0	-3.8	–	–	–	–	–	–	–	–
1954-5	96.0	-5.0	92.0	-8.9	–	–	–	–	–	–	–	–
1955-6	105.0	9.4	105.0	14.1	–	–	–	–	–	–	–	–
1956-7	111.0	5.7	112.0	6.7	–	–	–	–	–	–	–	–
1957-8	116.0	4.5	118.0	5.4	–	–	–	–	–	–	–	–
1958-9	121.0	4.3	125.0	5.9	–	–	–	–	–	–	–	–
1959-60	124.0	2.5	126.0	0.8	–	–	–	–	–	–	–	–
1960-1	126.0	1.6	126.0	0.0	–	–	–	–	–	–	–	–
1961-2	131.0	4.0	130.0	3.2	–	–	–	–	–	–	–	–
1962-3	134.0	2.3	135.0	3.8	–	–	–	–	–	–	–	–
1963-4	143.0	6.7	143.0	5.9	–	–	–	–	–	–	–	–
1964-5	159.0	11.2	162.0	13.3	–	–	–	–	–	–	–	–
1965-6	174.0	9.4	177.0	9.3	–	–	–	–	–	–	–	–
1966-7	200.0	14.9	210.0	18.6	–	–	–	–	–	–	–	–
1967-8	213.0	6.5	226.0	7.6	–	–	–	–	–	–	–	–
1968-9	207.0	-2.8	212.0	-6.2	170.0	–	183.0	–	–	–	–	–
1969-70	218.0	5.3	225.0	6.1	179.0	5.3	194.0	6.0	–	–	–	–
1970-1	224.0	2.8	226.0	0.4	184.0	2.8	195.0	0.5	–	–	–	–
1971-2	236.0	5.4	237.0	4.9	194.0	5.4	205.0	5.1	–	–	–	–
1972-3	263.0	11.4	273.0	15.2	216.0	11.3	236.0	15.1	–	–	–	–
1973-4	334.0	27.0	353.0	29.3	275.0	27.3	305.0	29.2	–	–	–	–
1974-5	390.0	16.8	416.0	17.8	321.0	16.7	359.0	17.7	–	–	–	–
1975-6	348.0	-10.8	343.0	-17.5	286.0	-10.9	296.0	-17.5	–	–	–	–
1976-7	379.0	8.9	384.0	12.0	312.0	9.1	332.0	12.2	–	–	–	–
1977-8	390.0	2.9	389.0	1.3	321.0	2.9	336.0	1.2	–	–	–	–
1978-9	404.0	3.6	395.0	1.5	332.0	3.4	341.0	1.5	–	–	–	–
1979-80	453.0	12.1	446.0	12.9	373.0	12.3	385.0	12.9	–	–	–	–
1980-1	510.0	12.6	506.0	13.5	420.0	12.6	437.0	13.5	–		–	–
1981-2	555.0	8.8	550.0	8.7	457.0	8.8	475.0	8.7	–	–	100.0	–
1982-3	–	–	–	–	502.0	9.8	522.0	9.9	100.0	–	100.0	–
1983-4	–	–	–	–	558.0	73.8	583.0	73.5	114.0	14.0	117.0	17.0
1984-5	–	–	–	–	586.0	5.0	600.0	2.9	120.0	5.3	120.0	2.6
1985-6	–	–	–	–	638.0	8.9	655.0	9.2	130.0	8.3	132.0	10.0
1986-7	–	–	–	–	686.0	7.5	707.0	7.9	138.0	6.2	142.0	7.6
1987-8	–	–	–	–	753.0	9.8	779.0	10.2	153.0	10.9	156.0	9.9
1988-9	–	–	–	–	818.0	8.6	169.0	-78.3	163.0	6.5	169.0	8.3
1989-90	–	–	–	–	177.0	-78.4	178.0	5.3	177.0	8.6	178.0	5.3
1990-1	–	–	–	–	201.0	13.6	207.0	16.3	201.0	13.6	207.0	16.3
1991-2	–	–	–	–	–	–	–	–	229.0	13.9	241.0	16.4
1992-3	–	–	–	–	–	–	–	–	243.0	6.1	253.0	5.0
1993-4	–	–	–	–	–	–	–	–	267.0	9.9	281.0	11.1
1994-5	–	–	–	–	–	–	–	–	293.0	9.7	311.0	10.7
1995-6	–	–	–	–	–	–	–	–	319.0	8.9	339.0	9.0
1996-7	–	–	–	–	–	–	–	–	351.0	10.0	373.0	10.0
1997-8	–	–	–	–	–	–	–	–	380.0	8.3	401.0	7.5
1998-9	–	–	–	–	–	–	–	–	414.0	8.9	445.0	11.0
1999-00	–	–	–	–	–	–	–	–	434.0	4.8	446.0	0.2
2000-1	–	–	–	–	–	–	–	–	445.0	2.5	446.0	0.0
2001-2	–	–	–	–	–	–	–	–	468.0	5.2	462.0	3.6
2002-3	–	–	–	–	–	–	–	–	487.0	4.1	–	–

(contd.)

TABLE VI(2) contd.
(A) Consumer Price Index for Industrial Workers: Point-to-Point and Average Annual Variation

Year	Annual average											
	1949=100				1960=100				1982=100			
	Total index	Annual change (per cent)	Food index	Annual change (per cent)	Total index	Annual change (per cent)	Food index	Annual change (per cent)	Total index	Annual change (per cent)	Food index	Annual change (per cent)
(1)	(14)	(15)	(16)	(17)	(18)	(19)	(20)	(21)	(22)	(23)	(24)	(25)
1950-1	101.0	–	–	–	–	–	–	–	–	–	–	–
1951-2	105.0	4.0	–	–	–	–	–	–	–	–	–	–
1952-3	104.0	-1.0	NA	–	–	–	–	–	–	–	–	–
1953-4	106.0	1.9	109.0	–	–	–	–	–	–	–	–	–
1954-5	99.0	-6.6	101.0	-7.3	–	–	–	–	–	–	–	–
1955-6	96.0	-3.0	92.0	-8.9	–	–	–	–	–	–	–	–
1956-7	107.0	11.5	105.0	14.1	–	–	–	–	–	–	–	–
1957-8	112.0	4.7	112.0	6.7	–	–	–	–	–	–	–	–
1958-9	118.0	5.4	118.0	5.4	–	–	–	–	–	–	–	–
1959-60	123.0	4.2	125.0	5.9	–	–	–	–	–	–	–	–
1960-1	124.0	0.8	126.0	0.8	100.0	–	100.0	–	–	–	–	–
1961-2	127.0	2.4	126.0	0.0	104.0	4.0	108.0	8.0	–	–	–	–
1962-3	131.0	3.1	131.0	4.0	108.0	3.8	113.0	4.6	–	–	–	–
1963-4	137.0	4.6	138.0	5.3	113.0	4.6	119.0	5.3	–	–	–	–
1964-5	157.0	14.6	162.0	17.4	129.0	14.2	140.0	17.6	–	–	–	–
1965-6	169.0	7.6	174.0	7.4	139.0	7.8	151.0	7.9	–	–	–	–
1966-7	191.0	13.0	198.0	13.8	157.0	12.9	171.0	13.2	–	–	–	–
1967-8	213.0	11.5	228.0	15.2	175.0	11.5	197.0	15.2	–	–	–	–
1968-9	212.0	-0.5	223.0	-2.2	174.0	-0.6	192.0	-2.5	–	–	–	–
1969-70	215.0	1.4	223.0	0.0	177.0	1.7	193.0	0.5	–	–	–	–
1970-1	226.0	5.1	233.0	4.5	186.0	5.1	202.0	4.7	–	–	–	–
1971-2	233.0	3.1	237.0	1.7	192.0	3.2	205.0	1.5	–	–	–	–
1972-3	251.0	7.7	258.0	8.9	207.0	7.8	223.0	8.8	–	–	–	–
1973-4	304.0	21.1	323.0	25.2	250.0	20.8	279.0	25.1	–	–	–	–
1974-5	385.0	26.6	414.0	28.2	317.0	26.8	358.0	28.3	–	–	–	–
1975-6	380.0	-1.3	396.0	28.2	313.0	-1.3	342.0	-4.5	–	–	–	–
1976-7	366.0	-3.7	367.0	-4.3	301.0	-3.8	317.0	-7.3	–	–	–	–
1977-8	394.0	7.7	399.0	-7.3	324.0	7.6	345.0	8.8	–	–	–	–
1978-9	402.0	2.0	400.0	8.7	331.0	2.2	346.0	0.3	–	–	–	–
1979-80	438.0	9.0	432.0	0.3	360.0	8.8	373.0	7.8	–	–	–	–
1980-1	487.0	11.2	485.0	21.3	401.0	11.4	419.0	12.3	–	–	–	–
1981-2	548.0	12.5	551.0	13.6	451.0	12.5	476.0	13.6	–	–	–	–
1982-3	590.0	7.7	588.0	6.7	486.0	7.8	508.0	6.7	100.0	–	100.0	–
1983-4	665.0	12.7	673.0	14.5	547.0	12.6	581.0	14.4	111.0	11.0	117.0	17.0
1984-5	707.0	6.3	703.0	4.5	582.0	6.4	607.0	4.5	118.0	6.3	122.0	4.3
1985-6	753.0	6.5	738.0	5.0	620.0	6.5	638.0	5.1	126.0	6.8	128.0	4.9
1986-7	820.0	8.9	810.0	9.8	674.0	8.7	700.0	9.7	137.0	8.7	141.0	10.2
1987-8	–	–	–	–	736.0	9.2	759.0	8.4	149.0	8.8	152.0	7.8
1988-9	–	–	–	–	802.0	9.0	839.0	10.5	163.0	9.4	169.0	11.2
1989-90	–	–	–	–	853.0	6.4	–	–	173.0	6.1	177.0	4.7
1990-1	–	–	–	–	951.0	11.5	–	–	193.0	11.6	199.0	12.4
1991-2	–	–	–	–	1080.0	13.6	–	–	219.0	13.5	230.0	15.6
1992-3	–	–	–	–	1183.0	9.5	–	–	240.0	9.6	254.0	10.4
1993-4	–	–	–	–	1272.0	7.5	–	–	258.0	7.5	272.0	7.1
1994-5	–	–	–	–	1400.0	10.1	–	–	279.0	8.1	297.0	9.2
1995-6	–	–	–	–	1543.0	10.2	–	–	313.0	12.2	337.0	13.5
1996-7	–	–	–	–	1686.0	9.3	–	–	342.0	9.3	369.0	9.5
1997-8	–	–	–	–	1804.0	7.0	–	–	366.0	7.0	388.0	5.1
1998-9	–	–	–	–	2041.0	13.1	–	–	414.0	13.1	445.0	14.7
1999-00	–	–	–	–	2110.0	3.4	–	–	428.0	3.4	446.0	0.2
2000-1	–	–	–	–	2189.0	3.7	–	–	444.0	3.7	453.0	1.6
2001-2	–	–	–	–	2283.0	4.3	–	–	463.0	4.3	446.0	-1.5
2002-3	–	–	–	–	–	–	–	–	482.0	4.1	–	–

* – for 1988-9 onwards, CPI-IW has been derived from the base of 1982=100 using the conversion factor (4.93).

Source:- Various issues of Economic Survey, Govt. of India & RBI Bulletin, Ministry of Labour Annual Report.

TABLE VI(2) contd.
(B): Consumer Price Index for Urban Non Manual Employees: Point-to-Point and Average Annual Variations

Year	1960=100				1984–5=100			
	General index (average)	Annual change (per cent)	General index (PTP)	Annual change (per cent)	General index (average)	Annual change (per cent)	General index (PTP)	Annual change (per cent)
(1)	(2)	(3)	(4)	(5)	(6)	(7)	(8)	(9)
1959–60	–	–	–	–	–	–	–	–
1960–1	100.0	–	–	–	–	–	–	–
1961–2	104.0	4.0	–	–	–	–	–	–
1962–3	108.0	3.8	–	–	–	–	–	–
1963–4	113.0	4.6	–	–	–	–	–	–
1964–5	124.0	9.7	–	–	–	–	–	–
1965–6	132.0	6.5	135.0	–	–	–	–	–
1966–7	146.0	10.6	151.0	11.9	–	–	–	–
1967–8	159.0	8.9	159.0	5.3	–	–	–	–
1968–9	161.0	1.3	161.0	1.3	–	–	–	–
1969–70	167.0	3.7	170.0	5.6	–	–	–	–
1970–1	174.0	4.2	174.0	2.4	–	–	–	–
1971–2	180.0	3.4	184.0	5.7	–	–	–	–
1972–3	192.0	6.7	199.0	8.2	–	–	–	–
1973–4	221.0	15.1	238.0	19.6	–	–	–	–
1974–5	270.0	22.2	277.0	16.4	–	–	–	–
1975–6	277.0	2.6	265.0	–4.3	–	–	–	–
1976–7	277.0	0.0	285.0	7.5	–	–	–	–
1977–8	296.0	6.9	297.0	4.2	–	–	–	–
1978–9	306.0	3.4	308.0	3.7	–	–	–	–
1979–80	330.0	7.8	343.0	11.4	–	–	–	–
1980–1	369.0	11.8	385.0	12.2	–	–	–	–
1981–2	413.0	11.9	423.0	9.9	–	–	–	–
1982–3	446.0	8.0	462.0	9.2	–	–	–	–
1983–4	492.0	10.3	505.0	9.3	92.0	–	–	–
1984–5	532.0	8.1	540.0	6.9	100.0	8.7	100.0	–
1985–6	568.0	6.8	584.0	8.1	107.0	7.0	110.0	10.0
1986–7	613.0	7.9	625.0	7.0	115.0	7.5	117.0	6.4
1987–8	668.0	9.0	686.0	9.8	126.0	9.6	129.0	10.3
1988–9	724.0	8.4	–	–	136.0	7.9	138.0	7.0
1989–90	–	–	–	–	145.0	6.6	149.0	8.0
1990–1	–	–	–	–	161.0	11.0	169.0	13.4
1991–2	–	–	–	–	183.0	13.7	192.0	13.6
1992–3	–	–	–	–	202.0	10.4	205.0	6.8
1993–4	–	–	–	–	216.0	6.9	222.0	8.3
1994–5	–	–	–	–	232.0	7.4	244.0	9.9
1995–6	–	–	–	–	259.0	11.6	264.0	8.2
1996–7	–	–	–	–	283.0	9.3	291.0	10.2
1997–8	–	–	–	–	302.0	6.7	312.0	7.2
1998–9	–	–	–	–	340.0	12.6	337.0	8.0
1999–00	–	–	–	–	352.0	3.5	357.0	5.9
2000–1	–	–	–	–	371.0	5.4	377.0	5.6
2001–2	–	–	–	–	390.0	5.1	395.0	4.8
2002–3			–	–	405.0	3.8	410.0	

TABLE VI(2) contd.
(C): Consumer Price Index for Agricultural Labourers: Point-to-Point and Average Annual Variations

Year	1960=100				1986-7=100			
	General index (average)	Annual change (per cent)	General index (PTP)	Annual change (per cent)	General index (average)	Annual change (per cent)	General index (PTP)	Annual change (per cent)
(1)	(10)	(11)	(12)	(13)	(14)	(15)	(16)	(17)
1959-60	–	–	–	–	–	–	–	–
1960-1	–	–	–	–	–	–	–	–
1961-2	–	–	–	–	–	–	–	–
1962-3	–	–	–	–	–	–	–	–
1963-4	–	–	–	–	–	–	–	–
1964-5	143.0	–	–	–	–	–	–	–
1965-6	153.0	7.0	156.0	–	–	–	–	–
1966-7	190.0	24.2	195.0	25.0	–	–	–	–
1967-8	206.0	8.4	193.0	-1.0	–	–	–	–
1968-9	187.0	-9.2	178.0	-7.8	–	–	–	–
1969-70	193.0	3.2	193.0	8.4	–	–	–	–
1970-1	192.0	-0.5	187.0	-3.1	–	–	–	–
1971-2	196.0	2.1	200.0	7.0	–	–	–	–
1972-3	225.0	14.8	229.0	14.5	–	–	–	–
1973-4	263.0	16.9	297.0	29.7	–	–	–	–
1974-5	368.0	39.9	373.0	25.6	–	–	–	–
1975-6	307.0	-16.6	279.0	-25.2	–	–	–	–
1976-7	360.0	17.3	311.0	11.5	–	–	–	–
1977-8	409.0	13.6	318.0	2.3	–	–	–	–
1978-9	317.0	-22.5	310.0	-2.5	–	–	–	–
1979-80	346.0	9.1	364.0	17.4	–	–	–	–
1980-1	395.0	14.2	419.0	15.1	–	–	–	–
1981-2	444.0	12.4	440.0	5.0	–	–	–	–
1982-3	467.0	5.2	488.0	10.9	–	–	–	–
1983-4	520.0	11.3	514.0	5.3	–	–	–	–
1984-5	521.0	0.2	517.0	0.6	–	–	–	–
1985-6	546.0	4.8	556.0	7.5	–	–	–	–
1986-7	572.0	4.8	573.0	3.1	–	–	–	–
1987-8	629.0	10.0	658.0	14.8	–	–	–	–
1988-9	708.0	12.6	729.0	10.8	–	–	–	–
1989-90	746.0	5.4	736.0	1.0	–	–	–	–
1990-1	803.0	7.6	858.0	16.6	–	–	–	–
1991-2	958.0	19.3	1046.0	21.9	–	–	–	–
1992-3	1076.0	12.3	1053.0	0.7	–	–	–	–
1993-4	1114.0	3.5	1175.0	11.6	–	–	–	–
1994-5	1247.0	11.9	1300.0	10.6	–	–	–	–
1995-6	1381.0	10.7	–	–	234.0	–	237.0	–
1996-7	1508.0	9.2	–	–	256.0	9.4	262.0	10.5
1997-8	1555.0	3.1	–	–	264.0	3.1	284.0	8.4
1998-9	1726.0	11.0	–	–	293.0	11.0	293.0	3.2
1999-00	1802.0	4.4	–	–	306.0	4.4	306.0	4.4
2000-1	1796.0	-0.3	–	–	305.0	-0.3	300.0	-2.0
2001-2	1820.0	1.3	–	–	309.0	1.3	309.0	3.0
2002-3	–	–	–	–	318.0	2.9	324.0	4.9

Notes: + – Though the base of the series is 1960-1 the indices are available from Sept. 1964. The annual average for 1964-5 is on 10 months period Sept. 1964 to June 1995- Indian Labour Journal, March 1982
PTP—Point-to-Point

Source: Various issues of Economic Survey, Govt. of India & RBI Bulletin.

TABLE VII(1)
Balance of Payments: 1990-1 to 2002-3

(US Dollar million)

	1990-1 PR			1991-2			1992-3			1993-4			1994-5		
	Receipts	Payments	Net	Receipts	Payments	Net	Receipts	Payments	Net	Receipts	Payments	Net	Receipts	Payments	Net
(1)	(2)	(3)	(4)	(5)	(6)	(7)	(8)	(9)	(10)	(11)	(12)	(13)	(14)	(15)	(16)
A) Current account (I+II)	25,941	35,621	-9680	27,768	28,946	-1178	28,203	31,729	-3526	34,002	35,160	-1158	42,409	45,778	-3369
I) Merchandise (FoB/CIF)	18,477	27,915	-9438	18,266	21,064	-2798	18,869	24,316	-5447	22,683	26,739	-4056	26,855	35,904	-9049
II) Invisibles (a+b+c)	7464	7706	-242	9502	7882	1620	9334	7413	1921	10,319	8421	2898	15,554	9874	5680
B) Total capital account	22,766	15,710	7056	23,334	19,424	3910	22,617	18,741	3876	28,955	20,060	8395	25,914	17,412	8502
1. Foreign investment (I+II)	113	10	103	151	18	133	589	32	557	4611	376	4235	5763	956	4807
In India (Ii+IIi)	113	10	103	151	18	133	589	32	557	4611	376	4235	5753	831	4922
Abroad (Iii+IIii)	—	—	—	—	—	—	—	—	—	—	—	—	10	125	-115
I. Direct	107	10	97	147	18	129	345	30	315	651	65	586	1351	8	1343
i) In India	—	—	—	—	—	—	—	—	—	—	—	—	—	—	—
Equity	—	—	—	—	—	—	—	—	—	—	—	—	—	—	—
Reinvested earnings	—	—	—	—	—	—	—	—	—	—	—	—	—	—	—
Other capital	—	—	—	—	—	—	—	—	—	—	—	—	—	—	—
ii) Abroad	—	—	—	—	—	—	—	—	—	—	—	—	—	—	—
Equity	—	—	—	—	—	—	—	—	—	—	—	—	—	—	—
Reinvested earnings	—	—	—	—	—	—	—	—	—	—	—	—	—	—	—
Other capital	—	—	—	—	—	—	—	—	—	—	—	—	—	—	—
II. Portfolio	6	0	6	4	—	4	244	2	242	3960	311	3649	4402	823	3579
i) In India	—	—	—	—	—	—	—	—	—	—	—	—	—	—	—
ii) Abroad	—	—	—	—	—	—	—	—	—	—	—	—	—	—	—
2. Loans	9432	3899	5533	9416	5437	3979	8671	8260	411	9971	8159	1812	10,930	7895	3035
a) External assistance	3397	1193	2204	4366	1335	3031	3302	1446	1856	3476	1580	1896	3193	1675	1518
(i) By India	—	6	-6	—	6	-6	—	3	-3	—	5	-5	2	10	-8
(ii) To India	3397	1187	2210	4366	1329	3037	3302	1443	1859	3476	1575	1901	3191	1665	1526
b) Commercial borrowings	4282	2028	2254	3152	1689	1463	1179	1545	-366	3015	2330	685	4249	3125	1124
i) By India	30	24	6	19	12	7	12	20	-8	102	24	78	97	3	94
ii) To India	4252	2004	2248	3133	1677	1456	1167	1525	-358	2913	2306	607	4152	3122	1030
c) Short term to India	1753	678	1075	1898	2413	-515	4190	5259	-1069	3480	4249	-769	3488	3095	393
3. Banking capital	10,106	9424	682	10,958	10,394	564	11,998	8172	3826	11,500	9237	2263	7020	7354	-334
a) Commercial banks	7960	7056	904	9065	8929	136	10,653	7723	2930	10,614	8956	1658	6449	7075	-626
i) Assets	425	789	-364	1335	1107	228	1234	161	1073	276	1120	-844	241	1203	-962
ii) Liabilities	187	456	-269	35	417	-382	231	375	-144	1483	191	1292	403	239	164
of which: Non-resident deposits	7348	5811	1537	7695	7405	290	9188	7187	2001	8850	7645	1205	5805	5633	172
b) Others	2146	2368	-222	1893	1465	428	1345	449	896	886	281	605	571	279	292
4. Rupee debt service	—	1193	-1193	—	1240	-1240	—	878	-878	—	1053	-1053	—	983	-983
5. Other capital	3117	1186	1931	2809	2335	474	1359	1399	-40	2873	1235	1638	2201	224	1977
C. Errors & omissions	132	—	132	—	133	-133	—	940	-940	800	—	800	654	—	654
D. Overall balance (A+B+C)	48,839	51,331	-2492	51,102	48,503	-2599	50,820	51,410	-590	63,757	55,220	8537	68,977	63,190	5787
E. Monetary movements	3136	644	2492	1245	459	786	1623	1033	590	321	8858	-8537	—	5787	-5787
i) I.M.F. 1858	644	1214	1245	459	786	1623	335	1288	321	134	187	—	1143	—
ii) Foreign exchange reserves	1278	—	1278	—	3385	-3375	—	698	-698	—	8724	-8724	—	4644	-4644

(contd.)

261

TABLE VII(1) contd.
Balance of Payments: 1990-1 to 2002-3

(US Dollar million)

	1990-1 PR			1991-2			1992-3			1993-4			1994-5		
	Receipts	Payments	Net	Receipts	Payments	Net	Receipts	Payments	Net	Receipts	Payments	Net	Receipts	Payments	Net
(1)	(17)	(18)	(19)	(20)	(21)	(22)	(23)	(24)	(25)	(26)	(27)	(28)	(29)	(30)	(31)
A) Current account (I+II)	49,987	55,886	-5899	55,538	60,157	-4619	58,924	64,424	-5500	60,068	64,106	-4038	67,854	72,552	-4698
I) Merchandise (FoB/CIF)	32,311	43,670	-11,359	34,133	48,948	-14,815	35,680	51,187	-15,507	34,298	47,544	-13,246	37,542	55,383	-17,841
II) Invisibles (a+b+c)	17,676	12,216	5460	21,405	11,209	10,196	23,244	13,237	10,007	25,770	16,562	9208	30,312	17,169	13,143
B) Total capital account	24,165	20,087	4078	36,191	24,185	12,006	39,292	29,448	9844	34,170	25,735	8435	40,531	30,087	10,444
1. Foreign investment (I+II)	5632	1028	4604	7824	1861	5963	9266	3913	5353	5892	3580	2312	12,240	7123	5117
In India (Ii+IIi)	5632	824	4794	7816	1663	6153	9169	3779	5390	5743	3331	2412	12,121	6930	5191
Abroad (Iii+IIii)	14	204	-190	8	198	-190	97	134	-37	149	249	-100	119	193	-74
I. Direct	2162	29	2133	2863	22	2841	3596	34	3562	2518	38	2480	2170	3	2167
i) In India															
Equity															
Reinvested earnings															
Other capital															
ii) Abroad															
Equity															
Reinvested earnings															
Other capital															
II. Portfolio	3456	795	2661	4953	1641	3312	5573	3745	1828	3225	3293	-68	9951	6927	3024
i) In India															
ii) Abroad															
2. Loans	11,332	9131	2201	17,720	12,925	4795	17,301	12,502	4799	14,771	10,353	4418	13,060	11459	1601
a) External assistance	2933	2066	867	3056	1955	1101	2885	2000	885	2726	1927	799	3074	2183	891
i) By India	0	16	-16	-	8	-8	-	22	-22	-	21	-21	0	10	-10
ii) To India	2933	2050	883	3056	1947	1109	2885	1978	907	2726	1906	820	3074	2173	901
b) Commercial borrowings	4262	2977	1285	7579	4723	2856	7382	3372	4010	7231	2864	4367	3207	2874	333
i) By India	10	0	10	8	-	8	11	-	11	124	135	-11	20	-	20
ii) To India	4252	2977	1275	7571	4723	2848	7371	3372	3999	7226	2864	4362	3187	2874	313
c) Short term to India	4137	4088	49	7085	6247	838	7034	7130	-96	4814	5562	-748	6779	6402	377
3. Banking capital	6453	5691	762	8018	5789	2229	8910	9803	-893	8197	6717	1480	10,659	8532	2127
a) Commercial banks	6172	5235	937	7632	5407	2225	8164	9424	-1260	6768	6434	334	10,259	7955	2304
i) Assets	867	1251	-384	755	1625	-870	580	2775	-2195	1344	6434	334	2653	1863	790
ii) Liabilities	376	158	218	102	357	-255	52	242	-190	4511	2741	-1397	201	227	-26
of which: Non-resident deposits	4929	3826	1103	6775	3425	3350	7532	6407	1125	4511	92,886	-88,375	7405	5865	1540
b) Others	281	456	-175	386	382	4	746	379	367	5300	3558	1742	400	577	-177
4. Rupee debt service	-	952	-952	-	727	-727	-	767	-767	1429	283	1146	-	711	-711
5. Other capital	748	3285	-2537	2629	2883	-254	3815	2463	1352	-	802	-802	4572	2262	2310
C. Errors & omissions	600	-	600	-	594	-594	167	-	167	3958	2801	1157	656	-	656
D. Overall balance (A+B+C)	74,752	75,973	-1221	91,729	6793	84,936	98,383	93,872	4511	32,818	24,253	8565	109,041	102,639	6402
E. Monetary movements	2936	1715	1221	-	6793	-6793	-	4511	-4511	-	305	-305	-	6402	-6402
i) I.M.F. 1858	-	-1715	-1715	-	975	-975	-	618	-618	-	-	-	-	260	-260
ii) Foreign exchange reserves	2936	-	2936	-	5818	-5818	-	3893	-3893	1935	5479	-3544	-	6142	-6142

(contd.)

TABLE VII(1) contd.
Balance of Payments: 1990-1 to 2002-3

(US Dollar million)

	2000-1 PR			2001-2 PR			2002-3		
	Receipts	Payments	Net	Receipts	Payments	Net	Receipts	Payments	Net
(1)	(32)	(33)	(34)	(35)	(36)	(37)	(38)	(39)	(40)
A) Current account (I+II)	79,680	83,270	-3590	81,605	80,823	782	96,037	92,329	3708
I) Merchandise (FoB/CIF)	44,894	59,264	-14,370	44,915	57,618	-12,703	53,000	65,474	-12,474
II) Invisibles (a+b+c)	34,786	24,006	10,780	36,690	23,205	13,485	43,037	26,855	16,182
B) Total capital account	55,542	45,524	10,018	47,108	36,535	10,573	49,888	37,250	12,638
1. Foreign investment (I+II)	15,981	10,119	5862	14,450	7758	6692	12,325	7770	4555
In India (Ii+Iii)	15,911	9122	6789	14,351	6200	8151	12,252	6613	5639
Abroad (Iii+IIIi)	70	170	-100	99	1558	-1459	73	1157	-1084
I. Direct	4121	849	3272	6235	1494	4741	4790	1179	3611
i) In India	4051	22	4029	6136	5	6131	4717	57	4660
Equity	2422	22	2400	4100	5	4095	2757	57	2700
Reinvested earnings	1350	–	1350	1646	–	1646	1498	–	1498
Other capital	279	–	279	390	–	390	462	–	462
ii) Abroad	70	827	-757	99	1489	-1390	73	1122	-1049
Equity	70	414	-344	99	669	-570	73	497	-424
Reinvested earnings	–	339	-339	–	699	-699	–	519	-519
Other capital	–	74	-74	–	121	-121	–	106	-106
II. Portfolio	11,860	9270	2590	8215	6264	1951	7535	6591	944
i) In India	11,860	9100	2760	8215	6195	2020	7535	6556	979
ii) Abroad	–	170	-170	–	69	-69	–	35	-35
2. Loans	22,797	18,545	4252	11,512	12,862	-1350	13,699	16,878	-3179
a) External assistance	2942	2532	410	3352	2235	1117	2773*	5233*	-2460*
i) By India	–	17	-17	–	87	-87	–	32	-32
ii) To India	2942	2515	427	3352	2148	1204	2773	5201	-2428
b) Commercial borrowings	9052	5315	3737	2696	4272	-1576	2737	4435	-1698
i) By India	7	2	5	3	–	3	9	–	9
ii) To India	9045	5313	3732	2693	4272	-1579	2728	4435	-1707
c) Short term to India	10,803	10,698	105	5464	6355	-891	8189	7210	979
3. Banking capital	12,772	11,961	811	17,526	11,934	5592	17,462	9219	8243
a) Commercial banks	12,452	11,567	885	17,041	11,656	5385	16,926	8973	7953
i) Assets	3009	-1468	4477	-1468	5051	2789	2262	6853	1990
ii) Liabilities	9443	6672	2317	2353	11,990	8867	3123	10,073	6983
of which: Non-resident deposits	8989	6672	2317	11,435	8681	2754	9580	6772	2808
b) Others	320	394	-74	485	278	207	536	246	290
4. Rupee debt service	–	617	-617	–	519	-519	–	474	-474
5. Other capital	3992	4282	-290	3620	3462	158	6402	2909	3493
C. Errors & omissions	–	572	-572	402	–	402	634	–	634
D. Overall balance (A+B+C)	135,222	129,366	5856	129,115	117,358	11,757	146,559	129,579	16,980
E. Monetary movements	–	5856	-5856	–	11,757	-11,757	–	16,980	-16,980
i) I.M.F. 1858	–	26	-26	–	–	–	–	–	–
ii) Foreign exchange reserves	–	5830	-5830	–	11,757	-11,757	–	16,980	-16,980

Notes: * Includes Repayment of US dollar 3035 million of government loans effected in Jan-Mar 2003   @ Data for 2002-03 are estimated as average of the previous two years   PR = Provisional. Data on Foreign Direct Investment have been revised since 2000-1 with expanded coverage to approach international best practices. These data, therefore, are not comparable with FDI data for previous years.

Sources: Reserve Bank of India BULLETINS- July 2003 and various previous issues Monograph on India's Balance of Payments, July 1993.

TABLE VII(2)

Indices of Real Effective Exchange Rate (REER) and Nominal Effective Exchange Rate (NEER) of the Indian Rupee

Year/Month	Reserve Bank of India's Indices									Government of India's Index (Base 1995=100)					
	36-country bilateral weights (Base: 1985=100)									Five-country index Trade-based weight (Base: 2001-2 = 100) (April-March)		NEER		REER	
	Export-based weights			Trade-based weights											
	REER	Per cent variation	NEER	Per cent variation	REER	Per cent variation	NEER	Per cent variation		NEER	REER	5-Country index	10-Country index	5-Country index	10-Country index
(1)	(2)	(3)	(4)	(5)	(6)	(7)	(8)	(9)		(10)	(11)	(12)	(13)	(14)	(15)
1991-2	61.36	-16.3	51.12	-22.8	64.20	-15.1	52.51	-21.9		179.74	114.89	143.92	142.40	105.88	105.57
1992-3	54.42	-11.3	42.30	-17.3	57.08	-11.1	43.46	-17.2		160.98	109.65	118.75	117.37	96.06	95.52
1993-4	59.09	8.6	43.48	2.8	61.59	7.9	44.69	2.8		136.64	97.96	110.21	111.36	95.51	96.80
1994-5	63.29	7.1	42.20	-2.9	66.04	7.2	43.37	-2.9		131.31	103.66	106.31	106.80	101.17	101.72
1995-6	60.94	-3.7	38.74	-8.2	63.62	-3.7	39.73	-8.4		119.84	100.21	97.57	97.35	97.99	97.75
1996-7	61.14	0.3	38.09	-1.7	63.81	0.3	38.97	-1.9		118.15	101.33	95.68	95.37	101.12	100.78
1997-8	63.76	4.3	38.93	2.2	67.02	5.0	40.01	2.7		118.17	103.68	95.05	96.52	105.19	106.40
1998-9	60.13	-5.7	35.32	-9.3	63.44	-5.3	36.34	-9.2		104.47	95.80	84.09	85.33	101.06	101.89
1999-00	59.7	-0.7	34.30	-2.9	63.29	-0.2	35.46	-2.4		101.41	94.77	81.40	83.95	99.68	102.08
2000-1	62.47	4.6	34.24	-0.2	66.53	5.1	35.52	0.2		100.80	98.72	80.37	84.45	99.08	103.04
2001-2	64.36	3.0	34.54	0.9	68.43	2.8	35.75	0.7		100.00	100.00	79.49	83.49	102.35	105.84
2002-3	67.97	5.6	35.41	2.5	72.84	6.4	37.05	3.6		93.99	95.89	na	na	na	na
2000-1															
April	62.23	1.7	34.69	0.4	66.29	1.9	36.01	0.6		na	na	81.79	85.67	99.89	103.65
May	63.07	1.3	35.18	1.4	67.21	1.4	36.53	1.4		na	na	82.91	87.23	101.10	105.33
June	61.34	-2.7	34.15	-2.9	65.30	-2.8	35.40	-3.1		na	na	80.52	84.15	97.92	101.44
July	61.68	0.5	34.31	0.5	65.65	0.5	35.57	0.5		na	na	80.76	84.48	98.21	101.74
August	61.15	-0.9	33.95	-1.0	65.15	-0.8	35.23	-1.0		na	na	79.97	84.11	97.82	101.76
September	61.98	1.3	34.24	0.8	66.08	1.4	35.56	0.9		na	na	80.54	85.17	99.74	104.28
October	63.26	2.1	34.27	0.1	67.53	2.2	35.64	0.2		na	na	80.14	85.04	99.87	104.67
November	63.09	-0.3	34.11	-0.5	67.30	-0.3	35.46	-0.5		na	na	79.66	84.49	99.37	104.08
December	62.52	-0.9	33.73	-1.1	66.57	-1.1	34.97	-1.4		99.28	98.80	79.04	83.14	98.48	102.54
January	62.6	0.1	33.79	0.2	66.51	-0.1	34.95	-0.1		99.01	98.39	79.08	82.53	97.01	100.56
February	62.89	0.5	34.05	0.8	66.89	0.6	35.23	0.8		99.74	98.77	79.50	83.24	98.64	102.29
March	63.81	1.5	34.46	1.2	67.86	1.5	35.66	1.2		100.77	99.98	80.23	84.13	100.39	104.08
2001-2															
April	64.36	0.9	34.71	0.7	68.39	0.8	35.91	0.7		101.39	100.79	80.69	84.76	101.33	105.13
May	64.33	-0.1	34.74	0.1	68.37	–	35.94	0.1		101.47	100.69	80.68	84.96	101.41	105.36
June	64.95	1.0	35.02	0.8	69.06	1.0	36.24	0.9		102.32	101.75	81.19	85.73	102.73	107.00
July	65.01	0.1	34.92	-0.3	69.11	0.1	36.14	-0.3		102.05	102.06	80.98	85.39	103.49	107.59

(contd.)

TABLE VII(2) contd.

(1)	(2)	(3)	(4)	(5)	(6)	(7)	(8)	(9)	(10)	(11)	(12)	(13)	(14)	(15)
August	63.89	-1.7	34.19	-2.1	67.91	-1.7	35.38	-2.1	100.19	100.36	79.68	83.53	102.10	105.63
September	62.77	-1.8	33.66	-1.6	66.74	-1.7	34.83	-1.6	98.01	97.98	78.10	81.90	100.27	103.71
October	63.21	0.7	33.65	0.0	67.19	0.7	34.81	-0.1	97.86	98.56	77.93	81.71	101.71	104.95
November	63.67	0.7	33.88	0.7	67.67	0.7	35.04	0.6	98.76	99.60	78.54	82.46	102.75	106.11
December	64.16	0.8	34.20	0.9	68.08	0.6	35.31	0.8	99.53	100.19	79.13	82.93	103.76	106.86
January	63.76	-0.6	34.24	0.1	67.58	-0.7	35.32	–	99.71	99.69	79.23	83.01	103.04	106.01
February	63.39	-0.6	34.17	-0.2	67.20	-0.6	35.25	-0.2	99.69	99.35	79.08	83.01	103.16	106.23
March	68.88	8.7	37.12	8.6	73.83	9.9	38.89	10.3	99.04	98.99	78.65	82.49	102.48	105.53
2002-3														
April	69.05	0.3	36.81	-0.8	74.10	0.4	38.55	-0.9	98.22	98.05	77.99(P)	81.65(P)	101.74(P)	104.58(P)
May	67.84	-1.8	36.09	-2.0	72.77	-1.8	37.79	-2.0	96.29	96.27	76.67(P)	79.95(P)	100.00(P)	102.41(P)
June (P)	67.47	-0.5	35.50	-1.6	72.39	-0.5	37.16	-1.7	94.72	95.79	75.54	78.37	99.90	101.80
July (P)	66.67	-1.2	34.87	-1.8	71.56	-1.1	36.52	-1.7	92.60	94.23	74.12	76.76	98.38	100.01
August (P)	67.95	1.9	35.30	1.2	72.96	1.9	36.98	1.3	93.60	95.87	74.86	77.67	100.23	102.10
September (P)	68.28	0.5	35.36	0.2	73.21	0.4	37.04	0.2	93.92	96.19	75.04	77.81	100.43	102.25
October (P)	68.75	0.7	35.61	0.7	73.66	0.6	37.27	0.6	94.48	96.78	75.51	78.21	100.75	102.46
November (P)	68.66	-0.1	35.49	-0.3	73.54	-0.2	37.14	-0.3	93.72	96.22	na	na	na	na
December (P)	67.88	-1.1	35.22	-0.8	72.65	-1.2	36.84	-0.8	93.47	95.47	na	na	na	na
January (P)	66.97	-1.3	34.74	-1.4	71.63	-1.4	36.32	-1.4	92.09	94.32	na	na	na	na
February (P)	67.64	1.0	34.91	0.5	72.21	0.8	36.42	0.3	92.25	94.92	na	na	na	na
March (P)	68.53	1.3	35.02	0.3	73.15	1.3	36.53	0.3	92.55	96.07	na	na	na	na
2003-4 (P)														
April	69.52	1.6	35.25	0.7	74.12	1.5	36.72	0.5	93.15	97.63	na	na	na	na
May	68.27	-1.8	34.52	-2.1	72.64	-2.0	35.88	-2.3	91.38	95.35	na	na	na	na
June	68.7	0.6	34.69	0.5	73.05	0.6	36.03	0.4	91.72	96.29	na	na	na	na
July (P)	70.06	2.0	35.44	2.2	74.53	2.0	36.84	2.2	93.69	98.23	na	na	na	na
August (P)	71.08	1.4	35.98	1.5	75.66	1.5	37.42	1.6	95.11	99.70	na	na	na	na
September (P)	70.95	-0.2	35.65	-0.9	75.55	-0.1	37.09	-0.9	94.40	99.78	na	na	na	na
October (P)	70.13	-1.2	35.21	-1.2	74.68	-1.2	36.64	-1.2	92.83	98.50	na	na	na	na
November (P)	70.02	-0.2	34.92	-0.8	74.52	-0.2	36.31	-0.9	92.42	98.28	na	na	na	na
December (P)	na	na	na	na	na	na	na	na	90.37	96.19	na	na	na	na
December 26 (P)	na	na	na	na	na	na	na	na	89.73	94.88	na	na	na	na
January 2 (P)	na	na	na	na	na	na	na	na	89.58	95.46	na	na	na	na
January 9 (P)	na	na	na	na	na	na	na	na	88.69	94.51	na	na	na	na
January 16 (P)	na	na	na	na	na	na	na	na	89.16	95.01	na	na	na	na

Notes: The indices on REER have been recalculated by the RBI from April 1994 onwards using the new WPI series with base year 1993-94=100.
The REER and NEER indices have been estimated using the common price index and the exchange rate for the EURO area w.e.f.01.03.2002. Thus representing 31 countries and the EURO. Columns 12 to15 are export weighted indices with weights based on direction of India's exports during 1992-97. The USA, Japan, the UK, Germany and France are included in the 5- country index and Netherlands, Italy, Belgium, Switzerland and Australia are included, in addition, in the 10-country index.
P—Provisional; na: not available; – nil or negligible.

Source: *Reserve Bank of India Bulletin*, February 2004 for columns 2 to 11 and *Economic Survey 2001-02 and 2002-03* for columns 12 to 15.

TABLE VII(3)

Foreign Exchange Rate for the Indian Rupee vis-à-vis Some Select Currencies (Indian Rupee per Currency): 1990-1 to 2002-3

(Per cent appreciation (+)/depreciation (-))

Countries	Currency	2002-3	2001-2	2000-1	1999-00	1998-9	1997-8	1996-7	1995-6	1994-5	1993-4	1992-3	1991-2	1990-1	1990-1 to 1996-7	1996-7 to 2002-3
(1)	(2)	(3)	(4)	(5)	(6)	(7)	(8)	(9)	(10)	(11)	(12)	(13)	(14)	(15)	(16)	(17)
Developing countries								End-period								
Argentina	Pesos	16.2287	16.5424	46.6633	43.6418	42.4512	39.5198	36.0905	34.3300	31.5000	31.5276	31.3869	26.0856	20.3844	-43.5	122.4
Bangladesh	Taka	0.2120	0.8428	0.8637	0.8553	0.8748	0.8531	0.8313	0.8373	0.7855	0.7794	0.8008	0.6638	0.5482	-34.1	292.1
Brazil	Reais	14.1813	20.9983	21.5726	24.9685	24.6400	34.7405	33.9093	34.7822	35.1563	34.3593	na	na	na	na	139.1
China	Yuan	5.7440	5.8956	5.6344	5.2689	5.1244	4.7710	4.3284	4.1193	3.7380	3.6024	5.4607	4.7353	3.7571	-13.2	-24.6
Colombia	Pesos	0.0165	0.0216	0.0202	0.0224	0.0277	0.0291	0.0339	0.0327	0.0358	0.0382	0.0373	0.0353	0.0328	-3.2	105.5
Indonesia	Rupiah for Rs 100	0.5338	0.5100	0.4485	0.5747	0.4885	0.4745	1.4845	1.4690	1.4196	1.4638	1.5080	1.2836	1.0155	-31.6	178.1
Israel	New Sheqalim	10.1451	10.4542	11.1260	10.8346	10.5181	10.9967	10.6843	11.0350	10.6132	10.5658	11.2825	10.7696	8.6776	-18.8	5.3
Kenya	Shillings	0.6367	0.6252	0.5994	0.5826	0.6537	0.6595	0.6564	0.5880	0.7233	0.4837	0.6860	0.8623	0.7377	12.4	3.1
Korea	Won	0.0389	0.0368	0.0351	0.0394	0.0346	0.0286	0.0400	0.0439	0.0408	0.0389	0.0393	0.0334	0.0271	-32.3	2.8
Malaysia	Ringgit	12.5132	12.8421	12.2737	11.4789	11.1658	10.8279	14.4857	13.5328	12.4172	11.7359	12.0370	10.0155	7.0779	-51.1	15.8
Mexico	Pesos	4.4074	5.4043	4.8899	4.7243	4.4589	4.6381	4.5510	4.5471	4.6202	9.3369	10.0820	8.3963	6.5817	44.6	3.3
Nigeria	Naira	0.3851	0.4221	0.4232	0.4357	0.4738	1.8048	1.6406	1.5685	1.4398	1.4262	1.2554	1.3980	2.2328	36.1	326.0
Pakistan	Rupees	0.8229	0.8117	0.7655	0.8422	0.9224	0.8990	0.8973	0.9945	1.0201	1.0285	1.1719	1.0364	0.8549	-4.7	9.0
Philippines	Pesos	0.8886	0.9541	0.9446	1.0623	1.0945	1.0652	1.3619	1.3105	1.2121	1.1380	1.2241	1.0200	0.7007	-48.5	53.3
Saudi Arabia	Riyals	12.6969	13.0307	12.4539	11.6475	11.3298	10.5474	9.5888	9.1669	8.4112	8.3765	8.3391	6.9132	5.2390	-45.4	-24.5
Singapore	Singapore $	26.9316	26.4858	25.9039	25.3767	24.4949	24.5953	24.8495	24.3821	22.1972	19.9911	19.0357	15.5917	10.9419	-56.0	-7.7
Sri Lanka	Rupees	0.5034	0.5102	0.5374	0.5963	0.6109	0.6300	0.6188	0.6338	0.6309	0.6394	0.6582	0.5986	0.4814	-22.2	22.9
Thailand	Baht	1.1097	1.1224	1.0417	1.1482	1.0921	1.0771	1.4086	1.3737	1.2581	1.2399	1.2293	1.0127	0.7708	-45.3	26.9
Turkey	Lira for Rs 100	na	0.0036	0.0046	0.0092	0.0146	0.0222	0.0378	0.0664	0.0888	0.2391	0.4049	0.5405	0.6967	1743.1	950.0
Industrialised countries																
Australia	Australian $	28.7012	25.9421	22.8070	26.4119	26.7012	26.2043	28.2432	26.7533	22.9320	21.9841	22.0421	19.8478	15.2094	-46.1	-1.6
Belgium*	Franc	51.8030	42.5718	41.1941	41.6699	45.5795	1.0365	1.0342	1.1321	1.1099	0.9126	0.9395	0.7662	0.5559	-46.4*	-12.0*
Canada	Canadian $	32.3623	30.6244	29.5676	30.0103	28.1142	27.8837	25.9409	25.1834	22.5161	22.6711	24.8409	21.7581	16.9328	-34.7	-19.8
France*	Franc	51.8369	42.5718	41.1941	41.6699	45.5795	6.3869	6.3631	6.8230	6.4962	5.4939	5.7000	4.6502	3.3735	-47.2*	-12.1*
Germany*	Deutsche Mark	51.8369	42.5718	41.1941	41.6699	45.5795	21.3883	21.4030	23.2635	22.7651	18.7620	19.3458	15.7606	11.4269	-46.6*	-12.1*
Italy*	Lire	51.8369	42.5718	41.1941	41.6699	45.5795	0.0217	0.0214	0.0219	0.0184	0.0195	0.0195	0.0209	0.0155	-28.6*	-12.1*
Japan	Yen	0.3957	0.3664	0.3743	0.4121	0.3524	0.2991	0.2895	0.3230	0.3525	0.3041	0.2684	0.1944	0.1391	-52.0	-26.8
Netherlands*	Guidars	51.8030	42.5718	41.1941	41.6699	45.5795	18.9849	18.9980	20.7872	20.3567	16.6951	17.2019	14.0029	10.1453	-46.6*	-12.0*
Switzerland	Francs	35.1259	28.9776	26.9331	26.1385	28.5301	25.9680	24.7450	28.8439	27.6534	22.2482	20.8896	17.2773	13.4384	-45.7	-29.6
UK	Pound	75.1174	69.4522	66.4853	69.5783	68.3759	66.3639	68.5082	52.3670	50.8095	46.4966	46.9543	45.0279	34.0505	-50.3	-8.8
USA	US $	47.5500	48.8000	46.6400	43.6200	42.4300	39.5000	35.9100	34.3300	31.5000	31.3700	31.2300	25.8600	19.6200	-45.4	-24.5

(contd.)

TABLE VII(3)

(1)	(2)	(3)	(4)	(5)	(6)	(7)	(8)	(9)	(10)	(11)	(12)	(13)	(14)	(15)	(16)	(17)
								Period average								
Developing countries																
Argentina	Pesos	14.3886	38.8523	45.7084	43.3557	42.0833	37.1769	35.5186	33.4673	31.4292	31.4681	26.6057	24.7615	29.2368	-17.7	146.9
Bangladesh	Taka	0.8360	0.8401	0.8638	0.8717	0.8850	0.8308	0.8408	0.8269	0.7803	0.7872	0.6772	0.6565	0.5081	-39.6	0.6
Brazil	Reais	15.1325	19.7735	24.0767	23.8689	31.8292	33.8634	34.7196	35.3031	39.1494	na	na	na	na	na	129.4
China	Yuan	5.8483	5.7623	5.5188	5.2347	5.0807	4.4845	4.2731	4.0212	3.6714	4.8262	4.7265	4.5546	3.6572	-14.4	-26.9
Colombia	Pesos	0.0181	0.0207	0.0211	0.0234	0.0284	0.0306	0.0340	0.0350	0.0376	0.0357	0.0336	0.0367	0.0335	-1.5	87.8
Indonesia	Rupiah for Rs 100	0.5380	0.4603	0.5065	0.5771	0.4271	0.7962	1.5020	1.4706	1.4396	1.4917	1.2915	1.2428	0.9604	-36.1	179.2
Israel	New Sheqalim	10.1067	11.0219	11.1494	10.4712	10.7340	10.5738	10.9408	11.0092	10.4087	10.9033	10.2729	10.4406	8.7940	-19.6	8.3
Kenya	Shillings	0.6171	0.6069	0.5892	0.5950	0.6660	0.6176	0.6297	0.6108	0.6235	0.4816	0.7637	0.8591	0.7589	20.5	2.0
Korea	Won	0.0366	0.0366	0.0391	0.0370	0.0324	0.0327	0.0430	0.0434	0.0393	0.0389	0.0335	0.0329	0.0251	-41.6	17.5
Malaysia	Ringgit	12.7384	12.5510	12.0225	11.4037	10.8537	11.6454	14.1980	13.3682	12.1725	12.0456	10.3802	8.9921	6.6297	-53.3	11.5
Mexico	Pesos	4.8020	5.1857	4.7948	4.5998	4.4165	4.6122	4.6207	4.9147	7.7052	10.0183	8.5058	8.0553	6.2291	34.8	-3.8
Nigeria	Naira	0.3915	0.4247	0.4379	0.4526	1.1099	1.6976	1.6222	1.5292	1.4286	1.4260	1.3372	2.2981	2.1318	31.4	314.4
Pakistan	Rupees	0.8183	0.7683	0.8211	na	0.9248	0.8869	0.9462	1.0293	1.0230	1.0762	1.0377	1.0039	0.8191	-13.4	15.6
Philippines	Pesos	0.9254	0.9263	0.9858	1.0950	1.0413	1.1239	1.3523	1.2887	1.2171	1.1321	1.0440	0.9074	0.6996	-48.3	46.1
Saudi Arabia	Riyals	12.9255	12.7353	12.1991	11.5712	11.2316	9.9221	9.4795	8.9365	8.3839	8.3750	7.0525	6.5471	4.7927	-49.4	-26.7
Singapore	Singapore $	27.3712	26.3138	26.2953	25.5899	25.0326	23.9932	25.1511	23.7289	21.0641	19.5843	16.2014	14.3940	10.0931	-59.9	-8.1
Sri Lanka	Rupees	0.5021	0.5214	0.5705	0.6064	0.6349	0.6181	0.6331	0.6403	0.6332	0.6430	0.5868	0.5844	0.4466	-29.5	26.1
Thailand	Baht	1.1330	1.0702	1.1007	1.1406	1.0826	1.0132	1.3925	1.3392	1.2540	1.2397	1.0396	0.9590	0.7051	-49.4	22.9
Turkey	Lira for Rs 100	na	0.0036	0.0067	0.0091	0.0145	0.0209	0.0374	0.0648	0.0885	0.2391	0.3425	0.5118	0.6373	1604.0	938.9
Industrial countries																
Australia	Australian $	27.2332	24.5242	25.4605	27.9504	26.1329	26.6049	27.9927	25.1736	23.2975	21.4904	18.9865	18.9485	14.0780	-49.7	2.8
Belgium*	Franc	47.9158	42.1360	41.4221	44.7065	1.1719	1.0151	1.1106	1.1382	0.9760	0.8235	0.8193	0.7086	0.5527	-45.6*	-97.6*
Canada	Canadian $	31.2670	30.4655	30.3841	29.4549	27.9707	26.4924	26.0882	24.4541	22.7636	23.9404	21.4763	21.3003	15.4715	-40.7	-16.6
France*	Franc	47.9158	42.1360	41.4221	44.7065	7.2101	6.2329	6.7543	6.7500	5.8373	5.4622	4.9806	4.2886	3.3777	-45.8*	-85.0*
Germany*	Deutsche Mark	47.9158	42.1360	41.4221	44.7065	24.1751	20.9437	22.8698	23.4004	20.1036	18.7171	16.8710	14.5798	11.3850	-45.6*	-49.5*
Italy*	Lire	47.9158	42.1360	41.4221	44.7065	0.0245	0.0213	0.0228	0.0208	0.0196	0.0195	0.0201	0.0195	0.0153	-28.2*	-99.9*
Japan	Yen	0.3968	0.3812	0.4134	0.3885	0.3285	0.3028	0.3152	0.3470	0.3160	0.2908	0.2116	0.1839	0.1270	-59.7	-20.6
Netherlands*	Guidars	47.9158	42.1360	41.4221	44.7065	21.4429	18.5996	20.3922	20.8949	17.9242	16.6752	14.9844	12.9476	10.1056	-45.7*	-55.2*
Switzerland	Francs	32.7045	28.1828	26.9186	27.9034	29.2689	25.4335	27.3567	28.6217	23.8712	21.4164	18.6180	16.6670	13.3954	-51.0	-16.4
UK	Pound	74.8163	68.2784	67.5734	69.8414	69.5458	60.9916	56.3256	52.3998	48.8361	47.1939	44.6856	42.5303	33.1670	-41.1	-24.7
USA	US $	48.4060	47.6938	45.6855	43.334	42.062	37.158	35.501	33.467	31.398	31.364	26.411	24.519	17.948	-49.4	-26.7

Note: * In case of Belgium, France, Germany, Netherlands and Italy ,Euro currency came into existence with effect from January 1, 1998; in their cases per cent appreciation or depreciation worked out is for the period 1990–1 to 1997-8 and 1998-9 to 2002-3 for the purpose of comparability.

Source: International Financial Statistics, IMF, Various Issues

TABLE VIII(1)
State-Wise Population: 1951–2001 (in Million)

State/UTs	2001	Decadal growth (%)	1991	Decadal growth (%)	1981	Decadal growth (%)	1971	Decadal growth (%)	1961	Decadal growth (%)	1951	Decadal growth (%)
(1)	(2)	(3)	(4)	(5)	(6)	(7)	(8)	(9)	(10)	(11)	(12)	(13)
India	1027.01	21.3	846.39	23.9	683.33	24.7	548.16	24.8	439.23	21.6	361.09	13.3
Andhra Pradesh	75.73	13.9	66.51	24.2	53.55	23.1	43.50	20.9	35.98	15.6	31.12	14.0
Arunachal Pradesh	1.09	26.2	0.87	36.8	0.63	35.0	0.47	38.9	0.34	–	–	
Assam	26.64	18.8	22.41	24.2	18.04	23.4	14.63	35.0	10.84	35.0	8.03	19.9
Bihar	82.88	28.4	64.53	-7.7	69.92	24.1	56.35	21.3	46.45	19.8	38.78	10.3
Goa	1.34	14.9	1.17	16.1	1.01	26.7	0.80	34.7	0.59	7.9	0.55	1.1
Gujarat	50.60	22.5	41.31	21.2	34.09	27.7	26.70	29.4	20.63	26.9	16.26	18.7
Haryana	21.08	28.1	16.46	27.4	12.92	28.8	10.04	32.2	7.59	33.8	5.67	7.6
Himachal Pradesh	6.08	17.5	5.17	20.8	4.28	23.7	3.46	23.0	2.81	17.9	2.39	5.4
Jammu and Kashmir	10.07	29.0	7.80	30.3	5.99	29.7	4.62	29.7	3.56	9.4	3.25	10.4
Karnataka	52.73	17.2	44.98	21.1	37.14	26.7	29.30	24.2	23.59	21.6	19.40	19.4
Kerala	31.84	9.4	29.10	14.3	25.45	19.2	21.35	26.3	16.90	24.8	13.55	22.8
Madhya Pradesh	60.39	24.3	48.57	-8.0	52.79	26.7	41.65	28.7	32.37	24.2	26.07	8.7
Maharashtra	96.75	22.6	78.94	25.7	62.78	24.5	50.41	27.5	39.55	23.6	32.00	19.3
Manipur	2.39	30.0	1.84	29.3	1.42	32.4	1.07	37.6	0.78	34.9	0.58	12.9
Meghalaya	2.31	29.9	1.78	32.9	1.34	32.0	1.01	31.6	0.77	26.9	0.61	9.0
Mizoram	0.89	29.1	0.69	39.7	0.49	48.8	0.33	24.8	0.27	35.7	0.20	28.1
Nagaland	1.99	64.4	1.21	56.1	0.78	50.2	0.52	39.8	0.37	73.2	0.21	12.1
Orissa	36.71	15.9	31.66	20.1	26.37	20.2	21.95	25.0	17.55	19.8	14.65	6.4
Punjab	24.29	19.8	20.28	20.8	16.79	23.9	13.55	21.7	11.14	21.5	9.16	-4.6
Rajasthan	56.47	28.3	44.01	28.4	34.26	33.0	25.77	27.8	20.16	26.2	15.97	15.2
Sikkim	0.54	33.0	0.41	28.5	0.32	50.5	0.21	29.6	0.16	17.4	0.14	13.1
Tamil Nadu	62.11	11.2	55.86	15.4	48.41	17.5	41.20	22.3	33.69	11.8	30.12	14.7
Tripura	3.19	15.7	2.76	34.2	2.06	31.7	1.56	36.6	1.14	78.7	0.64	24.6
Uttar Pradesh	166.05	25.8	132.00	19.1	110.86	25.5	88.34	19.8	73.76	16.7	63.22	11.8
West bengal	80.22	-88.3	688.08	1160.7	54.58	23.2	44.31	26.9	34.93	32.8	26.30	13.2
Uttranchal	8.48	19.2	7.11	–	–	–	–	–	–	–	–	–
Jharkhand	26.91	23.2	21.84	–	–	–	–	–	–	–	–	–
Chhatisgarh	20.80	18.1	17.62	–	–	–	–	–	–	–	–	–
Union Territories												
Andaman & Nicobar	0.36	26.7	0.28	48.7	0.19	64.3	0.12	-82.0	0.64	106.5	0.31	-8.8
Chandigarh	0.90	40.3	0.64	42.0	0.45	75.9	0.26	114.2	0.12	-50.0	0.24	4.3
Dadra & Nagar Haveli	0.22	59.4	0.14	32.7	0.10	40.5	0.07	27.6	0.06	38.1	0.04	5.0
Daman and Diu	0.16	54.9	0.10	29.1	0.08	25.4	0.06	70.3	0.04	-24.5	0.05	14.0
Delhi	13.78	46.3	9.42	51.5	6.22	55.2	4.01	50.7	2.66	52.5	1.74	90.0
Lakshadweep	0.06	17.3	0.05	30.0	0.04	25.0	0.03	33.3	0.02	14.3	0.02	16.7
Pondicherry	0.97	20.5	0.81	33.8	0.60	28.0	0.47	27.9	0.37	16.4	0.32	11.2

Source: Census of India 2001, Provisional Population Totals, Paper 1 of 2001 and Census of India 1991 Final Population totals, Paper 1 of 1992 Vol. II.

TABLE VIII(2)
State-Wise: Rural and Urban Population of India: 1951–2001 (in Million)

State/UTs	2001		1991		1981		1971		1961		1951	
	Rural	Urban	Rural	Urban	Rural	Urban	Rural	Urban	Rural	Urban	Rural	Urban
(1)	(2)	(3)	(4)	(5)	(6)	(7)	(8)	(9)	(10)	(11)	(12)	(13)
India	741.66	285.36	628.69	217.61	523.87	159.46	439.05	109.11	360.30	78.94	298.64	62.44
Andhra Pradesh	55.22	20.50	48.62	17.89	41.06	12.49	35.10	8.40	29.71	6.28	25.69	5.42
Arunachal Pradesh	0.48	0.06	0.75	0.11		0.04	0.45	0.02	0.34	–	–	–
Assam	23.25	3.39	19.93	2.49	16.26	1.78	13.34	1.29	10.06	0.78	7.68	0.35
Bihar	74.20	8.68	75.02	11.35	61.20	8.72	50.72	5.63	42.53	3.91	36.16	2.63
Goa	0.68	0.67	0.69	0.48	0.69	0.32	0.59	0.20	0.50	0.09	0.48	0.07
Gujarat	31.70	18.90	27.06	14.25	23.48	10.60	19.20	7.50	15.32	5.32	11.84	4.43
Haryana	14.97	6.11	12.41	4.06	10.10	2.83	8.26	1.77	6.28	1.31	4.71	0.97
Himachal Pradesh	5.48	0.60	4.72	0.45	3.96	0.33	3.22	0.24	2.63	0.18	2.23	0.15
Jammu and Kashmir	7.57	2.51	5.88	1.84	4.73	1.26	3.76	0.86	2.97	0.59	2.80	0.46
Karnataka	34.81	17.92	31.07	13.91	26.41	10.73	22.18	7.12	18.32	5.27	14.95	4.45
Kerala	23.57	8.27	21.42	7.68	20.68	4.77	17.81	3.47	14.35	2.55	11.72	1.83
Madhya Pradesh	44.28	16.10	50.84	15.34	41.59	10.59	34.87	6.79	27.75	4.63	22.94	3.13
Maharashtra	55.73	41.02	48.40	30.54	40.79	21.99	34.70	15.71	28.39	11.16	22.80	9.20
Manipur	1.82	0.57	1.33	0.51	1.05	0.38	0.93	0.14	0.71	0.07	0.58	0.03
Meghalaya	1.85	0.45	1.45	0.33	1.09	0.24	0.87	0.15	0.65	0.12	0.55	0.06
Mizoram	0.45	0.44	0.37	0.32	0.37	0.12	0.30	0.04	0.25	0.01	0.19	0.01
Nagaland	1.64	0.35	1.00	0.21	0.66	0.12	0.47	0.05	0.35	0.02	0.21	0.00
Orissa	31.21	5.50	27.43	4.24	23.26	3.11	20.10	1.85	16.44	1.11	14.05	0.59
Punjab	16.04	8.25	14.29	5.99	12.14	4.65	10.34	3.22	8.57	2.57	7.17	1.99
Rajasthan	43.27	13.21	33.94	10.07	27.05	7.21	21.22	4.54	16.87	3.28	13.02	2.96
Sikkim	0.48	0.06	0.37	0.04	0.27	0.05	0.19	0.02	0.16	0.07	0.14	0.03
Tamil Nadu	34.87	27.24	36.78	19.08	32.46	15.95	28.73	12.47	24.70	8.99	22.79	7.33
Tripura	2.65	0.54	2.34	0.42	1.83	0.23	1.39	0.16	1.04	0.10	0.60	0.04
Uttar Pradesh	131.54	34.51	111.51	27.61	90.96	19.90	75.95	12.39	64.28	9.48	54.59	8.63
West bengal	57.74	22.49	49.37	18.71	40.13	14.45	33.35	10.97	26.39	8.54	20.02	6.28
Uttranchal	6.31	2.17	–	–	–	–	–	–	–	–	–	–
Jharkhand	20.92	5.99	–	–	–	–	–	–	–	–	–	–
Chhatisgarh	16.62	4.18	–	–	–	–	–	–	–	–	–	–
Union Territories												
Andaman & Nicobar	0.24	0.12	0.21	0.08	0.14	0.05	0.09	0.03	0.05	0.01	0.02	0.01
Chandigarh	0.09	0.81	0.07	0.58	0.03	0.42	0.02	0.23	0.02	0.10	0.02	0.00
Dadra & Nagar Haveli	0.17	0.05	0.13	0.01	0.10	0.01	0.07	0.00	0.06	0.00	0.04	0.00
Daman and Diu	0.10	0.06	0.05	0.05	0.05	0.03	0.04	0.02	0.02	0.01	0.03	0.02
Delhi	0.96	12.82	0.92	8.47	0.45	5.77	0.42	3.66	0.30	2.36	0.31	1.44
Lakshadweep	0.03	0.03	0.02	0.03	0.02	0.02	0.03	0.00	0.02	0.00	0.02	0.00
Pondicherry	0.33	0.65	0.30	0.52	0.29	0.32	0.27	0.20	0.28	0.09	0.32	0.00

Source: Census of India 2001, Provisional Population Totals, Part 1 of 2001 and Census of India 1991, Final Population Totals, Paper-1 of 1992 Vol-II.

TABLE VIII(3)
State-Wise: Sex Ratio (females per 1000 males)

State/UTs	2001	1991	1981	1971	1961	1951	1941	1931	1921	1911	1901
(1)	(2)	(3)	(4)	(5)	(6)	(7)	(8)	(9)	(10)	(11)	(12)
India	933	927	934	930	941	946	945	950	955	964	972
Andhra Pradesh	978	972	975	977	981	986	980	987	993	992	985
Arunachal Pradesh	901	859	862	861	894	na	na	na	na	na	na
Assam	932	923	910	896	869	868	875	874	896	915	919
Bihar	921	907	948	957	1005	1000	1002	995	1020	1051	1061
Goa	960	967	975	981	1066	1128	1084	1088	1120	1108	1091
Gujarat	921	934	942	934	940	952	941	945	944	946	954
Haryana	861	865	870	867	868	871	869	844	844	835	867
Himachal Pradesh	970	976	973	958	938	912	890	897	890	889	884
Jammu and Kashmir	900	896	892	878	878	873	869	865	870	876	882
Karnataka	964	960	963	957	959	966	960	965	969	981	983
Kerala	1058	1036	1032	1016	1022	1028	1027	1022	1011	1008	1004
Madhya Pradesh	920	912	921	920	932	945	946	947	949	967	972
Maharashtra	922	934	937	930	936	941	949	947	950	966	978
Manipur	978	958	971	980	1015	1036	1055	1065	1041	1029	1037
Meghalaya	975	955	954	942	937	949	966	971	1000	1013	1036
Mizoram	938	921	919	946	1009	1041	1069	1102	1109	1120	1113
Nagaland	909	886	863	871	933	999	1021	997	992	993	973
Orissa	972	971	981	988	1001	1022	1053	1067	1086	1056	1037
Punjab	874	882	879	865	854	844	836	815	799	780	832
Rajasthan	922	910	919	911	908	921	906	907	896	908	905
Sikkim	875	878	835	863	904	907	920	967	970	951	916
Tamil Nadu	986	974	977	978	992	1007	1012	1027	1029	1042	1044
Tripura	950	945	946	943	932	904	886	885	885	885	874
Uttar Pradesh	898	876	882	876	907	908	907	903	908	916	938
West bengal	934	917	911	891	878	865	852	890	905	925	945
Uttranchal	964	936	936	940	947	940	907	913	916	907	918
Jharkhand	941	922	940	945	960	961	978	989	1002	1021	1032
Chhatisgarh	990	985	996	998	1008	1024	1032	1043	1041	1039	1046
Union Territories											
Andaman & Nicobar	846	818	760	644	617	625	574	495	303	352	318
Chandigarh	773	790	769	749	652	781	763	751	743	720	771
Dadra & Nagar Haveli	811	952	974	1007	963	946	925	911	940	967	960
Daman and Diu	709	969	1062	1099	1169	1125	1080	1088	1143	1040	995
Delhi	821	827	808	801	785	768	715	722	733	793	862
Lakshadweep	947	943	975	978	1020	1043	1018	994	1027	987	1063
Pondicherry	1001	979	985	989	1013	1030	na	na	1053	1058	na

Sourcce: Census of India 2001, Provisional Population Totals, Part 1 of 2001.

TABLE VIII(4)
State-Wise: Literacy Rate: 1951 to 2001 (in Per cent)

State/UTs	2001			1991			1981			1971			1961			1951		
	Persons	Male	Female	Persons	Male	Female	Persons	Male	Female	Persons	Male	Female	Persons	Male	Female	Persons	Male	Female
(1)	(2)	(3)	(4)	(5)	(6)	(7)	(8)	(9)	(10)	(11)	(12)	(13)	(14)	(15)	(16)	(17)	(18)	(19)
India	65.4	75.9	54.2	52.2	64.1	39.3	43.6	56.4	29.8	34.5	39.5	18.7	28.3	34.40	12.9	18.3	24.9	7.9
Male-female gap	(21.7)			(24.8)			(26.6)			(24.0)			(25.1)			(18.3)		
Andhra Pradesh	61.1	70.9	51.2	44.1	55.1	32.7	35.7	46.8	24.2	24.6	33.1	15.8	21.2	30.20	12.0	13.2	19.7	6.5
Arunachal Pradesh	54.7	64.1	44.2	41.6	51.5	29.7	25.5	35.1	14.0	11.3	17.8	3.7	47.9	na	na	na	na	na
Assam	64.3	71.9	56.0	52.9	61.9	43.0	na	na	na	28.7	*	*	33.0	37.30	16.0	18.3	27.4	7.9
Bihar	47.5	60.3	33.6	38.5	52.5	22.9	32.0	46.6	16.5	19.9	30.6	8.7	21.8	29.80	6.9	12.2	20.5	3.8
Goa	82.3	88.9	75.5	75.5	83.6	67.1	64.7	76.0	55.2	na	54.3	35.1	36.2	41.10	19.1	23.0	32.3	13.5
Gujarat	70.0	80.5	58.6	61.3	73.1	48.6	52.2	65.1	38.5	35.8	46.1	24.8	30.5	41.10	19.1	23.1	32.3	13.5
Haryana	68.6	79.3	56.3	55.9	69.1	40.5	43.9	58.5	26.9	26.9	37.2	14.9	24.1	27.20	6.2	7.7	12.6	2.4
Himachal Pradesh	77.1	86.0	68.1	63.9	75.4	52.1	51.2	64.3	37.7	32	43.1	20.2	24.9	17.00	4.3	na	na	na
Jammu and Kashmir	54.5	65.8	41.8	na	na	na	32.7	44.2	19.6	18.6	*	*	13.0			na	na	na
Karnataka	67.0	76.3	57.5	56.0	67.3	44.3	46.2	58.7	33.2	31.5	48.6	27.8	29.8	36.10	14.2	19.3	29.1	9.2
Kerala	90.9	94.2	87.9	89.8	93.6	86.2	81.6	87.7	75.7	60.4	74.0	64.5	55.1	55.00	38.9	40.7	50.2	31.5
Madhya Pradesh	64.1	76.8	50.3	44.2	58.4	28.9	34.2	48.4	19.0	22.1	32.7	10.9	20.5	27.00	6.7	9.8	16.2	3.2
Maharashtra	77.3	86.3	67.5	64.9	76.6	52.3	55.8	69.7	41.0	39.2	51.0	26.4	35.1	42.00	16.8	20.9	31.4	9.7
Manipur	68.9	77.9	59.7	59.9	71.6	47.6	49.6	64.1	34.6	32.9	46.0	19.5	36.0	45.10	15.9	11.4	20.8	2.4
Meghalaya	63.3	66.1	60.4	49.1	53.1	44.9	42.0	46.6	37.2	29.5	34.1	24.6	na	na	na	na	na	na
Mizoram	88.5	90.7	86.1	82.3	85.6	78.6	74.3	79.4	68.6	na	60.5	46.7	20.4	24.00	11.3	10.4	15.0	5.7
Nagaland	67.1	71.8	61.9	61.6	67.6	54.8	50.2	58.5	40.3	27.4	35.0	18.7	25.2	34.70	8.6	15.8	27.3	4.5
Orissa	63.6	76.0	51.0	49.1	63.1	34.7	41.0	56.5	25.1	26.2	38.3	13.9	31.5	33.00	14.1	15.2	21.0	8.5
Punjab	70.0	75.6	63.6	58.5	65.7	50.4	48.1	55.5	39.6	33.7	40.4	25.9	18.1	23.70	5.8	8.9	14.4	3.0
Rajasthan	61.0	76.5	44.3	38.6	55.0	20.4	30.1	44.8	14.0	19.1	28.7	8.5	14.2	19.60	4.3	7.3	12.8	1.3
Sikkim	69.7	76.7	61.5	56.9	65.7	46.7	41.6	53.0	27.4	17.7	*	*	36.4	44.50	18.2	20.8	31.7	10.0
Tamil Nadu	73.5	82.3	64.6	62.7	73.8	51.3	54.4	68.1	40.4	39.5	51.8	26.9	24.3	29.60	10.2	15.5	22.3	8.0
Tripura	73.7	81.5	65.4	60.4	70.6	49.7	50.1	61.5	38.0	31.0	40.2	21.2	20.7	27.30	7.0	10.8	17.4	3.6
Uttar Pradesh	57.4	70.2	43.0	41.6	55.7	25.3	33.3	47.4	17.2	21.7	31.5	10.6	20.7	27.30	7.0	10.8	17.4	3.6
West bengal	69.2	77.6	60.2	57.7	67.8	46.6	48.6	59.9	36.1	33.2	42.8	22.4	34.5	40.10	17.0	24.0	34.2	12.2
Uttranchal	72.3	84.0	60.3	–	–	–	–	–	–	–	–	–	–	–	–	–	–	–
Jharkhand	54.1	67.9	39.4	–	–	–	–	–	–	–	–	–	–	–	–	–	–	–
Chhatisgarh	65.2	77.9	52.4	–	–	–	–	–	–	–	–	–	–	–	–	–	–	–
Union Territories																		
Andaman & Nicobar	81.2	86.1	75.3	73.0	79.0	65.5	63.2	70.3	53.2	43.6	–	–	40.1	42.40	19.4	25.8	34.2	12.3
Chandigarh	81.8	85.7	76.7	77.8	82.0	72.3	74.8	78.9	69.3	61.6	–	–	55.1	na	na	na	na	na
Dadra & Nagar Haveli	60.0	73.3	43.0	40.7	53.6	27.0	32.7	44.7	20.4	15.0	–	–	11.6	14.70	4.1	4.0	na	na
Daman and Diu	81.1	88.4	70.4	71.2	82.7	59.4	59.9	74.5	46.5	44.8	–	–	34.9	na	na	22.9	na	na
Delhi	81.8	87.4	75.0	75.3	82.0	67.0	71.9	79.3	62.6	56.6	–	–	62.0	60.80	42.5	38.4	43.0	32.3
Lakshadweep	87.5	93.2	81.6	81.8	90.2	72.9	68.4	81.2	55.3	43.7	–	–	27.2	35.80	11.0	15.2	25.6	5.3
Pondicherry	81.5	88.9	74.1	74.7	83.7	65.6	65.1	77.1	53.0	46.0	–	–	43.7	50.40	24.6	na	na	na

Note: * Some of the figures for these states are unavailable due to unorganisation of states according to present classifications. Therefore figures for Tamil Nadu, Karnataka, Meghalaya, Mizoram, Arunachal Pradesh and haryana are unavailable. They are to be seen as Mysore State for Karnataka, Madras Presidency for Tamil Nadu, Punjab includes present days Haryana; similarly for Assam and other North-eastern states. The 1971 census figure for Goa is inclusive of Daman and Diu as Goa had not converted to Statehood at the time under consideration.

Source: Registrar General of India, Various Census Reports.

Table VIII(5)
State-Wise Infant Mortality Rate: 1961, 1981, 1991 and 2001 (per thousand)

State/UTs	2001			1991			1981			1961		
	Persons	Male	Female	Persons	Male	Female	Persons	Male	Female	Persons	Male	Female
(1)	(2)	(3)	(4)	(5)	(6)	(7)	(8)	(9)	(10)	(11)	(12)	(13)
India	71	na	na	77	79	74	115	122	108	115	122	108
Andhra Pradesh	66	na	na	55	67	51	91	100	82	91	100	82
Arunachal Pradesh	44	na	na	91	111	103	126	141	111	126	141	111
Assam	78	na	na	92	96	87	–	–	–			
Bihar	67	na	na	75	62	89	94	95	94	94	95	94
Goa	36	na	na	51	56	48	90	87	93	57	60	56
Gujarat	64	na	na	78	74	82	115	120	110	84	81	84
Haryana	69	na	na	52	57	54	126	132	119	94	87	119
Himachal Pradesh	64	na	na	82	84	81	143	160	126	92	101	89
Jammu & Kashmir	45	na	na	na	na	na	108	115	99	78	78	78
Karnataka	58	na	na	74	81	53	81	87	74	77	74	79
Kerala	16	na	na	42	45	41	54	61	48	52	55	48
Madhya Pradesh	97	na	na	133	131	136	150	158	140	150	158	140
Maharashtra	49	na	na	74	72	76	119	131	106	92	96	89
Manipur	25	na	na	28	29	27	32	31	33	32	31	33
Meghalaya	52	na	na	80	79	82	79	81	76	79	81	76
Mizoram	23	na	na	53	51	56	83	94	70	69	73	65
Nagaland	na	na	na	51	51	52	68	76	58	68	76	58
Orissa	98	na	na	125	129	111	163	172	153	115	119	111
Punjab	54	na	na	74	81	53	127	138	114	77	74	79
Rajasthan	83	na	na	87	94	79	141	146	135	114	114	114
Sikkim	52	na	na	60	58	62	127	135	118	96	105	87
Tamil Nadu	53	na	na	54	55	51	104	114	93	86	89	82
Tripura	49	na	na	82	81	84	130	143	116	111	106	116
Uttar Pradesh	85	na	na	99	98	104	130	131	128	130	131	128
West bengal	53	na	na	62	75	51	95	103	57	95	103	57
Union Territories												
Andaman & Nicobar	30	na	na	69	71	61	95	114	76	77	78	66
Chandigarh	32	na	na	48	50	47	118	141	96	53	53	53
Dadra & Nagar Haveli	61	na	na	81	84	73	117	149	82	98	102	93
Daman and Diu	na	na	na	56	61	50	90	87	93	57	60	56
Delhi	51	na	na	54	55	51	100	108	92	67	66	70
Lakshadweep	30	na	na	91	100	78	132	170	88	118	124	88
Pondicherry	21	na	na	34	32	35	84	100	68	73	77	68

Source: Economic Survey:2002-3 and National Human Development Report 2001, Planning Commission.

TABLE VIII(6)
Human Development Index for India by State 1981, 1991 and 2001

States/UTs	HDI 1981									HDI 1991								HDI 2001	
	Rural		Urban		Combined		Gender disparity index			Rural		Urban		Combined		Gender disparity index		Combined	
	Value	Rank	Value	Rank	Value	Rank	Value	Rank		Value	Rank	Value	Rank	Value	Rank	Value	Rank	Value	Rank
(1)	(2)	(3)	(4)	(5)	(6)	(7)	(8)	(9)		(10)	(11)	(12)	(13)	(14)	(15)	(16)	(17)	(18)	(19)
Andhra Pradesh	0.262	25	0.425	23	0.298	23	0.744	10		0.344	23	0.473	29	0.377	23	0.801	23	0.416	10
Arunachal Pradesh	0.228	28	0.419	24	0.242	31	0.537	28		0.300	28	0.572	15	0.328	29	0.776	28	*	
Assam	0.261	26	0.380	28	0.272	26	0.462	32		0.326	26	0.555	19	0.348	26	0.575	30	0.386	14
Bihar	0.220	30	0.378	29	0.237	32	0.471	30		0.286	30	0.460	31	0.308	32	0.469	32	0.367	15
Goa	0.422	5	0.517	10	0.445	5	0.785	2		0.534	3	0.658	3	0.575	4	0.775	13	*	
Gujarat	0.315	14	0.458	18	0.360	14	0.723	6		0.380	18	0.532	23	0.431	17	0.714	22	0.479	6
Haryana	0.332	13	0.465	17	0.360	15	0.536	24		0.409	15	0.562	17	0.443	16	0.714	17	0.509	5
Himachal Pradesh	0.374	10	0.600	1	0.398	10	0.783	4		0.442	12	0.700	1	0.469	13	0.858	4	*	
Jammu & Kashmir	0.301	17	0.468	16	0.337	19	0.584	19		0.364	22	0.575	14	0.402	21	0.740	25	*	
Karnataka	0.295	18	0.489	14	0.346	16	0.707	20		0.367	21	0.523	24	0.412	19	0.753	11	0.478	7
Kerala	0.491	1	0.544	6	0.500	2	0.872	1		0.576	1	0.628	9	0.591	3	0.825	2	0.638	1
Madhya Pradesh	0.209	32	0.395	26	0.245	30	0.664	25		0.282	32	0.491	28	0.328	30	0.662	28	0.394	12
Maharashtra	0.306	15	0.489	15	0.363	13	0.740	15		0.403	16	0.548	21	0.452	15	0.793	15	0.523	4
Manipur	0.440	2	0.553	5	0.461	4	0.802	3		0.503	7	0.618	12	0.536	9	0.815	3	*	
Meghalaya	0.293	20	0.442	21	0.317	21	0.799	12		0.332	24	0.624	10	0.365	24	0.807	12	*	
Mizoram	0.381	9	0.558	4	0.411	8	0.502	18		0.464	10	0.648	5	0.548	7	0.770	6	*	
Nagaland	0.295	19	0.519	8	0.328	20	0.783	16		0.442	13	0.633	7	0.486	11	0.729	21	*	
Orissa	0.252	27	0.368	31	0.257	27	0.547	27		0.328	25	0.469	30	0.345	28	0.639	27	0.404	11
Punjab	0.386	8	0.494	13	0.411	9	0.688	14		0.447	11	0.566	16	0.475	12	0.710	19	0.537	2
Rajasthan	0.216	31	0.386	27	0.256	28	0.650	17		0.298	29	0.492	27	0.347	27	0.692	16	0.424	9
Sikkim	0.302	16	0.515	11	0.342	18	0.643	23		0.398	17	0.618	11	0.425	18	0.647	20	*	
Tamil Nadu	0.289	21	0.445	19	0.343	17	0.710	9		0.421	14	0.560	18	0.466	14	0.813	9	0.531	3
Tripura	0.264	23	0.498	12	0.287	24	0.422			0.368	20	0.551	20	0.389	22	0.531	29	*	
Uttar Pradesh	0.227	29	0.398	25	0.255	29	0.447	29		0.284	31	0.444	32	0.314	31	0.520	31	0.388	13
West Bengal	0.264	24	0.427	22	0.305	22	0.556	26		0.370	19	0.511	26	0.404	20	0.631	26	0.472	8
Andaman & Nicobar Islands	0.335	12	0.575	2	0.394	11	0.645	21		0.528	5	0.653	4	0.574	5	0.857	1	*	
Chandigarh	0.437	4	0.565	3	0.550	1	0.719	7		0.501	8	0.694	2	0.674	1	0.764	7	*	
Dadra & Nagar Haveli	0.269	22	0.268	32	0.276	25	0.888	11		0.310	27	0.519	25	0.361	25	0.832	14	*	
Daman & Diu	0.409	6	0.518	9	0.438	6	0.760	5		0.492	9	0.629	8	0.544	8	0.714	8	*	

(contd.)

TABLE VIII(6) contd.

(1)	(2)	(3)	(4)	(5)	(6)	(7)	(8)	(9)	(10)	(11)	(12)	(13)	(14)	(15)	(16)	(17)	(18)	(19)
Delhi	0.439	3	0.531	7	0.495	3	0.595	22	0.530	4	0.635	6	0.624	2	0.690	10	*	
Lakshadweep	0.395	7	0.371	30	0.434	7	0.688	8	0.520	6	0.545	22	0.532	10	0.680	24	*	
Pondicherry	0.338	11	0.443	20	0.386	12	0.753	13	0.556	2	0.591	13	0.571	6	0.783	5	*	
All India	0.263		0.442		0.302		0.620		0.340		0.511		0.381		0.676		0.472	

Notes: * Not available for the year 2001.

1 The HDI is a composite of variables capturing attainments in three dimensions of human development viz, economic, educational and health. These have been captured by per capita monthly expenditure adjusted for inequality; a combination of literacy rate and intensity of formal education; and a combination of life expectancy at age 1 and infant mortality rate. See the Technical Note in the source for the estimation methodology and other details.

2 For sake of completeness, for some variables used in estimating the indices, the data for small States/Uts have been estimated/assumed following, in general, principles of physical contiguity or similarity in socio-economic or demographic profile. The details are availble in the Technical Note contained in the source.

3 The Gender Disparity Index is estimated as proportion of female attainments to that of male for a common set of variables. The variable used to capture economic attainments is worker population ratio which is different from the variable used to capture economic attainment in the HDI. The details are availbale in the Technical Note of the source.

4 The HDI for 2001 has been estimated only for a few selected States for which some data, including the Census 2001, was available. The assumptions that have been made for HDI 2001 are indicated in the Technical Appendix contained in the source.

Source: Planning Commission (2002): National Human Development Report, 2001, March.

Table IX(1)
Poverty Estimates-Statewise Headcount Ratio

Sl. no.	States	1973–4	1977–8	1983	1987–8	1993–4	1999–2000
(1)	(2)	(3)	(4)	(5)	(6)	(7)	(8)
1	Jammu & Kashmir	40.83	38.97	24.24	23.82	25.17	3.48
2	Goa	44.26	37.23	18.90	24.52	14.92	4.40
3	Chandigarh	27.96	27.32	23.79	14.67	11.35	5.75
4	Punjab	28.15	19.27	16.18	13.20	11.77	6.16
5	Himachal Pradesh	26.39	32.45	16.40	15.45	28.44	7.63
6	Delhi	49.61	33.23	26.22	12.41	14.69	8.23
7	Haryana	35.36	29.55	21.37	16.64	25.05	8.74
8	Kerala	59.79	52.22	40.42	31.79	25.43	12.72
9	Gujarat	48.15	41.23	32.79	31.54	24.21	14.07
10	Rajasthan	46.14	37.42	34.46	35.15	27.41	15.28
11	Lakshadweep	59.68	52.79	42.36	34.95	25.04	15.60
12	Andhra Pradesh	48.86	39.31	28.91	25.86	22.19	15.77
13	Dadra & Nagar Haveli	46.55	37.20	15.67	67.11	50.84	17.14
14	Mizoram	50.32	54.38	36.00	27.52	25.66	19.47
15	Karnataka	54.47	48.78	38.24	37.53	33.16	20.04
16	Andaman & Nicobar Islands	55.56	55.42	52.13	43.89	34.47	20.99
17	Tamil Nadu	54.94	54.79	51.66	43.39	35.03	21.12
18	Pondicherry	53.82	53.25	50.06	41.46	37.40	21.67
19	Maharashtra	53.24	55.88	43.44	40.41	36.86	25.02
20	All India	54.88	51.32	44.48	38.86	35.97	26.10
21	West Bengal	63.43	60.52	54.85	44.72	35.66	27.02
22	Manipur	49.96	53.72	37.02	31.35	33.78	28.54
23	Uttar Pradesh	57.07	49.05	47.07	41.46	40.85	31.15
24	Nagaland	50.81	56.04	39.25	34.43	37.92	32.67
25	Arunachal Pradesh	51.93	58.32	40.88	36.22	39.35	33.47
26	Meghalaya	50.20	55.19	38.81	33.92	37.92	33.87
27	Tripura	51.00	56.88	40.03	35.23	39.01	34.44
28	Assam	51.21	57.15	40.47	36.21	40.86	36.09
29	Sikkim	50.86	55.89	39.71	36.06	41.43	36.55
30	Madhya Pradesh	61.78	61.78	49.78	43.07	42.52	37.43
31	Bihar	61.91	61.55	62.22	52.13	54.96	42.60
32	Orissa	66.18	70.07	65.29	55.58	48.56	47.15

Sl. no.	States	1973–4			1999–2000			Adjusted poverty ratios: 1999–2000 55th round (1999–2000)	
		Rural	Urban	Combined	Rural	Urban	Combined	Rural	Urban
(1)	(2)	(3)	(4)	(5)	(6)	(7)	(8)	(9)	(10)
1	Jammu & Kashmir	45.51	21.32	40.83	3.97	1.98	3.48		
2	Goa	46.85	37.69	44.26	1.35	7.52	4.40		
3	Chandigarh	27.96	27.96	27.96	5.75	5.75	5.75		
4	Punjab	28.21	27.96	28.15	6.35	5.75	6.16	5.9	6.3
5	Himachal Pradesh	27.42	13.17	26.39	7.94	4.63	7.63	18.9	4.5
6	Delhi	24.44	52.23	49.61	0.40	9.42	8.23		6.5
7	Haryana	34.23	40.18	35.36	8.27	9.99	8.74	12.7	9.5
8	Kerala	59.19	62.74	59.79	9.38	20.27	12.72	12.6	18.7
9	Gujarat	46.35	52.57	48.15	13.17	15.59	14.07	15.4	16.0
10	Rajasthan	44.76	52.13	46.14	13.74	19.85	15.28	19.6	22.8

(contd.)

Table IX(1) contd.

(1)	(2)	(3)	(4)	(5)	(6)	(7)	(8)	(9)	(10)
11	Lakshadweep	59.19	62.74	59.68	9.38	20.27	15.60		
12	Andhra Pradesh	48.41	50.61	48.86	11.05	26.63	15.77	14.9	27.7
13	Dadra & Nagar Haveli	46.85	37.69	46.55	17.57	13.52	17.14		
14	Mizoram	52.67	36.92	50.32	40.04	7.47	19.47		
15	Karnataka	55.14	52.53	54.47	17.38	25.25	20.04	25.7	25.5
16	Andaman & Nicobar Islands	57.43	49.40	55.56	20.55	22.11	20.99		
17	Tamil Nadu	57.43	49.40	54.94	20.55	22.11	21.12	19.9	24.4
18	Pondicherry	57.43	49.40	53.82	20.55	22.11	21.67		
19	Maharashtra	57.71	43.87	53.24	23.72	26.81	25.02	29.2	28.1
20	All India	56.44	49.01	54.88	27.09	23.62	26.10	30.2	24.7
21	West Bengal	73.16	34.67	63.43	31.85	14.86	27.02	37.1	19.5
22	Manipur	52.67	36.92	49.96	40.04	7.47	28.54		
23	Uttar Pradesh	56.53	60.09	57.07	31.22	30.89	31.15	33.7	30.4
24	Nagaland	52.67	36.92	50.81	40.04	7.47	32.67		
25	Arunachal Pradesh	52.67	36.92	51.93	40.04	7.47	33.47		
26	Meghalaya	52.67	36.92	50.20	40.04	7.47	33.87		
27	Tripura	52.67	36.92	51.00	40.04	7.47	34.44		
28	Assam	52.67	36.92	51.21	40.04	7.47	36.09	44.1	8.3
29	Sikkim	52.67	36.92	50.86	40.04	7.47	36.55		
30	Madhya Pradesh	62.66	57.65	61.78	37.06	38.44	37.43	36.4	37.9
31	Bihar	62.99	52.96	61.91	44.30	32.91	42.60	49.2	33.8
32	Orissa	67.28	55.62	66.18	48.01	42.83	47.15	47.3	41.4

Sources: (i) Planning Commission (2003): *Five Year Plan 2002–2007*, Volume III.
(ii) Angus Deaton (2002): Adjusted Indian Poverty Estimates for 1999–2000 in *Sarvekshana*, Vol. XXIV, No. 2&3, 85th Issue October 2000–March 2001.

TABLE IX(2)
Annual Growth Rate of Employment By Agricultural and Non-Agricultural Sectors, 1950-1 to 1999-2000

Period	Employment growth (per cent per annum)			Employment growth in	
	Total	Males	Females	Agricultural sector	Non-agricultural sector
Inter census/Survey dates					
April 1951 to April 1961	1.57	1.75	1.2	1.49	1.83
April 1961 to April 1973	1.8	1.63	2.12	1.61	2.38
April 1973 to January 1978	2.74	2.54	3.25	1.88	5.05
January 1978 to July 1983	2.36	2.28	2.53	1.72	3.85
July 1983 to January 1988	1.59	1.87	1.05	0.38	4.07
January 1988 to January 1994	2.41	2.54	2.14	2.33	2.55
January 1994 to January 2000	0.82	1.19	0.03	-0.49	2.98
Long periods					
1950-1 to 1999-2000	1.85	1.9	1.73	1.36	2.91
1950-1 to 1964-5	1.63	1.72	1.44	1.53	1.97
1964-5 to 1980-1	2.16	2.02	2.45	1.71	3.36
1980-1 to 1999-2000	1.74	1.94	1.33	0.95	3.23
Shorter periods					
1950-1 to 1960-1	1.58	1.75	1.2	1.5	1.82
1960-1 to 1970-1	1.79	1.64	2.11	1.6	2.35
1970-1 to 1980-1	2.37	2.25	2.63	1.77	3.95
1980-1 to 1990-1	2.02	2.14	1.77	1.15	3.82
1990-1 to 1999-2000	1.43	1.71	0.84	0.74	2.59

Source: Sivasubramonian, S (2004): *The Sources of Economic Growth in India: 1950-1 to 1999-2000* (OUP), p. 68.

TABLE IX(3)
Number of Workers and Worker-Population Ratios
A: Number of Workers (in Terms of Usual Status) By Sex and Rural-Urban Residence, 1951 to 1999–2000

(in millions)

Refrence Date/Source	All-India			Rural India			Urban India		
	Persons	Males	Females	Persons	Males	Females	Persons	Males	Females
(1)	(2)	(3)	(4)	(5)	(6)	(7)	(8)	(9)	(10)
1 April 1951, Census 1951	161.39	108.55	52.84	–	–	–	–	–	–
1 April 1961, Census 1961	188.68	129.17	59.51	162.25	106.75	55.5	26.43	22.42	4.01
1 April 1973, NSS 27th Rd (1972–73)	233.81	156.9	76.91	194.8	125.2	69.6	39.01	31.7	7.31
1 January 1973, NSS 32nd Rd (1977–8)	265.87	176.79	89.08	217.21	138.41	78.8	48.66	38.38	10.28
1 July 1983, NSS 38th Rd (1983)	302.32	200.13	102.19	243.94	153.49	90.45	58.38	46.64	11.74
1 Janaury 1988, NSS 43rd Rd (1987–8)	324.61	217.5	107.11	257.67	164.67	93	66.94	52.83	14.11
1 January 1994, NSS 50th Rd (1993–4)	374.39	252.76	121.63	291.95	187.66	104.29	82.44	65.1	17.34
1 January 2000, NSS 55th Rd (1999–2000)	393.19	271.37	121.82	298.05	195	103.05	95.14	76.37	18.77

B: Worker Population Ratios by Sex and Rural–Urban Residence, 1951 to 1999–2000

Year	Source	All-India			Rural India			Urban India		
		Persons	Males	Females	Persons	Males	Females	Persons	Males	Females
1951	Census	39.1	53.9	23.4	39.5	53.5	25	37.1	56.4	14.7
1961	Census	43	57.1	28	45.1	58.2	31.4	33.5	52.4	11.1
1971	Census	34	52.7	13.9	36.1	53.6	15.5	29.6	48.9	7.1
1972–3	NSS 27th Rd	41.3	53.5	28.2	43.5	54.5	31.8	33.1	5.1	13.4
1977–8	NSS 32th Rd	42.2	54.2	29.3	44.4	55.2	33.1	34.4	50.8	15.6
1983	NSS 38th Rd	42.2	53.8	29.6	44.6	54.7	34	34.3	51.2	15.1
1987	NSS 43rd Rd	41.1	53.1	28.1	43.4	53.9	32.3	33.9	50.6	15.2
1991	Census	37.5	51.6	22.3	40	52.5	26.7	30.2	48.9	9.2
1993–4	NSS 50th Rd	42	54.45	28.6	44.4	55.3	32.8	34.7	52	15.4
1999–2000	NSS 55th Rd	39.7	52.7	25.9	41.7	53.1	29.9	33.7	51.8	13.9

Source: Sivasubramonian, S (2004): The Sources of Economic Growth in India: 1950–1 to 1999–2000 (OUP), p.63 and p 68.

TABLE IX(4)
Macro Scenario on Employment and Sectoral Employment Growth
A: Past and Present Macro-scenario on Employment and Unemployment (CDS Basis) (person years)

	Million			Growth per annum (%)	
	1983	1993–4	1999–00	1983 to 1993–4	1993–4 to 1999–00
All-India					
Population	718.20	894.01	1003.97	2.00	1.95
Labour force	261.33	335.97	363.33	2.43	1.31
Workforce	239.57	315.84	336.75	2.7	1.07
Unemployment rate	(8.30)	(5.99)	(7.32)		
No. of unemployed	21.76	20.13	26.58	−0.08	4.74
Rural					
Population	546.61	658.83	727.5	1.79	1.67
Labour force	204.18	255.38	270.39	2.15	0.96
Workforce	187.92	241.04	250.89	2.4	0.67
Unemployment rate	(7.96)	(5.61)	(7.21)		
No. of unemployed	16.26	14.34	19.5	−1.19	5.26
Urban					
Population	171.59	234.98	276.47	3.04	2.74
Labour force	57.15	80.60	92.95	3.33	2.40
Workforce	51.64	74.80	85.84	3.59	2.32
Unemployment rate	(9.64)	(7.19)	(7.65)		
No. of unemployed	5.51	5.80	7.11	0.49	3.45

B: Sectoral Employment Growth (CDS Basis)

Sector	Employment (in million)				Annual growth (%)			
	1983	1987–8	1993–4	1999–2000	1983 to 1987–8	1987–8 to 1993–4	1983 to 1993–4	1993–4 to 1999–2000
Agriculture	151.35	163.82	190.72	190.94	1.77	2.57	2.23	0.02
Manufacturing								
Mining and quarrying	1.74	2.40	2.54	2.26	7.35	1.00	3.68	−1.91
Manufacturing	27.69	32.53	35.00	40.79	3.64	1.23	2.26	2.58
Electricity, gas and water supply	0.83	0.94	1.43	1.15	2.87	7.19	5.31	−3.55
Construction	7.17	11.98	11.02	14.95	12.08	−1.38	4.18	5.21
Services								
Trade, hotels and restaurent	18.17	22.53	26.88	37.54	4.89	2.99	3.80	5.72
Transport, storage and communication	6.99	8.05	9.88	13.65	3.21	3.46	3.35	5.53
Financial, insurance real estate and business services	2.10	2.59	3.37	4.62	4.72	4.50	4.60	5.40
Community, social and personal services	23.52	27.55	34.98	30.84	3.57	4.06	3.85	−2.08
All sectors	239.57	272.39	315.84	336.75	2.89	2.50	2.67	1.07

Source: Economic Survey 2002–3.

TABLE IX(5)
Growth Of Employment: Statewise and Rural and Urban in the 1980s and 1990s

(Percent per annum)

States/UTs	Combined							Rural							Urban					
	1983 to 1993–4			1993–4 to 1999-2000				1983 to 1993–4			1993–4 to 1999-2000				1983 to 1993–4			1993–4 to 1999-2000		
	Male	Female	Persons	Male	Female	Persons		Male	Female	Persons	Male	Female	Persons		Male	Female	Persons	Male	Female	Persons
(1)	(2)	(3)	(4)	(5)	(6)	(7)		(8)	(9)	(10)	(11)	(12)	(13)		(14)	(15)	(16)	(17)	(18)	(19)
Andhra Pradesh	2.1	2.7	2.4	1.6	0.3	1.1		1.7	2.5	2.0	1.3	0.1	0.8		3.5	4.2	3.7	2.4	1.6	2.2
Arunachal Pradesh	–	–	–	0.5	-0.7	0.0		–	–	–	-0.4	-1.4	-0.8		–	–	–	4.7	10.7	5.6
Assam	1.3	3.2	1.6	2.5	2.3	2.5		1.4	3.1	1.7	2.5	2.1	2.4		0.8	3.5	1.0	2.2	6.2	2.7
Bihar	1.8	-1.7	0.9	2.3	3.0	2.5		1.9	-1.8	0.9	2.1	2.9	2.3		1.3	-1.4	0.9	3.4	4.7	3.6
Goa	1.7	-3.0	0.1	2.6	-4.1	0.8		0.0	-4.7	-1.8	2.1	-4.0	0.4		4.3	1.4	3.5	3.1	-4.4	1.5
Gujarat	2.4	1.6	2.1	2.1	2.2	2.1		2.0	1.2	1.7	1.8	2.4	2.0		3.2	3.6	3.3	2.6	0.7	2.3
Haryana	2.5	4.7	3.1	1.9	-3.1	0.6		2.2	4.3	2.8	2.0	-3.0	0.5		3.1	7.5	3.8	1.8	-3.7	0.8
Himachal Pradesh	2.8	3.0	2.9	1.4	1.5	1.4		2.9	3.0	2.9	1.4	1.6	1.5		2.0	4.8	2.6	2.0	-3.1	0.8
Jammu & Kashmir	1.7	5.9	2.9	2.2	-1.2	1.1		1.5	5.8	2.9	2.3	-0.4	1.3		2.4	6.7	3.1	2.1	-9.8	0.3
Karnataka	2.2	2.4	2.3	2.0	0.8	1.6		2.0	2.7	2.3	1.8	0.3	1.2		2.7	0.6	2.2	2.5	3.9	2.8
Kerala	2.0	-1.2	0.9	1.6	1.4	1.6		1.1	-2.3	-0.1	1.0	0.8	0.9		4.9	3.3	4.4	3.2	3.3	3.2
Madhya Pradesh	2.4	1.7	2.2	1.9	1.5	1.8		2.2	1.6	1.9	1.4	1.4	1.4		3.2	3.7	3.3	3.5	2.3	3.3
Maharashtra	2.1	2.3	2.2	1.8	-0.2	1.0		1.8	1.9	1.9	1.3	-0.2	0.6		2.6	4.2	2.9	2.5	-0.5	1.9
Manipur	3.6	2.9	3.3	3.2	-0.3	2.0		3.2	2.8	3.1	2.1	-2.2	0.6		4.5	3.0	3.9	5.6	5.0	5.4
Meghalaya	3.1	4.0	3.5	2.3	3.0	2.6		3.0	3.9	3.4	3.1	2.9	3.0		3.9	4.6	4.0	-1.4	3.3	-0.1
Mizoram	3.1	20.5	6.3	2.9	5.9	4.0		-0.8	3.3	0.4	5.0	2.1	–		9.8	12.7	10.6	5.0	6.8	5.6
Nagaland	19.7	34.5	22.4	4.6	15.9	8.6		–	–	–	4.6	15.4	8.7		2.6	6.9	3.2	4.7	20.2	8.0
Orissa	1.8	2.9	2.1	1.5	1.0	1.3		1.6	2.7	2.0	1.2	0.7	1.0		2.6	6.7	3.3	3.3	4.0	3.4
Punjab	1.8	-1.4	1.0	1.5	6.1	2.6		1.5	-1.5	0.6	1.2	6.0	2.5		2.6	-0.4	2.1	2.0	6.5	2.6
Rajasthan	2.6	2.4	2.5	2.2	0.5	1.5		2.4	2.5	2.5	2.0	0.4	1.4		3.1	1.6	2.8	2.8	0.8	2.4
Sikkim	2.9	0.6	2.3	1.4	9.1	3.4		3.5	0.8	2.8	1.4	9.0	3.4		-1.0	-1.7	-1.1	1.6	9.4	3.0
Tamil Nadu	1.6	2.0	1.8	1.4	-0.3	0.8		1.4	1.8	1.6	1.1	-0.7	0.4		2.2	2.9	2.4	1.8	1.1	1.6
Tripura	3.3	10.4	4.3	2.7	-5.5	1.4		2.9	10.6	3.9	2.7	-5.7	1.4		5.7	9.4	6.3	2.5	-4.6	1.3
Uttar Pradesh	2.3	1.1	2.0	1.8	1.4	1.7		2.2	0.8	1.8	1.4	1.3	1.4		2.7	4.1	2.9	3.5	2.3	3.3
West Bengal	2.4	2.1	2.4	1.6	-0.8	1.1		2.7	1.9	2.5	1.7	-0.6	1.2		1.8	3.1	2.0	1.3	-1.3	0.8
Andaman & Nicobar Is.	3.9	12.9	6.1	2.4	-8.0	-0.7		4.0	13.1	6.6	2.1	-11.1	-2.0		3.5	12.0	4.7	3.0	4.4	3.3
Chandigarh	3.7	5.0	3.9	2.5	-1.1	1.8		6.2	0.0	5.3	8.6	10.9	8.9		3.4	5.3	3.8	1.6	-2.1	0.9
Dadra & Nagar Haveli	4.5	3.4	4.0	3.5	-2.0	1.2		3.3	2.9	3.1	3.7	-1.7	1.4		–	–	–	2.0	-10.1	-0.6
Daman & Diu	4.2	-2.7	1.8	4.8	7.0	5.4		3.7	-2.6	1.3	4.1	5.7	4.6		4.8	-2.9	2.6	5.6	9.5	6.5
Delhi	4.1	3.2	3.9	2.7	4.2	2.9		8.1	0.1	6.6	6.7	-11.2	5.2		3.7	3.7	3.7	2.2	5.5	2.6
Lakshadweep	–	–	–	3.8	11.0	5.2		–	–	–	1.2	2.8	1.5		–	–	–	5.6	16.2	7.8
Pondicherry	3.4	1.4	2.8	3.5	3.0	3.4		-0.1	-1.2	-0.5	1.1	1.0	1.1		6.1	4.4	5.6	4.7	4.4	4.6
All India	2.2	1.7	2.1	1.9	0.9	1.6		2.0	1.5	1.8	1.6	0.8	1.3		2.8	3.2	2.9	2.6	1.5	2.4

Note: 1. Growth in employment has been estimated as compound annual growth in the persons employed in the age group 15 years and above on the usual principal and subsidiary status.
2. Work Force Participation Rates assumed to be the same for Goa and Daman & Diu for 1983.
3. 1983 NSSO survey excludes Arunachal Pradesh, Lakshadweep, Dadar & Nagar Haveli (Urban) and Nagaland (Rural).

Source: 1. The 38th, 50th and the 55th Rounds of the NSSO on Employment and Unemployment Situation in India
2. Census of India, 1981 & 1991 and Report of the Technical Group on Population Projections, RGI, 1996.

TABLE X(1)

Rank of States in Descending order of Per Capita NSDP and GSDP (Three-Yearly Annual Averages)

Rank	State	Per capita NSDP at 1980-1 prices: annual averages for 1980-1 to 1982-3	Rank	State	Per capita NSDP at 1980-1 prices: annual averages for 1990-1 to 1992-3	Rank	State	Per capita NSDP at 1993-4 prices: annual averages for 1993-4 to 1995-6	Rank	State	Per capita NSDP at 1993-4 prices: annual averages for 1998-9 to 2000-1
(1)	(2)	(3)	(4)	(5)	(6)	(7)	(8)	(9)	(10)	(11)	(12)
1.	Punjab	2818	1.	Punjab	3829	1.	Punjab	12,834	1.	Punjab	14,881
2.	Maharashtra	2452	2.	Maharashtra	3573	2.	Maharashtra	12,521	2.	Maharashtra	14,732
3.	Haryana	2419	3.	Haryana	3476	3.	Haryana	11,426	3.	Haryana	13,681
4.	Gujarat	2011	4.	Gujarat	2704	4.	Gujarat	10,993	4.	Gujarat	13,163
5.	West Bengal	1727	5.	Tamil Nadu	2290	5.	Tamil Nadu	9686	5.	Tamil Nadu	12,315
6.	Himachal Pradesh	1718	6.	Himachal Pradesh	2240	6.	Kerala	8401	6.	Karnataka	11,257
	Average for all states	1595	7.	West Bengal	2236	7.	Himachal Pradesh	8387	7.	Himachal Pradesh	10,529
	All-India NDP(CSO)	1672	8.	Karnataka	2193	8.	Karnataka	8101	8.	Kerala	10,141
7.	Karnataka	1563		Average for all states	2132	9.	Andhra Pradesh	7757	9.	Andhra Pradesh	9534
8.	Tamil Nadu	1555		All-India NDP(CSO)	2264		Average for all states	7694	10.	West Bengal	9307
9.	Andhra Pradesh	1504	9.	Andhra Pradesh	2078		All-India NDP(CSO)	8234		Average for all states	9245
10.	Kerala	1487	10.	Rajasthan	1891	10.	West Bengal	7114		All-India NDP(CSO)	10,139
11.	Assam	1374	11.	Kerala	1858	11.	Rajasthan	6844	11.	Rajasthan	8466
12.	Madhya Pradesh	1369	12.	Uttar Pradesh	1631	12.	Madhya Pradesh	6631	12.	Madhya Pradesh	7520
13.	Uttar Pradesh	1299	13.	Madhya Pradesh	1617	13.	Assam	5737	13.	Assam	5933
14.	Orissa	1265	14.	Assam	1559	14.	Uttar Pradesh	5156	14.	Uttar Pradesh	5633
15.	Rajasthan	1261	15.	Orissa	1463	15.	Orissa	4921	15.	Orissa	5206
16.	Bihar	933	16.	Bihar	1106	16.	Bihar	3045	16.	Bihar	3294

(contd.)

TABLE X(1) contd.
Rank of States in Descending order of Per Capita GSDP (Three-yearly Annual Averages)

Rank	State	Per capita GSDP at 1980–1 prices: annual averages for 1980–1 to 1982–3	Rank	State	Per capita GSDP at 1980–1 prices: annual averages for 1990–1 to 1992–3	Rank	State	Per capita GSDP at 1993–4 prices: annual averages for 1993–4 to 1995–6	Rank	State	Per capita GSDP at 1993–4 prices: annual averages for 1998–9 to 2000–1
(1)	(2)	(3)	(4)	(5)	(6)	(7)	(8)	(9)	(10)	(11)	(12)
1.	Punjab	3174	1.	Punjab	4286	1.	Punjab	14,405	1.	Maharashtra	16,865
2.	Haryana	2705	2.	Maharashtra	3931	2.	Maharashtra	14,019	2.	Punjab	16,848
3.	Maharashtra	2695	3.	Haryana	3843	3.	Haryana	13,021	3.	Gujarat	15,779
4.	Gujarat	2280	4.	Gujarat	3118	4.	Gujarat	12,661	4.	Haryana	15,716
5.	Himachal Pradesh.	1888	5.	Tamil Nadu	2579	5.	Tamil Nadu	10,823	5.	Tamil Nadu	13,859
6.	West Bengal	1871	6.	Himachal Pradesh	2507	6.	Himachal Pradesh	9454	6.	Karnataka	12,619
	Average for all states	1776	7.	Karnataka	2462	7.	Kerala	9266	7.	Himachal Pradesh	12,027
	All-India GDP(CSO)	1857	8.	West Bengal	2448	8.	Karnataka	9054	8.	Kerala	11,304
7.	Tamil Nadu	1743		Average for all states	2393	9.	Andhra Pradesh	8681	9.	Andhra Pradesh	10,665
8.	Karnataka	1739		All-India GDP(CSO)	2538		Average for all states	8672		Average for all states	10,510
9.	Kerala	1683	9.	Andhra Pradesh	2312		All-India GDP(CSO)	9234		All-India GDP(CSO)	11,433
10.	Andhra Pradesh.	1673	10.	Kerala	2158	10.	West Bengal	7844	10.	West Bengal	10,236
11.	Madhya Pradesh.	1529	11.	Rajasthan	2129	11.	Rajasthan	7749	11.	Rajasthan	9569
12.	Assam	1485	12.	Madhya Pradesh	1882	12.	Madhya Pradesh	7479	12.	Madhya Pradesh	8495
13.	Uttar Pradesh	1449	13.	Uttar Pradesh	1833	13.	Assam	6476	13.	Assam	6762
14.	Rajasthan	1416	14.	Assam	1719	14.	Uttar Pradesh	5877	14.	Uttar Pradesh	6500
15.	Orissa	1371	15.	Orissa	1639	15.	Orissa	5682	15.	Orissa	6236
16.	Bihar	1080	16.	Bihar	1291	16.	Bihar	3349	16.	Bihar	3656

Source: EPWRF (2003): Domestic Product of States of India.

TABLE X(2)
Trends in Statewise Bank Deposits and Credit and Credit-Deposit Ratios

(Amount in rupees lakh)
(C-D ratio in per cent)

S. no.	Name of the district	All-India 2002 Deposits	Credit	C-D ratio	1992 Deposits	Credit	C-D ratio	1982 Deposits	Credit	C-D ratio
	(1)	(2)	(3)	(4)	(5)	(6)	(7)	(8)	(9)	(10)
	Northern Region	25,670,471	14,431,388	56.2	4,919,863	2,512,115	51.1	1,111,278	777,719	70.0
1	Haryana	2,342,553	1,024,789	43.7	449,360	248,423	55.3	93,092	69,616	74.8
2	Himachal Pradesh	866,799	202,891	23.4	161,710	56,398	34.9	30,559	13,143	43.0
3	Jammu & Kashmir	1,162,145	428,024	36.8	209,170	105,883	50.6	47,603	22,960	48.2
4	Punjab	5,123,484	2,141,368	41.8	1,134,056	483,946	42.7	276,766	124,069	44.8
5	Rajasthan	3,159,332	1,529,831	48.4	635,899	353,614	55.6	124,043	87,012	70.1
6	Chandigarh	880,357	904,714	102.8	163,644	121,381	74.2	40,092	67,175	167.6
7	Delhi	12,135,801	8,199,771	67.6	2,166,024	1,142,470	52.7	499,123	393,744	78.9
	North-Eastern Region	1,831,232	497,713	27.2	382,648	178,599	46.7	77,270	32,088	41.5
8	Arunachal Pradesh	75,678	11,936	15.8	17,685	3938	22.3	1716	326	19.0
9	Assam	1,151,519	365,590	31.7	247,712	124,685	50.3	56,993	24,102	42.3
10	Manipur	63,404	16,751	26.4	11,984	8074	67.4	2152	906	42.1
11	Meghalaya	195,233	35,817	18.3	39,757	8427	21.2	6614	1497	22.6
12	Mizoram	49,312	12,997	26.4	10,673	2700	25.3	1207	263	21.8
13	Nagaland	104,990	13,479	12.8	23,233	10,083	43.4	3069	1337	43.6
14	Tripura	191,096	41,143	21.5	31,604	20,692	65.5	5519	3657	66.3
	Eastern Region	14,542,557	5,471,117	37.6	3,437,295	1,701,003	49.5	873,737	489,910	56.1
15	Bihar	2,983,254	636,830	21.3	1,016,110	375,058	36.9	229,916	98,349	42.8
16	Jharkhand	1,908,408	478,298	25.1						
17	Orissa	1,833,661	816,335	44.5	316,130	217,980	69.0	63,009	47,932	76.1
18	Sikkim	81,051	12,934	16.0	10,322	2472	23.9	1022	166	16.2
19	West Bengal	7,689,700	3518,118	45.8	2,088,100	1,103,320	52.8	578,675	343,131	59.3
20	Andaman & Nicobar Isl	46,484	8603	18.5	6633	2173	32.8	1115	332	29.8
	Central Region	15,271,522	5,180,681	33.9	3,177,132	1,511,143	47.6	714,991	342,023	47.8
21	Chhattisgarh	948,964	417,696	44.0						
22	Madhya Pradesh	3,316,234	1,544,891	46.6	868,345	529,784	61.0	167,540	97,452	58.2
23	Uttar Pradesh	9,852,010	2,943,982	29.9	2,308,787	981,359	42.5	547,451	244,571	44.7
24	Uttaranchal	1,154,316	274,111	23.7						
	Western Region	29,661,556	23,633,751	79.7	6,845,629	3,984,760	58.2	1,326,765	978,119	73.7
25	Goa	803,180	203,172	25.3	169,743	49,034	28.9	43,100$	17,210$	39.9$
26	Gujarat	6,528,428	2,882,011	44.1	1,390,515	728,161	52.4	357,015	185,617	52.0
27	Maharashtra	22,254,602	20,538,117	92.3	5,277,062	3,205,383	60.7	926,468	775,058	83.7
28	Dadra & Nagar Haveli	27,072	5654	20.9	1933	809	41.9	182	234	128.6
29	Daman & Diu	48,275	4797	9.9	6376	1373	21.5			
	Southern Region	25,361,993	16,384,658	64.6	4,948,159	3,782,962	76.5	1,120,082	887,335	79.2
30	Andhra Pradesh	6,378,853	3,950,556	61.9	1,246,155	998,542	80.1	286,272	197,925	69.1
31	Karnataka	6,295,312	3,879,343	61.6	1,120,735	861,061	76.8	270,083	214,673	79.5
32	Kerala	5,166,705	2,236,709	43.3	960,769	497,004	51.7	205,287	139,197	67.8
33	Tamil Nadu	7,328,940	6,257,841	85.4	1,581,238	1,407,977	89.0	349,734	330,889	94.6
34	Lakshadweep	7312	580	7.9	1183	155	13.1	172	16	9.3
35	Pondicherry	184,871	59629	32.3	38,079	18,223	47.9	8534	4635	54.3
	All-India	112,339,332	65,599,308	58.4	23,710,723	13,670,582	57.7	5,224,123	3,507,194	67.1

Notes: $ Includes Daman & Diu.
Data for 1992 & 2002 relate to end-March and those for 1982, to end-December.
Source: Reserve Bank of India: Basic Statistical Returns of Scheduled Commercial Banks in India, Various Issues.

TABLE X(3)
Trends in Districtwise Deposits and Credit and Credit-Deposit Ratios
PUNJAB

(Amount in rupees lakh)
(C-D ratio in per cent)

S. no.	Name of the district	2002 Deposits	Credit	C-D ratio	1992 Deposits	Credit	C-D ratio	1982 Deposits	Credit	C-D ratio
(1)		(2)	(3)	(4)	(5)	(6)	(7)	(8)	(9)	(10)
1	Amritsar	606,074	189,906	31.3	147,691	55,209	37.4	38,292	17,013	44.4
2	Bathinda	127,198	57,463	45.2	42,964	29,710	69.2	8986	8034	89.4
3	Faridkot	58,084	23,991	41.3	61,581	31,132	50.6	14,251	9611	67.4
4	FatehgarhSahib	67,000	40,343	60.2						
5	Ferozpur	127,216	82,149	64.6	38,963	26,235	67.3	9881	9275	93.9
6	Gurdaspur	256,719	67,128	26.1	61,725	20,008	32.4	14,155	6309	44.6
7	Hoshiarpur	383,190	55,736	14.5	83,672	16,243	19.4	19,410	4653	24.0
8	Jalandhar	1,126,348	208,931	18.5	253,550	50,768	20.0	65,607	16,958	25.8
9	Kapurthala	312,566	48,535	15.5	56,576	12,621	22.3	13,887	3869	27.9
10	Ludhiana	845,216	890,726	105.4	197,066	142,743	72.4	48,810	25,723	52.7
11	Mansa	29,383	22,265	75.8						
12	Moga	117,627	37,835	32.2						
13	Muktsar	60,907	32,971	54.1						
14	Nawanshahar	197,955	21,637	10.9						
15	Patiala	386,683	188,672	48.8	101,013	52,996	52.5	23,614	12,598	53.3
16	Rupnagar	244,062	79,738	32.7	43,539	15,747	36.2	9046	3415	37.8
17	Sangrur	177,255	93,344	52.7	45,719	30,533	66.8	10,827	6611	61.1
	Punjab Total	5,123,483	2,141,370	41.8	1,134,059	483,945	42.7	276,766	124,069	44.8

Source & Notes: As in Table X(2).

RAJASTHAN

(Amount in rupees lakh)
(C-D ratio in per cent)

S. no.	Name of the district	2002 Deposits	Credit	C-D ratio	1992 Deposits	Credit	C-D ratio	1982 Deposits	Credit	C-D ratio
	(1)	(2)	(3)	(4)	(5)	(6)	(7)	(8)	(9)	(10)
1	Ajmer	203,500	61,015	30.0	39,843	18,763	47.1	8875	5107	57.5
2	Alwar	125,376	63,015	50.3	29,434	18,027	61.2	5862	5289	90.2
3	Banswara	56,947	17,497	30.7	10,544	5973	56.6	1662	1364	82.1
4	Baran	25,931	15,404	59.4	5237	4491	85.8			
5	Barmer	37,879	15,346	40.5	7472	3405	45.6	1059	535	50.5
6	Bharatpur	70,217	48,654	69.3	17,281	16,686	96.6	3559	3570	100.3
7	Bhilwara	82,914	82,217	99.2	16,286	17,368	106.6	2745	4111	149.8
8	Bikaner	106,880	41,877	39.2	23,951	11,187	46.7	6105	2157	35.3
9	Bundi	27,866	18,097	64.9	6826	6087	89.2	1089	961	88.2
10	Chittaurgarh	78,356	28,417	36.3	15,242	7881	51.7	2838	1714	60.4
11	Churu	76,651	23,884	31.2	17,206	5475	31.8	3770	1034	27.4
12	Dausa	32,647	12,887	39.5	5550	2276	41.0			
13	Dholpur	21,441	12,038	56.1	4700	2763	58.8	860	419	48.7
14	Dungarpur	47,770	9893	20.7	8794	2592	29.5	1412	394	27.9
15	Ganganagar	99,227	66,564	67.1	37,648	29,255	77.7	7544	5995	79.5
16	Hanumangarh	50,546	35970	71.2						
17	Jaipur	806,781	545,375	67.6	152,497	83,894	55.0	29,186	25,010	85.7
18	Jaisalmer	15,676	6197	39.5	3389	1139	33.6	489	84	17.2
19	Jalor	31,473	11,103	35.3	5338	2046	38.3	829	953	115.0
20	Jhalawar	26,986	11,974	44.4	5045	3888	77.1	1076	781	72.6
21	Jhunjhunun	92,751	20,869	22.5	20,274	6444	31.8	4618	1906	41.3
22	Jodhpur	219,557	85,880	39.1	44,909	20,755	46.2	9229	5034	54.5
23	Karauli	27,708	10,473	37.8						
24	Kota	142,263	70,249	49.4	29,207	25,437	87.1	7641	6134	80.3
25	Nagaur	77,312	21,344	27.6	16,745	6558	39.2	3399	2489	73.2
26	Pali	73,966	23,975	32.4	14,365	6586	45.8	2479	2912	117.5
27	Rajsamand	45,031	14,768	32.8	8910	2769	31.1			
28	Sawai Madhopur	34,078	14,597	42.8	14,526	8081	55.6	2571	847	32.9
29	Sikar	106,563	26,416	24.8	20,619	6960	33.8	3753	1505	40.1
30	Sirohi	52,420	16,062	30.6	8817	2971	33.7	1712	825	48.2
31	Tonk	36,929	14,280	38.7	7177	4194	58.4	1146	614	53.6
32	Udaipur	225,691	83,496	37.0	38,068	19,661	51.6	8535	5268	61.7
	Rajasthan total	3,159,333	1,529,833	48.4	635,900	353,612	55.6	124,043	87,012	70.1

Source & notes: As in Table X(2).

ASSAM

(Amount in rupees lakh)
(C-D ratio in per cent)

S. no.	Name of the district	2002 Deposits	2002 Credit	2002 C-D ratio	1992 Deposits	1992 Credit	1992 C-D ratio	1982 Deposits	1982 Credit	1982 C-D ratio
(1)		(2)	(3)	(4)	(5)	(6)	(7)	(8)	(9)	(10)
1	Barpeta	34,737	11,349	32.7	5206	3188	61.2			
2	Bongaigaon	32,148	12,972	40.4	5306	2803	52.8			
3	Cachar	73,437	16,001	21.8	1,4091	5552	39.4	4123	1220	29.6
4	Darrang	22,584	8295	36.7	4935	2636	53.4	3270	937	28.7
5	Dhemaji	7715	2390	31.0	1507	911	60.5			
6	Dhubri	23,456	5996	25.6	4669	2322	49.7			
7	Dibrugarh	91,664	27,578	30.1	2,1749	9371	43.1	16,063	5579	34.7
8	Goalpara	16,106	5407	33.6	3288	1478	45.0	3181	2086	65.6
9	Golaghat	24,098	6444	26.7	4885	3054	62.5			
10	Hailakandi	12,070	2110	17.5	2286	1116	48.8			
11	Jorhat	62,618	24,539	39.2	1,6453	5867	35.7			
12	Kakrojhar	18,465	6575	35.6	2974	1265	42.5			
13	Kamrup	383,587	147,467	38.4	8,5446	46,827	54.8	20,113	10,618	52.8
14	Karbi Anglong	16,363	3117	19.0	3456	1840	53.2	431	125	29.0
15	Karimganj	31,247	4951	15.8	6144	2965	48.3			
16	Lakhimpur	18,185	6852	37.7	4317	2817	65.3	878	250	28.5
17	Morigaon	12,198	4393	36.0	1808	1350	74.7			
18	Nagaon	63,098	14,211	22.5	1,3699	6882	50.2	2952	991	33.6
19	Nalbari	23,628	10,781	45.6	3801	2883	75.8			
20	North Cachar Hills	10,162	872	8.6	2851	406	14.2	460	41	8.9
21	Sibsagar	52,298	10,858	20.8	1,1181	4360	39.0	5522	2255	40.8
22	Sonitpur	52,648	14,929	28.4	1,0461	4649	44.4			
23	Tinsukia	69,006	17,504	25.4	1,7200	10,142	59.0			
	Assam total	1,151,518	365,591	31.7	24,7713	124,684	50.3	56,993	24,102	42.3

Source & notes: As in Table X(2).

BIHAR

(Amount in rupees lakh)
(C-D ratio in per cent)

S. no.	Name of the district	2002			1992			1982		
		Deposits	Credit	C-D ratio	Deposits	Credit	C-D ratio	Deposits	Credit	C-D ratio
1	Araria	27,771	10,385	37.4	5501	3220	58.5			
2	Aurangabad	58,552	10,217	17.4	11,176	4231	37.9	2267	541	23.9
3	Banka	27,729	6398	23.1	4925	2644	53.7			
4	Begusarai	72,034	17,522	24.3	14,139	6612	46.8	2957	1334	45.1
5	Bhabua				6966	3846	55.2			
6	Bhagalpur	102,298	23,681	23.1	23,207	10,035	43.2	6080	2424	39.9
7	Bhojpur	115,222	16,392	14.2	24,438	6716	27.5	8656	2067	23.9
8	Bokaro				45,433	10,211	22.5			
9	Buxar	60,042	10,993	18.3	13,478	4924	36.5			
10	Darbhanga	89,570	17,425	19.5	19,180	7717	40.2	4061	1634	40.2
11	Deoghar				10,385	3412	32.9			
12	Dhanbad				67,591	17,735	26.2	31,208	9989	32.0
13	Dhumka				9213	3101	33.7			
14	Garhwa				3008	1610	53.5			
15	Gaya	136,414	23,668	17.4	30,115	10,228	34.0	7543	2516	33.4
16	Gopalganj	74,245	12,057	16.2	12,318	3857	31.3	2000	962	48.1
17	Giridih				13,338	5490	41.2	4826	1167	24.2
18	Godda				4657	1978	42.5			
19	Gumla				8596	2561	29.8			
20	Hazaribag				40,308	11,733	29.1	8556	2392	28.0
21	Jamui	31,077	6566	21.1	5799	2714	46.8			
22	Jehanabad	46,300	6623	14.3	9442	3389	35.9			
23	Kaimur	34,787	10,790	31.0						
24	Katihar	43,442	16,148	37.2	7886	6207	78.7	1673	780	46.6
25	Khagaria	21,544	6475	30.1	4907	2490	50.7	672	682	101.5
26	Kishanganj	15,193	6355	41.8	2482	1826	73.6			
27	Lohardagga				2561	1306	51.0			
28	Lakhisarai	27,347	4056	14.8						
29	Madhepura	21,239	8827	41.6	3924	2830	72.1	503	598	118.9
30	Madhubani	64,865	15,734	24.3	13,249	7154	54.0	2519	1556	61.8
31	Munger	66,382	9158	13.8	23,823	7139	30.0	6250	1751	28.0
32	Muzaffarpur	149,475	35,042	23.4	34,659	14,864	42.9	8629	3224	37.4
33	Nalanda	84,860	13,410	15.8	16,567	7224	43.6	2976	1519	51.0
34	Nawada	37,496	7098	18.9	8158	3663	44.9	1281	1215	94.8
35	Palamu				14,593	4610	31.6	2737	1076	39.3
36	Paschimi Champaran	53,714	22,425	41.7	11,723	6636	56.6	3141	2129	67.8
37	Passchimi Singhbhum				25257	4829	19.1			
38	Patna	744,950	159,140	21.4	166,336	55,345	33.3	45,044	22,280	49.5
39	Purbi Champaran	79,154	20,347	25.7	16,022	8645	54.0			
40	Purbi Singhbhum				64,719	21,580	33.3			
41	Purnia	44,237	17,694	40.0	8207	5842	71.2	3526	2890	82.0
42	Purva Champaran							3020	2314	76.6
43	Ranchi				70,411	31851	45.2	20,207	10,861	53.7
44	Rohtas	93,981	21,230	22.6	24,145	9063	37.5	7567	5797	76.6
45	Saharsa	28,169	7715	27.4	4064	2173	53.5	1595	862	54.0
46	Sahebganj				9014	2579	28.6			
47	Samastipur	92,438	22,940	24.8	18,353	7699	41.9	3003	1786	59.5
48	Santhal Parganas							5483	1599	29.2
49	Saran	135,413	17,727	13.1	27,840	9838	35.3	4671	1581	33.8
50	Singhbhum							19442	5135	26.4
51	Sheikhpura	15,317	2319	15.1						
52	Sheohar	4199	1260	30.0						
53	Sitamarhi	42,725	12,017	28.1	9443	6343	67.2	1933	1270	65.7
54	Siwan	132,776	14,994	11.3	24,578	6082	24.7	3555	1328	37.4
55	Supaul	20,303	7774	38.3	3799	2700	71.1			
56	Vaishali	87,993	14,230	16.2	16,180	6579	40.7	2335	1090	46.7
	Bihar total	2,983,253	636,832	21.3	1,016,113	375,061	36.9	229,916	98,349	42.8

Source & notes: As in Table X(2).

(Amount in rupees lakh)
(C-D ratio in per cent)

S. no.	JHARKHAND Name of the district	Deposits 2002	Credit	C-D ratio	CHHATTISGARH Name of the district	Deposits	2002 Credit	C-D ratio	UTTARANCHAL Name of the District	Deposits	2002 Credit	C-D ratio
	(1)	(2)	(3)	(4)	(5)	(6)	(7)	(8)	(9)	(10)	(11)	(12)
1	Bokaro (B)	211,704	82,638	39.0	Bastar (MP)	32,407	9290	28.7	Almora (UP)	54,809	6902	12.6
2	Chatra	21,837	3720	17.0	Bilaspur (MP)	92,173	26,833	29.1	Bageshwar	15,050	2458	16.3
3	Deoghar (B)	55,722	13,131	23.6	Dantewada	15,854	10,108	63.8	Chamoli (UP)	27,846	4133	14.8
4	Dhanbad (B)	288,897	37,970	13.1	Dhamtari	17,626	8189	46.5	Champawat	13,767	2189	15.9
5	Dumka (B)	54,252	11,043	20.4	Durg (MP)	208,908	63,670	30.5	Dehradun (UP)	485,148	96,445	19.9
6	Garhwa (B)	22,114	5732	25.9	Janjir-champa	32,945	7336	22.3	Garhwal	85,141	10,027	11.8
7	Giridih (B)	76,990	16,223	21.1	Jashpur	20,226	3219	15.9	Haridwar (UP)	173,026	42,601	24.6
8	Godda (B)	27,558	6059	22.0	Kanker	12,010	3164	26.3	Nainital (UP)	100,675	24,665	24.5
9	Gumla (B)	37,303	7040	18.9	Kawardha	6825	1896	27.8	Pithoragarh (UP)	38,398	6379	16.6
10	Hazaribagh (B)	156,435	22,705	14.5	Korba	58,682	14,366	24.5	Rudra Prayag	11,960	1965	16.4
11	Koderma	28,845	4371	15.2	Koriya	41,825	5580	13.3	TehriGarhwal (UP)	51,442	6261	12.2
12	Lohardagga (B)	11,872	2651	22.3	Mahasamund	15,719	6361	40.5	Udhamsingh Nagar	84,273	66,427	78.8
13	Pakur	12,664	3467	27.4	Raigarh (MP)	33,901	12,917	38.1	Uttar Kashi (UP)	12,782	3661	28.6
14	Palamu (B)	73,168	13,769	18.8	Raipur (MP)	264,145	215,243	81.5				
15	Paschimi Singhbhum (B)	99,564	19,839	19.3	Rajnandgaon (MP)	38,300	14,675	38.3				
16	Purbi Singhbhum (B)	336,930	120,654	35.8	Surguja (MP)	57,418	14,849	25.9				
17	Ranchi (B)	366,951	102,413	27.9								
18	Sahebganj (B)	25,602	4874	19.0								
	Jharkhand total	1,908,408	478,299	25.1	Chhatisgarh Total	948,964	417,696	44.0	Uttaranchal Total	1,154,317	274,113	23.7

Source & Notes: As in Table X(2).

ORISSA

(Amount in rupees lakh)
(C-D ratio in per cent)

S. no.	Name of the district	2002			1992			1982		
		Deposits	Credit	C-D ratio	Deposits	Credit	C-D ratio	Deposits	Credit	C-D ratio
	(1)	(2)	(3)	(4)	(5)	(6)	(7)	(8)	(9)	(10)
1	Angul	67,381	21,495	31.9						
2	Balasore							2475	1596	64.5
3	Balangir	28,309	14,190	50.1	6541	5594	85.5	1298	2139	164.8
4	Baleshwar	69,870	42,043	60.2	16,206	14,439	89.1			
5	Bargarh	23,872	22,495	94.2						
6	Bhadrak	35,525	13,545	38.1						
7	Boudh	6395	3379	52.8						
8	Cuttack	185,144	73,668	39.8	67,533	45,055	66.7	12629	10115	80.1
9	Deogarh	5335	1773	33.2						
10	Dhenkanal	45,946	19,550	42.5	17,748	8535	48.1	2570	1295	50.4
11	Gajapati	12,990	3982	30.7						
12	Ganjam	169,699	49,750	29.3	29,045	15,980	55.0	6031	2647	43.9
13	Jagatsinghpur	105,680	17,107	16.2						
14	Jajpur	55,414	23,668	42.7						
15	Jharsuguda	31,601	11,324	35.8						
16	Kalahandi	29,224	17,526	60.0	4973	5787	116.4	1122	1500	133.7
17	Kendrapara	44,289	11,460	25.9						
18	Keonjhar	50,093	22,193	44.3	8262	6462	78.2	1341	1096	81.7
19	Khurda	396,561	206,134	52.0						
20	Koraput	39,346	19,919	50.6	12,899	10,768	83.5	2851	4299	150.8
21	Malkangiri	7490	2968	39.6						
22	Mayurbhanj	69,562	62,259	89.5	10,218	6504	63.7	2026	1329	65.6
23	Nawapara	11,336	4425	39.0						
24	Nayagarh	20,198	10,532	52.1						
25	Nowrangpur	10,103	7145	70.7						
26	Phulabani	12,476	5463	43.8	3183	2356	74.0	614	510	83.1
27	Puri	65,142	29,516	45.3	82,272	64,528	78.4	16,909	13,869	82.0
28	Rayagada	23,398	10,333	44.2						
29	Sambalpur	64,652	26,998	41.8	25,841	15,798	61.1	5814	4001	68.8
30	Sonepur	8715	3905	44.8						
31	Sundergarh	137,918	57,589	41.8	31,411	16,175	51.5	7329	3536	48.2
	Orissa total	1,833,664	816,334	44.5	316,132	217,981	69.0	63,009	47,932	76.1

Source & notes: As in Table X(2).

WEST BENGAL

(Amount in rupees lakh)
(C-D ratio in per cent)

S. no.	Name of the district	2002 Deposits	2002 Credit	2002 C-D ratio	1992 Deposits	1992 Credit	1992 C-D ratio	1982 Deposits	1982 Credit	1982 C-D ratio
(1)		(2)	(3)	(4)	(5)	(6)	(7)	(8)	(9)	(10)
1	Bankura	106,820	22,609	21.2	20,745	7951	38.3	4060	1024	25.2
2	Barddhaman	540,415	109,806	20.3	126,881	42,450	33.5			
3	Birbhum	113,373	32,247	28.4	21,092	9343	44.3	4706	1626	34.6
4	Burdwan							33,078	9970	30.1
5	Dakshin Dinajpur	28,282	10,640	37.6						
6	Darjiling	167,510	50,127	29.9	32,382	12,342	38.1	7502	2404	32.0
7	Haora	358,715	62,072	17.3	83,663	24,196	28.9	24,344	5032	20.7
8	Hugli	332,227	52,458	15.8	74,096	23,660	31.9	21,179	4088	19.3
9	Jalpaiguri	133,144	35,382	26.6	25,002	10,542	42.2	7250	3144	43.4
10	Koch Bihar	54,140	17,554	32.4	10,226	6242	61.0	2297	1108	48.2
11	Kolkata	3,920,066	2,778,358	70.9	1,321,329	842,764	63.8	388,088	296,721	76.5
12	Maldah	81,862	25,406	31.0	14,383	7758	53.9	2622	1455	55.5
13	Medinipur	365,718	79,431	21.7	72,923	29,199	40.0	12,971	2829	21.8
14	Murshidabad	136,572	34,329	25.1	25,773	11,066	42.9	5606	1804	32.2
15	Nadia	176,290	38,804	22.0	34,914	11,417	32.7	7934	2423	30.5
16	North 24 Parganas	815,099	104,810	12.9	146,095	36,487	25.0			
17	Puruliya	84,988	14,447	17.0	17,068	5963	34.9	3565	809	22.7
18	South 24 Parganas	232,921	33,740	14.5	48,901	14,735	30.1			
19	24 Parganas	50,777	7482	14.7						
20	Uttar Dinajpur	41,560	15,898	38.3						
21	West Dinajpur	12,623	7206	57.1	2696	1212	45.0			
	West Bengal total	7,689,702	3,518,118	45.8	2,088,096	1,103,321	52.8	578,675	343,131	59.3

Source & notes: As in Table X(2).

MADHYA PRADESH

(Amount in rupees lakh)
(C-D ratio in per cent)

S. no.	Name of the district	2002 Deposits	2002 Credit	2002 C-D ratio	1992 Deposits	1992 Credit	1992 C-D ratio	1982 Deposits	1982 Credit	1982 C-D ratio
	(1)	(2)	(3)	(4)	(5)	(6)	(7)	(8)	(9)	(10)
1	Balaghat	32,637	11,625	35.6	6004	3202	53.3	1412	837	59.3
2	Bastar				10,787	5680	52.7	2011	1049	52.2
3	Barwani	26,605	16,398	61.6						
4	Betul	54,006	14,421	26.7	10,977	3463	31.5	1775	578	32.6
5	Bhind	43,029	13,405	31.2	9239	4074	44.1	1693	663	39.2
6	Bhopal	471,847	230,771	48.9	108,642	54,753	50.4	18,303	10,432	57.0
7	Bilaspur				39097	14,442	36.9	6197	3237	52.2
8	Chhatarpur	45,617	13,439	29.5	8537	4081	47.8	1666	1008	60.5
9	Chhindwara	83,344	22,309	26.8	17,991	6459	35.9	2906	1308	45.0
10	Damoh	27,609	11,840	42.9	5291	3923	74.1	979	509	52.0
11	Datia	22,462	8436	37.6	3747	1715	45.8	687	435	63.3
12	Dewas	47,649	32,508	68.2	9635	10,313	107.0	1846	2597	140.7
13	Dhar	54,937	29,503	53.7	10,589	7789	73.6	1548	1091	70.5
14	Durg				41,336	22,496	54.4	8181	3366	41.1
15	Dindori	6446	1815	28.2						
16	EastNimar	62,036	28,792	46.4	14,932	10,798	72.3	3454	2214	64.1
17	Guna	53,696	28,953	53.9	10,361	7134	68.9	1579	789	50.0
18	Gwalior	219,955	77,628	35.3	48,393	29,145	60.2	12245	6410	52.3
19	Harda	17,703	7524	42.5						
20	Hoshangabad	57,975	24,668	42.5	16,180	10,558	65.3	3769	2297	60.9
21	Indore	529,535	410,914	77.6	108,787	87,907	80.8	22,430	14,314	63.8
22	Jabalpur	272,570	104,378	38.3	69,105	52,067	75.3	16,457	7951	48.3
23	Jhabua	26,411	9377	35.5	4580	3562	77.8	847	634	74.9
24	Katni	52,002	13,836	26.6						
25	Mandla	19,978	6345	31.8	4629	2603	56.2	918	513	55.9
26	Mandsaur	40,433	19,505	48.2	13,749	7322	53.3	3029	1902	62.8
27	Morena	45,657	26,609	58.3	12,086	8066	66.7	2251	1560	69.3
28	Narsimhapur	31,397	14,542	46.3	8140	5484	67.4	1442	844	58.5
29	Neemuch	34,322	8167	23.8						
30	Panna	20,278	6250	30.8	3752	1635	43.6	655	274	41.8
31	Raigarh				9180	5574	60.7	1714	825	48.1
32	Raisen	25,741	20,248	78.7	5481	5458	99.6	929	1143	123.0
33	Rajgarh	31,225	21,077	67.5	5086	4383	86.2	836	672	80.4
34	Raipur				42,858	28,346	66.1	9049	5702	63.0
35	Rajnandgaon				8389	5489	65.4	1569	1035	66.0
36	Ratlam	74,845	26,051	34.8	16,148	9729	60.2	3253	2566	78.9
37	Rewa	96,281	25,928	26.9	18,442	7680	41.6	2689	1458	54.2
38	Sagar	85,521	29,662	34.7	18,626	10,790	57.9	4140	1679	40.6
39	Satna	81,719	25,950	31.8	16,956	9859	58.1	2718	2199	80.9
40	Sehore	35,479	19,021	53.6	7648	6313	82.5	1408	1023	72.7
41	Seoni	27,871	8859	31.8	5554	2964	53.4	1030	443	43.0
42	Shahdol	58,109	9037	15.6	17,253	4458	25.8	2433	792	32.6
43	Shajapur	30,102	20,000	66.4	5733	4972	86.7	1091	832	76.3
44	Sheopur	8921	5459	61.2						
45	Shivpuri	40,134	15,008	37.4	7390	4189	56.7	1186	651	54.9
46	Sidhi	65,275	10,952	16.8	15,548	3617	23.3	1447	784	54.2
47	Surguja				18,142	4556	25.1	2823	922	32.7
48	Tikamgarh	31,650	6876	21.7	5232	2465	47.1	875	772	88.2
49	Ujjain	114,905	60,629	52.8	28,280	24,593	87.0	6441	4256	66.1
50	Umaria	33,803	5926	17.5						
51	Vidisha	35,684	21,500	60.3	7295	6151	84.3	1371	1365	99.6
52	West Nimar	38,836	18,750	48.3	12,537	9530	76.0	2258	1521	67.4
	Madhya Pradesh total	3316,237	1,544,891	46.6	868,344	529787	61.0	167,540	97,452	58.2

Source & notes: As in Table X(2).

APPENDIX TABLES 291

UTTAR PRADESH

(Amount in rupees lakh)
(C-D ratio in per cent)

S. no.	Name of the district	2002			1992			1982		
		Deposits	Credit	C-D ratio	Deposits	Credit	C-D ratio	Deposits	Credit	C-D ratio
	(1)	(2)	(3)	(4)	(5)	(6)	(7)	(8)	(9)	(10)
1	Agra	379,269	107,383	28.3	80,130	36,500	45.6	23,245	11,888	51.1
2	Aligarh	214,941	61,345	28.5	48,128	18,464	38.4	11,352	5149	45.4
3	Allahabad	437,161	83,869	19.2	105,248	31,326	29.8	23,677	9796	41.4
4	Almora	13,593	3197	23.5	2440	643	26.4			
5	Ambedkar Nagar	64,624	14,560	22.5						
6	Auraiya	33,978	5471	16.1						
7	Azamgarh	191,677	26,516	13.8	37,033	9831	26.5	8136	2839	34.9
8	Baghpat	45,278	10,780	23.8						
9	Bahraich	56,497	20,171	35.7	17,421	9787	56.2	3400	1595	46.9
10	Ballia	144,849	20,127	13.9	31,125	8652	27.8	6347	1850	29.1
11	Balrampur	48,007	14,223	29.6						
12	Banda	37,159	13,323	35.9	11,455	5586	48.8	2023	973	48.1
13	Barabanki	82,416	28,160	34.2	17,347	7207	41.5	3198	1763	55.1
14	Bareilly	198,093	63,630	32.1	43,801	19,292	44.0	10,882	4358	40.0
15	Basti	73,074	27,697	37.9	21,692	8827	40.7	5181	2876	55.5
16	Bijnor	124,697	56,091	45.0	30,456	14,678	48.2	6856	2917	42.5
17	Budaun	62,921	29,659	47.1	15,389	8895	57.8	3303	1343	40.7
18	Bulandshahr	138,140	35,884	26.0	37,685	15,117	40.1	9229	3630	39.3
19	Chamoli	5751	1091	19.0	728	191	26.2			
20	Chandauli	60,346	13,877	23.0						
21	Chitrakoot	19,706	7205	36.6						
22	Dehra Dun	92,570	17,056	18.4	52,436	4745	9.0			
23	Deoria	122,143	23,280	19.1	39,055	13,654	35.0	6668	3857	57.8
24	Etah	80,964	25,361	31.3	16,670	7903	47.4	3992	2904	72.7
25	Etawah	53,722	12,986	24.2	20,341	7507	36.9	4579	1892	41.3
26	Faizabad	108,657	25,202	23.2	36,101	12,920	35.8	8442	2503	29.6
27	Farrukhabad	64,979	19,869	30.6	24,742	12,524	50.6	6227	2793	44.9
28	Fatehpur	61,768	13,406	21.7	12,773	5354	41.9	2498	918	36.7
29	Firozabad	88,611	25,854	29.2	19,129	7293	38.1			
30	Garhwal	16,818	2963	17.6	2358	695	29.5			
31	Gautam Buddha Nagar	442,886	93,812	21.2						
32	Ghaziabad	407,642	158,895	39.0	120,221	58,416	48.6	20,295	15,886	78.3
33	Ghazipur	156,474	22,352	14.3	31,297	8804	28.1	5310	1760	33.1
34	Gonda	91,211	22,035	24.2	31,053	10,611	34.2	4816	1923	39.9
35	Gorakhpur	289,154	69,610	24.1	60,979	18,780	30.8	14,381	6114	42.5
36	Hamirpur	26,255	11,007	41.9	11,930	5335	44.7	2250	850	37.8
37	Hardoi	80,600	25,480	31.6	17,119	7885	46.1	3446	1887	54.8
38	Haridwar	40,706	9844	24.2						
39	Hathras	60,042	21,273	35.4						
40	Jalaun	51,761	18,624	36.0	12,813	6764	52.8	2390	1440	60.3
41	Jaunpur	203,061	34,101	16.8	40,480	11,024	27.2	5821	1767	30.4
42	Jhansi	130,276	34,124	26.2	28,417	8900	31.3	6849	1859	27.1

(contd.)

UTTAR PRADESH (contd.)

	(1)	(2)	(3)	(4)	(5)	(6)	(7)	(8)	(9)	(10)
43	Jyotiba Phule Nagar	44,849	19,584	43.7						
44	Kanauj	42,606	14,241	33.4						
45	Kanpur City	712,552	219,096	30.7	172,063	100,538	58.4	52,988	28,035	52.9
46	Kanpur Dehat	64,152	19,753	30.8	14,517	8244	56.8			
47	Kaushambi	31,422	6395	20.4						
48	Kushi Nagar	74,751	24,563	32.9						
49	Lakhimpur Kheri	84,916	38,673	45.5	18,999	15,541	81.8	3944	2582	65.5
50	Lalitpur	27,083	9657	35.7	6176	3046	49.3	1524	551	36.2
51	Lucknow	1153,873	420,666	36.5	214,460	101,626	47.4	52,657	30,387	57.7
52	Maharajganj	51,936	17,823	34.3	10,983	4934	44.9			
53	Mahoba	18,727	6838	36.5						
54	Mainpuri	56,800	18,201	32.0	11,923	4823	40.5	3721	2014	54.1
55	Mathura	144,399	43,097	29.8	30,948	11,732	37.9	7361	3647	49.5
56	Mau	89,582	12,207	13.6	17,251	4737	27.5			
57	Meerut	303,812	112,909	37.2	87,061	40,446	46.5	23,337	9591	41.1
58	Mirzapur	87,535	31,696	36.2	22,523	10,428	46.3	10,268	6370	62.0
59	Moradabad	218,762	94,397	43.2	57,594	33,036	57.4	15,131	7734	51.1
60	Muzaffarnagar	178,063	76,677	43.1	46,003	26,564	57.7	12,757	6030	47.3
61	Nainital	43,366	24,988	57.6	10,775	5871	54.5			
62	Pilibhit	48,103	22,032	45.8	11,188	8490	75.9	3159	2377	75.2
63	Pithoragarh	8183	2225	27.2	1179	385	32.7			
64	Pratapgarh	107,798	18,282	17.0	20,582	6401	31.1	3329	910	27.3
65	Rai Bareli	98,623	19,737	20.0	19,642	9491	48.3	3654	2248	61.5
66	Rampur	49,167	27,564	56.1	13,063	9689	74.2	2803	1994	71.1
67	Saharanpur	151,942	64,706	42.6	38,627	21,110	54.7	19,107	8318	43.5
68	Sant Kabir Nagar	36,099	7520	20.8						
69	Sant Ravidas Nagar	85,998	43,617	50.7						
70	Shahjahanpur	86,933	36,707	42.2	17,972	9917	55.2	3858	2284	59.2
71	Shravasti	19,863	6252	31.5						
72	Sidharthanagar	49,914	12,439	24.9	9775	3089	31.6			
73	Sitapur	91,840	25,193	27.4	23,633	10,487	44.4	4999	2305	46.1
74	Sonbhadra	80,810	22,486	27.8	18,603	8043	43.2			
75	Sultanpur	120,247	31,254	26.0	24,516	9341	38.1	3588	2078	57.9
76	Tehri Garhwal	8926	1633	18.3	1389	420	30.2			
77	Unnao	102,355	19,321	18.9	20,859	5981	28.7	3830	1250	32.6
78	Uttar Kashi	6134	780	12.7	570	219	38.4			
79	Varanasi	403,459	103,159	25.6	123,754	52,016	42.0	28,768	11,367	39.5
	Uttar Pradesh total	9,852,010	2,943,984	29.9	2,308,792	981,363	42.5	547,451	24,4571	44.7

Source & notes: As in Table X(2).

GUJARAT

(Amount in rupees lakh)
(C-D ratio in per cent)

S. no.	Name of the district	2002 Deposits	2002 Credit	2002 C-D ratio	1992 Deposits	1992 Credit	1992 C-D ratio	1982 Deposits	1982 Credit	1982 C-D ratio
(1)		(2)	(3)	(4)	(5)	(6)	(7)	(8)	(9)	(10)
1	Ahmedabad	1,533,528	1,175,344	76.6	358,241	216,244	60.4	83,024	59,062	71.1
2	Amreli	65,566	25,322	38.6	12,917	5504	42.6	4114	1166	28.3
3	Anand	390,668	53,897	13.8						
4	Banaskantha	57,269	24,737	43.2	12,817	7485	58.4	3846	1194	31.0
5	Bharuch	132,857	68,261	51.4	27,748	25,963	93.6	6704	9364	139.7
6	Bhavnagar	222,746	100,398	45.1	47,628	27,251	57.2	13,313	6555	49.2
7	Dahod	39,034	9616	24.6						
8	Dangs	5032	927	18.4	965	413	42.8	249	112	45.0
9	Gandhinagar	212,311	73,601	34.7	25,697	15,277	59.5	4784	5736	119.9
10	Jamnagar	241,069	52,410	21.7	50,838	18,415	36.2	14,622	4696	32.1
11	Junagadh	167,157	43,621	26.1	62,575	24,723	39.5	16,621	6316	38.0
12	Kachchh	501,591	50,395	10.0	83,679	11,176	13.4	23,386	2925	12.5
13	Kheda	192,432	30,346	15.8	119,717	60,943	50.9			
14	Kaira	27,429	8819	32.2						
15	Mahesana	92,957	27,546	29.6	38,325	20,623	53.8	11,632	4777	41.1
16	Narmada	12,141	3306	27.2						
17	Navsari	323,352	27,970	8.7						
18	Panch Mahals	67,729	23,363	34.5	21,852	14,355	65.7	4872	2204	45.2
19	Patan	64,449	18,547	28.8						
20	Porbandar	134,949	37,567	27.8						
21	Rajkot	413,313	112,945	27.3	85,512	33,808	39.5	22,624	9122	40.3
22	Sabarkantha	68,347	25,944	38.0	12,890	7536	58.5	3741	1955	52.3
23	Surat	576,071	242,962	42.2	143,310	65,380	45.6	31,484	14,781	46.9
24	Surendranagar	67,498	25,567	37.9	13,094	6829	52.2	4672	2036	43.6
25	Vadodara	810,316	569,694	70.3	173,744	129,523	74.5	53,914	35,546	65.9
26	Valsad	136,044	57,726	42.4	98,968	36,714	37.1	25,984	9251	35.6
	Gujarat total	6,528,426	2882,012	44.1	1,390,517	728,162	52.4	357,015	185,617	52.0

Source & notes: As in Table X(2).

MAHARASHTRA

(Amount in rupees lakh)
(C-D ratio in per cent)

S. no.	Name of the district	2002			1992			1982		
		Deposits	Credit	C-D ratio	Deposits	Credit	C-D ratio	Deposits	Credit	C-D ratio
	(1)	(2)	(3)	(4)	(5)	(6)	(7)	(8)	(9)	(10)
1	Ahmednagar	116,618	70,034	60.1	31,913	26,131	81.9	8582	8311	96.8
2	Akola	47,533	35,303	74.3	16,945	13,441	79.3	4851	3456	71.2
3	Amravati	95,635	36,680	38.4	26,148	15,458	59.1	6275	3863	61.6
4	Aurangabad	158,841	115,417	72.7	30,549	23,629	77.3	5954	5770	96.9
5	Bhandara	63,584	30,079	47.3	14,519	9512	65.5	2988	1581	52.9
6	Bid	48,208	28,118	58.3	10,724	6235	58.1	2282	1849	81.0
7	Buldhana	38,497	29,973	77.9	10,419	7980	76.6	2957	2621	88.6
8	Chandrapur	108,449	32,029	29.5	24,934	10,928	43.8	5189	2313	44.6
9	Dhule	45,771	26,091	57.0	18,095	14,252	78.8	4525	2920	64.5
10	Gadchiroli	21,253	7728	36.4	3159	1442	45.6			
11	Greater Mumbai	16,857,703	17,626,036	104.6	4,166,607	2,548,963	61.2	651,549	612,798	94.1
12	Hingoli	15,321	8835	57.7						
13	Jalgaon	125,971	79,929	63.5	32,128	19,264	60.0	8610	5566	64.6
14	Jalna	37,501	31,489	84.0	7528	7064	93.8	1501	1595	106.3
15	Kolhapur	169,517	114,031	67.3	39,829	32,099	80.6	11,433	8881	77.7
16	Latur	56,276	32,307	57.4	10,298	6958	67.6			
17	Nagpur	495,282	234,034	47.3	120,394	68,148	56.6	26,978	13,428	49.8
18	Nanded	68,240	41,649	61.0	14,534	11,078	76.2	3554	2960	83.3
19	Nandurbar	20,583	11,264	54.7						
20	Nasik	238,465	130,170	54.6	53,596	37,110	69.2	13,345	8004	60.0
21	Osmanabad	30,546	12,926	42.3	7081	4070	57.5	3271	2518	77.0
22	Parbhani	33,640	21,469	63.8	10,624	7990	75.2	2535	2271	89.6
23	Pune	1,473,927	882,781	59.9	257,859	172,599	66.9	70,501	44,312	62.9
24	Raigad	172,908	45,405	26.3	34,270	10,955	32.0	7889	3000	38.0
25	Ratnagiri	111,687	31,649	28.3	25,312	6176	24.4	5877	1594	27.1
26	Sangli	121,140	78,713	65.0	32,892	22,803	69.3	8459	5110	60.4
27	Satara	124,535	60,478	48.6	32,452	19,938	61.4	8129	5212	64.1
28	Sindhudurg	58,394	17,960	30.8	14,917	3631	24.3	3741	889	23.8
29	Solapur	132,608	91,105	68.7	35,627	25,681	72.1	10,798	7466	69.1
30	Thane	1,045,666	507,277	48.5	164,465	53,558	32.6	37,761	12,945	34.3
31	Wardha	45,064	25,599	56.8	13,722	8229	60.0	3259	1759	54.0
32	Washim	14,118	9217	65.3						
33	Yavatmal	61,121	32,342	52.9	15,519	10,058	64.8	3675	2066	56.2
	Maharashtra total	22,254,602	20,538,117	92.3	5,277,059	3,205,380	60.7	926,468	775,058	83.7

Source & notes: As in Table X(2).

ANDHRA PRADESH

(Amount in rupees lakh)
(C-D ratio in per cent)

S. no.	Name of the district	2002 Deposits	2002 Credit	2002 C-D ratio	1992 Deposits	1992 Credit	1992 C-D ratio	1982 Deposits	1982 Credit	1982 C-D ratio
(1)		(2)	(3)	(4)	(5)	(6)	(7)	(8)	(9)	(10)
1	Adilabad	119,058	50,209	42.2	21,485	7098	33.0	2870	1817	63.3
2	Anantapur	197,926	88,821	44.9	39,588	23,433	59.2	7735	5404	69.9
3	Chittoor	289,390	115,110	39.8	51,088	33,023	64.6	10,875	6626	60.9
4	Cuddapah	148,491	73,211	49.3	26,721	19,505	73.0	6582	4902	74.5
5	East Godavari	288,204	187,895	65.2	69,267	47,478	68.5	26,929	10,598	39.4
6	Guntur	305,244	229,419	75.2	74,219	59,861	80.7	20,181	16,722	82.9
7	Hyderabad	2,207,899	1,485,362	67.3	357,534	362,253	101.3	78,348	55,034	70.2
8	Karimnagar	226,600	74,206	32.7	44,381	20,256	45.6	6187	3672	59.4
9	Khammam	105,098	44,144	42.0	23,145	12,501	54.0	4547	3956	87.0
10	Krishna	339,003	189,935	56.0	80,969	57,613	71.2	20,684	11,977	57.9
11	Kurnool	160,812	88,984	55.3	34,603	27,085	78.3	8887	7339	82.6
12	Mahbubnagar	100,757	62,849	62.4	22,846	15,105	66.1	3966	3750	94.6
13	Medak	115,068	170,764	148.4	21,261	24,487	115.2	3064	4715	153.9
14	Nalgonda	93,860	65,069	69.3	19,746	14,213	72.0	3964	4281	108.0
15	Nellore	145,839	101,499	69.6	33,745	27,548	81.6	9064	9475	104.5
16	Nizamabad	126,008	62,141	49.3	26,941	16,075	59.7	4525	4889	108.0
17	Prakasam	154,600	104,334	67.5	40,067	30,220	75.4	10,879	8352	76.8
18	Ranga Reddy	293,776	136,735	46.5	34,216	45,383	132.6	4040	4139	102.5
19	Srikakulam	93,879	52,262	55.7	18,444	10,246	55.6	4093	2533	61.9
20	Visakhapatnam	433,355	301,060	69.5	102,035	66,867	65.5	23,660	9032	38.2
21	Vizianagaram	72,939	33,182	45.5	15,013	10,238	68.2	3562	3079	86.4
22	Warangal	166,888	79,781	47.8	34,280	22,590	65.9	6037	4885	80.9
23	West Godavari	194,154	153,585	79.1	54,562	45,463	83.3	15,593	10,748	68.9
	Andhra Pradesh total	6,378,854	3,950,557	61.9	1,246,156	998,541	80.1	286,272	197,925	69.1

Source & notes: As in Table X(2).

KARNATAKA

(Amount in rupees lakh)
(C-D ratio in per cent)

S. no.	Name of the district	2002 Deposits	2002 Credit	2002 C-D ratio	1992 Deposits	1992 Credit	1992 C-D ratio	1982 Deposits	1982 Credit	1982 C-D ratio
	(1)	(2)	(3)	(4)	(5)	(6)	(7)	(8)	(9)	(10)
1	Bagalkote	91,801	50,911	55.5						
2	Bangalore Rural	72,178	31,368	43.5	12,456	10,990	88.2			
3	Bangalore Urban	3,264,935	2,198,829	67.3	495,474	412,898	83.3			
4	Bangalore							111,486	106,394	95.4
5	Belgaum	257,222	128,091	49.8	61,441	37,315	60.7	16,373	10,090	61.6
6	Bellary	102,970	83,266	80.9	21,410	24,163	112.9	5,662	6906	122.0
7	Bidar	45,324	24,425	53.9	9980	7125	71.4	1548	1210	78.2
8	Bijapur	78,465	52,220	66.6	30,123	19,917	66.1	6888	4413	64.1
9	Chamarajanagar	24,272	14,840	61.1						
10	Chikmagalur	86,482	93,930	108.6	19,093	17,702	92.7	5714	4950	86.6
11	Chitradurga	51,588	35,482	68.8	23,196	21,209	91.4	8340	4883	58.5
12	Dakshin Kannada	447,534	179,160	40.0	138,991	75,122	54.0	35,356	19,340	54.7
13	Davangere	68,652	60,392	88.0						
14	Dharwad	198,900	114,750	57.7	57,722	37,392	64.8	15,259	9628	63.1
15	Gadag	39,315	23,579	60.0						
16	Gulbarga	124,631	68,624	55.1	27,110	18,188	67.1	4699	3335	71.0
17	Hassan	93,009	67,014	72.1	19,352	16,812	86.9	5429	3956	72.9
18	Haveri	40,511	31,351	77.4						
19	Kodagu	69,777	57,886	83.0	18,527	10,947	59.1	4894	3395	69.4
20	Kolar	93,040	48,535	52.2	21,322	15,723	73.7	5121	3475	67.9
21	Koppal	34,668	35,005	101.0						
22	Mandya	61,278	36,916	60.2	12,261	11,203	91.4	3542	2294	64.8
23	Mysore	274,166	142,553	52.0	55,138	46,473	84.3	15,460	12,196	78.9
24	Raichur	57,766	45,939	79.5	21,718	22,699	104.5	4595	4415	96.1
25	Shimoga	124,478	82,049	65.9	26,043	28,126	108.0	7603	7115	93.6
26	Tumkur	99,709	54,853	55.0	23,212	15,811	68.1	5433	3512	64.6
27	Udipi	268,646	77,363	28.8						
28	Uttar Kannada	123,995	40,014	32.3	26,164	11,247	43.0	6681	3166	47.4
	Karnataka total	6,295,312	3,879,345	61.6	1,120,733	861,062	76.8	270,083	214,673	79.5

Source & notes: As in Table X(2).

KERALA

(Amount in rupees lakh)
(C-D ratio in per cent)

S. no.	Name of the district	2002 Deposits	2002 Credit	2002 C-D ratio	1992 Deposits	1992 Credit	1992 C-D ratio	1982 Deposits	1982 Credit	1982 C-D ratio
	(1)	(2)	(3)	(4)	(5)	(6)	(7)	(8)	(9)	(10)
1	Alapuzha	373,934	121,117	32.4	70,466	28,214	40.0			
2	Alleppey							24,684	9480	38.4
3	Cannur	287,079	107,005	37.3	52,709	21,158	40.1	15,005	9937	66.2
4	Ernakulam	881,286	556,133	63.1	162,911	139,314	85.5	39,532	39,102	98.9
5	Idukki	51,560	48,905	94.9	11,233	9799	87.2	2155	2409	111.8
6	Kasaragod	94,910	46,899	49.4	16,242	9791	60.3			
7	Kollam	321,033	148,198	46.2	68,002	53,010	78.0			
8	Kottayam	385,643	156,784	40.7	73,048	32,062	43.9	15,805	9364	59.2
9	Kozhikode	267,848	157,923	59.0	53,406	39,085	73.2	11,368	9766	85.9
10	Malappuram	255,212	87,175	34.2	44,068	18,649	42.3	7927	5471	69.0
11	Palakkad	241,591	108,874	45.1	47,592	21,963	46.1			
12	Palghat							12,251	6967	56.9
13	Pathanamthitta	548,888	85,227	15.5	98,286	13,211	13.4			
14	Quilon							19,481	16,175	83.0
15	Thiruvananthapuram	778,237	374,660	48.1	136,897	60,180	44.0			
16	Thrissur	655,094	193,124	29.5	120,384	40,507	33.6	25,400	11,281	44.4
17	Trivandrum							30,441	17,117	56.2
18	Wayanad	24,392	44,685	183.2	5525	10,058	182.0	1238	2128	171.9
	Kerala total	5,166,707	2,236,709	43.3	960,769	497,001	51.7	205,287	139,197	67.8

Source & notes: As in Table X(2).

TAMIL NADU

(Amount in rupees lakh)
(C-D ratio in per cent)

S. no.	Name of the district	2002 Deposits	Credit	C-D ratio	1992 Deposits	Credit	C-D ratio	1982 Deposits	Credit	C-D ratio
	(1)	(2)	(3)	(4)	(5)	(6)	(7)	(8)	(9)	(10)
1	Ariyalur	15,111	10,704	70.8						
2	Anna				20,528	20,249	98.6			
3	Chingleput							13,466	9722	72.2
4	Chengai—M.G.R.				67,021	48,255	72.0			
5	Chidambaranar				29,336	18,345	62.5			
6	Chennai	2,932,731	3,548,459	121.0	699,261	713,226	102.0	148,304	170,305	114.8
7	Coimbatore	785,812	834,393	106.2	156,924	157,367	100.3	32,434	32,070	98.9
8	Cuddalore	138,843	52,663	37.9						
9	Dharmapuri	87,637	59,191	67.5	17,219	20,260	117.7	3447	3667	106.4
10	Dindigul	105,067	72,891	69.4						
11	Erode	249,077	162,960	65.4						
12	Kamarajar				23,362	27,061	115.8			
13	Kancheepuram	234,631	79,871	34.0						
14	Kanyakumari	153,517	59,831	39.0	30,531	15,188	49.7	6124	3422	55.9
15	Karur	88,199	53,186	60.3						
16	Madurai	284,989	156,697	55.0	62,564	57,684	92.2	20,610	19,085	92.6
17	Nagapattinam	106,177	31,789	29.9	36,848	16,142	43.8			
18	Namakkal	138,547	64,923	46.9						
19	Nilgiri	69,851	40,199	57.5	18,107	14,756	81.5	4421	6189	140.0
20	North Arcot							11,270	9468	84.0
21	P.T. Thirumagan				18,435	9846	53.4			
22	Periyar				53,069	37,756	71.1	12,736	7628	59.9
23	Perambalur	25,786	13,357	51.8						
24	Pudukottai	54,222	23,437	43.2	10,935	8651	79.1	2790	1832	65.7
25	Ramanathapuram	55,090	20,202	36.7	11,368	5332	46.9	12,477	10,237	82.0
26	Salem	214,414	154,784	72.2	74,440	57,127	76.7	16,532	11,489	69.5
27	Sivaganga	91,743	29,189	31.8						
28	South Arcot				44,401	33,079	74.5	10,029	8238	82.1
29	T. Kattabomman				41,529	20,722	49.9			
30	T.V. Malai-Sambuvarayar				13,990	13,877	99.2			
31	Thanjavur	169,411	80,805	47.7	37,265	23,705	63.6	19,313	8999	46.6
32	Theni	44,592	36,713	82.3						
33	Thiruvallur	180,236	70,516	39.1						
34	Thiruvarur	67,272	20,690	30.8						
35	Tiruchirapalli	271,221	118,367	43.6	75,816	58,190	76.8	18,342	16,908	92.2
36	Tirunelveli	207,272	77,248	37.3				17,439	11,630	66.7
37	Tiruvannamalai	57,602	34,794	60.4						
38	Toothukudi	134,126	77,903	58.1						
39	Vellore	172,312	90,307	52.4						
40	Vellore-Ambedkar				38,290	31,160	81.4			
41	Villupuram	70,342	64,485	91.7						
42	Virudhunagar	123,114	117,287	95.3						
	Tamil Nadu total	7328,944	6,257,841	85.4	1,581,239	1,407,978	89.0	349,734	330,889	94.6

Source & notes: As in Table X(2).